T0252614

Constrained Clustering

Advances in Algorithms,
Theory, and Applications

Chapman & Hall/CRC
Data Mining and Knowledge Discovery Series

SERIES EDITOR

Vipin Kumar
University of Minnesota
Department of Computer Science and Engineering
Minneapolis, Minnesota, U.S.A

AIMS AND SCOPE

This series aims to capture new developments and applications in data mining and knowledge discovery, while summarizing the computational tools and techniques useful in data analysis. This series encourages the integration of mathematical, statistical, and computational methods and techniques through the publication of a broad range of textbooks, reference works, and handbooks. The inclusion of concrete examples and applications is highly encouraged. The scope of the series includes, but is not limited to, titles in the areas of data mining and knowledge discovery methods and applications, modeling, algorithms, theory and foundations, data and knowledge visualization, data mining systems and tools, and privacy and security issues.

PUBLISHED TITLES

UNDERSTANDING COMPLEX DATASETS: Data Mining with Matrix Decompositions
David Skillicorn

COMPUTATIONAL METHODS OF FEATURE SELECTION
Huan Liu and Hiroshi Motoda

CONSTRAINED CLUSTERING: Advances in Algorithms, Theory, and Applications
Sugato Basu, Ian Davidson, and Kiri L. Wagstaff

Chapman & Hall/CRC
Data Mining and Knowledge Discovery Series

Constrained Clustering

Advances in Algorithms, Theory, and Applications

Edited by

Sugato Basu • Ian Davidson
Kiri L. Wagstaff

CRC Press
Taylor & Francis Group
Boca Raton London New York

CRC Press is an imprint of the
Taylor & Francis Group, an **informa** business

A CHAPMAN & HALL BOOK

Chapman & Hall/CRC
Taylor & Francis Group
6000 Broken Sound Parkway NW, Suite 300
Boca Raton, FL 33487-2742

© 2009 by Taylor & Francis Group, LLC
Chapman & Hall/CRC is an imprint of Taylor & Francis Group, an Informa business

No claim to original U.S. Government works
Printed in the United States of America on acid-free paper
10 9 8 7 6 5 4 3 2 1

International Standard Book Number-13: 978-1-58488-996-0 (Hardcover)

Library of Congress Cataloging-in-Publication Data

Constrained clustering : advances in algorithms, theory, and applications / editors, Sugato Basu, Ian Davidson, Kiri Wagstaff.
    p. cm. -- (Chapman & Hall/CRC data mining and knowledge discovery series)
Includes bibliographical references and index.
    ISBN 978-1-58488-996-0 (hardback : alk. paper)
    1. Cluster analysis--Data processing. 2. Data mining. 3. Computer algorithms. I. Basu, Sugato. II. Davidson, Ian, 1971- III. Wagstaff, Kiri. IV. Title. V. Series.

QA278.C63 2008
519.5'3--dc22
                                2008014590

Visit the Taylor & Francis Web site at
http://www.taylorandfrancis.com

and the CRC Press Web site at
http://www.crcpress.com

Thanks to my family, friends and colleagues especially Joulia, Constance and Ravi. – Ian

I would like to dedicate this book to all of the friends and colleagues who've encouraged me and engaged in idea-swapping sessions, both about constrained clustering and other topics. Thank you for all of your feedback and insights! – Kiri

Dedicated to my family for their love and encouragement, with special thanks to my wife Shalini for her constant love and support. – Sugato

Foreword

In 1962 Richard Hamming wrote, "The purpose of computation is insight, not numbers." But it was not until 1977 that John Tukey formalized the field of exploratory data analysis. Since then, analysts have been seeking techniques that give them better understanding of their data. For one- and two-dimensional data, we can start with a simple histogram or scatter plot. Our eyes are good at spotting patterns in a two-dimensional plot. But for more complex data we fall victim to the curse of dimensionality; we need more complex tools because our unaided eyes can't pick out patterns in thousand-dimensional data.

Clustering algorithms pick up where our eyes leave off: they can take data with any number of dimensions and cluster them into subsets such that each member of a subset is near the other members in some sense. For example, if we are attempting to cluster movies, everyone would agree that *Sleepless in Seattle* should be placed near (and therefore in the same cluster as) *You've Got Mail*. They're both romantic comedies, they've got the same director (Nora Ephron), the same stars (Tom Hanks and Meg Ryan), they both involve falling in love over a vast electronic communication network. They're practically the same movie. But what about comparing *Charlie and the Chocolate Factory* with *A Nightmare on Elm Street*? On most dimensions, these films are near opposites, and thus should not appear in the same cluster. But if you're a Johnny Depp completist, you know he appears in both, and this one factor will cause you to cluster them together.

Other books have covered the vast array of algorithms for fully-automatic clustering of multi-dimensional data. This book explains how the Johnny Depp completist, or any analyst, can communicate his or her preferences to an automatic clustering algorithm, so that the patterns that emerge make sense to the analyst; so that they yield insight, not just clusters. How can the analyst communicate with the algorithm? In the first five chapters, it is by specifying constraints of the form "these two examples should (or should not) go together." In the chapters that follow, the analyst gains vocabulary, and can talk about a taxonomy of categories (such as romantic comedy or Johnny Depp movie), can talk about the size of the desired clusters, can talk about how examples are related to each other, and can ask for a clustering that is different from the last one.

Of course, there is a lot of theory in the basics of clustering, and in the refinements of constrained clustering, and this book covers the theory well. But theory would have no purpose without practice, and this book shows how constrained clustering can be used to tackle large problems involving textual, relational, and even video data. After reading this book, you will have the tools to be a better analyst, to gain more insight from your data, whether it be textual, audio, video, relational, genomic, or anything else.

Dr. Peter Norvig
Director of Research
Google, Inc.
December 2007

Editor Biographies

Sugato Basu is a senior research scientist at Google, Inc. His areas of research expertise include machine learning, data mining, information retrieval, statistical pattern recognition and optimization, with special emphasis on scalable algorithm design and analysis for large text corpora and social networks. He obtained his Ph.D. in machine learning from the computer science department of the University of Texas at Austin. His Ph.D. work on designing novel constrained clustering algorithms, using probabilistic models for incorporating prior domain knowledge into clustering, won him the Best Research Paper Award at KDD in 2004 and the Distinguished Student Paper award at ICML in 2005. He has served on multiple conference program committees, journal review committees and NSF panels in machine learning and data mining, and has given several invited tutorials and talks on constrained clustering. He has written conference papers, journal papers, book chapters, and encyclopedia articles in a variety of research areas including clustering, semi-supervised learning, record linkage, social search and routing, rule mining and optimization.

Ian Davidson is an assistant professor of computer science at the University of California at Davis. His research areas are data mining, artificial intelligence and machine learning, in particular focusing on formulating novel problems and applying rigorous mathematical techniques to address them. His contributions to the area of clustering with constraints include proofs of intractability for both batch and incremental versions of the problem and the use of constraints with both agglomerative and non-hierarchical clustering algorithms. He is the recipient of an NSF CAREER Award on Knowledge Enhanced Clustering and has won Best Paper Awards at the SIAM and IEEE data mining conferences. Along with Dr. Basu he has given tutorials on clustering with constraints at several leading data mining conferences and has served on over 30 program committees for conferences in his research fields.

Kiri L. Wagstaff is a senior researcher at the Jet Propulsion Laboratory in Pasadena, CA. Her focus is on developing new machine learning methods, particularly those that can be used for data analysis onboard spacecraft, enabling missions with higher capability and autonomy. Her Ph.D. dissertation, "Intelligent Clustering with Instance-Level Constraints," initiated work in the machine learning community on constrained clustering methods. She has developed additional techniques for analyzing data collected by instruments on the EO-1 Earth Orbiter, Mars Pathfinder, and Mars Odyssey. The applications range from detecting dust storms on Mars to predicting crop yield on

Earth. She is currently working in a variety of machine learning areas including multiple-instance learning, change detection in images, and ensemble learning. She is also pursuing a Master's degree in Geology at the University of Southern California, and she teaches computer science classes at California State University, Los Angeles.

Contributors

Charu Aggarwal
IBM T. J. Watson Research Center
Hawthorne, New York, USA

Arindam Banerjee
Dept. of Computer Science and Eng.
University of Minnesota Twin Cities
Minneapolis, Minnesota, USA

Aharon Bar-Hillel
Intel Research
Haifa, Israel

Boaz Ben-moshe
Dept. of Computer Science
Simon Fraser University
Burnaby, Vancouver, Canada

Kristin P. Bennett
Dept. of Mathematical Sciences
Rensselaer Polytechnic Institute
Troy, New York, USA

Indrajit Bhattacharya
IBM India Research Laboratory
New Delhi, India

Jean-Francois Boulicaut
INSA-Lyon
Villeurbanne Cedex, France

Paul S. Bradley
Apollo Data Technologies
Bellevue, Washington, USA

Joachim M. Buhmann
ETH Zurich
Zurich, Switzerland

Rich Caruana
Dept. of Computer Science
Cornell University
Ithaca, New York, USA

David Cohn
Google, Inc.
Mountain View, California, USA

Ayhan Demiriz
Dept. of Industrial Eng.
Sakarya University
Sakarya, Turkey

Marie desJardins
Dept. of Computer Science and EE
University of Maryland Baltimore County
Baltimore, Maryland, USA

Martin Ester
Dept. of Computer Science
Simon Fraser University
Burnaby, Vancouver, Canada

Julia Ferraioli
Bryn Mawr College
Bryn Mawr, Pennsylvania, USA

Byron J. Gao
Dept. of Computer Science
Simon Fraser University
Burnaby, Vancouver, Canada

Stephen C. Gates
IBM T. J. Watson Research Center
Hawthorne, New York, USA

Rong Ge
Dept. of Computer Science
Simon Fraser University
Burnaby, Vancouver, Canada

Lise Getoor
Dept. of Computer Science and
UMIACS
University of Maryland
College Park, Maryland, USA

Joydeep Ghosh
Dept. of Elec. and Computer Eng.
University of Texas at Austin
Austin, Texas, USA

David Gondek
IBM T. J. Watson Research Center
Hawthorne, New York, USA

Jiawei Han
Dept. of Computer Science
University of Illinois
Urbana-Champaign, Illinois, USA

Alexander G. Hauptmann
School of Computer Science
Carnegie Mellon University
Pittsburgh, Pennsylvania, USA

Tomer Hertz
Microsoft Research
Redmond, Washington, USA

Zengjian Hu
Dept. of Computer Science
Simon Fraser University
Burnaby, Vancouver, Canada

Nicole Immorlica
Dept. of Computer Science
Northwestern University
Evanston, Illinois, USA

Anil K. Jain
Dept. of Computer Science and Eng.
Michigan State University
East Lansing, Michigan, USA

Laks V. S. Lakshmanan
Dept. of Computer Science
University of British Columbia
Vancouver, Canada

Tilman Lange
ETH Zurich
Zurich, Switzerland

Martin H. Law
Dept. of Computer Science and Eng.
Michigan State University
East Lansing, Michigan, USA

Todd K. Leen
Dept. of Computer Science and Eng.
Oregon Graduate Institute
Beaverton, Oregon, USA

Zhengdong Lu
Dept. of Computer Science and Eng.
Oregon Graduate Institute
Beaverton, Oregon, USA

James MacGlashan
Dept. of Computer Science and EE
University of Maryland Baltimore County
Baltimore, Maryland, USA

Andrew Kachites McCallum
Dept. of Computer Science
University of Massachusetts Amherst
Amherst, Massachusetts, USA

Raymond T. Ng
Dept. of Computer Science
University of British Columbia
Vancouver, Canada

Satoshi Oyama
Dept. of Social Informatics
Kyoto University
Kyoto, Japan

Ruggero G. Pensa
ISTI-CNR
Pisa, Italy

Céline Robardet
INSA-Lyon
Villeurbanne Cedex, France

Noam Shental
Dept. of Physics of Complex Systems
Weizmann Institute of Science
Rehovot, Israel

Katsumi Tanaka
Dept. of Social Informatics
Kyoto University
Kyoto, Japan

Anthony K. H. Tung
Dept. of Computer Science
National University of Singapore
Singapore

Daphna Weinshall
School of Computer Science and Eng.
and the Center for Neural Comp.
The Hebrew University of Jerusalem
Jerusalem, Israel

Anthony Wirth
Dept. of Computer Science
and Software Eng.
The University of Melbourne
Melbourne, Victoria, Australia

Rong Yan
IBM T. J. Watson Research Center
Hawthorne, New York, USA

Jie Yang
School of Computer Science
Carnegie Mellon University
Pittsburgh, Pennsylvania, USA

Philip Yu
IBM T. J. Watson Research Center
Hawthorne, New York, USA

Jian Zhang
Dept. of Statistics
Purdue University
West Lafayette, Indiana, USA

List of Tables

List of Figures

Contents

Chapter 1

Introduction

Sugato Basu

Google, Inc., `sugato@google.com`

Ian Davidson

University of California, Davis, `davidson@cs.ucdavis.edu`

Kiri L. Wagstaff

Jet Propulsion Laboratory, California Institute of Technology
`kiri.wagstaff@jpl.nasa.gov`

1.1 Background and Motivation

Clustering is an important tool for data mining, since it can identify major patterns or trends without any supervisory information such as data labels. It can be broadly defined as the process of dividing a set of objects into clusters, each of which represents a meaningful sub-population. The objects may be database records, nodes in a graph, words, images, or any collection in which individuals are described by a set of features or distinguishing relationships. Clustering algorithms identify coherent groups based on a combination of the assumed cluster structure (e.g., Gaussian distribution) and the observed data distribution. These methods have led to new insights into large data sets from a host of scientific fields, including astronomy [5], bioinformatics [13], meteorology [11], and others.

However, in many cases we have access to additional information or domain knowledge about the types of clusters that are sought in the data. This supplemental information may occur at the object level, such as class labels for a subset of the objects, complementary information about "true" similarity between pairs of objects, or user preferences about how items should be grouped; or it may encode knowledge about the clusters themselves, such as their position, identity, minimum or maximum size, distribution, etc.

The field of *semi-supervised* or *constrained* clustering grew out of the need to find ways to accommodate this information when it is available. While it is possible that a fully unsupervised clustering algorithm might naturally find a solution that is consistent with the domain knowledge, the most interesting cases are those in which the domain knowledge suggests that the default solution is not the one that is sought. Therefore, researchers began exploring principled methods of enforcing desirable clustering properties.

Initial work in this area proposed clustering algorithms that can incorporate pairwise constraints on cluster membership or learn problem-specific distance metrics that produce desirable clustering output. Subsequently, the research area has greatly expanded to include algorithms that leverage many additional kinds of domain knowledge for the purpose of clustering. In this book, we aim to provide a current account of the innovations and discoveries, ranging from theoretical developments to novel applications, associated with constrained clustering methods.

1.2   Initial Work: Instance-Level Constraints

A clustering problem can be thought of as a scenario in which a user wishes to obtain a partition Π_X of a data set X, containing n items, into k clusters ($\Pi_X = \pi_1 \cup \pi_2 \ldots \cup \pi_k$, $\bigcap \pi_i = \emptyset$). A *constrained clustering* problem is one in which the user has some pre-existing knowledge about their desired Π_X. The first introduction of constrained clustering to the machine learning and data mining communities [16, 17] focused on the use of instance-level constraints. A set of instance-level constraints, C, consists of statements about pairs of instances (objects). If two instances should be placed into the same cluster, a must-link constraint between them is expressed as $c_=(i,j)$. Likewise, if two instances should not be placed into the same cluster, $c_{\neq}(i,j)$ expresses a cannot-link constraint. When constraints are available, rather than returning partition Π_X that best satisfies the (generic) objective function used by the clustering algorithm, we require that the algorithm adapt its solution to accommodate C.

These instance-level constraints have several interesting properties. A collection of must-link constraints encodes an equivalence relation (symmetric, reflexive, and transitive) on the instances involved. The transitivity property permits additional must-link constraints to be inferred from the base set [4, 17]. More generally, if we produce a graph in which nodes represent instances and edges represent must-link relationships, then any must-link constraint that joins two connected components will entail an additional must-link constraint between all pairs of items in those components. Formally:

Observation 1 *Transitive Inference of Must-Link Constraints.* Let G_M *be the must-link graph for data set* X, *with a node for each* $x_i \in X$ *and an edge between nodes* i *and* j *for each* $c_=(i,j)$ *in* C. *Let* CC_1 *and* CC_2 *be two connected components in this graph. If there exists a must-link constraint*

$c_=(x, y)$, where $x \in CC_1$ and $y \in CC_2$, then we can infer $c_=(a, b)$ for all $a \in CC_1, b \in CC_2$.

In contrast, the cannot-link constraints do not encode an equivalence relation; it is not the case that $c_{\neq}(i, j)$ and $c_{\neq}(j, k)$ implies $c_{\neq}(i, k)$. However, when must-link and cannot-link constraints are combined, we can infer additional cannot-link constraints from the must-link relation.

Observation 2 ***Transitive Inference of Cannot-Link Constraints.*** *Let G_M be the must-link graph for data set X, with a node for each $x_i \in X$ and an edge between nodes i and j for each $c_=(i, j)$ in C. Let CC_1 and CC_2 be two connected components in this graph. If there exists a cannot-link constraint $c_{\neq}(x, y)$, where $x \in CC_1$ and $y \in CC_2$, then we can infer $c_{\neq}(a, b)$ for all $a \in CC_1, b \in CC_2$.*

The full set of constraints can be used in a variety of ways, including enforcing individual constraints and using them to learn a problem-specific distance metric.

1.2.1 Enforcing Pairwise Constraints

As noted above, the most interesting cases occur when the constraints are not consistent with the default partition obtained in the absence of any supervisory information. The first work in this area proposed a modified version of COBWEB [10] that strictly enforced pairwise constraints [16]. It was followed by an enhanced version of the widely used k-means algorithm [14] that could also accommodate constraints, called COP-KMEANS [17]. Table 1.1 reproduces the details of this algorithm. COP-KMEANS takes in a set of must-link $(C_=)$ and cannot-link $(C_{\neq})$ constraints. The essential change from the basic k-means algorithm occurs in step (2), where the decision about where to assign a given item x_i is constrained so that no constraints in C are violated. The satisfying condition is checked by the VIOLATE-CONSTRAINTS function. Note that it is possible for there to be no solutions that satisfy all constraints, in which case the algorithm exits prematurely.

When clustering with hard constraints, the goal is to minimize the objective function subject to satisfying the constraints. Here, the objective function is the vector quantization error, or variance, of the partition.

Problem 1 ***Clustering with Hard Constraints to Minimize Variance.*** *Given a set of data X, a distance function $D(x, y)$, a set of must-link constraints $C_=$, a set of cannot-link constraints $C_{\neq}$, and the desired number of clusters k, find Π_X (represented as a collection of k cluster centers μ_i) that minimizes*

$$V = \sum_{i=1...k} \sum_{x \in \pi_i} D(x, \mu_i),$$

TABLE 1.1: Constrained k-means algorithm for hard constraints

---

COP-KMEANS (data set X, number of clusters k, must-link constraints $C_= \subset X \times X$, cannot-link constraints $C_{\neq} \subset X \times X$)

1. Let $\mu_1 \ldots \mu_k$ be the k initial cluster centers.
2. For each instance $x_i \in X$, assign it to the closest cluster c such that VIOLATE-CONSTRAINTS$(x_i, c, C_=, C_{\neq})$ is false. If no such cluster exists, fail (return $\{\}$).
3. Update each cluster center μ_i by averaging all of the instances x_j that have been assigned to it.
4. Iterate between (2) and (3) until convergence.
5. Return $\{\mu_1 \ldots \mu_k\}$.

VIOLATE-CONSTRAINTS (instance x_i, cluster c, must-link constraints $C_=$, cannot-link constraints $C_{\neq}$)

1. For each $c_=(i, j) \in C_=$: If $x_j \notin c$, return true.
2. For each $c_{\neq}(i, j) \in C_{\neq}$: If $x_j \in c$, return true.
3. Otherwise, return false.

---

subject to the constraints $\forall c_=(x, y) \in C_=, \exists i : x, y \in \pi_i$ and $\forall c_{\neq}(x, y) \in C_{\neq}, \not\exists i : x, y \in \pi_i$.

Note that there is no assumption that the constraints help improve the objective function value obtained by the algorithm. That is, if Π_X^* is the partition that minimizes the objective function of the clustering algorithm, the constraints may be violated by Π_X^*. The algorithm's objective function provides a bias toward good clusterings, while the constraints **bias** the algorithm toward a smaller subset of good clusterings with an additional desirable property.

Consider the illustrative example shown in Figure 1.1. There are two reasonable ways to partition the data into two clusters: by weight or by height. An unsupervised clustering algorithm will ideally select one of these as the result, such as the weight-clustering in Figure 1.1a. However, we may prefer clusters that are separated by height. Figure 1.1b shows the result of clustering with two must-link constraints between instances with similar heights, and one cannot-link constraint between two individuals with different heights.

A drawback of the COP-KMEANS approach is that it may fail to find a satisfying solution even when one exists. This happens because of the greedy fashion in which items are assigned; early assignments can constrain later ones due to potential conflicts, and there is no mechanism for backtracking. Further, the constraints must be 100% accurate, since they will all be strictly

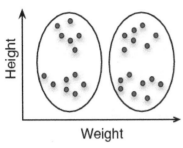
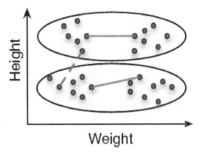

(a) No constraints: Clusters by weight   (b) 3 constraints: Clusters by height

FIGURE 1.1: Illustrative example: Clustering ($k = 2$) with hard pairwise constraints. Must-link constraints are indicated with solid lines, and cannot-link constraints are indicated with dashed lines.

enforced. Later work explored a constrained version of the EM clustering algorithm [15]. To accommodate noise or uncertainty in the constraints, other methods seek to satisfy as many constraints as possible, but not necessarily all of them [2, 6, 18]. Methods such as the MPCK-means algorithm permit the specification of an individual weight for each constraint, addressing the issue of variable per-constraint confidences [4]. MPCK-means imposes a penalty for constraint violations that is proportional to the violated constraint's weight.

1.2.2 Learning a Distance Metric from Pairwise Constraints

Another fruitful approach to incorporating constraints has arisen from viewing them as statements about the "true" distance (or similarity) between instances. In this view, a must-link constraint $c_=(i,j)$ implies that x_i and x_j should be close together, and a cannot-link constraint $c_{\neq}(i,j)$ implies that they should be sufficiently far apart to never be clustered together. This distance may or may not be consistent with the distance implied by the feature space in which those instances reside. This can happen when some of the features are irrelevant or misleading with respect to the clustering goal. Therefore, several researchers have investigated how a better distance metric can be learned from the constraints, specific to the problem and data at hand. Several such metric learning approaches have been developed; some are restricted to learning from must-link constraints only [1], while others can also accommodate cannot-link constraints [12, 19]. The HMRF-KMeans algorithm fuses both of these approaches (direct constraint satisfaction and metric learning) into a single probabilistic framework [2].

This problem can be stated as follows:

Problem 2 *Learning a Distance Metric from Constraints. Given a*

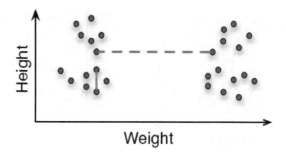

FIGURE 1.2: Illustrative example: Data shown in the modified feature space implied by the distance metric learned from two constraints.

set of data X, a set of must-link constraints $C_=$, and a set of cannot-link constraints $C_{\neq}$, find a distance metric D that minimizes

$$\sum_{c_=(x,y)} D(x,y)$$

and maximizes

$$\sum_{c_{\neq}(x,y)} D(x,y).$$

Figure 1.2 shows an example of using two constraints to learn a modified distance metric for the same data as shown in Figure 1.1. There is a must-link constraint between two items of different height and a cannot-link constraint between two items of different weight. The new distance metric compresses distance in the "height" direction and extends distance in the "weight" direction. A regular, unsupervised, clustering algorithm can be applied to the data with this new distance metric, and it will with high probability find a clustering that groups items of similar weight together.

1.3   Advances Contained in This Book

Since the initial work on constrained clustering, there have been numerous advances in methods, applications, and our understanding of the theoretical properties of constraints and constrained clustering algorithms. This book brings together several of these contributions and provides a snapshot of the current state of the field.

1.3.1   Constrained Partitional Clustering

The first five chapters of the book investigate ways in which instance-level, pairwise constraints can be used in ways that extend their original use in COBWEB and k-means clustering.

In "Semi-supervised Clustering with User Feedback," David Cohn, Rich Caruana, and Andrew K. McCallum propose an *interactive* approach to constrained clustering in which the user can iteratively provide constraints as feedback to refine the clusters towards the desired concept. Like active learning, this approach permits human effort to be focused on only those relationships that the algorithm cannot correctly deduce on its own. The results indicate that significant improvements can be made with only a few well chosen constraints. There has been further work on active learning for constraint selection in semi-supervised clustering [3], which is not included in this book.

Several methods have been proposed for incorporating pairwise constraints into EM clustering algorithms. In "Gaussian Mixture Models with Equivalence Constraints," Noam Shental, Aharon Bar-Hillel, Tomer Hertz, and Daphna Weinshall present two such algorithms, one for must-link and one for cannot-link constraints. In each case, the specified constraints restrict the possible updates made at each iteration of the EM algorithm, aiding it to converge to a solution consistent with the constraints. In "Pairwise Constraints as Priors in Probabilistic Clustering," Zhengdong Lu and Todd K. Leen describe an EM algorithm, penalized probabilistic clustering, that interprets pairwise constraints as *prior probabilities* that two items should, or should not, be assigned to the same cluster. This formulation permits both hard and soft constraints, allowing users to specify background knowledge even when it is uncertain or noisy. In "Clustering with Constraints: A Mean-Field Approximation Perspective," Tilman Lange, Martin H. Law, Anil K. Jain, and J. M. Buhmann extend this approach by introducing a weighting factor, η, that permits direct control over the *relative influence* of the constraints and the original data. This parameter can be estimated heuristically or specified by the user.

In "Constraint-Driven Co-Clustering of 0/1 Data," Ruggero G. Pensa, Celine Robardet, and Jean-Francois Boulicaut describe how pairwise constraints can be incorporated into *co-clustering* problems, where the goal is to identify clusters of items and features simultaneously. Co-clustering is often applied to "0/1" data, in which the features are binary (or Boolean) and denote the presence or absence of a given property. The authors also introduce *interval constraints*, which specify that a given cluster should include items with values within a given interval (for a feature with real-valued or otherwise rankable values).

1.3.2 Beyond Pairwise Constraints

The next five chapters of the book consider other types of constraints for clustering, distinct from pairwise must-link and cannot-link constraints.

In "On Supervised Clustering for Creating Categorization Segmentations," authors Charu Aggarwal, Stephen C. Gates, and Philip Yu consider the problem of using *a pre-existing taxonomy* of text documents as supervision in improving the clustering algorithm, which is subsequently used for classifying text documents into categories. In their experiments, they use the Yahoo! hierarchy as prior knowledge in the supervised clustering scheme, and demonstrate that the automated categorization system built by their technique can achieve equivalent (and sometimes better) performance compared to manually built categorization taxonomies at a fraction of the cost.

The chapter "Clustering with Balancing Constraints" by Arindam Banerjee and Joydeep Ghosh considers a scalable algorithm for creating balanced clusters, i.e., clusters of comparable sizes. This is important in applications like direct marketing, grouping sensor network nodes, etc. The *cluster size balancing constraints* in their formulation can be used for clustering both offline/batch data and online/streaming data. In "Using Assignment Constraints to Avoid Empty Clusters in k-Means Clustering," Ayhan Demiriz, Kristin P. Bennett, and Paul S. Bradley discuss a related formulation, where they consider constraints to prevent empty clusters. They incorporate explicit *minimum cluster size constraints* in the clustering objective function to ensure that every cluster contains at least a pre-specified number of points.

The chapter "Collective Relational Clustering" by Indrajit Bhattacharya and Lise Getoor discusses constrained clustering in the context of the problem of entity resolution (e.g., de-duplicating similar reference entries in the bibliographic database of a library). In their formulation, the similarity function between two clusters in the algorithm considers both the average attribute-level similarity between data instances in the clusters and *cluster-level relational constraints* (i.e., aggregate pairwise relational constraints between the constituent points of the clusters).

Finally, in "Non-Redundant Data Clustering," David Gondek considers a problem setting where *one possible clustering of a data set is provided as an input constraint*, and the task is to cluster the data set into groups that are different from the given partitioning. This is useful in cases where it is easy to find the dominant partitioning of the input data (e.g., grouping images in a face database by face orientation), but the user may be interested in biasing the clustering algorithm toward explicitly avoiding that partitioning and focusing on a non-dominant partitioning instead (e.g., grouping faces by gender).

1.3.3 Theory

The use of instance level constraints and clustering poses many computational challenges. It was recently proven that clustering with constraints raised an intractable feasibility problem [6, 8] for simply finding *any* clustering that satisfies all constraints via a reduction from graph coloring. It was later shown that attempts to side-step this feasibility problem by pruning constraint sets, or exactly or even approximately calculating k and trying to repair infeasible solutions, also lead to intractable problems [9]. Some progress has been made on generating easy to satisfy constraint sets [7] for k-means style clustering. The two chapters in this section have taken an alternative approach of carefully crafting useful variations of the clustering under the traditional constraints problem, and they provide approximation algorithms with useful performance guarantees.

In "Joint Cluster Analysis of Attribute Data and Relationship Data," Martin Ester, Rong Ge, Byron Gao, Zengjian Hu, and Boaz Ben-moshe introduce the Connected k-Center (CkC) problem, a variation of the k-Center problem with the internal connectedness constraint that any two entities in a cluster must be connected by an internal path. Their problem formulation offers the distinct advantage of taking into account attribute and relationship data. In addition, the k-Center problem is more amenable to theoretical analysis than k-means problems. After showing that the CkC problem is intractable, they derive a constant factor approximation algorithm, develop the heuristically inspired NetScan algorithm, and empirically show its scalability.

In "Correlation Clustering," Nicole Immorlica and Anthony Wirth explore the problem of clustering data with only constraints (advice) and *no* description of the data. Their problem formulation studies agreement with the possibly inconsistent advice in both a minimization and maximization context. In this formulation, k need not be specified a priori but instead can be directly calculated. The authors present combinatorial optimization and linear programming approximation algorithms that have O(log n) and factor 3 approximation guarantees. They conclude their chapter by showing several applications for correlation clustering including consensus clustering.

1.3.4 Applications

The initial applications of clustering with constraints were successful examples of the benefits of using constraints typically generated from labeled data. Wagstaff et al. illustrated their use for noun phrase coreference resolution and GPS lane finding [16, 17]. Basu et al. illustrated their use for text data [2, 4]. The authors in this section have greatly extended the application of clustering with constraints to relational, bibliographic, and even video data.

In "Interactive Visual Clustering for Relational Data," Marie desJardins, James MacGlashan, and Julia Ferraioli use constraints to interactively cluster relational data. Their interactive visual clustering (IVC) approach presents the data using a spring-embedded graph layout. Users can move groups of instance to form initial clusters after which constrained clustering algorithms are used to complete the clustering of the data set.

Two chapters focus on important problems relating to publication data. In "Distance Metric Learning from Cannot-be-linked Example Pairs, with Application to Name Disambiguation," Satoshi Oyama and Katsumi Tanaka provide a distance metric learning approach that makes use of cannot-link constraints to disambiguate author names in the DBLP database. They propose a problem formulation and a subsequent algorithm that is similar to support vector machines. They conclude their chapter by providing experimental results from the DBLP database. In "Privacy-Preserving Data Publishing: A Constraint-Based Clustering Approach," Anthony K. H. Tung, Jiawei Han, Laks V. S. Lakshmanan, and Raymond T. Ng build on their earlier published work on using existential constraints to control cluster size and aggregation level constraints to bound the maximum/minimum/average/sum of an attribute. Here, they apply this approach to privacy-preserving data publishing by using the existential and aggregation constraints to express privacy requirements.

Finally, in "Learning with Pairwise Constraints for Video Object Classification," Rong Yan, Jian Zhang, Jie Yang, and Alexander G. Hauptmann illustrate discriminative learners with constraints and their application to video surveillance data. They propose a discriminatory learning with constraints problem that falls under the rubric of regularized empirical risk minimization. They provide non-convex and convex loss functions that make use of constraints and derive several algorithms for these loss functions such as logistic regression and support vector machines. They provide a striking example of using constraints in streaming video by illustrating that automatically generated constraints can be easily created from the data in the absence of human labeling.

1.4   Conclusion

In the years since constrained clustering was first introduced as a useful way to integrate background knowledge when using the k-means clustering algorithm, the field has grown to embrace new types of constraints, use other clustering methods, and increase our understanding of the capabilities and limitations of this approach to data analysis. We are pleased to present so many of these advances in this volume, and we thank all of the contributors for putting in a tremendous amount of work. We hope readers will find this collection both interesting and useful.

There are many directions for additional work to extend the utility of constrained clustering methods. A persistent underlying question is the issue of where constraint information comes from, how it can be collected, and how much it should be trusted; the answer likely varies with the problem domain, and constrained clustering methods should accommodate constraints of differing provenance, value, and confidence. Like other semi-supervised learning methods, constrained clustering also raises interesting questions about the roles of the user and the algorithm; how much responsibility belongs to each? We look forward to the next innovations in this arena.

Acknowledgments

We thank Douglas Fisher for his thoughtful and thought-provoking comments, which contributed to the content of this chapter. We also thank the National Science Foundation for the support of our own work on constrained clustering via grants IIS-0325329 and IIS-0801528. The first author would additionally like to thank Google, IBM, and DARPA for supporting some of his work through their research grant, fellowship program, and contract #NBCHD030010 (Order-T310), respectively.

1.5   Notation and Symbols

The following table summarizes the notation that we shall use throughout this book.

Sets of Numbers	
$\mathbb{N}$	the set of natural numbers, $\mathbb{N} = \{1, 2, \dots\}$
$\mathbb{R}$	the set of reals
$[n]$	compact notation for $\{1, \dots, n\}$
$x \in [a, b]$	interval $a \leq x \leq b$
$x \in (a, b]$	interval $a < x \leq b$
$x \in (a, b)$	interval $a < x < b$
$|C|$	cardinality of a set C
Data	
$\mathcal{X}$	the input domain
d	(used if $\mathcal{X}$ is a vector space) dimension of $\mathcal{X}$
m	number of underlying classes in the labeled data
k	number of clusters (can be different from m)
l, u	number of labeled, unlabeled training examples
n	total number of examples, $n = l + u$
i, j	indices, often running over $[n]$ or $[k]$
x_i	input data point $x_i \in \mathcal{X}$
y_j	output cluster label $y_j \in [K]$
X	a sample of input data points, $X = \{X_l \cup X_u\}$
Y	output cluster labels, $Y = (y_1, \dots, y_n)$ and $Y = \{Y_l \cup Y_u\}$
Π_X	k block clustering (set partition) on X: $\{\pi_1, \pi_2 \dots \pi_k\}$
μ_i	the center of cluster π_i
$D(x, y)$	distance between points x and y
X_l	labeled part of X, $X_l = (x_1, \dots, x_l)$
Y_l	part of Y where labels are specified, $Y_l = (y_1, \dots, y_l)$
X_u	unlabeled part of X, $X_u = (x_{l+1}, \dots, x_{l+u})$
Y_u	part of Y without labels, $Y_u = (y_{l+1}, \dots, y_{l+u})$
C	set of constraints
W	weights on constraints
$C_=$	conjunction of must-link constraints
$C_{\neq}$	conjunction of cannot-link constraints
$c_=(i, j)$	must-link constraint between x_i and x_j
$c_{\neq}(i, j)$	cannot-link constraint between x_i and x_j
$w_=(i, j)$	weight on must-link constraint $c_=(i, j)$
$w_{\neq}(i, j)$	weight on cannot-link constraint $c_{\neq}(i, j)$
Kernels	
$\mathcal{H}$	feature space induced by a kernel
Φ	feature map, $\Phi : \mathcal{X} \to \mathcal{H}$
K	kernel matrix or Gram matrix, $K_{ij} = k(x_i, x_j)$

Vectors, Matrices, and Norms

1	vector with all entries equal to one
I	identity matrix
$A^\top$	transposed matrix (or vector)
A^{-1}	inverse matrix (in some cases, pseudo-inverse)
$\mathbf{tr}\,(A)$	trace of a matrix
$\mathbf{det}\,(A)$	determinant of a matrix
$\langle \mathbf{x}, \mathbf{x}' \rangle$	dot product between $\mathbf{x}$ and $\mathbf{x}'$
$\|\cdot\|$	2-norm, $\|\mathbf{x}\| := \sqrt{\langle \mathbf{x}, \mathbf{x} \rangle}$
$\|\cdot\|_p$	p-norm , $\|\mathbf{x}\|_p := \left(\sum_{i=1}^{N} |x_i|^p \right)^{1/p}$, $N \in \mathbb{N} \cup \{\infty\}$
$\|\cdot\|_\infty$	∞-norm , $\|\mathbf{x}\|_\infty := \sup_{i=1}^{N} |x_i|$, $N \in \mathbb{N} \cup \{\infty\}$

Functions

$\ln$	logarithm to base e
$\log_2$	logarithm to base 2
f	a function, often from $\mathcal{X}$ or $[n]$ to $\mathbb{R}$, $\mathbb{R}^M$ or $[M]$
$\mathcal{F}$	a family of functions
$L_p(\mathcal{X})$	function spaces, $1 \le p \le \infty$

Probability

$\mathrm{P}\{\cdot\}$	probability of a logical formula
$\mathrm{P}(C)$	probability of a set (event) C
$p(x)$	density evaluated at $x \in \mathcal{X}$
$\mathbf{E}\,[\cdot]$	expectation of a random variable
$\mathbf{Var}\,[\cdot]$	variance of a random variable
$\mathcal{N}(\mu, \sigma^2)$	normal distribution with mean μ and variance σ^2

Graphs

g	graph $\mathbf{g} = (V, E)$ with nodes V and edges E
$\mathcal{G}$	set of graphs
W	weighted adjacency matrix $(\mathbf{W}_{ij} \ne 0 \Leftrightarrow (i,j) \in E)$
D	(diagonal) degree matrix of a graph, $\mathbf{D}_{ii} = \sum_j W_{ij}$
$\mathcal{L}$	normalized graph Laplacian, $\mathcal{L} = \mathbf{D}^{-1/2} \mathbf{W} \mathbf{D}^{-1/2}$
L	un-normalized graph Laplacian, $L = \mathbf{D} - \mathbf{W}$

Miscellaneous

I_A	characteristic (or indicator) function on a set A i.e., $I_A(x) = 1$ if $x \in A$ and 0 otherwise
δ_{ij}	Kronecker δ ($\delta_{ij} = 1$ if $i = j$, 0 otherwise)
δ_x	Dirac δ, satisfying $\int \delta_x(y) f(y) dy = f(x)$
$O(g(n))$	a function $f(n)$ is said to be $O(g(n))$ if there exist constants $C > 0$ and $n_0 \in \mathbb{N}$ such that $|f(n)| \le Cg(n)$ for all $n \ge n_0$
$o(g(n))$	a function $f(n)$ is said to be $o(g(n))$ if there exist constants $c > 0$ and $n_0 \in \mathbb{N}$ such that $|f(n)| \ge cg(n)$ for all $n \ge n_0$
rhs/lhs	shorthand for "right/left hand side"
w.r.t.	with regard to
∎	the end of a proof

References

[1] A. Bar-Hillel, T. Hertz, N. Shental, and D. Weinshall. Learning a Mahalanobis metric from equivalence constraints. *Journal of Machine Learning Research*, 6:937–965, 2005.

[2] S. Basu, M. Bilenko, and R. J. Mooney. A probabilistic framework for semi-supervised clustering. In *Proceedings of the Tenth ACM SIGKDD International Conference on Knowledge Discovery and Data Mining*, pages 59–68, Seattle, WA, 2004.

[3] Sugato Basu, Arindam Banerjee, and Raymond J. Mooney. Active semi-supervision for pairwise constrained clustering. In *Proceedings of the Fourth SIAM International Conference on Data Mining (SDM-04)*, pages 333–344, April 2004.

[4] M. Bilenko, S. Basu, and R. J. Mooney. Integrating constraints and metric learning in semi-supervised clustering. In *Proceedings of the Twenty-First International Conference on Machine Learning*, pages 11–18, 2004.

[5] P. Cheeseman and J. Stutz. Bayesian classification (autoclass): Theory and results. In *Advances in Knowledge Discovery and Data Mining*, pages 153–180. Morgan Kaufmann, 1996.

[6] I. Davidson and S. S. Ravi. Clustering with constraints: Feasibility issues and the k-means algorithm. In *Proceedings of the 2005 SIAM International Conference on Data Mining*, pages 138–149, Newport Beach, CA, 2005.

[7] I. Davidson and S. S. Ravi. Generating easy sets of constraints for clustering. In *Proceedings of the 2006 AAAI Conference*, Boston, MA, 2006.

[8] I. Davidson and S. S. Ravi. The complexity of non-hierarchical clustering with instance and cluster level constraints. *Data Mining and Knowledge Discovery*, 14:25–61, 2007.

[9] I. Davidson and S. S. Ravi. Intractability and clustering with constraints. In *Proceedings of the 2007 ICML Conference*, Corvallis, OR, 2007.

[10] D. Fisher. Knowledge acquisition via incremental conceptual clustering. *Machine Learning*, 2:139–172, 1987.

[11] S. J. Gaffney, A. W. Robertson, P. Smyth, S. J. Camargo, and M. Ghil. Probabilistic clustering of extratropical cyclones using regression mixture models. Technical Report UCI-ICS 06-02, Bren School of Information and Computer Sciences, University of California, Irvine, January 2006.

[12] D. Klein, S. D. Kamvar, and C. D. Manning. From instance-level constraints to space-level constraints: Making the most of prior knowledge in data clustering. In *Proceedings of the Nineteenth International Conference on Machine Learning*, pages 307–313, 2002.

[13] N. Ling and Q. Yang. Special issue on machine learning and bioinformatics-part 1. *IEEE/ACM Transactions on Computational Biology and Bioinformatics*, 2(2), 2005.

[14] J. B. MacQueen. Some methods for classification and analysis of multivariate observations. In *Proceedings of the Fifth Symposium on Math, Statistics, and Probability*, volume 1, pages 281–297, Berkeley, CA, 1967. University of California Press.

[15] N. Shental, A. Bar-Hillel, T. Hertz, and D. Weinshall. Computing Gaussian mixture models with EM using equivalence constraints. In *Advances in Neural Information Processing Systems 16*, 2004.

[16] K. Wagstaff and C. Cardie. Clustering with instance-level constraints. In *Proceedings of the Seventeenth International Conference on Machine Learning*, pages 1103–1110, 2000.

[17] K. Wagstaff, C. Cardie, S. Rogers, and S. Schroedl. Constrained k-means clustering with background knowledge. In *Proceedings of the Eighteenth International Conference on Machine Learning*, pages 577–584, 2001.

[18] K. L. Wagstaff. *Intelligent Clustering with Instance-Level Constraints*. PhD thesis, Cornell University, August 2002.

[19] E. P. Xing, A. Y. Ng, M. I. Jordan, and S. Russell. Distance metric learning, with application to clustering with side-information. In *Advances in Neural Information Processing Systems 15*, 2003.

Chapter 2

Semi-Supervised Clustering with User Feedback

David Cohn

Google, Inc., `cohn@google.com`

Rich Caruana

Cornell University, `caruana@cs.cornell.edu`

Andrew Kachites McCallum

University of Massachusetts, Amherst, `mccallum@cs.umass.edu`

Abstract   We present an approach to clustering based on the observation that "it is easier to criticize than to construct." Our approach of *semi-supervised clustering* allows a user to iteratively provide feedback to a clustering algorithm. The feedback is incorporated in the form of constraints, which the clustering algorithm attempts to satisfy on future iterations. These constraints allow the user to guide the clusterer toward clusterings of the data that the user finds more useful. We demonstrate semi-supervised clustering with a system that learns to cluster news stories from a Reuters data set.[1]

2.1   Introduction

Consider the following problem: you are given 100,000 text documents (e.g., papers, newsgroup articles, or web pages) and asked to group them into classes or into a hierarchy such that related documents are grouped together. You are not told what classes or hierarchy to use or what documents are related. Your job is simply to create this taxonomy so that the documents can be browsed and accessed efficiently, either by yourself or by other people. While

---

[1] This work was originally circulated as an unpublished manuscript [4] when all the authors were at Justsystem Pittsburgh Research Center.

you may have some criterion in mind, you would probably be hard-pressed to express it algorithmically.

This problem is ubiquitous. The web has created a number of new examples of it, but it can be found in many fields that don't involve the web, as well as with many different types of "documents." Librarians, astronomers, biologists — practically everyone tasked with creating a taxonomy from data faces this problem in one form or another.

We propose the following iterative solution to this problem:

1. Give the 100,000 documents to an unsupervised clustering algorithm and have it cluster them.

2. Browse the resulting clusters and tell the system which clusters you like, and which clusters you don't like. Don't do this for all the clusters, just for some of the ones you browsed. Provide feedback to the system by saying *"This document doesn't belong in here," "Move this document to that cluster,"* or *"These two documents shouldn't be (or should be) in the same cluster."*

   Don't do this for all, or even many, of the documents; only for the few that look most out of place.

3. After your critique, re-cluster the documents, allowing the clustering algorithm to modify the the distance metric parameters to try to find a new clustering that satisfies the constraints you provided in the critique.

4. Repeat this until you are happy with the clustering.

This solution is distinct from both traditional supervised and unsupervised learning. Unsupervised clustering takes an unlabeled collection of data and, without intervention or additional knowledge, partitions it into sets of examples such that examples within clusters are more "similar" than examples between clusters. Much work in unsupervised clustering is dedicated to the problem of manually engineering similarity criteria that yield good partitioning of data for a given domain.

Supervised learning, on the other hand, assumes that the class structure or hierarchy already is known. It takes a set of examples with class labels, and returns a function that maps examples to class labels. The goal of supervised learning is to learn mappings that are accurate enough to be useful when classifying new examples, and perhaps to learn mappings that allow users to understand the relationships between the data and the labels, such as which features are important.

Semi-supervised clustering falls between the extremes of totally unsupervised clustering and totally supervised learning. The main goal of our approach to semi-supervised clustering is to allow a human to "steer" the clustering process so that examples can be partitioned into a useful set of clusters with minimum time and human effort. A secondary goal of semi-supervised clustering is to give the user a way to interact and play with the data so that they can understand it better.[2]

Our approach to semi-supervised clustering assumes that the human user has in their mind criteria that enable them to evaluate the quality of a clustering. It does not assume that the user is conscious of what they think defines a good clustering but that, as with art, they will "know it when they see it." Most importantly, semi-supervised clustering never expects a user to write a function that *defines* the clustering criterion. Instead, the user *interacts* with the clustering system, which attempts to learn a criterion that yields clusters the user is satisfied with. As such, one of the primary challenges of semi-supervised clustering is finding ways to elicit and make use of user feedback during clustering.

The remainder of this chapter describes one simple, illustrative way in which this may be accomplished. Other challenges that need to be addressed by future research on semi-supervised clustering are briefly described in the discussion section.

2.1.1   Relation to Active Learning

Semi-supervised clustering with user feedback is closely related to active learning [5]. In the most common form of active learning, a learning system attempts to identify which data points, if labeled by a human, would be most informative. In semi-supervised clustering, the *human* selects the data points, and puts on them a wide array of possible *constraints* instead of labels. These two key differences point toward some situations in which the semi-supervised approach is preferable.

1. In some clustering problems the desired similarity metric may be so different from the default that traditional active learning would make many inefficient queries. This problem also arises when there are many different plausible clusterings. Although less automated, a human browsing the data would do less work by selecting the feedback data points themself.

2. The intuitive array of possible constraints are easier to apply than labels, especially when the final clusters are not known in advance.

3. The very act of human browsing can lead to the discovery of what clusters are desired. Semi-supervised learning can thus be seen as a method of data exploration and pattern discovery, efficiently aided by cluster-based summarization.

---

[2]Demiriz et al. [7] independently introduced a semi-supervised clustering model similar to the one we describe here. The main distinction between our work and theirs is our use of iterative feedback to acquire labelings; Demiriz et al. assume that all available labels are given a priori.

However, the distinction with active learning is subjective. As we will see in Section 2.5.1, our system could easily be viewed as a practical application of learning by counterexamples [1] – one of the earliest and most powerful forms of active learning studied in the theory community.

Hybrid active-semi-supervised systems are also plausible. In situations with a large number of data points and data types that are difficult to browse, one could imagine a system that combines some of the automated selection of active learning with the human browsing of semi-supervised clustering. The active learner could make many disparate hypotheses about the underlying labels and present the examples that would be most indicative of each.

2.2 Clustering

Formally, clustering is the process of partitioning a data set into subsets such that all members of a given subset are "similar" according to some distance measure D. We will denote the distance between two examples x_1 and x_2 as $D(x_1, x_2)$. We can generalize this to refer to $D(y_1, y_2)$, the distance between two cluster centers, or $D(y_1, x_1)$, the distance between a cluster center and an example.

The two most popular approaches to clustering are agglomerative clustering and prototype-based clustering. In agglomerative clustering, each datum is initially placed in its own cluster. The clusters that are most similar (according to D) are iteratively merged, until the desired number of clusters is reached, or some limit on data likelihood or distortion is exceeded (see Hofmann and Buhmann [14] for an in-depth treatment of agglomerative clustering).

In prototype-based clustering, the final number of clusters is usually set a priori, and the corresponding prototypes are found using some form of Expectation Maximization (EM) [8]. Each prototype is initialized to some position (in our case, a randomly weighted sample of the training points). Examples are assigned to prototypes according to their similarity to each prototype (the assignment may be 0-1 or fractional, depending on the algorithm). Prototypes are then adjusted to maximize the data likelihood, or, equivalently, minimize the data distortion. The assignment/adjustment process is repeated until no significant changes result (see Meilă and Heckerman [17] for concise review of prototype-based clustering).

In the present chapter, we adopt a statistical prototype-based approach, resulting from the naive Bayes model of document generation [16].[3] Given a

---

[3] We reiterate that the approach described in this chapter is only for the point of exploration and illustration; the approach is, in theory, applicable to almost any clustering algorithm.

vocabulary V, a document is assumed to be a "bag of words" generated from a multinomial distribution θ. In this model, the probability of document x is

$$P(x) = \prod_{t_j \in V} P(t_j|\theta)^{N(t_j,x)},$$

where $P(t_j|\theta)$ is the parameterized probability of term t_j being generated, and $N(t_j, x)$ is the number of times t_j appears in the document. Each document x forms an estimate of a multinomial distribution θ_x; likewise, each cluster of documents π forms an estimate θ_π composed from the θ_x of its constituent documents.[4]

For clustering we assume that, instead of being produced by a single multinomial distribution, each of the observed documents was drawn from one of distributions $\theta_{\pi_1}, \theta_{\pi_2}, \ldots, \theta_{\pi_k}$, corresponding to the unknown distribution of clusters $\pi_1, \pi_2, \ldots, \pi_k$:

$$P(x) = \sum_i P(\pi_i)P(x|\pi_i) = \sum_i P(\pi_i) \prod_{t_j \in V} P(t_j|\theta_{\pi_i})^{N(t_j,x)}.$$

Our task is to estimate values for $P(\pi_i)$ and θ_{π_i}, which will in turn allow us to estimate cluster memberships $P(\pi_i|x)$ by Bayes rule:

$$P(\pi_i|x) = P(x|\pi_i)P(\pi_i)/P(x). \tag{2.1}$$

We find estimates for $P(\pi_i)$ and θ_{π_i} via the standard procedure for EM, beginning with randomized estimates of θ_{π_i} drawn as a weighted sample from the observations. Then, for each cluster π_i and document x, we compute $P(x|\theta_{\pi_i})$ and apply Equation 2.1 to compute $P(\pi_i|x)$. Each cluster is given partial ownership of a document proportional to $P(\pi_i|x)$. The parameters θ_{π_i} are recomputed as the weighted sum of their component documents, and the process is repeated. The algorithm is guaranteed to converge to a locally optimal clustering (see, e.g., MacKay [15] or Meilă and Heckerman [17] for details).

2.3   Semi-Supervised Clustering

The goodness of any clustering depends on how well the metric D matches the user's (perhaps unknown) internal model of the target domain. We propose allowing the user to impose their model on the metric via the clustering

---

[4]The estimates for term probabilities are derived from the relative term frequencies in the documents. Following McCallum and Nigam [16], we smooth with a LaPlacean prior to avoid zero term probabilities.

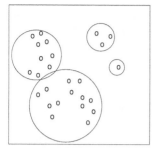 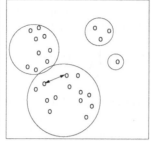 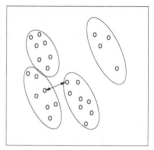

FIGURE 2.1: Illustration of semi-supervised clustering. Given an initial clustering, the user specifies two points that should not have been placed in the same cluster. The system warps its metric, allowing it to find a clustering that respects the constraint.

algorithm, by having the user provide the algorithm with feedback, and allowing it to alter the metric so as to accommodate that feedback. Not only is it easier to critique than to construct, but the user's criticism can take many forms — specifying that a particular example does/doesn't belong in a particular cluster, that two examples do/don't belong in the same cluster, or that a particular cluster is good (and should be preserved) or bad (and should be split up).

Feedback may be incorporated into the metric as constraints to be respected by the clustering algorithm. Consider two examples, x_1 and x_2, that are constrained by the user feedback to be in separate clusters. When the clustering algorithm attempts a partitioning which places x_1 and x_2 in the same cluster, the metric may be altered to increase the distance between x_1 and x_2 until one or the other of them falls in a different cluster (Figure 2.1). Other constraints may be implemented similarly, shrinking the distance between some example and a cluster prototype, or increasing the distance between a cluster prototype and all the examples assigned to it.

2.3.1 Implementing Pairwise Document Constraints

In this probabilistic setting, the natural measure of dissimilarity between two documents, x_1 and x_2, is the probability that they were generated by the same multinomial. From Pereira et al. [19], this is proportional to the *KL divergence to the mean* of their multinomial distributions:

$$D_{KLM}(x_1, x_2) = |x_1| D_{KL}(\theta_{x_1}, \theta_{x_1, x_2}) + |x_2| D_{KL}(\theta_{x_2}, \theta_{x_1, x_2}),$$

where $|x|$ is the length of document x, $D_{KL}(\theta_1, \theta_2)$ is the standard Kullback-Leibler divergence of θ_1 to θ_2, and θ_{x_1, x_2} is a distribution such that

$$P(t_j | \theta_{x_1, x_2}) = (P(t_j | \theta_{x_1}) + P(t_j | \theta_{x_2})) / 2.$$

The advantage of this measure is that it is symmetric, unlike standard KL divergence.

To implement our constraints, we augment the standard KL divergence $D(\theta_{x_1}, \theta_{x_2})$ with a weighting function

$$D'_{KL}(\theta_{x_1}, \theta_{x_2}) = \sum_{t_j \in V} \gamma_j \cdot P(t_j|\theta_{x_1}) \log \left(\frac{P(t_j|\theta_{x_2})}{P(t_j|\theta_{x_1})} \right)$$

where γ_j may be interpreted as indicating the importance of t_j for distinguishing x_1 and x_2. Then, given a constraint that x_1 and x_2 must be in separate clusters, we can warp the metric by computing

$$\frac{\partial D'_{KLM}(x_1, x_2)}{\partial \gamma_j} = |x_1| P(t_j|\theta_{x_1}) \log \left(\frac{P(t_j|\theta_{x_1 x_2})}{P(t_j|\theta_{x_1})} \right) +$$
$$|x_2| P(t_j|\theta_{x_2}) \log \left(\frac{P(t_j|\theta_{x_1 x_2})}{P(t_j|\theta_{x_2})} \right)$$

and hillclimbing over γ to increase the effective distance between the two. This gradient tells us the direction to move the γ's in order to increase (or decrease) the separation between two documents. (In the current experiments we constrain the γ's to be positive, but it might be interesting to relax this and allow some γ's to become negative.)

These γ's are incorporated back into the E-step of clustering algorithm as weights attached to the individual term frequencies:

$$P(x|\pi_i) = \prod_{t_j \in V} P(t_j|\theta_{\pi_i})^{\gamma_j N(t_j, x)}.$$

Intuitively, a small γ_j reduces the effect of t_j's presence or absence on document likelihood, effectively scaling its effect on the document's divergence from its cluster center. As such, we are able to inject a learned distance metric directly into the clustering algorithm.

2.3.2 Other Constraints

Other constraints described in the previous section may be similarly implemented by hillclimbing over the example-to-cluster and cluster-to-cluster distance. Note that the linear warping we describe will not guarantee that all constraints can be satisfied; some clusterings desired by the user may be non-convex and unrealizable in the space of models supported by naive Bayes. In this case, the hillclimbing will converge to a weighting that provides a local minimum of constraint violations. Local or nonlinear warpings of the distance metric, such as the ones described by Friedman [11] and Yianilos [21] may be of use in these situations.

2.4   Experiments

In this section, we illustrate the semi-supervised approach on a small document clustering problem. We use a set of 25 documents each from five Reuters topic areas: business, health, politics, sports, and tech. Starting from five randomly initialized prototypes, the EM-based clustering algorithm described in the previous sections finds clusters that maximize data likelihood.

Each time clustering converges, we add a constraint. We simulate a human user by identifying two documents from the same cluster whose sources are different Reuters topics, and constrain them to be in different clusters.[5] For each unsatisfied constraint, we reweight the divergence by a fixed number of hillclimbing steps, re-initialize the cluster prototypes, and repeat the EM training.

2.4.1   Clustering Performance

Figure 2.2 compares the performance of supervised, unsupervised, and semi-supervised learning. For unsupervised and semi-supervised learners, we plot cluster purity: the fraction of examples that would be classified correctly if all examples were assigned the majority label in each cluster. For the supervised learner, we plot both cluster purity and classification accuracy (generalization).

After only a few constraints have been added, cluster purity increases sharply over that of unsupervised clustering. It is not clear, however, how to fairly compare the performance of semi-supervised clustering with that of fully supervised clustering: constraints do not exactly correspond to labeled examples, and it is uncertain what constitutes a proper test set. In supervised learning, documents used for training are traditionally excluded from the test set, since their labels are already known. But the semi-supervised model clusters (and is tested on) the entire corpus, so it is also reasonable to gauge it against a supervised learner tested the same way. In the figure we show the cluster purity of supervised learning on the training set as well as its generalization to an independent test set.

The semi-supervised learner reaches its asymptotic performance after about 10 constraints have been added; the supervised learners require between 3 and 6 times more labeled examples to reach that level of performance.[6] It is in-

---

[5]A fully-operational semi-supervised clustering system would benefit from a graphical user interface that permits efficient browsing of the current clusters and supports easy specification of user constraints. See the discussion of Scatter/Gather later in this chapter.

[6]To assure ourselves that metric-warping alone wasn't responsible for the performance disparity, we also incorporated metric warping into the supervised clusterer, shrinking the divergence between a document and its assigned cluster. The addition resulted in no significant performance improvement.

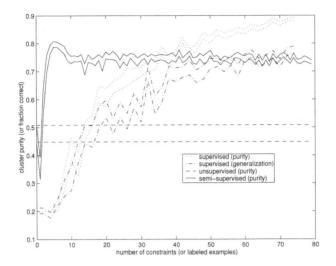

FIGURE 2.2: Learning curves for supervised, unsupervised, and semi-supervised clustering. For supervised clustering, cluster purity (measured on the train set) and generalization (measured on an independent test set) are plotted against the number of labeled examples; for semi-supervised clustering, purity is plotted against the number of constraints. Averages over 10 runs each, with the upper and lower lines indicating error bars at one standard deviation. See text for details.

teresting to note that the performance of the semi-supervised learner actually begins to decrease after roughly 20 constraints have been added. The Reuters data set contains many documents that appear under more than one topic (an identical article on Microsoft, for example, appears under both *business* and *tech*). We hypothesize that, in an attempt to separate these unseparable documents, the learner is pushing its term weightings to unhealthy extremes.

Experiments on a larger data set consisting of 20,000 USENET articles suggest that semi-supervised clustering is just as effective with large data sets. More importantly, these experiments show that semi-supervised clustering is able to cluster the same data according to different orthogonal criteria. This data set contains articles on four subjects: aviation simulators, real aviation, auto simulators, and real autos. Semi-supervised clustering can cluster the simulators and real groups together (e.g., aviation simulators and real aviation) or the auto and aviation groups together (e.g., aviation simulators and auto simulators) depending on the feedback provided by the user. In both cases it does so at about 80% accuracy with 10 constraints. When the distance metric is not adjusted, the same constraints give an average of only 64% accuracy. (Purely unsupervised clustering achieves only about 50% accuracy.)

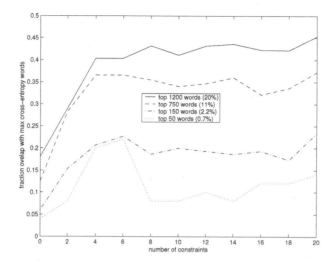

FIGURE 2.3: Fraction overlap of the top n weighted terms with top n terms ranked by information gain on fully-supervised data. As the number of constraints increases, there is increasing correlation with terms that strongly affect class conditional probabilities. Note that this overlap is achieved with far fewer constraints than the number of labels in the fully-supervised data.

2.4.2 Learning Term Weightings

Adjusting γ_j warps the metric by adjusting the resolving power of term t_j, essentially identifying which terms are most useful for distinguishing documents. If γ_j is large, small disparities in the frequency of t_j become important and will tend to separate documents; if γ_j is small, large disparities in frequency will be ignored.

Empirically, this behavior is borne out on the Reuters experiments. Terms that subjectively appear highly relevant for distinguishing topics, such as *Iraq*, *economy*, *weapons* and *council* are given large weightings. We computed the information gain of t_j using all document labels [18], and compared it with γ_j. Figure 2.3 shows the overlap between the top-weighted $n\%$ terms in the vocabulary with the same terms ranked by information gain. After about a dozen constraints, semi-supervised clustering learns term weightings with moderate overlap to the term weightings learned by supervised learning from all 125 document labels.

2.5   Discussion

This chapter only scratches the surface of semi-supervised clustering with user feedback. There are still many issues to be addressed; we touch on a few of these next.

2.5.1   Constraints vs. Labels

When applying supervised learning to classification problems, it is assumed that the users know the target classes and have labeled examples from each target class. In many interesting problems, this is an unrealistic assumption. A semi-supervised system allows users to give label-like information to the learner without having to know labels. Although user feedback in semi-supervised clustering serves a similar role as class labels serve in supervised learning, comparing supervised learning with semi-supervised clustering is an apples–to–oranges comparison. Semi-supervised clustering usually will be applied to problems where labels are not readily available. However, evaluating clustering systems is difficult and usually subjective. We compare the performance of semi-supervised clustering to supervised learning using a labeled data set principally to avoid this subjectivity.

The performance disparity between supervised and semi-supervised clustering is surprising. While we have argued that it is easier to provide constraints than labels, constraints also provide less information than labels. Constraints don't require the user to know the correct label (or even what labels exist!) — only the relationship among pairs or sets of labels. There are only 125 possible labels in the small Reuters data set, but thousands of possible separation constraints. Yet empirically, even with very few constraints, the semi-supervised learner is able to perform surprisingly well.

One explanation is in the connection to active learning. As a means of user feedback, the addition of a constraint indicates a problem and effectively acts as a counterexample for the present clustering. Counterexamples are a powerful tool for doing active learning, which, in some situations, are much more efficient than learning from randomly labeled examples [1]. As such, the user, by iteratively directing the clusterer's attention toward points that are incorrectly clustered, gives a semi-supervised clustering system the many advantages of an active learning system.

2.5.2   Types of User Feedback

As we have discussed, there are many different types of feedback that users might provide to a semi-supervised clustering system. One type of feedback is the constraints on individual data points and clusters we used earlier. But many other forms of feedback might prove useful as well. For example, a user might tell the system that the current clustering is too coarse or too fine. Or the user might point to a cluster and indicate that the cluster is bad without saying how it is bad. Similarly, a user might indicate that a cluster is good, suggesting that future re-clusterings of the data should attempt to maintain this cluster. Users might also give feedback that is not cluster specific, such as telling the system that the entire clustering looks bad and that the next clustering should be very different.

Some types of user feedback may require adaptive clustering that cannot be easily handled by the γ weighting scheme we used above. For example, we considered an approach to finding good—but qualitatively different—clusterings of the same data by exploiting EM's *weakness* for getting trapped in local minima. Different local minima may capture qualitatively different ways of clustering the data, one of which may better match the user's internal preference function than the deepest minima the system can find. In the long run we hope to develop a general framework for representing user feedback about clusters.

2.5.3 Other Applications

We believe there are many applications of feedback-driven semi-supervised clustering. Imagine a Yahoo! hierarchy for web pages that allows the user to tailor the hierarchy to better match their own interests by providing feedback while browsing. Similarly, consider an automatic e-mail system in which a user allows the system to cluster e-mail into related mailboxes instead of manually specifying the mailboxes. Semi-supervised feedback would allow the user to tailor mailbox clusters to fit their (possibly changing) needs. As a different example, consider a user clustering proteins into homology groups (groups of proteins with similar structures). Large proteins have complex structures and could be clustered many different ways. A feedback-driven semi-supervised clustering system would allow the user to explore many different ways the proteins might be clustered and to find clusterings most suitable to their purposes.

2.5.4 Related Work

The core operation of semi-supervised clustering involves learning a distance metric, of which a great deal of work has been done for classification problems (see Hastie and Tibshirani [13] for an overview); more recently, researchers have begun applying these techniques to clustering and other forms of machine learning (see, e.g., Xing et al. [20]).

As indicated earlier, our model is most similar to the work of Demiriz et al. They report how a fixed set of labeled examples may be used to bias a clustering algorithm; we investigate how a user, interacting with the system, may efficiently guide the learner to a desired clustering.

In the time since this work was first presented, there has been a great deal of research in improving clusterings by the (semi-supervised) learning of a distance measure. Instead of attempting a complete list of references here, we refer the reader the references in Chapter 1 and to the other, more recent contributions in this volume.

Our technique of incorporating user feedback is a cousin to relevance feedback, a technique for information retrieval [2]. Given a query and initial set of retrieved documents, relevance feedback asks the user to tag documents as being more or less relevant to the query being pursued. As the process is iterated, the retrieval system builds an increasingly accurate model of what the user is searching for.

The question of how a user (or teacher) may best select examples to help a learner identify a target concept is the focus of much work in computational learning theory. See Goldman and Kearns [12] for a detailed treatment of the problem.

The Scatter/Gather algorithm [6] is an interactive clustering algorithm designed for information retrieval. The system provides an initial clustering of data. When the user selects a subset of the clusters for further examination, the system gathers their components and regroups them to form new clusters. Scatter/Gather aims at pursuing and finding structure in a small part of a corpus. This makes it an interesting complement to our approach: Scatter/Gather may provide an effective means for browsing and focusing on clusters of interest, and semi-supervised learning may be an effective means of improving the quality of those clusters.

Note that we do not compare our performance to that of other purely unsupervised clustering systems such as AutoClass [3], COBWEB [9], or Iterative Optimization [10]. The contribution of our work is not to introduce a new clustering *algorithm*, but an approach that allows user feedback to guide the clustering. While we have illustrated our approach on a relatively simple system, we believe it is equally applicable to more sophisticated algorithms, and expect that it will provide similar improvements over the unsupervised variants.

References

[1] Dana Angluin. Learning regular sets from queries and counterexamples. *Information and Computation*, 75(2):87–106, 1987.

[2] Chris Buckley and Gerard Salton. Optimization of relevance feedback weights. In *Proceedings of the 18th Annual International Association for Computing Machinery (ACM) Special Interest Group on Informa-*

tion Retrieval Conference on Research and Development in Information Retrieval, pages 351–357. ACM Press, 1995.

[3] Peter Cheeseman, James Kelly, Matthew Self, John Stutz, Will Taylor, and Don Freeman. Autoclass: A Bayesian classification system. In *Readings in Knowledge Acquisition and Learning: Automating the Construction and Improvement of Expert Systems*, pages 431–441. Morgan Kaufmann, 1993.

[4] David Cohn, Rich Caruana, and Andrew McCallum. Semi-supervised clustering with user feedback. Unpublished manuscript (later released as Cornell University Technical Report TR2003-1892), 1999.

[5] David Cohn, Zoubin Ghahramani, and Michael I. Jordan. Active learning with statistical models. *Journal of Artificial Intelligence Research*, 4:129–145, 1996.

[6] Douglass R. Cutting, Jan O. Pedersen, David Karger, and John W. Tukey. Scatter/gather: A cluster-based approach to browsing large document collections. In *Proceedings of the 15th Annual International Association for Computing Machinery (ACM) Special Interest Group on Information Retrieval Conference on Research and Development in Information Retrieval*, pages 318–329, 1992.

[7] A. Demiriz, K. P. Bennett, and M. J. Embrechts. Semi-supervised clustering using genetic algorithms. In *Proceedings of Artificial Neural Networks in Engineering*, 1999.

[8] A. P. Dempster, N. M. Laird, and D. B. Rubin. Maximum likelihood from incomplete data via the em algorithm. *Journal of the Royal Statistical Society Series B (Methodological)*, 39(1):1–38, 1977.

[9] Doug H. Fisher. Knowledge acquisition via incremental conceptual clustering. *Machine Learning*, 2:139–172, 1987.

[10] Doug H. Fisher. Iterative optimization and simplification of hierarchical clusterings. *Journal of Artificial Intelligence Research*, 4:147–180, 1996.

[11] Jerome Friedman. Flexible metric nearest neighbor classication. Technical Report 113, Stanford University, Department of Statistics, 1994.

[12] Sally A. Goldman and Michael J. Kearns. On the complexity of teaching. *Journal of Computer and System Sciences*, 50(1):20–31, 1995.

[13] Trevor Hastie and Rob Tibshirani. Discriminant adaptive nearest neighbor classification. *Institute of Electrical and Electronics Engineers (IEEE) Transactions on Pattern Analysis and Machine Intelligence*, 18:607–616, 1996.

[14] Thomas Hofmann and Joachim M. Buhmann. Pairwise data clustering by deterministic annealing. *Institute of Electrical and Electronics*

Engineers (IEEE) Transactions on Pattern Analysis and Machine Intelligence, 19(1):1–14, 1997.

[15] David J.C. MacKay. *Information Theory, Inference and Learning Algorithms*. Cambridge University Press, 2003.

[16] Andrew McCallum and Kamal Nigam. A comparison of event models for naive Bayes text classification. In *Workshop on Learning for Text Categorization at the 15th Conference of the American Association for Artificial Intelligence*, 1998.

[17] Marina Meilă and David Heckerman. An experimental comparison of several clustering and initialization methods. In *Proceedings of the 14th Conference on Uncertainty in Artificial Intelligence (UAI 98*, pages 386–395. Morgan Kaufmann, 1998.

[18] Tom M. Mitchell. *Machine Learning*. McGraw-Hill, 1997.

[19] Fernando Pereira, Naftali Tishby, and Lillian Lee. Distributional clustering of English words. In *Proceedings of the 31st Annual Meeting on Association for Computational Linguistics*, pages 183–190. Association for Computational Linguistics, 1993.

[20] Eric P. Xing, Andrew Y. Ng, Michael I. Jordan, and Stuart Russell. Distance metric learning with application to clustering with side-information. In S. Becker, S. Thrun, and K. Obermayer, editors, *Advances in Neural Information Processing Systems 15*, pages 505–512. MIT Press, 2003.

[21] Peter N. Yianilos. Metric learning via normal mixtures. Technical report, NEC Research Institute, 1995.

Chapter 3

Gaussian Mixture Models with Equivalence Constraints

Noam Shental

Weizmann Institute of Science, `noam.shental@weizmann.ac.il`

Aharon Bar-Hillel

Intel Research, `aharon.bar-hillel@intel.com`

Tomer Hertz

Microsoft Research, `hertz@microsoft.com`

Daphna Weinshall

The Hebrew University of Jerusalem Israel, `daphna@cs.huji.ac.il`

Abstract   Gaussian Mixture Models (GMMs) have been widely used to cluster data in an unsupervised manner via the Expectation Maximization (EM) algorithm. In this chapter we suggest a semi-supervised EM algorithm that incorporates equivalence constraints into a GMM. Equivalence constraints provide information about pairs of data points, indicating whether the points arise from the same source (a must-link constraint) or from different sources (a cannot-link constraint). These constraints allow the EM algorithm to converge to solutions that better reflect the class structure of the data. Moreover, in some learning scenarios equivalence constraints can be gathered automatically while they are a natural form of supervision in others. We present a closed form EM algorithm for handling must-link constraints, and a generalized EM algorithm using a Markov network for incorporating cannot-link constraints. Using publicly available data sets, we demonstrate that incorporating equivalence constraints leads to a considerable improvement in clustering performance. Our GMM-based clustering algorithm significantly outperforms two other available clustering methods that use equivalence constraints.

3.1 Introduction

Mixture models are a powerful tool for probabilistic modelling of data, which have been widely used in various research areas such as pattern recognition, machine learning, computer vision, and signal processing [13, 14, 18]. Such models provide a principled probabilistic approach to cluster data in an unsupervised manner [24, 25, 30, 31]. In addition, their ability to represent complex density functions has also made them an excellent choice in density estimation problems [20, 23].

Mixture models are usually estimated using the efficient Expectation Maximization (EM) algorithm [12, 31], which converges to a local maximum of the likelihood function. When the component densities arise from the exponential family, the EM algorithm has closed form update rules, which make it very efficient. For this reason it is not surprising that most of the literature on mixture models has focused on Gaussian mixtures (GMMs). When such mixtures are used to cluster data, it is usually assumed that each class is represented as a single Gaussian component within the mixture.[1]

Since GMMs can be estimated in unsupervised and supervised settings, they have also been adapted to semi-supervised scenarios. In these scenarios, we are provided with an unlabeled data set and with some additional side-information. The two most common types of side-information considered in the literature are partial labels and equivalence constraints (see Section 3.5 for more details).

The additional side-information provided can help the algorithm to uncover the underlying class structure in the data. Furthermore, when the data originates from the assumed mixture model, side-information can be used to alleviate local maxima problems, often encountered in EM, by constraining the search space of the algorithm. More interestingly, in cases where the data distribution does not correspond to class labels, equivalence constraints may help steer the EM algorithm toward the required solution. Incorporating equivalence constraints modifies the likelihood objective function, which EM seeks to maximize, thus allowing the algorithm to choose clustering solutions that would have been rejected by an unconstrained EM algorithm due to their relatively low likelihood score. Two illustrative examples of this advantage are shown in Fig. 3.1.

In this chapter we suggest a semi-supervised EM algorithm for a GMM that incorporates equivalence constraints. An equivalence constraint determines whether a pair of data points were generated by the same source (must-link constraint) or by different sources (cannot link constraint). Equivalence constraints carry *less* information than explicit labels of the original data points.

---

[1]When this assumption does not hold, it is possible to model the data using a hierarchical mixture model in which each class is represented using a set of models within the mixture.

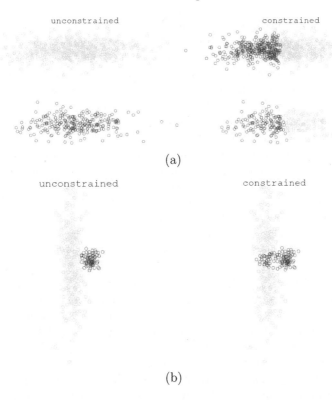

(a)

(b)

FIGURE 3.1: Two illustrative examples that demonstrate the benefits of incorporating equivalence constraints into the EM algorithm. (a) The data set consists of two *vertically aligned* non-Gaussian classes (each consisting of two halves of a Gaussian distribution). Left: Given no additional information, the unconstrained EM algorithm identifies two *horizontal* Gaussian classes, and this can be shown to be the maximum likelihood solution (with log likelihood of -3500 vs. log likelihood of -2800 for the solution shown on the right). Right: Using additional side-information in the form of equivalence constraints between the right and left halves of the Gaussians modifies the likelihood function, and the constrained EM algorithm obtains a vertical partition as the most likely solution. (b) The data set consists of two Gaussian classes (horizontal and vertical) with partial overlap. Left: Without constraints the most likely solution consists of two *non*-overlapping sources. Right: Using class relevant constraints the correct model with overlapping classes was obtained as the most likely solution. In all plots only the class assignments of *unconstrained* points are shown.

This can be seen by observing that a set of labeled points can be easily used to extract a set of equivalence constraints: any pair of points with identical labels form a must-link constraint, while any pair of points with different labels form a cannot-link constraint. The opposite is not true. Transforming equivalence constrains into labels can only be done when the entire set of pairwise constraints are provided, a requirement that is usually far from being fulfilled. However, unlike labels, in some scenarios equivalence constraints can be extracted automatically or with a minimal amount of supervision (see Section 3.4 for more details). In such cases, we show that equivalence constraints may provide significantly better data clustering.

Our semi-supervised EM algorithm uses an unlabeled data set augmented by equivalence constraints. The formulation allows to incorporate both must-link and cannot-link constraints. As we will show, the equivalence constraints are used to limit the space of possible assignments of the hidden variables in the E step of the algorithm. An important advantage of this approach is that the probabilistic semantics of the EM procedure allows for the introduction of equivalence constraints in a principled manner, unlike several other heuristic approaches to this problem.

While introducing must-link constraints is fairly straightforward, the introduction of cannot-link constraints is more complex and may require some approximations. We therefore begin by presenting the case of must-link constraints (Section 3.2.2) and then proceed to the case of cannot-link constraints (Section 3.2.3). We then discuss the case in which both types of constraints are provided (Section 3.2.4). Experimental results of our algorithm are presented in Section 3.3 using a number of data sets from the UCI repository and a large database of facial images [15]. The algorithm's performance is compared with two previously suggested constrained clustering algorithms: constrained k-means (COP k-means) [37] and constrained complete linkage [28]. Our experiments show that the constrained EM algorithm provides significantly better clustering results when compared with these two algorithms. Section 3.4 provides some important motivations for semi-supervised learning using equivalence constraints and briefly discusses its relation to semi-supervised learning from *partial labels*. Section 3.5 discusses some related work on constrained clustering. Finally, Section 3.6 provides a short discussion of the method's advantages and limitations and the relation between constrained clustering and distance learning algorithms.[2]

3.2 Constrained EM: The Update Rules

A Gaussian mixture model (GMM) is a parametric statistical model that assumes the data originates from a weighted sum of several Gaussian sources.

---

[2]A Matlab implementation of the algorithm can be obtained from http://www.cs.huji.ac.il/~daphna.

More formally, a GMM is given by: $p(x|\Theta) = \Sigma_{l=1}^{M}\alpha_l p(x|\theta_l)$ where M denotes the number of Gaussian sources in the GMM, α_l denotes the weight of each Gaussian, and θ_l denotes its respective parameters.

EM is often the method of choice for estimating the parameter set of the model (Θ) using unlabeled data [12]. The algorithm iterates between two steps:

- E-step: Calculate the expectation of the log-likelihood over all possible assignments of data points to sources.

- M-step: Maximize the expectation by differentiating w.r.t the current parameters.

Equivalence constraints modify the E-step in the following way: Instead of summing over *all* possible assignments of data points to sources, we sum only over assignments that comply with the given constraints. For example, if points x_i and x_j form a must-link constraint, we only consider assignments in which both points are assigned to the *same* Gaussian source. On the other hand, if these points form a cannot-link constraint, we only consider assignments in which each of the points is assigned to a *different* Gaussian source.

It is important to note that there is a basic difference between must-link and cannot-link constraints: While must-link constraints are transitive (i.e., a group of pairwise must-link constraints can be merged using transitive closure), cannot-link constraints are not transitive. The outcome of this difference is expressed in the complexity of incorporating each type of constraints into the EM formulation. Therefore, we begin by presenting a formulation for must-link constraints (Section 3.2.2) and then move on to cannot-link constraints (Section 3.2.3). We conclude by presenting a unified formulation for both types of constraints (Section 3.2.4).

3.2.1 Notations

The following notations are used:

- $p(x) = \sum_{l=1}^{M} \alpha_l \, p(x|\theta_l)$ denotes our GMM. Each $p(x|\theta_l)$ is a Gaussian parameterized by $\theta_l = (\mu_l, \Sigma_l)$, where μ_l is the distribution's center and Σ_l its covariance matrix. $\{\alpha_l\}$ are the mixing coefficients and $\sum_{l=1}^{M} \alpha_l = 1$.

- X denotes the set of all points, $X = \{x_i\}_{i=1}^{n}$.

- Y denotes the assignment of all points to sources.

- E_C denotes the event $\{Y$ complies with the constraints$\}$.

- A *chunklet* denotes a small subset of constrained points that originate from the same source (i.e., that are must-linked to one another).

3.2.2 Incorporating Must-Link Constraints

In this setting we are given a set of unlabeled data points and a set of must-link constraints. Since must-link constraints may be grouped using transitive closure, we obtain a set of *chunklets*. Hence the data set is initially partitioned into chunklets. Note that unconstrained points can be described as chunklets of size one.

- Let $\{X_j\}_{j=1}^{L}$ denote the set of all chunklets, and $\{Y_j\}_{j=1}^{L}$ denote the set of assignments of chunklet points to sources.

- The points that belong to a certain chunklet are denoted $X_j = \{x_j^1, \ldots, x_j^{|X_j|}\}$, where $X = \bigcup_j X_j$.

In order to write down the likelihood of a given assignment of points to classes, a probabilistic model of how chunklets are obtained must be specified. We consider two such models:

1. A source is sampled i.i.d according to the prior distribution over sources, and then points are sampled i.i.d from that source to form a chunklet.

2. Data points are first sampled i.i.d from the full probability distribution. From this sample, pairs of points are randomly chosen according to a uniform distribution. In case both points in a pair belong to the same source a must-link constraint is formed (and a cannot-link if formed when they belong to different sources). Chunklets are then obtained using transitive closure over the sampled must-link constraints.

The first assumption is justified when chunklets are automatically obtained from sequential data with the Markovian property. The second sampling assumption is justified when equivalence constraints are obtained via *distributed learning*. (For more details regarding these two scenarios see Section 3.4.) When incorporating these sampling assumptions into the EM algorithm, different algorithms emerge: With the first assumption we obtain closed-form update rules for all of the GMM parameters. When the second sampling assumption is used there is no closed-form solution for the sources' weights. We therefore derive the update rules under the first sampling assumption, and then briefly discuss the second sampling assumption.

3.2.2.1 Update Equations When Chunklets are Sampled i.i.d.

In order to derive the update equations of our constrained GMM model, we must compute the expectation of the log likelihood, which is defined as:

$$
\mathbf{E}\left[\log(p(X, Y|\Theta^{new}, E_C))|X, \Theta^{old}, E_C\right]
$$
$$
= \sum_Y \log(p(X, Y|\Theta^{new}, E_C)) \cdot p(Y|X, \Theta^{old}, E_C) \quad (3.1)
$$

In (3.1) $\sum_Y$ denotes the summation over all assignments of points to sources: $\sum_Y \equiv \sum_{y_1=1}^{M} \cdots \sum_{y_n=1}^{M}$. In the following discussion we shall also reorder the sum according to chunklets: $\sum_Y \equiv \sum_{Y_1} \cdots \sum_{Y_L}$, where $\sum_{Y_j}$ stands for $\sum_{y_1^j} \cdots \sum_{y_{|X_j|}^j}$.

Calculating the Posterior probability $p(Y|X, \Theta^{old}, E_C)$: Using Bayes rule we can write

$$p(Y|X, \Theta^{old}, E_C) = \frac{p(E_C|Y, X, \Theta^{old})\, p(Y|X, \Theta^{old})}{\sum_Y p(E_C|Y, X, \Theta^{old})\, p(Y|X, \Theta^{old})} \qquad (3.2)$$

From the definition of E_C it follows that

$$p(E_C|Y, X, \Theta^{old}) = \prod_{j=1}^{L} \delta_{Y_j}$$

where $\delta_{Y_j} \equiv \delta_{y_1^j, \ldots, y_{|X_j|}^j}$ equals 1 if all the points in chunklet i have the same source, and 0 otherwise.

Using the assumption of chunklet independence we have:

$$p(Y|X, \Theta^{old}) = \prod_{j=1}^{L} p(Y_j|X_j, \Theta^{old})$$

Therefore (3.2) can be rewritten as:

$$p(Y|X, \Theta^{old}, E_C) = \frac{\prod_{j=1}^{L} \delta_{Y_j}\, p(Y_j|X_j, \Theta^{old})}{\sum_{Y_1} \cdots \sum_{Y_L} \prod_{j=1}^{L} \delta_{Y_j}\, p(Y_j|X_j, \Theta^{old})} \qquad (3.3)$$

The complete data likelihood $p(X, Y|\Theta^{new}, E_C)$: This likelihood can be written as:

$$p(X, Y|\Theta^{new}, E_C) = p(Y|\Theta^{new}, E_C)\, p(X|Y, \Theta^{new}, E_C)$$
$$= p(Y|\Theta^{new}, E_C) \prod_{i=1}^{n} p(x_i|y_i, \Theta^{new})$$

where the last equality is due to the independence of data points, given the assignment to sources. Using Bayes rule and the assumption of chunklet independence, we can write:

$$p(Y|\Theta^{new}, E_C) = \frac{\prod_{j=1}^{L} \delta_{Y_j}\, p(Y_j|\Theta^{new})}{\sum_{Y_1} \cdots \sum_{Y_L} \prod_{j=1}^{L} \delta_{Y_j}\, p(Y_j|\Theta^{new})}$$

Using the notation $Z \equiv \sum_{Y_1} \cdots \sum_{Y_L} \prod_{j=1}^{L} \delta_{Y_j} \, p(Y_j | \Theta^{new})$, the likelihood can be rewritten as:

$$p(X, Y | \Theta^{new}, E_C) = \frac{1}{Z} \prod_{j=1}^{L} \delta_{Y_j} \, p(Y_j | \Theta^{new}) \prod_{i=1}^{n} p(x_i | y_i, \Theta^{new}) \qquad (3.4)$$

The first sampling assumption introduced means that a chunklet's source is sampled once for all the chunklet's points, i.e., $p(Y_j | \Theta^{new}) = \alpha_{Y_j}$. Under this sampling assumption, Z—the normalizing constant—equals 1. Therefore, the resulting log likelihood is

$$\log \, p(X, Y | \Theta^{new}, E_C) =$$

$$\sum_{j=1}^{L} \sum_{x_i \in X_j} \log \, p(x_i | y_i, \Theta^{new}) + \sum_{j=1}^{L} \log(\alpha_{Y_j}) + \sum_{j=1}^{L} \log(\delta_{Y_J})$$

Maximizing the expected log likelihood: We substitute (3.3) and (3.4) into (3.1) to obtain (after some manipulations) the following expression:

$$\mathbf{E} \left[\log(p(X, Y | \Theta^{new}, E_C)) | X, \Theta^{old}, E_C \right] =$$

$$\sum_{l=1}^{M} \sum_{j=1}^{L} p(Y_j = l | X_j, \Theta^{old}) \sum_{x_i \in X_j} \log \, p(x_i | l, \Theta^{new}) + \sum_{l=1}^{M} \sum_{j=1}^{L} p(Y_j = l | X_j, \Theta^{old}) \, \log \, \alpha_l$$

$$(3.5)$$

where the chunklet posterior probability is:

$$p(Y_j = l | X_j, \Theta^{old}) = \frac{\alpha_l^{old} \prod_{x_i \in X_j} p(x_i | y_i^j = l, \Theta^{old})}{\sum_{m=1}^{M} \alpha_m^{old} \prod_{x_i \in X_j} p(x_i | y_i^j = m, \Theta^{old})}$$

In order to find the update rule for each parameter, we differentiate (3.5) with respect to μ_l, Σ_l, and α_l, to get the following update equations:

$$\alpha_l^{new} = \frac{1}{L} \sum_{j=1}^{L} p(Y_j = l | X_j, \Theta^{old})$$

$$\mu_l^{new} = \frac{\sum_{j=1}^{L} \bar{X}_j p(Y_j = l | X_j, \Theta^{old}) |X_j|}{\sum_{j=1}^{L} p(Y_j = l | X_j, \Theta^{old}) |X_j|}$$

$$\Sigma_l^{new} = \frac{\sum_{j=1}^{L} \Sigma_{jl}^{new} p(Y_j = l | X_j, \Theta^{old}) |X_j|}{\sum_{j=1}^{L} p(Y_j = l | X_j, \Theta^{old}) |X_j|}$$

$$\text{for } \Sigma_{jl}^{new} = \frac{\sum_{x_i \in X_j} (x_i - \mu_l^{new})(x_i - \mu_l^{new})^T}{|X_j|}$$

where $\bar{X}_j$ denotes the sample mean of the points in chunklet j, $|X_j|$ denotes the number of points in chunklet j, and Σ_{jl}^{new} denotes the sample covariance matrix of the jth chunklet of the lth class.

As can be readily seen, the update rules above effectively treat each chunklet as a single data point weighted according to the number of elements in it.

3.2.2.2 Update Equations When Constrained Points are Sampled i.i.d.

We now derive the update equations under the assumption that the data points are sampled i.i.d. and that chunklets are selected only afterward.

The difference between the two sampling assumptions first appears in the prior probabilities, which must be changed to $p(Y_j|\Theta^{new}) = \prod_{i=1}^{|X_j|} p(y_j^i = l|\Theta^{new}) = \alpha_{Y_j}^{|X_j|}$. We therefore have:

$$p(Y|\Theta^{new}, E_C) = \frac{\prod_{j=1}^{L} \alpha_{Y_j}^{|X_j|}}{\prod_{j=1}^{L} \sum_{m=1}^{M} \alpha_m^{|X_j|}} \tag{3.6}$$

and the expected log likelihood becomes:

$$\sum_{l=1}^{M} \sum_{j=1}^{L} p(Y_j = l|X_j, \Theta^{old}) \sum_{x_i \in X_j} \log\, p(x_i|l, \Theta^{new})$$

$$+ \sum_{l=1}^{M} \sum_{j=1}^{L} p(Y_j = l|X_j, \Theta^{old}) \, |X_j| \, \log\, \alpha_l - \sum_{j=1}^{L} \log\left(\sum_{m=1}^{M} \alpha_m^{|X_j|}\right) \tag{3.7}$$

The main difference between (3.5) and (3.7) lies in the last term, which can be interpreted as a "normalization" term. Differentiating (3.7) with respect to μ_l and Σ_l readily provides the same update equations as before, but now the posterior takes a slightly different form:

$$p(Y_j = l|X_j, \Theta^{old}) = \frac{(\alpha_l^{old})^{|X_j|} \prod_{x_i \in X_j} p(x_i|y_i^j = l, \Theta^{old})}{\sum_{m=1}^{M} (\alpha_m^{old})^{|X_j|} \prod_{x_i \in X_j} p(x_i|y_i^j = m, \Theta^{old})}$$

A problem arises with the derivation of the update equations for the sources' weights α_l. In order to calculate α_l^{new}, we need to differentiate (3.7) subject to the constraint $\sum_{l=1}^{M} \alpha_l = 1$. Due to the "normalization" term we cannot obtain a closed-form solution, and we must resort to using a Generalized EM (GEM) scheme where the maximum is found numerically.

3.2.3 Incorporating Cannot-Link Constraints

As mentioned earlier, incorporating cannot-link constraints is inherently different and much more complicated than incorporating must-link constraints.

This difficulty can be related to the fact that unlike must-link constraints, cannot-link constraints are not transitive. For example if points x_i and x_j are known to belong to *different* classes and points x_j and x_k are also known to belong to *different* classes, points x_i and x_k may or may not belong to the same class. Hence cannot-link constraints are given as a set $C_{\neq} = \{c_{\neq}(a_i^1, a_i^2)\}_{i=1}^P$ of index pairs corresponding to P negatively constrained pairs.

Similarly to the case of must-link constraints (in Equation (3.4)), the complete data likelihood is

$$p(X, Y | \Theta, E_{C_{\neq}}) = \frac{1}{Z} \prod_{c_{\neq}(a_i^1, a_i^2)} (1 - \delta_{y_{a_i^1}, y_{a_i^2}}) \prod_{i=1}^n p(y_i | \Theta) p(x_i | y_i, \Theta) \quad (3.8)$$

The product over δ in (3.4) is replaced by the product over $(1 - \delta)$ here, and the normalizing constant is now given by

$$Z \equiv \sum_{y_1} \cdots \sum_{y_n} \prod_{C_{\neq}} (1 - \delta_{y_{a_j^1}, y_{a_j^2}}) \prod_{i=1}^n p(y_i | \Theta).$$

In the following derivations we start with the update rules of μ_l and Σ_l, and then discuss how to update α_l, which once again poses additional difficulties.

Deriving the update equations for μ_l and Σ_l

Following exactly the same derivation as in the case of must-link constraints, we can write down the update equations of μ_l and Σ_l:

$$\mu_l^{new} = \frac{\sum_{i=1}^n x_i p(y_i = l | X, \Theta^{old}, E_{C_{\neq}})}{\sum_{i=1}^n p(y_i = l | X, \Theta^{old}, E_{C_{\neq}})}$$

$$\Sigma_l^{new} = \frac{\sum_{i=1}^n \widehat{\Sigma_{il}} p(y_i = l | X, \Theta^{old}, E_{C_{\neq}})}{\sum_{i=1}^n p(y_i = l | X, \Theta^{old}, E_{C_{\neq}})}$$

where $\widehat{\Sigma_{il}} = (x_i - \mu_l^{new})(x_i - \mu_l^{new})^T$ denotes the sample covariance matrix.

The difficulty lies in estimating the probabilities $p(y_i = l | X, \Theta^{old}, E_{C_{\neq}})$, which are calculated by marginalizing the following expression:

$$p(Y | X, \Theta^{old}, E_{C_{\neq}}) = \quad (3.9)$$

$$\frac{\prod_{c_{\neq}(a_i^1, a_i^2)} (1 - \delta_{y_{a_i^1}, y_{a_i^2}}) \prod_{i=1}^n p(y_i | x_i, \Theta^{old})}{\sum_{y_1} \cdots \sum_{y_n} \prod_{c_{\neq}(a_i^1, a_i^2)} (1 - \delta_{y_{a_i^1}, y_{a_i^2}}) \prod_{i=1}^n p(y_i | x_i, \Theta^{old})}$$

It is not feasible to write down an explicit derivation of this expression for a general constraints graph, since the probability of a certain assignment of point x_i to source l depends on the assignment of all other points sharing a cannot-link constraint with x_i. However, since the dependencies enforced by the constraints are local, we can describe (3.8) as a product of local components, and therefore it can be readily described using a Markov network.

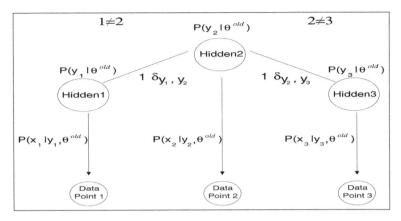

FIGURE 3.2: An illustration of the Markov network required for incorporating cannot-link constraints. Data points 1 and 2 have a cannot-link constraint, and so do points 2 and 3.

A Markov network is a graphical model defined by a graph $g = (V, E)$, whose nodes $v \in V$ represent a random variable and whose edges E represent the dependencies between the different nodes. In our case the graph contains observable nodes which correspond to the observed data points $\{x_i\}_{i=1}^n$, and discrete hidden nodes $\{y_i\}_{i=1}^n$ (see Fig. 3.2). The variable y_i describes the index of the Gaussian source of point x_i. Each observable node x_i is connected to its hidden node y_i by a directed edge, holding the potential $p(x_i|y_i, \Theta)$. Each hidden node y_i also has a local prior potential of the form of $p(y_i|\Theta)$. A cannot-link constraint between data points x_i and x_j is represented by an *undirected* edge between their corresponding hidden nodes y_i and y_j, having a potential of $(1 - \delta_{y_i, y_j})$. These edges prevent both hidden variables from having the same value.

The mapping of our problem into the language of graphical models makes it possible to use efficient inference algorithms. We use Pearl's junction tree algorithm [34] to compute the posterior probabilities. The complexity of the junction tree algorithm is exponential in the induced-width of the graph, hence for practical considerations the number of cannot-link constraints should be limited to $O(n)$.[3] Therefore, in order to achieve scalability to large sets of constraints, we must resort to approximations; in our implementation we specifically replaced the graph by its minimal spanning tree.

---

[3]The general case with $O(n^2)$ constraints is NP-hard, as the graph coloring problem can be reduced to it.

Deriving the update equations for α_l

The derivation of the update rule of $\alpha_l = p(y_i = l|\Theta_{new}, E_{C_{\neq}})$ is more intricate due to the normalization factor Z. In order to understand the difficulties, note that maximizing the expected log-likelihood with respect to α_l is equivalent to maximizing:

$$\mathcal{I} = -\log(Z) + \sum_{m=1}^{M}[\sum_{i=1}^{n} p(y_i = m|X, \Theta, E_{C_{\neq}})]\log(\alpha_m)$$

where the normalization factor Z is:

$$Z = p(E_{C_{\neq}}|\Theta) = \sum_{Y} p(Y|\Theta)p(E_{C_{\neq}}|Y) \tag{3.10}$$

$$= \sum_{y_1}\cdots\sum_{y_n}\prod_{i=1}^{n}\alpha_{y_i}\prod_{c_{\neq}(a_i^1,a_i^2)}(1 - \delta_{y_{a_i^1},y_{a_i^2}})$$

The gradient of this expression w.r.t. α_l is given by

$$\frac{\partial\mathcal{I}}{\partial\alpha_l} = -\frac{1}{Z}\frac{\partial Z}{\partial\alpha_l} + \frac{\sum_{i=1}^{n}p(y_i = l|X, \Theta, E_{C_{\neq}})}{\alpha_l} \tag{3.11}$$

Equating (3.11) to zero (subject to the constraint $\sum_{l=1}^{M}\alpha_l = 1$) does not have a closed form solution, and once again we must use the numerical GEM procedure. The new difficulty, however, lies in estimating (3.11) itself; although the posterior probabilities have already been estimated using the Markov network, we still need to calculate Z and its derivatives.

We considered three different approaches for computing Z and its derivatives. The first, naive approach is to ignore the first term in (3.11). Thus we are left only with the second term, which is a simple function of the expected counts. This function is identical to the usual EM case, and the update has the regular closed form:

$$\alpha_l^{new} = \frac{\sum_{i=1}^{n}p(y_i = l|X, \Theta^{old})}{n}$$

Our second approach is to perform an exact computation of Z and $\frac{\partial Z}{\partial\alpha}$ using additional Markov networks. A third approach is to use a pseudo-likelihood approximation. The description of the last two approaches is left to the appendix.

3.2.4 Combining Must-Link and Cannot-Link Constraints

Both types of constraints can be incorporated into the EM algorithm using a single Markov network by a rather simple extension of the network described

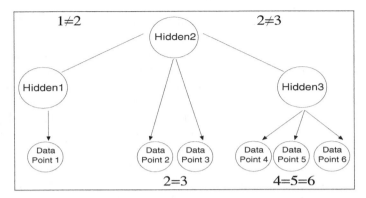

FIGURE 3.3: An illustration of the Markov network required for incorporating both cannot-link and must-link constraints. Data points 1 and 2 have a cannot-link constraint, and so do points 2 and 4. Data points 2 and 3 have a must-link constraint, and so do points 4, 5, and 6.

in the previous section. Assume we have, in addition to the cannot-link constraints, a set $\{X_j\}_{j=1}^{L}$ of chunklets containing points known to share the same label.[4] The likelihood becomes

$$p(X, Y | \Theta, E_C) = \frac{1}{Z} \prod_j \delta_{Y_j} \prod_{c \neq (a_i^1, a_i^2)} (1 - \delta_{y_{a_i^1}, y_{a_i^2}}) \prod_{i=1}^{n} p(y_i | \Theta) p(x_i | y_i, \Theta)$$

where δ_{Y_j} is 1 iff all the points in chunklet X_j have the same label, as defined in Section 3.2.2.1. Since the probability is non-zero only when the hidden variables in the chunklet are identical, we can replace the hidden variables of each chunklet $h_{i_1} \cdots h_{i_{|c_i|}}$ with a single hidden variable. Hence in the Markov network implementation points in a must-link constraint share a hidden father node (see Fig. 3.3). The EM procedure derived from this distribution is similar to the one presented earlier, with a slightly modified Markov network and normalizing constant.

3.3 Experimental Results

In order to evaluate the performance of our constrained EM algorithms, we compared them to two alternative clustering algorithms that use equivalence

---

[4]In this section, must-link constraints are sampled in accordance with the second sampling assumption described in Section 3.2.2.

constraints: the constrained k-means algorithm (COP k-means) [37] and the constrained complete-linkage algorithm [28]. We tested all three algorithms using several data sets from the UCI repository and a facial database.

In our experiments we simulated a "distributed learning" scenario in order to obtain side-information. In this scenario, we obtain equivalence constraints using the help of n teachers. Each teacher is given a random selection of K data points from the data set, and is then asked to partition this set of points into equivalence classes. The constraints provided by the teachers are gathered and used as equivalence constraints.

Each algorithm was tested in three modes: *basic*—using no side-information; *must-link*—using only must-link constraints; and *combined*—using both must-link and cannot-link constraints. Specifically we compared the performance of the following variants:

(a) k-means—*basic* mode.

(b) k-means—*must-link* mode [37].

(b) k-means—*combined* mode [37].

(d) complete-linkage—*basic* mode.

(e) complete-linkage—*must-link* mode [28].

(f) complete-linkage—*combined* mode [28].

(g) constrained-EM —*basic* mode.

(h) constrained-EM—*must-link* mode.

(i) constrained-EM—*combined* mode.

The number of constrained points was determined by the number of teachers n and the size of the subset K that was given to each teacher. By controlling the product nK we modified the total amount of side-information available. For a fair comparison, all of the algorithms that require initial conditions, were given the same initial conditions, which were randomly sampled without using the available equivalence constraints. Clustering solutions were evaluated using a combined measure of precision P and recall R scores given by $f_{\frac{1}{2}} = \frac{2PR}{R+P}$.

3.3.1 UCI Data Sets

The results over several UCI data sets are shown in Fig. 3.4. We experimented with two conditions: using "little" side-information (approximately 15% of the data points are constrained), and using "much" side-information (approximately 30% of the points are constrained).[5]

---

[5] With the protein and ionosphere data sets we used more side-information: protein: 80% and 50%, ionosphere: 75% and 50%.

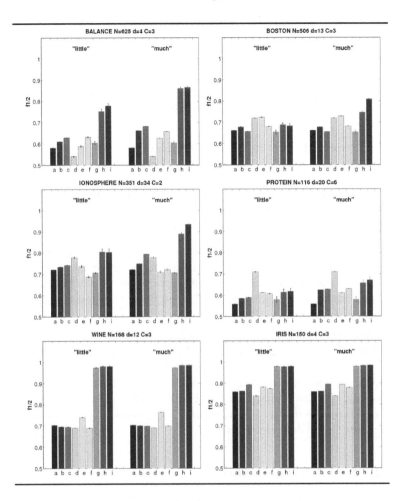

FIGURE 3.4: Combined precision and recall scores ($f_{\frac{1}{2}}$) of several cluster-ing algorithms over 6 data sets from the UCI repository. Results are pre-sented for the following algorithms: (a) k-means, (b) constrained k-means using only must-link constraints, (c) constrained k-means using both must-link and cannot-link constraints, (d) complete linkage, (e) complete linkage using must-link constraints, (f) complete linkage using both must-link and cannot-link constraints, (g) regular EM, (h) EM using must-link constraints, and (i) EM using both must-link and cannot-link constraints. In each panel results are shown for two cases, using 15% of the data points in constraints (left bars) and 30% of the points in constraints (right bars). The results were averaged over 100 realizations of constraints. Also shown are the names of the data sets used and some of their parameters: N—the size of the data set; C—the number of classes; d—the dimensionality of the data.

Several effects can be clearly seen:

- The performance of the EM algorithms is generally better than the performance of the respective k-means and complete-linkage algorithms. In fact, our constrained EM outperforms the constrained k-means and the constrained complete-linkage algorithms on all databases.

- As expected, introducing side-information in the form of equivalence constraints improves the results of both k-means and the EM algorithms, though curiously this is not always the case with the constrained complete-linkage algorithm. As the amount of side-information increases, the algorithms that make use of it tend to improve.

- Most of the improvement can be attributed to the must-link constraints, and can be achieved using our closed form EM version. In most cases adding the cannot-link constraints contributes a small but significant improvement over results obtained when using only must-link constraints.

It should be noted that most of the UCI data sets considered so far contain only two or three classes. Thus in the distributed learning setting a relatively large fraction of the constraints were must-link constraints. In a more realistic situation, with a large number of classes, we are likely to gather more cannot-link constraints than must-link constraints. This is an important point in light of the results in Fig. 3.4, where the major boost in performance was due to the use of must-link constraints.

3.3.2 Facial Image Database

In order to consider the multi-class case, we conducted the same experiment using a subset of the Yale facial image data set [15], which contains a total of 640 images, including 64 frontal pose images of 10 different subjects. Some example images from the data set are shown Fig. 3.5. In this database the variability between images of the same person is due mainly to different lighting conditions. We automatically centered all the images using optical flow. Images were then converted to vectors, and each image was represented using the first 60 principal components coefficients. The task was to cluster the facial images belonging to these 10 subjects.

Our results are summarized in Fig. 3.5. As before, our constrained EM algorithms substantially outperform the regular EM algorithms and the other constrained clustering algorithms used. Due to the random selection of images given to each of the n teachers, mostly cannot-link constraints were obtained. However, even though there was only a small number of must-link constraints, most of the boost in performance was obtained using these constraints.

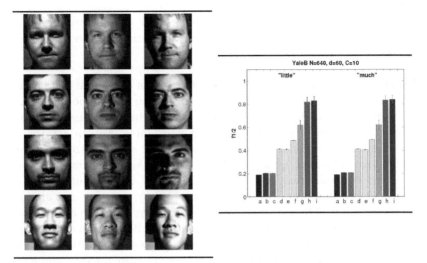

FIGURE 3.5: Left: Examples from the subset of pictures we used from the Yale database, which contains 640 frontal face images of 10 individuals taken under different lighting conditions. Right: Combined precision and recall scores of several clustering algorithms over the Yale facial data set. The results are presented using the same format as in Fig. 3.4, representing an average of more than 1000 realizations of constraints. Percentage of data in constraints was 50% (left bars) and 75% (right bars). It should be noted that when using 75% of the data in constraints, the constrained k-means algorithm failed to converge in more than half of its runs.

3.4 Obtaining Equivalence Constraints

In contrast to explicit labels that are usually provided by a human instructor, in some scenarios equivalence constraints may be extracted with minimal effort or even automatically. Two examples of such scenarios are described below:

- **Temporal continuity**—In this scenario, we consider cases where the data are inherently sequential and can be modeled by a Markovian process. In these cases we can automatically obtain must-link constraints by considering a set of samples that are temporally close to one another. In some cases, we can also use this scenario to obtain cannot-link constraints. For example, in a movie segmentation task, the objective may be to find all the frames in which the same actor appears [9]. Due to the continuous nature of most movies, faces extracted from successive frames in roughly the same location can be assumed to come from the same person, and thus provide a set of must-link constraints.[6] Yan et al. [40] have presented an interesting application of video object classification using this approach.

- **Distributed learning**—Anonymous users of a retrieval system can be asked to help annotate the data by providing information about small portions of the data that they see.[7] We can use these user annotations to define equivalence constraints. For example, we can ask the users of an image retrieval engine to annotate the set of images retrieved as an answer to their query [3]. Thus, each of these cooperative users will provide a collection of small sets of images that belong to the same category. Moreover, different sets provided by the same user are known to belong to different categories. Note however that we cannot use the explicit labels provided by the different users because we cannot assume that the subjective labels of each user are consistent with one another: A certain user may label a set of images as "F-16" images, and another user may label another set of F-16 images as "Airplane" images.

3.5 Related Work

As noted in the introduction, two types of semi-supervised clustering algorithms have been considered in the literature: algorithms that incorporate some additional labeled data and algorithms that incorporate equivalence constraints. Miller and Uyar [32] and Nigam et al. [33] have both suggested enhancements of the EM algorithm for a GMM that incorporates labeled data. Several other works have proposed augmentations of other classical clustering algorithms to incorporate labeled data [8, 10, 11, 16, 26, 29, 41].

Incorporating equivalence constraints has been suggested for almost all classical clustering algorithms. Cohn et al. (see Chapter 2) were perhaps the first to suggest a semi-supervised technique trained using equivalence constraints for clustering of text documents. The suggested method applies equivalence constraints in order to learn a distance metric based on a weighted Jensen-Shannon divergence. The latter is then used in the EM algorithm.

Klein et al. [28] introduced equivalence constraints into the complete-linkage algorithm by a simple modification of the similarity matrix provided as input to the algorithm. Wagstaff et al. [37] suggested the COP k-means algorithm, which is a heuristic approach for incorporating both types of equivalence constraints into the k-means algorithm (see Chapter 1, Table 1.1). Basu et al. [5]

---

[6]This is true as long as there is no scene change, which can be robustly detected [9].

[7]This scenario may also be called *generalized relevance feedback*.

suggested a constrained clustering approach based on a Hidden Markov Random Field (HMRF) and can incorporate various distortion measures. An additional approach was suggested by Bilenko et al. [7] who introduced the MPCK-means algorithm that includes a metric learning step in each clustering iteration.

Kamvar et al. [27] introduced pairwise constraints into spectral clustering by modifying the similarity matrix in a similar way to that suggested in Klein et al. [28]. This work is also closely related to the work of Yu and Shi [41]. An alternative formulation was presented by De Bie et al. [6] who incorporated a separate label constraint matrix into the objective function of a spectral clustering algorithm such as the normalized-cut [36]. Motivated by the connection between spectral clustering and graph-cut algorithms, Bansal et al. [1] have suggested a general graph-based algorithm incorporating both must-link and cannot-link constraints. Finally, the constrained EM algorithm has been successfully used as a building block of the *DistBoost* algorithm, which learns a non-linear distance function using a semi-supervised boosting approach [21, 22].

3.6 Summary and Discussion

In this chapter we have shown how equivalence constraints can be incorporated into the computation of a Gaussian Mixture Model (GMM). When using must-link constraints, we provided an efficient closed form solution for the update rules and demonstrated that using must-link constraints can significantly boost clustering performance. When cannot-link constraints are added, the computational cost increases since a Markov network is used as an inference tool, and we must defer to approximation methods. Our experiments show that although most of the improvement in performance is obtained from the must-link constraints alone, the contribution of the cannot-link constraints is still significant.

We conjecture that must-link constraints may be more valuable than cannot-link constraints for two reasons. First, from an information related perspective must-link constraints are more informative than cannot-link constraints. To see this, note that if the number of classes in the data is m, then a must-link constraint $c_=(i, j)$ allows only m possible assignments of points i and j (out of m^2 assignments for an unconstrained pair of points), while a cannot-link constraint allows $m(m-1)/2$ such assignments. Hence for $m > 2$ the reduction in uncertainty due to a must-link constraint is much larger than for a cannot-link one. A second (and probably more important) reason concerns the estimation of the $d \times d$ covariance matrix of the Gaussian sources. In many cases a source that is represented in a d-dimensional input space actually lies in a lower k-

dimensional manifold where $k \ll d$. In these cases, estimating the covariance matrix of the source boils down to identifying these k dimensions. Must-link constraints are better suited for this task, since they directly provide information regarding the k relevant dimensions, whereas cannot-link constraints can only be used to identify non-relevant dimensions, whose number is much larger (since $k \ll d$). This may also explain why the superiority of must-link constraints over cannot-link constraints is more pronounced for data sets with a large number of classes that are represented in a high-dimensional space, as in the Yale facial image data set.

While this work has focused on incorporating equivalence constraints into a clustering algorithm, there are other possible ways in which these constraints may be used to improve clustering performance. Many clustering algorithms are distance based, i.e., their only input are pairwise distances between data points. Therefore, another approach that has recently received growing attention is to use the constraints to learn a distance function over the input space [2, 4, 6, 7, 17, 19, 21, 35, 38, 39]. While both constrained clustering algorithms and distance learning algorithms have been shown to significantly improve clustering performance, the question of whether these approaches are interchangeable or whether combining them would provide an additional advantage remains open.

3.7 Appendix: Calculating the Normalizing Factor Z and its Derivatives when Introducing Cannot-Link Constraints

Recall that when cannot-link constraints are introduced, the update rule for α_l does not have a closed form solution. This follows from the fact that maximizing the expected log-likelihood with respect to α_l requires maximizing

$$\mathcal{I} = -\log(Z) + \sum_{m=1}^{M}[\sum_{i=1}^{n} p(y_i = m|X, \Theta, E_{C_{\neq}})]\log(\alpha_m)$$

where the normalization factor Z is:

$$Z = p(E_{C_{\neq}}|\Theta) = \sum_{Y} p(Y|\Theta)p(E_{C_{\neq}}|Y)$$

$$= \sum_{y_1}\cdots\sum_{y_n}\prod_{i=1}^{n}\alpha_{y_i}\prod_{c_{\neq}(a_i^1,a_i^2)}(1-\delta_{y_{a_i^1},y_{a_i^2}})$$

The gradient of this expression w.r.t. α_l is given by

$$\frac{\partial\mathcal{I}}{\partial\alpha_l} = -\frac{1}{Z}\frac{\partial Z}{\partial\alpha_l} + \frac{\sum_{i=1}^{n}p(y_i = l|X, \Theta, E_{C_{\neq}})}{\alpha_l}$$

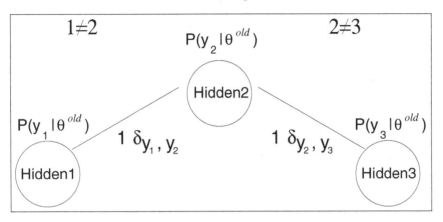

FIGURE 3.6: An illustration of the Markov network required for calculating Z for the case where data points 1 and 2 have a cannot-link constraint, as do points 2 and 3.

which requires the computation of Z and its derivatives. We now present an exact solution and an approximate solution for these computations.

3.7.1 Exact Calculation of Z and $\frac{\partial Z}{\partial \alpha_l}$

When comparing (3.10) and (3.8), we can see that Z can be calculated as the evidence in a Markov network. This network has a similar structure to the former network: it contains the same hidden nodes and local potentials, but lacks the observable nodes (see Fig 3.6). Computing Z now amounts to the elimination of all the variables in this "prior" network. In order to calculate $\frac{\partial Z}{\partial \alpha_l}$ we have to differentiate the distribution represented by the prior network with respect to α_l and sum over all possible network states. This gradient calculation can be done simultaneously with the calculation of Z as described below.

The prior network contains two types of factors: edge factors of the form $\delta_{y_{i_1}, y_{i_2}}$ and node factors of the form $(\alpha_1, \ldots, \alpha_M)$. In the gradient calculation process, we calculate M gradient factors (one for each gradient component) for every factor in the prior network. Thus in effect we have $M + 1$ replicas of the original prior network: the original network and M gradient networks.

The l-th gradient factor holds the gradient $\frac{\partial}{\partial \alpha_l} f(x_{i_1}, \ldots, x_{i_m})$ for the various values of $x_{i_1}, \ldots, x_{i_m}$. These factors are initialized as follows:

- Edge gradient factors are initialized to zero, since $\delta_{y_{i_1}, y_{i_2}}$ does not depend on α_l.

- Node factors take the form of $e_l = (0, \ldots, 1, \ldots, 0)$ with 1 in the lth entry and 0 otherwise.

Using this data structure, variables are eliminated according to a predefined (heuristically determined) elimination order. In the elimination step of variable x the factors and gradient factors containing that variable are eliminated, resulting in a prior network factor over x's neighbors and the M gradient factors of this factor. If we denote the factors containing x as $\{f_j(x)\}_{j=1}^k$, the resulting prior network factor is computed by standard variable elimination, i.e., by summing out x from $\prod_{j=1}^k f_j(x)$. The l-th gradient factor is computed by summing out x from $\frac{\partial}{\partial \alpha_l} \prod_{j=1}^k f_j(x)$. This last expression can be computed from already known factors (regular and gradient factors of $\{f_j(x)\}_{j=1}^k$) since

$$\frac{\partial}{\partial \alpha_k} \prod_{j=1}^k f_j(x) = \sum_{i=1}^k [\frac{\partial}{\partial \alpha_k} f_i(x)] \prod_{j \neq i} f_j(x)$$

The computation of a new gradient factor requires only the usual operations of factor product and marginalization, as well as factor summation. Since we compute M gradient elements, the cost of the above procedure is $O(M^{d+1})$, where d is the induced width of the network. We project the gradient to the weights plane $\sum_l \alpha_l = 1$ and use it in a gradient ascent process. The step size is determined using a line search. Since the gradient computation is done many times in each EM round, this method can be very slow for complicated constraint graphs.

3.7.2 Approximating Z Using the Pseudo-Likelihood Assumption

Z can be approximated under the assumption that the cannot-link constraints are mutually exclusive. Denote the number of cannot-link constraints by c. If we now assume that all pairs of constrained points are disjoint, the number of unconstrained points is $u = n - 2c$. Assume, without loss of generality, that the unconstrained data points are indexed by $1 \ldots u$, and the remaining points are ordered so that constrained points are given successive indices (e.g., points $u + 1$ and $u + 2$ are in a cannot-link constraint). Now Z can be decomposed as follows:

$$Z = \sum_{y_1} \cdots \sum_{y_n} \prod_{i=1}^n \alpha_{y_i} \prod_{c \neq (a_i^1, a_i^2)} (1 - \delta_{y_{a_i^1}, y_{a_i^2}})$$

$$= \sum_{y_1} \alpha_{y_1} \cdots \sum_{y_u} \alpha_{y_u}$$

$$\cdot \sum_{y_{u+1}} \sum_{y_{u+2}} \alpha_{y_{u+1}} \alpha_{y_{u+2}} (1 - \delta_{y_{u+1}, y_{u+2}}) \cdots \sum_{y_{n-1}} \sum_{y_n} \alpha_{y_{n-1}} \alpha_{y_n} (1 - \delta_{y_{n-1}, y_n})$$

$$= (1 - \sum_{i=1}^M \alpha_i^2)^c \tag{3.12}$$

This expression for Z may be easily differentiated and can be used in a GEM scheme. Although the assumption is not valid in most cases, it seems to yield a good approximation for sparse networks. We empirically compared the three approaches presented. As can be expected, the results show a trade-off between speed and accuracy. However, the average accuracy loss caused by ignoring or approximating Z seems to be small. The pseudo-likelihood approximation seems to give good accuracy at a minimal speed cost, and so we used it in our experiments.

References

[1] Nikhil Bansal, Avrim Blum, and Shuchi Chawla. Correlation clustering. In *43rd Symposium on Foundations of Computer Science (FOCS 2002)*, pages 238–247, 2002.

[2] Aharon Bar-Hillel, Tomer Hertz, Noam Shental, and Daphna Weinshall. Learning distance functions using equivalence relations. In *Proceedings of the International Conference on Machine Learning (ICML)*, pages 11–18, 2003.

[3] Aharon Bar-Hillel, Tomer Hertz, Noam Shental, and Daphna Weinshall. Learning a mahalanobis metric from equivalence constraints. *Journal of Machine Learning Research*, 6:937–965, 2005.

[4] Aharon Bar-Hillel and Daphna Weinshall. Learning distance function by coding similarity. In *Proceedings of the International Conference on Machine Learning (ICML)*, pages 65–72, 2006.

[5] Sugato Basu, Mikhail Bilenko, and Raymond J. Mooney. A probabilistic framework for semi-supervised clustering. In *Proceedings of the International Conference on Knowledge Discovery and Data Mining (KDD)*, pages 59–68, 2004.

[6] T. De Bie, J. Suykens, and B. De Moor. Learning from general label constraints. In *Proceedings of the Joint IAPR International Workshops on Syntactical and Structural Pattern Recognition (SSPR 2004) and Statistical Pattern Recognition (SPR 2004)*, pages 671–679, Lisbon, August 2003.

[7] M. Bilenko, S. Basu, and R. Mooney. Integrating constraints and metric learning in semi-supervised clustering. In *Proceedings of the International Conference on Machine Learning (ICML)*, pages 81–88, 2004.

[8] A. Blum and S. Chawla. Learning from labeled and unlabeled data using graph mincuts. In *Proceedings of the International Conference on Machine Learning (ICML)*, pages 19–26. Morgan Kaufmann, San Francisco, CA, 2001.

[9] J. S. Boreczky and L. A. Rowe. Comparison of video shot boundary detection techniques. *SPIE Storage and Retrieval for Still Images and Video Databases IV*, 2664:170–179, 1996.

[10] Y. Boykov, O. Veksler, and R. Zabih. Fast approximate energy minimization via graph cuts. In *Proceedings of the International Conference on Computer Vision (ICCV)*, pages 377–384, 1999.

[11] Ayhan Demiriz, Mark Embrechts, and Kristin P. Bennet. Semisupervised clustering using genetic algorithms. In *Artificial Neural Networks in Engineering (ANNIE'99)*, pages 809–814, 1999.

[12] A. P. Dempster, N. M. Laird, and D. B. Rubin. Maximum likelihood from incomplete data via the EM algorithm. *Journal of the Royal Statistical Society (B)*, 39:1–38, 1977.

[13] R. O. Duda, P. E. Hart, and D. G. Stork. *Pattern Classification*. Wiley-Interscience Publication, 2000.

[14] K. Fukunaga. *Statistical Pattern Recognition*. Academic Press, San Diego, 2nd edition, 1990.

[15] A. Georghiades, P. N. Belhumeur, and D. J. Kriegman. From few to many: Generative models for recognition under variable pose and illumination. *IEEE International Conference on Automatic Face and Gesture Recognition*, pages 277–284, 2000.

[16] G. Getz, N. Shental, and E. Domany. Semi-supervised learning—a statistical physics approach. In *Proceedings of the Workshop on Learning with Partially Classified Training Data, International Conference on Machine Learning (ICML)*, pages 37–44, 2005.

[17] Amir Globerson and Sam Roweis. Metric learning by collapsing classes. In *Advances in Neural Information Processing Systems (NIPS)*, pages 451–458, 2005.

[18] Ben Gold and Nelson Morgan. *Speech and Audio Signal Processing*. John Wiley and Sons, Inc, 2000.

[19] Jacob Goldberger, Sam Roweis, Geoff Hinton, and Ruslan Salakhutdinov. Neighbourhood component analysis. In *Advances in Neural Information Processing Systems (NIPS)*, pages 513–520, 2004.

[20] T. Hastie and R. Tibshirani. Discriminant analysis by gaussian mixtures. *Journal of the Royal Statistical Society (B)*, 58:155–176, 1996.

[21] Tomer Hertz, Aharon Bar-Hillel, and Daphna Weinshall. Boosting margin based distance functions for clustering. In *Proceedings of the International Conference on Machine Learning (ICML)*, pages 393–400, 2004.

[22] Tomer Hertz, Aharon Bar Hillel, and Daphna Weinshall. Learning a kernel function for classification with small training samples. In *Proceedings of the International Conference on Machine Learning (ICML)*, pages 401–408, 2006.

[23] G. Hinton, P. Dayan, and M. Revow. Modelling the manifolds of images of handwritten digits. *IEEE Transactions on Neural Networks*, 8:65–74, 1997.

[24] A. K. Jain and R. Dubes. *Algorithms for Clustering Data*. Prentice Hall, Englewood Cliffs, N.J., 1988.

[25] A. K. Jain, R. Duin, and J. Mao. Statistical pattern recognition: A review. *IEEE Transactions on Pattern Analysis and Machine Intelligence (PAMI)*, 22:4–38, January 2000.

[26] T. Joachims. Transductive learning via spectral graph partitioning. In *Proceedings of the International Conference on Machine Learning (ICML)*, pages 290–297, 2003.

[27] Sepandar D. Kamvar, Dan Klein, and Christopher D. Manning. Spectral learning. In *Proceedings of the Eighteenth International Joint Conference on Artificial Intelligence*, pages 561–566, 2003.

[28] D. Klein, S. Kamvar, and C. Manning. From instance-level constraints to space-level constraints: Making the most of prior knowledge in data clustering. In *Proceedings of the International Conference on Machine Learning (ICML)*, pages 307–314, 2002.

[29] Tilman Lange, Martin H. Law, Anil K. Jain, and Joachim Buhmann. Learning with constrained and unlabelled data. In *Proceedings of the Conference on Computer Vision and Pattern Recognition (CVPR)*, pages 20–25, 2005.

[30] G. McLachlan and K. Basford. *Mixture Models: Inference and Application to Clustering*. Marcel Dekker, New York, 1988.

[31] G. McLachlan and D. Peel. *Finite Mixture Models*. John Wiley and Sons, 2000.

[32] D. Miller and S. Uyar. A mixture of experts classifier with learning based on both labelled and unlabelled data. In M. C. Mozer, M. I. Jordan, and T. Petsche, editors, *Advances in Neural Information Processing Systems (NIPS)*, pages 571–578. MIT Press, 1997.

[33] K. Nigam, A. K. McCallum, S. Thrun, and T. M. Mitchell. Learning to classify text from labeled and unlabeled documents. In *Proceedings of Association for the Advancement of Artificial Intelligence (AAAI)*, pages 792–799, Madison, US, 1998. AAAI Press, Menlo Park, US.

[34] J. Pearl. *Probabilistic Reasoning in Intelligent Systems: Networks of Plausible Inference*. Morgan Kaufmann Publishers, Inc., 1988.

[35] N. Shental, T. Hertz, D. Weinshall, and M. Pavel. Adjustment learning and relevant component analysis. In A. Heyden, G. Sparr, M. Nielsen, and P. Johansen, editors, *Proceedings of the European Conference on Computer Vision (ECCV)*, volume 4, pages 776–792, 2002.

[36] J. Shi and J. Malik. Normalized cuts and image segmentation. *IEEE Transactions on Pattern Analysis and Machine Intelligence (PAMI)*, 22(8):888–905, 2000.

[37] K. Wagstaff, C. Cardie, S. Rogers, and S. Schroedl. Constrained k-means clustering with background knowledge. In *Proceedings of the International Conference on Machine Learning (ICML)*, pages 577–584. Morgan Kaufmann, San Francisco, CA, 2001.

[38] Kilian Weinberger, John Blitzer, and Lawrence Saul. Distance metric learning for large margin nearest neighbor classification. In Y. Weiss, B. Schölkopf, and J. Platt, editors, *Advances in Neural Information Processing Systems (NIPS)*, pages 1473–1480, Cambridge, MA, 2006. MIT Press.

[39] E. P. Xing, A. Y. Ng, M. I. Jordan, and S. Russell. Distance metric learning with application to clustering with side-information. In *Advances in Neural Information Processing Systems*, volume 15, pages 521–528. MIT Press, 2002.

[40] Rong Yan, Jian Zhang, Jie Yang, and Alexander Hauptmann. A discriminative learning framework with pairwise constraints for video object classification. In *Proceedings of the Conference on Computer Vision and Pattern Recognition (CVPR)*, volume 2, pages 284–291, 2004.

[41] S. X. Yu and J. Shi. Grouping with bias. In *Advances in Neural Information Processing Systems (NIPS)*, pages 1327–1334, 2001.

Chapter 4

Pairwise Constraints as Priors in Probabilistic Clustering

Zhengdong Lu

Oregon Graduate Institute, `zhengdon@csee.ogi.edu`

Todd K. Leen

Oregon Graduate Institute, `tleen@csee.ogi.edu`

Abstract   We extend Gaussian mixture models (GMM) in a simple and natural way to accommodate prior belief that pairs of items should, or should not, be assigned to the same cluster. We incorporate beliefs about pairwise cluster assignments into the GMM by expressing those beliefs as Bayesian priors over the assignment of data points to clusters. The priors can express either hard constraints (items A and B must, or must not, be assigned to the same cluster), or merely preferences for certain assignments. The strengths of the preferences are under user control. The priors penalize each cluster assignment according to both the number and the strength of assignments preferences it violates. We provide an expectation-maximization (EM) algorithm for parameter fitting. Experiments on artificial and real problems show that cluster assignment preferences expressed in the training data are effectively incorporated into the GMM parameters; clustering on test data is improved with respect to the standard GMM.

4.1 Introduction

While clustering is usually executed completely unsupervised, there are circumstances in which we have prior belief (with varying degrees of certainty) that pairs of samples should (or should not) be assigned to the same cluster. More specifically, we specify the must-link $(C_=)$ and cannot-link $(C_{\neq})$, as defined in Chapter 1.

Our interest in such problems was kindled when we tried to manually segment a satellite image by grouping small image clips from the image. One finds that it is often hard to assign the image clips to different "groups" since we do not know clearly the characteristic of each group, or even how many classes we should have. In contrast, it is much easier to compare two image clips and to decide how much they look alike and thus how likely they should be in one cluster. Another example is in information retrieval. Cohn et al. [6] suggested that in creating a document taxonomy, the expert critique is often in the form "these two documents shouldn't be in the same cluster." The last example is continuity, which suggests that neighboring pairs of samples in a time series or in an image are likely to belong to the same class of object, is also a source of clustering preferences [1, 19]. We would like these preferences to be incorporated into the cluster structure so that the assignment of out-of-sample data to clusters captures the concept(s) that give rise to the preferences expressed in the training data.

Some work has been done on adapting traditional clustering methods, such as k-means, to incorporate pairwise relations [2, 9, 21]. These models are based on hard clustering, and the clustering preferences are expressed as *hard pairwise constraints* that *must* be satisfied. Some other authors [3, 20] extended their models to deal with soft pairwise constraints, where each constraint is assigned a weight. The performance of those constrained k-means algorithms is often not satisfactory, largely due to the incapability of k-means to model non-spherical data distribution in each class.

Shental et al. [16] proposed a Gaussian mixture model (GMM) for clustering that incorporates hard pairwise constraints. However, the model cannot be naturally generalized to soft constraints, which are appropriate when our knowledge is only clustering preferences or carries significant uncertainty. Motivated in part to remedy this deficiency, Law et al. [11, 12] proposed another GMM-based model to incorporate soft constraints. In their model, virtual groups are created for samples that are supposed to be in one class. The uncertainty information in pairwise relations is there expressed as the soft membership of samples to the virtual group. This modeling strategy is cumbersome to model samples shared by different virtual groups. Moreover, it cannot handle the prior knowledge that two samples are in different clusters. Other efforts to make use of the pairwise relations include changing the metric in feature space in favor of the specified relations [6, 22] or combining the metric learning with constrained clustering [4].

In this chapter, we describe a soft clustering algorithm based on GMM that expresses clustering preferences (in the form of pairwise relations) in the *prior probability on assignments of data points to clusters*. Our algorithm naturally accommodates both *hard constraints* and *soft preferences* in a framework in which the preferences are expressed as a Bayesian prior probability that pairs of points should (or should not) be assigned to the same cluster. After training with the expectation-maximization (EM) algorithm, the information expressed as a prior on the cluster assignment of the training data is successfully encoded in the means, covariances, and cluster priors in the GMM. Hence the model generalizes in a way consistent with the prior knowledge. We call the algorithm penalized probabilistic clustering (PPC). Experiments on artificial and real-world data sets demonstrate that PPC can consistently improve the clustering result by incorporating reliable prior knowledge.

4.2 Model

Penalized probabilistic clustering (PPC) begins with a standard M-component GMM

$$P(x|\Theta) = \sum_{k=1}^{M} \pi_k \, P(x|\theta_k)$$

with the parameter vector $\Theta = \{\pi_1, \ldots, \pi_M, \theta_1, \ldots, \theta_M\}$. Here, π_k and θ_k are, respectively, the prior probability and parameters of the kth Gaussian component. We augment the data set $X = \{x_i\}$, $i = 1 \ldots N$ with (latent) cluster assignments $Z = \{z(x_i)\}, i = 1, \ldots, N$ to form the familiar *complete data* (X, Z). The complete data likelihood is

$$P(X, Z|\Theta) = P(X|Z, \Theta)P(Z|\Theta),$$

where $P(X|Z, \Theta)$ is the probability of X conditioned on Z

$$P(X|Z, \Theta) = \prod_{i=1}^{N} P(x_i|\theta_{z_i}). \tag{4.1}$$

4.2.1 Prior Distribution on Cluster Assignments

We incorporate our clustering preferences by manipulating the *prior probability* $P(Z|\Theta)$. In the standard Gaussian mixture model, the prior distribution on cluster assignments Z is trivial:

$$P(Z|\Theta) = \prod_{i=1}^{N} \pi_{z_i}.$$

We incorporate our clustering preferences through a weighting function $g(Z)$ that has large values when the assignment of data points to clusters Z conforms to our preferences and low values when Z conflicts with our preferences. We can thus define the penalized prior as proportional to the product of the original prior and the weighting factor:

$$P_p(Z|\Theta, G) \equiv \frac{(\prod_i \pi_{z_i}) g(Z)}{\sum_Z (\prod_j \pi_{z_j}) g(Z)} = \frac{1}{\Omega} (\prod_i \pi_{z_i}) g(Z), \qquad (4.2)$$

where $\Omega = \sum_Z (\prod_j \pi_{z_j}) g(Z)$ is the normalization constant. Note that in equation (4.2), we use $P_p(\cdot)$ for the penalized prior, thus we can distinguish it from the standard one. This notation convention will be used throughout this chapter.

The likelihood of the data, *given a specific cluster assignment Z*, is independent of the cluster assignment preferences:

$$P(X, Z|\Theta, G) = P(X|Z, \Theta) P(Z|\Theta, G). \qquad (4.3)$$

From equations (4.1), (4.2), and (4.3), the complete data likelihood is

$$P_p(X, Z|\Theta, G) = P(X|Z, \Theta) \frac{1}{\Omega} \prod_i \pi_{z_i} g(Z) = \frac{1}{\Omega} P(X, Z|\Theta) g(Z),$$

where $P(X, Z|\Theta)$ is the complete data likelihood for a *standard* GMM. The data likelihood is the sum of complete data likelihood over all possible Z, that is, $L(X|\Theta) = P_p(X|\Theta, G) = \sum_Z P_p(X, Z|\Theta, G)$, which can be maximized with the EM algorithm. Once the model parameters are fit, we do soft clustering according to the posterior probabilities for new data $P(k|x, \Theta)$. (Note that cluster assignment preferences are *not* expressed for the new data, only for the training data.)

4.2.2 Pairwise Relations

Pairwise relations provide a special case of the framework discussed above. The weighting factor given to the cluster assignment Z is:

$$g(Z) = \prod_{i \neq j} \exp(w(i, j) \, \delta_{z_i z_j}), \qquad (4.4)$$

where $w(i, j)$ is the weight associated with sample pair (x_i, x_j), with

$$w(i, j) \in [-\infty, \infty], \; w(i, j) = w(j, i).$$

The weight $w(i, j)$ reflects our preference for assigning x_i and x_j into one cluster: We use $w(i, j) > 0$ if $(i, j) \in C_=$, $w(i, j) < 0$ when $(i, j) \in C_{\neq}$, and $w(i, j) = 0$ if no constraint is specified for x_i and x_j. The absolute value

$|w(i,j)|$ reflects the strength of the preference. The prior probability with the pairwise relations is

$$P(Z|\Theta, G) = \frac{1}{\Omega} \prod_i \pi_{z_i} \prod_{i \neq j} \exp(w(i,j)\, \delta_{z_i z_j}). \qquad (4.5)$$

From equations (4.4) and (4.5), the weighting factor $g(Z)$ is large when the pairwise constraints expressed through $W = \{w(i,j)\}$ are satisfied by the cluster assignment Z.

The model described above provides a fairly flexible framework that encompasses standard GMM and several other constrained clustering models as special cases. Most obviously, when we let $w(i,j) = 0$ for all i and j, we have $g(Z) = 1$ for all Z, hence the complete likelihood reduces to the standard one:

$$P_p(X, Z|\Theta, G) = \frac{1}{\Omega} P(X, Z|\Theta) g(Z) = P(X, Z|\Theta).$$

In the other extreme with $|w(i,j)| \to \infty$, assignments Z that violate constraint between x_i and x_j have zero prior probability, since for those assignments

$$P_p(Z|\Theta, G) = \frac{\prod_k \pi_{z_k} \prod_{i \neq j} \exp(w(i,j)\, \delta_{z_i z_j})}{\sum_Z \prod_l \pi_{z_l} \prod_{m \neq n} \exp(w(m,n)\, \delta_{z_m z_n})} \to 0.$$

Then the relations become *hard constraints*, while the relations with $|w(i,j)| < \infty$ are called *soft preferences*. When all the specified pairwise relations are hard constraints, the data likelihood becomes

$$P_p(X, Z|\Theta, G) = \frac{1}{\Omega} \prod_{ij \in C_=} \delta_{z_i z_j} \prod_{ij \in C_{\neq}} (1 - \delta_{z_i z_j}) \prod_{i=1}^{N} \pi_{z_i} P(x_i|\theta_{z_i}). \qquad (4.6)$$

It is straightforward to verify that equation (4.6) is essentially the same with the complete data likelihood given by [16]. In Appendix A, we give a detailed derivation of equation (4.6) and hence the equivalence of two models. When only hard constraints are available, we simply implement PPC based on equation (4.6). In the remainder of this chapter, we will use W to denote the prior knowledge on pairwise relations, that is,

$$P_p(X, Z|\Theta, G) \equiv P_p(X, Z|\Theta, W) = \frac{1}{\Omega} P(X, Z|\Theta) \prod_{i \neq j} \exp(w(i,j)\, \delta_{z_i z_j}). \quad (4.7)$$

4.2.3 Model Fitting

We use the EM algorithm [7] to fit the model parameters Θ:

$$\Theta^* = \arg\max_{\Theta} L(X|\Theta, W).$$

The expectation step (E-step) and maximization step (M-step) are

$$\texttt{E-step: } Q(\Theta, \Theta^{(t-1)}) = E_{Z|X}(\log P_p(X, Z|\Theta, W)|X, \Theta^{(t-1)}, W)$$

$$\texttt{M-step: } \Theta^{(t)} = \arg\max_{\Theta} Q(\Theta, \Theta^{(t-1)}).$$

In the M-step, the optimal mean and covariance matrix of each component is:

$$\mu_k = \frac{\sum_{j=1}^{N} x_j P_p(k|x_j, \Theta^{(t-1)}, W)}{\sum_{j=1}^{N} P_p(k|x_j, \Theta^{(t-1)}, W)}$$

$$\Sigma_k = \frac{\sum_{j=1}^{N} P_p(k|x_j, \Theta^{(t-1)}, W)(x_j - \mu_k)(x_j - \mu_k)^T}{\sum_{j=1}^{N} P_p(k|x_j, \Theta^{(t-1)}, W)}.$$

The update of the prior probability of each component is more difficult due to the normalizing constant Ω in the data likelihood

$$\Omega = \sum_{Z} \left(\prod_{k=1}^{N} \pi_{z_k} \prod_{i \neq j} \exp(w(i,j)\, \delta_{z_i z_j}) \right).$$

We need to find

$$\pi \equiv \{\pi_1, \ldots, \pi_m\} = \arg\max_{\pi} \sum_{l=1}^{M} \sum_{i=1}^{N} \log \pi_l P_p(l|x_i, \Theta^{(t-1)}, W) - \log \Omega(\pi), \quad (4.8)$$

which, unfortunately, does not have a closed-form solution in general.[1] In this chapter, we use a rather crude approximation of the optimal π instead. First, we estimate the values of $\log \Omega(\pi)$ on a grid $H = \{\hat{\pi}^n\}$ on the simplex defined by

$$\sum_{k=1}^{M} \pi_k = 1, \ \pi_k \geq 0.$$

Then in each M-step, we calculate the value of $\sum_{l=1}^{M} \sum_{i=1}^{N} \log \hat{\pi}_l^n P_p(l|x_i, \Theta^{(t-1)}, W)$ for each node $\hat{\pi}^n \in H$ and find the node $\hat{\pi}^*$ that maximizes the function defined in equation (4.8):

$$\hat{\pi}^* = \arg\max_{\hat{\pi}^n \in H} \sum_{l=1}^{M} \sum_{i=1}^{N} \log \hat{\pi}_l^n P_p(l|x_i, \Theta^{(t-1)}, W) - \log \Omega(\hat{\pi}^n).$$

We use $\hat{\pi}^*$ as the approximate solution of equation (4.8). In this chapter, the resolution of the grid is set to be 0.01. Although it works very well for all experiments in this chapter, we notice that the search over grid will be

---

[1][16] pointed out that with a different sampling assumption, a closed-form solution for equation (4.8) exists when only hard must-links are available. See Section 4.4.

fairly slow for $M > 5$. Shental et al. [17] proposed to find optimal π using gradient descent and approximate $\Omega(\pi)$ by pretending all specified relations are disjoint (see Section 4.3.1). Although this method is originally designed for hard constraints, it can be easily adapted for PPC. This will not be covered in this chapter.

It is important to note that with a non-trivial w, the cluster assignment of samples are no longer independent of each other, consequently the posterior estimation of each sample cannot be done separately. This fact brings extra computational problem and will be discussed later in Section 4.3.

4.2.4 Selecting the Constraint Weights

4.2.4.1 Example: How the Weight Affects Clustering

The weight matrix W is crucial to the performance of the PPC. Here we give an example demonstrating how the weight of pairwise relations affects the clustering process. Figure 4.1 (a) shows the two-dimensional data sampled from four spherical Gaussians centered at (-1,-1), (-1,1), (1,-1), and (1,1). We intend to group the data into two classes, as indicated by the symbols. Besides the data set, we also have 20 pairs correctly labeled as must-links and cannot-links, as shown in Figure 4.1 (b). We try to fit the data set with a two-component GMM. Figure 4.1 (c) and (d) give the density contour of the two possible models on the data. Without any pairwise relations specified, we have an approximately equal chance to get each GMM model. After incorporating pairwise relations, the EM optimization process is biased toward the intended one. The weights of pairwise relations are given as follows

$$
w(i,j) = \begin{cases} w & (x_i, x_j) \in C_= \\ -w & (x_i, x_j) \in C_{\neq} \\ 0 & \text{otherwise,} \end{cases}
$$

where $w \geq 0$ measures the certainty of all specified pairwise constraints. In Figure 4.2, we give three runs with the *same* initial model parameters but different weight for constraints.

For each run, we give snapshots of the model after 1, 3, 5, and 20 EM iterations. The first row is the run with $w = 0$ (standard GMM). The search ends up with a model that violates our prior knowledge of class membership. The middle row is the run with w set to 1.3, with the same poor initial condition; the model fitting process still goes to the wrong one again, although at a slower pace. In the bottom row, we increase w to 3; this time the model converges to the one we intend.

4.2.4.2 Choosing Weight w Based on Prior Knowledge

There are some occasions we can translate our prior belief on the relations into the weight W. Here we assume that the pairwise relations are labeled

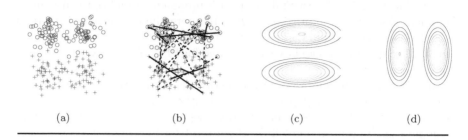

| (a) | (b) | (c) | (d) |

FIGURE 4.1: The influence of constraint weight on model fitting. (a) Artificial data set. (b) Must-links (solid lines) and cannot-links (dotted line). (c) and (d) The probability density contour of two possible fitted models.

by an oracle but contaminated by flipping noise before they are delivered to us. For each labeled pair (x_i, x_j), there is thus a certainty value $0.5 \leq \gamma_{ij} \leq 1$ equal to the probability that pairwise relation is *not* flipped.[2] Our prior knowledge would include those specified pairwise relations and their certainty values $\Gamma = \{\gamma_{ij}\}$.

This prior knowledge can be *approximately* encoded into the weight w by letting

$$
w(i,j) = \begin{cases} \frac{1}{2}\log(\frac{\gamma_{ij}}{1-\gamma_{ij}}) & (x_i, x_j) \text{ is specified as must-linked} \\ -\frac{1}{2}\log(\frac{\gamma_{ij}}{1-\gamma_{ij}}) & (x_i, x_j) \text{ is specified as cannot-linked} \\ 0 & \text{otherwise.} \end{cases} \tag{4.9}
$$

The details of the derivation are in Appendix B. It is obvious from equation (4.9) that for a specified pairwise relation (x_i, x_j), the greater the certainty value γ_{ij}, the greater the absolute value of weight $w(i,j)$.

Note that the weight designed this way is not necessarily optimal in terms of classification accuracy, as will be demonstrated by experiment in Section 4.5.1. The reason is twofold. First, equation (4.9) is derived based on a (possibly crude) approximation. Second, Gaussian mixture models, as classifiers, are often considerably biased from true class distribution of data. As a result, even if the PPC prior $P(Z|\Theta, W)$ faithfully reflects the truth, it does not necessarily lead to the best classification accuracy. Nevertheless, equation (4.9) gives a good initial guidance for choosing the weight. Our experiments in Section 4.5.1 show that this design often yields superior classification accuracy than simply using the hard constraints or ignoring the pairwise relations (standard GMM).

This weight design scheme is directly applicable when pairwise relations are labeled by domain experts and the certainty values are given at the same

---

[2]We only consider the certainty value > 0.5, because a pairwise relation with certainty $\gamma_{ij} < 0.5$ can be equivalently treated as its opposite relation with certainty $1 - \gamma_{ij}$.

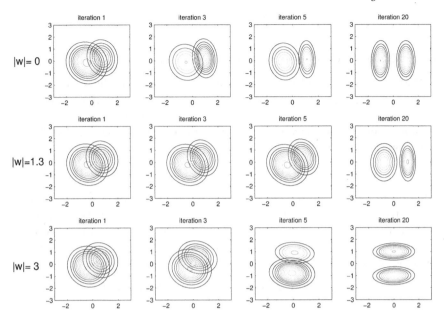

FIGURE 4.2: The contour of probability density fit on data with different weight given to pairwise relations. Top row: $w = 0$; Middle row: $w = 1.3$; Bottom row: $w = 3$.

time. We might also *estimate* the flipping noise parameters from historical data or from available statistics. For example, we can derive soft pairwise relations based on spatial or temporal continuity among samples. That is, we add soft must-links to all adjacent pairs of samples, assuming the flipping noise explaining all the adjacent pairs that are actually *not* in one class. We further assume that the flipping noise each pair follows the same distribution. Accordingly we assign the same weight to all adjacent pairs. Let q denote the probability that the label on an adjacent pair is flipped. We might be able to estimate q from labeled instances of a similar problem, for example, segmented images or time series. The maximum likelihood (ML) estimation of q is given by simple statistics:

$$\tilde{q} = \frac{\text{the number of adjacent pairs that are not in the same class}}{\text{the number of all adjacent pairs}}.$$

We give an application of this idea in Section 4.5.2.

4.3 Computing the Cluster Posterior

Both the M-step and the final clustering require the cluster membership posterior. Computing this posterior is simple for the standard GMM since each data point x_i is assigned to a cluster independently. The pairwise constraints bring extra relevancy in assignment among samples involved. From equation (4.7), if $w(i,j) \neq 0$,

$$P_p(z_i, z_j | x_i, x_j, \Theta, W) \neq P_p(z_i | x_i, \Theta, W) P_p(z_j | x_j, \Theta, W).$$

This relevancy can be further extended to any two pair x_i and x_j that are connected by a path of nonzero weights. Clearly $P_p(X, Z | \theta, W)$ can be best described as a undirected graphical model, and the exact inference of the posterior must be based on the maximal connected subgraphs (MCS). The inference of sample x_i in a MCS T based on a brute force marginalization is

$$P_p(z_i = k | X, \Theta, W) = \sum_{Z_T | z_i = k} P_p(Z_T | X_T, \Theta, W),$$

which requires time complexity $O(M^{|T|})$. This calculation can get prohibitively expensive if $|T|$ is very big.

We will first give some special cases with easy inference, then we will discuss Gibbs sampling and mean field approximation as two approximate inference models used for estimating the posterior. Other methods for complicated graphical model inference, such as (loopy) belief propagation, are also proposed to solve this kind of problem [15].

4.3.1 Two Special Cases with Easy Inference

Apparently the inference is easy when we limit ourselves to small MCS. Specifically, when $|T| \leq 2$, the pairwise relations are *disjoint*. With disjoint constraints, the posterior probability for the whole data set can be given in closed-form with $O(N)$ time complexity. Moreover, the evaluation of the normalization factor $\Omega(\pi)$ is simple:

$$\Omega(\pi) = (1 - \sum_{k=1}^{M} \pi_k^2)^{|C=|} (\sum_{k=1}^{M} \pi_k^2)^{|C \neq|}.$$

The optimization of π in M-step can thus be achieved with little cost. Sometimes disjoint relations are a natural choice: they can be generated by picking up sample pairs from the sample set and labeling the relations *without replacement*. More generally, we can avoid the expensive computation in posterior inference by breaking large MCS into small ones. To do this, we need to deliberately ignore some pairwise constraints. In Section 4.5.2, Experiment 2 is an application of this idea.

The second simplifying situation is when we have only hard must-links ($w(i,j) = +\infty$ or 0). Since must-link is an equivalence relation, we group the data set into several equivalence classes (called chunklets). Each chunklet can be treated as a single sample. That is, assume x_i is in chunklet T, we then have

$$P_p(z_i = k|x_i, \Theta, W) = P_p(Z_T = k|x_T, \Theta, W) = \frac{\prod_{j \in T} \pi_k P(x_j|\theta_k)}{\sum_{k'} (\prod_{j \in T} \pi_{k'} P(x_j|\theta_{k'}))}.$$

Similar ideas have been proposed independently in [4, 16, 21]. This case is useful when we are sure that a group of samples are from one source [16].

For more general cases where the exact inference is computationally prohibitive, we propose to use Gibbs sampling [14] and the mean field approximation [8] to estimate the posterior probability. This will be discussed in Section 4.3.2 and Section 4.3.3.

4.3.2 Estimation with Gibbs Sampling

In Gibbs sampling, we estimate $P_p(z_i|X, \Theta, W)$ as a sample mean

$$P_p(z_i = k|X, \Theta, W) = E(\delta_{z_i k}|X, \Theta, W) \approx \frac{1}{S} \sum_{t=1}^{S} \delta_{z_i^{(t)} k},$$

where the sum is over a sequence of S samples from $P(Z|X, \Theta, G)$ generated by the Gibbs MCMC. The tth sample in the sequence is generated by the usual Gibbs sampling technique:

- Pick $z_1^{(t)}$ from distribution $P_p(z_1|z_2^{(t-1)}, z_3^{(t-1)}, ..., z_N^{(t-1)}, X, w, \Theta)$

- Pick $z_2^{(t)}$ from distribution $P_p(z_2|z_1^{(t)}, z_3^{(t-1)}, ..., z_N^{(t-1)}, X, w, \Theta)$
  ...

- Pick $z_N^{(t)}$ from distribution $P_p(z_N|z_1^{(t)}, z_2^{(t)}, ..., z_{N-1}^{(t)}, X, w, \Theta)$

For pairwise relations it is helpful to introduce some notation. Let Z_{-i} denote an assignment of data points to clusters that leave out the assignment of x_i. Let $U(i)$ be the indices of the set of samples that participate in a pairwise relation with sample x_i, $U(i) = \{j : w(i,j) \neq 0\}$. Then we have

$$P_p(z_i|Z_{-i}, X, \Theta, W) \propto P(x_i, z_i|\Theta) \prod_{j \in U(i)} \exp(2w(i,j)\,\delta_{z_i z_j}). \quad (4.10)$$

The time complexity of each Gibbs sampling pass is $O(NnM)$, where n is the maximum number of pairwise relations a sample can be involved in. When W is sparse, the size of $U(i)$ is small, thus calculating $P_p(z_i|Z_{-i}, X, \Theta, W)$ is fairly cheap and Gibbs sampling can effectively estimate the posterior probability.

4.3.3 Estimation with Mean Field Approximation

Another approach to posterior estimation is to use mean field theory [8, 10]. Instead of directly evaluating the intractable $P_p(Z|X, \Theta, W)$, we try to find a tractable mean field approximation $Q(Z)$. To find a $Q(Z)$ close to the true posterior probability $P_p(Z|X, \Theta, W)$, we minimize the Kullback-Leibler divergence between them, i.e.,

$$\min_Q \text{KL}(Q(Z)|P_p(Z|X, \Theta, W)),$$

which can be recast into:

$$\max_Q [H(Q) + E_Q\{\log P_p(Z|X, \Theta, W)\}], \tag{4.11}$$

where $E_Q\{\cdot\}$ denotes the expectation with respect to Q. The simplest family of variational distribution is one where all the latent variables $\{z_i\}$ are independent of each other:

$$Q(Z) = \prod_{i=1}^{N} Q_i(z_i).$$

With this $Q(Z)$, the optimization problem in equation (4.11) does not have a closed-form solution, nor is it a convex problem. Instead, a locally optimal Q can be found iteratively with the following update equations

$$Q_i(z_i) \leftarrow \frac{1}{\Omega_i} \exp(E_Q\{\log P_p(Z|X, \Theta, W)|z_i\}) \tag{4.12}$$

for all i and $z_i \in \{1, 2, \cdots, M\}$. Here $\Omega_i = \sum_{z_i} \exp(E_Q\{\log P_p(Z|X, \Theta, W)|z_i\})$ is the local normalization constant. For the PPC model, we have

$$\exp(E_Q\{\log P_p(Z|X, \Theta, W)|z_i\}) = P(z_i|x_i, \Theta) \exp(\sum_{j \neq i} w(i, j)Q_j(z_i)).$$

Equation (4.12), collectively for all i, are the *mean field equations*. Evaluation of mean field equations requires at most $O(NnM)$ time complexity, which is the same as the time complexity of one Gibbs sampling pass. Successive updates of equation (4.12) will converge to a local optimum of equation (4.11). In our experiments, the convergence usually occurs after about 20 iterations, which is much less than the number of passes required for Gibbs sampling.

4.4 Related Models

Prior to our work, different authors have proposed several constrained clustering models based on k-means, including the seminal work by Wagstaff and colleagues [20, 21], and its successor [2, 3, 4]. These models generally fall into two classes. The first class of algorithms [2, 21] keep the original k-means cost function (reconstruction error) but confine the cluster assignments to be consistent with the specified pairwise relations. The problem can be casted into the following constrained optimization problem

$$\min_{Z,\mu} \sum_{i=1}^{N} ||x_i - \mu_{z_i}||^2$$

$$\text{subject to} \quad z_i = z_j, \text{ if } (x_i, x_j) \in C_=$$
$$z_i \neq z_j, \text{ if } (x_i, x_j) \in C_{\neq},$$

where $\mu = \{\mu_1, \cdots, \mu_M\}$ is the cluster centers. In the second class of algorithms, cluster assignments that violate the pairwise relations are allowed, but will be penalized. They employ a modified cost function [3]:

$$J(\mu, Z) = \frac{1}{2} \sum_{i=1}^{N} ||x_i - \mu_{z_i}||^2 + \sum_{(i,j) \in C_=} a_{ij}(z_i \neq z_j) + \sum_{(i,j) \in C_{\neq}} b_{ij}(z_i = z_j),$$

$$(4.13)$$

where a_{ij} is the penalty for violating the must-link between (x_i, x_j) and b_{ij} is the penalty when the violated pairwise relation is a cannot-link. It can be shown that both classes of algorithms are special cases of PPC with spherical Gaussian components and proper setting of radius and w (see Appendix C).

There are two weaknesses shared by the constrained k-means model. The first is their limited modeling capability inherited from the standard k-means. This weakness can be alleviated with the extra information from the pairwise constraints [20], but it often takes a lot of pairwise constraints to really achieve decent results when the distribution of class cannot be naturally modeled by k-means. As the second weakness, the hard clustering nature of constrained k-means often requires a combinatorial optimization of the cluster assignments, which is usually not trivial and often intractable. To cope with that, various ways have been proposed to obtain a suboptimal solution [2, 3, 21].

To overcome the limitation of constrained k-means, several authors proposed probabilistic constrained clustering models based on Gaussian mixture. The models proposed by Shental et al. [16, 17] address the situation where pairwise relations are hard constraints. The authors partition the whole data set into a number of chunklets consisting of samples that are (hard) must-linked to each other.[3] They discuss two sampling assumptions:

- Assumption 1: Chunklet X_i is generated i.i.d from component k with prior π_k [17], and the complete data likelihood is

$$P(X, Y | \Theta, E_\Omega) = \frac{1}{\Omega} \prod_{ij \in C_{\neq}} (1 - \delta_{z_i z_j}) \cdot \prod_{l=1}^{L} \{\pi_{z_l} \prod_{x_i \in X_l} P(x_i | \theta_{z_l})\},$$

---

[3]If a sample is not must-linked to any other samples, it comprises a chunklet by itself.

where E_Ω denotes the specified constraints.

- Assumption 2: Chunklet X_i is generated from component k with prior $\propto \pi_k^{|X_i|}$, where $|X_i|$ is the number of samples in X_i [17]. The complete data likelihood is:

$$P(X, Y|\Theta, E_\Omega) = \frac{1}{\Omega} \prod_{ij \in C_{\neq}} (1 - \delta_{z_i z_j}) \cdot \prod_{l=1}^{L} \{ \pi_{z_l}^{|X_l|} \prod_{x_i \in X_l} P(x_i | \theta_{z_l}) \} \quad (4.14)$$

$$= \frac{1}{\Omega} \prod_{ij \in C_{=}} \delta_{z_i z_j} \prod_{ij \in C_{\neq}} (1 - \delta_{z_i z_j}) \prod_{i=1}^{N} \pi_{z_i} P(x_i | \theta_{z_i}). \quad (4.15)$$

In Appendix A we show that when using Assumption 2, the model expressed in equations (4.14)-(4.15) is equivalent to PPC with only hard constraints (as expressed in equation (4.6)). It is suggested in [17] that Assumption 1 might be appropriate, for example, when chunklets are generated from temporal continuity. When pairwise relations are generated by labeling sample pairs picked from the data set, Assumption 2 might be more reasonable. Assumption 1 allows a closed-form solution in the M-step, including a solution for π, in each EM iteration [17].

To incorporate the uncertainty associated with pairwise relations, Law et al. [11, 12] proposed to use soft group constraints. To model a must-link between any sample pair (x_i, x_j), they create a group l and express the strength of the must-link as the membership of x_i and x_j to group l. This strategy works well for some simple situations, for example, when the pairwise relations are disjoint (as defined in Section 4.3.1). However, it is awkward if samples are shared by multiple groups, which is unavoidable when samples are commonly involved in multiple relations. Another serious drawback of the group constraints model is its inability to model cannot-links. Due to these obvious limitations, we omit the empirical comparison of this model to PPC in the following experiments section.

4.5 Experiments

The experiments section consists of two parts. In Section 4.5.1, we empirically evaluate the influence of randomly generated constraints on the clustering result when using PPC and compare it with other constrained clustering algorithms. In Section 4.5.2, we address real-world problems, where the constraints are derived from our prior knowledge. Also in this section, we demonstrate the approaches to reduce computational complexity, as described in Section 4.3.

Following are some abbreviations we will use throughout this section: *soft-PPC* for PPC with soft constraints, *hard-PPC* for PPC with hard constraints (implemented based on equation (4.6)), *soft-CKmeans* for the k-means with soft constraints [3] and *hard-CKmeans* for the k-means with hard constraints [21]. The Gaussian mixture model with hard constraints [16, 17] will be referred to as constrained-EM.

4.5.1 Artificial Constraints

In this section, we discuss the influence of pairwise relations on PPC's clustering. Due to the equivalence between hard-PPC and constrained-EM algorithm [17], we will not repeat the experiments with correct constraints and hard constraints in Chapter 3. Instead, we consider the more general situation where pairwise constraints are noisy, and thus justify the use of soft-PPC. The weights of soft-PPC are designed based on the strategy described in Section 4.2.4. The result is compared to hard-PPC and other semi-supervised clustering models.

Constraint Selection: We chose to limit our discussion to the disjoint pairwise relations, and leave the more complicated cases to Section 4.5.2. As discussed in Section 4.3.1, the disjoint pairwise relations, hard or soft, allow fast solution in the maximization step in each EM iteration. The pairwise relations are generated as follows – we randomly pick two samples from the data set without replacement. If the two have the same class label, we then add a must-link constraint between them; otherwise, we add a cannot-link constraint. After the constraints are chosen, we add noise to all the constraints by randomly flipping each pairwise relation with a certain probability $q \leq 0.5$. For the soft-PPC model, the weight $w(i, j)$ to each specified pairwise relation is given as follows:

$$w(i,j) = \begin{cases} \frac{1}{2}\log(\frac{1-q}{q}) & (x_i, x_j) \text{ specified as must-link} \\ -\frac{1}{2}\log(\frac{1-q}{q}) & (x_i, x_j) \text{ specified as cannot-link.} \end{cases} \quad (4.16)$$

For soft-CKmeans, we give equal weights to all the specified constraints. Because there is no guiding rule in literature on how to choose weight for soft-CKmeans model, we simply use the weight that yields the highest classification accuracy.

Performance Evaluation: We try PPC (with the number of components equal to the number of classes) with various numbers of pairwise relations. For comparison, we also give results of standard GMM, standard k-means, hard-CKmeans [21], and hard-PPC. For each clustering result, a confusion matrix is built to compare it to the true labeling. The classification accuracy is calculated as the ratio of the sum of diagonal elements to the number of all samples. The reported classification accuracy is averaged over 100 different realizations of pairwise relations.

Experiment 1: Artificial Constraints

In this experiment, we evaluate the performance of soft-PPC with noisy constraints on three two-dimensional artificial data sets and three UCI data sets. The three two-dimensional artificial data sets (Figure 4.3) are designed to highlight PPC's superior modeling flexibility over constrained k-means.[4] In each example, there are 200 samples in each class. We perform the same experiments on three UCI data sets: the Iris data set has 150 samples and three classes, 50 samples in each class; the Waveform data set has 5000 samples and three classes, around 1700 samples in each class; the Pendigits data set includes four classes (digits 0, 6, 8, 9), each with 750 samples.

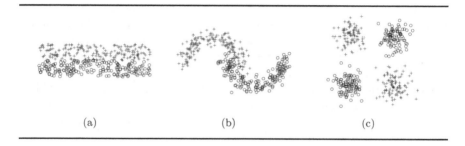

(a)   (b)   (c)

FIGURE 4.3: Three artificial data sets, with class denoted by symbols.

On each data set, we randomly generate a number of disjoint pairwise relations to have 50% of the data involved. In this experiment, we try two different noise levels with q set to 0.15 and 0.3. Figure 4.4 compares the classification accuracies given by the maximum likelihood (ML) solutions[5] of different models. The accuracy for each model is averaged over 20 random realizations of pairwise relations. On all data sets except artificial data set 3, soft-PPC with the designed weight gives higher accuracy than hard-PPC and standard GMM on both noise levels. On artificial data set 3, when $q = 0.3$ hard-PPC gives the best classification accuracy.[6] Soft-PPC apparently gives superior classification accuracy to the k-means models on all six data sets, even though the weight of soft-CKmeans is optimized. Figure 4.4 also shows

---

[4]Some authors [4, 6, 22] combined standard or constrained k-means with metric learning based on pairwise relations, and reported improvement on classification accuracy. This will not be discussed in this chapter.

[5]We choose the one with the highest data likelihood among 100 runs with different random initialization. For k-means models, including soft-CKmeans and hard-CKmeans, we use the solutions with the smallest cost.

[6]Further experiment shows that on this data, soft-PPC with the optimal w (> the one suggested by equation (4.16)) is still slightly better than hard-PPC.

that it can be harmful to use hard constraints when pairwise relations are noisy, especially when the noise is significant. Indeed, as shown by Figure 4.4 (d) and (f), hard-PPC can yield accuracy even worse than standard GMM.

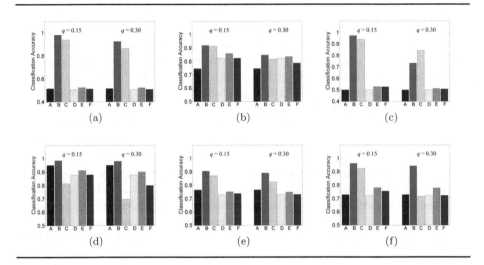

FIGURE 4.4: Classification accuracy with noisy pairwise relations. We use all the data in clustering. In each panel, **A**: standard GMM; **B**: soft-PPC; **C**: hard-PPC; **D**: standard k-means; **E**: soft-CKmeans with optimal weight; **F**: hard-CKmeans.

4.5.2 Real-World Problems

In this section, we present two examples where pairwise constraints are from domain experts or common sense. Both examples are about image segmentation based on Gaussian mixture models. In the first problem (Experiment 2), hard pairwise relations are derived from image labeling done by a domain expert. In the second problem, soft pairwise relations are generated based on spatial continuity.

Experiment 2: Hard Cannot-Links from Partial Class Information

The experiment in this subsection shows the application of pairwise constraints on partial class information. For example, consider a problem with six classes $A, B, ..., F$. The classes are grouped into several class sets: $C_1 = \{A, B, C\}, C_2 = \{D, E\}, C_3 = \{F\}$. The samples are partially labeled in the sense that we are told which class set a sample is from, but not which specific class it is from. We can logically derive a cannot-link constraint between any pair of samples known to belong to different class sets, while no must-link constraint can be derived if each class set has more than one class in it.

Figure 4.5 (a) is a 120x400 region from a Greenland ice sheet from NASA Langley DAAC [7] [18]. Each pixel has intensities from seven spectrum bands. This region is labeled into snow areas and non-snow areas, as indicated in Figure 4.5 (b). The snow areas may contain samples from several classes of interest: ice, melting snow, and dry snow, while the non-snow areas can be bare land, water, or cloud. The labeling from an expert contains incomplete but useful information for further segmentation of the image. To segment the image, we first divide it into 5x5x7 blocks (175 dim vectors). We use the first 50 principal components as feature vectors. Our goal is then to segment the image into (typically > 2) areas by clustering those feature vectors. With PPC, we can encode the partial class information into cannot-link constraints.

For hard-PPC, we use half of the data samples for training and the rest for test. Hard cannot-link constraints (only on training set) are generated as follows: for each block in the non-snow area, we randomly choose (without replacement) six blocks from the snow area to build cannot-link constraints. By doing this, we achieve cliques with size seven (1 non-snow block + 6 snow blocks). As in Section 4.5.1, we apply the model fit with hard-PPC to the test set and combine the clustering results on both data sets into a complete picture. Clearly, the clustering task is non-trivial for any $M > 2$. A typical clustering result of 3-component standard GMM and 3-component PPC are shown as Figure 4.5 (c) and (d) respectively. Standard GMM gives a clustering that is clearly in disagreement with the human labeling in Figure 4.5 (b). The hard-PPC segmentation makes far fewer mis-assignments of snow areas (tagged white and gray) to non-snow (black) than does the GMM. The hard-PPC segmentation properly labels almost all of the non-snow regions as non-snow. Furthermore, the segmentation of the snow areas into the two classes (not labeled) tagged white and gray in Figure 4.5 (d) reflects subtle differences in the snow regions captured by the gray-scale image from spectral channel 1, as shown in Figure 4.5 (a).

Experiment 3: Soft Links from Continuity

In this subsection, we will present an example where soft constraints come from continuity. As in the previous experiment, we try to do image segmentation based on clustering. The image is divided into blocks and rearranged into feature vectors. We use a GMM to model those feature vectors, with each Gaussian component representing one texture. However, standard GMM

---

[7]We use the first seven MoDerate Resolution Imaging Spectroradiometer (MODIS) Channels with bandwidths as follows (in nm): Channel 1: 620-670, Channel 2: 841-876, Channel 3: 459-479, Channel 4: 545-565, Channel 5: 1230-1250, Channel 6: 1628-1652, Channel 7: 2105-2155.

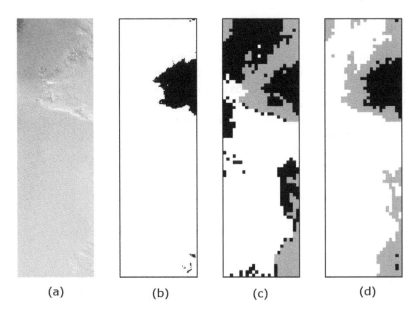

FIGURE 4.5: Clustering with hard constraints derived from partial labeling. (a) Gray-scale image from the first spectral channel 1. (b) Partial label given by an expert; black pixels denote non-snow areas and white pixels denote snow areas. Clustering result of standard GMM (c) and PPC (d). (c) and (d) are colored according to image blocks' assignment.

often fails to give good segmentations because it cannot make use of the spatial continuity of the image, which is essential in many image segmentation models, such as random field [5]. In our algorithm, the spatial continuity is incorporated as the soft must-link preferences with uniform weight between each block and its neighbors. As described in Section 4.2.4, the weight w of the soft must-link can be given as

$$w = \frac{1}{2} \log(\frac{1-q}{q}), \tag{4.17}$$

where q is the ratio of softly-linked adjacent pairs that are not in the same class. Usually q is given by an expert or estimated from segmentation results of similar images. In this experiment, we assume we already know the ratio q, which is calculated from the label of the image.

The *complete* data likelihood is

$$P_p(X, Z|\Theta, W) = \frac{1}{\Omega} P(X, Z|\Theta) \prod_i \prod_{j \in U(i)} \exp(w \, \delta_{z_i z_j}),$$

where $U(i)$ means the neighbors of the ith block. The EM algorithm can be roughly interpreted as iterating on two steps: (1) estimating the texture description (parameters of mixture model) based on segmentation, and (2) segmenting the image based on the texture description given by step 1. Since exact calculation of the posterior probability is intractable due to the large clique containing all samples, we have to resort to approximation methods. In this experiment, both the Gibbs sampling (see Section 4.3.2) and the mean field approximation (see Section 4.3.3) are used for posterior estimation. For Gibbs sampling, equation (4.10) is reduced to

$$P_p(z_i|Z_{-i}, X, \Theta, W) \propto P(x_i, z_i|\Theta) \prod_{j \in U(i)} \exp(2w\, \delta_{z_i z_j}).$$

The mean field equation (4.12) is reduced to

$$Q_i(z_i) \leftarrow \frac{1}{\Omega_i} P(x_i, z_i|\Theta) \prod_{j \in U(i)} \exp(2w\, Q_j(z_i)).$$

The image shown in Figure 4.6 (a) is built from four Brodatz textures.[8] This image is divided into 7x7 blocks and then rearranged to 49-dim vectors. We use those vectors' first five principal components as the associated feature vectors. A typical clustering result of 4-component standard GMM is shown in Figure 4.6 (b). For soft-PPC, the soft must-links with weight w calculated from equation (4.17) are added between each block and its four neighbors. Figure 4.6 (c) and (d) are the clustering result of 4-component soft-PPC with Gibbs sampling and mean field approximation, respectively. One run with Gibbs sampling takes around 160 minutes on a PC with Pentium 4, 2.0 G HZ processor whereas the algorithm using the mean field approximation takes only 3.1 minutes. Although mean field approximation is about 50 times faster than Gibbs sampling, the clustering results are comparable according to Figure 4.6. Comparing to the result given by standard GMM, soft-PPC with both approximation methods achieves significantly better segmentation after incorporating spatial continuity.

4.6   Discussion

Despite its success shown above, PPC has its limitations. First, PPC often needs a substantial *proportion* of samples involved in pairwise relations to give good results. Indeed, if we have the number of relations fixed and keep adding samples without any new relations, the algorithm will finally degenerate into unsupervised learning (clustering). To overcome this, one can instead design semi-supervised clustering algorithms based on discriminative models. Efforts

---

[8]Downloaded from http://sipi.usc.edu/services/database/Database.html, April 2004.

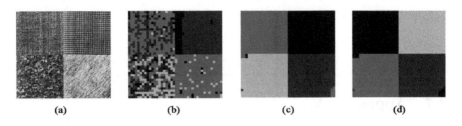

(a)   (b)   (c)   (d)

FIGURE 4.6: Clustering on the Brodatz texture data. (a) Texture combination. (b) Clustering result of standard GMM. (c) Clustering result of soft-PPC with Gibbs sampling. (d) Clustering result of soft-PPC with mean field approximation. (b)-(d) are shaded according to the blocks assignments to clusters.

in that direction include using support vector machines (see Chapter 17) or Gaussian process classifiers [13] while considering the pairwise constraints some kind of observation or labeling. Second, since PPC is based on the Gaussian mixture model, it works well in the situation where the data in each class can be approximated by a Gaussian distribution. When this condition is not satisfied, PPC could lead to poor results. One way to alleviate this weakness is to use multiple clusters to model one class [23]. Third, in choosing the weight matrix W, although our design works well in some situations, it is not clear how to set the weight for a more general situation.

To address the computational difficulty caused by large cliques, we propose two approximation methods: Gibbs sampling and mean field approximation. We also observe Gibbs sampling can be fairly slow for large cliques. One way to address this problem is to use fewer sampling passes (and thus a cruder approximate inference) in the early phase of EM training, and gradually increase the number of sampling passes (and a finer approximation) when EM is close to convergence. By doing this, we may be able to achieve a much faster algorithm without sacrificing too much precision. For the mean field approximation, the bias brought by the independence assumption among $Q_i(\cdot)$ could be severe for some problems. We can ameliorate this, as suggested by [8], by retaining more sub-structure of the original graphical model (for PPC, it is expressed in W), while still keeping the computation tractable.

Acknowledgments

Portions of this work were variously supported by NASA Collaborative Agreement NCC 2-1264, and NSF grants ITR CCF-0082736 and ITR OCI-

---

4.7 Appendix A

In this part of appendix, we prove that when $|w(i,j)| \to \infty$ for each specified pair (x_i, x_j), the complete likelihood of PPC can be written as in equation (4.6), and thus equivalent to the model proposed by [16].

In the model proposed by [16], the complete likelihood is written as:

$$P(X, Z|\Theta, E_\Omega) = \frac{1}{\Omega} \prod_{c_i} \delta_{y_{c_i}} \prod_{a_i^1 \neq a_i^2} (1 - \delta_{y_{a_i^1}, y_{a_i^2}}) \prod_{i=1}^{N} P(z_i|\Theta) P(x_i|z_i, \Theta)$$

$$= \frac{1}{\Omega} \prod_{c_i} \delta_{y_{c_i}} \prod_{a_i^1 \neq a_i^2} (1 - \delta_{y_{a_i^1}, y_{a_i^2}}) P(X, Z|\Theta)$$

where E_Ω stands for the pairwise constraints, $\delta_{y_{c_i}}$ is 1 iff all the points in the chunklet c_i have the same label, and (a_i^1, a_i^2) is the index of the sample pair with hard cannot-link between them. This is equivalent to

$$P(X, Z|\Theta, E_\Omega) = \begin{cases} \frac{1}{\Omega} P(X, Z|\Theta) & Z \text{ satisfies all the constraints;} \\ 0 & \text{otherwise.} \end{cases} \quad (4.18)$$

In the corresponding PPC model with hard constraints, we have

$$w(i,j) = \begin{cases} +\infty & (i,j) \in C_= \\ -\infty & (i,j) \in C_{\neq} \\ 0 & \text{otherwise.} \end{cases}$$

According to equations (4.3) and (4.18), to prove $P(X, Z|\Theta, E_\Omega) = P_p(X, Z|\Theta, W)$, we only need to prove $P_p(Z|\Theta, W) = 0$ for all the Z that violate the constraints, that is

$$P_p(Z|\Theta, W) = \frac{\prod_k \pi_{z_k} \prod_{i \neq j} \exp(w(i,j)\, \delta_{z_i z_j})}{\sum_Z \prod_l \pi_{z_l} \prod_{m \neq n} \exp(w(m,n)\, \delta_{z_m z_n})} = 0.$$

First let us assume Z violates one must-link between pair (α, β) $(w(\alpha, \beta) = +\infty)$, we have

$$z_\alpha \neq z_\beta \Rightarrow \delta_{z_\alpha z_\beta} = 0 \Rightarrow \exp(w(\alpha, \beta)\, \delta_{z_\alpha z_\beta}) = 1.$$

We assume the constraints are consistent. In other words, there is at least one Z that satisfies all the constraints. We can denote one such Z by Z^*. We also assume each component has a positive prior probability. It is straightforward to show that

$$P_p(Z^*|\Theta, W) > 0.$$

Then it is easy to show

$$
\begin{aligned}
P_p(Z|\Theta, W) &= \frac{\prod_k \pi_{z_k} \prod_{i \neq j} \exp(w(i,j)\, \delta_{z_i z_j})}{\sum_Z \prod_l \pi_{z_l} \prod_{m \neq n} \exp(w(m,n)\, \delta_{z_m, z_n})} \\
&\leq \frac{\prod_k \pi_{z_k} \prod_{i \neq j} \exp(w(i,j)\, \delta_{z_i z_j})}{\prod_k \pi_{z_k^*} \prod_{i \neq j} \exp(w(m,n)\, \delta_{z_i^* z_j^*})} \\
&= \left(\prod_k \frac{\pi_{z_k}}{\pi_{z_k^*}} \prod_{(i,j) \neq (\alpha, \beta)} \frac{\exp(w(i,j)\, \delta_{z_i z_j})}{\exp(w(i,j)\, \delta_{z_i^* z_j^*})}\right) \frac{\exp(2w(\alpha,\beta)\, \delta_{z_\alpha z_\beta})}{\exp(2w(\alpha,\beta)\, \delta_{z_\alpha^* z_\beta^*})} \\
&= \left(\prod_k \frac{\pi_{z_k}}{\pi_{z_k^*}} \prod_{(i,j) \neq (\alpha, \beta)} \frac{\exp(w(i,j)\, \delta_{z_i z_j})}{\exp(w(i,j)\, \delta_{z_i^* z_j^*})}\right) \frac{1}{\exp(2w(\alpha,\beta)\, \delta_{z_\alpha^* z_\beta^*})}.
\end{aligned}
$$

Since Z^* satisfies all the constraints, we must have

$$\prod_{(i,j) \neq (\alpha, \beta)} \frac{\exp(w(i,j)\, \delta_{z_i z_j})}{\exp(w(i,j)\, \delta_{z_i^* z_j^*})} \leq 1.$$

So we have

$$P_p(Z|\Theta, W) \leq \left(\prod_k \frac{\pi_{z_k}}{\pi_{z_k^*}}\right) \frac{1}{\exp(2w(\alpha,\beta)\, \delta_{z_\alpha^* z_\beta^*})}.$$

When $w(\alpha, \beta) \to +\infty$, we have

$$\frac{1}{\exp(2w(\alpha,\beta)\, \delta_{z_\alpha^* z_\beta^*})} \to 0$$

and then $P_p(Z|\Theta, W) \leq (\prod_k \frac{\pi_{z_k}}{\pi_{z_k^*}}) \frac{1}{\exp(2w(\alpha,\beta)\, \delta_{z_\alpha^* z_\beta^*})} \to 0$. The cannot-link case can be proven in a similar way.

■

4.8 Appendix B

In this appendix, we show how to derive weight w from the certainty value γ_{ij} for each pair (x_i, x_j). Let E denote those original (noise-free) labeled pairwise relations and $\tilde{E}$ the noisy version delivered to us. If we know the original pairwise relations E, we only have to consider the cluster assignments that are consistent with E and neglect the others, that is, the prior probability of Z is

$$P(Z|\Theta, E) = \begin{cases} \frac{1}{\Omega_E} P(Z|\Theta) & Z \text{ is consistent with } E \\ 0 & \text{otherwise,} \end{cases}$$

where Ω_E is the normalization constant for E: $\Omega_E = \sum_{Z: \text{ consistent with } E} P(Z|\Theta)$. Since we know $\tilde{E}$ and the associated certainty values $\Gamma = \{\gamma_{ij}\}$, we know

$$P(Z|\Theta, \tilde{E}, \Gamma) = \sum_E P(Z|\Theta, E, \tilde{E}, \Gamma) P(E|\tilde{E}, \Gamma) \qquad (4.19)$$

$$= \sum_E P(Z|\Theta, E) P(E|\tilde{E}, \Gamma). \qquad (4.20)$$

Let $E(Z) \equiv$ the unique E that is consistent with Z, from equation (4.20) we know

$$P(Z|\Theta, \tilde{E}, \Gamma) = P_p(Z|\Theta, E(Z)) P(E(Z)|\tilde{E}, \Gamma)$$

$$= \frac{1}{\Omega_E} P(Z|\Theta) P(E(Z)|\tilde{E}, \Gamma) = \frac{1}{\Omega_E} P(E(Z)|\tilde{E}, \Gamma) P(Z|\Theta).$$

If we ignore the variation of Ω_E over E, we can get an approximation of $P(Z|\Theta, \tilde{E}, \Gamma)$, denoted as $P_a(Z|\Theta, \tilde{E}, \Gamma)$:

$$P_a(Z|\Theta, \tilde{E}, \Gamma) = \frac{1}{\Omega_a} P(Z|\Theta) P(E(Z)|\tilde{E}, \Gamma)$$

$$= \frac{1}{\Omega_a} P(Z|\Theta) \prod_{i<j} \gamma_{ij}^{H_{ij}(\tilde{E}, z_i, z_j)} (1 - \gamma_{ij})^{1 - H_{ij}(\tilde{E}, z_i, z_j)}$$

where Ω_a is the new normalization constant: $\Omega_a = \sum_Z P(Z|\Theta) P(E(Z)|\tilde{E}, \Gamma)$ and

$$H_{ij}(\tilde{E}, z_i, z_j) = \begin{cases} 1 & (z_i, z_j) \text{ is consistent with } \tilde{E} \\ 0 & \text{otherwise} \end{cases}.$$

We argue that $P_a(Z|\Theta, \tilde{E}, \Gamma)$ is equal to a PPC prior probability $P_p(Z|\Theta, W)$ with

$$w(i, j) = \begin{cases} \frac{1}{2} \log(\frac{\gamma_{ij}}{1 - \gamma_{ij}}) & (z_i, z_j) \text{ is specified as must-linked in } \tilde{E} \\ -\frac{1}{2} \log(\frac{\gamma_{ij}}{1 - \gamma_{ij}}) & (z_i, z_j) \text{ is specified as cannot-linked in } \tilde{E} \\ 0 & \text{otherwise.} \end{cases}$$

This can be easily proven by verifying

$$\frac{P_p(Z|\Theta, W)}{P_a(Z|\Theta, \tilde{E}, \Gamma)} = \frac{\Omega_a}{\Omega_w} \prod_{i<j, w(i,j) \neq 0} \gamma_{ij}^{\text{sign}(w(i,j)) - 1} (1 - \gamma_{ij})^{-\text{sign}(w(i,j))} = \text{constant.}$$

Since both $P_a(Z|\Theta, \tilde{E}, \Gamma)$ and $P_p(Z|\Theta, W)$ are normalized, we know

$$P_a(Z|\Theta, \tilde{E}, \Gamma) = P_p(Z|\Theta, W).$$

4.9 Appendix C

In this appendix, we show how to derive the k-means model with soft and hard constraints from PPC.

C.1 From PPC to K-means with Soft Constraints

The adapted cost function for k-means with soft constraints is:

$$J(\mu, Z) = \frac{1}{2} \sum_{i=1}^{N} ||x_i - \mu_{z_i}||^2 + \sum_{(i,j) \in C_=} a_{ij}(z_i \neq z_j) + \sum_{(i,j) \in C_{\neq}} b_{ij}(z_i = z_j) \quad (4.21)$$

where μ_k is the center of the kth cluster. Equation (4.13) can be rewritten as

$$J(\mu, Z) = \frac{1}{2} \sum_{i=1}^{N} ||x_i - \mu_{z_i}||^2 - \sum_{ij} w(i,j)\delta_{z_i z_j} + C, \quad (4.22)$$

with $C = -\sum_{(i,j) \in C_=} a_{ij}$ is a constant and

$$w(i,j) = \begin{cases} a_{ij} & (i,j) \in C_= \\ -b_{ij} & (i,j) \in C_{\neq} \\ 0 & \text{otherwise.} \end{cases}$$

The clustering process includes minimizing the cost function $J(\mu, Z)$ over both the model parameters $\mu = \{\mu_1, \mu_2, ..., \mu_M\}$ and cluster assignment $Z = \{z_1, z_2, ..., z_N\}$. The optimization is usually done iteratively with modified Linde-Buzo-Gray (LBG) algorithm. Assume we have the PPC model, where the matrix w is the same as in equation (4.22). We further constrain each Gaussian component to be spherical with radius σ. The complete data likelihood for the PPC model is

$$P(X, Z|\Theta, W) = \frac{1}{\Omega} \prod_{i=1}^{N} \{\pi_{z_i} \exp(-\sum_{i=1}^{N} \frac{||x_i - \mu_{z_i}||^2}{2\sigma^2})\} \prod_{mn} \exp(w(m,n)\delta_{z_m z_n}),$$

$$(4.23)$$

where Ω is the normalizing constant and μ_k is the mean of the kth Gaussian component. To build its connection to the cost function in equation (4.22), we consider the following scaling:

$$\sigma \to \alpha\sigma, \quad w(i,j) \to w(i,j)/\alpha^2. \quad (4.24)$$

The complete data likelihood with the scaling parameters α is

$$P_\alpha(X, Z|\Theta, W) = \frac{1}{\Omega(\alpha)} \prod_{i=1}^{N} \{\pi_{z_i} \exp(-\sum_{i=1}^{N} \frac{||x_i - \mu_{z_i}||^2}{2\alpha^2\sigma^2})\} \prod_{mn} \exp(\frac{w(m,n)}{\alpha^2}\delta_{z_m z_n}).$$

$$(4.25)$$

It can be shown that when $\alpha \to 0$, the maximum data likelihood will dominate the data likelihood

$$\lim_{\alpha \to 0} \frac{\max_Z P_\alpha(X, Z|\Theta, W)}{\sum_Z P_\alpha(X, Z|\Theta, W)} = 1. \tag{4.26}$$

To prove equation (4.26), we first show that when α is small enough, we have

$$\arg\max_Z P_\alpha(X, Z|\Theta, W) = Z^* \equiv \arg\min_Z \{\sum_{i=1}^N \frac{||x_i - \mu_{z_i^*}||^2}{2} - \sum_{mn} w(m, n)\delta_{z_m^* z_n^*}\}. \tag{4.27}$$

Proof of equation (4.27): Assume Z' is any cluster assignment different than Z^*. We only need to show that when α is small enough,

$$P_\alpha(X, Z^*|\Theta, W) > P_\alpha(X, Z'|\Theta, W). \tag{4.28}$$

To prove equation (4.28), we notice that

$$\log P_\alpha(X, Z^*|\Theta, W) - \log P_\alpha(X, Z'|\Theta, W)$$
$$= \sum_{i=1}^N (\log \pi_{z_i^*} - \log \pi_{z_i'}) + \frac{1}{\alpha^2}\{\sum_{i=1}^N (\frac{||x_i - \mu_{z_i'}||^2}{2} - \frac{||x_i - \mu_{z_i^*}||^2}{2}) -$$
$$\sum_{mn} w(m, n)(\delta_{z_m' z_n'} - \delta_{z_m^* z_n^*})\}.$$

Since $Z^* = \arg\min_Z \{\sum_{i=1}^N \frac{||x_i - \mu_{z_i^*}||^2}{2} - \sum_{mn} w(m, n)\delta_{z_m^* z_n^*}\}$, we have

$$\sum_{i=1}^N (\frac{||x_i - \mu_{z_i'}||^2}{2} - \frac{||x_i - \mu_{z_i^*}||^2}{2}) - \sum_{mn} w(m, n)(\delta_{z_m' z_n'} - \delta_{z_m^* z_n^*}) > 0.$$

Let $\varepsilon = \sum_{i=1}^N (\frac{||x_i - \mu_{z_i'}||^2}{2} - \frac{||x_i - \mu_{z_i^*}||^2}{2}) - \sum_{mn} w(m, n)(\delta_{z_m' z_n'} - \delta_{z_m^* z_n^*})$, we can see that when α is small enough

$$\log P_\alpha(X, Z^*|\Theta, W) - \log P_\alpha(X, Z'|\Theta, W) = \sum_{i=1}^N (\log \pi_{z_i^*} - \log \pi_{z_i'}) + \frac{\varepsilon}{\alpha^2} 0. \tag{4.29}$$

∎

It is obvious from equation (4.29) that for any Z' different than Z^*

$$\lim_{\alpha \to 0} \log P_\alpha(X, Z^*|\Theta, W) - \log P_\alpha(X, Z'|\Theta, W)$$
$$= \lim_{\alpha \to 0} \sum_{i=1}^N (\log \pi_{z_i^*} - \log \pi_{z_i'}) + \frac{\varepsilon}{\alpha^2}$$
$$= +\infty,$$

or equivalently

$$\lim_{\alpha \to 0} \frac{P_\alpha(X, Z'|\Theta, W)}{P_\alpha(X, Z^*|\Theta, W)} = 0,$$

which proves equation (4.26). As the result of equation (4.26), when optimizing the model parameters we can equivalently maximize $\max_Z P_\alpha(X, Z|\Theta, W)$ over Θ. It is then a joint optimization problem

$$\max_{\Theta, Z} P_\alpha(X, Z|\Theta, W).$$

Following the same thought, we find the soft posterior probability of each sample (as in conventional mixture model) becomes hard membership (as in k-means). This fact can be simply proved as follows. The posterior probability of sample x_i to component k is

$$P_\alpha(z_i = k|X, \Theta, W) = \frac{\sum_{Z|z_i=k} P_\alpha(X, Z|\Theta, W)}{\sum_Z P_\alpha(X, Z|\Theta, W)}.$$

From equation (4.26), it is easy to see

$$\lim_{\alpha \to 0} P_\alpha(z_i = k|X, \Theta, W) = \begin{cases} 1 & z_i^* = k \\ 0 & \text{otherwise.} \end{cases}$$

The negative logarithm of the complete likelihood P_α is then:

$$\begin{aligned} J_\alpha(\Theta, Z) &= -\log P_\alpha(X, Z|\Theta, W) \\ &= -\sum_{i=1}^N \log \pi_{z_i} + \sum_{i=1}^N \frac{||x_i - \mu_{z_i}||^2}{2\alpha^2} - \sum_{mn} \frac{w(m,n)}{\alpha^2} \delta_{z_m z_n} + \log(\Omega(\alpha)) \\ &= -\sum_{i=1}^N \log \pi_{z_i} + \frac{1}{\alpha^2} \left(\sum_{i=1}^N \frac{||x_i - \mu_{z_i}||^2}{2} - \sum_{mn} w(m,n) \delta_{z_m z_n} \right) + C, \end{aligned}$$

where $C = \log \Omega(\alpha)$ is a constant. It is obvious that when $\alpha \to 0$, we can neglect the term $-\sum_{i=1}^N \log \pi_{z_i}$. Hence the only model parameters left for adjusting are the Gaussian means μ. We only have to consider the new cost function

$$\tilde{J}_\alpha(\mu, Z) = \frac{1}{\alpha^2} \left(\sum_{i=1}^N \frac{||x_i - \mu_{z_i}||^2}{2} - \sum_{mn} w(m,n) \delta_{z_m z_n} \right),$$

the optimization of which is obviously equivalent to equation (4.21). So we can conclude that when $\alpha \to 0$ in equation (4.24), the PPC model shown in equation (4.23) becomes a k-means model with soft constraints.

C.2 From PPC to K-means with Hard Constraints (COP-KMEANS)

COP-KMEANS is a hard clustering algorithm with hard constraints. The goal is to find a set of cluster centers μ and clustering result Z that minimizes the cost function

$$\sum_{i=1}^{N} ||x_i - \mu_{z_i}||^2, \quad (4.30)$$

while subject to the constraints

$$z_i = z_j, \text{ if } (x_i, x_j) \in C_= \quad (4.31)$$
$$z_i \neq z_j, \text{ if } (x_i, x_j) \in C_{\neq}. \quad (4.32)$$

Assume we have the PPC model with soft relations represented with the matrix w such that:

$$w(i,j) = \begin{cases} w & (x_i, x_j) \in C_= \\ -w & (x_i, x_j) \in C_{\neq} \\ 0 & \text{otherwise} \end{cases}$$

where $w > 0$. We further constrain each Gaussian component to be spherical with radius σ. The complete data likelihood for the PPC model is

$$P(X, Z|\Theta, W) = \frac{1}{\Omega} \prod_{i=1}^{N} \{\pi_{z_i} \exp(-\sum_{i=1}^{N} \frac{||x_i - \mu_{z_i}||^2}{2\sigma^2})\}$$
$$\prod_{(m,n) \in C_=} \exp(w\delta_{z_m z_n}) \prod_{(m',n') \in C_{\neq}} \exp(-w\delta_{z_{m'} z_{n'}}), \quad (4.33)$$

where μ_k is the mean of the kth Gaussian component. There are infinite ways to get equations (4.30)-(4.32) from equation (4.33), but we consider the following scaling with factor β:

$$\sigma \to \beta\sigma, \quad w(i,j) \to w(i,j)/\beta^3. \quad (4.34)$$

The complete data likelihood with the scaled parameters is

$$P_\beta(X, Z|\Theta, W) = \frac{1}{\Omega(\beta)} \prod_{i=1}^{N} \{\pi_{z_i} \exp(-\sum_{i=1}^{N} \frac{||x_i - \mu_{z_i}||^2}{2\beta^2\sigma^2})\}$$
$$\prod_{(m,n) \in C_=} \exp(\frac{w}{\beta^3}\delta_{z_m z_n}) \prod_{(m',n') \in C_{\neq}} \exp(-\frac{w}{\beta^3}\delta_{z_{m'} z_{n'}}). \quad (4.35)$$

As established in C.1, when $\beta \to 0$, the maximum data likelihood will dominate the data likelihood

$$\lim_{\beta \to 0} \frac{\max_Z P_\beta(X, Z|\Theta, W)}{\sum_Z P_\beta(X, Z|\Theta, W)} = 1.$$

As a result, when optimizing the model parameters Θ we can equivalently maximize $\max_Z P_\beta(X, Z|\Theta, W)$. Also, the soft posterior probability (as in conventional mixture model) becomes hard membership (as in k-means).

The negative logarithm of the complete likelihood P_β is then:

$$J_\beta(\Theta, Z) = -\sum_{i=1}^{N} \log \pi_{z_i} + C +$$

$$\frac{1}{\beta^2}(\sum_{i=1}^{N} \frac{||x_i - \mu_{z_i}||^2}{2} + \frac{1}{\beta}(\sum_{(m',n')\in C_{\neq}} w\delta_{z_{m'} z_{n'}} - \sum_{(m,n)\in C_=} w\delta_{z_m z_n})),$$

where $C = \log \Omega(\beta)$ is a constant. It is obvious that when $\beta \to 0$, we can neglect the term $-\sum_{i=1}^{N} \log \pi_{z_i}$. Hence we only have to consider the new cost function

$$\tilde{J}_\beta(\mu, Z) = \frac{1}{\beta^2}(\sum_{i=1}^{N} \frac{||x_i - \mu_{z_i}||^2}{2} + \frac{1}{\beta}(\sum_{(m',n')\in C_{\neq}} w\delta_{z_{m'} z_{n'}} - \sum_{(m,n)\in C_=} w\delta_{z_j, z_k})),$$

the minimization of which is obviously equivalent to the following equation since we can neglect the constant factor $\frac{1}{\beta^2}$:

$$\tilde{\tilde{J}}_\beta(\mu, Z) = \sum_{i=1}^{N} \frac{||x_i - \mu_{z_i}||^2}{2} + \frac{w}{\beta} J_c(Z),$$

where $J_c(Z) = \sum_{(m',n')\in C_{\neq}} \delta_{z_{m'} z_{n'}} - \sum_{(m,n)\in C_=} \delta_{z_m z_n}$ is the cost function term from pairwise constraints.

Let $S_Z = \{Z|z_i = z_j \text{ if } w(i,j) > 0; z_i \neq z_j \text{ if } w(i,j) < 0; \}$. We assume the pairwise relations are consistent, that is, $S_Z \neq \emptyset$. Obviously, all Z in S_Z achieve the same minimum value of the term $J_c(Z)$. That is

$$\forall Z \in S_Z, Z' \in S_Z \quad J_c(Z) = J_c(Z')$$
$$\forall Z \in S_Z, Z'' \notin S_Z \quad J_c(Z) < J_c(Z'').$$

It is obvious that when $\beta \to 0$, any Z that minimizes $\tilde{\tilde{J}}_\beta(\mu, Z)$ must be in S_Z. So the minimization of equation (4.35) can be finally cast into the following form:

$$\min_{Z,\mu} \sum_{i=1}^{N} ||x_i - \mu_{z_i}||^2$$
$$\text{subject to } Z \in S_Z,$$

which is apparently equivalent to equations (4.30)-(4.32). So we can conclude that $\beta \to 0$ in equation (4.34), the PPC model shown in equation (4.33) becomes a k-means model with hard constraints.

References

[1] C. Ambroise, M. Dang, and G. Govaert. Clustering of spatial data by the EM algorithm. In A. Soares, J. Gmez-Hernndez, and R. Froidevaux, editors, *Geostatistics for Environmental Applications*, volume 3, pages 493–504. Kluwer, 1997.

[2] S. Basu, A. Bannerjee, and R. Mooney. Semi-supervised clustering by seeding. In C. Sammut and A. Hoffmann, editors, *Proceedings of the Nineteenth International Conference on Machine Learning*, pages 19–26. Morgan Kaufmann, 2002.

[3] S. Basu, M. Bilenko, and R. Mooney. A probabilistic framework for semi-supervised clustering. In W. Kim, R. Kohavi, J. Gehrke, and W. Du-Mouchel, editors, *Proceedings of the Tenth Association of Computing Machinery SIGKDD International Conference on Knowledge Discovery and Data Mining*, pages 59–68. Association of Computing Machinery, 2004.

[4] M. Bilenko, S. Basu, and R. Mooney. Integrating constraints and metric learning in semi-supervised clustering. In C. Brodley, editor, *Proceedings of the Twenty-first International Conference on Machine Learning*, pages 11–18. Association of Computing Machinery, 2004.

[5] C. Bouman and M. Shapiro. A multiscale random field model for Bayesian image segmentation. *IEEE Transaction on Image Processing*, 3:162–177, March 1994.

[6] D. Cohn, R. Caruana, and A. McCallum. Semi-supervised Clustering with User Feedback. Technical Report TR2003-1892, Cornell University, 2003.

[7] A. Dempster, N. Laird, and D. Rubin. Maximum likelihood from incomplete data via the EM algorithm. *Journal of the Royal Statistical Society, Series B*, 39:1–38, 1977.

[8] T. Jaakkola. Tutorial on variational approximation methods. In C. Brodley, editor, *Proceedings of the Twenty-first International Conference on Machine Learning*, pages 11–18. Association of Computing Machinery, 2004.

[9] D. Klein, S. Kamvar, and C. Manning. From instance level to space-level constraints: Making the most of prior knowledge in data clustering.

In C. Sammut and A. Hoffmann, editors, *Proceedings of the Nineteenth International Conference on Machine Learning*, pages 307–313. Morgan Kaufmann, 2002.

[10] T. Lange, M. Law, A. Jain, and J. Buhmann. Learning with constrained and unlabelled data. In *Proceedings of the IEEE Computer Society Conference on Computer Vision and Pattern Recognition*, pages 730–737, 2005.

[11] M. Law, A. Topchy, and A. Jain. Clustering with soft and group constraints. In A. Fred, T. Caelli, R. Duin, A. Campilho, and D. Ridder, editors, *Joint International Association for Pattern Recognition International Workshop on Syntactical and Structural Pattern Recognition and Statistical Pattern Recognition*, pages 662–670. Springer-Verlag, 2004.

[12] M. Law, A. Topchy, and A. Jain. Model-based clustering with probabilistic constraints. In *Proceedings of Society for Industrial and Applied Mathematics Data Mining*, pages 641–645, 2005.

[13] Z. Lu and T. Leen. Semi-supervised clustering with pairwise constraints: A discriminative approach. In *Eleventh International Conference on Artificial Intelligence and Statistics*, 2007.

[14] R. Neal. Probabilistic inference using Markov Chain Monte Carlo methods. Technical Report CRG-TR-93-1, Computer Science Department, Toronto University, 1993.

[15] E. Segal, H. Wang, and D Koller. Discovering molecular pathways from protein interaction and gene expression data. *Bioinformatics*, 19:i264–i272, 2003.

[16] N. Shental, A. Bar-Hillel, T. Hertz, and D. Weinshall. Computing Gaussian mixture models with EM using side-information. Technical Report 2003-43, Leibniz Center for Research in Computer Science, 2003.

[17] N. Shental, A. Bar-Hillel, T. Hertz, and D. Weinshall. Computing Gaussian mixture models with EM using equivalence constraints. In L. Saul, Y. Weiss, and L. Bottou, editors, *Advances in Neural Information Processing System*, volume 16, pages 505–512. Cambridge, MA: MIT Press, 2004.

[18] A. Srivastava and J. Stroeve. Onboard detection of snow, ice and other geophysical processes using kernel methods. In *International Conference on Machine Learning 2003 Workshop on Machine Learning Technologies for Autonomous Space Sciences*, 2003.

[19] J. Theiler and G. Gisler. A contiguity-enhanced K-means clustering algorithm for unsupervised multispectral image segementation. In B. Javidi and D. Psaltis, editors, *Proceedings of Society of Photographic Instru-*

mentation Engineers, volume 3159, pages 108–118. Society of Photographic Instrumentation Engineers, 1997.

[20] K. Wagstaff. *Intelligent clustering with instance-level constraints.* PhD thesis, Cornell University, 2002.

[21] K. Wagstaff, C. Cardie, S. Rogers, and S. Schroedl. Constrained K-means clustering with background knowledge. In C. Brodley and A. Danyluk, editors, *Proceedings of the Eighteenth International Conference on Machine Learning*, pages 577–584. Morgan Kaufmann, 2001.

[22] E. Xing, A. Ng, M. Jordan, and S. Russell. Distance metric learning with applications to clustering with side information. In S. Becker, S. Thrun, and K. Obermayer, editors, *Advances in Neural Information Processing System*, volume 15, pages 505–512. Cambridge, MA: MIT Press, 2003.

[23] Q. Zhao and D. Miller. Mixture modeling with pairwise, instance-level class constraints. *Neural Computation*, 17:2482–2507, 2005.

Chapter 5

Clustering with Constraints: A Mean-Field Approximation Perspective

Tilman Lange

ETH Zurich, `tilman.lange@gmail.com`

Martin H. Law

Michigan State University, `lawhiu@cse.msu.edu`

Anil K. Jain

Michigan State University, `jain@cse.msu.edu`

Joachim M. Buhmann

ETH Zurich, `jbuhmann@inf.ethz.ch`

Abstract   Data clustering, the quest for natural group structure in data sets, is commonly addressed by modeling the expected class structure, where different models reflect different preferences (or lack thereof) for certain types of structures. The inclusion of *instance-level label constraints* in the inference allows the user to vaguely phrase what should belong to the same class and what should not, without the need to explicitly state what these classes are. Such constraint information can be regarded as a special type of side information whose integration in the inference and, thereby, fusion with the measurements can be beneficial for the finally discovered group structure.

We discuss an integration strategy for instance-level constraints by utilizing a hidden Markov Random Field formulation. The wide applicability of this model is mainly demonstrated for vectorial, parametric and outlined for pairwise, non-parametric clustering models. The computational complexity induced by the constraints in such models is addressed by way of a mean-field approximation. Furthermore, a weighting mechanism is introduced that controls the trade-off between constrained and unlabelled data. A model selection heuristic is employed to actually pick a sensible value of this trade-off parameter. Experiments shed light on the usefulness of this proposal—in the model-based setting—on various data sets. Most of the material in this chapter is based on the previous work in [20].

5.1 Introduction

Classification and grouping problems are abundant in many areas, such as computer vision (e.g., object categorization or low-level segmentation), data mining (e.g., document classification), or bio-informatics (e.g., protein function prediction). Often, a clear distinction is made between problems that are (i) supervised or (ii) unsupervised, the first involving only labelled, the latter only unlabelled data in the process of learning. *Semi-supervised* classification problems represent a hybrid setting where the labels of only a portion of the data set are available for training, and the unlabelled data, i.e., $p(x)$, is hoped to convey meaningful information about the joint data and label density $p(x, y)$. Therefore, the unlabelled data is, instead of being discarded, integrated in the learning process.

Instance-level constraints represent a "weaker" form of a priori knowledge about the desired grouping. A *must-link* constraint corresponds to the requirement that a specified set of objects should be assigned the same label, whereas the labels of objects participating in a *must-not-link* constraint should be different. Figure 5.1 illustrates the spectrum of different types of prior knowledge that can be included in the process of classifying data. The problem that is discussed here, grouping with instance-level constraints (see figure 5.1(c)), has also been termed *semi-supervised clustering* by some authors (see, e.g., [4]) in the literature. Must-link constraints are generally easier to model because they usually represent an equivalence relation – at least as long as such constraints are supposed to be strictly obeyed. Hence, they can be augmented, e.g., by constructing the transitive closure of constraints. This is illustrated in figure 5.2 and further discussed in chapter 1. Instance-level constraints are often simply called "constraints" if the context is clear. Constraints naturally arise in several settings, e.g., in interactive learning, where a potential non-expert user provides feedback about the success of learning in the form of constraints (an example for this is shown in figures 5.2(a) – 5.2(c), where the user input guides the image segmentation).

In this chapter, we adopt the perspective that constraints act on the latent label variables and, thereby, shall affect the probability of observing a certain label. This assumption leads to a Markov Random Field model acting on the latent variables. Computational intractability in this model is addressed by resorting to the mean-field approximation for approximate inference. We

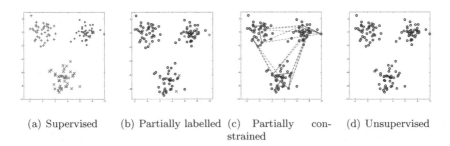

(a) Supervised   (b) Partially labelled   (c) Partially con-   (d) Unsupervised
strained

FIGURE 5.1: Spectrum between supervised and unsupervised learning. Points with labels have +, x or * shape while those without labels have circle shape. In (c), the must-link and must-not-link constraints are displayed as solid and dotted lines, respectively.

demonstrate the wide applicability of this approach ranging from exponential family mixtures to pairwise clustering approaches. As the inference of labels, in particular in an inductive context, is governed by the parameter θ of the underlying model, the approach taken here attempts to ensure that the constraints also affect the parameter estimation process by the introduction of an appropriate weighting mechanism. Experimental results demonstrate the effectiveness and robustness of our approach.

5.1.1 Related Work

A lot of work has already been devoted to semi-supervised learning (see, e.g., the recent surveys in [35, 43]) and its cousin learning with grouping constraints. We proceed with a brief overview. Work on semi-supervised learning is also covered here since the problems of learning with partial labels and with partial label constraints are strongly related and ideas for addressing one problem are often borrowed from approaches addressing the other.

A classical approach to semi-supervised learning assumes a generative model $p(x, y) = p(y)p(x|y)$, where the class-conditional density $p(x|y)$ is for example a Gaussian. An often employed method for fitting the model with labelled and unlabelled data ([27], p. 75) is to apply the Expectation-Maximization (EM) algorithm ([12], see also chapter 5.2), where the known labels enter the E-step update of the class posteriors: Instead of estimating an assignment probability, all probability mass is put on the actually observed class in the E-step. This type of technique has, e.g., been used for document classification [30]. In the approach to grouping with constraints presented in this work, a similar strategy is applied. In graph-based approaches (see, e.g., [3] or [44]), label-smoothness is enforced by utilizing a graph whose nodes are the labelled

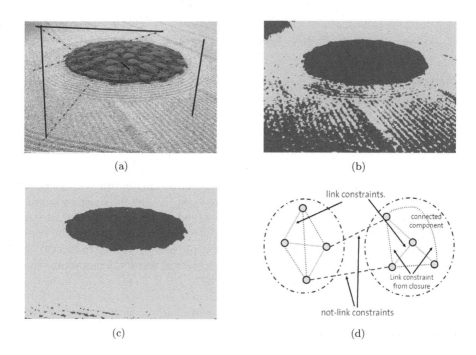

(a)   (b)

(c)   (d)

FIGURE 5.2: Pairwise instance-level constraints may arise from user input indicating what types of objects are supposed to be similar and which are not: (a) gives an example for the case of image segmentation; dashed lines indicate that the endpoints should not be grouped together, while solid lines indicate the opposite. Note that there is a misspecified not-link constraint. (b) The unconstrained segmentation of the image arbitrarily splits the image. (c) Already the few constraints specified in (a) help to improve the result and to render the segmentation more meaningful. In particular, the method of this chapter turns out to be robust w.r.t. errorneous constraints. (d) Sketches of the graph structure induced by pairwise constraints: the circles indicate connected components and, thereby, the possible augmentation to group level constraints.

and unlabelled examples and the edge weights reflect the similarity of pairs of objects. Approaches adopting this perspective usually rely on the so-called *cluster assumption*, which essentially states that highly similar points share the same label; thus, differently labelled but highly similar points will induce a high penalty. It should be clear that graph-based methods are non-parametric, discriminative, and transductive[1] in nature as they rely on a graph structure (solely) defined for $n_u + n_l$ objects.

Recently, there has been growing interest in the integration of link/not-link side information into the inference. Generally, one can distinguish between distance (editing)-based and constraint-based approaches. In [41], smoothness of the cluster labels is enforced, which utilizes a graph-based approach similar to those employed for transductive inference. In [19], the distance metric is modified in view of the constraints to propagate the effect of a constraint to the neighboring objects, which is also along the lines of connectivity-based regularization known from semi-supervised learning. However, this particular approach is not very robust, since a single constraint can provide a short-cut, which leads to significant changes in the distance matrix. In the worst, objects belonging to different classes are artificially made highly similar or even indistinguishable this way. A similar problem arises in ISOMAP-based embedding procedures when an erroneous "short-cut" is present. A slightly different constraint-based metric editing procedure has been proposed in [18]. Combining graph-based regularization with grouping models is one particular form of phrasing a hybrid criterion that integrates aspects of the (marginal) data density $p(x)$ and the assignment probabilities $p(y|x)$. [40] described a method that learns a Mahalanobis metric based on instance level constraints. In [36, 38, 39], for example, the subjects of inference are the *labels* of the objects. Hence, the setting bears a close similarity to the transductive learning setting as introduced by Vapnik [37]. From a probabilistic point of view, one specifies a prior on the class labels for points participating in constraints or for labelled points. Combinations of labels that violate the constraints or prior label information are either forbidden by having zero prior probability, or they are penalized by having small prior probability values (e.g., in [36] constraints are strictly enforced). Labels of originally unlabelled or unconstrained points are affected by the prior knowledge only indirectly by the parameter estimates. This, however, can lead to "discontinuous" label assignments: two points at exactly the same location, one endowed with constraint and one without, can be assigned different labels! A possible work-around for this problem represents the use of a constraint propagation mechanism, similar to graph Laplacian-based label propagation methods known from semi-supervised learning. In section 5.3.7, we adopt a different strategy to circumvent this problem. The approaches in [21, 22, 36] attempt to pro-

---

[1]Some work has been devoted to extend graph-based approaches to inductive settings, e.g., by way of nearest neighbor extension or the Nystrm approximation [11, 45].

vide a sampling model for constraints, which is fitted in an EM framework. The approach in [2], which can be regarded as an extension of the early work in [38, 39], phrases the problem of integrating pairwise constraints as a constrained k-means problem that integrates the metric learning ideas from the work by [40]. Inference for this approach is based on the iterated conditional mode (ICM) and, therefore, gets easily stuck in poor local minima. Markov Random Field (MRF) approaches have been independently developed in [24], [42], and [20] and are closely related to each other. In particular, the work in [42] relies on the same inference technique, the mean field approximation [31], as our approach in [20], which is described in the following sections.

5.2   Model-Based Clustering

Let $\mathcal{X} \subseteq \mathbb{R}^l$ be the space of measurements under consideration. A common strategy in clustering is to *explain* the group structure by a so-called *mixture model* [27]: the basic idea is to model the data density $p(x)$ as marginalized joint density $\sum_\nu p(x, \nu)$ where the marginalization is with respect to the so-called *latent* class variable Y. Viewed differently, the marginal density of x may be written as $p(x) = \sum_{\nu=1}^k \gamma_\nu p_\nu(x)$, where γ_ν, $\sum_{\nu \in [k]} \gamma_\nu = 1$, denotes *mixing proportions* and $p_\nu(x)$ *class conditional densities*.

Usually, a parametric family is fixed, of which the true (but unknown) class conditional density is assumed to be a member. We denote by θ_ν the parameter vectors that index models $p(x; \theta_\nu)$ for $p_\nu(x)$ in the chosen family. Given an unlabelled sample, $X_u = (x_i)_{i \in [n]}$, the unknown parameters γ and $\boldsymbol{\theta} = (\theta_\nu)_{\nu \in [k]}$ have to be estimated. The maximum likelihood (ML) [10] strategy minimizes the negative log-likelihood of the data as a function of the parameters

$$\min_{\gamma, \boldsymbol{\theta}} \mathcal{L}(\gamma, \boldsymbol{\theta}) := -\sum_{i \in [n]} \log \left(\sum_{\nu \in [k]} \gamma_\nu p(x_i; \theta_\nu) \right). \tag{5.1}$$

The Expectation-Maximization (EM) algorithm ([12]) is a commonly employed heuristic for determining the ML estimate. Some details on the rationale underlying EM are required in the following: Let X be the *observed* random variable and Y the unobserved (label) variable. By Bayes rule

$$\log \sum_\nu \gamma_\nu p(x_i; \theta_\nu) = \log \gamma_{y_i} p(x_i; \theta_{y_i}) - \log p(y_i | x_i; \gamma, \boldsymbol{\theta}) \tag{5.2}$$

w.r.t. the unobserved y_i. Hence,

$$\mathcal{L}(\gamma, \boldsymbol{\theta}) = -\sum_i \log \gamma_{y_i} p(x_i; \theta_{y_i}) + \sum_i \log p(y_i | x_i; \gamma, \boldsymbol{\theta}).$$

Let $\{\mathbf{p}_i\}$ be a set of n distributions defined on the range of Y (in the clustering case on $[k]$). Now, taking expectations w.r.t. $\mathbf{p}_i$ in equation (5.2) gives

$$-\log p(x_i; \gamma, \boldsymbol{\theta}) = -\mathbf{E}_{\mathbf{p}_i} \log p(x_i, Y; \gamma, \boldsymbol{\theta}) + \mathbf{E}_{\mathbf{p}_i} \log p(Y | x_i; \gamma, \boldsymbol{\theta})$$
$$\leq -\mathbf{E}_{\mathbf{p}_i} \log p(x_i, Y; \gamma, \boldsymbol{\theta}) + \mathbf{E}_{\mathbf{p}_i} \log p_i(Y), \tag{5.3}$$

where equality is obtained iff $\mathbf{p}_i = p(\cdot | x_i; \gamma, \boldsymbol{\theta})$. Taking sums on both sides, one gets

$$\mathcal{L}(\gamma, \boldsymbol{\theta}) \leq \mathcal{L}(\gamma, \boldsymbol{\theta}) + \sum_{i \in [n]} d_{\mathrm{KL}}(\mathbf{p}_i \| p(\cdot | x_i; \gamma, \boldsymbol{\theta})) \tag{5.4}$$

and, thus, one has obtained an upper bound $\tilde{\mathcal{L}}$ on $\mathcal{L}$:

$$\tilde{\mathcal{L}}(\gamma, \boldsymbol{\theta}; \{\mathbf{p}_i\}) = -\sum_{i \in [n]} \sum_{\nu \in [k]} (p_i(\nu) \log p(x_i; \theta_\nu) \gamma_\nu - p_i(\nu) \log p_i(\nu)).$$

The EM algorithm is a minimization-minimization algorithm: For fixed $\gamma^{(m)}$, $\boldsymbol{\theta}^{(m)}$, find the $\mathbf{p}_i^{(m)}$ minimizing the bound in equation (5.3). This *Estimation step (E-step)* is Bayes' rule, i.e.,

$$\mathbf{p}_i^{(m)}(\nu) \leftarrow \frac{p(x_i; \theta_\nu^{(m)}) \gamma_\nu^{(m)}}{\sum_{a \in [k]} p(x_i; \theta_a^{(m)}) \gamma_a^{(m)}},$$

since this choice minimizes the KL-divergence $d_{\mathrm{KL}}(\mathbf{p}_i^{(m)} \| p(\cdot | x_i; \gamma^{(m)}, \boldsymbol{\theta}^{(m)}))$ and turns the inequality into an equality. In the M-step (*Maximization step*) one re-estimates the parameters γ and $\boldsymbol{\theta}$ by minimizing the bound $\tilde{\mathcal{L}}$, for fixed $\mathbf{p}_i^{(m)}$, $i \in [n]$. Interesting terms are $-\sum_i \sum_\nu p_i^{(m)}(\nu) \log(\gamma_\nu)$ and $-\sum_i \sum_\nu p_i^{(m)}(\nu) \log(p(x_i; \theta_\nu))$. The solution for γ is

$$\gamma^{(m+1)} = \frac{1}{n} \sum_i \mathbf{p}_i^{(m)}. \tag{5.5}$$

Determining $\boldsymbol{\theta}^{(m+1)}$ on the basis of the $\tilde{\mathcal{L}}$ also leads to a convex minimization, if the densities $p(x; \theta_\nu)$ are log-concave, which is the case for the exponential family (c.f. [1]).

REMARK 5.1   Many model classes used in practice for $p_\nu(x)$ are elements of the so-called exponential family [1]:

$$p(x; \theta) = h(x) \exp \left(\chi(\theta)^\top T(x) - A(\theta) \right). \tag{5.6}$$

Here, $\eta := \chi(\theta)$ is called *natural parameter*, $T(\cdot)$ is the *sufficient statistic*, and $A(\theta)$ is known as the *cumulant generating* or *log-partition* function. The function T can be defined on any domain as long as it maps the input to a vector of fixed, finite dimension. An important aspect of the exponential family is its (strict) log-concavity in its parameter. Therefore, maximum likelihood parameter estimation is feasible. In particular, there is a unique minimizer for strictly convex $-\log p(x;\theta)$. Many parametric distributions belong to the exponential family, e.g., the multivariate Gaussian, the Dirichlet, the multinomial, the Poisson distribution, and so forth. $\Box$

Solving $\nabla_{\theta}\tilde{\mathcal{L}} \overset{!}{=} 0$ yields optimal parameter estimates for fixed assignment probabilities.

In Gaussian mixture models, the class conditional density follows a Gaussian distribution with mean $\boldsymbol{\mu}_{\nu}$ and co-variance matrix $\boldsymbol{\Sigma}_{\nu}$:

$$p(x; \boldsymbol{\mu}_{\nu}, \boldsymbol{\Sigma}_{\nu}) = \frac{1}{(2\pi)^{(d/2)}|\boldsymbol{\Sigma}_{\nu}|^{1/2}} \exp\left(-\frac{1}{2}(x - \boldsymbol{\mu}_{\nu})^{\top}\boldsymbol{\Sigma}_{\nu}^{-1}(x - \boldsymbol{\mu}_{\nu})\right).$$

Since, the Gaussian density, as a member of the exponential family, is (strictly) log-concave, it is sufficient to look for the zero crossings of the gradient, i.e. $\nabla_{\theta}\tilde{\mathcal{L}} \overset{!}{=} 0$. For the Gaussian case, the derivation has been performed, e.g., in [5]. The algorithm as well as the parameter estimates are summarized in algorithm 1. The k-means cost function [25] can be derived from the negative log-likelihood of Gaussian mixture model with vanishing covariance $\boldsymbol{\Sigma}_{\nu} = \epsilon\mathbf{I}_{l}$ for $\epsilon \to 0$ and equal class priors $\gamma_{\nu} = \frac{1}{k}$.

Iterating the EM two-step procedure until convergence will yield *locally* optimal parameter estimates $\tilde{\gamma}$ and $\tilde{\theta}$ with respect to the original cost function $\mathcal{L}$ ([28]). Once the parameter estimates have been obtained, the maximum a-posteriori class assignments can be computed in order to arrive at a k-clustering.

5.3 A Maximum Entropy Approach to Constraint Integration

In the following, we focus on model-based, generative grouping methods as briefly described in the previous section. For the biggest part of this section, we assume that the data generation process can be explained sufficiently well by a mixture of class-conditional densities, which are members of the exponential family. The ME strategy adopted here can also be applied to the pairwise

---

Algorithm 1 The EM algorithm for Gaussian mixture models

1: Initialize $\boldsymbol{\gamma}^{(0)}$, $\boldsymbol{\theta}^{(0)}$.

2: $m \leftarrow 0$;

3: **while** not converged **do**

4:     Determine *class posteriors* $p_i^{(m)}(\nu) := p(\nu|x_i; \boldsymbol{\gamma}^{(m)}, \boldsymbol{\theta}^{(m)})$ by Bayes rule.

5:     Update parameters: $\boldsymbol{\gamma}^{(m+1)}$ according to eq. (5.5). For mean and covariance:

$$\boldsymbol{\mu}_\nu^{(m+1)} = \frac{\sum_i p_i(\nu) x_i}{\sum_i p_i(\nu)} \tag{5.7}$$

$$\boldsymbol{\Sigma}_\nu^{(m+1)} = \frac{\sum_i p_i(\nu)(x_i - \boldsymbol{\mu}_\nu^{(m+1)})(x_i - \boldsymbol{\mu}_\nu^{(m+1)})^\top}{\sum_i p_i(\nu)} \tag{5.8}$$

6:     $m \leftarrow m + 1$;

7: **end while**

---

grouping models to integrate constraints into the inference. We sketch this option as well.

5.3.1   Integration of Partial Label Information

In model-based classification, a classical approach to combining labelled and unlabelled data consists of integrating the labelled data into the E-step, where class assignment probabilities are estimated. The underlying rationale requires that the estimated parameters yield high likelihood for *both* labelled and unlabelled data [7]. In *supervised* model-based classification, the ML principle applied to the labelled data X_l tells us to choose the parameters $\boldsymbol{\gamma}$ and $\boldsymbol{\theta}$ that minimize $\mathcal{L}_{X_l}(\boldsymbol{\gamma}, \boldsymbol{\theta}) = -\sum_{(x_i, y_i) \in X_l} \log p(x_i, y_i; \gamma_{y_i}, \theta_{y_i})$, where $p(x_i, y_i; \gamma_{y_i}, \theta_{y_i}) = \gamma_{y_i} p(x_i; \theta_{y_i})$. The integration of partially labelled and unlabelled data can be achieved by considering the hybrid objective function

$$\min_{\boldsymbol{\gamma}, \boldsymbol{\theta}} \left[\mathcal{L}_{X_u}(\boldsymbol{\gamma}, \boldsymbol{\theta}) + \mathcal{L}_{X_l}(\boldsymbol{\gamma}, \boldsymbol{\theta}) \right]. \tag{5.9}$$

According to Section 5.2, an EM-based procedure can be used to optimize the relaxed cost function $\tilde{\mathcal{L}}_{X_u}(\boldsymbol{\gamma}, \boldsymbol{\theta}; \{\mathbf{p}_i\}) + \mathcal{L}_{X_l}(\boldsymbol{\gamma}, \boldsymbol{\theta})$. Here, $\tilde{\mathcal{L}}_{X_u}$ is used to denote the usual EM relaxation for the unlabelled data known from the previous section. For the labelled data, no posterior probability needs to be estimated since the label was actually observed. The label information enters the inference in the E-step updates where the class posteriors for labelled objects x_i are set to $\mathbb{I}\{y_i = \nu\}$. The observed labels may, hence, be viewed as constraints on the class assignment probability $p(\nu|x; \boldsymbol{\gamma}, \boldsymbol{\theta})$.

5.3.2 Maximum-Entropy Label Prior

The maximum entropy approach described in this section attempts to integrate *pairwise* instance-level constraints into the inference in a way similar to the integration of partially labelled data just described. Our perspective is that specifying constraints amounts to specifying a partially *object-specific* prior model for the assignment of constrained data to different classes. This contrasts the sampling paradigm underlying a standard mixture model. For constraints, the first step of the sampling process (i.e., the label sampling) is no longer object independent but depends also on the labels of other objects participating in constraints.

Let X_c be the set of all data points that participate in at least one constraint. The class labels y are regarded as latent variables; the constraints are supposed to act on the probabilities characterizing the latent variable. For a given labelling y, a constraint violation occurs whenever the latent variables in a constraint have a different (the same) value while they are supposed to be the same (different). In mathematical terms, a must-link constraint is *violated*, whenever $c_=(i,j)\mathbb{I}\{y_i \neq y_j\} = 1$; similarly, a must-not-link is not satisfied if $c_{\neq}(i,j)\mathbb{I}\{y_i = y_j\} = 1$. Both quantities can be used in order to *penalize* constraint violations.

By specifying constraints, a preference for or against certain labellings of the constrained data is expressed. However, we have to take the possibility of faulty grouping constraints into account. Hence, strictly enforcing constraints may render the learning problem infeasible (which actually happens for one of the approaches discussed in [36]). In order to turn the constraint information into a prior on the assignment variables for the data in X_c, we apply Jaynes' maximum entropy (ME) principle: Find the prior distribution $p(y) = p(y_1, \ldots, y_n)$ for the group labels of the data points $x_i \in X_c$ such that the entropy $H(p) = -\sum_{y \in [k]^n} p(y) \log p(y)$ is maximized while the *expected* number of constraint violations,

$$\mathbf{E}_{P_{Y^n}}\left[\sum_{i,j \in [n]} c_=(i,j)\mathbb{I}\{Y_i \neq Y_j\}\right] =$$

$$\sum_{y_1=1}^{k} \cdots \sum_{y_n=1}^{k} p(y) \sum_{i,j \in [n]} (c_=(i,j)\mathbb{I}\{y_i \neq y_j\}) \leq \kappa^+,$$

$$\mathbf{E}_{P_{Y^n}}\left[\sum_{i,j \in [n]} c_{\neq}(i,j)\mathbb{I}\{Y_i = Y_j\}\right] =$$

$$\sum_{y_1=1}^{k} \cdots \sum_{y_n=1}^{k} p(y) \sum_{i,j \in [n]} (c_{\neq}(i,j)\mathbb{I}\{y_i = y_j\}) \leq \kappa^-,$$

is bounded by κ^+ for positive and κ^- for negative constraints. Instead of working with the constraints κ^+ and κ^-, we consider the Lagrangian, yielding the modified problem:

$$
\begin{aligned}
\min_{p \in \mathcal{P}_{k^n}} \ & -H(p) \\
& +\lambda^+ \mathbf{E}_p[\textstyle\sum_{i,j \in [n]} c_=(i,j)\mathbb{I}\{Y_i \neq Y_j\}] \\
& +\lambda^- \mathbf{E}_p[\textstyle\sum_{i,j \in [n]} c_{\neq}(i,j)\mathbb{I}\{Y_i = Y_j\}] \\
\text{s.t.} \quad & \textstyle\sum_{y_1=1}^{k} \cdots \sum_{y_n=1}^{k} p(y) = 1 \qquad p(y) \geq 0 \ \ \forall y \in [k]^n.
\end{aligned}
\tag{5.10}
$$

The regularization parameters λ^+ and λ^- control how strongly a constraint violation is actually penalized. The maximum entropy (minimum neg. entropy) problem just phrased is convex in the discrete distribution p since $-H(p)$ is a convex function of p ([9]), expectations are linear in p and the normalization constraint is affine. The solution to this inference problem can in fact be found by analytical means: Taking derivatives yields the stationary equation

$$
\log p(y) + 1 + \lambda^+ \sum_{i,j \in [n]} c_=(i,j)\mathbb{I}\{y_i \neq y_j\} + \lambda^- \sum_{i,j \in [n]} c_{\neq}(i,j)\mathbb{I}\{y_i = y_j\} + \xi \overset{!}{=} 0,
$$

where $\xi \in \mathbb{R}$ is the Lagrange multiplier belonging to the normalization constraint. The solution to the stationary equations is the so-called *Gibbs distribution* (e.g., [9]) known from statistical physics. In this case, it is given by

$$
p(y) = \frac{1}{Z} \prod_{i,j \in [n]} \exp\left(-\lambda^+ c_=(i,j)\mathbb{I}\{y_i \neq y_j\} - \lambda^- c_{\neq}(i,j)\mathbb{I}\{y_i = y_j\}\right), \tag{5.11}
$$

where Z is the normalization constant – also known as *partition function* – in which ξ was absorbed. This prior is intuitive: Depending on the choice of λ^+ and λ^-, constraint violations are more or less likely. For $\lambda^+ \to \infty, \lambda^- \to \infty$, the prior strictly enforces the constraints for the data in X_c. It is, therefore, reasonable to use a large value for λ^+ and λ^- whenever constraints correspond to true label information in product space. Generally, the prior puts low probability mass on labellings that violate instance-level grouping constraints: the more constraints are violated, the less likely is the labelling. The ME prior can be regarded as maximally non-committal with respect to fluctuations in the input (here: the constraint information!) since the ME principle assumes the least about the label information apart from the information derived from the constraints. It is this property that renders this approach to integrating constraints robust w.r.t. erroneously specified link/not-link information.

REMARK 5.2 In order to penalize constraint violations, we have chosen the 0-1 loss on pairs of labels. However, other loss functions, e.g., with a constraint-specific weighting, also fit into this framework: a loss of the form (here for violations of positive constraints)

$$c_=(i,j)w_{ij}\ell(y_i,y_j)$$

will also lead to a Gibbs distribution. A reasonable choice for w_{ij} represents, for example, a similarity-based penalty: the smaller $\|x_i - x_j\|_{\mathbf{A}}^2$, the higher the penalty induced by a link constraint violation, for example. Note, that $\mathbf{A}$ may be any positive semi-definite matrix $\mathbf{A} \succeq 0$, which defines a bilinear form. In particular, $\mathbf{A}$ could also be learned from the data. The loss function ℓ can be any loss function of the labels y_i and y_j, i.e., $\ell \colon [k]^2 \to \mathbb{R}$. For the sake of simplicity, however, we focus on the 0-1-loss here. $\quad\Box$

Note that we have not integrated classical class priors γ_ν as they arise in the standard mixture modelling setting so far. For problems, where uniform class priors are assumed, the prior in equation (5.11) is appropriate. In [20], different label sampling mechanisms have been assumed for unlabelled and constrained data, such that γ_ν is only estimated using the unlabelled data. In some cases, it may be, however, worthwhile to integrate global class priors γ also for the constrained objects (in the experiments uniform γ_ν are assumed, however). There are several ways with which this can be achieved: In theory, class priors, that act on both constrained and unconstrained objects, can be added without much effort. The additional term

$$-\sum_{i\in[n]} \mathbf{E}_p \left[\log \gamma_{Y_i}\right]$$

which quantifies the cross-entropy between class priors γ_ν and per-object marginal class probability for class ν and object i as obtained from $\sum_{y:y_i=\nu} p(y)$ for each (fixed) $i \in [n]$. Adding this constraint to the maximum entropy problem in equation (5.10), yields the modified Gibbs distribution

$$p(y;\gamma) = \frac{1}{Z(\gamma)} \prod_i \gamma_{y_i} \prod_{i,j} \exp\left(-\lambda^+ c_=(i,j)\mathbb{I}\{y_i \neq y_j\} - \lambda^- c_{\neq}(i,j)\mathbb{I}\{y_i = y_j\}\right),$$

$$(5.12)$$

which is parametrized now by γ and breaks down to the usual class priors if no constraints are given. That type of integration leads to the model used in [24]. The integration differs, however, from the model in [42], where constraints are artificially added to the already relaxed cost function, which implies a departure from the originally assumed probabilistic model.

5.3.3 Markov Random Fields and the Gibbs Distribution

The Gibbs labelling prior derived in the last section has an illuminating interpretation in terms of a Markov Random Field (MRF) (cf., e.g., [6]). So far measurements x have not been taken into account. The MRF perspective provides a sound way to integrate the actual measurements (x_i) into the model. This perspective covers also the approaches in [2, 24, 36].

In MRF terminology, the set of objects $V = [n]$ is also called a set of *sites*. A state is associated with each site being an element of a *state* or *phase* space. As we work with labels, the state space is simply $[k]$. The set of label random variables $\{Y_i\}_{i\in[n]}$ with domain $[k]$ defines a *random field* on $[n]$. Interesting random fields are equipped with a graph structure that reflects conditional (in-) dependencies and is encoded in what is commonly termed a *neighborhood system*: A neighborhood system is a family of subsets $\mathcal{N}_i$, $i \in [n]$, of $[n]$ such that $i \notin \mathcal{N}_i$ and $j \in \mathcal{N}_i \Rightarrow i \in \mathcal{N}_j$. In the case considered here, the neighborhood structure is induced by the constraint indicators $c_=(i,j)$ and $c_{\neq}(i,j)$: In terms of the underlying graph structure, there is a link between nodes i and j, if $c_=(i,j) + c_{\neq}(i,j) = 1$ assuming $c_=(i,i) = c_{\neq}(i,i) = 0$ and non-conflicting constraints, i.e., $\mathcal{N}_i = \{j \in [n] \mid c_=(i,j) + c_{\neq}(i,j) = 1\}$. A random field is a *Markov* random field if

$$\mathbf{P}\{Y_i = y_i \mid Y_{[n]\setminus i} = y_{[n]\setminus i}\} = \mathbf{P}\{Y_i = y_i \mid Y_{\mathcal{N}_i} = y_{\mathcal{N}_i}\}, \qquad (5.13)$$

where we have used the notation Y_A for a set $A \subseteq [n]$ to denote the tuple $(Y_i)_{i\in A}$. In words, equation (5.13) means that the probability of node i being in state y_i is independent of the state of the nodes *not* being in the neighborhood $\mathcal{N}_i$ of node i. Now, the Gibbs distribution in equation (5.12) defines a *Gibbs potential* on the neighborhood system $\{\mathcal{N}_i\}_{i\in[n]}$. The celebrated *Gibbs-Markov equivalence* (e.g., [6], p. 260) states that Gibbs fields are Markov fields.[2] Hence, the joint distribution in the MRF is the Gibbs distribution given in equation (5.12).

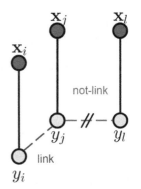

FIGURE 5.3: Hidden MRF on the labels: Observations made (data (x_i) and the constraints) are employed to make inferences about y.

In our case, the labels are hidden variables. The data itself, i.e., the measurements x_i, can be naturally integrated into the hidden MRF model. They provide what is often termed *evidence* in the literature, resulting in a term $\tilde{\psi}_i(x_i, y_i)$ (see fig. 5.3). In fact, the latter can absorb everything that only depends on a single object alone. In our context, this concerns the likelihood as well as the *global* class prior term. The pairwise couplings additionally lead to what is commonly referred to as compatibility terms $\psi_{ij}(y_i, y_j)$. The

---

[2]The converse direction can be obtained from the Hammersley-Clifford theorem, e.g., [6], p. 262.

graphical depiction in fig. 5.3 already indicates that independence of the measurements given their labels is assumed, i.e., $p(x_i, x_j | y_i, y_j) = p(x_j | y_j)p(x_i | y_i)$. More precisely, for the pairwise Markov random field, one gets for the *joint distribution* of data and labels

$$p(y, X; \boldsymbol{\gamma}, \boldsymbol{\theta}) = \frac{1}{Z(\boldsymbol{\gamma})} \prod_{i \in [n]} \tilde{\psi}_i(x_i, y_i) \prod_{i,j \in [n]} \psi_{ij}(y_i, y_j)$$

where $\psi_{ij}(y_i, y_j) = \exp(-(\lambda^+ c_=(i,j) - \lambda^- c_{\neq}(i,j))\mathbb{I}\{y_i \neq y_j\})$ and $\tilde{\psi}_i(x_i, y_i) = p(x_i; \theta_{y_i})\gamma_{y_i}$. Starting from the ME prior, we have arrived at a model for measurements and latent label variables that integrates the constraints.

5.3.4 Parameter Estimation

We assume that the class-conditional densities $p(x_i | \nu) \equiv p(x_i; \theta_\nu)$ are members of the (same class within the) exponential family. Following the rationale in Section 5.2, the parameters of the class priors and class-conditional densities need to be learned, where we follow the maximum likelihood principle here, i.e., $(\boldsymbol{\gamma}^*, \boldsymbol{\theta}^*) = \arg\min_{\boldsymbol{\gamma},\boldsymbol{\theta}} - \log \sum_y p(y, X; \boldsymbol{\gamma}, \boldsymbol{\theta})$ are to be identified. An EM perspective can be naturally adopted – similar to the case of partially labelled data sketched earlier. The standard EM relaxation still applies here, however, with respect to label vectors y in contrast to individual labels, i.e.,

$$\mathcal{L}(\boldsymbol{\gamma}; \boldsymbol{\theta}) = -\log \sum_{y \in [k]^n} p(y; \boldsymbol{\gamma}) \prod_i p(x_i; \theta_{y_i})$$

$$\leq - \sum_{y \in [k]^n} q(y) \left(\log p(y; \boldsymbol{\gamma}) \prod_i p(x_i; \theta_{y_i}) - \log q(y) \right)$$

$$=: \tilde{\mathcal{L}}(\boldsymbol{\gamma}, \boldsymbol{\theta}; q),$$

where $q \in \mathcal{P}_{k^n}$ is any distribution on $[k]^n$ and $p(y; \boldsymbol{\gamma})$ is the Gibbs distribution from equation (5.12). Clearly, equality holds iff $q(y) = p(y|X; \boldsymbol{\gamma}, \boldsymbol{\theta}) \propto p(y; \boldsymbol{\gamma}) \prod_i p(x_i; \theta_{y_i})$. Hence, standard EM amounts to iterating the steps

1. **E-step:** $\min_{q \in \mathcal{P}_{k^n}} d_{\mathrm{KL}}(q \| p(\cdot | X; \boldsymbol{\gamma}, \boldsymbol{\theta}))$ for fixed $\boldsymbol{\gamma}$ and $\boldsymbol{\theta}$.

2. **M-step:** $\min_{\boldsymbol{\gamma},\boldsymbol{\theta}} \tilde{\mathcal{L}}(\boldsymbol{\gamma}, \boldsymbol{\theta}; q)$ for fixed q.

Obviously, the constraints only implicitly influence the estimation of the parameters θ_ν in the second step, since the constraints enter the E-step. There are, however, two technical difficulties. In order to arrive at a proper probability distribution, the label posterior and, thereby, q needs to be normalized. The normalization constant, however, involves a sum over *all* possible (exponentially many) labellings in $[k]^n$, which does not factorize over individual objects as in the standard mixture model case due to the pairwise couplings introduced by the constraints. In [2], the authors avoid the need to compute the partition function by resorting to a different, more greedy hill climbing heuristic, the *iterative conditional mode (ICM)*. As the results in the experimental section indicate, such a procedure gets very easily stuck in poor local minima, which is particularly dangerous in the context of clustering with instance-level constraints. In order to use more sophisticated optimization techniques such as EM or DA, the label posteriors need to be marginalized in order to apply the standard estimates, which is costly due to the couplings.

The second problem arises in the M-step, once the parameters γ of the global class prior probability have to be estimated (cf., equation 5.12). In principle, a numerical minimization technique could be used for determining γ. However, such an approach also requires the gradient $\nabla_\gamma \tilde{\mathcal{L}}$, which unfortunately involves *expensive* marginalization over $p(y; \gamma)$. A different, heuristic yet more efficient strategy is sketched below. For uniform γ_ν, as used in the experiments, the parameter cancels out in the partition function and the prior from equation (5.11) is recovered. Similarly, the problem does not arise, if the constrained data is assumed to be independent of γ (as in [20]).

In order to keep the optimization tractable, we approximate the per-object posteriors in the E-step by the mean-field approximation [31] as described in the following section.

5.3.5 Mean-Field Approximation for Posterior Inference

By Bayes rule, the posterior probability of a labelling y can be written as

$$p(y|X; \gamma, \theta) \propto p(y; \gamma) \prod_i p(x_i; \theta_{y_i}).$$

In the mean-field approximation, one tries to identify a *factorial approximation*, the mean-field approximation $q(y) = \prod_i q_i(y_i)$ of the true posterior $p(y|X; \gamma, \theta)$ such that the Kullback-Leibler divergence between the approximate and true posterior distributions is minimized, i.e.,

$$\min_q d_{\mathrm{KL}}(q \| p(\cdot|X; \gamma, \theta)) = \min_q \sum_y q(y) \log \left(\frac{q(y)}{p(y|X; \gamma, \theta)} \right), \qquad (5.14)$$

such that $\sum_\nu q_i(\nu) = 1$, for all $i \in [n]$. Note that this is exactly the first step of the EM scheme sketched in the last section; however, q is constrained to the set of factorial distributions. Because the approximation is factorial, the computation of the marginalized posterior probabilities becomes feasible, and, hence, the partition function for q can be evaluated efficiently. The latter is a prerequisite for the tractable optimization of the model. Note that the KL divergence can be decomposed as

$$d_{\mathrm{KL}}(q\|p(\cdot|X;\boldsymbol{\gamma},\boldsymbol{\theta})) = -H(q) - \mathbf{E}_q\left[\log p(Y^n|X;\boldsymbol{\gamma},\boldsymbol{\theta})\right]$$

where $H(q)$ denotes the entropy of the mean-field approximation, Y^n is the the random variable of k-labellings of n objects, and $\mathbf{E}_q$ denotes the expectation w.r.t. q. Here, the negative entropy term decomposes into a sum over individual negative entropies $-H(q_i)$. We seek to minimize the expression in equation (5.14) by looking for stationary points w.r.t. each $q_i(\nu)$. Let $\rho_{ij} = \lambda^+ c_=(i,j) - \lambda^- c_{\neq}(i,j)$ and $\Delta_{\nu\mu} = 1 - \delta_{\nu\mu}$, where $\delta_{\nu\mu}$ is the Kronecker delta function. Using this convention, one can summarize the exponents in equation (5.12) by $\rho_{ij}\Delta_{\nu\mu}$ if $y_i = \nu$ and $y_j = \mu$. It should be emphasized that this approximation is only required for the constrained data, i.e., for (unconstrained) objects in X_u the approximation is exact. In the following, we use $h_i(\nu)$ as a shortcut for $-\log\gamma_\nu p(x_i;\theta_\nu)$.

Taking the derivative of equation (5.14) w.r.t. the approximate posteriors $q_i(\nu)$ and setting it to zero leads to the equation(s)

$$q_i(\nu) = \frac{1}{Z_i}\exp\left(-h_i(\nu) - \sum_{j\neq i}\sum_\mu q_j(\mu)\rho_{ij}\Delta_{\nu\mu}\right),$$

where

$$Z_i = \sum_{\nu\in[k]}\exp\left(-h_i(\nu) - \sum_{j\neq i}\sum_\mu q_j(\mu)\rho_{ij}\Delta_{\nu\mu}\right).$$

Since $\Delta_{\nu\mu} = 1$ iff $\mu \neq \nu$ and by taking cancellation into account, one can further simplify the expression for $q_i(\nu)$ to

$$q_i(\nu) = \frac{1}{Z_i}\exp\left(-h_i(\nu) + \sum_{j\neq i}q_j(\nu)\rho_{ij}\right).$$

Eventually, a factorial approximation of the marginal posterior probabilities has been derived. For the constrained data, these update equations can be used in the E-step for posterior probability estimation. These are fixed-point equations, that need to be iterated in order to arrive at meaningful estimates. Following [17], a sequential update scheme is employed in practice to ensure convergence.

Recall that the estimates for the class priors in the standard EM setting are the averages over class posterior probabilities as computed in the E-step. This suggests to heuristically estimate γ_ν as in equation (5.5), where mean-field estimates replace the standard per-object E-step posteriors. This amounts to dropping the term $\log Z(\boldsymbol{\gamma})$ in $-\sum_y q(y)\log p(y;\boldsymbol{\gamma})$. This heuristic is not required if the perspective of [20] is adopted.

5.3.6 A Detour: Pairwise Clustering, Constraints, and Mean Fields

Pairwise clustering algorithms expect data as input that characterize the mutual (dis-)similarity of the objects under consideration. (Dis-)Similarity data consists of pairwise *proximity* measurements d_{ij}, in the case of dissimilarities, between objects i and j, $i, j \in [n]$. $d \colon \mathcal{X}^2 \to \mathbb{R}_{\geq 0}$ is a *dissimilarity measure on* $\mathcal{X}$, if d is symmetric and for all $x, z \in \mathcal{X} : x = z \Rightarrow d(x, z) = 0$ where the converse is not necessarily true. In particular, d is not required to be a *metric*. For a sample $X = (x_i)$, the dissimilarities between x_i and x_j are typically summarized in a *dissimilarity matrix* $\mathbf{D} = (d(x_i, x_j))_{i,j \in [n]} \in \mathbb{R}^{n \times n}$. From vectorial data, one can easily derive both similarities and dissimilarities, e.g., by utilizing squared Euclidean distances in the feature space:

$$d_{ij} = \kappa(x_i, x_i) + \kappa(x_j, x_j) - 2\kappa(x_i, x_j) = \|\phi(x_i) - \phi(x_j)\|^2, \qquad (5.15)$$

where κ denotes a kernel function and ϕ the corresponding feature map. The pairwise clustering cost function ([17]) can be motivated from the kernel k-means cost function. The latter may be written as

$$\mathcal{H}^{\mathrm{kkm}}(\mathbf{K}; y) = \frac{1}{2} \sum_{\nu \in [k]} \sum_{i: y_i = \nu} \sum_{j: y_j = \nu} \frac{1}{n_\nu} (\kappa(x_i, x_i) + \kappa(x_j, x_j) - 2\kappa(x_i, x_j));$$

generalizing this definition to *arbitrary* dissimilarity matrices $\mathbf{D}$ leads to the definition of the pairwise clustering cost function

$$\mathcal{H}^{pw}(\mathbf{D}; y) = \frac{1}{2} \sum_{\nu \in [k]} \sum_{i: y_i = \nu} \sum_{j: y_j = \nu} \frac{d_{ij}}{n_\nu}.$$

In graph-theoretic terms, each cluster forms a clique whose cost contribution is weighted by the sum over all edge weights normalized by the number of nodes in the clique. Adopting a ME perspective (as in [17]), one obtains a Gibbs label posterior

$$p(y|\mathbf{D}) = \frac{1}{Z} \exp\left(-\beta \mathcal{H}^{pw}(\mathbf{D}; y)\right),$$

where β is the inverse temperature. Integration of constraints is straightforward in this model. It yields the modified Gibbs posterior:

$$p(y|\mathbf{D}) = \frac{1}{Z} \exp\left(-\beta \mathcal{H}^{pw}(\mathbf{D}; y)\right)$$
$$\prod_{i,j} \exp\left(-\lambda^+ c_=(i, j) \mathbb{I}\{y_i \neq y_j\} - \lambda^- c_{\neq}(i, j) \mathbb{I}\{y_i = y_j\}\right).$$

Applying the mean-field approximation to this problem (cf. [17] on details of the derivation and [33] for reasons why equation (26) in [17] is exact), results into approximate marginal posteriors

$$q_i(\nu) = \frac{1}{Z_i} \exp\left(\sum_{j\neq i} q_j(\nu)\rho_{ij}\right)$$

$$\exp\left(-\beta \frac{1}{\sum_{j\neq i} q_j(\nu) + 1} \sum_j q_j(\nu)d_{ij}\right)$$

$$\exp\left(\beta \frac{1}{2\sum_{j\neq i} q_j(\nu)} \sum_{j,j'} q_j(\nu)q_{j'}(\nu)d_{jj'}\right).$$

These fixed point equation can again be iteratively solved using the update strategy in [17]. The equivalence of k-means and pairwise clustering problems, as established using constant-shift embeddings in [33], implies that the k-means covers already the pairwise case, so that we stick with vectorial representation at the moment.

5.3.7 The Need for Weighting

So far, the pairwise grouping constraints have been embedded into the EM-based fitting of a mixture model. Analogous to the semi-supervised problem in equation (5.9), the overall negative log-likelihood $\mathcal{L}_X(\gamma, \theta)$, $X = X_u \cup X_c$, can be (roughly) decomposed into two cost terms:

$$\mathcal{L}_{X_u \cup X_c}(\gamma, \theta) = \mathcal{L}_{X_u}(\gamma, \theta) + \mathcal{L}_{X_c}(\gamma, \theta),$$

which are the costs induced by the unlabelled data $\mathcal{L}_{X_u}(\gamma, \theta)$ and those by the data in X_c, $\mathcal{L}_{X_c}(\gamma, \theta)$, i.e., induced by objects participating in ≥ 1 constraint. It is apparent that the constrained objects will have vanishingly small influence on the parameter estimates because $\mathcal{L}_{X_u}$ dominates the objective whenever $|X_c| \ll |X_u|$. This problem has already been noted in [7, 8, 20, 30] in the context of both semi-supervised and learning with constraints. Without modifying the model, one has the choice to either allow the decision of the model and the side information to de-couple or to simply ignore the side information about the labels, since the E-step estimate and the MAP estimate based on the parameters γ and θ alone may be different. This effect can be cured, however, by more strongly emphasizing the points for which constraints are given: Technically, this can be achieved by modifying the objective function to

$$\min_{\gamma, \theta} \mathcal{L}_\eta(\gamma, \theta) := \mathcal{L}_{X_u}(\gamma, \theta) + \eta \mathcal{L}_{X_c}(\gamma, \theta),$$

where $\eta \in [0, \infty)$ controls the influence of the objects participating in a constraint. For $\eta = 0$ the constrained objects do not play a role at all while for $\eta \to \infty$, the unlabelled data is not taken into consideration at all. For $\eta \in \mathbb{N}$, this corresponds to replicating objects participating in a constraint η times. For $\eta = 1$, the original formulation is recovered. The parameter η enters the EM relaxation in a straightforward way. The E-step remains, however, unaffected from this modification, since the mean-field approximation is not required for unlabelled (and unconstrained) objects. However, parameter estimates will be affected.

It is now natural to ask what is exactly the influence of the data replication on the parameter estimates and, thereby, of the data participating in constraints. To this end, the class-conditional density is restricted to the exponential family briefly discussed in section 5.2. Recall, that an exponential family density has the form

$$p(x; \theta_\nu) = p_0(x) \exp \left(\theta_\nu^\top T(x) - A(\theta_\nu) \right),$$

where θ_ν is the natural parameter, p_0 some appropriate (parameter independent) measure, and $A(\theta_\nu)$ the log-partition function. In addition to that, $T(x)$ is a minimal sufficient statistic. In the parameter estimation step of the EM procedure given above, the bound $\tilde{\mathcal{L}}_\eta$ on $\mathcal{L}_\eta$ introduced by the EM relaxation becomes (while taking into account that for $x_i \in X_u$ factorial marginals are exact)

$$\tilde{\mathcal{L}}_\eta(\gamma, \theta; q) = - \sum_{\nu \in [k]} \sum_{x_i \in X_u} q_i(\nu) \log p(x_i; \theta_\nu) \gamma_\nu$$
$$- \eta \sum_{\nu \in [k]} \sum_{x_i \in X_c} q_i(\nu) \log p(x_i; \theta_\nu) \gamma_\nu$$
$$- \eta \sum_{y \in [k]^n} q(y) \log \frac{\prod_{ij} \psi_{ij}(y_i, y_j)}{Z(\gamma)}$$
$$+ \sum_{y \in [k]^n} q(y) \log q(y). \qquad (5.16)$$

Taking derivatives w.r.t. the natural parameter θ_ν and solving the stationary equations yields

$$\sum_{x_i \in X_u} q_i(\nu) T(x_i) + \eta \sum_{x_i \in X_c} q_i(\nu) T(x_i) =$$
$$\sum_{x_i \in X_u} q_i(\nu) \nabla_{\theta_\nu} A(\theta_\nu) + \eta \sum_{x_i \in X_c} q_i(\nu) \nabla_{\theta_\nu} A(\theta_\nu).$$

Since $A(\theta_\nu)$ is the cumulant generating function, $\nabla_{\theta_\nu} A$ is the moment parameter. For minimal sufficient statistics $T(\cdot)$ and strictly convex $A(\theta)$, there is a bijection between the mean parameters of an exponential family density and the natural parameters. Thus, the mean parameter determines the density. In this context, the class-conditional densities are determined by a linear combination of maximum likelihood parameter estimates due to constrained and unconstrained data, since ML parameter estimation in exponential families amounts to matching the moment and natural parameters.

For a mixture of Gaussian class-conditional densities $\mathcal{N}(\boldsymbol{\mu}_\nu, \boldsymbol{\Sigma}_\nu)$ (compare Section 5.2) that is used for the experimental evaluation, one, therefore, straightforwardly arrives at the parameter estimates

$$\boldsymbol{\mu}_\nu = \frac{\sum_{x_i \in X_u} q_i(\nu) x_i + \eta \sum_{x_i \in X_c} q_i(\nu) x_i}{\sum_{x_i \in X_u} q_i(\nu) + \eta \sum_{x_i \in X_c} q_i(\nu)}$$

$$\boldsymbol{\Sigma}_\nu = \frac{\sum_{x_i \in X_u} q_i(\nu)(x_i - \boldsymbol{\mu}_\nu)(x_i - \boldsymbol{\mu}_\nu)^\top + \eta \sum_{x_i \in X_c} q_i(\nu)(x_i - \boldsymbol{\mu}_\nu)(x_i - \boldsymbol{\mu}_\nu)^\top}{\sum_{x_i \in X_u} q_i(\nu) + \eta \sum_{x_i \in X_c} q_i(\nu)}.$$

By dropping the log-partition function $\log Z(\boldsymbol{\gamma})$ in equation (5.16), the class priors can be estimated via the approximate marginal posteriors q_i by looking for the zero-crossings of $\nabla_\gamma \tilde{\mathcal{L}}_\eta(\boldsymbol{\gamma}, \boldsymbol{\theta})$. This yields for the global class priors again a linear combination due to unlabelled and constrained data, namely:

$$\gamma_\nu = \frac{\sum_{x_i \in X_u} q_i(\nu) + \eta \sum_{x_i \in X_c} q_i(\nu)}{|X_u| + \eta |X_c|}.$$

The role of the weighting parameter η becomes now obvious: η linearly scales the influence of the constrained data on the parameter estimates. Due to the normalization, the influence of the unlabelled data is scaled down at the same time.

REMARK 5.3 The mechanism for constraint integration introduced in this chapter can be easily extended to more complex models by means of kernel functions. A particularly elegant and, at the same time, straightforward extension is the following: Consider a Gaussian mixture model in feature space where the co-variance matrix $\boldsymbol{\Sigma}$ is common to all classes. According to [14, 15], the M-step of EM for estimating the mixture parameters can be rephrased as equivalent linear discriminant analysis (LDA) (cf. [13]) problem. For the latter, a kernel-based variant, termed *non-linear kernel discriminant analysis* has been proposed in [34], which turns the LDA problem into a sequence of regression problems. By means of this step, the mixture estimation can be straightforwardly kernelized. In particular, the maximum entropy label priors as well as the mean-field approximation remain applicable in this context as they rely on the unchanged E-step. $\quad\Box$

5.3.8 Selecting η

Introducing the weighting mechanism comes at the expense of an additional parameter, η, which has to be selected. The appropriate choice of η largely depends on what the user wants to achieve. Setting $\eta = 1$, one assigns equal importance to all data points. Departing from this puts more or less emphasis on the unlabelled or the constrained data. Such a weighting parameter is commonly encountered in semi-supervised learning. Unfortunately, no strategy is often devised on how to pick the appropriate parameter values. We briefly mention a heuristic procedure for determining η that is applicable if constrained data are not too scarce.[3]

In principle, one may think of applying a pure K-fold cross-validation (cf. [16]), which attempts to assess the error for various settings of η: Partition the data participating in at least one constraint into K blocks. For each block b and fixed η, apply the algorithm to the data in all blocks $b' \neq b$ and evaluate the number of constraint violations (i.e., the 0-1 loss in product space) on the held-out block b. The K estimates obtained in this way can be combined into a single estimate by averaging. Model selection could now be based on the corresponding error estimate obtained by cross-validation. However, as it is assumed that $|X_c| \ll |X_u|$, the estimate will be relatively unreliable as it has high variance. This has already been noted in [35] in the context of semi-supervised learning. Still, a reasonable estimate for η is required. The strategy that may be adopted is essentially a biased version of cross-validation: For hold-out sets of constrained data, one can identify the *smallest* η that minimizes the classification error on the withheld data. By means of this, the approach puts the most emphasis on the unlabelled data while attempting to maintain consistency (in a predictive sense) with the actually given constraints. If the constrained data is too scarce, one may switch to the (optimistically biased) in-sample estimate of the error. Intuitively, this method makes sense because not much is known about the label source except for the few samples participating in instance-level constraints. Clearly, the procedure lacks a thorough theoretical justification and, thus, remains a heuristic.

---

[3]Note that the coupling parameter η plays a different role compared to the Lagrange parameters λ^+ and λ^-: η controls the importance of constrained objects in X_c as opposed to objects in X_u, while the Lagrange parameters λ^+ and λ^- only affect the data in X_c. Whenever constraints are supposed to reflect real class information, λ^+ and λ^- should be large and kept constant – as done in the experimental section. Strictly speaking, the model selection strategy sketched here, does not apply in other cases.

5.4 Experiments

The approach described in the last section is applied to deterministic annealing (DA) [32] for Gaussian mixture models and squared error clustering, leading to a DA clustering algorithm with constraints. Class priors were chosen to be uniform in conjunction with the ME approach. This algorithm is tested on different synthetic and real-world data sets. The "clustering with constraints" algorithms[4] from [36] (abbreviated here by *GMM-Sh*), the hard-constraint version of penalized probabilistic clustering (PPC) from [24] (see below) and [2] are also run on all the data sets for comparison. For the algorithm in [2], both PCKMEANS and MPCKMEANS have been tested giving nearly identical results for all data sets. Thirteen different constraint penalty values ranging from 1 to 4000 are used for the algorithm in [2]; only the best result of their algorithms is reported. Note that for hard-constraint PPC (cf. [24]), the maximum clique size in the hMRF was assumed to be 2 in order to relate the quality of the MF approximation to a method of similar time complexity.[5] The version of PPC used in this chapter follows a different strategy of complexity reduction and is not to be confused with the Gibbs sampling approach also described in [24]. The latter was already related to our proposal in a recent study (cf. [29]).

To evaluate the results of the different methods, we use *F-scores*, i.e., the harmonic mean of precision and recall, to compare two classifications. The measure is briefly described since several authors use different F-measures in order to compare their results with a ground-truth solution. The F-measure employed here is based on a greedy matching (not a perfect matching) of the clusters in the two solutions under comparison. For a target labelling $t \in [k]^n$ and computed labelling $y \in [k']^n$, the assessment is based on the $k \times k'$ matrix with (ν, ν')-entry

$$a_{\nu\nu'} = |\{i \mid t_i = \nu\}| \cap |\{i \mid y_i = \nu'\}|, \qquad (5.17)$$

i.e., the number of objects that are in cluster ν of the target solution and at the same time in cluster ν' of the computed one. From this matrix, the cluster sizes are easily obtained by $\sum_{\nu} a_{\nu\nu'} = |\{i \mid y_i = \nu'\}| =: m_{\nu'}$ and

---

[4]Thanks to the authors for putting the implementation of their algorithms online: `http://www.cs.huji.ac.il/~tomboy/code/ConstrainedEM_plusBNT.zip` for [36] and `http://www.cs.utexas.edu/users/ml/risc/code/` for [2].

[5]By the Hammersley-Clifford theorem, this leads to an efficient factorization of the class posterior distribution depending at most on pairs of objects but may come at the expense of losing accuracy.

$\sum_{\nu'} a_{\nu\nu'} = |\{i \mid t_i = \nu\}| =: n_\nu$. The precision $p_{\nu\nu'}$ and recall $r_{\nu\nu'}$ per class-pair (ν, ν') are then simply

$$p_{\nu\nu'} = \frac{a_{\nu\nu'}}{m_{\nu'}} \text{ and } r_{\nu\nu'} = \frac{a_{\nu\nu'}}{n_\nu}. \tag{5.18}$$

The harmonic mean gives a local, per-cluster-pair score, i.e., $f_{\nu\nu'} = \frac{2p_{\nu\nu'}r_{\nu\nu'}}{p_{\nu\nu'}+r_{\nu\nu'}}$. In order to obtain a global, overall score, clusters in t and y are greedily matched. Hence, the total score becomes

$$F = \frac{1}{n} \sum_{\nu \in [k]} n_\nu \left(\max_{\nu' \in [k']} f_{\nu\nu'} \right), \tag{5.19}$$

which amounts to a greedy matching of clusters on the two solutions under comparison. Note that an F-score of one amounts to perfect agreement of two solutions.

Figure 5.4 shows a 2D synthetic data set with 200 points, together with an example set of constraints. Since the horizontal separation between the point clouds is smaller than the vertical separation, the two-cluster unsupervised solution is to group the data into "upper" and "lower" clusters. The structural bias provided here in the form of constraints, however, states that the data points should be grouped into "left" and "right" clusters. The constraints are generated by first sampling point pairs randomly and then converting each pair to either a link or not-link constraint according to its location. Due to the random sampling, the proportion of link and not-link constraints may vary. Different levels of constraint information are taken into account: 1%, 5%, 10%, 15%, 30%, or 50% of constraints are considered relative to the total number of samples in the data set in order to account for the construction of the transitive closure on constraint graphs. We run the proposed algorithm with $\lambda^+ = \lambda^- = 1000$ (since constraints presumably correspond to true label information here) and recover the desired boundary almost exactly (with at most one erroneous point) for *all* amounts of constraint information. In contrast to that, the desired boundary is recovered by the algorithms in [36], [24], and [2] only when 50% of constraints are present. The F-scores are shown in table 5.1. Note that a random grouping would have obtained a F-score of 0.5 on average in this case. In order to demonstrate the effect of misspecified constraints, we have randomly flipped 20% of the constraints for the 50% data set. The best result for the method in [36] is an F-score of 0.835. In contrast, the method proposed here behaves favorably: the misspecified constraints have hardly any effect on the decision boundary learnt and, hence, an F-score of 0.995 is obtained again. One may conclude that the proposal is more robust toward erroneous constraints in this case, thanks to the use of maximum entropy label priors.

The second experiment is about an ethnicity classification problem [23], where the goal is to decide whether a face image belongs to an Asian or not.

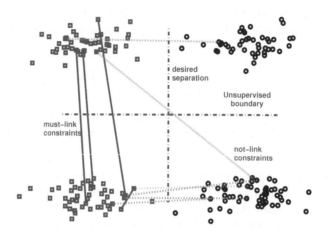

FIGURE 5.4: Synthetic data set. Solid lines: must-link constraints. Dashed lines: must-not-link constraints.

TABLE 5.1: F-scores on the toy data set.

	1%	5%	10%	15%	30%	50%
GMM-Sh	0.540	0.560	0.560	0.580	0.535	1.0
(M)PCKMEANS	0.540	0.545	0.535	0.590	0.535	1.0
hard PPC ($|T| \leq 2$)	0.535	0.545	0.55	0.53	0.535	1.0
Proposed	1.0	1.0	0.995	0.995	0.995	0.995

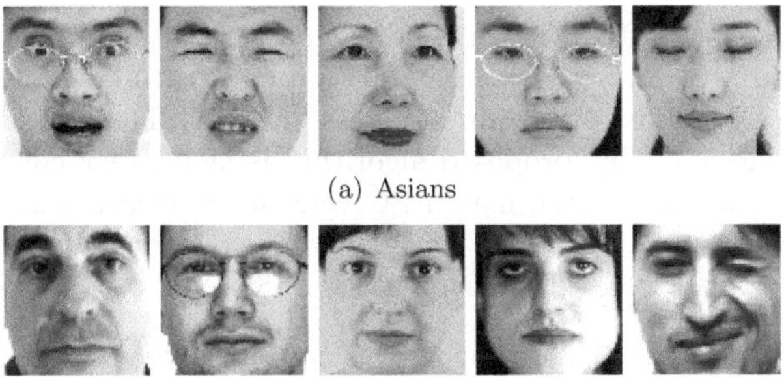

(a) Asians

(b) Non-Asians

FIGURE 5.5: Example face images in the face classification problem (from [20], ©2005 IEEE).

TABLE 5.2: F-scores on the ethnicity classification problem for different clustering-with-constraints algorithms.

	1%	10%	15%	30%
GMM-Sh	0.925	0.946	0.891	0.973
(M)PCKMEANS	0.568	0.565	0.570	0.809
hard PPC ($|T| \leq 2$)	0.653	0.59	0.570	0.811
Proposed	0.923	0.915	0.922	0.963

The data set consists of 2630 images with size 64×64 which were compiled from different databases, including the PF01 database,[6] the Yale database,[7] the AR database [26], and the non-public NLPR database.[8] Some example images are shown in Figure 5.5. A face image is represented by its first 30 eigenface coefficients. Again, different levels (1%, 10%, 15%, and 30%) of constraint information (derived from the known ground-truth labelling) are considered. The resulting F-scores of the algorithms under comparison are shown in table 5.2. The proposed algorithm significantly outperforms hard PPC variant taken from Lu et al. and the algorithm Basu et al. (the latter similarly perform), and is competitive with the algorithm by Shental et al.

The third experiment is based on three newsgroup data sets[9] used in [2]. To improve readability, the description of the data is briefly repeated. It consists of three data sets, each of which contains roughly 300 documents from three different topics. The topics are regarded as the classes to be recovered. Latent semantic indexing is used to transform the term frequency (TF) and inverse

---

[6]http://nova.postech.ac.kr/archives/imdb.html.

[7]http://cvc.yale.edu/projects/yalefaces/yalefaces.html.

[8]Provided by Dr. Yunhong Wang, National Laboratory for Pattern Recognition, Beijing.

[9]http://www.cs.utexas.edu/users/ml/risc/.

document frequency (IDF) normalized document vectors to a 20-dimensional feature vector. Again, we have access to a ground-truth labelling of the data, which we used to derive varying numbers of constraints. The F-scores are shown in table 5.3. The proposed algorithm is again very competitive: the method in [2] as well as the hard PPC version are clearly outperformed on most problem instances. Similar behavior can be observed on two of the three data sets in comparison with the approach in [36].

The final comparison experiment considers an artificial image segmentation problem. A Mondrian image (figure 5.6(a)) consisting of five regions is employed: three regions with strong texture and two regions of very noisy gray-level segments are to be identified. This 512-by-512 image is divided into a 101-by-101 grid. A 24-dimensional feature vector is extracted for each site: 12 features originate from a 12-bin histogram of gray-level values, while the remaining 12 correspond to the averages of Gabor filter responses for four orientations at three different scales (2, 4, and 8 pixels wavelength) at each site. The segment labels of different sites are generated from a ground-truth image. Since the texture information dominates the gray-value information, clustering with unlabelled data fails to recover the ground-truth information. This also holds true for the data set with 1% and 5% of the data in constraints (see figure 5.6(c)). The segmented image with 10% of sites in constraints is shown in figure 5.6(d). Here, the proposal almost perfectly identifies the ground-truth information, since the algorithm is able to distinguish between the gray-level segments. The F-scores for various algorithms are listed in table 5.4. The proposed method holds an edge when at least 10% of the data points are in constraints, and it can discover a good approximation to the desired segmentation with the least amount of constraint information. The quality gap is particularly large in this case. Furthermore, the approach in [36] had a very high running time, in particular for examples with a large number of constraints.

5.5 Summary

In this chapter, a model-based framework for integrating side information in the form of instance-level constraints into the inference was proposed. A similar integration strategy can, in principle, be applied to partially labelled data, so that partially labelled, partially constrained, and unlabelled data can be embedded in the learning process within a common framework. By introducing a weighting mechanism, inconsistent labelling rules can be avoided: Instead of only considering the posterior assignment probabilities, the infer-

TABLE 5.3: F-scores obtained for the newsgroup data sets (taken from [2]) with different numbers of constraints.

Data set		1%	10%	15%	30%
same-300	GMM-Sh	0.412	0.429	0.516	0.487
	(M)PCKMEANS	0.515	0.459	0.472	0.552
	hard PPC ($|T| \leq 2$)	0.481	0.468	0.47	0.483
	Proposed	0.491	0.588	0.527	0.507
similar-300	GMM-Sh	0.560	0.553	0.531	0.532
	(M)PCKMEANS	0.515	0.492	0.549	0.530
	hard PPC ($|T| \leq 2$)	0.48	0.474	0.492	0.509
	Proposed	0.54	0.54	0.53	0.514
diff-300	GMM-Sh	0.877	0.554	0.907	0.871
	(M)PCKMEANS	0.677	0.582	0.558	0.608
	hard PPC ($|T| \leq 2$)	0.485	0.476	0.498	0.520
	Proposed	0.533	0.658	0.571	0.594

TABLE 5.4: F-scores on the image segmentation task.

	1%	5%	10%	15%
GMM-Sh	0.830	0.831	0.840	0.829
(M)PCKMEANS	0.761	0.801	0.821	0.776
hard PPC ($|T| \leq 2$)	0.799	0.785	0.772	0.8165
Proposed	0.772	0.829	0.972	0.98

ence strategy systematically affects parameter estimates by allowing to control the influence of the constraint information. The combination approach also decouples the learning task; instead of worrying about how different types of information interact with each other, one can focus on building the most appropriate model for a single source of information (constraints in our case). To this end, we adopt the maximum entropy principle to derive a prior distribution for the assignment labels. This principle assumes the least about the label information apart from the information derived from the constraints and is, thereby, robust to erroneously specified constraint information. The mean-field approximation technique is adopted to keep the computation tractable, as the computation requirement in each iteration is similar to that of a standard EM iteration. This approach can be much more efficient than the algorithm in [36] in the case where the constraints lead to a large clique in the corresponding MRF on the set of label random variables. At the same time it yields superior inference results in comparison with standard ICM as employed in [2]. The factorial distribution due to mean-field approximation is a stationary point of the variational free energy and, thereby, aims at finding the best factorial distribution in terms of the Kullback-Leibler divergence to the true distribution. The use of deterministic annealing in our approach helps to avoid

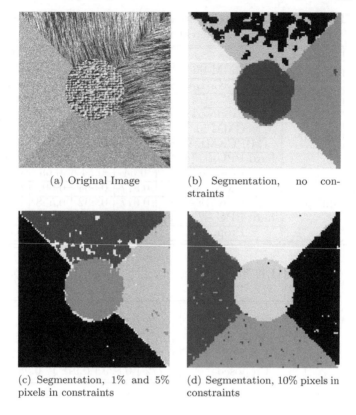

(a) Original Image

(b) Segmentation, no constraints

(c) Segmentation, 1% and 5% pixels in constraints

(d) Segmentation, 10% pixels in constraints

FIGURE 5.6: Results of image segmentation. (a): source image. (b) to (d): segmentation results with different numbers of constraints (from [20], ©2005 IEEE).

poor local minima; the latter can be the case for the ICM technique used in [2]. This feature of our proposal is particularly valuable in clustering with constraints, where the energy landscape may lack the smoothness of standard clustering problems. Finally, it should be underscored that the approach has wide applicability covering many (also pairwise) grouping models as already indicated in the technical exposition.

References

[1] O. E. Barndorff-Nielsen. *Information and Exponential Families.* Wiley, New York, 1978.

[2] S. Basu, M. Bilenko, and R. J. Mooney. A probabilistic framework for semi-supervised clustering. In *Proceedings of the 10th ACM SIGKDD, International Conference on Knowledge Discovery and Data Mining (KDD)*, pages 59–68. ACM Press, 2004.

[3] M. Belkin and P. Niyogi. Laplacian eigenmaps for dimensionality reduction and data representation. *Neural Computation*, 15:1373–1396, 2003.

[4] M. Bilenko and S. Basu. A comparison of inference techniques for semi-supervised clustering with hidden Markov random fields. In *Proceedings of the ICML-2004 Workshop on Statistical Relational Learning and Its Connections to Other Fields (SRL-2004), Banff, Canada*, pages 17–22, 2004.

[5] J. A. Bilmes. A gentle tutorial of the em algorithm and its application to parameter estimation for Gaussian mixture and hidden Markov models. Technical Report TR-97-021, International Computer Science Institute and Computer Science Division, Department of Electrical Engineering and Computer Science, U.C. Berkeley, April 1998.

[6] P. Bremaud. *Markov Chains – Gibbs Fields, Monte Carlo Simulation, and Queues.* Number 31 in Texts in Applied Mathematics. Springer, 1999.

[7] I. Cohen, F. G. Cozman, N. Sebe, M. C. Cirelo, and T. S. Huang. Semisupervised learning of classifiers: Theory, algorithms, and their application to human-computer interaction. *IEEE Transactions on Pattern Analysis and Machine Intelligence*, 26(12):1553–1567, December 2004.

[8] A. Corduneanu and T. Jaakkola. Continuation methods for mixing heterogeneous sources. In *Proceedings of the 18th Annual Conference on Uncertainty in Artificial Intelligence (UAI-02)*, San Francisco, CA, 2002. Morgan Kaufmann.

[9] T. M. Cover and J. A. Thomas. *Elements of Information Theory.* Wiley Series in Telecommunications. John Wiley & Sons, New York, 1991.

[10] H. Cramer. *Mathematical Methods of Statistics*. Princeton University Press, 1946.

[11] O. Delalleau, Y. Bengio, and N. L. Roux. Efficient non-parametric function induction in semi-supervised learning. In R. G. Cowell and Z. Ghahramani, editors, *Proceedings of the Tenth International Workshop on Artificial Intelligence and Statistics (AISTAT)*, pages 96–103. Society for Artificial Intelligence and Statistics, 2005.

[12] A. P. Dempster, N. M. Laird, and D. B. Rubin. Maximum likelihood from incomplete data via the EM algorithm. *Journal of the Royal Statistical Society, Series B*, 39(1):1–38, 1977.

[13] R. O. Duda, P. E. Hart, and D. G. Stork. *Pattern Classification*. John Wiley & Sons, 2000.

[14] T. Hastie and R. Tibshirani. Discriminant analysis by Gaussian mixtures. *Journal of the Royal Statistical Society, Series B*, 58:158–176, 1996.

[15] T. Hastie, R. Tibshirani, and A. Buja. Flexible discriminant and mixture models. In J. Kay and D. Titterington, editors, *Neural Networks and Statistics*. Oxford University Press, 1995.

[16] T. Hastie, R. Tibshirani, and J. Friedman. *The Elements of Statistical Learning: Data Mining, Inference and Prediction*. Springer Series in Statistics. Springer-Verlag, New York, 2001.

[17] T. Hofmann and J. M. Buhmann. Pairwise data clustering by deterministic annealing. *IEEE Transactions on Pattern Analysis and Machine Intelligence*, 19(1):1–14, January 1997.

[18] S. Kamvar, D. Klein, and C. D. Manning. Spectral learning. In *Proceedings of the Eighteenth International Joint Conference on Artificial Intelligence (IJCAI)*, pages 561–566, 2003.

[19] D. Klein, S. D. Kamvar, and C. D. Manning. From instance-level constraints to space-level constraints: Making the most of prior knowledge in data clustering. In *Proceedings of the Nineteenth International Conference on Machine Learning (ICML)*, pages 307–314, San Francisco, CA, 2002. Morgan Kaufmann Publishers Inc.

[20] T. Lange, M. H. C. Law, A. K. Jain, and J. M. Buhmann. Learning with constrained and unlabelled data. In *2005 IEEE Computer Society Conference on Computer Vision and Pattern Recognition (CVPR 2005), 20-26 June 2005, San Diego, CA, USA*, pages 731–738. IEEE Computer Society, 2005.

[21] M. H. Law, A. Topchy, and A. K. Jain. Clustering with soft and group constraints. In *Proceedings of the Joint IAPR International Workshops*

on Structural, Syntactic, and Statistical Pattern Recognition, pages 662–670, Lisbon, Portugal, August 2004.

[22] M. H. Law, A. Topchy, and A. K. Jain. Model-based clustering with probabilistic constraints. In *2005 Society for Industrial and Applied Mathematics (SIAM) International Conference on Data Mining (SDM)*, pages 641–645. SIAM, 2005.

[23] X. Lu and A. K. Jain. Ethnicity identification from face images. In *Proceedings of the Society of Photographic Instrumentation Engineers (SPIE)*, volume 5404, pages 114–123, 2004.

[24] Z. Lu and T. Leen. Semi-supervised learning with penalized probabilistic clustering. In *Advances in Neural Information Processing Systems (NIPS) 17*, pages 849–856. MIT Press, Cambridge, MA, 2005.

[25] J. MacQueen. Some methods for classification and analysis of multivariate observations. In L. M. LeCam and J. Neyman, editors, *Proceedings of the Fifth Berkeley Symposium on Mathematical Statistics and Probability*, volume 1, pages 281–297. University of California Press, 1967.

[26] A. Martinez and R. Benavente. The AR face database. Technical Report 24, CVC, 1998. `http://rvl1.ecn.purdue.edu/~aleix/aleix_face_DB.html`.

[27] G. McLachlan and D. Peel. *Finite Mixture Models*. John Wiley and Sons Inc., 2000.

[28] R. Neal and G. Hinton. A view of the em algorithm that justifies incremental, sparse, and other variants. In M. Jordan, editor, *Learning in Graphical Models*, pages 355–368. Kluwer Academic Publishers, 1998.

[29] B. Nelson and I. Cohen. Revisiting probabilistic models for clustering with pairwise constraints. Technical report, HP Laboratories, Palo Alto, 2007.

[30] K. Nigam, A. K. McCallum, S. Thrun, and T. Mitchell. Text classification from labeled and unlabeled documents using em. *Machine Learning*, 39:103–134, 2000.

[31] G. Parisi. *Statistical Field Theory*. Addison-Wesley, 1988.

[32] K. Rose, E. Gurewitz, and G. Fox. Vector quantization and deterministic annealing. *IEEE Transactions on Information Theory*, 38(4):1249–1257, 1992.

[33] V. Roth, J. Laub, M. Kawanabe, and J. M. Buhmann. Optimal cluster preserving embedding of nonmetric proximity data. *IEEE Transactions on Pattern Analysis and Machine Intelligence*, 25(12):1540–1551, December 2003.

[34] V. Roth and V. Steinhage. Nonlinear discriminant analysis using kernel functions. In S. A. Solla, T. K. Leen, and K.-R. Müller, editors, *Advances in Neural Information Processing Systems (NIPS) 12*, pages 568–574. MIT Press, 1999.

[35] M. Seeger. Learning with labelled and unlabelled data. Technical report, Institute for Adaptive and Neural Computation, University of Edinburgh, UK, 2001.

[36] N. Shental, A. Bar-Hillel, T. Hertz, and D. Weinshall. Computing Gaussian mixture models with EM using equivalence constraints. In S. Thrun, L. Saul, and B. Schölkopf, editors, *Advances in Neural Information Processing Systems (NIPS) 16*, Cambridge, MA, 2004. MIT Press.

[37] V. Vapnik. *The Nature of Statistical Learning Theory*. Springer-Verlag, 2nd edition, 1999.

[38] K. Wagstaff and C. Cardie. Clustering with instance-level constraints. In P. Langley, editor, *Proceedings of the Seventeenth International Conference on Machine Learning (ICML)*, pages 1103–1110. Morgan Kaufmann, 2000.

[39] K. Wagstaff, C. Cardie, S. Rogers, and S. Schroedl. Constrained k-means clustering with background knowledge. In C. E. Brodley and A. P. Danyluk, editors, *Proceedings of the Eighteenth International Conference on Machine Learning (ICML)*, pages 577–584. Morgan Kaufmann, 2001.

[40] E. P. Xing, A. Y. Ng, M. I. Jordan, and S. Russell. Distance metric learning, with application to clustering with side-information. In S. Becker, S. Thrun, and K. Obermayer, editors, *Advances in Neural Information Processing Systems (NIPS) 15*, pages 505–512, Cambridge, MA, 2003. MIT Press.

[41] S. X. Yu and J. Shi. Segmentation given partial grouping constraints. *IEEE Transactions on Pattern Analysis and Machine Intelligence*, 26(2):173–183, 2004.

[42] Q. Zhao and D. J. Miller. Mixture modelling with pairwise, instance-level class constraints. *Neural Computation*, 17(11):2482–2507, November 2005.

[43] X. Zhu. Semi-supervised learning literature survey. Technical Report 1530, Computer Sciences, University of Wisconsin-Madison, http://www.cs.wisc.edu/~jerryzhu/pub/ssl_survey.pdf, 2005.

[44] X. Zhu. *Semi-supervised learning with graphs*. PhD thesis, Carnegie Mellon University, 2005. CMU-LTI-05-192.

[45] X. Zhu, J. Lafferty, and Z. Gharamani. Semi-supervised learning: From Gaussian fields to Gaussian processes. Technical Report CMU-CS-03-175, Carnegie Mellon University, 2003.

Chapter 6

Constraint-Driven Co-Clustering of 0/1 Data

Ruggero G. Pensa

ISTI-CNR, `ruggero.pensa@isti.cnr.it`

Céline Robardet

INSA-Lyon, `celine.robardet@insa-lyon.fr`

Jean-François Boulicaut

INSA-Lyon, `jean-francois.boulicaut@insa-lyon.fr`

Abstract   We investigate a co-clustering framework (i.e., a method that provides a partition of objects and a linked partition of features) for binary data sets. So far, constrained co-clustering has been seldomly explored. First, we consider straightforward extensions of the classical instance level constraints (must-link, cannot-link) to express relationships on both objects and features. Furthermore, we study constraints that exploit sequential orders on objects and/or features. The idea is that we can specify whether the extracted co-clusters should involve or not contiguous elements (interval and non-interval constraints). Instead of designing constraint processing integration within a co-clustering scheme, we propose a local-to-global (L2G) framework. It consists of postprocessing a collection of (constrained) local patterns that have been computed beforehand (e.g., closed feature sets and their supporting sets of objects) to build a global pattern like a co-clustering. Roughly speaking, the algorithmic scheme is a k-means-like approach that groups the local patterns. We show that it is possible to push local counterparts of the global constraints on the co-clusters during the local pattern mining phase itself. A large part of the chapter is dedicated to experiments that demonstrate the added-value of our approach. Considering both synthetic data and real gene expression data sets, we discuss the use of constraints to get not only more stable but also more relevant co-clusters.

6.1 Introduction

Many data mining techniques have been proposed to support knowledge discovery from large 0/1 data sets, i.e., Boolean matrices whose rows denote objects and columns denote Boolean attributes recording object properties. Table 6.1(a) gives an example of such a matrix where, for instance, object t_2 only satisfies properties g_2 and g_5. In fact, many application domains provide such data sets: besides data sets that are intrinsically Boolean, they can be applied on categorical or numerical data sets as well. Indeed, a categorical feature that can have n different values can be transformed into n Boolean attributes, and continuous attributes can also be transformed into a set of Boolean attributes using discretization methods [14]. Just to name a few interesting application domains, objects can denote commercial transactions, WWW sessions, digital documents, or biological samples. Properties could then denote purchased items (i.e., a product belongs to the transaction or not), WWW resources (i.e., a resource has been uploaded or not during a session), keywords (i.e., a keyword is considered as a descriptor or not for the content of a document), or gene expression properties (e.g., a given gene has been found over-expressed or not in a biological sample).

Exploratory data analysis processes often make use of clustering techniques. This can be used to look for groups of similar objects according to some metrics. Properties can be considered as well. Many methods can provide relevant partitions on one dimension (say objects or properties) but they suffer from the lack of explicit cluster characterization, i.e., what are the properties that are shared by the objects of a same cluster. This has motivated the research on conceptual clustering and, among others, the design of co-clustering algorithms [24, 13, 9, 3]. The goal of a co-clustering task is to cluster simultaneously the rows and columns of the data matrix such that there is a one-to-one mapping that associates to a cluster of objects the cluster of properties that are mostly supported by these objects. An example of a co-clustering result on the data of Table 6.1(a) would be $\{\{\{t_1, t_3, t_4\}, \{g_1, g_3, g_4\}\}, \{\{t_2, t_5, t_6, t_7\}, \{g_2, g_5\}\}\}$. The first co-cluster indicates that the objects from cluster $\{t_1, t_3, t_4\}$ almost always share properties from cluster $\{g_1, g_3, g_4\}$. Also, properties in $\{g_2, g_5\}$ are characteristic of objects in $\{t_2, t_5, t_6, t_7\}$ (see Table 6.1(b)).

In the context of, for instance, WWW usage mining, this kind of pattern may help to identify communities, i.e., groups of users whose sessions give rise to almost the same uploading behavior. This is also useful in the context of gene expression data analysis where such co-clusters may provide putative synexpression groups of genes [5].

As clustering algorithms, co-clustering methods heuristically optimize an objective function (e.g., Goodman-Kruskal's τ coefficient [24] or the loss of mutual information [13]), the search space being too large to enable exhaustive

TABLE 6.1: A Boolean matrix **r** (a) and its associated co-clustering (b).

	g_1	g_2	g_3	g_4	g_5		g_1	g_3	g_4	g_2	g_5
t_1	1	0	1	1	0	t_1	1	1	1	0	0
t_2	0	1	0	0	1	t_3	1	1	1	0	0
t_3	1	0	1	1	0	t_4	0	1	1	0	0
t_4	0	0	1	1	0	t_2	0	0	0	1	1
t_5	1	1	0	0	1	t_5	1	0	0	1	1
t_6	0	1	0	0	1	t_6	0	0	0	1	1
t_7	0	0	0	0	1	t_7	0	0	0	0	1

(a) (b)

computation. In such a context, it is mandatory to take advantage of any available information to guide the search. Thus, a timely challenge is to support constrained co-clustering, where user-defined constraints can be used to reduce the search space.

Our contribution is twofold. First, we are not aware of previous work related to constrained co-clustering. Not only we extend the use of *must-link* and *cannot-link* constraints [27, 16, 4, 11, 10, 26] within a co-clustering task, but also we introduce new constraints that are useful when the object and/or property dimensions are ordered (e.g., when properties are measured at several time steps giving rise to objects that are ordered w.r.t. time). Thanks to our *interval* and *non-interval* constraints, it is possible to specify whether a collection of co-clusters has to be consistent w.r.t. as such a priori order. In this chapter, we will briefly describe an application of such constraints for gene expression data analysis. Our second contribution concerns the framework for computing the co-clusters. We recently proposed a generic method to compute co-clusters based on collections of local patterns which capture locally strong associations [21]. Such local patterns are obtained thanks to exhaustive search algorithms. Then, co-clustering is performed as an heuristic combination of these patterns using a k-means approach. We have shown that using this two-phases process leads to more robust co-clusters. We now exploit this idea within a constrained co-clustering setting, and we show that the local pattern identification step can guide the computation of constrained co-clusters. This chapter extends the preliminary results from [22]. Not only do we provide more technical details on constraint processing but also the experimental validation has been considerably extended.

The rest of the paper is organized as follows. Section 6.2 provides the problem setting, including the definition of the considered constraints. Section 6.3 recalls the framework from [21] and it introduces its extension toward constrained co-clustering. Section 6.4 concerns our experimental validation, including applications on real gene expression data sets. Section 6.5 concludes.

6.2 Problem Setting

The Boolean context to be mined is $\mathbf{r} \subseteq \mathcal{T} \times \mathcal{G}$, where $\mathcal{T} = \{t_1, \ldots, t_m\}$ is a set of objects and $\mathcal{G} = \{g_1, \ldots, g_n\}$ is a set of Boolean properties. We assume that $r_{ij} = 1$ if property g_j is satisfied by object t_i. For the sake of clarity, $\mathcal{D}$ will denote either $\mathcal{T}$ or $\mathcal{G}$. Let us now define the co-clustering task.

DEFINITION 6.1 Co-clustering task   *A co-clustering task delivers a partition $\Pi_\mathcal{T}$ of k clusters of objects $\{\pi_{\mathcal{T}1}, \ldots, \pi_{\mathcal{T}k}\}$ and a partition $\Pi_\mathcal{G}$ of k clusters of properties $\{\pi_{\mathcal{G}1}, \ldots, \pi_{\mathcal{G}k}\}$ with a bijective mapping denoted σ between both partitions:*

$$\sigma : \Pi_\mathcal{T} \to \Pi_\mathcal{G}$$

The computed co-clustering, denoted Π, is composed of k co-clusters $\{\pi_1, \ldots, \pi_k\}$ with $\pi_i = (\pi_{\mathcal{T}i}, \sigma(\pi_{\mathcal{T}i}))$.

Example 6.1
An example of co-clustering is presented in Table 6.1(b). It is composed of the two partitions:

$$\Pi_\mathcal{T} = \{\{t_1, t_3, t_4\}, \{t_2, t_5, t_6, t_7\}\}$$
$$\Pi_\mathcal{G} = \{\{g_1, g_3, g_4\}, \{g_2, g_5\}\}$$

The associated function σ is defined as:

$$\sigma(\{t_1, t_3, t_4\}) = \{g_1, g_3, g_4\}$$
$$\sigma(\{t_2, t_5, t_6, t_7\}) = \{g_2, g_5\}$$

$\square$

In such a framework, it makes sense to apply the standard must-link and cannot-link constraints on both object and property sets.

DEFINITION 6.2 Extended must-link and cannot-link constraints
An extended must-link constraint, denoted $c_{e=}(x_i, x_j, \Pi, \mathcal{D})$, specifies that two elements x_i and x_j of $\mathcal{D}$ have to belong to a same co-cluster from Π. An extended cannot-link constraint, denoted $c_{e\neq}(x_i, x_j, \Pi, \mathcal{D})$, specifies that x_i and x_j cannot belong to the same co-cluster of Π.

Assume now there exists a function $s : \mathcal{D} \to \mathbb{R}$ that associates a real value $s(x_i)$ to each element $x_i \in \mathcal{D}$. For instance, $s(x_i)$ can be a temporal or spatial measure related to x_i. For instance, in microarray data, where $\mathcal{T}$ is a set of DNA chips corresponding to biological experiments, and $\mathcal{G}$ is a set of genes,

$s(t_i)$ might be the time stamp for the experiment t_i. Such a function s enables us to define an order $\preceq$ on dimension $\mathcal{D}$ where $x_i \preceq x_j$ iff $s(x_i) \leq s(x_j)$. For the sake of simplicity, we consider that if a function s exists on dimension $\mathcal{D}$, then all its elements x_i are ordered. We can now introduce constraints that exploit an ordered set $\mathcal{D}$.

DEFINITION 6.3 Interval and non-interval constraints *Given an order ($\preceq$) on $\mathcal{D}$, an interval constraint on this dimension, denoted $c_{int}(\mathcal{D}, \Pi)$, enforces each cluster on $\mathcal{D}$ to be an interval: $\forall \ell = 1 \ldots k$, if $x_i, x_j \in \pi_{\mathcal{D}\ell}$ then $\forall x$ s.t. $x_i \preceq x \preceq x_j$, $x \in \pi_{\mathcal{D}\ell}$. A non-interval constraint denoted $c_{non-int}(\mathcal{D}, \Pi)$ specifies that clusters on $\mathcal{D}$ should not be intervals: $\forall \ell = 1 \ldots k$, $\exists x_i, x_j \in \pi_{\mathcal{D}\ell}, \exists x \in \mathcal{D}$ s.t. $x_i \preceq x \preceq x_j$, $x \notin \pi_{\mathcal{D}\ell}$.*

An interval constraint can be used to find clusters that are continuous intervals, while a non-interval constraint can be used to find clusters that are not intervals.

Example 6.2
Suppose that $\mathcal{G}$ is ordered such that $g_1 \preceq g_2 \preceq g_3 \preceq g_4 \preceq g_5$. Partition $\Pi_{\mathcal{G}} = \{\{g_1, g_3, g_4\}, \{g_2, g_5\}\}$ does not satisfy $c_{int}(\mathcal{D}, \Pi_{\mathcal{G}})$ since g_2 and g_5 belongs to $\pi_{\mathcal{G}2}$ but g_3 ($g_2 \preceq g_3 \preceq g_5$) does not belong to $\pi_{\mathcal{G}2}$.

$c_{non-int}(\mathcal{D}, \Pi_{\mathcal{G}})$ is an example of a satisfied constraint. ▯

One of the typical application domains that motivates the use of these constraints is temporal gene expression data analysis: objects are a given organism considered at several developmental steps and properties encode, for instance, the over-expression of genes. In such a context (see, e.g., [2, 8]), using interval constraints enables us to capture conjunctions of properties that characterize any single developmental period, while the use of non-interval constraints might point out interactions that are somehow time-independent.

6.3 A Constrained Co-Clustering Algorithm Based on a Local-to-Global Approach

In [21], we have proposed a generic co-clustering framework. The main idea is to compute a co-clustering not starting from the raw data but from local patterns that capture locally strong associations between sets of objects and sets of properties. Let us first consider the local-to-global (L2G) aspect of our proposal. We use the simple formalization introduced in [12] to support the discussion.

6.3.1   A Local-to-Global Approach

Many local pattern mining techniques (e.g., looking for frequent patterns, data dependencies) have been studied extensively the last decade (see, e.g., [20] for a recent survey on local pattern detection issues). Many mining tasks can be formalized as the computation of the theory $Th(\mathcal{L}, \mathbf{r}, q) = \{\phi \in \mathcal{L} \mid q(\phi, \mathbf{r})$ is true$\}$ where $\mathbf{r}$ is the data, $\mathcal{L}$ is a language of patterns, and $q(\phi, \mathbf{r})$ denotes the selection predicate of interesting patterns [19]. One crucial observation with this simple formalization is that the interestingness of a pattern can be tested independently of the other patterns (e.g., testing that a pattern is frequent enough can be done without looking at other solution patterns). For us, in such a context, it justifies that instances of this framework are called local pattern mining tasks.

However, many useful mining tasks are looking for models or global patterns (e.g., classifiers, clusterings) and can be formalized as the computation of sets of patterns that satisfy constraints. Let us assume that lower case letters such as ϕ denote individual patterns and that upper case ones such as Φ denote sets of patterns, a local-to-global mining task can be defined by the two following steps:

1. $L = Th(\mathcal{L}, \mathbf{r}, q)$

2. $M = Th(f(L), \mathbf{r}, p)$ where $f(L)$ is a transformation of L,

$$Th(f(L), \mathbf{r}, p) = \{\Phi \subseteq f(L) \mid p(\Phi, \mathbf{r}) \text{ is true}\}$$

In this context, the constraint q is said to be local as it applies on an individual pattern, whereas the constraint p is said global as it has to hold for a set of patterns. The popular association-based classification approach [17] is an obvious example of a L2G scheme: standard association rules are the local patterns (i.e., local constraints are the minimal frequency and minimal confidence constraints). The various proposals for building classifiers from them are then based on different global constraints on these collections of association rules. Clustering can be considered within a L2G framework as well.

6.3.2   The CDK-MEANS Proposal

The CDK-MEANS algorithm is our L2G proposal for co-clustering 0/1 data. It is closely related to subspace clustering and it exploits the many results that are available for local pattern extraction from large Boolean matrices.

Our language of patterns is the language of bi-sets and it is denoted $\mathcal{B}$:

$$\mathcal{B} \equiv \{(T, G) \mid T \subseteq \mathcal{T} \text{ and } G \subseteq \mathcal{G}\}$$

A bi-set $b = (T, G)$ is thus a couple made of a set of objects and a set of properties. Clearly, many interesting classes of bi-sets can be computed from a data set $\mathbf{r}$ given a selection predicate q. For instance, the selection predicate can enforce that the set of properties is a frequent itemset because the set of objects that share these properties has a size greater than a user-defined threshold [1]. We can use a more selective predicate and, for instance, restrict the bi-sets to the ones whose sets of properties are closed sets. In that case, we are looking for the well-known formal concepts (see, e.g., [7]). Many other interesting types of bi-sets could be considered, e.g., support envelopes [25] or the dense and relevant bi-sets [6]. Discussing the pros and cons of each type of local pattern is out of the scope of this chapter. Let us notice that we find in the literature (see the survey in [18]) various local pattern mining tasks that are named bi-clustering tasks as soon as both dimensions (objects and properties) are involved. In our case, we prefer to talk about a clustering only in the context of unsupervised classification and thus the computation of collections of clusters, not collections of local patterns whose interestingness can be evaluated based on individuals only.

The CDK-MEANS algorithm introduced in [21] computes

$$Th(\mathcal{B}, \mathbf{r}, p_{CDK}) = \{\Phi \subseteq \mathcal{B} \mid p_{CDK}(\Phi, \mathbf{r}) \text{ is true}\}$$

with Φ being a partition Π_B of a bi-set collection B ($\Pi_B : B \rightarrow \{1 \cdots k\}$) and

$$p_{CDK}(\Pi_B, \mathbf{r}) \quad \equiv \quad \Pi_B = \operatorname{argmin} \sum_{b_j \in B} d(b_j, \mu_{\Pi_B(b_j)})$$

The constraint p_{CDK} is the one used in the K-MEANS algorithm with d being a distance and $\mu_{\Pi_B(b_j)}$ being the centroid of the cluster that contains the bi-set b_j. Let us now introduce some notations to formally define these quantities.

First, we describe each bi-set b_j by its characteristic vector as follows:

$$< \mathbf{t}_j >, < \mathbf{g}_j > = < t_{j1}, \ldots, t_{jm} >, < g_{j1}, \ldots, g_{jn} >$$

where $t_{ji} = 1$ if $t_i \in T_j$ (0 otherwise) and $g_{ji} = 1$ if $g_i \in G_j$ (0 otherwise).

We are looking for k clusters of bi-sets $\{\pi_{B1}, \ldots, \pi_{Bk}\}$ ($\pi_{B\ell} \subseteq B$). Let us define the centroid of a cluster of bi-sets $\pi_{B\ell}$ as $\mu_\ell = < \tau_\ell >, < \gamma_\ell > = < \tau_{\ell 1}, \ldots, \tau_{\ell m} >, < \gamma_{\ell 1}, \ldots, \gamma_{\ell n} >$ where τ and γ are the usual centroid components:

$$\tau_{\ell i} = \frac{1}{|\pi_{B\ell}|} \sum_{b_j \in \pi_{B\ell}} t_{ji}, \quad \gamma_{\ell i} = \frac{1}{|\pi_{B\ell}|} \sum_{b_j \in \pi_{B\ell}} g_{ji}$$

We now define the distance used between a bi-set b_j and a centroid μ_ℓ:

$$d(b_j, \mu_\ell) = \frac{1}{2} \left(\frac{|\mathbf{t}_j \cup \boldsymbol{\tau}_\ell| - |\mathbf{t}_j \cap \boldsymbol{\tau}_\ell|}{|\mathbf{t}_j \cup \boldsymbol{\tau}_\ell|} + \frac{|\mathbf{g}_j \cup \boldsymbol{\gamma}_\ell| - |\mathbf{g}_j \cap \boldsymbol{\gamma}_\ell|}{|\mathbf{g}_j \cup \boldsymbol{\gamma}_\ell|} \right)$$

It is the mean of the weighted symmetrical differences of the set components. We assume $|\mathbf{t}_j \cap \boldsymbol{\tau}_\ell| = \sum_{i=1}^m a_i \frac{t_{ji} + \tau_{\ell i}}{2}$ and $|\mathbf{t}_j \cup \boldsymbol{\tau}_\ell| = \sum_{i=1}^m \frac{t_{ji} + \tau_{\ell i}}{2}$ where $a_i = 1$ if $t_{ji} \cdot \tau_{\ell i} \neq 0$, 0 otherwise. Intuitively, the intersection is equal to the

TABLE 6.2: CDK-MEANS pseudo-code

CDK-MEANS ($\mathbf{r}$ is a Boolean context, B is a collection of bi-sets in $\mathbf{r}$, k is the number of clusters, MI is the maximal iteration number.)

1. Let $\mu_1 \ldots \mu_k$ be the initial cluster centroids. $it := 0$.

2. Repeat

    (a) For each bi-set $b_j \in B$, assign it to cluster $\pi_{B\ell}$ s.t. $d(b_j, \mu_\ell)$ is minimal.

    (b) For each cluster $\pi_{B\ell}$, compute τ_ℓ and γ_ℓ.

    (c) $it := it + 1$.

3. Until centroids are unchanged or $it = MI$.

4. For each $t_i \in \mathcal{T}$ (resp. $g_i \in \mathcal{G}$), assign it to the first cluster $\pi_{\mathcal{T}\ell}$ (resp. $\pi_{\mathcal{G}\ell}$) s.t. $\tau_{\ell i} = \frac{1}{|\pi_{B\ell}|} \sum_{b_j \in \pi_{B\ell}} t_{ji}$ (resp. $\gamma_{\ell i} = \frac{1}{|\pi_{B\ell}|} \sum_{b_j \in \pi_{B\ell}} g_{ji}$) is maximum.

5. Return $\{\pi_{\mathcal{T}1} \ldots \pi_{\mathcal{T}k}\}$ and $\{\pi_{\mathcal{G}1} \ldots \pi_{\mathcal{G}k}\}$

---

mean between the number of common objects and the sum of their centroid weights. The union is the mean between the number of objects and the sum of their centroid weights. These measures are defined similarly on properties.

Objects t_i (resp. properties g_i) are assigned to one of the k clusters (say cluster ℓ) for which $\tau_{\ell i}$ (resp. $\gamma_{\ell i}$) is maximum. We can enable that a number of objects and/or properties belong to more than one cluster by controlling the size of the overlapping part of each cluster. Thanks to our definition of cluster membership determined by the values of τ_ℓ and γ_ℓ, we just need to adapt the cluster assignment step given some user-defined thresholds.

A simplified algorithm CDK-MEANS is given in Table 6.2: for the sake of brevity, we do not consider further cluster overlapping. It computes a co-clustering of $\mathbf{r}$ given a collection of bi-sets B extracted from $\mathbf{r}$ beforehand (e.g., collections of formal concepts). CDK-MEANS can provide the example co-clustering given in Section 6.1.

6.3.3 Constraint-Driven Co-Clustering

Let us now consider the L2G framework when some of the co-clustering constraints defined in Section 6.2 have been specified (i.e., besides the specification of the number of co-clusters and the implicit optimization constraint on the objective function, the global constraint might also contain must-link, cannot-link, interval, or non-interval constraints).

The key idea is that, to compute a co-clustering that satisfies the specified global constraints, we can exploit *local counterparts* of them, i.e., constraints that apply on local patterns (here, bi-sets) to select only part of them. For some constraints (e.g., must-link), the satisfaction of the local counterpart is sufficient to guarantee that the co-clusters satisfy the global constraint. In such cases, we say that the local constraint is automatically propagated to the global level. For other constraints, it happens that a new global constraint must be used in addition to the local counterpart. In such cases however, we consider new global constraints that are easier to check. Notice also that, given the state-of-the-art, evaluating local constraints can be extremely more efficient than checking for global ones, and quite efficient algorithms are available to compute bi-sets that satisfy, e.g., monotonic constraints (see Section 6.3.4). For instance, we use here D-MINER [7] to computate collections of formal concepts that satisfy size constraints on both object and property sets. Let us now provide more details on how we manage to process the different constraints.

- The *local counterpart* of a must-link constraint $c_{e=}(x_i, x_j, \Pi, \mathcal{D})$ consists in selecting bi-sets that contain either both x_i and x_j or none of them:

$$q_{must-link}(b, \mathbf{r}) \quad \equiv \quad (x_i \in b \wedge x_j \in b) \vee ((x_i \notin b \wedge x_j \notin b)$$

  As the coefficients of each object/property in each centroid μ_ℓ depends on the number of bi-sets containing this object/property, the coefficients corresponding to x_i and x_j are equal in each centroid. Consequently, x_i and x_j are assigned to the same cluster and thus the local counterpart of the must-link constraint is automatically propagated to the computed co-clusters.

- A necessary condition for the extended cannot-link constraint, is that B does not contain any bi-set violating the constraint. Indeed, the *local counterpart* of a cannot-link constraint $c_{e\neq}(x_i, x_j, \Pi, \mathcal{D})$ consists in selecting bi-sets that do not contain both x_i and x_j:

$$q_{cannot-link}(b, \mathbf{r}) \quad \equiv \quad \neg(x_i \in b \wedge x_j \in b)$$

  This condition does not ensure that the global cannot-link constraint is satisfied in the final co-clustering (it is not automatically propagated) and a further control is needed. In particular, in Step 2(a) of CDK-MEANS algorithm (see Table 6.2), before adding a bi-set containing x_i (resp. x_j) to a cluster, we should ensure that no bi-set containing x_j (resp. x_i) has been assigned to it earlier.

- For the interval and non-interval constraints, it is possible to directly use these constraints on each bi-set independently, i.e., as a local constraint. However, for the interval constraint, it might be too stringent in practice (i.e., too few bi-sets would satisfy the constraint), whereas for the non-interval one, it will not be selective enough (almost all the bi-sets would satisfy the constraint). For these reasons, we propose to relax the interval constraint and to strengthen the non-interval constraints as *local counterparts* of the global ones. These two new local constraints, respectively called max-gap and min-gap, are now defined.

DEFINITION 6.4 Max-gap and min-gap constraints   *Given an order on $\mathcal{D}$, a max-gap constraint on $\mathcal{D}$, denoted $c_{maxgap}(\mathcal{D}, \sigma, b)$, is satisfied by b w.r.t threshold σ iff, for each pair of consecutive elements $x_i, x_j \in b$ s.t. $x_i \prec x_j$, $|\{x_h \notin b, \text{ with } x_i \prec x_h \prec x_j\}| \leq \sigma$. A min-gap constraint, denoted $c_{mingap}(\mathcal{D}, \sigma, b)$, is satisfied by b w.r.t threshold σ iff, for each pair of consecutive elements $x_i, x_j \in b$ s.t. $x_i \prec x_j$, $|\{x_h \notin b, \text{ with } x_i \prec x_h \prec x_j\}| \geq \sigma$.*

Max-gap is used as a *local counterpart* of the interval constraint and min-gap as the non-interval one. Clearly, these local constraints do not ensure the satisfaction of c_{int} and $c_{non-int}$, but it supports the computation of more relevant co-clusters (see the experimental section).

Example 6.3
Suppose that $\mathcal{G}$ is ordered such that $g_1 \preceq g_2 \preceq g_3 \preceq g_4 \preceq g_5$. The bi-set $b = \{\{t_1, t_3, t_4\}, \{g_1, g_3, g_4\}\}$ satisfies $c_{maxgap}(\mathcal{G}, 1, b)$ but not $c_{maxgap}(\mathcal{G}, 0, b)$. It does not satisfy $c_{mingap}(\mathcal{G}, 1, b)$.   ☐

The modified version of the algorithm is sketched in Table 6.3 (modifications in bold). It uses the same greedy strategy as COP-KMEANS [27]. A slight difference is that, as we process local patterns (bi-sets), then it concerns only the sets of objects and properties that belong to the local patterns.

6.3.4   Discussion on Constraint Processing

To summarize, we can classify the constraints w.r.t. propagation issues.

1. Constraints that are automatically propagated from the local level to the global one (extended must-link).

2. Constraints that need a control to be propagated from the local level to the global one (extended cannot-link).

3. Constraints whose propagation to the local level to the global one is not ensured (interval and non-interval constraints).

Even if we cannot ensure the ultimate satisfaction for the interval and non-interval constraints, we show in our experimental validation (see Section 6.4) that using max-gap and min-gap local constraints enables us to produce clusters that tend to be intervals. One of the perspectives of this work is clearly

TABLE 6.3: Constrained CDK-MEANS pseudo-code

CDK-MEANS (**r** is a Boolean context, B is a collection of local patterns in **r**, k is the number of clusters, MI is the maximal iteration number, C **a set of constraints.**)

1. **Let $B' \subseteq B$ be the sub-collection satisfying all the local counterparts of the constraints in C (extended must-link and cannot-link, max-gap and min-gap).**

2. Let $\mu_1 \dots \mu_k$ be the initial cluster centroids. $it := 0$.

3. Repeat

   (a) For each local pattern $b_j \in B'$, assign it to cluster $\pi_{B\ell}$ s.t. $d(b_j, \mu_\ell)$ is minimum and **no cannot-link constraint is violated.**

   (b) For each cluster $\pi_{B\ell}$, compute $\boldsymbol{\tau}_\ell$ and $\boldsymbol{\gamma}_\ell$.

   (c) $it := it + 1$.

4. Until centroids are unchanged or $it = MI$.

5. For each $t_i \in \mathcal{T}$ (resp. $g_i \in \mathcal{G}$), assign it to the first cluster $\pi_{\mathcal{T}\ell}$ (resp. $\pi_{\mathcal{G}\ell}$) s.t. $\tau_{\ell i}$ (resp. $\gamma_{\ell i}$) is maximum.

6. Return $\{\pi_{\mathcal{T}1} \dots \pi_{\mathcal{T}k}\}$ and $\{\pi_{\mathcal{G}1} \dots \pi_{\mathcal{G}k}\}$

---

to enforce the propagation of these two constraints by introducing a control step in the iterative part of the algorithm (as for the extended cannot-link constraint).

When a constraint is too selective (too many bi-sets violate such a constraint), some objects and/or properties could not be represented in the collection used by our algorithm. The solution of a garbage cluster for each unclustered object/property is not always possible, specially when they are involved in cannot-link constraints. In fact, if a cannot-link constraint involving x_i and x_j is not satisfied by any bi-set (i.e., each time a bi-set contains x_i, it also contains x_j), the two objects/properties will not be contained in the final co-clustering. But they cannot be assigned to a garbage co-cluster, since a cannot-link constraint prevents this situation. If such a situation happens, our approach returns no solution. We say that the co-clustering is unfeasible. Notice that in this work we do not address the problem of the feasibility of conjunctions of must-link and cannot-link constraints (see [11] for a complete overview of the constraint feasibility problem).

As discussed earlier, the local counterpart of a global constraint is easier to check, especially when the local constraint is monotonic w.r.t. some specialization relation. In such cases, we can use efficient local pattern mining algorithms. For bi-set mining, we use D-MINER [7] that exploit such constraints.

DEFINITION 6.5 D-MINER **specialization and monotonicity**   *The specialization on bi-sets from $\mathcal{B}$ used by D-MINER is defined by $(T_1, G_1) \leq (T_2, G_2)$ iff $T_1 \subseteq T_2$ and $G_1 \subseteq G_2$. A constraint $\mathcal{C}$ is said anti-monotonic w.r.t. $\leq$ iff $\forall \alpha, \beta \in \mathcal{B}$ such that $\alpha \leq \beta$, $\mathcal{C}(\beta) \Rightarrow \mathcal{C}(\alpha)$. $\mathcal{C}$ is said monotonic w.r.t. $\leq$ iff $\forall \alpha, \beta \in \mathcal{B}$ such that $\alpha \leq \beta$, $\mathcal{C}(\alpha) \Rightarrow \mathcal{C}(\beta)$.*

D-MINER efficiently exploits both monotonic and anti-monotonic constraints. Consequently, if the local constraints used are conjunctions or disjunctions of monotonic constraints, they can be directly pushed during the local pattern mining step.

Let us now summarize how the local counterparts of the co-clustering constraints can be directly used during our bi-set mining step.

- The local counterparts of the extended must-link and cannot-link constraints require that some elements are included or not in bi-sets (see $q_{must-link}(b, \mathbf{r})$ and $q_{cannot-link}(b, \mathbf{r})$ constraints). Such constraints are monotonic while considering the specialization relation of Definition 6.5. Consequently, the local counterparts of these constraints can be represented by a conjunction and/or a disjunction of monotonic constraints that can be exploited by D-MINER.

- The min-gap constraint is anti-monotonic. Let $b_1 = (X_1, Y_1)$ and $b_2 = (X_2, Y_2)$ be two bi-sets s.t. $X_1 \subseteq X_2$. If we define $S_i = \{x_h \notin X_i | x_i \prec x_h \prec x_j\}$, we have $S_2 \subseteq S_1$. Consequently, if $|S_2| \geq \sigma$, i.e., $c_{maxgap}(\mathcal{D}, \sigma, b_2)$ is satisfied, then $|S_1| \geq \sigma$ and $c_{maxgap}(\mathcal{D}, \sigma, b_1)$ is satisfied as well.

- The max-gap constraint has no monotonicity properties. Let us consider the max-gap constraint $c_{maxgap}(D, 1, b)$ with $D = \{x_1, x_2, \ldots, x_n\}$. It is not satisfied by $X_1 = \{x_2, x_3, x_7\}$ but it is satisfied by $X_2 = \{x_2, x_3, x_5, x_7\}$ and one of its subset $X_0 = \{x_2, x_3\}$. Therefore, it is neither monotonic nor anti-monotonic. This constraint is thus checked after the execution of the bi-set mining algorithm, i.e., in a post-processing phase.

6.4   Experimental Validation

Let us first introduce some measures that are to be used in our experiments to evaluate the quality of co-clustering results. In the first batch of experiments, we show the interest in using pairwise constraints on both dimensions thanks to an application to a synthetic data set for which standard and unconstrained co-clustering approaches produce unstable results. Then we apply our framework on two real temporal gene expression data sets to illustrate the added-value of interval constraints. Finally, we discuss another application to another gene expression data set to illustrate how the interval and non-interval constraints can be used to supervise a co-clustering task to discover more stable co-clusters, which are more relevant as well.

6.4.1   Evaluation Method

A general criterion to evaluate clustering results consists of comparing the computed partition with a "correct" one. It means that data instances are already associated to some correct labels and that we want to quantify the agreement between computed labels and correct ones. A popular measure is the Rand index, which measures the agreement between two partitions of m elements. If $\mathbf{C} = \{C_1 \ldots C_s\}$ is our clustering structure and $\mathbf{P} = \{P_1 \ldots P_t\}$ is a predefined partition, each pair of data points is either assigned to the same cluster in both partitions or to different ones. Let a be the number of pairs belonging to the same cluster of $\mathbf{C}$ and to the same cluster of $\mathbf{P}$. Let b be the number of pairs whose points belong to different clusters of $\mathbf{C}$ and to different clusters of $\mathbf{P}$. The agreement between $\mathbf{C}$ and $\mathbf{P}$ can be estimated using

$$Rand(\mathbf{C}, \mathbf{P}) = \frac{a + b}{m \cdot (m - 1)/2}$$

It takes values between 0 and 1 and it is maximized when $s = t$ [23].

To evaluate the added-value of the interval constraint, we propose to measure the number of jumps within a partition.

DEFINITION 6.6 Jump number   *Given* $\mathcal{D} = \{x_1, \ldots, x_n\}$ *a set of ordered points and a cluster* $\pi_{\mathcal{D}\ell}$ *on these points, we have a jump given a number* $\nu > 1$, *if* $x_i \in \pi_{\mathcal{D}\ell}$, $x_{i+\nu} \in \pi_{\mathcal{D}\ell}$ *and* $\forall h$ *s.t.* $i < h < i + \nu$, $x_h \notin \pi_{\mathcal{D}\ell}$. *Let* J_ℓ *be the number of jumps within a cluster* $\pi_{\mathcal{D}\ell}$. *Given a partition* $\Pi_{\mathcal{D}} = \{\pi_{\mathcal{D}1}, \ldots, \pi_{\mathcal{D}k}\}$, *the jump number measure denoted* N_J *is then*

$$N_J = \sum_{\pi_{\mathcal{D}\ell} \in \Pi_{\mathcal{D}}} J_\ell$$

If $N_J = 0$, clusters are intervals. As the interval constraint is processed as a soft constraint, we average the N_J measure on a set of clustering instances (with random initialization) to measure the efficiency of the approach.

We also want to evaluate co-clustering quality by means of an internal criterion. An interesting measure for this purpose is the symmetrical Goodman and Kruskal's τ coefficient [15], which evaluates the proportional reduction in error given by the knowledge of $\Pi_\mathcal{T}$ on the prediction of $\Pi_\mathcal{G}$ and vice versa. Another measure is the loss in mutual information [13], which is the objective function that COCLUSTER tries to minimize. Both coefficients are evaluated on a contingency table **p**. Let p_{ij} be the frequency of relations between an object of a cluster $\pi_{\mathcal{T}i}$ and a property of a cluster $\pi_{\mathcal{G}j}$. Furthermore, we have $p_{i.} = \sum_j p_{ij}$ and $p_{.j} = \sum_i p_{ij}$. The Goodman-Kruskal's τ coefficient is defined as follows:

$$\tau = \frac{\frac{1}{2}\sum_i \sum_j \left(p_{ij} - p_{i.}p_{.j}\right)^2 \frac{p_{i.}+p_{.j}}{p_{i.}p_{.j}}}{1 - \frac{1}{2}\sum_i p_{i.}^2 - \frac{1}{2}\sum_j p_{.j}^2}$$

The mutual information, which computes the amount of information $\Pi_\mathcal{T}$ contains about $\Pi_\mathcal{G}$ is:

$$I(\Pi_\mathcal{T}, \Pi_\mathcal{G}) = \sum_i \sum_j p_{ij} \log \frac{p_{ij}}{p_{i.}p_{.j}}$$

Then, given two different co-clusterings $(\Pi_\mathcal{T}, \Pi_\mathcal{G})$ and $(\hat{\Pi}_\mathcal{T}, \hat{\Pi}_\mathcal{G})$, the loss in mutual information is given by:

$$I(\Pi_\mathcal{T}, \Pi_\mathcal{G}) - I(\hat{\Pi}_\mathcal{T}, \hat{\Pi}_\mathcal{G})$$

Finally, to evaluate the performances of our method, we use a comparison coefficient, which is the mean of the products between the number of needed iterations and the number of processed bi-sets, i.e.:

$$CC = \frac{\sum_i^N |B| \cdot NI_i}{N}$$

where, N is the number of executions, $|B|$ is the size of the local pattern collection computed beforehand, and NI_i is the number of iterations for the i-th execution.

6.4.2 Using Extended Must-Link and Cannot-Link Constraints

Let us use a synthetic data set, which intrinsically leads to unstable clustering. The goal is here to show how using must-link and cannot-link constraints can support the discovery of different co-clustering structures. This synthetic data set is some kind of idealized abstraction of temporal gene expression data (see Fig. 6.1 where the gray zones denote true values in the matrix). In this data set, the expression level of 20 genes changes during the 105 time points of the sampling period. It is easy to capture some cyclic behavior, since the first and the last time periods gives rise to similar patterns. Such a situation should produce quite unstable clustering results.

We have extracted a collection of formal concepts using D-MINER [7]. This collection (containing 85 formal concepts) has been used for all the experiments described in this section. When using the unconstrained version of

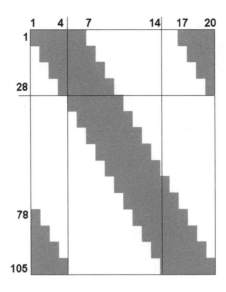

FIGURE 6.1: A synthetic data set.

CDK-MEANS or COCLUSTER [13] (with $k = 3$), the results clearly point out two kinds of co-clustering results (see Fig. 6.2(a) and Fig. 6.2(b) for co-clusterings **a** and **b**). The second co-clustering (Fig. 6.2(b)) emphasizes some cyclic behavior, since the first and the last groups of samples are in the same co-cluster. Such a structure is clearly missing in the first co-clustering (Fig. 6.2(a)). Notice that all the results produced by the random instances of the two algorithms are similar to one of these two co-clusterings. Table 6.4 provides the various results concerning the τ and I values, and the Rand coefficient values computed w.r.t. the two co-clusterings for both objects and properties.

Let us assume that we want to supervise the co-clustering process to discover co-clustering **a** or co-clustering **b**. For this purpose, we can use some extended must-link or/and cannot-link constraints to control the search. If we look at the two targeted co-clusterings, there are objects that always belong to the same cluster, while other objects and properties "change" clusters when moving from co-clustering **a** to co-clustering **b**. For instance, objects 1 to 21 are always in the same cluster (we say they are "stable"), while objects 22 to 35 change clusters in the second co-clustering (we say they are "unstable"). We list all possible pairs that are composed by one object belonging to the "stable" set and one object belonging to the "unstable" set. We construct a similar list for properties. Then, we pick a fixed number of pairs randomly and we compare the class labels (which are inferred from co-clusterings **a** and **a**) of each object (resp. property) inside the co-clustering we want to discover.

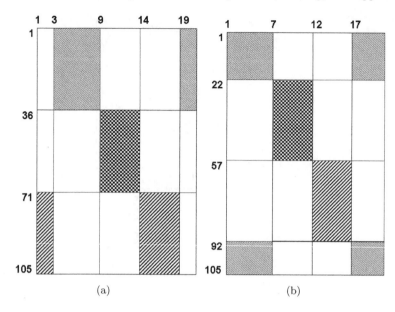

FIGURE 6.2: Two co-clusterings for the synthetic data from Fig. 6.1.

If the objects (resp. properties) share the same class label, we construct a must-link constraint. Otherwise, we construct a cannot-link constraint. In our experiments, we have computed the results for 100 randomly generated sets of 1 and 2 constraints for both objects and properties. For each set of constraints, we executed 25 randomly initialized instances of CDK-MEANS. Results are in Table 6.5 (for sets of 1 constraint) and Table 6.6 (for sets of 2 constraints). All the average Rand indexes are 1% to 9% better than the same indexes obtained by the unconstrained versions, for both our CDK-MEANS algorithm or COCLUSTER. It works for generated constraints over both the set of objects and the set of properties. Results are also slightly more stable w.r.t. unconstrained instances. It shows that even a few number of constraints enables us to obtain a co-clustering that is more stable w.r.t. initialization but also more relevant w.r.t. user expectation.

User-defined constraints can be derived from domain knowledge. Looking at the two co-clusterings (see Fig. 6.2(a) and Fig. 6.2(b)), we see that the first object is clustered together with the first property in **b** but not in **a**. Then, we can introduce an extended cannot-link constraint between the first object and the first property to drive CDK-MEANS toward the first type of co-clustering. In this case, the average Rand indexes w.r.t. to **a**, computed on both objects and properties, are both equal to 0.83 (i.e., 8% better than the one obtained by unconstrained co-clustering). Now, if we add an extended cannot-link constraint between the last object and the last property, then the

TABLE 6.4:   Co-clustering synthetic
data without constraints (25 trials).

	Cocluster	CDK-Means
τ	0.29±0.03	0.34±0.02
I	0.90±0.07	0.96±0.02
a-Rand($\mathcal{T}$)	0.74±0.07	0.78±0.11
a-Rand($\mathcal{G}$)	0.74±0.08	0.77±0.11
b-Rand($\mathcal{T}$)	0.75±0.07	0.77±0.10
b-Rand($\mathcal{G}$)	0.74±0.08	0.78±0.11

two scores rise respectively to 0.87 and 0.88.

Notice however that our framework has to be considered as an unsupervised method that is useful when we lack from detailed information about the data. When a large number of constraints is introduced, some conjunctions can remove an important number of local patterns. In this case, some objects and properties might disappear from the co-clustering process.

6.4.3   Time Interval Cluster Discovery

We have studied the impact of the interval constraint in two microarray data sets called malaria and drosophila. The first one [8] concerns the transcriptome of the intraerythrocytic developmental cycle of Plasmodium Falciparum, i.e., a causative agent of human malaria. The data provide the expression profile of 3719 genes in 46 biological samples. Each sample corresponds to a time point of the developmental cycle: it begins with merozoite invasion of the red blood cells, and it is divided into three main phases: the ring, trophozoite and schizont stages. The second data set is described in [2]. It concerns the gene expression of the Drosophila melanogaster during its life cycle. The expression levels of 3944 genes are evaluated for 57 sequential time periods divided into embryonic, larval, and pupal stages. The numerical gene expression data from [8] has been discretized by using one of the encoding methods described in [5]: for each gene g, we assigned the Boolean value 1 to those samples whose expression level was greater than X% of its max expression level. X was set to 25% for malaria and 35% for drosophila. The two matrices have been mined for formal concepts by using D-Miner [7].

We applied Cocluster algorithm [13] and the unconstrained version of CDK-Means with $k = 3$ to identify the three developmental stages. Since the initialization of both algorithms is randomized, we average all the measures obtained after 100 executions. We have measured the N_J coefficient, the Rand index w.r.t. to the correct partition that has been inferred from the literature, and the Goodman-Kruskal's coefficient to evaluate the co-clustering quality. Results are in Table 6.7.

There is a significant difference between the two data sets. In malaria, the average number of jumps (N_J) is already small with both algorithms. In

TABLE 6.5: Co-clustering synthetic data (1 pairwise constraint, 100 random constraint sets, 25 trials).

	A		B	
	$\mathcal{T}$	$\mathcal{G}$	$\mathcal{T}$	$\mathcal{G}$
τ	0.32±0.03	0.33±0.03	0.33±0.03	0.30±0.02
I	0.97±0.04	0.96±0.03	0.97±0.03	0.96±0.03
Rand($\mathcal{T}$)	0.81±0.10	0.80±0.10	0.83±0.10	0.80±0.09
Rand($\mathcal{G}$)	0.78±0.10	0.78±0.10	0.84±0.11	0.80±0.08

TABLE 6.6: Co-clustering synthetic data (2 pairwise constraints, 100 random constraint sets, 25 trials).

	A		B	
	$\mathcal{T}$	$\mathcal{G}$	$\mathcal{T}$	$\mathcal{G}$
τ	0.31±0.05	0.31±0.04	0.31±0.05	0.29±0.02
I	0.98±0.05	0.98±0.05	0.99±0.06	0.96±0.03
Rand($\mathcal{T}$)	0.82±0.10	0.80±0.10	0.83±0.10	0.80±0.08
Rand($\mathcal{G}$)	0.78±0.10	0.77±0.10	0.82±0.11	0.81±0.06

particular, if COCLUSTER enables us to get a good Goodman-Kruskal's coefficient, the co-clusters obtained by CDK-MEANS are more consistent with the biological knowledge (i.e., the partition has a higher Rand index). We notice that the number of comparisons is rather high. What we expect here, is that a constrained approach can obtain the same clustering results by using less computing resources. Instead, for drosophila, both algorithms fail in finding the correct partitioning w.r.t. the available biological knowledge. The number of jumps is in both cases high, while the Rand index is relatively low. In this case we expect to obtain better results with our constrained co-clustering approach.

We have defined the interval constraint on the biological condition dimension. Different levels of the max-gap constraint have been applied and we have studied the impact on the final partition by measuring the N_J coefficient, the Rand index, the Goodman-Kruskal's coefficient, and the average number of comparisons. Results are in Fig. 6.3 and Fig. 6.4, respectively for malaria and drosophila.

For malaria, the best results in terms of number of jumps (see Fig. 6.3(a))

TABLE 6.7: Co-clustering without interval constraints (100 trials).

Data Set	COCLUSTER			CDK-MEANS			
	N_J	*Rand*	τ_S	N_J	*Rand*	τ_S	CC
malaria	0.85	0.761	0.494	0.3	0.877	0.438	3.063M
drosophila	6.39	0.692	0.513	4.29	0.601	0.424	1.652M

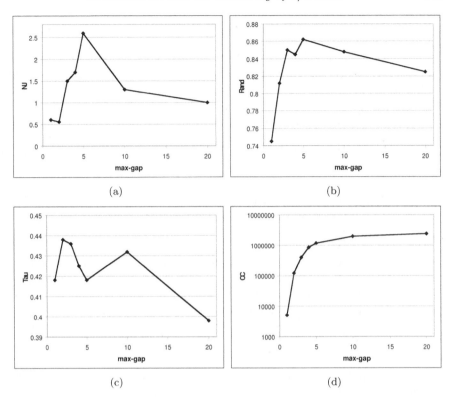

FIGURE 6.3: Jump number (a), Rand index (b), Goodman-Kruskal's coefficient (c) and comparison coefficient (d) on malaria.

are for a max-gap constraint of 1 and 2. When max-gap = 2, the Rand index (Fig. 6.3(b)) is higher, and the Goodman-Kruskal's coefficient (Fig. 6.3(c)) is maximum (and similar to the one obtained without constraint, see Table 6.7). An important observation is that the average comparison numbers (Fig. 6.3(d)) for these values of the max-gap constraint are sensibly reduced (by a factor of 8, for max-gap = 3, up to 28 for max-gap = 2). When max-gap is set to 1, the average comparison number is about 1/1000 of the one obtained without specifying any constraint. When max-gap is 5, we obtain a rather bad N_J index, but the Rand coefficient is max (and similar to the one obtained without constraint). An optimal choice in this context seems to be max-gap = 2: it sensibly reduces the computational time, and it produces good clustering results. We notice also that our definition of the max-gap constraint works for open time intervals. By setting an open time interval constraint, we are always able to obtain a circular sequence of intervals, i.e., capturing typical developmental life cycles.

For drosophila, the improvements are more obvious. Unconstrained clustering results have shown that good partitions (with a high Goodman-Kruskal's coefficient) contain a lot of jumps. With a max-gap constraint of 2 or 3, we can sensibly reduce the number of jumps (Fig. 6.4(a)) and it increases the quality of the partition (Fig. 6.4(b)) w.r.t. the available biological knowledge. The fact that for these max-gap values, the Goodman-Kruskal's coefficient is minimum (Fig. 6.4(c)), indicates that the partition that better satisfies the constraints is not necessarily the "best" one. Moreover, the average number of comparisons (Fig. 6.4(d)) is reduced by 60 (max-gap = 2) and 30 (max-gap = 3).

6.4.3.1 Using Non-Interval Constraints

We have shown how interval constraints can support the discovery of time interval clusters. Within some data (e.g., malaria), an unconstrained approach already gives perfect intervals, and then the question is: is it possible to discover different gene associations that hold between time points belonging to different intervals? To answer this question, we applied the non-interval constraint to the gene expression data concerning adult time samples of the drosophila melanogaster life cycle. Indeed, time samples from t_1 to t_{10} concern the first days of male adult individual life cycle while time samples from t_{11} to t_{20} concern female individuals.

When we apply CDK-MEANS (with $k = 2$) without specifying any constraint, the two intervals $t_1, \ldots, t_{10}$ and $t_{11}, \ldots, t_{20}$ are well identified in the 100 executions. Then, we obtain almost exactly a co-cluster of males and a co-cluster of females and the average jump number is low. Moreover, the Goodman-Kruskal's coefficient and the loss in mutual information appears rather stable (see cdk:unconst result on Table 6.8). We computed these coefficients on the 100 co-clusterings returned by COCLUSTER and we noticed a significant instability (see Table 6.8). It seems that there are two optimum points for which the two measures are distant. For 56 runs, we got a high τ coefficient (mean 0.5605), for the other 44 ones the τ coefficient was sensibly smaller (mean 0.1156). If we consider each group of results separately, the standard deviation is significantly smaller. It means that these two results are two local optima for the COCLUSTER heuristics. Furthermore, the first group of solutions reflects the male and female repartition of the individuals, while in the second group each cluster contains both male and female individuals. The average Rand value is 0.69 and the standard deviation is 23% of the mean. Also the jump number has a high and unstable value. Then, we tried to specify a min-gap constraint on the collection of formal concepts to enforce the discovery of non interval clusters. Even for small values of the min-gap constraint, the average Rand value is high, while the standard deviation is lower (12% of the mean for min-gap = 2, 4% for min-gap = 3) w.r.t. COCLUSTER results. The cdk:nonint row in Table 6.8 summarizes the more stable (w.r.t. the τ coefficient) results obtained with min-gap = 10. We

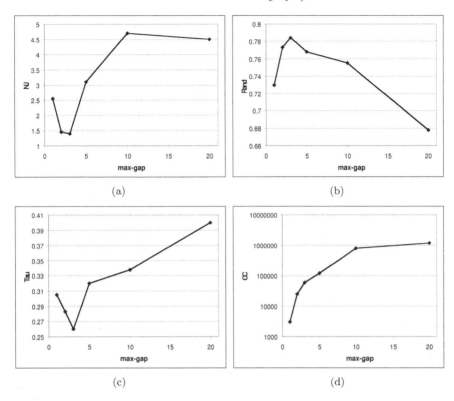

FIGURE 6.4: Jump number (a), Rand index (b), Goodman-Kruskal's coefficient (c) and comparison coefficient (d) on drosophila.

also tested whether an interval constraint could influence the stability of the co-clustering. Setting max-gap = 5 enables to get more stable co-clusterings where the Rand index is always equal to one (see cdk:int results in Table 6.8). These results show that, by specifying an interval or a non-interval constraint, the user gets some control on the shape of the co-clusters. An algorithm like COCLUSTER has sometimes found co-clusters where the sex of the individual is the major discriminative parameter. At some moment, it has captured something else. Our thesis is that a biologist might be able to have a kind of supervision on such a process. Moreover, using constraints also speeds up the co-clustering construction because we have to process a reduced collection of local patterns.

When using a co-clustering approach, it seems natural to consider both constraints on objects and on properties. In this section we have shown that even a few number of must-link and cannot-link constraints can support the computation of more stable co-clusterings. When a bijection exists between

TABLE 6.8:   Clustering adult drosophila individuals.

bi-part.	inst.	τ mean	std.dev	Rand mean	std.dev	N_J mean	std.dev
co:MF	56	0.5605	0.0381	0.82	0.06	0.25	0.61
co:mixed	44	0.1156	0.0166	0.51	0.02	7.52	2.07
co:overall	100	0.3648	0.2240	0.69	0.16	3.45	3.90
cdk:unconst	100	0.4819	0.0594	0.88	0.04	1.00	0.20
cdk:int	100	0.4609	0.0347	1.00	0.00	0.00	0.00
cdk:nonint	100	0.1262	0.0761	0.53	0.04	6.94	1.93

a partition of objects and a partition of properties (as for CDK-MEANS), it makes sense to set constraints that involve both objects and properties. In our framework, this extension is quite natural, and it opens new possibilities in popular applications such as document analysis and gene expression data analysis. We have also illustrated the added-value of interval constraints. In gene expression data analysis, we often have temporal information about data. With standard (co-)clustering algorithms, there are no simple possibilities to exploit this temporal information. With a systematic approach in two different gene expression data, we were able to improve clustering results and to propose ways to control the clustering results based on domain knowledge. Here again, we can exploit such facilities across many other application domains.

6.5   Conclusion

Co-clustering is an interesting conceptual clustering approach. Improving co-cluster relevancy remains a difficult task in real-life exploratory data analysis processes. First, it is hard to capture subjective interestingness aspects, e.g., the analyst's expectation given her/his domain knowledge. Next, when these expectations can be declaratively specified, using them during the computational process is challenging. We have shown that it was possible to use a simple but powerful generic co-clustering framework based on local patterns. Several types of constraints on co-clusters have been considered, including new constraints when at least one of the dimensions is ordered. Applications on temporal gene expression data analysis have been sketched. Many other applications rely on ordered data analysis and might benefit from such constrained co-clustering approaches. Notice also that extended must-link and cannot-link constraints can be handled efficiently by our framework. A short-term perspective is to formalize the properties of the global constraints (i.e., constraints on co-clusterings), which can be, more or less automatically, transformed into local level constraints. Looking for propagation strategies that might enable to enforce interval constraints on every computed co-cluster is also on our research agenda.

Acknowledgments

This work was performed when Ruggero G. Pensa was a research fellow at University of Saint-Etienne (France). This research is partially funded by EU contract IQ FP6-516169 (FET arm of the IST program).

References

[1] R. Agrawal, H. Mannila, R. Srikant, H. Toivonen, and A. I. Verkamo. Fast discovery of association rules. In *Advances in Knowledge Discovery and Data Mining*, pages 307–328. AAAI Press, 1996.

[2] M. N. Arbeitman, E. E. Furlong, F. Imam, E. Johnson, B. H. Null, B. S. Baker, M. A. Krasnow, M. P. Scott, R. W. Davis, and K. P. White. Gene expression during the life cycle of drosophila melanogaster. *Science*, 297:2270–2275, 2002.

[3] A. Banerjee, I. Dhillon, J. Ghosh, S. Merugua, and D. Modha. A generalized maximum entropy approach to bregman co-clustering and matrix approximation. *Journal of Machine Learning Research*, 8:1919–1986, 2007.

[4] S. Basu, M. Bilenko, and R. J. Mooney. A probabilistic framework for semi-supervised clustering. In *Proceedings of the Tenth ACM SIGKDD International Conference on Knowledge Discovery and Data Mining*, pages 59–68, Seattle, USA, 2004.

[5] C. Becquet, S. Blachon, B. Jeudy, J.-F. Boulicaut, and O. Gandrillon. Strong association rule mining for large gene expression data analysis: A case study on human SAGE data. *Genome Biology*, 12:1–16, 2002.

[6] J. Besson, C. Robardet, and J-F. Boulicaut. Mining a new fault-tolerant pattern type as an alternative to formal concept discovery. In *Proceedings of the Fourteenth International Conference on Conceptual Structures*, volume 4068 of *Lecture Notes in Computer Science*, pages 144–157, Aalborg, Denmark, July 2006. Springer.

[7] J. Besson, C. Robardet, J.-F. Boulicaut, and S. Rome. Constraint-based concept mining and its application to microarray data analysis. *Intelligent Data Analysis*, 9(1):59–82, 2005.

[8] Z. Bozdech, M. Llinás, B. Lee Pulliam, E. D. Wong, J. Zhu, and J. L. DeRisi. The transcriptome of the intraerythrocytic developmental cycle of plasmodium falciparum. *Public Library of Science Biology*, 1(1):1–16, 2003.

[9] H. Cho, I. S. Dhillon, Y. Guan, and S. Sra. Minimum sum-squared residue co-clustering of gene expression data. In *Proceedings of the 2004 SIAM International Conference on Data Mining*, pages 114–125, Lake Buena Vista, USA, 2004.

[10] I. Davidson and S. S. Ravi. Agglomerative hierarchical clustering with constraints: Theoretical and empirical results. In *Proceedings of the Ninth European Conference on Principles and Practice of Knowledge Discovery in Databases*, volume 3721 of *Lecture Notes in Computer Science*, pages 59–70, Porto, Portugal, 2005. Springer.

[11] I. Davidson and S. S. Ravi. Clustering with constraints: Feasibility issues and the k-means algorithm. In *Proceedings of the 2005 SIAM International Conference on Data Mining*, pages 138–149, Newport Beach, USA, 2005.

[12] L. De Raedt and A. Zimmermann. Constraint-based pattern set mining. In *Proceedings of the 2007 SIAM International Conference on Data Mining*, Minneapolis, USA, 2007.

[13] I. S. Dhillon, S. Mallela, and D. S. Modha. Information-theoretic co-clustering. In *Proceedings of the Ninth ACM SIGKDD International Conference on Knowledge Discovery and Data Mining*, pages 89–98, Washington, USA, 2003.

[14] W. D. Fisher. On grouping for maximum homogeneity. *Journal of the American Statistical Association*, 53:789–798, 1958.

[15] L. A. Goodman and W. H. Kruskal. Measures of association for cross classification. *Journal of the American Statistical Association*, 49:732–764, 1954.

[16] D. Klein, S. D. Kamvar, and C. D. Manning. From instance-level constraints to space-level constraints: Making the most of prior knowledge in data clustering. In *Proceedings of the Nineteenth International Conference on Machine Learning*, pages 307–314, Sydney, Australia, 2002. Morgan Kaufmann.

[17] B. Liu, W. Hsu, and Y. Ma. Integrating classification and association rule mining. In *Proceedings of the Fourth ACM SIGKDD International*

Conference on Knowledge Discovery and Data Mining, pages 80–86. AAAI Press, 1998.

[18] S. C. Madeira and A. L. Oliveira. Biclustering algorithms for biological data analysis: A survey. *IEEE/ACM Transactions on Computational Biology and Bioinformatics*, 1(1):24–45, 2004.

[19] H. Mannila and H. Toivonen. Levelwise search and borders of theories in knowledge discovery. *Data Mining and Knowledge Discovery*, 1(3):241–258, 1997.

[20] K. Morik, J-F. Boulicaut, and A. Siebes, editors. *Local Pattern Detection, International Seminar, Dagstuhl Castle, Germany, April 12-16, 2004, Revised Selected Papers*, volume 3539 of *Lecture Notes in Computer Science*. Springer, 2005.

[21] R. G. Pensa, C. Robardet, and J.-F. Boulicaut. A bi-clustering framework for categorical data. In *Proceedings of the Ninth European Conference on Principles and Practice of Knowledge Discovery in Databases*, volume 3721 of *Lecture Notes in Artificial Intelligence*, pages 643–650, Porto, Portugal, October 2005. Springer.

[22] R. G. Pensa, C. Robardet, and J-F. Boulicaut. Towards constrained co-clustering in ordered 0/1 data sets. In *Proceedings of the Sixteenth International Symposium on Methodologies for Intelligent Systems*, volume 4203 of *Lecture Notes in Computer Science*, pages 425–434, Bari, Italy, 2006. Springer.

[23] W. M. Rand. Objective criteria for the evaluation of clustering methods. *Journal of the American Statistical Association*, 66(336):846–850, 1971.

[24] C. Robardet and F. Feschet. Efficient local search in conceptual clustering. In *Discovery Science: Proceedings of the Fourth International Conference DS 2001*, volume 2226 of *Lecture Notes in Computer Science*, pages 323–335, Washington, USA, November 2001. Springer.

[25] M. Steinbach, P-N. Tan, and V. Kumar. Support envelopes: A technique for exploring the structure of association patterns. In *Proceedings of the Tenth ACM SIGKDD International Conference on Knowledge Discovery and Data Mining*, pages 296–305, Seattle, USA, 2004.

[26] K. Wagstaff. Value, cost, and sharing: Open issues in constrained clustering. In *Knowledge Discovery in Inductive Databases: the Fifth International Workshop, KDID 2006 Berlin, Germany, September 18, 2006 Revised Selected and Invited Papers*, volume 4747 of *Lecture Notes in Computer Science*, pages 1–10. Springer, 2007.

[27] K. Wagstaff, C. Cardie, S. Rogers, and S. Schrödl. Constrained k-means clustering with background knowledge. In *Proceedings of the*

Eighteenth International Conference on Machine Learning, pages 577–584, Williamstown, USA, 2001. Morgan Kaufmann.

Chapter 7

On Supervised Clustering for Creating Categorization Segmentations

Charu Aggarwal

IBM T. J. Watson Research Center, charu@us.ibm.com

Stephen C. Gates

IBM T. J. Watson Research Center, scgates@us.ibm.com

Philip Yu

IBM T. J. Watson Research Center, psyu@us.ibm.com

Abstract   In this paper, we discuss the merits of using supervised clustering for coherent categorization modeling. Traditional approaches for document classification on a predefined set of classes are often unable to provide sufficient accuracy because of the difficulty of fitting a manually categorized collection of records in a given classification model. This is especially the case for domains such as text in which heterogeneous collections of Web documents have varying styles, vocabulary, and authorship. Hence, this paper investigates the use of clustering in order to create the set of categories and its use for classification. We will examine this problem from the perspective of text data. Completely unsupervised clustering has the disadvantage that it has difficulty in isolating sufficiently fine-grained classes of documents relating to a coherent subject matter. In this chapter, we use the information from a pre-existing taxonomy in order to supervise the creation of a set of related clusters, though with some freedom in defining and creating the classes. We show that the advantage of using supervised clustering is that it is possible to have some control over the range of subjects that one would like the categorization system to address, but with a precise mathematical definition of how each category is defined. An extremely effective way then to categorize documents is to use this a priori knowledge of the definition of each category. We also discuss a new technique to help the classifier distinguish better among closely related clusters.

7.1 Introduction

In this chapter, we consider the problem of supervised clustering and its relationship to automated categorization. Such a system has several applications, such as the construction of recommendation systems or providing the ability to categorize very large libraries of text collections on the Web in an automated way. We assume that a pre-existing sample of records with the associated classes is available in order to provide the supervision to the categorization system. We will examine the problem from the perspective of text categorization.

Several text classifiers have recently been proposed, such as those discussed in [3, 4, 5, 13, 14]. These classifiers have shown excellent results on document collections such as the *Reuters* dataset or the US patent database [4] and to a somewhat lesser extent on the Web with the *Yahoo!* taxonomy. Categorization of Web documents has proven to be especially difficult because of the widely varying style, authorship and vocabulary in different documents.

Most of the above-mentioned categorizations are created using manual categorizations by subject experts. The apparent inaccuracy of classification methods on large document collections is a result of the fact that a large heterogeneous collection of manually categorized documents is usually a poor fit for any given classification model. Thus, it is interesting to investigate the construction of categorization systems which relax the restriction imposed by predefined sets of classes. We study the use of clustering in order to create the categories. Once such a set of categories has been obtained, it is easy to perform the categorization by using the same distance measures as were used to perform the clustering. The initially available document taxonomy can provide sufficient supervision in creating a set of categories which can handle similar subjects as the original, but with some freedom in choosing exactly how to define and create the classes. As long as the final application of the categorization system does not restrict us to the use of a fixed set of class labels, this approach may provide considerable advantage because of the tight integration of the measures which are used for clustering and classification.

The fact that we actually know the model used to construct each partition in the clustering ensures that we can theoretically obtain a perfect accuracy on this categorization. Therefore the quality of categorization depends completely on the quality and coherence of each cluster in the new taxonomy, rather than the accuracy of a training procedure on the original taxonomy. Thus, if the supervised clustering procedure can create a new set of classes which are qualitatively comparable to the original taxonomy (in terms of human perception and judgment), the accuracy of the overall categorization system is substantially improved.

The use of clustering for providing browsing capabilities has been espoused in earlier work by Cutting et. al [6, 7]. Other work on clustering algorithms for text data may be found in [2, 8, 11, 19, 20, 21]. These methods do not use any kind of supervision from a pre-existing set of classes, and are attractive for creation of a small number of clusters such as fifty or so, though the clustering rapidly degrades in quality when there is a need to find more fine-grained partitions. Typically, when categories are related sufficiently such that some documents can be considered to be related to both, unsupervised clustering methods are unable to create distinct sets of classes for such categories. The use of a pre-existing manual categorization helps in the creation of a new set of clusters, so that we have some control over the range of subjects that we would like the categorization system to address. The resulting set of clusters may contain additional, new or similar classes to the original taxonomy, and may be quite different in terms of the distribution of the documents among the different classes.

In this chapter, we will use an earlier scan of the *Yahoo!* taxonomy in order to study our categorization system. This is one of many hierarchical organizations of documents which are built by manual categorizations of documents. This is also one of the larger categorizations of documents which are currently available, and hence was a good choice for our study.

This paper is organized as follows. In section 7.2, we will discuss the details of the cluster generation and categorization. In section 7.3, we provide an intuitive discussion of the observed behavior of the engine. A conclusion and summary is provided in section 7.4.

7.2   A Description of the Categorization System

In this section, we will provide a description of our categorization system including feature selection, clustering, and classification. We will first begin with the definitions and notations which we will need for further development of our ideas.

7.2.1   Some Definitions and Notations

In order to represent the documents, we used the vector space model [17]. In the vector space model, it is assumed that each document can be represented as as *term vector* of the form $\bar{a} = (a_1, a_2, \ldots a_n)$. Each of the terms a_i has a weight w_i associated with it, where w_i denotes the normalized frequency of the word in the vector space. A well-known normalization technique is the cosine normalization. In cosine normalization, the weight w_i of the term i is computed as follows:

$$w_i = \frac{tf_i \cdot idf_i}{\sqrt{\sum_{i=1}^{n}(tf_i \cdot idf_i)^2}} \tag{7.1}$$

Here the value of tf_i denotes the *term frequency* of a_i, whereas the value of idf_i denotes the *inverse document frequency*. The inverse document frequency is the inverse of the number of documents in which a word is present in the training data set. Thus, less weight is given to words which occur in larger number of documents, ensuring that the commonly occurring words are not given undue importance.

The similarity between two documents may be measured by calculating the *cosine* similarity between the documents. A *centroid* of a set of documents is defined by a concatenation of the documents in the set. Thus a centroid of a set of documents is a meta document which contains all the terms in that set with the appropriate term frequencies added. A *damped centroid* (or pseudo-centroid) of a set of documents is defined in the same way as the centroid, except that in this case a damping function is applied to the frequencies of the terms in each document before adding them together. The damping function ensures that the repeated presence of a word in a single document does not affect the pseudo-centroid of the entire cluster excessively. Thus, the pseudo-centroid is often a much more stable representation of a central point in a cluster of documents as compared to the centroid.

A projection of a document is defined by setting the term frequencies (or weights) of some of the terms in the vector representation of the document to zero. These are the terms which are said to be *projected out*. We will use the process of projection frequently in the course of the supervised clustering algorithm. Each cluster is represented by a seed vector containing only a certain maximum number of projected words. The aim in projection is to isolate a relatively small vocabulary which describes the subject matter of a cluster well, while filtering out the non-relevant features for that class. We use an incremental process of gradually finding the best set of projected words, while simultaneously refining the clusters, so as to gradually converge to an optimum feature set for each cluster.

7.2.2 Feature Selection

Our first phase was to perform the feature selection in such a way so that only the more differentiating words are used in order to perform the clustering. Note that in unsupervised clustering methods, where a pre-existing taxonomy is not used, the feature selection is somewhat rudimentary in which only *stop words* (very commonly occurring words in the English language) are removed. In this case, since more information is available, we use it in order to prune the feature set further and bias the clustering process to use words which are discriminatory with respect to the original class labels. We use a number called the *normalized gini index* of a word in order to calculate its importance in the clustering process.

Let there be K classes $C_1, C_2 \ldots C_K$ at the lowest level in the original taxonomy. Let $f_1, f_2 \ldots f_K$ be the number of occurrences of that word in each of the K classes, and let $n_1 \ldots n_K$ be the total word count for the documents in each of the K classes. Thus, the *fractional presence* of a word in a particular class is given by f_i/n_i. We define the *skew fraction* of a word for class i by $\frac{f_i/n_i}{\sum_{i=1}^{K} f_i/n_i}$. We shall denote this skew fraction by p_i. Note that if the word is very noisy, and is very evenly distributed among the different classes, then the skew fraction for the word is likely to be approximately $1/K$ for many classes.

The normalized gini index of a word with skew fractions $p_1 \ldots p_K$ is given by $1 - \sqrt{\sum_{i=1}^{K} p_i^2}$. If the word is distributed evenly across the different classes, then the gini index is $1 - 1/\sqrt{K}$. This is the maximum possible value of the gini index. On the other hand, when the word is highly correlated with particular categories and is very skewed in its distribution, then the normalized gini index is much lower.

For our feature selection phase, we calculated the normalized gini index of each word in the lexicon in order to calculate its significance to the lexicon. All those words whose gini index was higher than a predefined value were removed from contention. Thus, the removal of these words ensures the use of a much better set of features than the simple stopword removal of unsupervised clustering techniques. In subsequent phases of clustering and categorization, only the reduced feature set was used for all analysis.

7.2.3 Supervised Cluster Generation

The clustering algorithm uses a seed-based technique in order to create the clusters. Traditional clustering methods have often used seed-based algorithms in order to serve as an anchor point for the creation of the clusters. In other words, seeds form an implicit representation of the cluster partitioning in which each item to be categorized is assigned to its closest seed based on some distance (or similarity) measure. In the context of information retrieval, a seed is a meta-document which can be considered as a pseudo-representation of a central point in a given cluster. Most of the current clustering algorithms discussed in [2, 6, 7, 11] are based on finding a set of seeds in order to define the implicit partitions.

Since the focus of the algorithm is on *supervised clustering*, we started off with a set of seeds which are representative of the classes in the original taxonomy. Thus, the supervision is derived with the choice of a particular set of seeds. These representative seeds are constructed by finding the damped centroids (or pseudo-centroids) of the corresponding classes. This choice of starting point (and features picked) ensures the inclusion of supervision information from the old taxonomy, but the subsequent clustering process is

Algorithm *TClus(D)*
begin
  S = Initial set of seed meta-documents;
  iteration := 0;
  words = *Initial_Value*1;
  threshold = *Initial_Value*2;
  minimum = *Initial_Value*3;
  while *not(termination-criterion)*
  do begin
    (S, D) =*Assign*(S, D);
    S =*Project*$(S, words)$;
    S =*Merge*$(S, threshold)$;
    S =*Kill*$(S, minimum)$;
    iteration := *iteration* + 1;
    words = *words* * θ;
    { θ is a number which is less than 1, and
      indicates the rate at which the number of
      projected dimensions in each seed reduces }
  end
end

FIGURE 7.1: The clustering algorithm

Algorithm *Assign(Pseudo-centroids: S, Documents: D)*
begin
  Initialize each of the clusters $C_1 \ldots C_K$ to *null*;
  { Note that the clusters $C_1 \ldots C_K$ correspond to the pseudo-centroids $s_1 \ldots s_K$ in S }
  for each document $d \in D$ **do**
  begin
    Calculate the cosine of d to each pseudo-centroid in S;
    Find the pseudocentroid s_i, which is most similar to d;
    if $cosine(s_i, d) < OutlierThreshold$ **then**
      begin
      { d is removed from D as an outlier }
      $D = D - \{d\}$;
      end
    else
      Add d to cluster C_i;
  end
  for each $s_i \in S$ **do**
    redefine $s_i \in S$ to the pseudo-centroid of cluster C_i;
  return(S, D);
end

FIGURE 7.2: Assigning documents to pseudo-centroids

Algorithm *Project(Pseudo-centroids: S, Words: l)*
begin
  for each $s_i \in S$ **do**
  begin
    Retain the l terms in the pseudo-centroid s_i with
    maximum weight, setting the weight of all other terms to 0;
  end
end

FIGURE 7.3: Projecting out the less important terms

Algorithm *Merge(PseudoCentroids: S, MergingThreshold: t)*
begin
  for each pair of pseudo-centroids $s_i, s_j \in S$ **do**
    calculate $cos[ij] = cosine(s_i, s_j)$;
  Construct a graph with one node for each pseudo-centroid;
  for each pair s_i, s_j of pseudo-centroids **do**
    if $cos[ij] > t$ **then** add an edge between the nodes for s_i and s_j;
  for each connected component of the graph, concatenate the
    metadocuments for the corresponding pseudo-centroids in order
    to create a new pseudo-centroid. Let S be the new set of
    pseudo-centroids formed out of these connected components;
  return(S)
end

FIGURE 7.4: Merging very closely related clusters

Algorithm *Kill(Pseudo-centroids: S, MinimumLimit: l)*
begin
  for each pseudo-centroid $s_i \in S$ such that the
  associated cluster C_i has less than l documents, discard the
  corresponding pseudo-centroids from S ($S = S - \{s_i\}$);
  return(S);
end

FIGURE 7.5: Removal of poorly defined clusters

independent of any further supervision. Providing this level of independence is critical in the construction of a much more refined set of classes, which are based purely upon content. One of the aspects of the algorithm is that it projects out some of the words in order to represent the seeds. Thus, each seed consists of a vector in which the number of words with a non-zero weight is restricted to a predefined maximum. This vector of words is indicative of the subject material which is most relevant to that cluster. The algorithm starts with a projected dimensionality of about 500 words, and gradually reduces it in each iteration as the clusters get more refined, and a smaller number of words are required in order to isolate the subject of the documents in that cluster. This technique of representing clusters by using both the documents and the projected dimensions in order to represent a cluster is referred to as *projected clustering* [1], and is an effective technique for the creation of clusters for very high dimensional data. The idea of using truncation for speeding up document clustering has been discussed in [19], though our focus for using projections is different, and is designed in order to improve the quality of the clustering by iteratively refining the dimensions and clusters. Thus, the projected clustering technique merges the problem of finding the best set of documents and features for a cluster into one framework. More details on the advantages of using projected clustering for very high dimensional data may be found in [1]. The basic framework of the clustering algorithm is illustrated in Figure 7.1. The following four steps (detailed in Figures 7.2-7.5) are applied iteratively in order to converge to the final set of clusters in the taxonomy. We assume that the set of seeds available to the algorithm at any stage is denoted by S and the documents which are being clustered by the algorithm are denoted by D.

(1) **Document Assignment:** (Figure 7.2) In each iteration, we assign the documents to their closest seed in S. The similarity of each document to its closest seed is calculated using the cosine measure. Thus, a new partition of the documents in D is created by the set of seeds S. After the assignment process, the old set of seeds S are discarded, and the new pseudo-centroid of each partition is added to S as a seed. The procedure returns the new set of seeds S after the assignment of documents to seeds. Those documents which are not close enough to any of the seeds may be permanently discarded as outliers. Thus the document set D is pruned in conjunction with the formation of clusters, so that documents which do not fit well in any category are quickly removed.

(2) **Project:** (Figure 7.3) In each iteration, we project out the words with the least weight from the pseudo-centroids of the previous iteration. This ensures that only the terms which are frequently occurring within a cluster of documents are used for the assignment process. The number of terms which are projected out in each iteration is such that the number of non-zero weight terms reduces by a geometric factor in each iteration. We denote this geometric factor by θ. The use of an iterative

projection technique is useful in finding the words which are most representative of the subject material of a cluster. This is because in the first few iterations, when the clusters are not too refined, a larger number of dimensions need to be retained in the projection in order to avoid premature loss of information. In later iterations, the clusters become more refined and it is possible to project down to a fewer number of words.

(3) **Merge:** (Figure 7.4) In each iteration, we merge all the clusters where the similarity of the seeds in the corresponding partitions is higher than a predefined value (denoted by *threshold*). The merging process is implemented using a simple single linkage method [18]. Each cluster is represented by a node in an undirected graph, and an edge is added between the two nodes if the similarity of the seeds of the corresponding clusters is larger than the predefined threshold value. Each connected component in this graph is then treated as a supercluster. In other words, the documents in each connected component are assigned to a single cluster. The set of pseudo-centroids of this reduced set of clusters is returned by the procedure. Although the simple linkage process is somewhat naive, it is very fast and effective for high values of the threshold similarity.

(4) **Kill:** (Figure 7.5) In each iteration, we discard all those seeds from S such that the number of documents in the corresponding clusters is less than a predefined number. This predefined parameter is denoted by *minimum* in Figure 7.1. These documents either get re-distributed to other clusters or get classified as outliers in later iterations.

These procedures are applied iteratively in order to create the clusters. In the initialization process we started off with a projected dimensionality of 500 words, and reduced the number of words by a factor of 70% ($\theta = 0.7$) in each iteration. When the number of projected dimensions in the seed of each cluster was 200, we terminated the clustering process.

7.2.4 Categorization Algorithm

The definition of each cluster ensures that it is possible to categorize any test document very easily by assigning it to the class for which the corresponding seed is the closest. As in the case of the clustering, the cosine measure is used in order to perform the classification.

An important feature which we added to our categorization process was a method for distinguishing between very closely related subjects. This issue has been discussed earlier by Chakrabarti et. al [4] for building hierarchical categorization models. Here, we discuss this issue in the context of a flat set of clusters which are defined in terms of their seed vectors.

Algorithm *Classify(TestDocument: T)*
begin
  Use cosine measure to find the k closest seeds $\{S_1 \ldots S_k\}$
               to the test document T;
  for $i = 1$ **to** k *domination*$[i] = 0$;
  for $i = 1$ **to** k **do**
    for $j = (i + 1)$ **to** k **do**
    begin
      if $(cosine(S_i - S_j, T) > cosine(S_j - S_i, T))$ **then**
      domination$[i] = $ *domination*$[i] + 1$;
      else
      domination$[j] = $ *domination*$[j] + 1$;
    end
    end
  Rank order the k categorizations in decreasing order of *domination*$[i]$;
end

FIGURE 7.6: The classification algorithm

This is required because even a supervised clustering technique may not provide perfect subject isolation, and a small percentage[1] of the documents do get clustered with documents from a closely related (though slightly inaccurate) category. Even though a theoretical accuracy of 100% can be obtained by reporting the cluster label for the most similar seed, it may sometimes be desirable to correct for the errors in the clustering process by using a context-sensitive comparison method.

We build a *domination matrix* on a subset of the universe of categories, such that we know that all of these categories are good candidates for being the best match. As we will see, the simplicity of this process ensures that speed is not compromised by the use of the flat organization of clusters.

The first step in the algorithm is to find the k closest cluster seeds to the test document. The similarity of each cluster to the test document is calculated by using the cosine measure of the test document to the seed corresponding to each cluster. The value of k is a user-chosen parameter, and is typically a small number compared to the total number of nodes in the taxonomy. These k categories are the candidates for the best match and may often contain a set of closely related subjects. This ranking process is designed to re-rank these categories more appropriately.

In order to understand the importance of distinguishing among closely related subjects, let us consider the seeds for two nodes in the taxonomy: **Business Schools** and **Law Schools**. Recall that our process of projection limits the number of words in each seed to only words which are relevant to the corresponding categories. Some examples of words (with non-zero weights)

---

[1]See empirical section for details.

which could be represented in the seed vector of each of these categories are as follows:

(1) **Business Schools:** business (35), management (31), school (22), university (11), campus (15), presentation (12), student (17), market (11), operations (10) ...

(2) **Law Schools:** law (22), university (11), school (13), examination (15), justice (17), campus (10), courts (15), prosecutor (22), student (15) ...

A document in the generic category of schools is likely to contain all of the words such as university and school. Thus both these categories may be among the k closest seeds for the document. In order to establish the relative closeness of two categories to a given document more accurately, we need to ignore the contributions of the words common to both categories to the cosine measure. In other words, we need to compare the closeness based on the words which are *not* common in the seed vector of both categories. This is done by performing a *relative seed subtraction* operation on the seed vectors of each of the categories. The seed subtraction operation is defined as follows: Let S_1 and S_2 be two seed vectors. Then, the seed $S_1 - S_2$ is obtained by taking the seed S_1 and setting the weight of all those words which are common to S_1 and S_2 to 0.

We say that the seed S_1 dominates the seed S_2 under the following conditions:

• The (cosine) similarity of S_1 to the test document T is larger than the similarity of S_2 to T by at least a predefined threshold referred to as the *domination threshold*.

• The (cosine) similarity of S_1 to T is not larger than the similarity of S_2 to T by the predefined threshold, but the similarity of $(S_1 - S_2)$ to T is larger than the similarity of $(S_2 - S_1)$ to T.

The use of a domination threshold ensures that it is only possible to reorder seeds whose similarity to the test document are very close together. This is because it is primarily in these cases that the differences in the contributions of the common words tends to be a result of noise, rather than any actual pattern of difference in the frequencies of the (common) words in the seeds for the two categories. For each pair of the closest k seeds to the test document, we compute the domination matrix, which is the pairwise domination of each seed over the other. In order to rank order the k candidate seeds, we compute the *domination number* of each seed. The *domination number* of a seed is equal to the number of seeds (among the remaining $(k-1)$ seeds) that it dominates. The k seeds are ranked in closeness based on their domination number; ties are broken in favor of the original ordering based on cosine measure. The algorithm for returning the ranked set of k categorizations is illustrated in Figure 7.6.

It is obvious that the best matching category is more likely to be contained among the top k categories based on cosine measure, than only the closest category based on this measure. (If the clustering is perfect then it suffices to use $k = 1$.) The re-ranking process is then expected to rank this category highly among the k choices. If there are a total of K classes created by the clustering algorithm, then the categorization algorithm needs to perform $O(K + k^2)$ cosine similarity calculations. Further, since the projected dimensionality of each seed is restricted to a few hundred words, each similarity calculation can be implemented efficiently. Thus, the categorization system is extremely fast because of its simplicity, and scales almost linearly with the number of classes. This feature is critical for its use in performing automated categorization of large libraries of documents.

7.3 Performance of the Categorization System

The assessment of the performance of a categorization system based on supervised clustering presents new challenges. Existing benchmarks, such as the well-known Reuters set, are designed principally to test the performance of a new classifier against an predefined set of classes; i.e., the class label for each document is defined externally, and the goal is to measure the accuracy in terms of this "expert" classification. However, when a new set of classes are created, such as by our clustering, these categories may not have a precise correspondence to the original set of classes, and an accuracy measurement with respect to this new set is meaningless.

We know that since the classifier uses the same similarity model as the clustering system does, the key issues are clustering quality and classifier speed. Another point to understand is that the use of supervised clustering to create the new set of categories makes it difficult to apply the standard synthetic data models and techniques [15, 16] which are used for evaluating unsupervised clustering; therefore, our discussion of the performance of the system is primarily an intuitive one based on real data.

As indicated earlier, we used a scan of the *Yahoo!* taxonomy from November 1996. This taxonomy contained a total of 167,193 Web documents, over a lexicon of approximately 700,000 words. The unusually large size of this lexicon is a result of the fact that many of the words in Web document collections tend to be non-standard words which could be misspellings or creative variations on standard words. Such words are so sparse, that they do not have much of a role to play in the clustering process. Only 87,000 words occurred in 7 or more documents in the entire collection. We truncated the *Yahoo!* tree taxonomy to obtain a set of 1500 classes corresponding to higher level nodes. The purpose was to use the lowest level nodes in the taxonomy which contained at least 50 or more documents. (Otherwise, it is difficult to use such sparsely populated nodes for any kind of reasonable categorization or clustering.) The slight shortening and variation of names illustrated in Figure 7.7 from the actual *Yahoo!* names is because of this truncation. The total number of categories at the leaf level of this truncated *Yahoo!* taxonomy was about 1500.

We first performed unsupervised clustering of the data by using an improved variation of the algorithm discussed in [19].[2] We found about 1000 clusters from the original set of documents. Although unsupervised clustering was able to group together similar documents in each cluster, it was unable to perform the fine-grained level of subject isolation that one would expect from such a large number of clusters. For example, a cluster was formed such that it contained constituent documents were drawn from *Yahoo!* categories related to computer-generated art, hand-crafted arts, artists, painting, sculpture, museums, and architecture. Although these documents shared considerable similarity in the subject material and vocabulary, the overall subject material in the documents was relatively generic (art), and it was difficult to find the level of fine-grained subject isolation that is available in the *Yahoo!* taxonomy. Almost all the clusters found using the unsupervised clustering technique provided categories in which the overall subject was as generic as a top level category of the hierarchical *Yahoo!* organization. This is consistent with our earlier observation that unsupervised methods are often unable to create a sufficiently fine-grained subject isolation.

In our implementation of the supervised clustering algorithm we first calculated the gini index of the different words in the clusters and removed about 10,000 words with the highest gini index. We also removed the very infrequently occurring words in order to remove misspellings and creative variations on ordinary words. Specifically, we removed all those words which occurred in less than 7 documents out of the original training data set of 167,193 Web documents. At this stage, we were left with a lexicon of about 77,000 words. We found that the use of the *idf* normalization actually decreased the quality of the clustering, and therefore we used only the term frequencies in order to represent the weights of the terms in the vector-space representation of the documents.[3] We restricted the number of words in the pseudo-centroid of each cluster to about 200. The algorithm started with about 500 projected words in each seed, and successively removed words from the seed, until a maximum of about 200 words was obtained in each seed. The value of the seed reduction factor θ was 0.7. The value of the parameter *minimum* used to decide when to kill a cluster was 8. The value of the merging threshold (the parameter *threshold* in Figure 7.1) was 0.95. The algorithm required a total

---

[2]We omit the exact details of the implementation of this algorithm, since it is beyond the scope of this paper.

[3]The fact that *idf* normalizations reduce cluster quality has also been observed in earlier work [19].

Category	*Yahoo!* **Categories of constituent documents**
1. Wine	@Entertainment@Drinks_and_...@Wine (28) @Business_...@Companies@Drinks@...@Wine@Wineries (9) @Business_...@Companies@Drinks@...@Wine@Other (2) @Entertainment@Magazines@Other (2)
2. Fitness	@Health@Fitness (29) @Business_...@Companies@Health@Fitness (7) @Recreation@Sports@Other (3) @Business_...@Companies@Sports@Other (3) @Business_...@Products_Services@Magazines@Sports (3)
3. Health Org.	@Health@Medicine@Organizations (39) @Health@Medicine@Other (16) @Health@Other (4) @Education@Other (3) @Business_...@Organizations@Public_Interest_Groups@Other (3) @Business_...@Companies@Health@Other (3) @Business_...@Companies@Books@Titles@Other (2)
4. N. Parks	@Recreation@...@Parks@National_Parks... (37) @Recreation@Outdoors@Other (8) @Recreation@Travel@Regional@US_States@Other (7) @Business_...@Travel@Tour_Operators@Adventure (7) @Recreation@Travel@Regional@Countries@Other (2) @Business_...@Travel@Lodging@Regional@...@Canada (2)
5. S. Trek	@News_And_Media@...@Science_FF&H@Star_Trek@Other (120) @Entertainment@Movies_And_Films@Actors_And_Actresses (13) @Entertainment@Science_FF&H (4) @Entertainment@....@Science_FF&H@Other (4) @Entertainment@Humor_Jokes_And_Fun@Other (3) @Recreation@Hobbies_And_Crafts@Collecting (3)

FIGURE 7.7: Some examples of constituent documents in each cluster

of 3 hours to complete on a 233 MHz AIX machine with 100 MB of memory. We obtained a total of 1167 categories in a flat taxonomy.

We labeled the nodes by examining the constituent *Yahoo!* categories in this set of newly created clusters. Typically, the clustering did a very excellent job in grouping together documents from very closely related categories in the *Yahoo!* taxonomy in a creative way, so as to result in a coherent subject for each cluster. This kind of grouping differs from the case of unsupervised clustering in terms of providing much cleaner subject isolation. We have illustrated some examples of the clusters obtained in Figure 7.7. In the right hand column of the table, we have illustrated the constituent documents in each *Yahoo!* category in the cluster. In order to give a flavor of how well the clustering performed, we provide some interesting observations for these examples:

1. Wine: The cluster for wine was constructed by picking out documents from the wine segment of the *@Entertainment* and *@Business_And_Economy* subcategories of *Yahoo!*. Two of the documents in the category were also drawn from a *Yahoo!* category on magazines, but in both the cases, we found that the documents were magazine articles related to wine. Although the original *Yahoo!* categorization was accurate, the actual content of the page cannot be directly related to the topic of magazines, without prior knowledge of the meta-information that the document is a magazine article. Thus, the training phase of a classifier on the *Yahoo!* taxonomy would not be helped by the presence of such a document in the category on magazines.

2. Fitness: Most of the documents in the **Fitness** category were drawn from either fitness, health or sports related categories from the *Yahoo!* taxonomy. Again, these categories occurred in widely separated branches of the *Yahoo!* hierarchy. This is an example of a case where the clustering was able to pick out specific documents from interrelated categories which were more general than the topic of fitness. The presence of very closely related documents in many widely separated branches of a hierarchy is somewhat detrimental to the performance of a hierarchical classifier because it becomes more difficult to distinguish nodes at the higher levels of the taxonomy.

3. Health Organizations: This cluster consisted of documents from commercial health related categories, non-commercial health related categories, and education related categories, which were related to the general topic of health organizations.

4. National Parks: In the original *Yahoo!* categorization, many of the documents on parks fall under the travel, tourism, and outdoors category. Correspondingly, the clustering grouped together Web pages which were closely related to the subject material of parks but drawn from these very distinct *Yahoo!* categories. Again, the presence of documents on parks in travel related categories of *Yahoo!* may often confuse classifiers, since this subject is only peripherally related to the topic of travel and tourism in general.

5. Star Trek: The clustering was able to pick out documents from various *Yahoo!* categories, which dealt with different aspects of Star Trek including the categories on television shows, motion pictures, actors and actresses, and collectibles. Two documents were also drawn from the Humor category of *Yahoo!* which had Star Trek related material in them.

In many cases, we found a correspondence between some original *Yahoo!* class and the final class which was created by the supervised clustering technique. However, the documents in these categories were often quite different and more directly related to the actual content of the page. Manual categorizations take into account factors which are not reflected in the content of a given document. Although this is often desirable to effectively index documents, it does not help provide the ability to train classifiers accurately. The redistribution of such documents to clusters which are more related on content provides a cleaner set of classes from the perspective of a content-based classification engine. (See, for example, the case for the category of **Wine** above.) In all cases, we found that the projected set of words for a cluster corresponded very closely with its subject.

7.3.1 Categorization

We ran the classifier and reported the three best categories as the results. The domination threshold used for 0.025. We found that the use of the domination matrix approach caused a different ranking (from the original ranking of the categories based on cosine measure) in about 8% to 9% of the cases. In order to provide a flavor of the performance of categorization, we provide some examples of the classifications which were reported in Figure 7.8. One interesting observation was that when we tested documents which were related to multiple subjects in the taxonomy, the classifier was able to get the different related subjects as the first, second, and third categories. As an example (see Figure 7.8), when we tested a Web page containing a compilation of lawyer jokes, the classifier was able to pick out both the closely related subjects (lawyer and jokes) among its different choices. Another similar example was (3) in Figure 7.8, where a humorous narrative on the Web was categorized to belong to both fiction and humor related categories.

When we tested the classifier on the homepage of the 1999 Conference on Knowledge Discovery and Data Mining, we found that the top three categories provided some interesting information: (1) The document was related to a computer conference. (2) The document was related to computer science. (3) The document was related to artificial intelligence. Since there is no category on data mining conferences, the classifier finds the closest set of general categories which are related to data mining conferences. Thus, each of the first, second, and third categories provide different pieces of relevant information about this document.

We observed this kind of behavior by the categorization system on a very regular basis. Another example was a page of documentation on the Winsock Protocol, in which case it provided the categories of Internet Software Proto-

Example	Comments
www.wpi.edu/tanis/lawyer.html: **Title:** Canonical List of Lawyer Jokes **First Category:** Jokes **Second Category:** Individual Attorneys **Third Category:** Misc. Humor, Jokes and Fun	Since there is no category on lawyer jokes, the classifier finds the categories most closely related to both attorneys and jokes.
www.doubleclick.com/advertisers: **Title:** Solutions for Advertisers **First Category:** Misc. Advertising (Commercial) **Second Category:** Misc. Marketing (Commercial) **Third Category:** Direct Marketing (Commercial)	Can distinguish pages about advertising from pages containing advertising
www.pliant.org/personal/ **TomErickson/hawaii.html:** **Title:** The Key **First Category:** Web Science, Fantasy, Horror **Second Category:** Misc. Humor Jokes and Fun **Third Category:** Jokes	This is a humorous narrative on the Web by a scientist.
www.crstat.com/default.htm: **Title:** Charles River Strategies Inc. **First Category:** Management Consulting **Second Category:** Market Research **Third Category:** Infor. Tech. Consulting	Charles River Strategies is "the industry's prominent firm focussed on integrated end-user channel marketing strategy"
research.microsoft.com/datamine/kdd99: **Title:** Conference on Data Mining **First Category:** Computer Conferences **Second Category:** Misc. Computer Science **Third Category:** Artificial Intelligence	Finds all topics in computer science and artificial intelligence which) are related to data mining and knowledge discovery
users.neca.com/vmis/wsockexp.htm: **Title:** Getting back to the basics **First Category:** Misc. Internet Software Protocols **Second Category:** Microsoft Windows 95 **Third Category:** Internet Documentation	A page of documentation on the Winsock Protocol
www.software.ibm.com/ad/vajava: **Title:** IBM Visual Age for Java **First Category:** Object-Oriented Prog. Tools **Second Category:** Prog. Languages (Commercial) **Third Category:** Software Consulting (Commercial)	The word object-oriented is not mentioned on the page

FIGURE 7.8: Some examples of classifier performance

Case	Percentage of Instances
Better than *Yahoo!*	9%
Not as good as *Yahoo!*	10%
Both were equally correct	77%
Neither is correct	4%
Unknown	1%

FIGURE 7.9: Survey results

cols, Windows 95, and Internet Information and Documentation as relevant categories. Again, we see that although there is no category in the taxonomy which relates to documentation on the Winsock Protocol, the classifier is able to find categories, all of which are closely related to some aspect of the document. The other property which we noted about the classifier was that it was often able to infer peripherally related subjects as its second and third choices. For example, the first choice for the page on IBM Visual Age for Java was on Object Oriented Programming Tools, the second choice was on Programming Languages, and the third choice was on software consulting. Clearly, the first choice was a very exact match, whereas the second and third choices were peripherally related. It was very rare that the classifier reported totally unrelated choices for any subject.

The simplicity of the classifier ensured that it was extremely fast in spite of the very large number of classes used. The classifier required about two hours to categorize about 160,000 documents. This averaged at about 45 milliseconds per categorization. This does not include the time for parsing and tokenizing the document. In fact, the parsing procedure dominated the overall time for categorization (0.1 seconds for parsing). Since most text categorization techniques would need to parse the document anyway, this indicates that our categorization system is within a reasonable factor of the best possible overall speed of parsing and subsequent classification.

7.3.2 An Empirical Survey of Categorization Effectiveness

It is hard to provide a direct comparison of our technique to any other classification method by using a measure such as classification accuracy. This is because our algorithm does not use the original set of classes, but it actually defines the categories on its own. Therefore, the accuracy of such a classifier is high, whereas the actual quality of categorization is defined by clustering quality. Therefore, we need to provide some way to measure the clustering effectiveness.

Since the entire thrust of our supervised clustering algorithm was to facilitate the generation of a set of good clusters (in terms of human judgment) from a manually created taxonomy of real web pages, it is also impossible to use the traditional synthetic data techniques (used for unsupervised clustering algorithms) in order to test the effectiveness of our technique. Thus, we need to find some way of quantifying the results of our clustering technique on a real data set such as *Yahoo!*.

We used a survey technique by using input from external survey respondents in order to measure the quality of the clustering. We sampled 141 documents from the clusters obtained by our algorithm, and asked respondents to indicate how well the corresponding subject labels defined it with respect to the original *Yahoo!* categorization. Specifically, for each document, we asked respondents to indicate one of the following five choices: (1) *Yahoo!* categorization was better, (2) Our categorization was better, (3) Both were similar, (4) Neither were correct, (5) Do not know. The results of our survey are indicated in Figure 7.9.

One of the interesting aspects of the results in Figure 7.9 is that the quality of our categorization was as good as *Yahoo!* for 77% of the documents. Out of this 77%, the two categorizations reported the same label in 88% of the cases, while the remaining were judged to be qualitatively similar. Among the remaining documents, the opinions were almost evenly split (10%:9%) as to whether *Yahoo!* or our scheme provided a better categorization. For the 10% of the cases in which our clustering algorithm provided a categorization which was not as good as *Yahoo!*, we found that most of these instances belonged to one of two kinds:

(1) Neither categorization was particularly well suited, though the page was better categorized in *Yahoo!*. Typically, the content of the page did not reflect either category well, though some more meta-understanding of the page was required in order to accurately classify it. An example of such a page was *http://nii.nist.gov*, which discusses the United States Information Infrastructure Virtual Library. The web page discusses the National Information Infrastructure ("information superhighway"), which is an interconnection of computers and telecommunication networks, services, and applications. The document was present in the *Yahoo!* category on Government, though we clustered it along with telecommunication documents. The fact that the document is government related is meta-information, which cannot be automatically derived from its content. We assert that the effective categorization of such documents may be difficult for any system which is based purely on content.

(2) Our algorithm inserted the document in a closely related cluster, though the original *Yahoo!* categorization was slightly more accurate. This was a more common event than case (1). For example, a URL (*http://www.i-channel.com*) from the *Yahoo!* category on Cable Networks was grouped with miscellaneous documents on television by our clustering algorithm. Another URL (*http://fluxnet.com*) from the *Yahoo!* category on Rock Music CDS and Tapes was categorized by our algorithm in the general Rock Music topic. Most of these categorizations (though less accurate) were good enough to not be considered unreasonable.

Another way of interpreting the survey results is that that our automated (supervised) scheme provided clusters which were as good as or better than the *Yahoo!* partitions in $77 + 9 = 86\%$ of the cases, whereas the vice versa was true for $77 + 10 = 87\%$ of the cases. Among the 10% of the documents, in which *Yahoo!* was judged better, a substantial fraction belonged to case (2) above, in which the documents were inserted in a reasonably good cluster although not quite as accurately as its classification in *Yahoo!*. To summarize, the respondents found little or no quality difference in the (manual) categorization of *Yahoo!* versus our supervised cluster creation. At the same time, an ability of express each category in a structured way is a key advantage from the perspective of a classifier. Thus, the perceived accuracy of the overall categorization system is expected to be much higher, and the benefits of the use of supervised clustering are apparent.

7.4 Conclusions and Summary

In this chapter, we proposed methods for building categorization systems by using supervised clustering. We also discussed techniques for distinguishing closely related classes in the taxonomy. We built such a categorization system using a set of classes from the *Yahoo!* taxonomy, and using them as a base in order to create the supervised clusters. We showed that the supervised clustering created a new set of classes which were surveyed to be as good as the original set of classes in the *Yahoo!* taxonomy, but which are naturally suited to automated categorization. The result is a system which has much higher overall quality of categorization. Combined with the low cost of an automated categorization scheme compared to a manual scheme, such a system is likely to have wide applicability to large document repositories.

References

[1] Aggarwal C. C., Procopiuc C., Wolf J. L., Yu P. S., Park J.-S. A framework for finding projected clusters in high dimensional spaces. *Proceedings of the ACM SIGMOD Conference on Management of Data*, pp. 61–72, 1999.

[2] Anick P., Vaithyanathan S. Exploiting clustering and phrases for context-based information retrieval. *Proceedings of the ACM SIGIR Conference on Research and Development in Information Retrieval*, pp. 314–323, 1997.

[3] Apte C., Damerau F., Weiss S. M. Automated learning of decision rules for text categorization. *IBM Research Report* RC 18879.

[4] Chakrabarti S., Dom B., Agrawal R., Raghavan P. Using taxonomy, discriminants, and signatures for navigating in text databases. *Proceedings of the Very Large Databases Conference*, pp. 446–455, August 1997, Athens, Greece. *Extended Version:* Scalable feature selection, classification and signature generation for organizing text databases into hierar-

chical topic taxonomies. *Very Large Databases Journal*, 7: pp. 163–178, 1998.

[5] Chakrabarti S., Dom B., Indyk P. Enhanced hypertext categorization using hyperlinks. *Proceedings of the ACM SIGMOD Conference on Management of Data*, pp. 307–318, 1998.

[6] Cutting D. R., Karger D. R., Pedersen J. O., Tukey J. W. Scatter/Gather: A cluster-based approach to browsing large document collections. *Proceedings of the ACM SIGIR Conference on Research and Development in Information Retrieval*, pp. 318–329, 1992.

[7] Cutting D. R., Karger D. R., Pedersen J. O. Constant interaction-time Scatter/Gather browsing of very large document collections. *Proceedings of the ACM SIGIR Conference on Research and Development in Information Retrieval*, pp. 318–329, 1993.

[8] Douglas Baker L., McCallum A. K. Distributional clustering of words for text classification. *Proceedings of the ACM SIGIR Conference on Research and Development in Information Retrieval*, pp. 96–103, 1998.

[9] Frakes W. B., Baeza-Yates R. *Information Retrieval: Data Structures and Algorithms*. Prentice Hall, Englewood Cliffs, New Jersey.

[10] Jain A. K., Dubes R. C. *Algorithms for Clustering Data*. Prentice Hall, Englewood Cliffs, New Jersey.

[11] Hearst M. A., Pedersen J. O. Re-examining the cluster hypothesis: Scatter/Gather on retrieval results. *Proceedings of the ACM SIGIR Conference on Research and Development in Information Retrieval*, pp. 76–84, 1996.

[12] Ji X., Xu W. Document clustering with prior knowledge. *Proceedings of the ACM SIGIR Conference on Research and Development in Information Retrieval*, pp. 405–412, 2006.

[13] Koller D., Sahami M. Hierarchically classifying documents using very few words. *International Conference on Machine Learning*, pp. 170–178, 1997.

[14] Lam W., Ho C. Y. Using a generalized instance set for automatic text categorization. *Proceedings of the ACM SIGIR Conference on Research and Development in Information Retrieval*, pp. 81–88, 1998.

[15] Lewis D. D. Naive (Bayes) at forty: The independence assumption in information retrieval. *Proceedings of the European Conference on Machine Learning*, pp. 4–15, 1998.

[16] Nigam K., McCallum A., Thrun S., Mitchell T. Learning to classify text from labeled and unlabeled documents. *Proceedings of the Fifteenth*

National Conference on Artificial Intelligence and Tenth Innovative Applications of Artificial Intelligence Conference, pp. 792–299, 1998.

[17] Salton G., McGill M. J. *Introduction to Modern Information Retrieval.* McGraw Hill, New York, 1983.

[18] Sibson R. SLINK: An optimally efficient algorithm for the single link cluster method. *Computer Journal*, 16:30–34, 1973.

[19] Schutze H., Silverstein C. Projections for efficient document clustering. *Proceedings of the ACM SIGIR Conference on Research and Development in Information Retrieval*, pp. 74–81, 1997.

[20] Silverstein C., Pedersen J. O. Almost-constant time clustering of arbitrary corpus sets. *Proceedings of the ACM SIGIR Conference on Research and Development in Information Retrieval*, pp. 60–66, 1997.

[21] Zamir O., Etzioni O. Web document clustering: A feasibility demonstration. *Proceedings of the ACM SIGIR Conference on Research and Development in Information Retrieval*, pp. 46–53, 1998.

Chapter 8

Clustering with Balancing Constraints

Arindam Banerjee

University of Minnesota, Twin Cities, `banerjee@cs.umn.edu`

Joydeep Ghosh

University of Texas at Austin, `ghosh@ece.utexas.edu`

Abstract   In many applications of clustering, solutions that are balanced, i.e., where the clusters obtained are of comparable sizes, are preferred. This chapter describes several approaches to obtaining balanced clustering results that also scale well to large data sets. First, we describe a general scalable framework for obtaining balanced clustering that first clusters only a small subset of the data and then efficiently allocates the rest of the data to these initial clusters while simultaneously refining the clustering. Next, we discuss how frequency sensitive competitive learning can be used for balanced clustering in both batch and on-line scenarios, and illustrate the mechanism with a case study of clustering directional data such as text documents. Finally, we briefly outline balanced clustering based on other methods such as graph partitioning and mixture modeling.

8.1   Introduction

Several chapters in this book describe how to incorporate constraints stemming from additional information about the data into the clustering process. For example, prior information about known labels or about the knowledge that certain pairs of points have or do not have the same label, are translated into "must-link" and "cannot-link" constraints (see Chapter 1). In contrast, in this chapter we deal with a constraint that typically comes from the desiderata or needs of the end-application. This constraint is that the clusters be all of comparable sizes, i.e., the solution be *balanced*. Here "size" of a cluster typically refers to the number of data points in that cluster. In cases where each point may have a weight/value attached to it, for example the points represent customers and a point's weight is the monetary value of that customer, size can alternatively refer to the net weight of all points in a cluster.

In general, the natural clusters in the data may be of widely varying sizes. Moreover, this variation may not be known beforehand and balanced solutions may not be important. However, for several real-life applications, having a balancing requirement helps in making the clusters actually useful and actionable. Thus this imposition comes from the associated application/business needs rather than from the inherent properties of the data. Indeed, it may be specified simply based on the end-goals even without examining the actual data.

Let us now look at some specific applications where a balanced solution is desired:

- Direct Marketing [48, 52]: A direct marketing campaign often starts with segmenting customers into groups of roughly equal size or equal estimated revenue generation, (based on, say, market basket analysis, demographics, or purchasing behavior at a web site), so that the same number of sales teams, marketing dollars, etc., can be allocated to each segment.

- Category Management [39]: Category management is a process that involves managing product categories as business units and customizing them on a store-by-store basis to satisfy customer needs. A core operation in category management, with important applications for large retailers, is to group products into categories of specified sizes such that they match units of shelf space or floor space. Another operation key to large consumer product companies such as Procter & Gamble, is to group related stock keeping units (SKUs) in bundles of comparable revenues or profits. In both operations the clusters need to be refined on an on-going basis because of seasonal difference in sales of different products, consumer trends, etc. [26].

- Clustering of Documents [3, 32]: In clustering of a large corpus of documents to generate topic hierarchies, balancing greatly facilitates *browsing/navigation* by avoiding the generation of hierarchies that are highly skewed, with uneven depth in different parts of the hierarchy "tree" or having widely varying number of documents at the leaf nodes. Similar principles apply when grouping articles in a web site [32], portal design, and creation of domain specific ontologies by hierarchically grouping concepts.

- Balanced Clustering in Energy Aware Sensor Networks [20, 25]: In distributed sensor networks, sensors are clustered into groups, each represented by a sensor "head," based on attributes such as spatial location, protocol characteristics, etc. An additional desirable property, often imposed as an external soft constraint on clustering, is that each group consume comparable amounts of power, as this makes the overall network more reliable and scalable.

In all the examples the balancing constraint is soft. It is not important to have clusters of exactly the same size but rather to avoid very small or very large clusters. A cluster that is too small may not be useful, e.g., a group of otherwise very similar customers that is too small to provide customized solutions for. Similarly a very large cluster may not be differentiated enough to be readily actionable. Thus balancing may be sought even though the "natural" clusters in the data are quite imbalanced. Additionally, even the desired range of the number of clusters sought, say 5 to 10 in a direct marketing application, may come from high level "business" requirements rather than from data properties. For these reasons, the most appropriate number and nature of clusters determined from a purely data-driven perspective may not match the number obtained from a need-driven one. In such cases, constrained clustering can yield solutions that are of poorer quality when measured by a data-centric criterion such as "average dispersion from cluster representative" (kmeans objective function), even though these same solutions are more preferable from the application viewpoint. Nevertheless, a positive, seemingly surprising result, empirically illustrated later in this chapter, is that even for fairly imbalanced data, a versatile approach to balanced clustering provides comparable, and sometimes better, results as judged by the unconstrained clustering objective function. Thus such balanced solutions are then clearly superior if the benefit of meeting the constraints is also factored in. The advantage is largely because balancing provides a form of regularization that seems to avoid low-quality local minima stemming from poor initialization.

A variety of approaches to obtaining balanced clusters have been proposed. These include (i) techniques such as clustering via graph partitioning where balance is an integral part of the clustering formulation [30, 48]; (ii) formulations where balancing is encouraged by adding a constraint within an optimization framework [51, 54], and (iii) hierarchical approaches that encourage balanced results while progressively merging or splitting clusters [46]. Given the space constraints in this chapter, we shall focus on a general framework for scaling up balanced clustering algorithms capable of working with any representative-based clustering algorithm, such as KMeans (Section 8.2). Other methods are briefly described in Section 8.4, which also provides references for further details.

The framework presented in Section 8.2 can provably guarantee a prespecified minimum number of points per cluster, which can be valuable in several application domains, especially when the number of clusters is large and it is desirable to avoid very small or empty clusters. The framework first clusters a representative sample of the data, and then allocates the rest of the points to these initial clusters by solving a generalization of the stable marriage problem, followed by refinements that satisfy the balancing constraints.

Several practical applications can benefit from a soft balancing approach that produces approximately balanced clusters, but does not necessarily have provable balancing guarantees. Further, since several applications accumulate data over time, it is important to be able to generate online balanced clustering based on a sequence of data points. Section 8.3 describes a family of such methods based on frequency sensitive competitive learning, applicable to both batch and online settings, along with a case study of balanced text clustering. In Section 8.4, we briefly outline other methods for balanced clustering, with particular emphasis on graph partitioning and mixture modeling-based methods. Sections 8.2 and 8.3 are largely adapted from [6] and [5], respectively, and these works can be referenced by the interested reader for details. We conclude in Section 8.5 with a brief discussion on future directions.

8.2   A Scalable Framework for Balanced Clustering

In this section we describe a general framework for partitional clustering with a user-specified degree of balancing, which can be provably guaranteed. The proposed method can be broken down into three steps: (1) sampling, (2) clustering of the sampled set, and (3) populating and refining the clusters while satisfying the balancing constraints. For N points and k clusters, the overall complexity of the method is $O(kN \log N)$.

8.2.1   Formulation and Analysis

Let $\mathcal{X} = \{\mathbf{x}_1, \mathbf{x}_2, \cdots, \mathbf{x}_N\}, \mathbf{x}_i \in \mathbb{R}^d, \forall i$ be a set of N data points to be clustered. Let $d : \mathbb{R}^d \times \mathbb{R}^d \mapsto \mathbb{R}_+$ be a given distance function between any two points in $\mathbb{R}^d$. The goal is to find a disjoint k-partitioning $\{S_h\}_{h=1}^k$ of $\mathcal{X}$ and a corresponding set of k cluster representatives $M = \{\boldsymbol{\mu}_h\}_{h=1}^k$ in $\mathbb{R}^d$ for a given k such that the clustering objective function[1]

$$L(\{\boldsymbol{\mu}_h, S_h\}_{h=1}^k) = \sum_{h=1}^k \sum_{\mathbf{x} \in S_h} d(\mathbf{x}, \boldsymbol{\mu}_h) \qquad (8.1)$$

is minimized under the constraint that $|S_h| \geq m, \forall h$, for a given m with $mk \leq N$. The sampling-based method assumes that for the (unknown) *optimal*

---

[1]Weighted objects can be simply catered to by incorporating these weights in both the cost and the size constraint expressions. Weights have not been shown to keep the exposition simple.

partitioning $\{S_h^*\}_{h=1}^k$,

$$\min_h \frac{|S_h^*|}{N} \geq \frac{1}{l} \qquad (8.2)$$

for some integer $l \geq k$. In other words, if samples are drawn uniformly at random from the set $\mathcal{X}$, the probability of picking a sample from any particular optimal partition is at least $\frac{1}{l}$. $l = k$ if and only if $|S_h^*| = N/k, \forall h$, so that the optimal partitions are all of the same size. Further, the distance function d is assumed to be well-behaved in the following sense: Given a set of points $\mathbf{x}_i, \cdots, \mathbf{x}_n$, there is an efficient way of finding the representative $\boldsymbol{\mu} = \arg\min_c \sum_{i=1}^n d(\mathbf{x}_i, c)$. For a very large class of "distance" measures called Bregman divergences, which includes the squared Euclidean distance as well as KL-divergence as special cases, the optimal representative is simply the mean of the cluster and hence can be readily computed [7]. For cosine distance, the representative is again the mean, but scaled to unit length [4]. Therefore the assumption regarding the distance function is not very restrictive.

The above balanced clustering formulation can be efficiently solved in three steps, as outlined below:

Step 1: Sampling of the given data: The given data is first sampled in order to get a small representative subset of the data. The idea is to exploit (8.2) and compute the number of samples one must must draw from the original data in order to get a good representation from each of the optimal partitions in the sampled set with high probability. By extending the analysis of the so-called Coupon Collector's problem [37] one can show the following [6]: If X is the random variable for the number of samples to be drawn from $\mathcal{X}$ to get at least s points from each partition, $E[X] \leq sl \ln k + O(sl)$, where $E[X]$ is the expectation of X. Further, if $n = csl \ln k \approx cE[X]$ samples are drawn from $\mathcal{X}$ (where c is an appropriately chosen constant), then at least s samples are obtained from each optimal partition with probability at least $(1 - \frac{1}{k^c})$. To better understand the result, consider the case where $l = k = 10$, and say we want at least $s = 50$ points from each of the partitions. Table 8.1 shows the total number of points that need to be sampled for different levels of confidence.

Note that if the k optimal partitions are of equal size and $csk \ln k$ points are sampled uniformly at random, the expected number of points from each partition is $cs \ln k$. Thus the underlying structure is expected to be preserved in this smaller sampled set and the chances of wide variations from this behavior is very small. For example, for the 99.99% confidence level in Table 8.1, the average number of samples per partition is 127, which is only about 2.5 times the minimum sample size that is desired, irrespective of the total number of points in $\mathcal{X}$, which could be in the millions for example.

Step 2: Clustering of the sampled data: The second step involves clustering the set of n sampled points, $\mathcal{X}_s$. The only requirement from this stage is to obtain a k-partitioning of $\mathcal{X}_s$ and have a representative $\boldsymbol{\mu}_h, h = 1, \cdots, k$ corresponding to each partition. There are several clustering formulations

TABLE 8.1: Number of samples required to achieve a given confidence level for k = 10 and s = 50.

d	1	2	3	4	5
Confidence, $100(1 - \frac{1}{k^c})\%$	90.000	99.000	99.900	99.990	99.999
Number of Samples, n	1160	1200	1239	1277	1315

that satisfy this requirement, e.g., clustering using Bregman divergences [7] for which the optimal representatives are given by the centroids, clustering using cosine-type similarities [4, 17] for which the optimal representatives are given by the ℓ_2-normalized centroids, convex clustering [36] for which the optimal representatives are given by generalized centroids, etc. Since the size of the sampled set is much less than that of the original data, one can use slightly involved algorithms as well, without much blow-up in overall complexity.

Step 3: Populating and refining the clusters: After clustering the n point sample from the original data $\mathcal{X}$, the remaining $(N - n)$ points need to be assigned to the clusters, satisfying the balancing constraint. This can be achieved in two phases: *Populate*, where the points that were not sampled, and hence do not currently belong to any cluster, are assigned to the existing clusters in a manner that satisfies the balancing constraints while ensuring good quality clusters; and *Refine*, where iterative refinements are done to improve on the clustering objective function while satisfying the balancing constraints all along. Both phases can be applied irrespective of what clustering algorithm was used in the second step, as long as there is a way to represent the clusters. In fact, the third step is the most critical step and the first two steps can be considered a good way to initialize the populate-refine step.

Let n_h be the number of points in cluster h, so that $\sum_{h=1}^{k} n_h = n$. Let $\mathcal{X}_u$ be the set of $(N - n)$ non-sampled points. The final clustering needs to have at least m points per cluster to be feasible. Let $b = \frac{mk}{N}$, where $0 \leq b \leq 1$ since $m \leq N/k$, be the *balancing fraction*. For any assignment of the members of $\mathcal{X}$ to the clusters, let $\ell_i \in \{1, \ldots, k\}$ denote the cluster assignment of $\mathbf{x}_i$. Further, let $S_h = \{\mathbf{x}_i \in \mathcal{X} | \ell_i = h\}$.

In *Populate*, we just want a reasonably good feasible solution so that $|S_h| \geq m, \forall h$. Hence, since there are already n_h points in S_h, we need to assign $[m - n_h]_+$ more points to S_h, where $[x]_+ = \max(x, 0)$. Ideally, each point in $\mathcal{X}_u$ should be assigned to the nearest cluster so that $\forall \mathbf{x}_i, d(\mathbf{x}_i, \mu_{\ell_i}) \leq d(\mathbf{x}_i, \mu_h), \forall h$. Such assignments will be called *greedy* assignments. However, this need not satisfy the balancing constraint. So, we do the assignment of all the points as follows: (i) Exactly $[m - n_h]_+$ points are assigned to cluster $h, \forall h$, such that for each $\mathbf{x}_i$ that has been assigned to a cluster, *either* it has been assigned to its nearest cluster, *or* all clusters h' whose representatives $\mu_{h'}$ are nearer to $\mathbf{x}_i$ than its own representative μ_{ℓ_i} already have the required number of points $[m - n_{h'}]_+$, all of which are nearer to $\mu_{\mathbf{h'}}$ than $\mathbf{x}_i$; and (ii) the remaining points are greedily assigned to their nearest clusters. The assignment condition in (i) is motivated by the stable marriage problem that tries to get a stable match of n men and n women, each with his/her preference list for marriage over the other set [27]. The populate step can be viewed as a generalization of the standard stable marriage setting in that there are k clusters that want to "get married," and cluster h wants to "marry" at least $[m - n_h]_+$ points. Hence, an assignment of points to clusters that satisfies condition in (i) is called a *stable* assignment and the resulting clustering is called *stable*.

In *Refine*, feasible iterative refinements are done starting from the clustering obtained from the first part until convergence. Note that at this stage, each point $\mathbf{x}_i \in \mathcal{X}$ is in one of the clusters and the balancing constraints are satisfied, i.e., $|S_h| \geq m, \forall h$. There are two ways in which a refinement can be done, and we iterate between these two steps and the updating of the cluster representative: (i) Points that can be moved to a cluster whose representative is nearer than their current representative, without violating the balancing constraint, are all safely re-assigned; and (ii) groups of points in different clusters, which can only be simultaneously re-assigned in conjunction with other re-assignments to reduce the cost without violating the constraints, are obtained based on strongly connected components of the possible assignment graph, and all such group re-assignments are done.

After all the individual and group reassignments are made, the cluster representatives are re-estimated. Using the re-estimated means, a new set of re-assignments are possible and the above two steps are performed again. The process is repeated until no further updates can be done, and the refinement algorithm terminates.

8.2.2   Experimental Results

We now present results on two high-dimensional text data sets to judge both clustering quality and balancing. The Newsgroup data set (news20) is a widely used compilation of documents from 20 usenet newsgroups, having naturally balanced clusters with approximately 1000 documents per newsgroup. We tested our algorithms on not only the original data set, but on a variety of subsets with differing characteristics to explore and understand the behavior of the balanced clustering algorithms. The Yahoo data set (yahoo) is a collection of 2340 Yahoo news articles belonging one of 20 different Yahoo categories, with cluster sizes ranging from 9 to 494. The data set helps in studying the effect of forcing balanced clustering in naturally unbalanced data.

Six algorithms are compared:

- Standard KMeans applied to the L_2 normalized version of the data, which makes a fairer comparison for text (applying KMeans on the original sparse high-dimensional data gives very poor results [17].)

- SPKMeans, the spherical kmeans algorithm [17] (see Section 8.3) that uses cosine similarity between data points and cluster representatives and has been shown to give good results on several benchmark text data sets [4, 17].

- SPKpr, a balanced clustering method that uses SPKMeans as the base clustering algorithm and uses both the populate (p) and refine (r) steps.

For lesion studies, three variants are considered in which one or more components of the proposed framework are missing.

- SPKpnr uses SPKMeans as the base clustering algorithm. It uses the populate (p) step, but does not refine (nr) the resulting clusters. The algorithm satisfies any given balancing constraints but need not give good results since the feasible solution is not refined.

- SPKgpnr also uses SPKMeans for clustering. It uses a greedy populate (gp) scheme where every point is assigned to the nearest cluster. Further, no refinements (nr) are done after the greedy populate step. Clearly, this algorithm is not guaranteed to satisfy balancing constraints.

- SPKgpr uses SPKmeans as the base clustering algorithm. It uses greedy populate (gp) to put points into clusters, but performs a full refinement (r) after that. The algorithm is not guaranteed to satisfy the balancing constraints since the populate step is greedy and the refinements do not start from a feasible clustering.

In a tabular form, the four algorithms can be presented as follows:

	No Refine	Refine	Balancing
Greedy Populate	SPKgpnr	SPKgpr	No Guarantee
Populate	SPKpnr	SPKpr	Guaranteed

Performance of the algorithms are evaluated using one measure for the quality of clustering and two measures for balance of cluster sizes. Since class labels are available for both data sets, a suitable indicator quality of clustering (without regard for balancing) is *normalized mutual information* (NMI) [47], which measures the agreement of the assigned cluster labels and the true class labels from the confusion matrix of the assignments. A value of 1 for NMI indicates perfect agreement. Quality of balancing is evaluated using two measures: (i) the *standard deviation in cluster sizes* (SDCS) and (ii) the *ratio between the minimum to expected* (RME) cluster sizes. The second measure highlights situations where some very small or empty clusters are obtained. All reported results have been averaged over 10 runs. All algorithms were started with the same random initialization for a given run to ensure fairness of comparison. Moreover, each run was started with a *different* random initialization.

Figure 8.1 shows the results on news20. Recollect that this is a typical high-dimensional text clustering problem where the true clusters are balanced. As shown in Figure 8.1(a), the balanced algorithms SPKpr and SPKpnr perform as good as SPKMeans, whereas the unconstrained algorithms SPKgpr and SPKgpnr do not perform as well. Clearly, the balancing constraints resulted in better results. KMeans does not perform as well as the other algorithms. Under a stricter balancing requirement in Figure 8.1(b), as before, SPKgpr performs marginally better than SPKpr, but the latter satisfies the balancing constraints. The same behavior is observed for SPKgpnr and its corresponding SPKpnr. Note that among the two balancing algorithms, SPKpr performs much better than SPKpnr, thereby showing the value of the refinement step. The same is observed for the unbalanced algorithms as well. Figure 8.1(c) shows the variation in NMI across balancing constraints for the right number of clusters. We note that the refined algorithms perform much better, although the constraints do decrease the performance by a little amount. Interestingly, both KMeans and SPKmeans achieve very low minimum balancing fraction. Figure 8.1(d) shows the standard deviation in cluster sizes. The balancing algorithms achieve the lowest standard deviations, as expected. Figures 8.1(e) and 8.1(f) show the minimum-to-average ratio of cluster sizes. Clearly, the balancing algorithms respect the constraints whereas the ratio gets really low for the other algorithms. For a large number of clusters, almost all the unconstrained algorithms start giving zero-sized clusters.

Figure 8.2 shows the results on yahoo. This is a very different data set from the previous data sets since the natural clusters are highly unbalanced with cluster sizes ranging from 9 to 494. The comparison on most measures of performance look similar to that of other data sets. The major difference is in the minimum-to-average ratio shown in Figures 8.2(e) and (f). As expected, the balanced algorithms SPKpr and SPKpnr respect the constraints. The other algorithms (except KMeans) start getting zero-sized clusters for quite low values of clusters. Also, as the balancing requirement becomes more strict (as in Figure 8.2(f)), the disparity between the balanced and other algorithms become more pronounced. Surprisingly, even for such an unbalanced data, the balanced algorithms, particularly SPKpr, perform almost as good as the unconstrained algorithms (Figure 8.2(c)).

Overall, the results show that the sampling based balanced clustering method is able to guarantee balancing properties with little or no compromise in matching cluster to class labels.

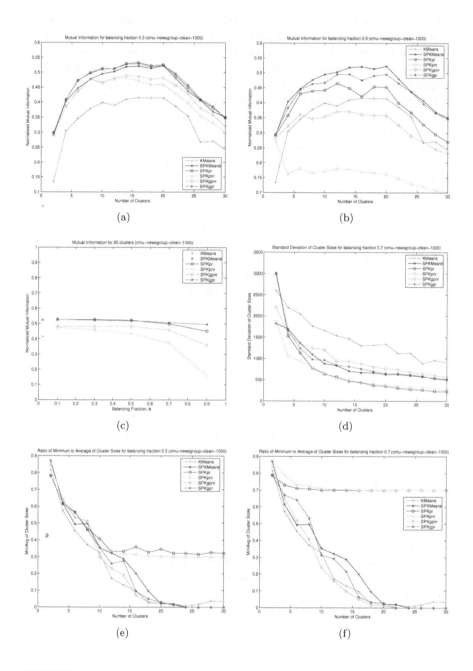

FIGURE 8.1: Results of applying the sampling based scalable balanced clustering framework on the news20 data set.

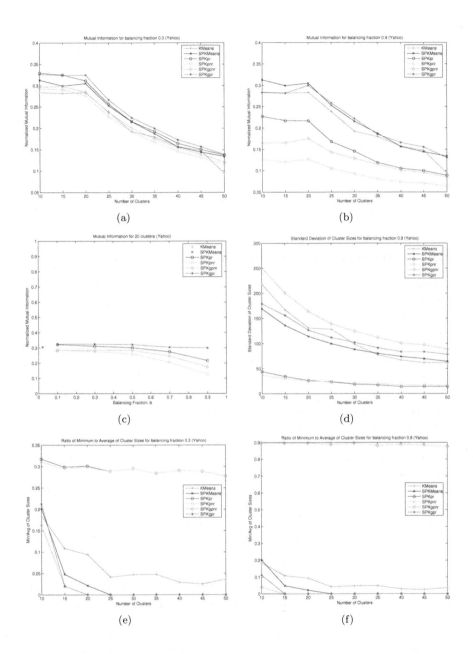

FIGURE 8.2: Results of applying the sampling based scalable balanced clustering framework on the yahoo data set.

8.3 Frequency Sensitive Approaches for Balanced Clustering

An alternative approach to obtain balanced clustering is via frequency sensitive competitive learning (FSCL) methods for clustering [1], where clusters of larger sizes are penalized so that points are less likely to get assigned to them. Such an approach can be applied both in the batch as well as in the online settings [5]. Although frequency sensitive assignments can give fairly balanced clusters in practice, there is no obvious way to guarantee that every cluster will have at least a pre-specified number of points. In this section, we first outline the basic idea in FSCL, and then discuss a case study in balanced clustering of directional data, with applications in text clustering.

8.3.1 Frequency Sensitive Competitive Learning

Competitive learning techniques employ winner-take-all mechanisms to determine the most responsive cell to a given input [22, 23, 44]. If this cell or exemplar then adjusts its afferent weights to respond even more strongly to the given input, the resultant system can be shown to perform unsupervised clustering. For example, the non-normalized competitive learning version of Rumelhart and Zipser [44], essentially yields an on-line analogue of the popular KMeans clustering algorithm. In its simplest form, one initializes k cluster prototypes or representatives, then visits the data points in arbitrary sequence. Each point is assigned to the nearest prototype (the "winner") which in turn moves a bit in the direction of the new point to get even closer to its most recent member. The kinship to KMeans is obvious. There are also soft competitive learning methods with multiple winners per input [53], that can be viewed as on-line analogues of soft batch-iterative clustering algorithms such as fuzzy c-means [10] as well as the expectation-maximization (EM)-based approach to clustering data modeled as a mixture of Gaussians [11].

To address the problem of obtaining clusters of widely varying sizes, a "conscience" mechanism was proposed for competitive learning [14] that made frequently winning representatives less likely to win in the future because of their heavier conscience. This work was followed by the notable frequency sensitive competitive learning (FSCL) method [1, 18]. FSCL was originally formulated to remedy the problem of under-utilization of parts of a codebook in vector quantization. In FSCL, the competitive computing units are penalized in proportion to the frequency of their winning, so that eventually all units participate in the quantization of the data space. Specifically, [1] proposed that each newly examined point $\mathbf{x}$ be assigned to the cluster h^* where $h^* = \arg\min_h \left\{ n_h \|\mathbf{x} - \boldsymbol{\mu}_h\|^2 \right\}$, and n_h is the number of points currently in the hth cluster with representative $\boldsymbol{\mu}_h$. Thus highly winning clusters, which have higher values of n_h, are discouraged from attracting new inputs. This also has the benefit of making the algorithm less susceptible to poor initialization. Convergence properties of the FSCL algorithm to a local minima have been studied by approximating the final phase of the FSCL by a diffusion process described by a Fokker-Plank equation [19].

Alternatively, suppose we initially start with a data model that is a mixture of identity co-variance Gaussians. Points are now sequentially examined. Each considered point is assigned to the most likely Gaussian (hard assignments), and simultaneously *shrink* the covariance of this Gaussian in proportion to the number of points that have been assigned to it so far. In this case one can show that the assignment rule will be [5]:

$$h^* = \arg\min_h \left\{ n_h \|\mathbf{x} - \boldsymbol{\mu}_h\|^2 + d \ln n_h \right\}. \tag{8.3}$$

Note that the empirically proposed FSCL method [1] only considers $n_h \|x - \boldsymbol{\mu}_h\|^2$ while a more formal treatment of the idea results in an extra second term, namely $d \ln n_h$.

8.3.2 Case Study: Balanced Clustering of Directional Data

In this section we show how the FSCL principle can applied to problems for which the domain knowledge indicates that data is directional [33]. For example, existing literature on document clustering often normalize the document vectors to unit length after all other preprocessing have been carried out. The cosine of the angle between two such normalized vectors then serves as the similarity measure between the two documents that they represent. Normalization prevents larger documents from dominating the clustering results. Normalization of high-dimensional vectors before clustering is also fruitful for market basket data analysis if one is interested in, say, grouping customers based on the similarities between the percentages of their money spent on the various products.

A suitable generative model for directional data sets is a mixture of von Mises-Fisher (vMF) distributions [33]. The vMF is an analogue of the Gaussian distribution on a hypersphere [4, 33] in that it is the maximum entropy distribution on the hypersphere when the first moment is fixed [29] under the constraint that the points are on a unit hypersphere. The density of a d-dimensional vMF distribution is given by

$$f(\mathbf{x}; \boldsymbol{\mu}, \kappa) = \frac{1}{Z_d(\kappa)} \exp\left(\kappa \mathbf{x}^T \boldsymbol{\mu}\right), \tag{8.4}$$

where $\boldsymbol{\mu}$ represents the mean direction vector of unit L_2 norm and κ is the concentration around the mean, analogous to the mean and covariance for the multivariate Gaussian distribution. The normalizing coefficient is

$$Z_d(\kappa) = (2\pi)^{d/2} I_{d/2-1}(\kappa)/\kappa^{d/2-1}, \tag{8.5}$$

where $I_r(y)$ is the modified Bessel function of the first kind and order r [35].

Suppose one applies expectation maximization (EM) to maximize the likelihood of fitting a mixture of vMF distributions to the data, assuming the same κ for each mixture component. Consider a special case where the E-step assigns each data point to the most likely vMF distribution to have generated it. This results in the simple assignment rule: $h^* = \arg\max_h \mathbf{x}^T \boldsymbol{\mu}_h$. The M-step, which involves computing the $\boldsymbol{\mu}_h, h = 1, \cdots, k$ using the current assignments of the data, results in updating the cluster means according to:

$$\boldsymbol{\mu}_h = \frac{\sum_{\mathbf{x} \in S_h} \mathbf{x}}{\| \sum_{\mathbf{x} \in S_h} \mathbf{x} \|}. \tag{8.6}$$

Hence the EM iterations become identical to the spherical kmeans (SPKMeans) algorithm, introduced by Dhillon et al. [17], and shown to be far superior to regular KMeans for document clustering. One can further show that the objective function to be minimized by this algorithm can be expressed as:

$$L(\{\boldsymbol{\mu}_h, S_h\}_{h=1}^k) = \frac{1}{n} \sum_{h=1}^k \sum_{\mathbf{x} \in S_h} \mathbf{x}^T \boldsymbol{\mu}_h. \tag{8.7}$$

L can be interpreted as the average *cosine similarity* (cosine of the angle) between any vector $\mathbf{x}$ and its cluster representative $\boldsymbol{\mu}_h$. It serves as an intrinsic measure of cluster quality and will be called the SPKMeans objective function.

A frequency sensitive version of the above method can be constructed by making κ inversely proportional to the number of points assigned to the corresponding distribution rather than keeping it constant. Thus, if n_h is the number of points assigned to S_h, then we set $\kappa_h \propto 1/n_h$. Thus, if a point $\mathbf{x}$ is such that $\mathbf{x}^T \boldsymbol{\mu}_1 = \mathbf{x}^T \boldsymbol{\mu}_2$ but $n_{h_1} < n_{h_2}$, then $\mathbf{x}$ has a higher likelihood of having been generated from S_{h_1} than S_{h_2} in the frequency sensitive setting. Hence, the likelihood of points going to clusters having fewer number of points increases and this implicitly discourages poor local solutions having empty clusters or clusters having a very small number of points. In [5] a hard assignment variant of EM was applied to such a frequency sensitive version of mixture of vMF distributions to obtain three algorithms:

- fs-SPKMeans, which is a direct extension of SPKMeans using frequency sensitive assignments;

- pifs-SPKMeans, a partially incremental version of fs-SPKMeans where the effective number of points per cluster are updated incrementally after processing every point and the mean of every cluster is updated in batch once in every iteration (after processing all the points); and

- fifs-SPKMeans, which is a fully incremental version of fs-SPKMeans where both the effective number of points per cluster and the cluster means are updated after processing every point.

All these algorithms need to know the number of points to be processed up-front and hence are applicable to static batch data. But suppose we are faced with streaming data and have limited storage available. Such situations are typical of non-stationary environments requiring continuous on-line adaptation [41]. The need for clustering streaming, normalized data is encountered, for example, for real-time incremental grouping of news stories or message alerts that are received on-line. For constructing a balanced, online variant of SPKMeans, we first note that a non-normalized mean $\boldsymbol{\mu}^{(t+1)}$ of $(t+1)$ data points can be written as a recursion in terms of $\boldsymbol{\mu}^{(t)}$ [50] as follows:

$$\boldsymbol{\mu}^{(t+1)} = \boldsymbol{\mu}^{(t)} + \frac{1}{t+1}(\mathbf{x}_{t+1} - \boldsymbol{\mu}^{(t)}) \, . \tag{8.8}$$

If the data is obtained from a stationary process, i.e., the parameters of the underlying generative model do not change with time, then $\boldsymbol{\mu}^{(t)}$, as computed by the above recursion will converge, and do not need updating after sufficiently large t. However, typical streaming data is non-stationary. There are two popular approaches taken in such cases: (i) If the data characteristics change abruptly, then such breakpoints can be detected, and a model is fitted for each segment (regime) between two successive breakpoints, assuming stationarity within such segments. Piecewise autoregressive modeling is an example of such an approach. (ii) If the data characteristics vary slowly over time, the problem may be addressed by discounting the past. In particular, a recursion can be used that keeps an exponentially decaying window over the history of observations and maintains the effective count c_{t+1} of the history rather than the exact $(t+1)$. More precisely, the approximate recursion for the mean [50] is given by:

$$\tilde{\boldsymbol{\mu}}^{(t+1)} = \tilde{\boldsymbol{\mu}}^{(t)} + \frac{1}{c_{t+1}}(\mathbf{x}_{t+1} - \tilde{\boldsymbol{\mu}}^{(t)}),$$

where $c_{t+1} = (1 - 1/L)c_t + 1$ and L is a large number [38, 42, 50]. Note that this exponential decay factor of $(1 - 1/L)$ ensures that c_{t+1} converges from below to L. Thus, after the "cold start" period is over, the history maintained in the computation has an effective length L. The choice of L depends on the degree of non-stationarity, and a fundamental trade-off between resolution and memory depth is encountered [40]. One can take a similar approach for approximating the normalized mean. Now, to make the frequency sensitive version of SPKMeans applicable to streaming data, as before, we want to make $\kappa_h \propto 1/n_h$. However, the number of points to be processed, n_h is unknown and may be unbounded. Using an exponential decay recursion for n_h so that $\tilde{n}_h^{(t+1)} = (1 - 1/L)\tilde{n}_h^{(t)} + 1$ and $\tilde{n}_h^{(0)} = 0$, one obtains [5]:

$$\tilde{\boldsymbol{\mu}}_h^{(t+1)} = \frac{\tilde{\boldsymbol{\mu}}_h^{(t)} + \frac{1}{\tilde{n}_h^{(t+1)}}(\mathbf{x}_{t+1} - \tilde{\boldsymbol{\mu}}_h^{(t)})}{\|\tilde{\boldsymbol{\mu}}_h^{(t)} + \frac{1}{\tilde{n}_h^{(t+1)}}(\mathbf{x}_{t+1} - \tilde{\boldsymbol{\mu}}_h^{(t)})\|}, \tag{8.9}$$

Also, the most likely distribution to have generated a particular point $\mathbf{x}_i$ is given by

$$h^* = \arg\max_h \frac{1}{\tilde{n}_h^{(t)}} \left\{ \mathbf{x}^T \tilde{\boldsymbol{\mu}}_h^{(t)} + 1 - \frac{\tilde{n}_h^{(t)}}{Ld} \log \tilde{n}_h^{(t)} \right\} . \qquad (8.10)$$

Using these results, algorithm sfs-SPKMeans, a variant of frequency sensitive SPKMeans applicable to streaming data, can be constructed.

8.3.3 Experimental Results

Let us now look at how the balanced variants of SPKMeans compare with the original version, using the same two data sets as in Section 8.2.2. In addition to the metrics used to gauge cluster quality and balancing in Section 8.2.2, we use an additional intrinsic measure of cluster quality, namely the SPKMeans *objective function* (SOF) value (8.7). Note that using this measure favors SPKMeans which optimizes this measure, while all the proposed methods attempt to optimize modified versions of this objective that also weave in balancing constraints. As before, all the results presented are averaged over 10 runs. The initial k means of the SPKMeans were generated by computing the mean of the entire data and making k small random perturbations to this mean [16]. For stability and repeatability, the frequency sensitive algorithms were initialized at points of local minima of the SPKMeans objective function.

8.3.3.1 Experiments with Batch Algorithms

For news20, fs-SPKMeans and fifs-SPKMeans show very similar behavior (Figure 8.3). pifs-SPKMeans has a high bias toward balancing, whereas SPKMeans has no explicit mechanism for balancing. All the algorithms achieve their individual highest values of the NMI at $k = 20$, which is the correct number of clusters (Figure 8.3(a)). At $k = 20$, fifs-SPKMeans and fs-SPKMeans perform better than the other two in terms of the NMI, and also show good balancing. For lower values of k, pifs-SPKMeans performs worse than the other three, which have quite similar behavior. For much higher values of k, SPKMeans has significantly higher values of NMI compared to the three proposed approaches, since it starts generating zero-sized clusters (Figure 8.3(d)) thereby maintaining the objective as well as NMI at a reasonable value. On the other hand, since none of the proposed algorithms generate zero-sized clusters, their performance in terms of NMI suffers. As seen from Figures 8.3(c),(d), pifs-SPKMeans has the most bias toward balancing, thereby achieving the lowest SDCS and the highest RME values for the entire range of k over which experiments were performed. It is interesting to note that fs-SPKMeans and fifs-SPKMeans seem to follow a middle ground in terms of cluster balancing and quality biases. Surprisingly, the SOF values for the proposed algorithms are equal or greater than those achieved by SPKMeans.

As mentioned earlier, yahoo is highly imbalanced in the true class sizes.

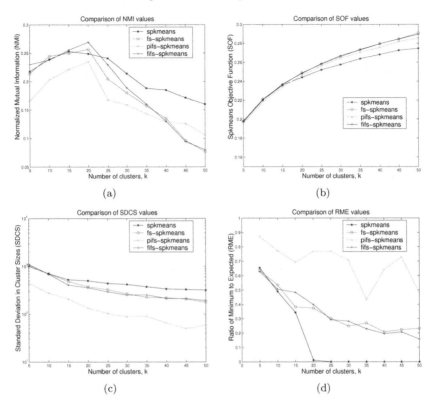

FIGURE 8.3: Comparison between the static frequency sensitive versions of spherical k-means on the News20 data: (a) the normalized mutual information values, (b) the SPKMeans objective function values, (c) the standard deviation in cluster sizes, and (d) the ratio of the minimum to expected cluster size values.

Hence, results on this data set show how the proposed algorithms handle the data when their balancing bias is not going to help. It is interesting to see that the performance of the algorithms in terms of the NMI is quite similar to what was observed for news20. As before fs-SPKMeans and fifs-SPKMeans perform very similarly and the NMI values they achieve deteriorate for values of k greater than 20, the correct number of clusters (Figure 8.4(a)). pifs-SPKMeans performs poorly in terms on the NMI because of its high bias toward balancing that does not help in this particular data set. It also performs slightly worse than the other algorithms in terms of the SOF values (Figure 8.4(b)). However, as before, it consistently gives the lowest SDCS (Figure 8.4(c)) and highest RME values (Figure 8.4(d)). SPKMeans maintains a reasonable value of the NMI even for large values of k by generating empty clusters. It is interesting to note that due to the fact that the natural clusters are not at all balanced, fs-SPKMeans and fifs-SPKMeans give quite low values of RME, but never actually give a zero-sized cluster in the range of k over which experiments were performed. Again, these two algorithms seem to have a good balance between the biases and can respond quite well to the underlying nature of the data set.

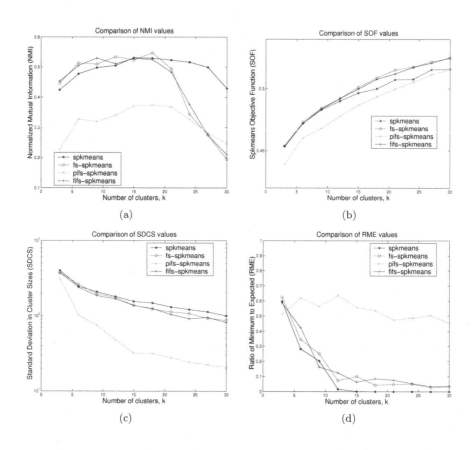

FIGURE 8.4: Comparison between the static frequency sensitive versions of spherical k-means on the Yahoo20 data: (a) the normalized mutual information values, (b) the SPKMeans objective function values, (c) standard deviation in cluster sizes, and (d) the ratio of the minimum to expected cluster size values.

Summary of Results: Both fs-SPKMeans and fifs-SPKMeans perform admirably when the value of k chosen is in the neighborhood of the number of classes in the data. They are comparable to or superior than SPKMeans in terms of cluster quality, and superior in terms of balancing. This result is particularly remarkable for yahoo, where the underlying classes have widely varying priors. This is indicative of the beneficial effect of the regularization provided by the soft balancing constraint. However, if k is chosen to be much larger than the number of natural clusters, SPKMeans has an advantage since it starts generating zero-sized clusters, while the others are now hampered by their proclivity to balance cluster sizes. On the other hand, if balancing is very critical, then pifs-SPKMeans is the best choice, but it has to compromise to some extent on cluster quality in order to achieve its superior balancing. So the choice of algorithm clearly depends on the nature of the data set and the clustering goals, but, in general, both fs-SPKMeans and fifs-SPKMeans are attractive even when balancing is not an objective.

8.3.3.2   Experiments with the Streaming Algorithm

The experiments with streaming algorithms were done by artificially "streaming" the static data sets. The data points are presented sequentially to the sfs-SPKMeans algorithm, repeating the process as many times as necessary in order to simulate streaming data. We call a sequence of showing every document in the selected data set once as an *epoch*, and the algorithm is run over multiple epochs until it converges or some preset maxEpoch value is reached. We now present results corresponding to two choices of L—100 and 1000. The corresponding algorithms are referred to as sfs100-SPKMeans and sfs1000-SPKMeans, respectively. Note that both of these values of L are less than the data set sizes. This means that sfs-SPKMeans has less effective memory than the static algorithms. In fact, such a low effective memory handicaps the streaming algorithm as compared to the static ones which use all the data to update their parameters. As we shall see, the streaming algorithm actually performs reasonably well even with this handicap. Additional results with other values of L are given in [5].

In news20, the streaming algorithms perform significantly better than the static ones in terms of the NMI (Figure 8.5(a)). The reason for this surprising result appears to be that since the natural clusters in the data are perfectly balanced and the streaming algorithms are biased toward balanced clustering, they get the correct structure in the data due to their bias. Further, the streaming approach is possibly avoiding bad local minima that affects the performance of KMeans and variants. Among the streaming algorithms, infs100-SPKMeans performs marginally better than infs1000-SPKMeans though the differences are not always significant. The SOF values for the static algorithms are significantly better than those achieved by the streaming algorithms (Figure 8.5(b)). There is no significant difference in the SDCS for the various algorithms (Figure 8.5(c)). The frequency sensitive algorithms perform better than SPKMeans in terms of the RME values, and the streaming algorithms give higher values of RME than fs-SPKMeans (Figure 8.5(d)).

In yahoo, the static algorithms seem to achieve higher values of NMI than

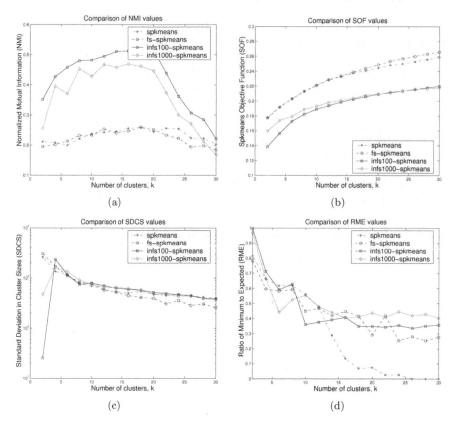

FIGURE 8.5: Comparison between streaming and static algorithms on the News20 data: (a) the normalized mutual information values, (b) the SPKMeans objective function values, (c) the standard deviation in cluster sizes, and (d) the ratio of the minimum to the expected cluster size values.

the streaming ones (Figure 8.6(a)). In the trade-off between balancing and cluster quality, the streaming algorithms seem to give more importance to the balancing aspect whereas the static ones seem to give higher priority to the cluster quality. The streaming algorithms, being biased toward the balancing criterion, perform poorly in terms of the NMI in this data set that has highly unbalanced natural clusters. Due to this bias, they give significantly better RME values as compared to the static algorithms (Figure 8.6(d)). Like news20, the SOF values achieved by the static algorithms are significantly better than those by the streaming ones (Figure 8.6(b)). Also, similar to news20, there is not much difference in the SDCS across all the algorithms (Figure 8.6(c)).

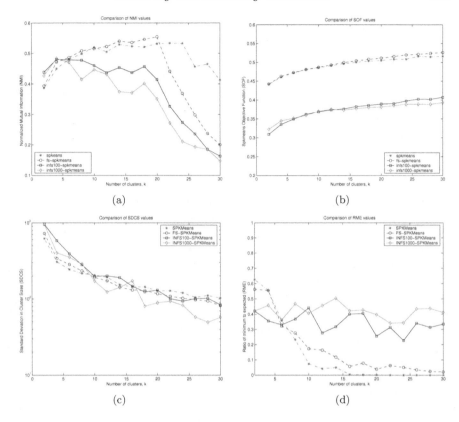

FIGURE 8.6: Comparison between streaming and static algorithms on the Yahoo20 data: (a) the normalized mutual information values, (b) the SPKMeans objective function values, (c) the standard deviation in cluster sizes, and (d) the ratio of minimum to the expected cluster size values.

8.4 Other Balanced Clustering Approaches

In this section, we first briefly comment on the balancing properties of commonly used clustering approaches and then discuss alternative approaches for balanced clustering.

We begin by noting that widely used clustering algorithms based on KMeans, expectation maximization (EM), and variants do not have any explicit way to guarantee that there is at least a certain minimum number of points per cluster, though, in theory, they have an implicit way of preventing highly skewed clusters [31]. For extreme situations when both the input dimensionality and the number of clusters is high, several researchers [9, 17, 24] have observed that KMeans and related variants quite often generate some clusters that are extremely small or even empty. Note that such imbalances arise in the assignment step, since the step of updating means does not directly govern cluster size. The cluster assignment step can be modified by solving a minimum cost flow problem satisfying constraints [9] on the cluster sizes, as was done in [20] to obtained balanced groupings in energy-aware sensor networks. However this approach is $O(N^3)$ and thus has poor scaling properties.

Agglomerative clustering methods also do not provide any guarantees on balancing. Complete link agglomerative clustering as well as Ward's method produce more compact clusters as compared to the single link or nearest neighbor agglomerative methods, but these clusters could be of widely varying sizes. Note that any agglomerative clustering method can be readily adapted so that once a cluster reaches a certain size in the bottom-up agglomeration process, it can be removed from further consideration. However, this may significantly impact cluster quality. Moreover, agglomerative clustering methods have a complexity of $\Omega(N^2)$ and hence do not scale well.

In contrast, certain top-down or divisive clustering methods tend to provide more balanced solutions. Most notable in this category is bisecting kmeans [46] which recursively partitions the current largest cluster into two clusters by solving a 2-means problem. If one ensures that the final split results in two clusters of the same size, then one can show that the largest cluster is no more than twice the size of the second largest one. However, no statement can be made of the smallest cluster size.

A pioneering study of constrained clustering in large databases was presented by Tung et al. [51]. They describe a variety of constraints that may be imposed on a clustering solution, but subsequently focus solely on a balancing constraint on certain key objects called pivot objects. They start with any clustering (involving *all* the objects) that satisfies the given constraints. This solution is then refined so as to reduce the clustering cost, measured as net dispersion from nearest representatives, while maintaining the constraint satisfaction. The refinement proceeds in two steps: pivot movement and deadlock resolution, both of which are shown to be NP-hard. They propose to scale their approach by compressing the objects into several tight "micro-clusters" [12] where possible, in a pre-clustering stage, and subsequently doing clustering at the micro-cluster level. Since this is a coarse grain solution, an option of finer grain resolution needs to be provided by allowing pivot points to be shared among multiple micro-clusters. This last facility helps to improve solution quality, but negates some of the computational savings in the process.

8.4.1 Balanced Clustering by Graph Partitioning

Of the very wide variety of approaches that have been proposed for clustering [21, 28], methods based on graph partitioning form the only general category that provides soft balancing. A clustering problem can be converted into a problem of graph partitioning as follows [30, 48]: A weighted graph is constructed whose vertices are the data points. An edge connecting two vertices has a weight proportional to the similarity between the corresponding data points. Thus vertices that represent very similar points are more strongly connected. The choice of the similarity measure quite often depends on the problem domain, e.g., Jaccard coefficient for market-baskets, normalized dot products for text, etc. If a pairwise distance value, d, is available instead of similarity, s, then it can be converted into a similarity value using a suitable inverse, monotonic relationship such as: $s = e^{-d^2}$ or $s = \frac{1}{1+d}$ [49]. Alternatively one can apply multi-dimensional scaling to the data to get an embedding into a low-dimensional vector space from which the distances can be obtained.

The weighted graph is then partitioned into k disjoint subgraphs by removing a set of edges, known as the "cut." The basic objective function is to minimize the size of this cut, which is calculated as the sum of the weights of all edges belonging to the cut. This tends to retain highly similar points in the same partition, which is also the objective of clustering. The simple min-cut objective has no balancing constraint, and may produce cuts that isolate a very small subset of the points from the rest, but are not of high quality from a clustering viewpoint. The balanced clustering objective functions based on graph partitioning are typically a normalized variant of the simple min-cut objective that ensures that the different partitions are comparable in size. Several ways of normalizing the cut using this added penalty are surveyed in [15], which also shows how graph clustering methods are related to kernel k-means. Note that the penalty term incorporated into the min-cut problem in order to obtain useful solutions explicitly provides a soft balancing constraint.

A case study of applying graph partitioning to balanced clustering of market baskets is given in [48]. In this work, the need for balancing came from a domain requirement of obtaining groups of customers so that (i) each group has about the same number of customers, or (ii) each group represents comparable revenue amounts. Both types of constraints were obtained through a suitable formulation of the efficient hierarchical "min-cut" algorithm, METIS [30], and a simple visualization scheme was used to show the balanced nature of the clusterings obtained.

Overall, graph partitioning or spectral clustering methods often give very good results, but they involve $\Omega(N^2)$ complexity in both memory requirements and computational complexity, since the size of the similarity matrix itself is N^2. In some situations, a similarity threshold can be used, so entries with similarity values less than the threshold are zeroed out. If the resultant graph is highly sparse, then more efficient storage and computational methods are available.

8.4.2 Model-Based Clustering with Soft Balancing

In model-based clustering, one estimates k probabilistic models from the N *objects* to be clustered, with each model representing a cluster. Perhaps the most well-known model-based technique is to fit a mixture of k multivariate Gaussians to a set of vectors using the EM algorithm. Here each Gaussian represents a cluster. But model-based clustering is a very general and versatile framework, catering to a wide variety of data types/datasets so long as reasonable probabilistic models are known for them [8, 13, 34, 54, 55]. For example, certain sets of strings are well-characterized using a mixture of hidden Markov models. For this reason, this section uses the term "objects" rather than "data points" for the entities being clustered.

When assigning object x to cluster y, the goal is to maximize the expected log-likelihood

$$L = \sum_{x} P(x) \sum_{y} P(y|x) \log p(x|\lambda_y), \tag{8.11}$$

where λ_y represents (the parameters of) model y [31]. Directly maximizing (8.11) over $P(y|x)$ and λ_y leads to a generic model-based k-means algorithm which iterates between the following two steps:

$$P(y|x) = \begin{cases} 1, \ y = \arg\max_{y'} \log p(x|\lambda_{y'}); \\ 0, \ \text{otherwise}, \end{cases} \tag{8.12}$$

and

$$\lambda_y = \arg\max_{\lambda} \sum_{x} P(y|x) \log p(x|\lambda_y) . \tag{8.13}$$

To make the data assignment step soft, one adds entropy terms to (8.11) [43], to get a modified objective: $L_1 = L + T \cdot H(Y|X) - T \cdot H(Y) = L - T \cdot I(X;Y)$, where $I(X;Y)$ is the mutual information between the set X of all objects and the set Y of all cluster indices. The parameter T is a Lagrange multiplier used to trade-off between maximizing the average log-likelihood L and minimizing the mutual information between X and Y, and can be interpreted as "temperature" using an analogy with deterministic annealing [43]. The net effect of the added term is to modify the assignment update to:

$$P(y|x) = \frac{P(y)p(x|\lambda_y)^{\frac{1}{T}}}{\sum_{y'} P(y)p(x|\lambda_{y'})^{\frac{1}{T}}}, \tag{8.14}$$

which now fractionally assigns each object to each cluster.

In [55], a simple but effective and efficient soft balancing strategy was proposed for the general soft model-based clustering framework described above. The key idea was to add another penalty that constrains the expected number of data objects in each cluster to be equal, rather than constraining the actual number of data objects in each cluster to be equal. In the resulting algorithm, the temperature parameter controls both the softness of clustering as well as that of balancing, and provides a useful knob for users to adjust the level of balancing.

The soft balancing constraints are expressed as:

$$\sum_x P(y|x) = \frac{N}{K}, \ \forall y \ , \tag{8.15}$$

and the modified Lagrangian is

$$L_2 = L_1 + \sum_x \xi_x \left(\sum_y P(y|x) - 1\right) + \sum_y \eta_y \left(\sum_x P(y|x) - M\right) , \tag{8.16}$$

where ξ_x and η_y are Lagrange multipliers. The resulting assignment step is now:

$$P(y|x) = \frac{P(y)\left[e^{\eta_y} p(x|\lambda_y)\right]^{\frac{1}{T}}}{\sum_{y'} P(y')\left[e^{\eta_{y'}} p(x|\lambda_{y'})\right]^{\frac{1}{T}}} . \tag{8.17}$$

For balanced clustering, it makes sense to set $P(y)$ to be $1/K$, which eliminates $P(y)$ from (8.17). Substituting (8.17) into (8.15) and some algebra results in an iterative formula for $\beta_y = e^{\eta_y}$ [55]:

$$\log \beta_y^{(t+1)} = T \cdot \log\left(\frac{N}{K}\right) - T \cdot \log\left(\sum_x \frac{e^{\frac{1}{T}\log p(x|\lambda_y)}}{\sum_{y'} e^{\frac{1}{T}\left(\log \beta_{y'}^{(t)} + \log p(x|\lambda_{y'})\right)}}\right), \tag{8.18}$$

where t is the iteration number, and $\log()$ is taken to avoid possible problems with very small likelihood values. For speedier computation, an annealing approach can be taken for computing $\log \beta_y$. That is, one starts from a high temperature (e.g., $T = 0.1$) and quickly lowers the temperature toward $T = 0.01$. At every temperature a small number of iterations are run after initializing $\log \beta_y$'s using the values computed from the previous temperature.

Compared to hard balancing, soft balancing for model-based clustering can be solved exactly and efficiently using the iterative strategy described above. If we fix the maximum number of iterations, the time complexity for computing $\log \beta$'s is $O(KN)$. Detailed derivations and experimental results that show the impact of temperature on balancing as well as on cluster quality can be found in [55].

8.5 Concluding Remarks

Obtaining a balanced solution is an explicit goal in certain clustering applications, irrespective of the underlying structure of the data. In other cases, obtaining clusters of comparable sizes is not a stated objective, but some amount of balancing helps in countering poor initializations in iterative clustering algorithms that converge only to a local optimum. In this chapter we covered a variety of methods for achieving scalable, balanced clustering. It will be instructive to carry out a detailed empirical comparison of the different approaches across different types data sets to further understand the strengths of each approach.

Another important issue that was not covered, however, is how to determine the appropriate number of clusters. This model selection issue in clustering has been extensively studied. Techniques range from information theoretic criteria [2, 45] for model comparison to purely Bayesian approaches such as reversible jump MCMC. But there is no universally accepted solution [28]. Moreover, not much work is available on model selection within a balanced clustering framework. One promising approach is to adapt competitive learning variants that add new clusters if need be as more data is encountered (see [53] and references cited therein). Alternatively, one can first obtain solutions for different values of k and then select a suitable one based on an appropriate model selection criterion that is modified to include a balancing criterion.

Acknowledgments

This research was supported in part by the Digital Technology Center Data Mining Consortium (DDMC) at the University of Minnesota, Twin Cities, and NSF grants IIS-0307792 and III-0713142.

References

[1] S. C. Ahalt, A. K. Krishnamurthy, P. Chen, and D. E. Melton. Competitive learning algorithms for vector quantization. *Neural Networks*, 3(3):277–290, 1990.

[2] H. Akaike. A new look at statistical model identification. *IEEE Transactions on Automatic Control*, AU-19:716–722, 1974.

[3] R. Baeza-Yates and B. Ribeiro-Neto. *Modern Information Retrieval*. Addison Wesley, New York, 1999.

[4] A. Banerjee, I. Dhillon, J. Ghosh, and S. Sra. Clustering on the unit

hypersphere using von Mises-Fisher distributions. *Journal of Machine Learning Research*, 6:1345–1382, 2005.

[5] A. Banerjee and J. Ghosh. Frequency sensitive competitive learning for balanced clustering on high-dimensional hyperspheres. *IEEE Transactions on Neural Networks*, 15(3):702–719, May 2004.

[6] A. Banerjee and J. Ghosh. Scalable clustering algorithms with balancing constraints. *Data Mining and Knowledge Discovery*, 13:265–295, Nov 2006.

[7] A. Banerjee, S. Merugu, I. Dhillon, and J. Ghosh. Clustering with Bregman divergences. *Journal of Machine Learning Research*, 6:1705–1749, 2005.

[8] J. D. Banfield and A. E. Raftery. Model-based Gaussian and non-Gaussian clustering. *Biometrics*, 49:803–821, 1993.

[9] K. Bennet and E. Bredensteiner. Duality and geometry in svm classifiers. In *Proceedings of the 17th International Conference on Machine Learning*, 2000.

[10] J. C. Bezdek and S. K. Pal. *Fuzzy Models for Pattern Recognition*. IEEE Press, Piscataway, NJ, 1992.

[11] J. A. Blimes. A gentle tutorial of the EM algorithm and its application to parameter estimation for Gaussian mixture and hidden Markov models. Technical report, UC Berkeley, April 1998.

[12] P. S. Bradley, U. M. Fayyad, and C. Reina. Scaling clustering algorithms to large databases. In *Proceedings of the 4th ACM SIGKDD International Conference on Knowledge Discovery and Data Mining*, pages 9–15, 1998.

[13] I. V. Cadez, S. Gaffney, and P. Smyth. A general probabilistic framework for clustering individuals and objects. In *Proceedings of the 6th ACM SIGKDD International Conference on Knowledge Discovery and Data Mining*, pages 140–149, Aug 2000.

[14] D. deSieno. Adding conscience to competitive learning. In *IEEE Annual International Conference on Neural Networks*, pages 1117–1124, 1988.

[15] I. Dhillon, Y. Guan, and B. Kulis. A unified view of kernel k-means, spectral clustering and graph clustering. In *UTCS Technical Report TR-04-05*, 2005.

[16] I. S. Dhillon, J. Fan, and Y. Guan. Efficient clustering of very large document collections. In R. Grossman, C. Kamath, V. Kumar, and R. Namburu, editors, *Data Mining for Scientific and Engineering Applications*. Kluwer Academic Publishers, 2001.

[17] I. S. Dhillon and D. S. Modha. Concept decompositions for large sparse text data using clustering. *Machine Learning*, 42(1):143–175, 2001.

[18] A. S. Galanopoulos and S. C. Ahalt. Codeword distribution for frequency sensitive competitive learning with one-dimensional input data. *IEEE Transactions on Neural Networks*, 7(3):752–756, 1996.

[19] A. S. Galanopoulos, R. L. Moses, and S. C. Ahalt. Diffusion approximation of frequency sensitive competitive learning. *IEEE Transactions on Neural Networks*, 8(5):1026–1030, Sept 1997.

[20] S. Ghiasi, A. Srivastava, X. Yang, and M. Sarrafzadeh. Optimal energy aware clustering in sensor networks. *Sensors*, 2:258–269, 2002.

[21] J. Ghosh. Scalable clustering. In N. Ye, editor, *The Handbook of Data Mining*, pages 247–277. Lawrence Erlbaum, 2003.

[22] S. Grossberg. Adaptive pattern classification and universal recoding: 1. Parallel development and coding of neural feature detectors. *Biological Cybernetics*, 23:121–134, 1976.

[23] S. Grossberg. Competitive learning: From interactive action to adaptive resonance. *Cognitive Science*, 11:23–63, 1987.

[24] Y. Guan, A. Ghorbani, and N. Belacel. Y-means: A clustering method for intrusion detection. In *Proceedings Canadian Conference on Electrical and Computer Engineering*, pages 1083–1086, May 2003.

[25] G. Gupta and M. Younis. Load-balanced clustering of wireless networks. In *Proceedings IEEE International Conference on Communications*, volume 3, pages 1848–1852, May 2003.

[26] G. K. Gupta and J. Ghosh. Detecting seasonal trends and cluster motion visualization for very high dimensional transactional data. In *Proceedings First SIAM Conference on Data Mining*, pages 115–129, 2001.

[27] D. Gusfield and R. W. Irving. *The Stable Marriage Problem: Structure and Algorithms*. MIT Press, Cambridge, MA, 1989.

[28] A. K. Jain and R. C. Dubes. *Algorithms for Clustering Data*. Prentice Hall, New Jersey, 1988.

[29] J. N. Kapur and H. K. Kesavan. *Entropy Optimization Principles with Applications*. Academic Press, 1992.

[30] G. Karypis and V. Kumar. A fast and high quality multilevel scheme for partitioning irregular graphs. *SIAM Journal on Scientific Computing*, 20(1):359–392, 1998.

[31] M. Kearns, Y. Mansour, and A. Ng. An information-theoretic analysis of hard and soft assignment methods for clustering. In *Proceedings of the*

13th Annual Conference on Uncertainty in Artificial Intelligence (UAI), pages 282–293, 1997.

[32] P. J. Lynch and S. Horton. *Web Style Guide: Basic Design Principles for Creating Web Sites*. Yale University Press, 2002.

[33] K. V. Mardia. Statistics of directional data. *Journal of the Royal Statistical Society, Series B (Methodological)*, 37(3):349–393, 1975.

[34] G. McLachlan and K. Basford. *Mixture Models: Inference and Applications to Clustering*. Marcel Dekker, New York, 1988.

[35] N. W. McLachlan. *Bessel Functions for Engineers*. Oxford University Press, 1955.

[36] D. Modha and S. Spangler. Feature weighting in k-means clustering. *Machine Learning*, 52(3):217–237, 2003.

[37] R. Motwani and P. Raghavan. *Randmized Algorithms*. Cambridge University Press, 1995.

[38] R. M. Neal and G. E. Hinton. A view of the EM algorithm that justifies incremental, sparse, and other variants. In M. I. Jordan, editor, *Learning in Graphical Models*, pages 355–368. MIT Press, 1998.

[39] Neilson Marketing Research. *Category Management: Positioning Your Organization to Win*. McGraw-Hill, 1993.

[40] J. C. Principe, J.-M. Kuo, and S. Celebi. An analysis of the gamma memory in dynamic neural networks. *IEEE Transactions on Neural Networks*, 5:331–337, March 1994.

[41] V. Ramamurti and J. Ghosh. On the use of localized gating in mixtures of experts networks. In *(invited paper), SPIE Conference on Applications and Science of Computational Intelligence, SPIE Proceedings, Volume 3390*, pages 24–35, Orlando, FL, April 1998.

[42] V. Ramamurti and J. Ghosh. Structurally adaptive modular networks for nonstationary environments. *IEEE Transactions on Neural Networks*, 10(1):152–160, 1999.

[43] K. Rose. Deterministic annealing for clustering, compression, classification, regression, and related optimization problems. *Proceedings of the IEEE*, 86(11):2210–39, 1998.

[44] D. E. Rumelhart and D. Zipser. Feature discovery by competive learning. *Cognitive Science*, 9:75–112, 1985.

[45] G. Schwatz. Estimating the dimension of a model. *The Annals of Statistics*, 6(2):461–464, 1978.

[46] M. Steinbach, G. Karypis, and V. Kumar. A comparison of document clustering techniques. In *KDD Workshop on Text Mining*, 2000.

[47] A. Strehl and J. Ghosh. Cluster ensembles – a knowledge reuse framework for combining partitionings. *Journal of Machine Learning Research*, 3(3):583–617, 2002.

[48] A. Strehl and J. Ghosh. Relationship-based clustering and visualization for high-dimensional data mining. *INFORMS Journal on Computing*, 15(2):208–230, 2003.

[49] A. Strehl, J. Ghosh, and R. Mooney. Impact of similarity measures on web-page clustering. In *Proceedings of the 7th National Conference on Artificial Intelligence: Workshop of AI for Web Search*, pages 58–64. AAAI, July 2000.

[50] H. G. C. Traven. A neural network approach to statistical pattern classification by "semiparametric" estimation of probability density functions. *IEEE Transactions on Neural Networks*, 2(3):366–377, 1991.

[51] A. K. H. Tung, R. T. Ng, L. V. S. Laksmanan, and J. Han. Constraint-based clustering in large databses. In *Proceedings of the International Conference on Database Theory (ICDT'01)*, Jan 2001.

[52] Y. Yang and B. Padmanabhan. Segmenting customer transactions using a pattern-based clustering approach. In *Proceedings of the Third IEEE International Conference on Data Mining*, pages 411–419, Nov 2003.

[53] Y. J. Zhang and Z. Q. Liu. Self-splitting competitive learning: A new on-line clustering paradigm. *IEEE Transactions on Neural Networks*, 13(2):369–380, March 2002.

[54] S. Zhong and J. Ghosh. Scalable, balanced, model-based clustering. In *Proceedings of the 3rd SIAM Conference on Data Mining*, pages 71–82, April 2003.

[55] S. Zhong and J. Ghosh. A unified framework for model-based clustering. *Journal of Machine Learning Research*, 4:1001–1037, 2003.

Chapter 9

Using Assignment Constraints to Avoid Empty Clusters in k-Means Clustering

Ayhan Demiriz

Sakarya University, `ademiriz@gmail.com`

Kristin P. Bennett

Rensselaer Polytechnic Inst., `bennek@rpi.edu`

Paul S. Bradley

Apollo Data Technologies, `paul@apollodatatech.com`

Abstract   We consider practical methods for adding constraints to the k-means clustering algorithm in order to avoid local solutions with empty clusters or clusters having very few points. We often observe this phenomena when applying k-means to data sets where the number of dimensions is $d \geq 10$ and the number of desired clusters is $k \geq 20$. Moreover, recent studies have shown successful formulations of various other types of constraints. Particularly, must-link and cannot-link types constraints have been studied in several papers. An appropriate objective function needs to be constructed to find clusters that satisfy minimum capacity, must-link and cannot-link pairwise constraints at the same time. Obviously, it requires an analysis of the applicability and the level of complexity of the constraint types.

We propose explicitly adding k constraints to the underlying clustering optimization problem requiring that each cluster have at least a minimum number of points in it, i.e., minimum capacity. We then investigate the resulting cluster assignment step. Numerical tests on real data sets indicate that the constrained approach is less prone to poor local solutions, producing a better summary of the underlying data. We also successfully formulate extended optimization models to cover other types of assignment constraints, specifically pairwise assignment constraints as well.

9.1   Introduction

The k-means clustering algorithm [16] has become a workhorse for the data analyst in many diverse fields. One drawback to the algorithm occurs when it is applied to data sets with n data points in $d \geq 10$ dimensional real space $\mathbb{R}^d$ and the number of desired clusters is $k \geq 20$. In this situation, the k-means algorithm often converges with one or more clusters which are either empty or summarize very few data points (i.e., one data point). Preliminary tests on clustering sparse 300-dimensional web-browsing data indicate that k-means frequently converges with truly empty clusters. For $k = 50$ and $k = 100$, on average 4.1 and 12.1 clusters are empty.

Incorporating prior knowledge, whether in the form of firmly defining the number of non-empty clusters or pairwise relationships, is very essential in partially supervised clustering. Like the general clustering problem, the partially supervised clustering problem can also be posed as an optimization problem. With partial supervision, the underlying clustering model can be used to prevent poor local solutions.

We propose explicitly adding k constraints to the underlying clustering optimization problem requiring that cluster h contain at least τ_h points. We focus on the resulting changes to the k-means algorithm and compare the results from standard k-means and the proposed constrained k-means algorithms. Empirically, for modest values of τ_h, solutions are obtained that better summarize the underlying data.

Since clusters with very few or no data points may be artifacts of poor local minima, typical approaches to handling them within the standard k-means framework include re-running the algorithm with new initial cluster centers or checking the cluster model at algorithm termination, resetting empty clusters, and re-running the algorithm. Our approach avoids the additional computation of these heuristics which may still produce clusters with too few points. In addition to providing a well-posed mathematical way to avoid small clusters, this work can be generalized to other constraints ensuring desirable clustering solutions (e.g., outlier removal or specified groupings) and to expectation-maximization probabilistic clustering.

Alternatively, empty clusters can be regarded as desirable "natural" regularizers of the cluster model. This heuristic argument states that if the data does not "support" k clusters, then allowing clusters to go empty, and hence reducing the value of k, is a desirable side effect. But there are applications in which, given a value of k, one desires to have a cluster model with k non-empty clusters. These include the situation when the value of k is known a priori and applications in which the cluster model is utilized as a compressed version of a specific data set [5, 19].

A significant part of this chapter is based on our earlier work in [8]. However we extend our formulations in this chapter to cover pairwise assignment constraints and a new constraint on minimum capacity on labeled points assigned to each cluster. The remaining portion of the chapter is organized as follows. Section 9.2 formalizes the constrained clustering optimization problem and outlines the algorithm computing a locally optimal solution. The sub-problem of computing cluster assignments so that cluster h contains at least τ_h points is discussed in Section 9.3. Section 9.4 presents numerical evaluation of the algorithm in comparison with the standard k-means implementation on real data sets. We report results on both small and large data sets in Section 9.4. In addition to constrained k-means results, we report also constrained k-median results and compare them. In Section 9.5, we provide a wide variety of extensions to our base model to incorporate new types of assignment constraints and Section 9.6 concludes the chapter.

9.2 Constrained Clustering Problem and Algorithm

Given a data set $\mathcal{X} = \{x_i\}_{i=1}^n$ of n points in $\mathbb{R}^d$ and a number k of desired clusters, the k-means clustering problem is as follows. Find cluster centers $\mu_1, \mu_2, \ldots, \mu_k$ in $\mathbb{R}^d$ such that the sum of the 2-norm distance squared between each point x_i and its *nearest* cluster center μ_h is minimized. Specifically:

$$\min_{\mu_1,\ldots,\mu_k} \sum_{i=1}^n \min_{h=1,\ldots,k} \left(\frac{1}{2} \|x_i - \mu_h\|^2 \right). \tag{9.1}$$

By [10, Lemma 2.1], Problem (9.1) is equivalent to the following problem where the min operation in the summation is removed by introducing "selection" variables $T_{i,h}$:

$$\begin{aligned} \underset{\mu,T}{\text{minimize}} \quad & \sum_{i=1}^n \sum_{h=1}^k T_{i,h} \cdot \left(\frac{1}{2} \|x_i - \mu_h\|^2 \right) \\ \text{s.t.} \quad & \sum_{h=1}^k T_{i,h} = 1, \ i = 1, \ldots, n, \\ & T_{i,h} \geq 0, \ i = 1, \ldots, n, \ h = 1, \ldots, k. \end{aligned} \tag{9.2}$$

Note that $T_{i,h} = 1$ if data point x_i is closest to center μ_h and zero otherwise.

Problem (9.2), or equivalently (9.1), is solved by the k-means algorithm iteratively. In each iteration, Problem (9.2) is solved first for $T_{i,h}$ with the cluster centers μ_h fixed. Then, (9.2) is solved for μ_h with the assignment variables $T_{i,h}$ fixed. The stationary point computed satisfies the Karush-Kuhn-Tucker (KKT) conditions [17] for Problem (9.2), which are necessary for optimality.

k-Means Clustering Algorithm Given a database $\mathcal{X}$ of n points in $\mathbb{R}^d$ and cluster centers $\mu_{1,t}, \mu_{2,t}, \ldots, \mu_{k,t}$ at iteration t, compute $\mu_{1,t+1}, \mu_{2,t+1}, \ldots, \mu_{k,t+1}$ at iteration $t+1$ in the following 2 steps:

1. **Cluster Assignment.** For each data record $x_i \in \mathcal{X}$, assign x_i to cluster $h(i)$ such that center $\mu_{h(i),t}$ is nearest to x_i in the 2-norm.

2. **Cluster Update.** Compute $\mu_{h,t+1}$ as the mean of all points assigned to cluster h.

Stop when $\mu_{h,t+1} = \mu_{h,t}$, $h = 1, \ldots, k$, else increment t by 1 and go to step 1.

Suppose cluster h is empty when Algorithm 9.2 terminates, i.e., $\sum_{i=1}^{n} T_{i,h} = 0$. The solution computed by Algorithm 9.2 in this case satisfies the KKT conditions for Problem (9.2). Hence, it is plausible that the standard k-means algorithm may converge with empty clusters. In practice, we observe this phenomenon when clustering high-dimensional data sets with a large number of clusters.

The KKT conditions [17] for Problem (9.2) are:

$$\sum_{h=1}^{k} T_{i,h} = 1 \,\forall i, \; T_{i,h} \geq 0 \,\forall i, h,$$

$$\|x_i - \mu_h\|^2 = \min_{\tilde{h}=1,\ldots,k} \|x_i - \mu_{\tilde{h}}\|^2 \Leftrightarrow T_{i,h} \geq 0,$$

$$\sum_{i=1}^{n} T_{i,h} > 0 \Rightarrow \mu_h = \frac{\sum_{i=1}^{n} T_{i,h} x_i}{\sum_{i=1}^{n} T_{i,h}}$$

$$\sum_{i=1}^{n} T_{i,h} = 0 \Rightarrow \mu_h \text{ arbitrary.}$$

To avoid solutions with empty clusters, we propose explicitly adding constraints to Problem (9.2) requiring that cluster h contain at least τ_h data points, where $\sum_{h=1}^{k} \tau_h \leq n$. This yields the following constrained k-means problem:

$$\underset{\mu,T}{\text{minimize}} \quad \sum_{i=1}^{n}\sum_{h=1}^{k} T_{i,h} \cdot \left(\frac{1}{2}\|x_i - \mu_h\|^2 \right)$$

$$\sum_{i=1}^{n} T_{i,h} \geq \tau_h, \; h = 1, \ldots, k \qquad (9.3)$$

s.t.

$$\sum_{h=1}^{k} T_{i,h} = 1, \; i = 1, \ldots, n,$$

$$T_{i,h} \geq 0, \; i = 1, \ldots, n, \; h = 1, \ldots, k.$$

Like the classic k-means algorithm, we propose an iterative algorithm to solve (9.3).

Constrained k-Means Clustering Algorithm Given a database $\mathcal{X}$ of n points in $\mathbb{R}^d$, minimum cluster membership values $\tau_h \geq 0$, $h = 1, \ldots, k$ and cluster centers $\mu_{1,t}, \mu_{2,t}, \ldots, \mu_{k,t}$ at iteration t, compute $\mu_{1,t+1}, \mu_{2,t+1}, \ldots, \mu_{k,t+1}$ at iteration $t+1$ in the following 2 steps:

1. **Cluster Assignment.** Let $T_{i,h}^t$ be a solution to the following linear program with $\mu_{h,t}$ fixed:

$$\underset{T}{\text{minimize}} \quad \sum_{i=1}^{n}\sum_{h=1}^{k} T_{i,h} \cdot \left(\frac{1}{2}\|x_i - \mu_{h,t}\|^2 \right)$$

$$\sum_{i=1}^{n} T_{i,h} \geq \tau_h, \; h = 1, \ldots, k \qquad (9.4)$$

s.t.

$$\sum_{h=1}^{k} T_{i,h} = 1, \; i = 1, \ldots, n,$$

$$T_{i,h} \geq 0, \; i = 1, \ldots, n, \; h = 1, \ldots, k.$$

2. **Cluster Update.** Update $\mu_{h,t+1}$ as follows:

$$\mu_{h,t+1} = \begin{cases} \dfrac{\sum_{i=1}^{n} T_{i,h}^t x_i}{\sum_{i=1}^{n} T_{i,h}^t} & \text{if } \sum_{i=1}^{n} T_{i,h}^t > 0, \\[4mm] \mu_{h,t} & \text{otherwise.} \end{cases}$$

Stop when $\mu_{h,t+1} = \mu_{h,t}$, $h = 1, \ldots, k$, else increment t by 1 and go to step 1.

Like the traditional k-means approach, the constrained k-means algorithm iterates between solving (9.3) in $T_{i,h}$ for fixed μ_h, then solving (9.3) in μ_h for fixed $T_{i,h}$. We end this section by with a finite termination result similar to [9, Theorem 7].

PROPOSITION 9.1

The constrained k-means algorithm 9.2 terminates in a finite number of iterations at a cluster assignment that is locally optimal. Specifically, the objective function of (9.3) cannot be decreased by either reassignment of a point to a different cluster, while maintaining $\sum_{i=1}^{n} T_{i,h} \geq \tau_h$, $h = 1, \ldots, k$, or by defining a new cluster center for any of the clusters.

PROOF At each iteration, the cluster assignment step cannot increase the objective function of (9.3). The cluster update step will either strictly decrease the value of the objective function of (9.3) or the algorithm will terminate since

$$\mu_{h,t+1} = \arg\min_{\mu} \sum_{i=1}^{n} \sum_{h=1}^{k} T_{i,h}^{t} \cdot \left(\frac{1}{2} \|x_i - \mu_h\|^2 \right)$$

is a strictly convex optimization problem with a unique global solution. Since there are a finite number of ways to assign n points to k clusters so that cluster h has at least τ_h points, since Algorithm 9.2 does not permit repeated assignments, and since the objective of (9.3) is strictly non-increasing and bounded below by zero, the algorithm must terminate at some cluster assignment that is locally optimal. □

Although our problem formulation is given for the constrained k-means algorithm, by utilizing a 1-norm cost function and using a 1-norm distance metric for the cluster assignment and update steps we can readily extend our formulation to run the constrained k-median algorithm. In the next section we discuss solving the linear program sub-problem in the cluster assignment step of Algorithm 9.2 as a minimum cost network flow problem.

9.3 Cluster Assignment Sub-Problem

The form of the constraints in the cluster assignment sub-problem (9.4) make it equivalent to a minimum cost flow (MCF) linear network optimization problem [6]. This is used to show that the optimal cluster assignment will place each point in exactly one cluster and can be found using fast network

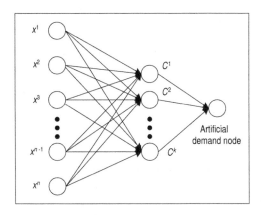

FIGURE 9.1: Equivalent minimum cost flow formulation of (9.4).

simplex algorithms. In general, a MCF problem has an underlying graph structure. Let $\mathcal{N}$ be the set of nodes. Each node $i \in \mathcal{N}$ has associated with it a value b_i indicating whether it is a supply node ($b_i > 0$), a demand node ($b_i < 0$), or a transshipment node ($b_i = 0$). If $\sum_{i \in \mathcal{N}} b_i = 0$, the problem is feasible (i.e., the sum of the supplies equals the sum of the demands). Let $\mathcal{A}$ be the set of directed arcs. For each arc $(i, j) \in \mathcal{A}$, the variable $y_{i,j}$ indicates the amount of flow on the arc. Additionally, for each arc (i, j), the constant $c_{i,j}$ indicates the cost of shipping one unit flow on the arc. The MCF problem is to minimize $\sum_{(i,j) \in \mathcal{A}} c_{i,j} \cdot y_{i,j}$ subject to the sum of the flow leaving node i minus the sum of flow incoming is equal to b_i. Specifically, the general MCF is:

$$\underset{y}{\text{minimize}} \quad \sum_{(i,j) \in \mathcal{A}} c_{i,h} \cdot y_{i,j}$$

$$\text{s.t.} \quad \sum_{j} y_{i,j} - \sum_{j} y_{j,i} = b_i, \forall i \in \mathcal{N}$$

$$0 \leq y_{i,j} \leq u_{i,j}, \forall (i,j) \in \mathcal{A}.$$

Let each data point x_i correspond to a supply node with supply $= 1$ ($b_{x_i} = 1$). Let each cluster μ_h correspond to a demand node with demand $b_{\mu_h} = -\tau_h$. Let there be an arc in $\mathcal{A}$ for each (x_i, μ_h) pair. The cost on arc (x_i, μ_h) is $\|x_i - \mu_h\|^2$. To satisfy the constraint that the sum of the supplies equals the sum of the demands, we need to add an artificial demand node a with demand $b_a = -n + \sum_{h=1}^{k} \tau_h$. There are arcs from each cluster node μ_h to a with zero cost. There are no arcs to or from the data point nodes x_i to the artificial node a. See Figure 9.1. Specifically, let $\mathcal{N} = \{x_i, i = 1, \ldots, n\} \cup \{\mu_h, h = 1, \ldots, k\} \cup \{a\}$. Let $\mathcal{A} = \{(x_i, \mu_h), x_i, \mu_h \in \mathcal{N}\} \cup \{(\mu_h, a), \mu_h \in \mathcal{N}\}$. With these identifications and the costs, supplies, and demands above, (9.4) has an equivalent MCF formulation. This equivalence allows us to state the following proposition that integer values of $T_{i,h}$ are optimal for (9.4).

PROPOSITION 9.2
If each τ_h, $h = 1, \ldots, k$ is an integer, then there exists an optimal solution of (9.4) such that $T_{i,h} \in \{0, 1\}$.

PROOF Consider the equivalent MCF formulation of (9.4). Since $b_{x_i} = 1, \forall x_i \in \mathcal{N}$, $b_{\mu_h} = -\tau_h$, and $b_a = -n + \sum_{h=1}^{k} \tau_h$ are all integers, it follows from [6, Proposition 2.3] that an optimal flow vector y is integer-valued. The optimal cluster assignment values $T_{i,h}$ correspond y_{x_i,μ_h} and, since each node x_i has 1 unit of supply, the maximum value of $T_{i,h}$ at a solution is 1. ☐

Hence, we are able to obtain optimal $\{0, 1\}$ assignments without having to solve a much more difficult integer programming problem. In addition to deriving the integrality result of Proposition 9.2, the MCF formulation allows one to solve (9.4) via codes specifically tailored to network optimization [6]. These codes usually run 1 or 2 orders of magnitude faster than general linear programming (LP) codes.

9.4   Numerical Evaluation

We conducted two different sets of experiments on machine learning benchmark data sets provided in [1]. In the first set of experiments, we report results using two real data sets: the Johns Hopkins Ionosphere data set and the Wisconsin Diagnostic Breast Cancer data set (WDBC) [1]. The results from the first set of experiments are also reported in [8].

The Ionosphere data set contains 351 data points in $\mathbb{R}^{33}$ and values along each dimension were normalized to have mean 0 and standard deviation 1. The WDBC data set subset consists of 683 normalized data points in $\mathbb{R}^9$. The values of τ_h (denoted by τ) were set equally across all clusters. The ILOG CPLEX 6.5 LP solver was used for cluster assignment. For initial cluster centers sampled uniformly on the range of the data, k-means produced at least 1 empty cluster in 10 random trials on WDBC for $k \geq 30$ and on Ion for $k \geq 20$. Figures 9.2 and 9.3 give the results for initial clusters chosen randomly from the data set. This simple technique can eliminate many empty clusters. Figure 9.2 shows the frequency with which the standard k-means algorithm 9.2 converges to clusters having fewer than τ points.

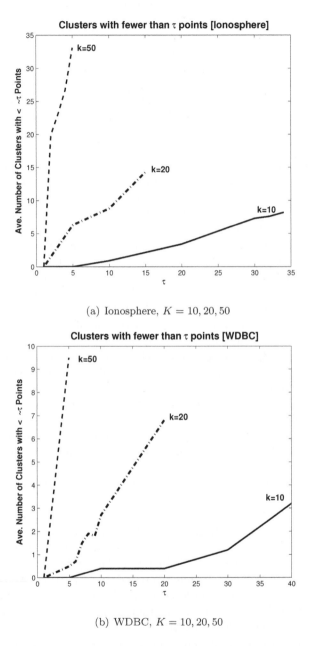

(a) Ionosphere, $K = 10, 20, 50$

(b) WDBC, $K = 10, 20, 50$

FIGURE 9.2: Average number of clusters with fewer than τ data points computed by the standard k-means algorithm 9.2.

The effect on the quality of the clustering by the constraints imposed by the constrained k-means Algorithm 9.2 is quantified by the ratio of the average objective function of (9.1) computed at the constrained k-means solution over that of the standard k-means solution. Adding constraints to any minimization problem can never decrease the **globally** optimal objective value. Thus we would expect this ratio to be greater than 1. Surprisingly the constrained k-means algorithm frequently found better local minima (ratios less than 1) than did the standard k-means approach. This might be due to a local solution with a large cluster, some other clusters with few points, and/or even empty clusters. Note that the same starting points were used for both algorithms. Results are summarized in Figure 9.3. Notice that for a fixed k, solutions computed by constrained k-means are equivalent to standard k-means for small τ-values. For large τ-values, the constrained k-means solution is often inferior to those of standard k-means. In this case, to satisfy the τ-constraints, the algorithm must group together points which are far apart resulting in a higher objective value. For a given data set, superior clustering solutions are computed by the constrained k-means algorithm when τ is chosen in conjunction with k. For small values of k (e.g., $k = 5$) we observe ratios < 1 up to $\tau = 50$ (maximum tested) on Ionosphere. For $k = 20$, we begin to see ratios > 1 for $\tau = 10$. Similar results are observed on WDBC.

For given values of k and τ_h, $h = 1, \ldots, k$, an effort is made so that the τ_h constraints are satisfied by the initial cluster centers and the final cluster centers computed by k-means. Initial cluster centers where chosen by randomly selecting k data points. If the number of points in cluster h is $< \tau_h$, then a new set of initial cluster centers are chosen. This is repeated until the thresholds τ_h, $h = 1, \ldots, k$ are satisfied or until 50 sets of initial centers have been tried. The k-means Algorithm 9.2 is applied. If, at convergence, the τ_h thresholds are not satisfied, and the entire initialization procedure is repeated (at most 10 times). The initial centers used for k-means are then also used to initialize constrained k-means. With this initialization strategy, for all values of k and $\tau_h > 1$ tested, k-means often converges with clusters violating the τ_h constraints.

The second set of experiments was run over a higher-dimensional data set derived from web-browsing behavior to a large internet portal. The browsing history for a group of 10,144 randomly selected users to 300 of the most popular news category stories was generated. This data set can be viewed as 10,144 data points in $\mathbb{R}^{300}$. We refer to this data set as the "Web Data Set." In order to handle this larger data set, we modify our original MATLAB code and utilize MOSEK 4.0 as the linear programming solver [18], which can be seamlessly integrated with MATLAB.

In addition to running k-means and constrained k-means algorithms, we also report results from k-median [10] and constrained k-median algorithms by using the 1-norm distance metric as mentioned in Section 9.2. The k-median clustering algorithm uses the median value in updating the cluster centers instead of using the average in the case of the k-means algorithm. Since we

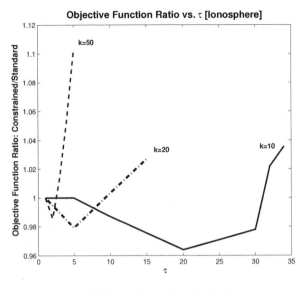

(a) Ionosphere, $K = 10, 20, 50$

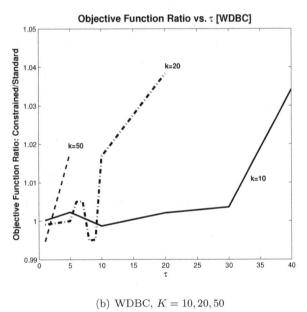

(b) WDBC, $K = 10, 20, 50$

FIGURE 9.3: Average ratio of objective function (9.1) computed at the constrained k-means solution over that of the standard k-means solution versus τ.

TABLE 9.1: k-Means and Constrained k-means Results on Web Data Set for $k=20$

τ	k-means			Constrained k-means	
	Objective ($\pm \sigma$)	Time (Sec.)	No. of Empty Clusters ($\pm \sigma$)	Objective ($\pm \sigma$)	Time (Sec.)
10	396037 ± 59297	104.9	8.7 ± 1.89	574555 ± 13209	154.2
20	424178 ± 31575	102.1	8.5 ± 1.72	661215 ± 6367	140.5
30	377261 ± 59321	90.1	9.3 ± 2.31	710156 ± 8086	154.9

TABLE 9.2: k-Median and Constrained k-median Results on Web Data Set for $k=20$

τ	k-median			Constrained k-median	
	Objective ($\pm \sigma$)	Time (Sec.)	No. of Empty Clusters ($\pm \sigma$)	Objective ($\pm \sigma$)	Time (Sec.)
10	37783 ± 539	77.2	2.8 ± 1.48	38091 ± 1166	137.62
20	37989 ± 709	69.2	1.9 ± 1.79	38389 ± 1258	135.90
30	38140 ± 748	70.6	2.0 ± 1.49	38811 ± 878	133.46

used a larger data set, we modified the definition of the empty cluster to be one with 5 or fewer points. We ran the experiments on a Pentium M 1.60 GHz notebook with 768 MB of memory running under the Windows XP operating system. For brevity, we only set k equal to 20. We set τ to be 10, 20, and 30. Initial cluster centers were randomly picked from the data set. Thus, the initial starting point consists of clusters that contain at least 1 point. At algorithm termination, clusters containing 5 or fewer points are considered "empty" per the modified definition. For each τ value, we ran 10 random realizations of the data set. We report average values over these 10 runs in Tables 9.1 and 9.2.

Average objective values and times in seconds for both regular and constrained clustering methods and also the number of empty clusters are reported for k-means and k-median clustering in Tables 9.1 and 9.2, respectively. Corresponding standard deviations are reported after the $\pm$ operator. Notice that the k-means clustering algorithm ends up with approximately 9 empty clusters on average out of 20 initial clusters. On the other hand, k-median clustering algorithm results in around 2 empty clusters on average. Changing τ does not seriously affect the running time for both constrained clustering methods. Although the objective values of both constrained and regular k-median methods do not differ, we see a significant change in constrained k-means probably due to the empty or near empty clusters found in regular k-means methods. From the comparisons of standard deviations of the objective values from both regular and constrained k-means algorithms, we can conclude that although the standard k-means algorithm has lower average objective values, it has higher variations. This result directly indicates the volatility of the local solutions of the regular k-means algorithm.

These results may be a result of the following observations: (i) a data point might be closer to any other data point as the dimensionality of the space becomes very large; (ii) the k-means algorithm is more prone to be affected by "outliers" in the data set than the k-median algorithm since k-means minimizes the 2-norm squared distance, whereas k-median minimizes the 1-norm distance [7].

9.5 Extensions

Around the same time that our earlier work [8] was published, Wagstaff and Cardie proposed using pairwise constraints in clustering problems [20]. More specifically they proposed the usage of must-link and cannot-link types of constraints in a clustering framework. From an optimization point of view, it might be more challenging to add pairwise constraints into clustering problems in general since it might jeopardize convexity and the smoothness of the solution. The work of Wagstaff and Cardie was later applied to the GPS lane finding problem [21]. Another constraint type was first studied in [2]. The aim in [2] was to utilize a sampling based scalable clustering algorithm with balancing constraints to produce balanced clusters, which is important in some commercial applications. Chapter 8 of this book is also on balancing constraints. In this section, we basically review some prior work and develop certain optimization models to tackle new types of constraints.

Kleinberg and Tardos proposed some linear programming relaxations of the metric labeling problem in [14, 15]. Specifically they used pairwise relationships in assigning k labels (classes) to each of n objects. In their approach to metric labeling problem, they utilized a Markov random fields framework [14, 15].

We can easily extend their uniform metric labeling formulation to a 2-norm cost function as follows in the following optimization model. Approximations to Kleinberg and Tardos' model for the general metrics are studied in [11].

$$\underset{T}{\text{minimize}} \sum_{i=1}^{n} \sum_{h=1}^{k} T_{i,h} \cdot \left(\frac{1}{2} \|x_i - \mu_h\|^2 \right) + \sum_{(u,v) \in \mathcal{X}} w(u,v) \cdot \frac{1}{2} \sum_{h=1}^{k} |T_{u,h} - T_{v,h}|$$

s.t.
$$\sum_{h=1}^{k} T_{i,h} = 1, \ i = 1, \ldots, n,$$
$$T_{i,h} \geq 0, \ i = 1, \ldots, n, \ h = 1, \ldots, k.$$

$$(9.5)$$

The major difference in Problem 9.5 with the original clustering problem defined in Problem 9.2 is the fact that there is a cost w associated with pairing two objects u and v. Technically, we can easily incorporate both must-link and cannot-link pairwise constraints with an appropriate cost structure with this formulation. Intuitively, appropriate positive terms should be assigned to $w(u, v)$'s. Assigning a negative value would make the objective non-convex and more difficult to solve with ordinary linear programming approach. Since each point is assigned exactly to one cluster, the term $w(u,v) \cdot \frac{1}{2} \sum_{h=1}^{k} |T_{u,h} - T_{v,h}|$ will be equal to 0 when both points are assigned to the same cluster and non-zero otherwise.

Although a minimum might exist, an algorithm like Algorithm 9.2 may not be sufficient to find a solution and the convergence of such an algorithm may not be guaranteed. Therefore a near zero cost value should be assigned to w for a cannot-link pairwise relationship (constraint). We can assign prohibitively large cost values for the must-link constraints. In this case, we can argue that there exists an extreme point solution, yet we need to show that Algorithm 9.2 converges. However, a more elegant way of introducing constraints is needed. In the following model, we first introduce our constraints on the number of points assigned to each cluster to Kleinberg and Tardos' model proposed in [14, 15].

$$\underset{T}{\text{minimize}} \sum_{i=1}^{n} \sum_{h=1}^{k} T_{i,h} \cdot \left(\frac{1}{2} \|x_i - \mu_h\|^2 \right) + \sum_{(u,v) \in \mathcal{X}} w(u,v) \cdot \frac{1}{2} \sum_{h=1}^{k} |T_{u,h} - T_{v,h}|$$

s.t.
$$\sum_{h=1}^{k} T_{i,h} = 1, \ i = 1, \ldots, n,$$
$$\sum_{i=1}^{n} T_{i,h} \geq \tau_h, \ h = 1, \ldots, k,$$
$$T_{i,h} \geq 0, \ i = 1, \ldots, n, \ h = 1, \ldots, k.$$

Certainly, pairwise relationships can be introduced to Markov random fields models in various ways. Basu et al. used hidden Markov models in [3, 4] in a probabilistic way to introduce such constraints. In the following model, we introduce such pairwise assignment constraints in our mathematical programming model. Notice that cannot-link constraints can be added without violating the convexity. However care is needed for the must-link type constraints since they are in the form of absolute value that is non-convex.

$$\underset{T,\varepsilon}{\text{minimize}} \sum_{i=1}^{n}\sum_{h=1}^{k} T_{i,h} \cdot \left(\frac{1}{2}\|x_i - \mu_h\|^2\right) + \sum_{(u,v)\in\mathcal{X}} w(u,v) \cdot \frac{1}{2}\sum_{h=1}^{k}|T_{u,h} - T_{v,h}|$$

s.t.
$$\sum_{h=1}^{k} T_{i,h} = 1,\ i = 1,\ldots,n,$$
$$\sum_{i=1}^{n} T_{i,h} \geq \tau_h,\ h = 1,\ldots,k,$$
$$T_{i,h} + T_{j,h} \leq 1,\ \forall\ i,j \in C_{\neq}, h = 1,\ldots,k,$$
$$-\varepsilon_{i,j,h} \leq T_{i,h} - T_{j,h} \leq \varepsilon_{i,j,h},\ \forall\ i,j \in C_{=},$$
$$\sum_{h=1}^{k} \varepsilon_{i,j,h} = 0,\ \forall\ i,j \in C_{=},$$
$$T_{i,h} \geq 0,\ i = 1,\ldots,n,\ h = 1,\ldots,k.$$
$$\text{(9.6)}$$

In Problem 9.6, we basically introduce a new variable, ε, for the each must-link constraint. From a practical point of view, Problem 9.6 needs to be solved by introducing a regularizer as given below. Our aim in introducing the regularizer, ρ, is just to simplify the objective function and speedup the solution. By doing this, we basically soften the must-link constraints. They are no longer hard constraints meaning that some violations of this type of constraints are permitted given that they are below certain associated costs.

$$\underset{T,\varepsilon}{\text{minimize}} \sum_{i=1}^{n}\sum_{h=1}^{k} T_{i,h} \cdot \left(\frac{1}{2}\|x_i - \mu_h\|^2\right) + \rho \sum_{(i,j)\in C_{=}}\sum_{h=1}^{k} \varepsilon_{i,j,h}$$

s.t.
$$\sum_{h=1}^{k} T_{i,h} = 1,\ i = 1,\ldots,n,$$
$$\sum_{i=1}^{n} T_{i,h} \geq \tau_h,\ h = 1,\ldots,k,$$
$$T_{i,h} + T_{j,h} \leq 1,\ \forall\ i,j \in C_{\neq}, h = 1,\ldots,k,$$
$$-\varepsilon_{i,j,h} \leq T_{i,h} - T_{j,h} \leq \varepsilon_{i,j,h},\ \forall\ i,j \in C_{=},$$
$$T_{i,h} \geq 0,\ i = 1,\ldots,n,\ h = 1,\ldots,k.$$
$$\text{(9.7)}$$

After removing the cost function associated with $w(u,v)$ from Problem 9.6 and introducing a regularizer in Problem 9.7, the resulting mathematical programming model has become numerically more stable and an algorithm, such as Algorithm 9.2, can be devised to solve this problem. Considering the cannot-link constraints, such an algorithm will converge. By adding trans-shipment nodes, we can show that the problem is equivalent to MCF. Thus we will have an integer solution, i.e., the integrality constraints are satisfied too. On the other hand, considering the must-link constraints, we can show that the algorithm will converge but we no more have the integrality.

Our proposed framework in this section enables us to introduce new constraints to the clustering problem in general. Assume that we face a situation that point x_i must be in the same cluster with point x_j or in the same cluster with point x_g but not in the same cluster with both points x_j and x_g. This situation might arise in analyzing social networks data. Imagine one chooses to be a friend of another person from among two persons but cannot be a friend of both persons at the same time. We call this type of constraint OR type constraints and denote it by C_{OR}. We show in the following model how to represent such constraints.

$$\underset{T,\varepsilon}{\text{minimize}} \quad \sum_{i=1}^{n}\sum_{h=1}^{k} T_{i,h} \cdot \left(\frac{1}{2}\|x_i - \mu_h\|^2\right) + \rho \sum_{(i,j)\in C_=}\sum_{h=1}^{k} \varepsilon_{i,j,h}$$

$$\text{s.t.} \quad \begin{aligned} &\sum_{h=1}^{k} T_{i,h} = 1,\, i = 1,\ldots,n, \\ &\sum_{i=1}^{n} T_{i,h} \geq \tau_h,\, h = 1,\ldots,k, \\ &T_{i,h} + T_{j,h} \leq 1,\, \forall\, i,j \in C_{\neq},\, h = 1,\ldots,k, \\ &-\varepsilon_{i,j,h} \leq T_{i,h} - T_{j,h} \leq \varepsilon_{i,j,h},\, \forall\, i,j \in C_=, \\ &\sum_{h=1}^{k} |T_{i,h} - T_{j,h}| + |T_{i,h} - T_{g,h}| \leq 1,\, \forall\, i,j,g \in C_{OR}, \\ &T_{i,h} \geq 0,\, i = 1,\ldots,n,\, h = 1,\ldots,k. \end{aligned} \qquad (9.8)$$

In Problem 9.8, C_{OR} constraints are convex. However, we can still propose a relaxed form. Since C_{OR} constraints are also convex, the algorithm to find a solution for this problem will converge but we will not have the integrality.

Adding must-link and cannot-link types of constraints into the clustering model may decrease the quality of solution. Unexpected or even unwanted results may occur. In [12], two measures, namely informativeness and coherence, are proposed to understand the underlying effects of adding constraints to the clustering problem. Such measures surely help to evaluate the importance of the semi-supervised approach through constrained clustering. Certain types of clustering approaches can be deployed for the transduction problem as well such as graph cut methods. However, it is reported that after deploying such methods for the two-class transduction problem, the algorithm might very well result in one very small cluster [13]. Such results may require a new type of constraint, precisely the minimum number of labeled points falling into each cluster. We can readily add such constraints to Problem 9.8 as in the following formulation.

$$\underset{T,\varepsilon}{\text{minimize}} \sum_{i=1}^{n}\sum_{h=1}^{k} T_{i,h} \cdot \left(\frac{1}{2}\|x_i - \mu_h\|^2\right) + \rho \sum_{(i,j)\in C_=}\sum_{h=1}^{k} \varepsilon_{i,j,h}$$

s.t.
$$\sum_{h=1}^{k} T_{i,h} = 1, \ i = 1,\ldots,n,$$
$$\sum_{i=1}^{n} T_{i,h} \geq \tau_h, \ h = 1,\ldots,k,$$
$$\sum_{i\in l} T_{i,h} \geq \pi_h, \ h = 1,\ldots,k,$$
$$T_{i,h} + T_{j,h} \leq 1, \ \forall \ i,j \in C_{\neq}, h = 1,\ldots,k,$$
$$-\varepsilon_{i,j,h} \leq T_{i,h} - T_{j,h} \leq \varepsilon_{i,j,h}, \ \forall \ i,j \in C_=,$$
$$T_{i,h} \geq 0, \ i = 1,\ldots,n, \ h = 1,\ldots,k.$$

To simplify the model, we can just omit the other types of constraints and just focus on the minimum number of points (minimum capacity) for each cluster whether labeled or unlabeled. The following formulation is provided for that reason.

$$\underset{T}{\text{minimize}} \quad \sum_{i=1}^{n}\sum_{h=1}^{k} T_{i,h} \cdot \left(\frac{1}{2}\|x_i - \mu_h\|^2\right)$$

s.t.
$$\sum_{h=1}^{k} T_{i,h} = 1, \ i = 1,\ldots,n,$$
$$\sum_{i=1}^{n} T_{i,h} \geq \tau_h, \ h = 1,\ldots,k,$$
$$\sum_{i\in l} T_{i,h} \geq \pi_h, \ h = 1,\ldots,k,$$
$$T_{i,h} \geq 0, \ i = 1,\ldots,n, \ h = 1,\ldots,k.$$

(9.9)

We can easily show that Problem 9.9 is equivalent to MCF by adding trans-shipment nodes. Therefore, the solution will converge and we will have the integrality constraints satisfied. From a practical point of view, Problem 9.9 is simple, yet has the potential to be very useful in the area of semi-supervised learning.

9.6 Conclusion

The k-means algorithm can be extended to insure that every cluster contains at least a given number of points. Using a cluster assignment step with constraints, solvable by linear programming or network simplex methods, can guarantee a sufficient population within each cluster. A surprising result was that constrained k-means was less prone to local minima than traditional k-means. Thus adding constraints may be beneficial to avoid local minima even when empty clusters are permissible. Constrained clustering suggests many research directions. Robust clustering can be done by simply adding an "outlier" cluster with high fixed distance that gathers "outliers" far from true clusters. Constraints forcing selected data into the same cluster could be used to incorporate domain knowledge or to enforce consistency of successive cluster solutions on related data.

We show in this chapter that it is feasible to solve constrained clustering problems by using efficient linear programming based algorithms even for the large data sets. We extend our solution to solve the constrained k-median algorithm. Results from real data sets are reported.

In addition to our original constraints on the number of points assigned to each cluster, we propose some extensions to represent pairwise assignment constraints via mathematical programming models in this chapter. Further investigations are still needed for these extensions to prove that they converge and the results satisfy the integrality constraints. Notice that such integrality constraints are expected to be satisfied without using more complex mixed-integer models. Our aim in this chapter was to show that linear programming and network simplex models can be efficiently used in solving constrained clustering problems.

Acknowledgments

Some parts of the work for this chapter were completed when Ayhan Demiriz was visiting University College of London through funding from EU PASCAL Network of Excellence.

References

[1] A. Asuncion and D.J. Newman. UCI machine learning repository, 2007. University of California, Irvine, School of Information and Computer Sciences. http://www.ics.uci.edu/~mlearn/MLRepository.html.

[2] A. Banerjee and J. Ghosh. Scalable clustering algorithms with balancing constraints. *Journal of Data Mining and Knowledge Discovery*, 13(3):365–395, 2006.

[3] S. Basu, A. Banerjee, and R. J. Mooney. Active semi-supervision for pairwise constrained clustering. In *Proceedings of the SIAM International Conference on Data Mining (SDM-2004)*, pages 333–344, Lake Buena Vista, FL, April 2004.

[4] S. Basu, M. Bilenko, A. Banerjee, and R. J. Mooney. Probabilistic semi-supervised clustering with constraints. In O. Chapelle, B. Schölkopf, and A. Zien, editors, *Semi-Supervised Learning*, pages 73–102. MIT Press, 2006.

[5] K. P. Bennett, U. M. Fayyad, and D. Geiger. Density-based indexing for approximate nearest neighbor queries. In *Proceedings of 5th International Conference on Knowledge Discovery and Data Mining (KDD99)*, pages 233–243, New York, 1999. ACM Press.

[6] D. P. Bertsekas. *Linear Network Optimization*. MIT Press, Cambridge, MA, 1991.

[7] K. S. Beyer, J. Goldstein, R. Ramakrishnan, and U. Shaft. When is "nearest neighbor" meaningful? In *Database Theory - ICDT '99, 7th International Conference*, volume 1540 of *Lecture Notes in Computer Science*, pages 217–235, Jerusalem, Israel, January 1999. Springer.

[8] P. S. Bradley, K. P. Bennett, and A. Demiriz. Constrained k-means clustering. Technical Report MSR-TR-2000-65, Microsoft Research, May 2000.

[9] P. S. Bradley and O. L. Mangasarian. k-Plane clustering. *Journal of Global Optimization*, 16(1):23–32, 2000.

[10] P. S. Bradley, O. L. Mangasarian, and W. N. Street. Clustering via concave minimization. In M. C. Mozer, M. I. Jordan, and T. Petsche, editors, *Advances in Neural Information Processing Systems 9*, pages 368–374, Cambridge, MA, 1997. MIT Press.

[11] C. Chekuri, S. Khanna, J. Naor, and L. Zosin. A linear programming formulation and approximation algorithms for metric labeling problem. *SIAM Journal of Discrete Mathematics*, 18(3):608–625, 2005.

[12] I. Davidson, K. L. Wagstaff, and S. Basu. Measuring constraint-set utility for partitional clustering algorithms. In *Proceedings of the Tenth European Conference on Principles and Practice of Knowledge Discovery in Databases (PKDD)*, pages 115–126, September 2006.

[13] T. De Bie and N. Cristianini. Fast sdp relaxations of graph cut clustering, transduction, and other combinatorial problems. *Journal of Machine Learning Research*, 7:1409–1436, 2006.

[14] J. Kleinberg and É. Tardos. Approximation algorithms for classification problems with pairwise relationships: Metric labeling and Markov

random fields. In *Proceedings of the 40th Annual IEEE Symposium on the Foundations of Computer Science*, Los Alamitos, CA, October 1999. IEEE Computer Society Press.

[15] J. Kleinberg and É. Tardos. Approximation algorithms for classification problems with pairwise relationships: Metric labeling and Markov random fields. *Journal of the ACM*, 49(5):616–639, September 2002.

[16] J. B. MacQueen. Some methods for classification and analysis of multivariate observations. In *Proceedings of the Fifth Symposium on Math, Statistics, and Probability*, volume 1, pages 281–297, Berkeley, CA, 1967. University of California Press.

[17] O. L. Mangasarian. *Nonlinear Programming*. McGraw–Hill, New York, 1969. Reprint: SIAM Classic in Applied Mathematics 10, 1994, Philadelphia.

[18] MOSEK, 2007. http://www.mosek.com.

[19] J. Shanmugusundaram, U. M. Fayyad, and P. S. Bradley. Compressed data cubes for olap aggregate query approximation on continuous dimensions. In *Proceedings of 5th International Conference on Knowledge Discovery and Data Mining (KDD99)*, pages 223–232, New York, 1999. ACM Press.

[20] K. Wagstaff and C. Cardie. Clustering with instance-level constraints. In *Proceedings of the International Conference on Machine Learning (ICML)*, pages 1103–1110, 2000.

[21] K. Wagstaff, C. Cardie, S. Rogers, and S. Schroedl. Constrained k-means clustering with background knowledge. In *Proceedings of the International Conference on Machine Learning (ICML)*, pages 577–584, 2001.

Chapter 10

Collective Relational Clustering

Indrajit Bhattacharya

IBM India Research Laboratory, `indrajbh@in.ibm.com`

Lise Getoor

University of Maryland, `getoor@cs.umd.edu`

Abstract   In many clustering problems, in addition to attribute data, we have relational information, linking different data points. In this chapter, we focus on the problem of collective relational clustering that makes use of both attribute and relational information. The approach is collective in that clustering decisions are not taken in an independent fashion for each pair of data points. Instead, the different pairwise decisions depend on each other. The first set of dependencies is among multiple decisions involving the same data point. The other set of dependencies come from the relationships. Decisions for any two references that are related in the data are also dependent on each other. Hence, the approach is collective as well as relational. We focus on the entity resolution problem as an application of the clustering problem, and we survey different proposed approaches that are collective or make use of relationships. One of the approaches is an agglomerative greedy clustering algorithm where the cluster similarity measure combines both attributes and relationships in a collective way. We discuss the algorithmic details of this approach and identifying data characteristics that influence its correctness. We also present experimental results on multiple real-world and synthetic data sets.

10.1 Introduction

Often in clustering problems, in addition to the attributes describing the data items to be clustered, there are links among the items. These links are co-occurrence links indicating that the data items were observed together in, for example, a market basket, a text document, or some other relational context. Relational clustering approaches make use of both the attributes of the instances and the observed co-occurrences to do a better job at clustering.

In this chapter, we will describe a relational clustering approach to entity resolution. The goal of the entity resolution problem is to eliminate duplicates, by identifying database records that correspond to the same underlying entity. A significant amount of research has gone into this problem and it goes by many different names in different research fields — record linkage, merge/purge, reference reconciliation, object consolidation, and others. Let us illustrate the problem using a bibliographic example. Consider the following four papers from a digital repository of papers such as CiteSeer, DBLP, or PubMed:

1. W. Wang, C. Chen, A. Ansari, "A mouse immunity model"

2. W. Wang, A. Ansari, "A better mouse immunity model"

3. L. Li, C. Chen, W. Wang, "Measuring protein-bound fluxetine"

4. W. W. Wang, A. Ansari, "Autoimmunity in biliary cirrhosis"

There are many author references that look very similar. For example, it may not be clear if the three "Wang" names map to the same real-world author. The goal the entity resolution process is to correctly resolve which references correspond to the same real world entities and which ones do not.

In this chapter, we will motivate entity resolution as a clustering problem, where the goal is to partition the references in a database according to their underlying entities. What makes the setting different from the standard clustering problem is the presence of relationships between the references in the database. In our example, the different author references are not observed in isolation, but as part of co-author lists in papers. Such relationships between references occur in many different scenarios, such as person names occurring in the same email, names of people in the same household in census or survey data, names of products purchased by the same customer, etc. These relationships can be used as valuable information in the clustering process. Our focus is on *collective relational clustering*, where the references are assigned to clusters based on the cluster memberships of their related references. In our example, whether or not "W. Wang" in the first paper corresponds to the same author as "W. Wang" in the second paper depends on whether their co-author references named "A. Ansari" refer to the same author. So the clustering has to be done *collectively* over related references.

The rest of this chapter is structured as follows. First in Section 10.2 we formalize entity resolution as a clustering problem and survey various approaches that perform collective resolution and those that make use of relationships between references. Next, in Section 10.3, we present a greedy algorithm for collective relational clustering. We discuss the computational bottlenecks of the process and explain the different components that are integrated into an efficient algorithm. A question that arises naturally is whether relational clustering improves clustering accuracy over traditional approaches. We address this question in Section 10.4: identify the data characteristics that influence the accuracy of collective relational clustering. We present an experimental evaluation in Section 10.5, and finally conclude in Section 10.6.

10.2 Entity Resolution: Problem Formulation

In this section, we first describe the notation we use for describing the entity resolution problem. We are given a set of references $\mathcal{R} = \{r_i\}$, where each reference r has attributes $r.A_1, r.A_2, \ldots, r.A_k$. The references correspond to some set of unknown entities $\mathcal{E} = \{e_i\}$. We introduce the notation $r.E$ to refer to the entity to which reference r corresponds. The problem is to recover the hidden set of entities $\mathcal{E} = \{e_i\}$ and the entity labels $r.E$ for individual references given the observed attributes of the references. Let us now illustrate how our running example is represented in this notation. Figure 10.1 shows the different author references in the data. Each observed author name corresponds to a reference, so there are ten references r_1 through r_{10}. In this case, the names are the only attributes of the references, so for example $r_1.A$ is "W. Wang," $r_2.A$ is "C. Chen," and $r_3.A$ is "A. Ansari." The set of true entities $\mathcal{E}$ is {Ansari, Wang1, Wang2, Chen1, Chen2, Li} as shown using different colors for references corresponding to different entities. References r_1, r_4 and r_9 correspond to Wang1, so that $r_1.E = r_4.E = r_9.E = $ Wang1. Similarly, $r_3.E = r_5.E = r_{10}.E = $ Ansari, and $r_2.E = $ Chen1, and so on. In the rest of this chapter, we will say two references r and r' are co-referent to mean that they correspond to the same entity, i.e., $r.E = r'.E$.

The problem has a long history and goes back to [15]. Recently, Koudas et al. [20] presented an excellent tutorial on entity resolution approaches. Winkler [30] and Gu et al. [17] have also written extensive surveys. Entity resolution can be viewed as a pairwise decision problem over references, or, alternatively, as a clustering problem where an entity label (or, a cluster label) needs to be assigned to each reference. We discuss this is more detail in the rest of this section. We will focus on collective entity resolution approaches,

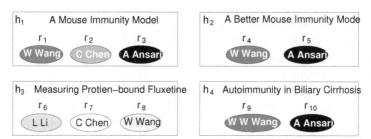

FIGURE 10.1: An example set of papers represented as references connected by hyper-edges. References are represented as ovals shaded according to their entities. Each paper is represented as a hyper-edge (shown as a rectangle) spanning multiple references.

and take a closer look at approaches that make use of relationships available in the data for entity resolution.

10.2.1   Pairwise Resolution

Entity resolution is often posed as a pairwise decision problem, where each pair of references is decided to be either a match or a non-match. The traditional focus has been on the design of similarity measures between attributes of references [11]. When references have multiple attributes, such as name, address, telephone number, etc., for person references, then the individual similarities may be combined to get the aggregated similarity $\text{sim}_A(r_i, r_j)$ is computed for each pair of references r_i, r_j. Then those pairs that have similarity above some threshold are considered co-referent. We use the abbreviation **A** to refer to this attribute-based approach to entity resolution. Considerable effort has gone into learning similarity measures between references [8]. Different aspects of the similarity measures, such as the parameters of individual measures (e.g., insert, delete, replace costs for edit-distance based measures) [26], the relevance of different attributes and the similarity threshold for detecting duplicates may be learned given sufficient labeled data. However, obtaining and preparing training data is often a problem. One way to address this issue is using active learning [27, 29].

In our example, the attribute-based pairwise approach **A** may allow us to decide that the "W. Wang" references (r_1, r_4) are co-referent. We may also decide using **A** that "W. Wang" and "W. W. Wang" (r_1, r_9) are co-referent, but not as confidently. However, pairwise decisions using attributes are often insufficient for entity resolution. In our example, **A** is almost certain to mark the two "W. Wang" references (r_1, r_8) as co-referent, which is incorrect.

10.2.2 Collective Resolution

The pairwise resolution approach does not directly address the entity resolution problem as we have described it. It does not aim to discover the underlying entities or the mapping from references to entities. Instead it determines whether or not two references map to the same underlying entity. One shortcoming of this approach is that it makes the pairwise decisions independently. An alternative approach to directly address the problem is to partition or cluster the references according to the underlying entities. We call this approach collective entity resolution since each pairwise decision takes into consideration other pairwise decisions. For example, two references "Jon Smith" and "J. H. Smith" are more likely to be co-referent if there exists a third reference "Jonathan H. Smith" that is co-referent with both of the first two references. The simplest approach is to take the transitive closure over the pairwise decisions. We refer to this naive attribute-based collective approach as **A***. This helps to improve recall, but often adversely affects precision. This can be illustrated using the following noun co-reference problem [23]. Imagine a segment of text that mentions "Mr. Powell," "Powell," and "she." Pairwise decisions may be able to resolve correctly that the first two mentions are co-referent, but they may wrongly decide because of proximity in the document that "Powell" and "she" are also co-referent. This may be avoided by considering that "Powell" has already been matched to "Mr. Powell," and that "Mr." and "she" are not consistent.

One possibility for collective resolution is to perform clustering on the pairwise decisions. In the correlation clustering approach [2, 10], the goal is to cluster the references by minimizing disagreement over the pairwise decisions. McCallum et al. [23] have proposed a model based on conditional random fields (CRF) for taking pairwise decisions collectively. The model leverages labeled data to learn edge-weights, and then the inference stage looks to partition the similarity graph into entity clusters based on edge-weights. Parag and Domingos [28] extend the CRF model by considering and leveraging dependencies across multiple attribute types. For example, we may be able to infer using author names and paper title that two paper citations correspond to the same underlying paper entity, even though their venue fields do not match significantly. For instance, one paper may have "SIGKDD 03" as the venue, while the other may have "Proc 9th ACM KDD." Since the two citations are co-referent, we know that their different-looking venue strings have to match. This information can now be used to match two other citations that have this same venue pair, but do not exactly match on the title field, for example. Such collective approaches have been shown to be superior to independent pairwise approaches in terms of resolution accuracy. However, the price paid is in terms of computational complexity. The joint decision problem cannot be solved exactly and approximate solutions are resorted to. Approximation schemes have been proposed for the correlation clustering problem [2], and the inference problem for the CRF-based models can be reduced to the correlation clustering problem [23] so that the same approximation algorithms can be utilized. Alternatively, approximate inference can be performed using the voted perceptron algorithm [12], as done in [28].

10.2.3 Entity Resolution Using Relationships

The attribute-based approaches that we have discussed so far assume that the different references in the data have been observed in isolation. However, in many scenarios, the references are not observed independently of each other. Many references are observed in the same context, or, in other words, co-occur with other references. Quite often, there is meaningful information in the co-occurrence relations. As examples, we can think of names of people and places occurring in the same document, names of products bought by the same customer, etc. We represent the co-occurrences in the data with a set of hyper-edges $\mathcal{H} = \{h_i\}$. Each hyper-edge h may have attributes as well, which we denote as $h.A_1, h.A_2, \ldots, h.A_l$, and we use $h.R$ to denote the set of references that it connects. A reference r can belong to zero or more hyper-edges and we use $r.H$ to denote the set of hyper-edges in which r participates. It is possible for multiple hyper-edges to share references. For example, if we have paper, author, and venue references, then a paper reference may be connected to multiple author references and also to a venue reference.

In our bibliographic example, there are four hyper-edges $\mathcal{H} = \{h_1, h_2, h_3, h_4\}$, one for each paper. The attributes of the hyper-edges in this domain are the paper titles; for example, $h_1.A_1 = $"A Mouse Immunity Model." The references r_1 through r_3 are associated with hyper-edge h_1, since they are the observed author references in the first paper. This is represented as $h_1.R = \{r_1, r_2, r_3\}$. Also, this is the only hyper-edge in which each of these references participate. So $r_1.H = r_2.H = r_3.H = \{h_1\}$. We can similarly represent the hyper-edge associations of the other references.

10.2.4 Pairwise Decisions Using Relationships

In most cases, the co-occurrences between references are not random, but are manifestations of meaningful relationships between entities in the underlying domain. For example, names of academic colleagues co-occur as author names in academic papers, and names of friends and acquaintances co-occur in bodies of emails. When reference co-occurrences occur as a result of meaningful relationships between underlying entities, they can be used to improve entity resolution performance in different ways. The simplest way to use co-occurrence relationships for entity resolution is to augment the pairwise similarity measures by considering the attributes of co-occurring references as well. For instance, to determine if two author references in two different papers are co-referent, we can additionally compare the names of their co-authors. In our running example, the naive use of relations for the references "W. Wang" and "W. W. Wang" would consider that both have co-authors with the name "A. Ansari." We refer to this approach as naive relational entity resolution **NR**.

A similar idea has been used in the context of matching in dimensional hierarchies [1]. To explain using an example from the paper, if two different country records with names "United States of America" and "US" have common names of states, such as "MO," "VA," and "PA," associated with them, then they are more likely to be the same country. On the other hand, though "UK" and "US" may be textually more similar, but they have no similarity in the names of the states that they are associated with. More formally, the dimensional hierarchy allows comparison of the children sets of two different records using co-occurrence. This structural similarity can then be combined with textual or attribute similarity to have a combined measure of similarity between records.

In the presence of a dimensional hierarchy, the co-occurrence relationships can be viewed as an ordered relationship. The same idea can be generalized for unordered relationships to define hyper-edge similarity $\text{sim}_H(h_i, h_j)$ between two hyper-edges h_i and h_j as the best pairwise attribute match between their references. Since the references in any hyper-edge are not ordered, each reference $r \in h_i$ can be matched to any reference $r' \in h_j$. Then, a simple linear combination of the attribute match $\text{sim}_A(r_i, r_j)$ and the hyper-edge match $\text{sim}_H(r_i, r_j)$ can be taken to get naive relational similarity for two references r_i and r_j:

$$\text{sim}_{NR}(r_i, r_j) = (1 - \alpha) \times \text{sim}_A(r_i, r_j) + \alpha \times \text{sim}_H(r_i, r_j), \quad 0 \le \alpha \le 1 \quad (10.1)$$

A more sophisticated way of incorporating relationships into the similarity measure has been explored by the RelDC algorithm [19]. It exploits path-based similarity over the connection graph between different entities in the database to determine the relational match between a reference and the multiple candidate possibilities for it. Consider an author reference with name "D. White" in a citation database that needs to be cleaned. The potential match candidates in the database for this reference are "Don White" at CMU and "Dave White" at Intel. Of these two, "Don White" has a paper with a researcher at MIT, while "Dave White" has no connection to MIT at all. On the other hand, the co-author of "D. White" is affiliated with MIT. This suggests that "D. Smith" is more likely to match with "Don White" than "Dave White." So, essentially, the RelDC approach goes beyond directly connected entities to define path-based similarity between an entity and a reference.

10.2.5 Collective Relational Entity Resolution

The naive relational approach **NR** takes relational information into account, but it still makes pairwise resolution decisions over references, independently of decisions for other pairs. For the two "Wang" references in the first two papers in our example, the two "C. Chen" co-author names match regardless of whether they refer to Chen1 or Chen2. The correct evidence to use here is that the "Chen"s are not co-referent. In such a setting, in order to resolve the "W. Wang" references, it is necessary to *resolve* the "C. Chen" references as well, and not just consider their name similarity. As with the attribute-based approach, an improvement is to take transitive closure over the pairwise decisions in **NR**. We represent this as **NR***. However, this clearly does not address our current problem adequately, since it does not capture dependency across hyper-edges. What we require here is collective relational entity resolution (**CR**), where resolution decisions for related references are not made independently, but instead one resolution decision affects other resolutions via hyper-edges.

We have proposed a probabilistic generative model for collective relational entity resolution based on LDA (latent Dirichlet allocation) [4] that identifies groups of related entities from the co-occurrences between the references, and then this group evidence is combined with the attribute evidence to partition the references into entities. Pasula et al. [25] have proposed a generative model for entity resolution over multiple types of entities. Culotta and McCallum [13] use a CRF-based model to capture dependency of resolution decisions for multiple types of entities connected by hyper-edges. While the attribute-based CRF models capture dependence using identical attribute values for different references, this model captures dependence over related references. The strength of the dependencies may be different for different types of records. For example, if two paper references are marked as co-referent, then their corresponding venue references are certain to be duplicates. On the other hand, if two venue references are marked as duplicates, then their corresponding paper references are more likely to be duplicates than before, but it is not a certainty. The CRF model can learn these different dependency patterns given sufficient training data. Dong et al. [14] make use of a similar dependency graph over multiple types of references. Instead of performing probabilistic inference, their algorithm propagates evidence from any resolution decision by iteratively updating the similarities of related references over the dependency network.

A very different approach to the collective relational clustering problem has been proposed by Long et al. [21]. They consider a matrix representation for multi-type relational data, which has one matrix to represent the attribute features for data of each type and one matrix for each pairwise relationship between types. They take a spectral view of the problem, where the goal is to find low dimensional embeddings over all data types simultaneously. The objective function to minimize is the distortion of the embedding aggregated over all attribute and relationship matrices. They show that this can be reduced to an eigen decomposition problem, which is solved using iterative techniques. Just as the cluster assignment for one reference propagates over relationships to influence the cluster assignment of other references in the earlier approaches, the spectral approach benefits from interactions between different types in the low dimensional subspaces.

Instead of computing and updating similarities between pairwise references, an alternative approach for performing collective resolution using relationships is to define a similarity measure between clusters of references that takes related clusters into account. We call this approach *collective relational clustering* [3, 6]. Assume a partitioning of references into *entity clusters* such that y_i denotes the cluster label of reference r_i, and $y_i \in [K]$. Then we may define the similarity of two cluster labels (or, clusters, in short) i and j as:

$$\text{sim}(i, j) = (1 - \alpha) \times \text{sim}_A(i, j) + \alpha \times \text{sim}_R(i, j), \qquad 0 \le \alpha \le 1 \qquad (10.2)$$

where $i, j \in [K]$, $\text{sim}_A()$ is the similarity of the attributes and $\text{sim}_R()$ is the relational similarity between the references in the two entity clusters. Note that the references in cluster j are those references r_i for which $y_i = j$. This similarity is dynamic in nature, which is one of the most important and interesting aspects of the collective approach. The similarity of two clusters depends on the current cluster labels of their neighbors, and therefore changes as their labels are updated. In our example, the similarity between "W. Wang" and "W. W. Wang" increases once the Ansari references are given the same cluster label.

The references in cluster j are connected to other references via hyper-edges. For collective clustering over hyper-edges, relational similarity considers the cluster labels of all these connected references. Recall that each reference r_i is associated with one or more hyper-edges in $\mathcal{H}$. Therefore, the set of hyper-edges $H(j)$ that we need to consider for a cluster label j is defined as

$$H(j) = \bigcup_{r_i \in \mathcal{R},\ y_i = j} \{h \in \mathcal{H} \mid r_i \in h.R\}$$

These hyper-edges connect j to other clusters j'. The relational similarity for two clusters needs to compare their connectivity patterns to other clusters.

For any cluster j, the set of other clusters to which j is connected via its hyper-edge set $H(j)$ form the neighborhood $Nbr(j)$ of cluster j:

$$Nbr(j) = \bigcup_{h \in H(j)} \{j' \mid j' = y_i \wedge r_i \in h.R\}$$

This defines the neighborhood as a set of related clusters. In our example in Figure 10.1, the neighborhood of the cluster for Wang1 consists of the clusters for Ansari and Chen1. For the relational similarity between two clusters, we look for commonness in their neighborhoods. This can be done in many different ways [6]. An option that works very well is Jaccard's co-efficient. For two sets A and B, the Jaccard's co-efficient is defined as

$$\text{Jaccard}(A, B) = \frac{|A \cap B|}{|A \cup B|}$$

Given the relational similarity measure between clusters, collective relational clustering can be performed efficiently in a greedy agglomerative fashion, as we describe in the next section.

The downside of using relational information for collective resolution is of course computational complexity. Collective resolution is already a hard problem, as we have discussed earlier. Here, we have significantly larger number of dependencies due to the hyper-edges. Clearly, finding the best partition into clusters is intractable, and approximate strategies are employed. For the CRF model, approximate inference is performed using either loopy belief propagation or relational agglomerative clustering [13]. In the **LDA-ER** model [4], we use a structured variant of Gibbs sampling, while Pasula et al. use Metropolis-Hastings sampling for inference in their generative model, with techniques to generate efficient proposals. Even approximate inference in joint probability models can be very slow in the presence of dependency over hyper-edges. Also, it is typically hard to put a bound on the number of iterations that the inference algorithms can take before converging. For our collective relational clustering algorithm, in contrast, it is possible to put a worst case complexity bound on performance, as we explain after describing the algorithm in the next section.

10.3   An Algorithm for Collective Relational Clustering

For the collective relational clustering problem, we can use a greedy agglomerative clustering algorithm that uses the similarity measure in (10.2) to find the closest cluster pair at each step and then merges them. The complexity of the algorithm arises from dependency of cluster similarities on the current neighbor clusters. As clusters evolve, the relevant similarity changes need to be efficiently computed and propagated over the hyper-edges. High level pseudo-code for the algorithm is provided in Figure 10.2. Next, we describe the different components that form the building blocks of the greedy algorithm, and then look at the overall computational complexity of the process.

Blocking to Find Potential Resolution Candidates: Unless the data sets are small, it is impractical to consider all possible pairs as potential candidates for merging. Apart from the scaling issue, most pairs checked by an $O(n^2)$ approach will be rejected since usually only about 1% of all pairs are true matches. Blocking techniques [18, 22, 24] are usually employed to rule out pairs which are certain to be non-matches. The goal is to separate references into possibly overlapping buckets and only pairs of references within each bucket are considered as potential matches. The relational clustering algorithm uses the blocking method as a black-box and any method that can quickly identify potential matches minimizing false negatives can be used. For n references, the bucketing algorithm runs in $O(nf)$ time, where a reference is assigned to at most f buckets.

1.	Find similar references using blocking
2.	Initialize clusters using bootstrapping
3.	For clusters i, j such that similar(i, j)
4.	Insert $\langle \mathrm{sim}(i, j), i, j \rangle$ into priority queue
5.	While priority queue not empty
6.	Extract $\langle \mathrm{sim}(i, j), i, j \rangle$ from queue
7.	If $\mathrm{sim}(i, j)$ less than threshold, then stop
8.	Merge i and j to new cluster $\widehat{ij}$
9.	Remove entries for i and j from queue
10.	For each cluster i' such that similar$(\widehat{ij}, i')$
11.	Insert $\langle \mathrm{sim}(\widehat{ij}, i'), \widehat{ij}, i' \rangle$ into queue
12.	For each cluster j' neighbor of $\widehat{ij}$
13.	For i' such that similar(j', i')
14.	Update $\mathrm{sim}(j', i')$ in queue

FIGURE 10.2: High-level description of the relational clustering algorithm.

Cluster Initialization: Each iteration of the relational clustering algorithm makes use of clustering decisions made in previous iterations. But if we begin with each reference in a distinct cluster, then initially there are no shared neighbors for references that belong to different hyper-edges. So the initial iterations of the algorithm have no relational evidence to depend on. To avoid this, we need to bootstrap the clustering algorithm such that each reference is not assigned to a distinct cluster. Specifically, if we are confident that some reference pair is co-referent, then they should be assigned to the same initial cluster. However, precision is crucial for the bootstrap process, since our algorithm cannot undo any of these initial merge operations. We use a bootstrap scheme that considers both attributes and relationships to determine bootstrap candidates. The bootstrapping scheme can be parameterized to account for different levels of ambiguity in data sets. After the bootstrap candidates are identified, the initial clusters are created using the union-find approach so that any two references that are bootstrap candidates are assigned to the same initial cluster.

Handling Cannot-Link Constraints: So far, we have considered shared relational neighborhoods between clusters as positive evidence that increases the similarity for a cluster pair. Additionally, the clustering setting can have negative or cannot-link constraints as well arising from relationships. For example, in many relational domains, two references appearing in the same hyper-edge *cannot* refer to the same entity. As a real bibliographic example, consider a paper with co-authors "M. Faloutsos," "P. Faloutsos," and "C. Faloutsos." Despite the similarity of the uncommon last name, in reality these references correspond to distinct author entities. In general, we can have a set of cannot-link constraints $C_{\neq}$ that the clusters need to satisfy. These can be taken into account by setting the similarity between two cluster pairs in (10.2) to zero if merging them violates any cannot-link constraint $c_{\neq}(i, j)$.

Merging Clusters and Updating Similarities: Once the similar clusters have been identified and bootstrapping has been performed, the algorithm iteratively merges the most similar cluster pair and updates similarities until the similarity drops below some specified threshold. This is shown in lines 5–14 of Figure 10.2. The similarity update steps for related clusters in lines 12–14 are the key steps that distinguish collective relational clustering from a traditional agglomerative clustering algorithm. In order to perform the update steps efficiently, indexes need to maintained for each cluster to record the list of all similar clusters and all neighboring clusters. All of the update operations from lines 9–14 can be performed efficiently using these lists. For example, updates for related clusters are done by first accessing the neighbor list and then traversing the similar list for each of them.

Complexity Analysis: As we have mentioned earlier, the computational challenge is a big issue for collective clustering with relationships. Now, we will briefly analyze how the different components handle the computational bottlenecks of the process. First, we look at how the number of similarity computations required in lines 3–4 of Figure 10.2 is reduced by the blocking method. We consider the worst case scenario where the bootstrapping approach does not reduce the number of clusters at all. We need to compare every pair of references within each bucket. But when n references are split over $O(n)$ buckets, using an optimistic estimate, we can show that only $O(n)$ similarity computations are required. However, it should be noted that a bad bucketing algorithm that assigns $O(n)$ references to any bucket will always lead to $O(n^2)$ comparisons.

Now, let us look at the time taken by each iteration of the algorithm. This depends on how the hyper-edges connect references in different buckets. When references in each bucket are connected to references in many other buckets, many update operations are required after every merge. In general, if any bucket is connected to b other buckets, each merge operation leads to $O(b)$ update/insert operations. Using a binary-heap implementation for the priority queue, the extract-max and each insert and update operation take $O(\log q)$ time, where q is the number of entries in the queue. So the total cost of each iteration of the algorithm is $O(b \log q)$. The total number of iterations that the algorithm may require is $O(q)$ in the worst case when the priority queue has q entries to start with. With each merge operation requiring $O(b \log q)$ time, the total cost of the iterative process is $O(qb \log q)$. A good initial bucketing leads to $O(n)$ entries in the queue to start with, so that the total cost of the algorithm can be bounded by $O(nb \log n)$. So we can see that it is possible to have an efficient implementation for the greedy agglomerative approach. Note that this does not lead to an optimal cluster assignment. But as we will see in the experimental section, it results in very good performance in practice.

To see how this compares against the attribute and naive relational baselines, observe that they need to take a decision for each pair of references in a bucket. This leads to a worst case analysis of $O(n)$ using the same assumptions as before. However, each similarity computation is more expensive for the naive relational approach (10.1) than the attribute-based approach, since the former requires a pairwise match to be computed between two hyperedges.

10.4 Correctness of Collective Relational Clustering

So far, we have discussed approaches and algorithms for collective relational clustering assuming that the use of relationships between references improves clustering accuracy. But is this a valid assumption? We now briefly discuss and analyze different scenarios to observe that clustering using relationships is beneficial when the data has certain characteristics.

For collective entity resolution using relational clustering, we have seen that the resolution performance of any entity becomes dependent on the resolution performance of related entities. The exact nature of this dependence hinges on both the attributes of the references in the data and the relationships between them. Let us first illustrate how the resolution accuracy of approaches that only use attributes depends on data characteristics. Consider a clustering algorithm that assigns two references to the same cluster if their attribute similarity is above some threshold δ, and to different clusters otherwise. The accuracy of this algorithm depends on the separation of references from different entities in terms of their attributes. More specifically, the recall for any entity will be high if its references are easily identifiable in terms of attributes, or, in other words, are at least as similar as the threshold δ. For instance, the multiple recorded names for any person should not be very different from each other. The other metric to consider is precision. The precision will be low if there is ambiguity across entities in terms of attributes, or, in other words, references from different entities have similarity larger than δ. For example, if different people have very similar names, this approach will not work well.

The collective relational clustering algorithm uses relational similarity in addition to attribute similarity for merging clusters. As a result, two clusters with low attribute similarity can still be merged if they have shared cluster neighborhoods. How this affects resolution accuracy depends on the nature of the relationships across entities in the underlying data. We may consider two different situations involving two related pairs of references. In Figure 10.3(a), we have two hyper-edges h_4 (Paper 4) and h_1 (Paper 1) con-

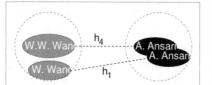 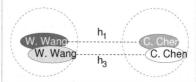

FIGURE 10.3: Illustration of (a) identifying relation and (b) ambiguous relation. Dashed lines represent co-occurrence relations.

necting the two "Wang-Ansari" pairs. Assume without loss of generality that the two "Ansari"s get clustered together first. As a result, the relational similarity between the "Wang"s increases leading to those getting clustered together subsequently. In this case, both the "Wang" and "Ansari" pairs are actually co-referent. So the relationships play an identifying role and propagate "good evidence," so that one correct clustering decision leads to another correct clustering decision. Here, recall for both the "Wang" and "Ansari" clusters increases as a result of using relationships collectively. However, in an alternative scenario, neither pair may be co-referent. In Figure 10.3(b), the "Wang" references map to different people, as do the two "Chen" references, but hyper-edge h_1 (Paper 1) connects the first "Wang-Chen" pair and h_3 (Paper 3) connects the other pair. In this case, the relational similarity of the two "Wang"s goes up as a result of the first incorrect merge of the two "Chen"s, and subsequently leads to a second incorrect merge. Here the relationships are ambiguous and propagate bad evidence from one incorrect clustering decision leading to another.

In general, we can show that recall increases in a geometric progression as a result of relational clustering, while precision goes down in a geometric progression, as higher neighborhood levels are considered [7]. How quickly the two progressions converge depend on the identifying and ambiguous nature of the attributes and relationships. Notably, whether or not there is an overall performance improvement depends on the fraction of attributes and relationships are ambiguous or play an identifying role. If the relationships and attributes are more of an identifying nature, then recall increases at a faster rate than the fall in precision, and performance increases overall. On the other hand, in the adverse situation, where a large fraction of the attributes and relationships are ambiguous, then clustering accuracy can actually degrade as a result of using relationships collectively.

10.5 Experimental Evaluation

We have evaluated the collective relational clustering algorithm for entity resolution on several real-world and synthetic data sets. Here, we present a snapshot of the results. The details are available elsewhere [6, 7]. Our real-world data sets involve publication information from several different scientific research areas. As in our running example, the goal is to use co-author relationships in the papers for author entity resolution. The **CiteSeer** data set contains 1,504 machine learning documents with 2,892 author references to 1,165 author entities. The data set was originally created by [16] and the version which we use includes the author entity ground truth provided by Aron Culotta and Andrew McCallum, University of Massachusetts, Amherst. The **arXiv** data set describes high energy physics publications. It was originally used in KDD Cup 2003.[1] It contains 29,555 papers with 58,515 references to 9,200 authors. The author entity ground truth for this data set was provided by David Jensen, University of Massachusetts, Amherst. Our third data set, describing biology publications, is the Elsevier **BioBase** data set[2] which was used in the IBM KDD-Challenge competition, 2005. It was created by selecting all Elsevier publications on "Immunology and Infectious Diseases" between years 1998 and 2001. It contains 156,156 publications with 831,991 author references. Unlike arXiv and CiteSeer that have complete as well as initialed author names, in BioBase all of the first names and middle names are abbreviated. In addition, the BioBase data set has other attributes which we use for resolution such as keywords, topic classification, language, country of correspondence, and affiliation of the corresponding author. There is a wide variety in the data with 20 languages, 136 countries, 1,282 topic classifications, and 7,798 keywords. For evaluating entity resolution accuracy on BioBase, we used 10,595 references having any one of 100 names that were hand labeled.

We compare *attribute-based entity resolution* (**A**), *naive relational entity resolution* (**NR**) that uses attributes of related references, and *collective relational entity resolution* (**CR**). For the first two algorithms, we also consider variants which perform transitive closures over the pairwise decisions (**A*** and **NR***).

In order to measure the performance of our algorithms, we consider the correctness of the pairwise co-reference decisions over all references. We evaluate the pairwise decisions using the F1 measure, which is the harmonic mean of precision and recall. For a fair comparison, we consider the best F1 for each of these algorithms over all possible thresholds for determining matches.

---

[1] http://www.cs.cornell.edu/projects/kddcup/index.html
[2] http://help.sciencedirect.com/robo/projects/sdhelp/about_biobase.htm

TABLE 10.1: Performance of different algorithms on the CiteSeer, arXiv, and BioBase data sets

	CiteSeer	arXiv	BioBase
A	0.980	0.974	0.568
A*	0.990	0.967	0.559
NR	0.981	0.975	0.710
NR*	0.991	0.972	0.753
CR	0.995	0.985	0.819

For comparing attributes, which is required for all of the algorithms, we use the *Soft TF-IDF* coupled with Jaro-Winkler similarity for names [9, 11] since it has been shown to perform well for name-based entity resolution. In the case of BioBase, where we had other multi-valued attributes to make use of besides names, we used TF-IDF similarity.

Table 10.1 gives an overview of the F1 results of the various algorithms on our three data sets. The numbers show that the attribute baselines perform remarkably well for CiteSeer and arXiv, but not as well for BioBase. The reason lies in the intrinsic hardness of the data sets. The number of ambiguous names in the first two data sets is very small. BioBase, in contrast, has many entities with identical or similar names, which are hard to resolve using attributes alone. The table shows that the effect of transitive closure on entity resolution performance also varies over the data sets. While it improves performance for both **A** and **NR** for CiteSeer and arXiv, in the case of BioBase, it helps **NR** but not **A**.

Most importantly, across all three data sets, the collective relational entity resolution algorithm (**CR**) performs the best. The gains for the less ambiguous domains are more modest, while in the most ambiguous domain, the gain is quite significant. In Figure 10.4(a), we show the precision-recall curves for the three algorithms on BioBase. The plots confirm that the benefits of **CR** are large in domains with high ambiguity such as BioBase. The performance improvements of **CR** over **NR** highlights the importance over considering the *identities* of related references rather than just their attributes.

Recall that **CR**, **NR**, and **NR*** involve a weighting parameter α for combining attribute and relational similarity. As mentioned earlier, the numbers in Table 10.1 record the best performance over different values of α for each of these algorithms. In Figure 10.4(b) we see how the performance of the different algorithms changes over different values of α for BioBase.

In our next experiment, we evaluate entity resolution performance over specific names. The goal is to evaluate how collective resolution accuracy changes as larger neighborhoods are considered for resolving the set of references in the database that have a particular name. For arXiv, we selected all 75 am-

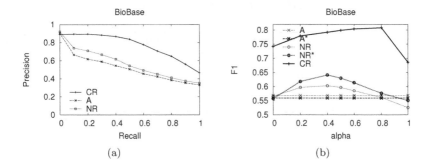

FIGURE 10.4: (a) Precision vs Recall and (b) F1 vs α for BioBase.

TABLE 10.2: Average entity resolution accuracy (F1) for different algorithms over 75 arXiv names and 100 BioBase names

	arXiv	BioBase
A	0.721	0.701
A*	0.778	0.687
NR	0.956	0.710
NR*	0.952	0.753
CR Level-1	0.964	0.813
CR Level-3	0.970	0.820

biguous names that correspond to more than one author entity. The number of true entities for the selected names varying from 2 to 11 (average 2.4). For BioBase, we selected the top 100 author names with the highest number of references. The average number of references for each of these 100 names is 106, and the number of entities for the selected names ranges from 1 to 100 (average 32). The average F1 scores over all names are shown in Table 10.2 for each algorithm in the two data sets. In BioBase, the improvement using **CR** is 21% over **A** and **NR**, 25% over **A***, and 13% over **NR***. As predicted by our analysis, most of the accuracy improvement comes from references that are directly connected. For 56 out of the 100 BioBase names, accuracy does not improve beyond directly connected references. For the remaining 44 names, the average improvement is 2%. However, for 8 of the most ambiguous names, accuracy improves by more than 5%, the biggest improvement being as high as 27% (from 0.67 to 0.85 F1). Such instances are fewer for arXiv, but the biggest improvement is 37.5% (from 0.727 to 1.0). On one hand, this shows that considering related records and resolving them collectively leads to

TABLE 10.3: Execution time of
different algorithms in CPU seconds

	CiteSeer	arXiv	BioBase
A	0.1	11.3	3.9
NR	0.1	11.5	19.1
CR	2.7	299.0	45.6

significant improvement in accuracy. On the other hand, it also demonstrates
that while there are potential benefits to considering higher order neighbors,
they fall off quickly beyond level 1. This is in keeping with the analysis of
collective resolution in Section 10.4 where we mentioned that accuracy levels
off in a geometric progression as we consider larger neighborhoods.

As we have seen, collective relational clustering improves entity resolution
performance over attribute-based baselines. However it is more expensive
computationally. Table 10.3 records the execution times in CPU seconds of
the baseline algorithms and **CR** on the three data sets. All execution times
are reported on a Dell Precision 870 server with 3.2 GHz Intel Xeon processor
and 3 GB of memory. As expected, **CR** takes more time than the baseline
but it is still quite fast. It takes less than 3 seconds for the 2,982 references
in CiteSeer and less than 5 minutes for the 58,515 references in arXiv. The
time recorded for BioBase in Table 10.3 is not for cleaning the entire data set.
Rather, it is the average time for collectively resolving references with each
of the 100 labeled names. The average number of "neighborhood" references
for each of the 100 instances in 5,510. Table 10.3 shows that the difference in
execution time between **CR** and the baselines is much smaller for BioBase.
One reason for this is that BioBase has many attributes in addition to author
name that the attribute-only baseline also need to take into account. Also,
the average number of authors per publication is 5.3 for BioBase as compared
to 1.9 for the other two data sets. This makes the naive relational approach
significantly more expensive than the attribute-only baseline.

10.5.1   Experiments on Synthetic Data

We have performed extensive experiments on synthetic data as well. They
allow us to focus on specific properties of the attributes and relations of the
references and the underlying domain entities, and to better understand how
different data characteristics affect the performance of our collective relational
clustering. We wrote a synthetic generator for reference data that allows us
to control different properties such as the number of entities and relationships, the size of relationships, the ambiguity of attributes and relationships

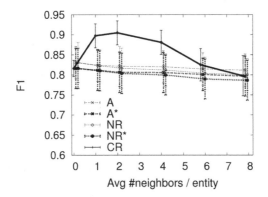

FIGURE 10.5: Performance of different entity resolution algorithms on data synthetically generated by varying the average number of neighbors per entity. Standard deviations are shown using error bars.

across entitie, etc.[3] The synthetic data generator is not tailored solely to bibliographic data, but can model general relationships between entities, as in social network data or email data.

Our experiments on synthetic data showed quite a few interesting trends. For example, we found that for the varying number of references in each hyper-edge, the performances of the attribute baselines (**A** and **A***) do not change, but the performance of **CR** improves with the increasing number of references per hyper-edge. In another experiment, we varied the percentage of ambiguous references in the data. The performances of all algorithms drop with increasing percentage of ambiguous references. However, the performance drop for **CR** is significantly slower than those for the attribute and naive relational baselines since the entity relationships help to make the algorithm more robust. As a result, the gap between **CR** and the baselines increases as the percentage of ambiguous references in the data increases.

Another interesting trend is shown in Figure 10.5. Here, we explored the impact of varying the number of relationships between the underlying entities. As expected, the performances of the attribute baselines (**A** and **A***) do not change significantly since they do not depend on the relationships. The performance of **CR** increases initially as the number of relationships increases. However it peaks when the average number of neighbors per entity is around 2 and then it starts falling off. In fact, it falls below the attribute-baseline when the neighborhood size increases to 8. This is an interesting result that shows that an increasing number of relationships does not always help collective entity resolution. As more relationships get added between entities,

---

[3] Available at http://www.cs.umd.edu/users/indrajit/ER

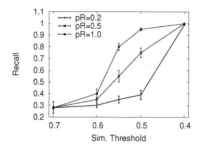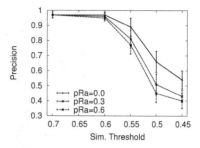

FIGURE 10.6: Effect of (a) identifying relations on recall and (b) ambiguous relations on precision for collective clustering. Error bars show standard deviation.

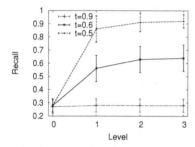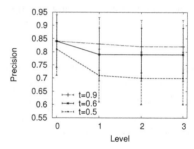

FIGURE 10.7: Change in (a) precision and (b) recall for increasing expansion levels in collective clustering. Error bars show standard deviation.

relationship patterns between entities are less informative, and may actually hurt performance.

Next, in Figure 10.6(a), we investigate the influence of identifying relationships on collective relational clustering using relational clustering. The plot shows recall at different similarity thresholds for three different levels of identifying relationships. The results confirm that recall increases progressively with more identifying relationships at all thresholds. The curves flatten out only when no further recall is achievable. Next, we observe the effect of ambiguous relations on precision of collective relational clustering. In Figure 10.6(b), we plot precision at different similarity thresholds for three different levels of ambiguous relationships. The plots confirm the progressive decrease in precision for all thresholds with higher ambiguity. This shows that more relations are not always helpful for collective relational clustering, but that the nature of the relationships is important.

Finally, we move on to the dependence of collective relational clustering on resolving related references. For this experiment, we performed localized collective clustering, focusing on the most ambiguous attribute value (that corresponds to the highest number of underlying entities) in the generated data. In Figure 10.7(a) and (b), we show how recall and precision change as neighbors that are farther away are considered and resolved. Recall improves with increasing neighborhood level, while precision decreases overall, as was predicted by our analysis. Importantly, recall increases at a significantly faster rate than the decrease in precision. In general, the rate of increase/decrease depends on the structural properties of the data, as we have shown in our analysis. In other experiments, we have seen different rates of change, but the overall trend remains the same. Our analysis also showed that precision and recall converge quickly over increasing neighborhood levels. This too is confirmed by the two plots where the curves flatten out by level 3.

10.6   Conclusions

In summary, we have discussed the collective relational clustering problem, where data points are partitioned into clusters such that the cluster assignment of any data point depends on the cluster assignments of all data points related to it. We considered entity resolution as the application area and, after reviewing different collective and relational approaches, presented a more detailed overview of one approach for collective relational clustering, where the similarity measure between clusters combines both attributes and relational evidence in a collective fashion. Given this similarity measure, we showed how it can be used by a greedy agglomerative algorithm for collective relational clustering. One of the challenges of using relationships collectively for clustering is computational complexity. We identified the computational bottlenecks, and looked at how these can be addressed efficiently. We also considered the issue of correctness of collective relational clustering, which has not received much attention in the literature, and showed how clustering accuracy, in terms of precision and recall, depends on specific characteristics of the data. We showed that while some relationships are good for recall, others hurt precision, and overall performance depends on the fraction of attributes and relationships that lead to ambiguity between clusters. We also showed how the impact of collective decisions on any cluster falls off as neighboring clusters at increasingly higher distances are considered. We evaluated the performance of collective relational clustering over multiple real-world and synthetic data sets and demonstrated that significant performance gains are achievable over traditional attribute-based and naive relational baselines. As expected, the price for improved performance is paid in terms of increased execution time over non-relational approaches, but the greedy approach scales well with increasing database size. Making use of relationships adaptively and efficiently is an ongoing challenge [5, 6]. In practical scenarios where accuracy is paramount, the improved performance can sufficiently compensate for the increase in execution time.

References

[1] Rohit Ananthakrishna, Surajit Chaudhuri, and Venkatesh Ganti. Eliminating fuzzy duplicates in data warehouses. In *The International Conference on Very Large Databases (VLDB)*, pages 586–597, Hong Kong, China, 2002.

[2] Nikhil Bansal, Avrim Blum, and Shuchi Chawla. Correlation clustering. *Machine Learning*, 56(1-3):89–113, 2004.

[3] Indrajit Bhattacharya and Lise Getoor. Iterative record linkage for cleaning and integration. In *The ACM SIGMOD Workshop on Research Issues on Data Mining and Knowledge Discovery (DMKD)*, pages 11–18, Paris, France, June 2004.

[4] Indrajit Bhattacharya and Lise Getoor. A latent dirichlet model for unsupervised entity resolution. In *The SIAM Conference on Data Mining (SIAM-SDM)*, pages 47–58, Bethesda, USA, 2006.

[5] Indrajit Bhattacharya and Lise Getoor. Query-time entity resolution. In *The ACM International Conference on Knowledge Discovery and Data Mining (SIGKDD)*, pages 529–534, Philadelphia, USA, 2006.

[6] Indrajit Bhattacharya and Lise Getoor. Collective entity resolution in relational data. *ACM Transactions on Knowledge Discovery from Data (TKDD)*, 1(1):5, March 2007.

[7] Indrajit Bhattacharya and Lise Getoor. Query-time entity resolution. *Journal of Artificial Intelligence Research (JAIR)*, 30:621–657, December 2007.

[8] Mikhail Bilenko and Raymond Mooney. Adaptive duplicate detection using learnable string similarity measures. In *The ACM International Conference on Knowledge Discovery and Data Mining (SIGKDD)*, pages 39–48, Washington, DC, USA, 2003.

[9] Mikhail Bilenko, Raymond Mooney, William Cohen, Pradeep Ravikumar, and Stephen Fienberg. Adaptive name matching in information integration. *IEEE Intelligent Systems*, 18(5):16–23, 2003.

[10] Moses Charikar, Venkatesan Guruswami, and Anthony Wirth. Clustering with qualitative information. In *Proceedings of the Annual IEEE Symposium on Foundations of Computer Science (FOCS)*, pages 524–533, 2003.

[11] William Cohen, Pradeep Ravikumar, and Stephen Fienberg. A comparison of string distance metrics for name-matching tasks. In *The IJCAI Workshop on Information Integration on the Web (IIWeb)*, pages 73–78, Acapulco, Mexico, August 2003.

[12] Michael Collins. Discriminative training methods for hidden Markov models: Theory and experiments with perceptron algorithms. In *Proceedings of the ACL-02 Conference on Empirical Methods in Natural Language Processing (EMNLP)*, pages 1–8, 2002.

[13] Aron Culotta and Andrew McCallum. Joint deduplication of multiple record types in relational data. In *Conference on Information and Knowledge Management (CIKM)*, pages 257–258, 2005.

[14] Xin Dong, Alon Halevy, and Jayant Madhavan. Reference reconciliation in complex information spaces. In *The ACM International Conference on Management of Data (SIGMOD)*, pages 85–96, Baltimore, USA, 2005.

[15] I. Fellegi and A. Sunter. A theory for record linkage. *Journal of the American Statistical Association*, 64:1183–1210, 1969.

[16] C. Lee Giles, Kurt Bollacker, and Steve Lawrence. CiteSeer: An automatic citation indexing system. In *The ACM Conference on Digital Libraries*, pages 89–98, Pittsburgh, USA, 1998.

[17] Lifang Gu, Rohan Baxter, Deanne Vickers, and Chris Rainsford. Record linkage: Current practice and future directions. Technical Report 03-83, CSIRO Mathematical and Information Sciences, Canberra, Australia, April 2003.

[18] Mauricio Hernández and Salvatore Stolfo. The merge/purge problem for large databases. In *The ACM International Conference on Management of Data (SIGMOD)*, pages 127–138, San Jose, USA, May 1995.

[19] Dmitri Kalashnikov, Sharad Mehrotra, and Zhaoqi Chen. Exploiting relationships for domain-independent data cleaning. In *The SIAM International Conference on Data Mining (SIAM SDM)*, pages 262–273, Newport Beach, USA, 2005.

[20] Nick Koudas, Sunita Sarawagi, and Divesh Srivastava. Record linkage: Similarity measures and algorithms (tutorial). In *Proceedings of the ACM SIGMOD International Conference on Management of Data (SIGMOD)*, pages 802–803, 2006.

[21] Bo Long, Zhongfei (Mark) Zhang, Xiaoyun Wú, and Philip S. Yu. Spectral clustering for multi-type relational data. In *Proceedings of the International Conference on Machine Learning (ICML)*, pages 585–592, 2006.

[22] Andrew McCallum, Kamal Nigam, and Lyle Ungar. Efficient clustering of high-dimensional data sets with application to reference matching. In *The International Conference on Knowledge Discovery and Data Mining (SIGKDD)*, pages 169–178, Boston, USA, August 2000.

[23] Andrew McCallum and Ben Wellner. Conditional models of identity uncertainty with application to noun coreference. In *The Annual Conference on Neural Information Processing Systems (NIPS)*, pages 905–912, Vancouver, Canada, 2004.

[24] Alvaro Monge and Charles Elkan. An efficient domain-independent algorithm for detecting approximately duplicate database records. In *The SIGMOD Workshop on Research Issues on Data Mining and Knowledge Discovery (DMKD)*, pages 23–29, Tuscon, USA, May 1997.

[25] Hanna Pasula, Bhaskara Marthi, Brian Milch, Stuart Russell, and Ilya Shpitser. Identity uncertainty and citation matching. In *The Annual Conference on Neural Information Processing Systems (NIPS)*, pages 1401–1408, Vancouver, Canada, 2003.

[26] Eric Ristad and Peter Yianilos. Learning string edit distance. *IEEE Transactions on Pattern Analysis and Machine Intelligence (PAMI)*, 20(5):522–532, 1998.

[27] Sunita Sarawagi and Anuradha Bhamidipaty. Interactive deduplication using active learning. In *The ACM International Conference on Knowledge Discovery and Data Mining (SIGKDD)*, pages 269–278, Edmonton, Canada, 2002.

[28] Parag Singla and Pedro Domingos. Object identification with attribute-mediated dependences. In *Proceedings of the European Conference on Principles and Practice of Knowledge Discovery in Databases (PKDD)*, pages 297–308, Porto, Portugal, 2005.

[29] Sheila Tejada, Craig Knoblock, and Steven Minton. Learning object identification rules for information integration. *Information Systems Journal*, 26(8):635–656, 2001.

[30] William Winkler. The state of record linkage and current research problems. Technical report, Statistical Research Division, U.S. Census Bureau, Washington, DC, USA, 1999.

Chapter 11

Non-Redundant Data Clustering

David Gondek

IBM Watson Research Center, `dgondek@us.ibm.com`

Abstract   As a discovery technique, clustering should avoid redundancies with existing knowledge about class structures or groupings and reveal novel, previously unknown aspects of the data. This setting is formally defined as a constrained clustering problem, referred to as "non-redundant clustering." A family of algorithms is derived which obtain high-quality clusterings while ensuring these clusterings are novel with respect to the existing knowledge. The algorithms are shown to allow for a range of data characteristics and may be used both when existing knowledge is available or in an exploratory manner to obtain successive novel clusterings. Experimental evaluations are used to evaluate and compare the algorithmic approaches on image, text, and synthetic data.

11.1 Introduction

Data contains multiple plausible clusterings. Constrained clustering techniques are used to control which of these multiple clusterings will be returned. While there are a range of techniques for guiding searches *toward* those solutions that bear certain characteristics known to be desired in advance, here we consider the problem of guiding searches *away from* known structures. In such a setting, an analyst specifies model-level characteristics of what is *not* desired. This is particularly useful in true exploratory settings where characteristics of the desired solution are not known in advance.

There are a range of settings in which non-redundant clustering is particularly useful. There is the straightforward application for domains where multiple clusterings exist. For instance, in document clustering of news stories, the documents may naturally cluster by topic, region, or source. Existing clustering techniques, even with random initializations, will typically return only one of these solutions. Non-redundant clustering allows an analyst to specify one or more of these clusterings which are not desired and should be avoided in the clustering solution. Importantly, it does this without characterizing the target solution. Under another setting we consider, the analyst may identify features (here, terms) which ought not be associated with the clustering. A successful non-redundant clustering algorithm should obtain a clustering which does not closely associate with this known structure. Another interesting application is when the known structure is the result of a previously run algorithm. This is particularly intriguing as it suggests a program of successive non-redundant clusterings, which would enumerate a number of plausible clusterings for the data. In a true exploratory setting where characteristics of the desired solution is not known in advance, enumeration is the only means by which one can explore the possible clusterings available. Finally, if supervision is available, as the approaches discussed here are based on well-known techniques, they may be easily combined to enhance performance on semi-supervised tasks. That is if one were classifying a set of news stories according to topic in a semi-supervised setting, by introducing the newsfeed source as known structure, topic classification performance can actually be improved.

11.2 Problem Setting

In this section, the non-redundant clustering problem is formally described, as first suggested in [24]. We begin by identifying the forms of known structure which may be used, briefly review some necessary concepts from information theory and cluster analysis, and then formally define the non-redundant clustering problem.

Known Structure

In the first case, a known categorization $(Z = \Pi_{\mathbf{X}}^{1})$ is given as known structure. This categorization may be the result of hand-labeled classification, it may be derived from the collection process (e.g., source websites of webpages), or it could be a classification obtained from supervised or unsupervised learning algorithms. The goal is to find a clustering which is novel with respect to this known categorization. Supervised information may be available in addition to known structure.

Noise Features

In the second case, a set of features are given as irrelevant, or "noise" features $(Z = \mathcal{NF})$. A clustering $\Pi_{\mathbf{X}}^{*}$ is desired with which the features $\mathcal{NF}$ are not correlated. Note that this notion of noise features differs from that presented in work such as [23] and [13]. In these works, noise features are defined as irrelevant features resulting from the learned structure. Instead, our use of the term *noise features* refers to features *desired* to appear noisy such that in any solution obtained, the $\mathcal{NF}$ features ought to appear as noise.

One setting in which this formulation is particularly relevant is those cases in which features bear semantic content. An obvious example would be that of text mining, where individual features (terms) contain semantic information about the document. An analyst could then select terms associated with the undesired structure (e.g., news source names). This approach is also useful in more specialized settings, in which it is known a priori that certain features dominate the structure of the data but this structure is not desired.

11.2.1 Background Concepts

The definition of non-redundant clustering and algorithms derived will make extensive use of several concepts from information theory. These are briefly reviewed here. For a full discussion of these concepts, see [3]. A crucial concept is that of *entropy*, which is a measure of the uncertainty of a random variable.

11.2.1.1 Shannon Information Entropy and Conditional Entropy

DEFINITION 11.1 *The* Shannon entropy, $H(X)$, *of a discrete random variable X is:*

$$H(X) = - \sum_{x \in \mathcal{X}} P(\mathbf{x}) \log_2 P(x).$$

Entropy has several properties which will be of use: entropy is non-negative, bounded $[H(X) \leq \log |\mathcal{X}|]$, and concave. The bound on entropy is reached when the distribution X is uniform. As a distribution becomes more peaked, the entropy decreases. The definition of entropy can be extended to address conditional distributions via the *conditional entropy*.

DEFINITION 11.2 *The* conditional entropy *of variable X conditioned on Y is given by:*

$$H(Y|X) = \sum_{x \in \mathcal{X}} \sum_{y \in \mathcal{Y}} P(x, y) \log P(y|x).$$

The conditional entropy expresses the uncertainty of variable X given that the value of Y is known. For instance, in the soft-clustering case where items are assigned to multiple clusters in probability, one may represent cluster membership as a probability $P(\mathbf{Y}|\mathbf{X})$. The conditional entropy $H(\mathbf{Y}|\mathbf{X})$

measures how soft the clustering is, with higher values meaning a "fuzzier" clustering.

11.2.1.2 Mutual Information and Relative Entropy

Mutual information describes how much information two variables convey about each other. Variables that are more dependent on each other have higher mutual information.

DEFINITION 11.3 *The* mutual information *of variables X and Y is given by:*

$$I(X;Y) = \sum_{x \in \mathcal{X}} \sum_{y \in \mathcal{Y}} P(x,y) \log \frac{P(x,y)}{P(x)P(y)}.$$

Often, mutual information is given in terms of the conditional probability:

$$I(X;Y) = \sum_{x \in \mathcal{X}} \sum_{y \in \mathcal{Y}} P(x,y) \log \frac{P(x|y)}{P(x)} = \sum_{y \in \mathcal{Y}} \sum_{x \in \mathcal{X}} P(x,y) \log \frac{P(y|x)}{P(y)}.$$

Mutual information may be written in terms of entropies:

$$I(X;Y) = H(X) - H(X|Y) = H(Y) - H(Y|X).$$

A number of useful properties follow: Mutual information is symmetric, $[I(X;Y) = I(Y;X)]$, non-negative, and bounded $[I(X;Y) \leq \min(H(X), H(Y))]$.

The definition of mutual information may be extended to any number of variables. Of particular use in non-redundant clustering will be the *conditional mutual information*, which is the mutual information of X and Y conditioned on Z. This measures how much incremental knowledge X offers about Y assuming that Z is already known.

DEFINITION 11.4 *The* conditional mutual information *of variables X and Y given Z is:*

$$I(X;Y|Z) = \sum_{x \in \mathcal{X}} \sum_{y \in \mathcal{Y}} \sum_{z \in \mathcal{Z}} P(x,y,z) \log \frac{P(x,y|z)}{P(x|z)P(y|z)}.$$

Another useful quantity is the *Kullback-Leibler (KL) divergence*, also known as the *relative entropy* which measures the divergence between two probability distributions:

DEFINITION 11.5 *The* Kullback-Leibler (KL) divergence *for distributions $P(x)$ and $Q(x)$ is:*

$$D_{KL}[p||q] = \sum_{x \in \mathcal{X}} P(x) \log \frac{P(x)}{Q(x)}.$$

The KL divergence is always non-negative and is equal to 0 if and only if $p = q$. Note that it is not a true metric as it is not symmetric and does not satisfy the triangle equality.

11.2.2 Multiple Clusterings

It is often the case that there exists multiple clusterings which are of high quality, i.e., obtain high values in the objective function. These may consist of minor variations on a single clustering or may include clusterings which are substantially dissimilar. Distinguishing between these two cases requires some notion of clustering similarity. Multiple techniques exist for determining the similarity or dissimilarity of clusterings. Many of these approaches were originally developed for use as external criteria for the *cluster validation* task, which seeks to measure the effectiveness of a clustering algorithm by comparing the results against a known clustering. Overviews of these methods are provided in [12] and [15] of which we review here the information-theoretic metric known as "variation of information," due to [15]. This is a true metric designed to measure the "distance" between two clusters, and will be used to justify our definition of "information-orthogonality."

11.2.2.1 Variation of Information

DEFINITION 11.6 *The* variation of information *between two clusterings* $\Pi_{\mathbf{X}}^1$ *and* $\Pi_{\mathbf{X}}^2$, $VI(\Pi_{\mathbf{X}}^1, \Pi_{\mathbf{X}}^2)$ *is defined as:*

$$VI(\Pi_{\mathbf{X}}^1, \Pi_{\mathbf{X}}^2) = H(\Pi_{\mathbf{X}}^1) + H(\Pi_{\mathbf{X}}^2) - 2I(\Pi_{\mathbf{X}}^1, \Pi_{\mathbf{X}}^2). \tag{11.1}$$

The definition in 11.1 can be rewritten as:

$$VI(\Pi_{\mathbf{X}}^1, \Pi_{\mathbf{X}}^2) = [H(\Pi_{\mathbf{X}}^1) - I(\Pi_{\mathbf{X}}^1; \Pi_{\mathbf{X}}^2)] + [H(\Pi_{\mathbf{X}}^2) - I(\Pi_{\mathbf{X}}^1; \Pi_{\mathbf{X}}^2)]$$
$$= H(\Pi_{\mathbf{X}}^1|\Pi_{\mathbf{X}}^2) + H(\Pi_{\mathbf{X}}^2|\Pi_{\mathbf{X}}^1),$$

which expresses the quantity as the sum of the conditional entropies. It can be shown that VI is a true metric, as it obeys the following three properties:

(i.) Non-negativity $VI(\Pi_{\mathbf{X}}^1, \Pi_{\mathbf{X}}^2) \geq 0$ with equality if and only if $\Pi_{\mathbf{X}}^1 = \Pi_{\mathbf{X}}^2$.

(ii.) Symmetry $VI(\Pi_{\mathbf{X}}^1, \Pi_{\mathbf{X}}^2) = VI(\Pi_{\mathbf{X}}^2, \Pi_{\mathbf{X}}^1)$.

(iii.) Triangle Inequality For clusterings $\Pi_{\mathbf{X}}^1, \Pi_{\mathbf{X}}^2, \Pi_{\mathbf{X}}^3$,

$$VI(\Pi_{\mathbf{X}}^1, \Pi_{\mathbf{X}}^2) + VI(\Pi_{\mathbf{X}}^2, \Pi_{\mathbf{X}}^3) \geq VI(\Pi_{\mathbf{X}}^1, \Pi_{\mathbf{X}}^3).$$

Further, VI is *bounded*, that is,

Boundedness

$$VI(\Pi_{\mathbf{X}}{}^1, \Pi_{\mathbf{X}}{}^2) \leq H(\Pi_{\mathbf{X}}{}^1) + H(\Pi_{\mathbf{X}}{}^2).$$

Boundedness follows by non-negativity of mutual information and is a consequence of the fact that the space of all clusterings is bounded.

11.2.3 Information Orthogonality

Now it is possible to formally define *information-orthogonality* for clusters. Note that this is intended to capture the orthogonality of clusterings and is not to be confused with the parameter information-orthogonality of [4]. In particular, we define:

DEFINITION 11.7 *Clusterings* $\Pi_{\mathbf{X}}{}^1$ *and* $\Pi_{\mathbf{X}}{}^2$ *are* information-orthogonal *with regard to X if and only if any of the following equivalent definitions:*

(i.) Original definition:

$$I(\Pi_{\mathbf{X}}{}^1, \Pi_{\mathbf{X}}{}^2; X) = I(\Pi_{\mathbf{X}}{}^1; X) + I(\Pi_{\mathbf{X}}{}^2; X). \qquad (11.2)$$

(ii.) Entropy formulation:

$$H(\Pi_{\mathbf{X}}{}^1, \Pi_{\mathbf{X}}{}^2) = H(\Pi_{\mathbf{X}}{}^1) + H(\Pi_{\mathbf{X}}{}^2).$$

(iii.) $\Pi_{\mathbf{X}}{}^1$ *and* $\Pi_{\mathbf{X}}{}^2$ *are independent:*

$$P(\Pi_{\mathbf{X}}{}^1, \Pi_{\mathbf{X}}{}^2) = P(\Pi_{\mathbf{X}}{}^1)P(\Pi_{\mathbf{X}}{}^2).$$

(iv.) The variation of information metric, $VI(\Pi_{\mathbf{X}}{}^1, \Pi_{\mathbf{X}}{}^2)$*, is maximal:*

$$VI(\Pi_{\mathbf{X}}{}^1, \Pi_{\mathbf{X}}{}^2) = H(\Pi_{\mathbf{X}}{}^1) + H(\Pi_{\mathbf{X}}{}^2).$$

Definition (i.) is the original definition and captures the idea of "orthogonality" in terms of mutual information. Definition (ii.) is an entropy formulation which has uses in developing objective functions for clustering algorithms. Definition (iii.) is a justification in terms of the cluster probabilities, which intuitively captures the notion of "information-orthogonality." And finally, in Definition (iv.), information-orthogonality implies the VI metric is maximal. By appeal to VI, it is clear that information-orthogonality satisfies our requirement for non-redundant clustering: informational-orthogonal clusters are as "distant" from one another as possible.

11.2.4   Non-Redundant Clustering

It is now possible to formally define the problem of *non-redundant clustering*. In the ideal case, non-redundant clustering seeks to find a high-quality clustering which is informational-orthogonal with respect to known structure.

DEFINITION 11.8   *The* **non-redundant clustering problem** *is given for data* $\mathcal{X}$, *known structure* Z, *and objective function* $\mathcal{L}$ *as:*

$$\max_{\Pi_{\mathbf{X}}^*} \mathcal{L}(\Pi_{\mathbf{X}}^*, \mathbf{X})$$
$$s.t. \quad \Pi_{\mathbf{X}}^* \text{ is a valid clustering,}$$
$$\Pi_{\mathbf{X}}^* \text{ and } Z \text{ are information-orthogonal.}$$

This definition is simply the general clustering problem with the addition of an information-orthogonality constraint. One way to intuitively explain the information-orthogonality constraint is using Definition 11.7(iii.), which implies

$$P(\mathbf{y}_i | z_j) = P(\mathbf{y}_i | z_k) \qquad \forall i, j, k.$$

This means that knowing the value of Z does not affect the probability of the cluster assignments in $\Pi_{\mathbf{X}}^*$. Thus, in the categorical case, possessing the known cluster assignment for an instance does not influence the solution cluster to which it is assigned. In that sense, the two clusterings are independent.

In practice, it may be the case that the information-orthogonality constraint is too strict. Informed by Definition 11.7(iv.) one may relax the non-redundant clustering problem by simply requiring that the VI be greater than some threshold δ.

DEFINITION 11.9   *The* **relaxed non-redundant clustering problem** *is given for data* $\mathbf{X}$, *known structure* Z, *and objective function* $\mathcal{L}$ *as:*

$$\max_{\Pi_{\mathbf{X}}^*} \mathcal{L}(\Pi_{\mathbf{X}}^*, \mathbf{X})$$
$$s.t. \quad \Pi_{\mathbf{X}}^* \text{ is a valid clustering,}$$
$$VI(\Pi_{\mathbf{X}}^*, Z) \geq \delta$$

This definition will be used to motivate two approaches for non-redundant clustering: conditional ensembles and the coordinated conditional information bottleneck.

11.3 Conditional Ensembles

Conditional ensembles [11] is a technique for obtaining non-redundant clusterings by independently clustering data conditioned on the known structure, and then combining the results. It can be motivated as follows. Suppose that there exists two strong orthogonal clusterings of data $\Pi_{\mathbf{X}}^1$ and $\Pi_{\mathbf{X}}^2$. Because $\Pi_{\mathbf{X}}^1$ and $\Pi_{\mathbf{X}}^2$ are informational-orthogonal, that means that $\Pi_{\mathbf{X}}^2$'s structure must be replicated *within* each of the k clusters $\Pi_{\mathbf{X}}^1$ clusters. Suppose $\Pi_{\mathbf{X}}^1$ is known side information and $\Pi_{\mathbf{X}}^2$ is not known. A straightforward method for accomplishing non-redundant clustering and discovering $\Pi_{\mathbf{X}}^2$ would be to perform clustering within each of the $\Pi_{\mathbf{X}}^1$ clusters. As the clustering structure of $\Pi_{\mathbf{X}}^1$ will not be significant within a single cluster of $\Pi_{\mathbf{X}}^1$, and the $\Pi_{\mathbf{X}}^2$ is the next most prominent structure, application of a clustering algorithm should produce a local version of $\Pi_{\mathbf{X}}^2$. Once local versions of $\Pi_{\mathbf{X}}^2$ are produced for each of the $\Pi_{\mathbf{X}}^1$ clusters, all that remains is to combine them into a coherent global solution. As it will turn out, this can be accomplished by using existing *ensemble clustering* methods which will be reviewed in the next section.

The framework is described in Figure 11.1, and consists of three stages: In the first stage, local clustering solutions are computed for all data points belonging to the same cluster of the given clustering. This results in one local clustering for every known cluster of the original clustering. The second stage extends these local solutions to create global clustering solutions. Note that in this stage, the characteristics of the clusters do not change. That is, in model-based or centroid-based approaches one would keep the model parameters or cluster centroids constant. For instance, with Expectation Maximization (EM), this stage corresponds to application of the E-step over all instances. With k-means, this stage corresponds to application of the assignment step over all instances. Finally, the global clustering solutions obtained from the local seeds are combined using an ensemble clustering method to produce the final coordinated clustering as explained in the next section.

Ensemble Clustering

Ensemble clustering deals with the problem of combining multiple clusterings to produce a combined clustering solution. This problem has received substantial attention (cf. [20, 22]) as a practical way of combining results from different clustering algorithms as well as a method to avoid overfitting by data resampling [16]. The goal is, given l clusterings $\{\Pi_{\mathbf{X}}^1, \ldots, \mathbf{Y}^l\}$ where each clustering $\Pi_{\mathbf{X}}^i$ partitions the data into k_i clusters, to find a combined clustering $\mathbf{Y}$ of k clusters. In our case, we are concerned with the combination step and not with the problem of how to generate the different clustering solutions as those are obtained via the first two steps of the CondEns algorithm.

Input: Data $\mathbf{X} = \{\mathbf{x}_1, \ldots, \mathbf{x}_n\}$, clustering $\Pi_{\mathbf{X}}{}^1 : \{\pi_{\mathbf{X}}{}^1_1, \ldots, \pi_{\mathbf{X}}{}^1_k\}$, number of clusters in target k in number of clusters k_j for each local clustering

Output: Clustering $\Pi_{\mathbf{X}}{}^* : \{\pi_{\mathbf{X}}{}^*_1, \ldots, \pi_{\mathbf{X}}{}^*_k\}$

1. Clustering

> Partition data set into local sets:
> $\mathbf{X}_j \equiv \{\mathbf{x}_i : i \in \mathbf{y}_j)\}, j = 1 \ldots, l.$
> Apply base clustering method to each $\mathbf{X}_j$ to find a local clustering
> $\tilde{\Pi}_{\mathbf{X}}{}^j : j = 1, \ldots k_1.$

2. Extension

> Extend each $\tilde{\Pi}_{\mathbf{X}}{}^j$ to a global clustering $\mathbf{Y}^j$ by assigning training instances in $\mathbf{X}_{\neq j}$, $m \neq j$ to one of the existing clusters
> $\Pi_{\mathbf{X}}{}^j : \{\mathbf{x}_1, \ldots, \mathbf{x}_n\} \to \{\pi_{\mathbf{X}1}, \ldots, \pi_{\mathbf{X}k_j}\}, j = 1 \ldots, l$

3. Combination

> Combine clustering solutions $\Pi_{\mathbf{X}}{}^j$ to form a consensus clustering:
> $\Pi_{\mathbf{X}}{}^* = \mathsf{Consens}(\mathbf{Y}^1, \ldots, \Pi_{\mathbf{X}}{}^l)$, where $\Pi_{\mathbf{X}}{}^*$ is a global clustering:
> $\Pi_{\mathbf{X}}{}^* : \{\mathbf{x}_1, \ldots, \mathbf{x}_n\} \to \{\pi_{\mathbf{X}1}, \ldots, \pi_{\mathbf{X}k}\}$

FIGURE 11.1: CondEns algorithm.

In [22], several techniques for obtaining a combined clustering solution are compared. The *median partition* technique, in particular, has the most attractive time complexity while achieving results on par with the other techniques studied. It can be motivated by the objective presented in [20]:

$$\Pi_{\mathbf{X}}{}^* = \arg\max_{\Pi_{\mathbf{X}}} \sum_{j=1}^{l} I(\Pi_{\mathbf{X}}; \Pi_{\mathbf{X}}{}^j).$$

Instead of optimizing the objective directly, [22] solves for a related quantity, the *generalized mutual information*. Generalized mutual information follows from the definition of generalized entropy for degree s:

$$H^s(\Pi_{\mathbf{X}}) = (2^{1-s} - 1)^{-1} \left(\sum_{j=1}^{l} P(\pi_{\mathbf{X}j})^s - 1 \right),$$

where $s > 0$ and $s \neq 1$. The generalized mutual information would then be:

$$I^s(\Pi_{\mathbf{X}}; \Pi_{\mathbf{X}}') = H^s(\Pi_{\mathbf{X}}') - H^s(\Pi_{\mathbf{X}}' | \Pi_{\mathbf{X}}). \tag{11.3}$$

One may consider the quadratic mutual information, where $s = 2$. This criterion is up to a factor of 2 equivalent to the *category utility function U* presented in [8]. Moreover, it was shown in [17] that maximization of Eq. (11.3) for a fixed number of target clusters is equivalent to the minimization of a squared-error criterion. The latter can be solved using standard approximation techniques such as k-means clustering. Following [22] we have obtained good results using the quadratic mutual information criterion and k-means clustering.

11.3.1 Complexity

The technique presented has attractive overall time complexity. For instance, in the case where k-means is used for the base clustering method, CondEns is typically faster than running simple k-means over the data set. This surprising result is due to the fact that CondEns first partitions the data set into smaller local sets. As the complexity of k-means clustering is typically superlinear in the number of instances [1, 6], the clustering step is more efficient. Further, the extension step consists of a single assignment iteration, and the combination step is a clustering over a dramatically smaller problem. Thus, the divide-and-conquer approach of CondEns achieves significant time savings over traditional k-means.

11.3.2 Conditions for Correctness

In this section, a theoretical analysis of sufficient conditions is provided for when a target clustering embedded in the data set can be recovered by the above algorithm. The analysis requires making a number of assumptions on the base clustering algorithm, the cluster combination scheme, and the relative dominance of the target clustering. These requirements are strong and may not be met in most realistic settings. However, they provide motivation for the proposed method and the analysis is valuable in explaining what factors impact the approach.

A crucial quantity to review in the current setting is the conditional mutual information, defined as

$$I(A; B|C) = H(A|C) - H(A|B, C),$$

where A, B, and C are random variables. We state a few useful facts about conditional mutual information that directly follow from this definition.

PROPOSITION 11.1

(a) $I(A; B|C) = I(B; A|C)$.
(b) $I(A; B|C) = I(A; B, C) - I(A; C)$.

(c) $I(A; B|C) - I(A; B) = I(A; C|B) - I(A; C)$.
(d) A is independent of $C|B$ if and only if $I(A; C|B) = 0$.

We will quantify the quality of a clustering as the mutual information between the feature representation and the cluster membership variable, i.e.,

$$Q(\mathbf{Y}) \equiv I(\mathbf{Y}; \mathbf{X}) = H(\mathbf{X}) - H(\mathbf{X}|\mathbf{Y}),$$

where H denotes the (conditional) entropy or the differential (conditional) entropy, dependent on the type of feature representation. An important property is that $\Pi_{\mathbf{X}}^2$ will be conditionally independent of any other random variable, given the input. In particular $\Pi_{\mathbf{X}}^2$ is independent of any given partitioning $\Pi_{\mathbf{X}}^1$, i.e., $\Pi_{\mathbf{X}}^2$ is independent of $\Pi_{\mathbf{X}}^1|\mathbf{X}$ or, equivalently $I(\Pi_{\mathbf{X}}^1; \Pi_{\mathbf{X}}^2|\mathbf{X}) = 0$, $\forall \Pi_{\mathbf{X}}^1$. Using the concept of information-orthogonality as defined, the following lemma results:

LEMMA 11.1
If $\Pi_{\mathbf{X}}^2$ and $\Pi_{\mathbf{X}}^1$ are information-orthogonal, then $I(\Pi_{\mathbf{X}}^1; \mathbf{X}) = I(\Pi_{\mathbf{X}}^1; \mathbf{X}|\Pi_{\mathbf{X}}^2)$ and $I(\Pi_{\mathbf{X}}^2; \mathbf{X}) = I(\Pi_{\mathbf{X}}^2; \mathbf{X}|\Pi_{\mathbf{X}}^1)$.

Using the chain rule for mutual information,

$$I(\Pi_{\mathbf{X}}^2, \Pi_{\mathbf{X}}^1; \mathbf{X}) = I(\Pi_{\mathbf{X}}^2; \mathbf{X}|\Pi_{\mathbf{X}}^1) + I(\Pi_{\mathbf{X}}^1; \mathbf{X})$$
$$= I(\Pi_{\mathbf{X}}^1; \mathbf{X}|\Pi_{\mathbf{X}}^2) + I(\Pi_{\mathbf{X}}^2; \mathbf{X}),$$

which when combined with (11.2) establishes that $I(\Pi_{\mathbf{X}}^2; \mathbf{X}) = I(\Pi_{\mathbf{X}}^2; \mathbf{X}|\Pi_{\mathbf{X}}^1)$ and $I(\Pi_{\mathbf{X}}^1; \mathbf{X}) = I(\Pi_{\mathbf{X}}^1; \mathbf{X}|\Pi_{\mathbf{X}}^2)$. ∎

For arbitrary clusterings C, Lemma 11.1 may not hold, however, the conditional independence from $\Pi_{\mathbf{X}}^1$ given $\mathbf{X}$ guarantees the following:

LEMMA 11.2
$I(\Pi_{\mathbf{X}}^2; \mathbf{X}|\Pi_{\mathbf{X}}^1) \leq I(\Pi_{\mathbf{X}}^2; \mathbf{X})$

Since $I(\Pi_{\mathbf{X}}^2; \Pi_{\mathbf{X}}^1|\mathbf{X}) = 0$, one obtains $I(\Pi_{\mathbf{X}}^2; \mathbf{X}|\Pi_{\mathbf{X}}^1) = I(\Pi_{\mathbf{X}}^2; \Pi_{\mathbf{X}}^1|\mathbf{X}) + I(\Pi_{\mathbf{X}}^2; \mathbf{X}) - I(\Pi_{\mathbf{X}}^2; \Pi_{\mathbf{X}}^1) = I(\Pi_{\mathbf{X}}^2; \mathbf{X}) - I(\Pi_{\mathbf{X}}^2; \Pi_{\mathbf{X}}^1) \leq I(\Pi_{\mathbf{X}}^2; \mathbf{X})$. ∎
An immediate implication of the two lemmata is the following corollary.

COROLLARY 11.1
If $\Pi_{\mathbf{X}}^{2*} = \arg\max_{\Pi_{\mathbf{X}}^2} I(\Pi_{\mathbf{X}}^2; \mathbf{X})$ and $\Pi_{\mathbf{X}}^{2*}$ is information-orthogonal to $\Pi_{\mathbf{X}}^1$, then $\Pi_{\mathbf{X}}^{2*} = \arg\max_{\Pi_{\mathbf{X}}^2} I(\Pi_{\mathbf{X}}^2; \mathbf{X}|\Pi_{\mathbf{X}}^1)$.

$I(\Pi_{\mathbf{X}}^{2*}; \mathbf{X}|\Pi_{\mathbf{X}}^1) = I(\Pi_{\mathbf{X}}^{2*}; \mathbf{X}) \geq I(\Pi_{\mathbf{X}}^2; \mathbf{X}) \geq I(\Pi_{\mathbf{X}}^2; \mathbf{X}|\Pi_{\mathbf{X}}^1)$ for all $\Pi_{\mathbf{X}}^2$.

∎

The main problem is that the bound in Lemma 11.2 holds only on the average. Namely, one may have a situation where $I(\Pi_{\mathbf{X}}^{2'}; \mathbf{X}|\Pi_{\mathbf{X}}^{1} = \pi_{\mathbf{X}_j}^{1}) > I(\Pi_{\mathbf{X}}^{2}; \mathbf{X}|\Pi_{\mathbf{X}}^{1} = \pi_{\mathbf{X}_j}^{1})$, despite the fact that $I(\Pi_{\mathbf{X}}^{2'}; \mathbf{X}|\Pi_{\mathbf{X}}^{1}) \leq I(\Pi_{\mathbf{X}}^{2}; \mathbf{X}|\Pi_{\mathbf{X}}^{1})$. As a relaxed condition, we can prove that a dominant, information-orthogonal clustering will also dominate all other clusterings in at least one group of $\Pi_{\mathbf{X}}^{1}$. We will require the following lemma:

LEMMA 11.3
There exists a $\Pi_{\mathbf{X}}^{2}$ where:

$$I(\Pi_{\mathbf{X}}^{2}; \mathbf{X}|\Pi_{\mathbf{X}}^{1}) = \sum_j P(\pi_{\mathbf{X}_j}^{1}) I(\Pi_{\mathbf{X}}^{2j}; \mathbf{X}|\Pi_{\mathbf{X}}^{1} = \pi_{\mathbf{X}_j}^{1}).$$

This lemma is proven by using the fact that $\Pi_{\mathbf{X}}^{1}$ is a partition, only the $\mathbf{X}^j$ participate in $I(\Pi_{\mathbf{X}}^{2j}; \mathbf{X}|\Pi_{\mathbf{X}}^{1} = \pi_{\mathbf{X}_j}^{1})$ and so in $\Pi_{\mathbf{X}}^{2}$ each $\mathbf{X}^j$ may be handled separately.

PROPOSITION 11.2
If $\Pi_{\mathbf{X}}^{2*}$ is information-orthogonal to $\Pi_{\mathbf{X}}^{1}$ and $I(\Pi_{\mathbf{X}}^{2*}; \mathbf{X}) > I(\Pi_{\mathbf{X}}^{2}; \mathbf{X})$ for all $\Pi_{\mathbf{X}}^{2} \in \mathcal{Y} - \{\Pi_{\mathbf{X}}^{2*}\}$, where $\diamond_{\mathbf{X}}\in$ is chosen such that for all $\Pi_{\mathbf{X}}^{2j} \equiv \arg\max_{\Pi_{\mathbf{X}}^{2}} I(\Pi_{\mathbf{X}}^{2}; \mathbf{X}|\Pi_{\mathbf{X}}^{1} = \pi_{\mathbf{X}_j}^{1})$, $\Pi_{\mathbf{X}}^{2j} \in \mathcal{Y}$, then there exists at least one group j^* such that $I(\Pi_{\mathbf{X}}^{2*}; \mathbf{X}|\Pi_{\mathbf{X}}^{1} = \pi_{\mathbf{X}_{j*}}^{1}) \geq I(\Pi_{\mathbf{X}}^{2}; \mathbf{X}|\Pi_{\mathbf{X}}^{1} = \pi_{\mathbf{X}_{j*}}^{1})$ for all $\Pi_{\mathbf{X}}^{2}$.

We first point out that there exists some $\Pi_{\mathbf{X}}^{2}$ such that $I(\Pi_{\mathbf{X}}^{2}; \mathbf{X}|\Pi_{\mathbf{X}}^{1}) = \sum_j P(\pi_{\mathbf{X}_j}^{1}) I(\Pi_{\mathbf{X}}^{2j}; \mathbf{X}|\Pi_{\mathbf{X}}^{1} = \pi_{\mathbf{X}_j}^{1})$. Such a $\Pi_{\mathbf{X}}^{2}$ is constructed such that the restriction of $\Pi_{\mathbf{X}}^{2}$ to the pre-images $\mathbf{X}^j$ of $\Pi_{\mathbf{X}}^{1}$ equals $\Pi_{\mathbf{X}}^{2j}$. Using the fact that $\Pi_{\mathbf{X}}^{1}$ is a partition, only those $\mathbf{X}^j$ participate in $I(\Pi_{\mathbf{X}}^{2j}; \mathbf{X}|\Pi_{\mathbf{X}}^{1} = \pi_{\mathbf{X}_j}^{1})$ and so in $\Pi_{\mathbf{X}}^{2}$ each $\mathbf{X}^j$ may be separately assigned to its $\Pi_{\mathbf{X}}^{2j}$. In conjunction with Lemma 11.2 this yields:

$$\sum_{j=1}^{l} P(\pi_{\mathbf{X}_j}^{1}) I(\Pi_{\mathbf{X}}^{2j}; \mathbf{X}|\Pi_{\mathbf{X}}^{1} = \pi_{\mathbf{X}_j}^{1}) = I(\Pi_{\mathbf{X}}^{2}; \mathbf{X}|\Pi_{\mathbf{X}}^{1}) \leq I(\Pi_{\mathbf{X}}^{2}; \mathbf{X}).$$

By assumption $I(\Pi_{\mathbf{X}}^{2}; \mathbf{X}) < I(\Pi_{\mathbf{X}}^{2*}; \mathbf{X})$ and with Lemma 11.1 one arrives at

$$I(\Pi_{\mathbf{X}}^{2}; \mathbf{X}) < I(\Pi_{\mathbf{X}}^{2*}; \mathbf{X}) = I(\Pi_{\mathbf{X}}^{2*}; \mathbf{X}|\Pi_{\mathbf{X}}^{1})$$
$$= \sum_{j=1}^{l} P(\pi_{\mathbf{X}_j}^{1}) I(\Pi_{\mathbf{X}}^{2*}; \mathbf{X}|\Pi_{\mathbf{X}}^{1} = \pi_{\mathbf{X}_j}^{1}).$$

If one now assumes that all $\Pi_{\mathbf{X}}^{2^j} \neq \Pi_{\mathbf{X}}^{2^*}$, then by the local optimality of $\Pi_{\mathbf{X}}^{2^j}$ one would get $I(\Pi_{\mathbf{X}}^{2^j}; \mathbf{X}|\Pi_{\mathbf{X}}^1 = \pi_{\mathbf{X}_j}^1) \geq I(\Pi_{\mathbf{X}}^{2^*}; \mathbf{X}|\Pi_{\mathbf{X}}^1 = \pi_{\mathbf{X}_j}^1)$ which contradicts the fact that

$$\sum_{j=1}^{l} P(\pi_{\mathbf{X}_j}^1) I(\Pi_{\mathbf{X}}^{2^j}; \mathbf{X}|\Pi_{\mathbf{X}}^1 = \pi_{\mathbf{X}_j}^1) < \sum_{j=1}^{l} P(\pi_{\mathbf{X}_j}^1) I(\Pi_{\mathbf{X}}^{2^*}; \mathbf{X}|\Pi_{\mathbf{X}}^1 = \pi_{\mathbf{X}_j}^1)$$

because of the non-negativity of the individual terms in the sum. Hence there has to be at least one index j^* so that $\Pi_{\mathbf{X}}^{2^*}$ is optimal for $\Pi_{\mathbf{X}}^1 = \pi_{\mathbf{X}_{j^*}}^1$. ∎

Thus, if the base clustering method uses a criterion analogous to the mutual information criterion to derive local clustering solutions and the target clustering is dominant and information-orthogonal to the given clustering, then the target clustering will be among the clustering solutions participating in the combination stage.

11.3.2.1 Summary

The CondEns approach provides a straightforward way of generating a non-redundant clustering given any of a number of common clustering techniques. It can accommodate a wide range of existing base clustering methods, and is straightforward to implement. Furthermore, as will be shown in the experiments section, the approach is quite effective in practice and shows remarkably good time complexity.

One drawback to the algorithm is that it requires categorical side information and so does not directly apply to situations where the side information is continuous. Another issue is that the optimization is broken into two stages so that in situations where there are multiple significant structures, the first stage may produce local solutions which are uncoordinated and difficult to combine.

11.4   Constrained Conditional Information Bottleneck

In the previous section the CondEns approach was introduced, which in its first step obtains local solutions and then combines the local solutions to produce a global solution. As mentioned, a drawback is that in practice, these local solutions may significantly disagree and result in a poor combined solution. To address this issue, one might wonder if it is possible to combine the two stages within a single-stage optimization. In such an approach, a single objective function would be offered wherein coherence is maintained among the local solutions while the search proceeds.

The coordinated conditional information bottleneck (CCIB) is designed to that purpose, featuring a single objective function which, when optimized, will produce non-redundant clusterings. The objective function must reward high quality clusterings and novelty with respect to the known clusterings while maintaining global coordination.

11.4.1 Coordinated Conditional Information Bottleneck

The CCIB formulation is an extension of the seminal work [21] on the information bottleneck (IB) framework and, among the different generalizations of IB proposed, is most closely related by motivation with the IB with side information [2] and by formulation with the parallel IB [7].

We desire an objective function which favors solutions that provide clusterings that describe the data, but are dissimilar with known structure. To avoid confusion, we will use F as a random variable over the feature space and $\mathbf{X}$ as a random variable over the set of instances. A natural quantity to consider is the conditional mutual information $I(\Pi_{\mathbf{X}}^{*}; F|Z)$. It describes how much information $\Pi_{\mathbf{X}}^{*}, Z$ convey jointly about relevant features F compared to the information provided by Z alone. Finding an optimal clustering solution should involve maximizing $I(\Pi_{\mathbf{X}}^{*}; F|Z)$.

In addition, we would like to avoid over-confidence in grouping objects together. Cluster assignment probabilities should reflect the uncertainty with which objects are assigned to clusters. One way to accomplish this is to explicitly control the fuzziness of the stochastic mapping $P_{\Pi_{\mathbf{X}}^{*}|X}$. The latter can be measured by the mutual information $I(\Pi_{\mathbf{X}}^{*}; X)$ between cluster and object identities. Here we would expect $I(\Pi_{\mathbf{X}}^{*}; X) = 0$, if objects are assigned to clusters with uniform probability, whereas $I(\Pi_{\mathbf{X}}^{*}; X)$ becomes maximal for non-stochastic mappings $P_{\Pi_{\mathbf{X}}^{*}|X}$. $I(\Pi_{\mathbf{X}}^{*}; X)$ also can be given a well-known interpretation in terms of the channel capacity required for transmitting probabilistic cluster assignments over a communication channel [21].

Combining both aspects, we define the optimal clustering as the solution to the following constrained optimization problem, the conditional information bottleneck (CIB), first introduced in [9]:

$$(\text{CIB}) \quad P_{\Pi_{\mathbf{X}}^{*}|X}^{*} = \arg \max_{P_{\Pi_{\mathbf{X}}^{*}|X} \in \mathcal{P}} I(\Pi_{\mathbf{X}}^{*}; Y|Z), \quad \text{where} \tag{11.4}$$

$$\mathcal{P} \equiv \{P_{\Pi_{\mathbf{X}}^{*}|X} : I(\Pi_{\mathbf{X}}^{*}; X) \leq c_{\max}\}. \tag{11.5}$$

This objective function captures that we are looking for probabilistic cluster assignments with a minimal fuzziness such that the relevant information jointly encoded in $\Pi_{\mathbf{X}}^{*}, Z$ is maximal.

11.4.2 Derivation from Multivariate IB

The conditional information bottleneck objective may also be derived using the multivariate information bottleneck framework presented in [7]. The multivariate information bottleneck is a technique for characterizing solutions for problems in which there are multiple partitions of the features (observed variables) or parameters (compression variables). Using Bayesian networks specifying the dependencies between these variables, information bottleneck-like objectives may be derived.

Two Bayesian networks, g_{in} and g_{out}, must be given, where g_{in} specifies the relation between the observed variables and the compression variables and g_{in} specifies the "relevant" information which is to be preserved. In our problem, which is of a form similar to the parallel information bottleneck described in [7], we obtain the g_{in} pictured in Figure 11.2(a) and the g_{out} pictured in Figure 11.2(b). The network g_{in} specifies that both $\Pi_{\mathbf{X}}^*$ and Z compress information about X. The network g_{out} specifies that $\Pi_{\mathbf{X}}^*$ and Z should preserve information about F.

(a) g_{in} (b) g_{out}

FIGURE 11.2: Multivariate information bottleneck: Bayesian networks.

Given networks g_{in} and g_{out}, and using the multi-information bottleneck principle presented in [7], a Lagrangian which enforces the dependencies specified by g_{in} and g_{out} may be derived. In particular, for our problem this Lagrangian, $\mathcal{L}^{(1)}$, would be

$$\mathcal{L}^{(1)} = I(X; \Pi_{\mathbf{X}}^*) + I(X; Z) - \beta I(F; \Pi_{\mathbf{X}}^*, Z).$$

This can be simplified, first using the fact that $I(X; Z)$ is constant and then expanding the information term:

$$\arg\min \mathcal{L}^{(1)} = \arg\min I(X; \Pi_{\mathbf{X}}^*) + I(X; Z) - \beta I(F; \Pi_{\mathbf{X}}^*, Z)$$
$$= \arg\min I(X; \Pi_{\mathbf{X}}^*) - \beta I(F; \Pi_{\mathbf{X}}^* | Z).$$

Thus, the final result obtained from application of the multivariate information bottleneck recovers our proposed conditional information bottleneck formulation.

As a side note, there are two methods proposed in [7] for obtaining Lagrangians. We have used the first method to derive the conditional information bottleneck formulation from $\mathcal{L}^{(1)}$ as above. The two methods differ in the form of input network g_{out} as well as the focus of the objectives produced.

The first, which produces $\mathcal{L}^{(1)}$, focuses on preserving the information in the dependencies of g_{out}, whereas the second, which produces $\mathcal{L}^{(2)}$, focuses on preserving information of independencies of g_{out}. The $g_{out}^{(b)}$, which would be used in the second method is pictured in Figure 11.3. This network specifies that X and F are independent given $\Pi_{\mathbf{X}}{}^*$, X and F are independent given Z, and Z and $\Pi_{\mathbf{X}}{}^*$ are independent. The corresponding Lagrangian, $\mathcal{L}^{(2)}$, would be:

$$\mathcal{L}^{(2)} = I(X; \Pi_{\mathbf{X}}{}^*) + I(X; Z) + \gamma\left(I(\Pi_{\mathbf{X}}{}^*; Z) - I(F; \Pi_{\mathbf{X}}{}^*, Z)\right),$$

which simplifies as before to yield:

$$\arg\min \mathcal{L}^{(2)} = \arg\min I(X; \Pi_{\mathbf{X}}{}^*) - \gamma\left(I(F; \Pi_{\mathbf{X}}{}^*|Z) - I(\Pi_{\mathbf{X}}{}^*; Z)\right).$$

We note that this second formulation $\mathcal{L}^{(2)}$ directly penalizes $I(\Pi_{\mathbf{X}}{}^*; Z)$ whereas the initial formulation $\mathcal{L}^{(1)}$ does not. The $\mathcal{L}^{(1)}$ formulation indirectly penalizes $I(\Pi_{\mathbf{X}}{}^*; Z)$ *through* F as it selects for $\Pi_{\mathbf{X}}{}^*$ which adds information about F that is not present in Z.

FIGURE 11.3: Alternate output network: $g_{out}^{(b)}$.

11.4.3 Coordinated CIB

While the conditional information reflects much of the intuition behind non-redundant data clustering, there still is a potential caveat in using Eq. (11.5): the solution of $\Pi_{\mathbf{X}}{}^*$ may lack global coordination. That is, clustering solutions obtained for different values z may not be in correspondence. The meaning of each cluster y_k is relative to a particular value z_i. The reason for this is that $I(\Pi_{\mathbf{X}}{}^*; F|Z)$ only measures the information conveyed by $\Pi_{\mathbf{X}}{}^*$ and Z in conjunction, but does not reflect how much relevant information $\Pi_{\mathbf{X}}{}^*$ provides on its own, i.e., without knowing Z. We call this problem the *cluster coordination problem*. One way to formally illustrate that the CIB does not address the coordination problem is via the following proposition:

PROPOSITION 11.3

Suppose $\Pi_{\mathbf{X}}{}^*$ and Z are finite random variables and define pre-image sets of $\Pi_{\mathbf{X}}{}^*$ by $z_r^{-1} = \{\mathbf{x} : \Pi_{\mathbf{X}}{}^*(\mathbf{x}) = z_r\}$. Assume that $P^*_{\Pi_{\mathbf{X}}{}^2|X}$ has been obtained *according to Eq. (11.5). Then one can chose arbitrary permutations π^{z_r} over $\Pi_{\mathbf{X}}{}^2$, one for every value z_r of $\Pi_{\mathbf{X}}{}^*$, and define permuted cluster assignments $P^{\pi}_{\Pi_{\mathbf{X}}{}^2|X}(c|x) \equiv P^*_{\Pi_{\mathbf{X}}{}^2|X}(\pi^{\Pi_{\mathbf{X}}{}^*(x_i)}(\pi_{\mathbf{X}}{}^*_j)|x_i)$ such that $P^{\pi}_{\Pi_{\mathbf{X}}{}^2|X}$ is also optimal for CIB.*

Intuitively this proposition states that by independently permuting cluster labels within each set z_r^{-1}, the optimality of the solution is not affected.

A solution to the CIB problem will effectively correspond to a subcategorization or a *local* refinement of the partition induced by Z. Generally, however, one is more interested in concepts or annotations $\Pi_{\mathbf{X}}{}^*$ that are consistent across the whole domain of objects. We propose to address this problem by introducing an additional constraint involving $I(\Pi_{\mathbf{X}}{}^*; f)$. This yields the following *coordinated conditional information bottleneck (CCIB)* formulation as introduced in [10]:

$$\text{(CCIB)} \quad P^*_{\Pi_{\mathbf{X}}{}^*|X} = \arg \max_{P_{\Pi_{\mathbf{X}}{}^*|X} \in \mathcal{P}} I(\Pi_{\mathbf{X}}{}^*; Y|Z), \quad \text{where}$$

$$\mathcal{P} \equiv \{P_{\Pi_{\mathbf{X}}{}^*|X} : I(\Pi_{\mathbf{X}}{}^*; X) \leq c_{\max}, I(\Pi_{\mathbf{X}}{}^*; F) \geq d_{\min}\}.$$

With $d_{min} > 0$ the CCIB favors clustering solutions that obey some global consistency across the sets z_r^{-1}.

11.4.4 Update Equations

11.4.4.1 Alternating Optimization

The formal derivation of an alternation scheme to compute an approximate solution for the CCIB is somewhat involved, but leads to very intuitive re-estimation equations [10]. One can compute probabilistic cluster assignments according to the following formula:

$$P(\pi_{\mathbf{X}}{}^*_j|x_i) \propto P(\pi_{\mathbf{X}}{}^*_j) \exp\left[\frac{\lambda}{\rho} \sum_f P(f|x_i) \log P(f|\pi_{\mathbf{X}}{}^*_j)\right] \quad (11.6)$$

$$\times \exp\left[\frac{1}{\rho} \sum_z P(z|x_i) \sum_f P(f|x_i, z) \log P(f|\pi_{\mathbf{X}}{}^*_j, z)\right],$$

where we have dropped all subscripts, since the meaning of the probability mass functions is clear from the naming convention for the arguments. The scalars $\rho \geq 0$ and $\lambda \geq 0$ are Lagrange multipliers enforcing the two inequality constraints; their values depend on $\Pi_{\mathbf{X}}{}^*_{\max}$ and $I_{\min}$. Notice that $P(f|\pi_{\mathbf{X}}{}^*_j)$ and $P(f|\pi_{\mathbf{X}}{}^*_j, z)$ appearing on the right-hand side of Eq. (11.6) implicitly depend on $P(\pi_{\mathbf{X}}{}^*_j|x_i)$. Iterating this equation is guaranteed to reach a fixed point corresponding to a local maximum of the CCIB criterion.

11.4.4.2   Finite Sample Considerations

So far we have tacitly assumed that the joint distribution P_{XFZ} is given. However, since this will rarely be the case in practice, it is crucial to be able to effectively deal with the finite sample case. Let us denote a sample set drawn i.i.d. by $\mathbf{X}_n = \{(x_i, f_i, z_i) : i = 1, \ldots, n\}$. We will first clarify the relationship between CCIB and likelihood maximization and then investigate particular parametric forms for the approximating distribution, leading to specific instantiations of the general scheme presented in the previous section.

11.4.4.3   Likelihood Maximization

A natural measure for the predictive performance of a model is the average conditional log-likelihood function

$$L(\mathbf{X}) = \frac{1}{n} \sum_{i=1}^{n} \sum_{c} P_{\Pi_{\mathbf{X}^*}|X}(\pi_{\mathbf{X}}^*(x_i)|x_i) \log \hat{P}_{F|\Pi_{\mathbf{X}^*},Z}(f(x_i)|\pi_{\mathbf{X}}^*(x_i), z(x_i)).$$

$$(11.7)$$

Here $\hat{P}_{F|\Pi_{\mathbf{X}^*},Z}$ is some approximation to the true distribution. This amounts to a two-stage prediction process, where x_i is first assigned to one of the clusters according to $P_{\Pi_{\mathbf{X}^*}|X}$ and then features are predicted using the distribution $\hat{P}_{F|\Pi_{\mathbf{X}^*},Z}(f_i|\pi_{\mathbf{X}}^*, z_i)$. Asymptotically one gets

$$L(\mathbf{X}) \xrightarrow{n \to \infty} \sum_{s,r} P_{\Pi_{\mathbf{X}^*},F,Z}(\pi_{\mathbf{X}}^*, f_s, z_r) \log \hat{P}_{F|\Pi_{\mathbf{X}^*},Z}(f_s|\pi_{\mathbf{X}}^*, z_r)$$

$$= -H(F|\Pi_{\mathbf{X}^*}, Z) - \mathbf{E}_{\Pi_{\mathbf{X}^*},Z}\left[KL(P_{F|\Pi_{\mathbf{X}^*},Z}||\hat{P}_{F|\Pi_{\mathbf{X}^*},Z})\right].$$

Provided that the estimation error (represented by the expected Kullback-Leibler divergence) vanishes as $n \to \infty$, maximizing the log-likelihood with respect to $P_{\Pi_{\mathbf{X}^*}|X}$ will asymptotically be equivalent to minimizing $H(F|\Pi_{\mathbf{X}^*}, Z)$ and thus to maximizing the conditional information $I(\Pi_{\mathbf{X}^*}; F|Z)$.

The practical relevance of the above considerations is that one can use the likelihood function Eq. (11.7) as the basis for computing a suitable approximation $\hat{P}_{F|\Pi_{\mathbf{X}^*},Z}$. For instance, if the latter is parameterized by some parameter θ, then one may compute the optimal parameter θ^* as the one that maximizes $L(\mathbf{X})$.

11.4.4.4   Categorical Background Knowledge

Considering the simplest case first, where Z is finite and its cardinality is small enough to allow estimating separate conditional feature distributions $P_{F|\Pi_{\mathbf{X}^*},Z}$ and $P_{F|Z}$ for every combination $(\pi_{\mathbf{X}}^*, z)$ and every z, respectively. As discussed before, the above probabilities may be estimated by conditional maximum likelihood estimation. For concreteness, we present and discuss the resulting update equations and algorithm for the special case of a multinomial sampling model for F, which is of importance in the context of text clustering applications. It is simple to derive similar algorithms for other sampling models such as Bernoulli, normal, or Poisson.

Denote by $\mathbf{x}_{is}$ observed feature frequencies for the i-th object and the j-th possible F-value and by $||x||_1$ the total number of observations for x_i. For instance, $\mathbf{x}_{is}$ may denote the number of times the j-th term occurs in the i-th document in the context of text clustering. Then we can define the relevant empirical distributions by

$$P(f_j|x_i) = P(f_j|x_i, z_r) \equiv \frac{\mathbf{x}_{is}}{||x||_1}, \ P(z|x_i) \equiv \delta(z, z(\mathbf{x}_i)).$$

The maximum likelihood estimates for given probabilistic cluster assignments can be computed according to

$$P(f_s|\pi_{\mathbf{X}}{}^*{}_j) = \frac{\sum_{i=1}^{n} P(\pi_{\mathbf{X}}{}^*{}_j|x_i)\mathbf{x}_{is}}{\sum_{i=1}^{n} P(\pi_{\mathbf{X}}{}^*{}_j|x_i)||x||_1},$$

$$P(f_s|\pi_{\mathbf{X}}{}^*{}_j, z_r) = \frac{\sum_{i=1}^{n} P(z_r|x_i)P(\pi_{\mathbf{X}}{}^*{}_j|x_i)\mathbf{x}_{is}}{\sum_{i=1}^{n} P(z_r|x_i)P(\pi_{\mathbf{X}}{}^*{}_j|x_i)||x||_1},$$

$$P(\pi_{\mathbf{X}}{}^*{}_j) = \frac{1}{n} \sum_{i=1}^{n} P(\pi_{\mathbf{X}}{}^*{}_j|x_i).$$

These equations need to be iterated in alternation with the re-estimation equation in Eq. (11.6), where the sum over f is replaced by a sum over the feature index s. We now discuss two special cases to illustrate the usefulness of the non-redundant data clustering algorithm.

11.4.4.5 Multinomial Features

We consider the case where features F are distributed according to a multinomial distribution. We propose to use the empirical feature counts or maximum likelihood estimates as a plug-in estimator for $P(F|\mathbf{X})$ and a uniform distribution over documents, which produces the iterative update equations of Figure 11.4.

11.4.4.6 Gaussian Features

We also consider the case that F is generated by Gaussians. In particular, assume F is vector-valued, distributed according to a multivariate Gaussian distribution with covariance matrix $\sigma^2 I$. The resulting update equations are shown in Figure 11.5.

11.4.4.7 Continuous-Valued Background Knowledge

A more general case involves background knowledge consisting of a vector $z \in \mathbb{R}^d$. This includes situations where Z might be a function of F or might

Initialized data probabilities

$$P(\mathbf{x}_i) = 1/n$$

$$P(z_r|\mathbf{x}_i) = \delta_{z_r \pi \mathbf{x}_j^1}$$

$$P(f_s|\mathbf{x}_i, z_j) = P(f_s|\mathbf{x}_i) = \frac{x_{is}}{||x||_1}$$

Iterative update equations
Auxiliary equations:

$$Q(\pi\mathbf{x}^*_j) = \frac{1}{n}\sum_{\mathbf{x}_i} P(\pi\mathbf{x}_j^2|\mathbf{x}_i)$$

$$Q(\pi\mathbf{x}^*_j, z_r) = \frac{1}{n}\sum_{\mathbf{x}_i:\pi\mathbf{x}_i^1=z_r} P(\pi\mathbf{x}^*_j|\mathbf{x}_i)$$

$$Q(\pi\mathbf{x}^*_j, f_s) = \frac{1}{||x||_1}\sum_{\mathbf{x}_i} x_{is}P(\pi\mathbf{x}^*_j|\mathbf{x}_i)$$

$$Q(\pi\mathbf{x}^*_j, f_s, z_r) = \frac{1}{||x||_1}\sum_{\mathbf{x}_i:\pi\mathbf{x}_i^1=z_r} x_{is}P(z_r|\mathbf{x}_i)$$

Membership equation:

$$P(\pi\mathbf{x}^*_j|\mathbf{x}_i) \propto Q(\pi\mathbf{x}^*_j)e^{\frac{1}{\rho}\sum_{s=1}^{d}\frac{x_{is}}{||x||_1}\log\frac{Q(\pi\mathbf{x}^*_j, f_s, Z_j)}{Q(Z_i, \pi\mathbf{x}^*_j)}}$$

FIGURE 11.4: Update equations for multinomial F, categorical $Z = \Pi_{\mathbf{X}}^1$.

consists of a subset of the features (so-called noise features). In order to obtain an estimate for $P(f|\pi_{\mathbf{X}}^*, z)$ one has to fit a regression model that predicts the relevant features F from the background knowledge Z for every cluster. If the response variable F is itself vector-valued, then we propose to fit regression models for every feature dimension separately.

The parametric form of the parametric regression function depends on the type and sampling model of the feature variable F. For instance, F may be a multivariate normal, a multinomial variable, or a vector of Bernoulli variables. In order to cover most cases of interest in a generic way, we propose to use of the framework of *generalized linear models* (GLMs) [14]. For a brief outline of what is involved in this process: We assume that the conditional mean of F can be written as a function of $\Pi_{\mathbf{X}}^*$ and Z in the following way $\mathbf{E}[F|\Pi_{\mathbf{X}}^*, Z] = \mu(\Pi_{\mathbf{X}}^*, Z) = h(\langle\theta, \phi(\Pi_{\mathbf{X}}^*, Z)\rangle)$, where h is the inverse link function and ϕ is a vector of predictor variables. Taking $h = $ id results in standard linear regression based on the independent variables $\phi(\Pi_{\mathbf{X}}^*, Z)$, but a variety of

Initialized data probabilities

$$P(x_i) = 1/n$$
$$P(z_r|x_i) = \delta(z_r, z(x_i))$$

Iterative update equations
Auxiliary equations:

$$Q(\pi_{\mathbf{X}}{}^*_j) = \frac{1}{n} \sum_{x_i} P(\pi_{\mathbf{X}}{}^*_j|x_i)$$

$$Q(\pi_{\mathbf{X}}{}^*_j, z_r) = \frac{1}{n} \sum_{x_i:z(x_i)=z_r} P(\pi_{\mathbf{X}}{}^*_j|x_i)$$

$$\theta_{\pi_{\mathbf{X}}{}^*_j} = \frac{\sum_{x_i:\pi_{\mathbf{X}}{}^*(x_i)=\pi_{\mathbf{X}}{}^*_j} f(x_i)}{\sum_{x_i:\pi_{\mathbf{X}}{}^*(x_i)=\pi_{\mathbf{X}}{}^*_j} 1}$$

$$\theta_{\pi_{\mathbf{X}}{}^*_j, z_r} = \frac{\sum_{x_i:\pi_{\mathbf{X}}{}^*(x_i)=\pi_{\mathbf{X}}{}^*, z(x_i)=z_r} f(x_i)}{\sum_{x_i:\pi_{\mathbf{X}}{}^*(x_i)=\pi_{\mathbf{X}}{}^*, z(x_i)=z_r} 1}$$

$$Q(f_s|z_r) = \exp\left[-\frac{1}{2\sigma^2} \|\theta_{\pi_{\mathbf{X}}{}^*} - f_s\|^2 + const \right]$$

$$Q(f_s|\pi_{\mathbf{X}}{}^*, z_r) = \exp\left[-\frac{1}{2\sigma^2} \|\theta_{\pi_{\mathbf{X}}{}^*, z_r} - f_s\|^2 + const \right]$$

Membership equation:

$$P(\pi_{\mathbf{X}}{}^*|x_i) \propto Q(\pi_{\mathbf{X}}{}^*) e^{-\frac{1}{\rho}(\|\theta_{\pi_{\mathbf{X}}{}^*, z_r} - F(x_i)\|^2 + \lambda\|\theta_{\pi_{\mathbf{X}}{}^*} - F(x_i)\|^2)}$$

FIGURE 11.5: Update equations for Gaussian f, categorical Z.

other (inverse) link functions can be used dependent on the application. The resulting iterative algorithm is shown in Figure 11.6.

In this general case, computing the quantities $P(f_s|\pi_{\mathbf{X}}{}^*_j) = P(f_s|\pi_{\mathbf{X}}{}^*_j; \eta)$ and $P(f_s|\pi_{\mathbf{X}}{}^*_j, z_r) = P(f_s|\pi_{\mathbf{X}}{}^*_j, z_r; \theta)$ requires estimating η and θ by maximizing the log-likelihood criterion in Eq. (11.7). The latter can be accomplished by standard model fitting algorithms for GLMs, which may themselves be iterative in nature.

11.4.5 Algorithms

11.4.5.1 Deterministic Annealing and Sequential Methods

We now address the issue of how to deal with the free parameters $\Pi_{\mathbf{X}}{}^*_{\max}$ and $I_{\min}$ of the CCIB or – equivalently – the Lagrange multipliers ρ and λ. No-

Initialize data probabilities

$$P(x_i) = 1/n$$

Iterative update equations
Update auxiliary equations:

$$Q(\pi_{\mathbf{X}}{}^*{}_j) = \frac{1}{n} \sum_{x_i} P(\pi_{\mathbf{X}}{}^*{}_j | x_i)$$

Update GLM

$$\forall j = 1 \ldots |F| :$$
$$\theta_j = \text{GLM-FIT}_h(Z, F_j, P(\Pi_{\mathbf{X}}{}^* | X))$$

Membership equation:

$$P(\pi_{\mathbf{X}}{}^*{}_j | x_i) \propto Q(\pi_{\mathbf{X}}{}^*)$$
$$\cdot exp[\frac{1}{\rho} \sum_{f_s} P(f_s | \pi_{\mathbf{X}}{}^*{}_j, z(x_i)) \log Q(f_s | \pi_{\mathbf{X}}{}^*{}_j, z(x_i); \theta)$$
$$+ \frac{\lambda}{\rho} \sum_{f_s} P(f_s | \pi_{\mathbf{X}}{}^*{}_j) \log Q(f_s | \pi_{\mathbf{X}}{}^*{}_j)]$$

FIGURE 11.6: Update equations for F distribution chosen via GLM link function h, non-categorical Z.

tice that the constraint $I(\Pi_{\mathbf{X}}{}^*; F) \geq I_{\min}$ leads to a Lagrangian function that additively combines two (conditional) mutual informations $I(\Pi_{\mathbf{X}}{}^*; F|Z) + \lambda I(\Pi_{\mathbf{X}}{}^*; F)$. It is often more natural to directly set λ which controls the trade-off between conditional and unconditional information maximization. Since the $I(\Pi_{\mathbf{X}}{}^*; F)$ term has been added to address the coordination problem, we will in practice typically chose $\lambda \leq 1$. As the performance of the algorithm is insensitive with respect to λ [10], it is reasonable to fix this parameter in practice.

The ρ parameter in Eq. (11.6) on the other hand directly controls the fuzziness of the assignments such that hard clusterings are computed in the limit of $\rho \to 0$. We consider two algorithmic approaches for setting ρ so as to obtain hard assignments: a sequential approach as discussed in [19] where ρ is set to 0 and equations derived, as well as using a well-known continuation method, deterministic annealing [18]. The sequential approach is shown in Figure 11.7. The deterministic annealing approach, shown in Figure 11.8 has two chief advantages: conceptually, non-zero values for ρ avoid over-confidence in assigning objects to clusters and thus addresses the crucial problem of over-fitting in learning from finite data. For instance, we may choose to select a value for ρ that maximizes the predictive performance on some held-out data set.

The second advantage is algorithmic in nature. The proposed alternating scheme is sensitive with respect to the choice of initial values. As a result of that, convergence to poor local optima may be a nuisance in practice, a problem that plagues many similar alternating schemes such as k-means, mixture modeling, and the sequential approach. However, a simple control strategy that starts with high entropy cluster assignments and then successively lowers the entropy of the assignments has proven to be a simple, yet effective, tool in practice to improve the quality of the solutions obtained (cf. [18, 21]). In analogy of a physical system, one may think of ρ in terms of a *computational temperature*.

We thus propose the following scheme: Starting with a large enough value for $\rho = \rho_0$, one alternates the update equations until convergence. Then one lowers ρ according to some schedule, for instance an exponential schedule $\rho \leftarrow b\rho$ with $b < 1$. The process terminates if the chosen ρ leads to a value for $I(\Pi_{\mathbf{X}}{}^*; X)$ that is close to the desired bound $I_{\max}$ or if cluster assignments numerically reach hard assignments.

11.4.5.2 Summary

The coordinated conditional information bottleneck provides a single objective function which encourages high-quality, coordinated solutions which are novel with respect to the known structure. From this objective, update equations were derived for a number of common settings. These update equations may then be used in a sequential or deterministic annealing approach to obtain solutions. An empirical analysis of the performance of these approaches as well as a comparison to the CondEns techniques will be discussed in the next section.

11.5 Experimental Evaluation

In this section, the proposed algorithms are evaluated on a range of data sets. First, a small image set is used as a proof of concept. Next, a more detailed analysis is performed over an ensemble of text data sets. Finally, synthetically generated data is considered as a controlled setting in which to compare the algorithms' behaviors.

Initialization:

- Construct $\Pi_{\mathbf{X}}^* \equiv X$:

    - $\Pi_{\mathbf{X}}^* \leftarrow$ random partition of X into K clusters
    - For $\pi_{\mathbf{X}}^*{}_i$ in $\Pi_{\mathbf{X}}^*$:
        * $P(\pi_{\mathbf{X}}^*{}_i) = \sum_{x_j \in \pi_{\mathbf{X}}^*{}_i} P(x_j)$
        * $P(y, \pi_{\mathbf{X}}^*{}_i, z_r) = \sum_{x_j \in \pi_{\mathbf{X}}^*{}_i} P(x_j)P(f|x_j)P(z_r|x_j) \;\; \forall f \in F, z_r \in Z$
        * $P(\pi_{\mathbf{X}}^*{}_i, z_r) = \sum_{x_j \in \pi_{\mathbf{X}}^*{}_i} P(x_j)P(z_r|x_j) \; \forall z_r \in Z$
        * $P(\pi_{\mathbf{X}}^*{}_i|x_j) = 1$ if $x_j \in \pi_{\mathbf{X}}^*{}_i$, 0 otherwise

Loop:

- For $t = 1 \ldots (N-1)$

    - randomly draw x_j to $\pi_{\mathbf{X}}^*{}_{from}(x_j)$
    - $\pi_{\mathbf{X}}^{*\prime}{}_{from} = \pi_{\mathbf{X}}^*{}_{from} \backslash \{x_j\}$
    - $\pi_{\mathbf{X}}^*{}_{to} = \arg\min_{\pi_{\mathbf{X}}^*{}_i} d(x_j, \pi_{\mathbf{X}}^*{}_i)$
    - $\pi_{\mathbf{X}}^{*\prime}{}_{to} = \pi_{\mathbf{X}}^*{}_{to} \cup \{x_j\}$
        * $P(\pi_{\mathbf{X}}^{*\prime}{}_{to}) = P(\pi_{\mathbf{X}}^*{}_{to}) + P(x_j)$
        * $P(\pi_{\mathbf{X}}^{*\prime}{}_{from}) = P(\pi_{\mathbf{X}}^*{}_{from}) - P(x_j)$
        * $P(\pi_{\mathbf{X}}^{*\prime}{}_{to}|x) = 1$
        * $P(\pi_{\mathbf{X}}^{*\prime}{}_{from}|x) = 0$
        * $P(\pi_{\mathbf{X}}^{*\prime}{}_{to}, z_r) = P(\pi_{\mathbf{X}}^*{}_{to}|z_r) + P(x_j|z_r) \; \forall f \in F$
        * $P(\pi_{\mathbf{X}}^{*\prime}{}_{from}, z_r) = P(\pi_{\mathbf{X}}^*{}_{from}|z_r) - P(x_j|z_r) \; \forall y \in F$
        * $P(f, \pi_{\mathbf{X}}^{*\prime}{}_{to}, z_r) = P(f, \pi_{\mathbf{X}}^*{}_{to}, z_r) + P(f, x_j, z_r) \; \forall f \in F, z_r \in Z$
        * $P(f, \pi_{\mathbf{X}}^{*\prime}{}_{from}, z_r) = P(f|\pi_{\mathbf{X}}^*{}_{from}, z_r) + P(f, x_j, z_r) \; \forall f \in F, z_r \in Z$

    - Replace $\pi_{\mathbf{X}}^*{}_{from}$ with $\pi_{\mathbf{X}}^{*\prime}{}_{from}$, $\pi_{\mathbf{X}}^*{}_{to}$ with $\pi_{\mathbf{X}}^{*\prime}{}_{to}$

FIGURE 11.7: Sequential method.

- initialize inverse temperature $\beta = \frac{1}{\rho} = \epsilon$

- initialize $P(\pi_{\mathbf{X}}^* | x_i)$ randomly

- Repeat:

    - Repeat:
        * iterate equations from Algorithm 11.4, 11.5, or 11.6 until converged
    - Until max change in $P_{\Pi_{\mathbf{X}^*}|X}(\pi_{\mathbf{X}}^*, x_i) < \epsilon$
    - increase inverse temperature: $\beta = b \cdot \beta$

- no change in $P(\pi_{\mathbf{X}}^* | x_i)$ and $\forall \pi_{\mathbf{X}}^*, x_i : P(\pi_{\mathbf{X}}^* | x_i) \in \{0, 1\}$

FIGURE 11.8: Deterministic annealing algorithm for non-redundant clustering.

11.5.1 Image Data Set

As a first proof-of-concept, consider a set of 369 face images with 40×40 grayscale pixels and gender annotations. We performed clustering with $K = 2$ clusters and a Gaussian noise model for the features. Initially, no background knowledge was used. All of 20 trials converged to the same clustering, suggesting that this clustering is the dominant structure in the data set. The precision score between the discovered clustering and the gender classification was 0.5122, i.e., the overlap is close to random. Examining the centroids of each cluster in Figure 11.9 shows the clustering which was obtained partitions the data into face-and-shoulder views and face-only views.

What is a non-redundant clustering with respect to this dominant clustering? The dominant clustering may be set as known structure and a non-redundant clustering algorithm (in this case, CCIB) used to obtain a novel clustering. Centroids for this clustering are in Figure 11.10. In this solution, the precision score for gender is substantially higher, at 0.7805. Confusion matrices for both clusterings are in Table 11.5.1. This confirms that the dominant structure found in the previous attempt has been avoided, revealing lower-order structure that is informative with respect to gender.

11.5.2 Text Data Sets

Textual data is a natural opportunity for applying non-redundant clustering as document sets typically have many plausible categorization schemes. In this section, performance is evaluated on several real-world text data sets. Each set may be partitioned according to either of two independent classification schemes. Experiments are performed using either one of these classifica-

C1  C2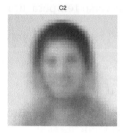

FIGURE 11.9: Centroids from initial clustering with no side information.

C1 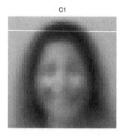 C2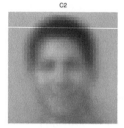

FIGURE 11.10: Centroids from second clustering using initial clustering as side information.

tion schemes as background knowledge. An algorithm is considered successful if it finds a clustering similar to the unknown classification scheme. Documents are represented by term frequency vectors that are assumed to follow a multinomial distribution. For all experiments described, $\lambda = 0.3$ is used (chosen based on results from evaluation on synthetic data) and k is set to the cardinality of the target categorization.

TABLE 11.1: Confusion matrices for face data.

	initial clustering		nonredundant clustering	
	female	male	female	male
y_1	140	144	105	1
y_2	45	40	80	183
	Precision = 0.5122		Precision = 0.7805	

11.5.2.1 The WebKB Data Set

We use the CMU 4 Universities WebKB data set as described in [5] which consists of webpages collected from computer science departments and has a classification scheme based on page type: ('course,' 'faculty,' 'project,' 'staff,' 'student') as well source university: ('Cornell,' 'Texas,' 'Washington,' 'Wisconsin'). Documents belonging to the 'misc' and 'other' categories, as well as the 'department' category which contained only 4 members, were removed, leaving 1087 pages remaining. Stopwords were removed, numbers were tokenized, and only terms appearing in more than one document were retained, leaving 5650 terms.

11.5.2.2 Reuters RCV-1

Additional data sets were derived from the Reuters RCV-1 news corpus which contains multiple labels for each document. We first select a number of topic labels *Topic* and region labels *Region* and then sample documents from the set of documents having labels {*Topic* × *Region*}. For ease of evaluation, those documents which contain multiple labels from *Topic* or multiple labels from *Region* were excluded. We selected labels which would produce high numbers of eligible documents and generated the following sets:

(i) *RCV1-ec5x6:* 5 of the most frequent subcategories of the ECAT (Economics) and 6 of the most frequent country codes were chosen: 5362 documents and 4052 terms.

(ii) *RCV1-top7x9:* ECAT (Economics), MCAT (Markets) and the 5 most frequent subcategories of the GCAT (General) topic and the 9 most frequent country codes were chosen: 4345 documents and 4178 terms.

As with the WebKB set, stopwords were removed, numbers were tokenized, and a term frequency cutoff was used to remove low-frequency terms.

11.5.2.3 Experimental Design

Tests are performed, assuming one of the categorizations is known and the results are evaluated according to how similar the solution is to the remaining, or *target*, categorization. The number of clusters, k is set to the number of categories in the target categorization. As the number of categories may differ between known and target categorizations, we use normalized mutual information (NMI) $[NMI(\Pi_{\mathbf{X}}; \mathbf{Y}) = (I(\Pi_{\mathbf{X}}; \mathbf{Y})/H(\mathbf{Y})]$ which, unlike precision, is well-defined for two clusterings with different k. We evaluate the CCIB and CondEns algorithms. We include results for daCCIB, the deterministic annealing version of CCIB, which is relatively fast. Results for seqCCIB, the sequential clustering version, are not included as it has been shown to typically underperform daCCIB on synthetic sets and takes considerably more time, rendering it impractical for data sets this large. CondEns-Kmeans and

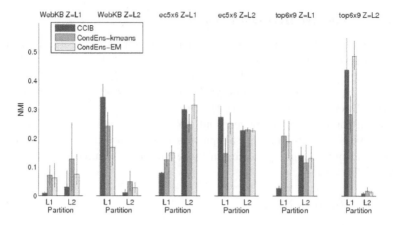

FIGURE 11.11: Results on text data sets: WebKB, ec5x6, top6x9. Each set has two known orthogonal labelings $\mathbf{Y}_1$ and $\mathbf{Y}_2$. Shaded bars show mean $NMI(\Pi_{\mathbf{X}}; \mathbf{Y})$ for $\mathbf{Y}_1$ and $\mathbf{Y}_2$ over 20 initializations. Error bars range from minimum to maximum score. As desired, solutions generally have that $NMII(\Pi_{\mathbf{X}}; \mathbf{Y}_2)$ is higher for $Z = \mathbf{Y}_2$ and $I(\mathbf{Y}; \mathbf{Y}_1)$ is higher for $Z = \mathbf{Y}_2$.

CondEns-EM are considered as they show better performance on synthetic sets and more favorable runtimes with respect to CondEns-IB. Each algorithm is evaluated for 20 random initializations on each data set.

11.5.2.4 Analysis of Text Data Results

Results of the CCIB and CondEns methods on the text data sets are shown in Figure 11.11. It is interesting to note that results generally improve as sets with more categories are considered. In all cases, the solutions found are more similar to the target classification than the known classification. The performance of the CondEns algorithm is competitive with CCIB across the data sets. We will focus on the performance of CondEns-EM which for the most part obtains better solutions than CondEns-Kmeans. Looking across the data sets, CondEns-EM outscores CCIB in mean performance on half of the sessions. Notably, the range of solutions obtained due to the sensitivity of CondEns-EM to initialization does not appear to help relative to daCCIB. That is, if one considers maximum scores, the relative performance still falls along the lines of mean scores. A key advantage to CondEns-EM, however, is that daCCIB ranges between 4.57x to 44.67x slower in runtime than CondEns-EM. So while the quality of solutions may not argue for one algorithm over the other, CondEns-EM boasts a substantial advantage in computational efficiency.

11.5.3 Evaluation Using Synthetic Data

By further evaluation of the algorithms on synthetically generated data, it is possible to more precisely gauge the algorithms' behaviors with respect to characteristics of the data. Of interest is the quality of solutions, sensitivity to initialization, and robustness with respect to the orthogonality assumption.

11.5.3.1 Generation

Two-dimensional synthetic data sets with two clusterings A and B are generated using a two-dimensional multinomial model. For the first dimension, which is associated with clustering A, for each of the clusters $p_1, \ldots p_k$, feature probabilities $\theta_{p1} \ldots \theta_{pk}$ are chosen to be equally spaced on the interval $[0,1]$. The feature probabilities for B are obtained by first taking $\theta'_{q1}, \ldots \theta'_{qk}$ equally spaced on the interval $[0,1]$. Next, these probabilities are associated with the θ_{pj} according to an orthogonality weight, α in the following expression: $\theta_{qj} = \alpha\theta_{qj} + (1 - \alpha)\theta_{pj}$. An instance is sampled by randomly selecting membership in $\{p_1, \ldots, p_k\}$ and $\{q_1, \ldots, q_k\}$ and sampling from the associated distributions. At $\alpha = 1$, A and B are orthogonal and as $\alpha \to 0$, the clusterings A and B become perfectly correlated.

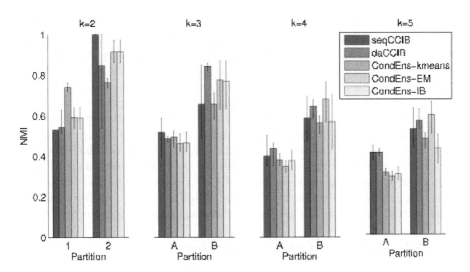

FIGURE 11.12: Results on synthetic sets with two natural clusterings A and B. A is assumed to be known and the algorithms are evaluated on how successfully they find solutions similar to B. Shaded bars show mean $NMI(\Pi_{\mathbf{X}}; A)$ and $NMI(\Pi_{\mathbf{X}}; B)$ for 10 random initializations each over 50 generated data sets. Error bars range from minimum to maximum score. As desired, solutions are substantially closer to B than A.

11.5.3.2   Experimental Setup

In the experiments, it is assumed that clustering A is known and supplied as categorical known structure, and evaluate the algorithms on their ability to discover clustering B. As the data set is multinomial, we consider performance of CCIB and CondEns.

In these experiments, for each of k = 2,3,4,5, 50 synthetic data sets consisting of 800 instances were generated and 10 random initializations of the algorithm were used. We evaluate results in terms of the best, mean, and worst performance over the 10 initializations and average these quantities over the 50 data sets. Results are presented for various settings of k in Figure 11.5.3.1.

11.5.3.3   Analysis of CCIB Algorithms

We first examine the results of the CCIB family of algorithms, focusing on their precision with respect to target partition B. First, and most importantly, we note that the algorithms obtain solutions more similar to target partitioning B than to known partitioning A, as desired. As a general trend, daCCIB outperforms seqCCIB for higher k, for $k = 3, 4, 5$ outperforming seqCCIB by 28.8%, 10.0%, and 7.6%, respectively. If one examines the max and min performance of each algorithm as indicated by the error bars in the graph, a crucial difference between the two algorithms becomes apparent: the deterministic annealing version is considerably less sensitive to initialization than the sequential clustering version. In fact, for $k > 2$, the range of solutions obtained by seqCCIB is at least 2x as great as that obtained by daCCIB. This stability is a well-known phenomenon attributed to deterministic annealing approaches which we see replicated throughout the experiments. Another important distinction between the two approaches is the runtime. For $k > 2$, the larger sets with more complicated structure, the complexity advantages of daCCIB become apparent. For $k = 3, 4, 5$ the seqCCIB algorithm is 10x, 19x, and 27x slower than daCCIB, respectively, a phenomenon which has been replicated throughout many experiments. For the CCIB family of algorithms, this set of experiments indicates that daCCIB consistently shows better mean performance, is more stable with respect to initialization, and has considerably better runtimes which are an order of magnitude better than seqCCIB.

11.5.3.4   Analysis of Condens Algorithms

Considering performance of the CondEns approaches, as with CCIB, performance decreases for higher k. Comparing the various base-clustering techniques, it is immediately apparent that k-means substantially underperforms the EM and IB techniques for low k. As k increases, the performance using k-means improves somewhat and attains the performance of IB, however, it never rivals the performance of EM. Examining the sensitivity to initialization as indicated by the error bars reveals that the range of precisions $Prec_B(C)$

obtained by CondEns-EM and CondEns-IB is larger than that of CondEns-Kmeans by approximately a factor of 2. While CondEns-Kmeans shows less sensitivity to initialization, this comes at a cost as the precisions obtained are substantially lower than CondEns-EM.

Across the CondEns techniques, the runtimes are of similar magnitudes. For $k = 2, 3, 4$, and 5, the CondEns-IB times take on average 12.5x, 9.1x, 7.0x, and 4.1x more time than CondEns-EM which shows that as k increases, the relative computational advantage of CondEns-EM versus CondEns-IB weakens. It is not surprising that CondEns-IB would require a longer runtime as the base clustering method, daIB, is a deterministic annealing technique while the base clustering method EM used in CondEns-EM does not use deterministic annealing and so should be considerably faster.

For the CondEns family, we conclude that CondEns-EM is the best performer of the three base clustering techniques considered, while also boasting runtimes which are comparable to CondEns-Kmeans and several times faster than CondEns-IB.

11.5.3.5 Analysis of CondEns and CCIB

Now comparing the CondEns and CCIB families, with a particular focus on daCCIB and CondEns-EM as they show the best mean precision and runtimes overall of their respective families. Looking at mean precision, $Prec_B(C)$, CondEns-EM slightly outscores daCCIB for $k = 2, 4$, and 5. Specifically, it outscores daCCIB by 8.0%, 5.3%, and 5.4%, respectively. For $k = 3$, daCCIB outscores CondEns-EM by 8.7%. Another difference emerges if the $Prec_A(C)$ scores are considered. These scores measure the similarity to the known, undesired, solution A. It is interesting to observe that as k increases, CondEns-EM actually finds solutions which are *less like* B than does daCCIB. By $k = 5$, the daCCIB solutions have average precisions with respect to the known categorization that are 41.65% higher than CondEns-EM. Another important distinction between the algorithms is the range of solutions obtained. This range is greater for CondEns-EM than daCCIB. This greater range manifests itself in the higher max $Prec_B(C)$ scores of CondEns-EM, which outscores daCCIB for $k = 3, 4$, and 5. It also is responsible for daCCIB having higher min $Prec_B(C)$ scores on the same values for k. Finally, examining the runtimes shows that CondEns-EM is consistently faster than daCCIB for all k considered. The average runtime for daCCIB is 62.5x, 7.4x, 5.3x, and 2.5x longer than CondEns-EM for $k = 1, 2, 3, 4$, respectively.

In conclusion, the mean performance of daCCIB and CondEns-EM are competitive, with daCCIB outperforming CondEns-EM on low k and CondEns-EM outperforming daCCIB on higher k. The range of solutions obtained by CondEns-EM, however, is consistently greater than that of daCCIB. Whether this is an advantage or disadvantage depends on the application being considered. On the one hand, it allows CondEns-EM to obtain some solutions which are better than all of those obtained by daCCIB, as evidenced by the max

$Prec_B(C)$ scores. On the other hand, it also means that CondEns-EM will obtain solutions worse than all of those obtained by daCCIB, as evidenced by the min $Prec_B(C)$ scores. Another important consideration to note is the $Prec_A(C)$ scores which favor CondEns-EM for the data sets with higher k. Finally, we find a consistent advantage in runtime for CondEns-EM versus daCCIB.

11.5.3.6 Orthogonality Assumption

We now evaluate the robustness of the CCIB and CondEns algorithms to weakening of the orthogonality assumption. As discussed in the generation procedure given in 11.5.3.1, orthogonality weight α controls the independence of the two partitions A and B. For $\alpha = 1$, partition membership is independent whereas for $\alpha = 0$ partition membership is completely dependent. Examples of data sets generated with various α are given in Figure 11.13. We evaluate both the CCIB and CondEns algorithms as α varies between 0 and 1.

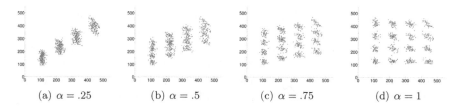

(a) $\alpha = .25$ (b) $\alpha = .5$ (c) $\alpha = .75$ (d) $\alpha = 1$

FIGURE 11.13: Relaxation of the orthogonality assumption: sample synthetic data sets for $k = 4$ with various α. $n = 800$ items, $m = 1100$ draws.

The mean precisions for the results of the algorithms for $\alpha = 1.0, 0.75, 0.50$, and 0.25 and where $k = 2, 3,$ and 4 are shown in Figure 11.14. The results show that CondEns-EM on average underperforms CCIB for orthogonal sets (high α). For lower α, however, the results favor CondEns At $k = 2$, for instance, with $\alpha = 0.25$, the mean precision $Prec_B(C)$ of CondEns-EM is 34.36% higher than that of daCCIB and the max precision is 41.86% higher than daCCIB. The advantage of CondEns-EM does decrease as k increases however, with a mean increase of 29.05% at $\alpha = 0.25, k = 3$ and a mean increase of 26.22% at $\alpha = 0.25, k = 4$. Sets with lower α share the characteristic that the undesired clustering A is a much higher quality clustering than B when measured over the entire set. This affects CCIB directly as it has a coordination term that favors clusterings which are high quality with respect to the entire set. CondEns, on the other hand, finds high quality clusterings independently within the pre-image sets. In those cases, B is still a higher quality clustering. This is a notable result as while rather strong orthogonal-

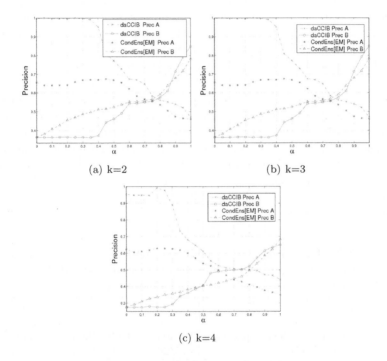

(a) k=2   (b) k=3

(c) k=4

FIGURE 11.14: CCIB vs. CondEns: Mean precision scores for $k = 2, 3, 4$ where the orthogonality constant α varies.

ity assumptions were made in the theoretical analysis, in these experiments CondEns is quite robust for less orthogonal sets.

11.5.3.7   Successive Non-Redundant Clusterings

A natural problem which arises in interactive settings is, after using non-redundant clustering to find a non-dominant clustering, what is the *next* non-dominant clustering? That is, how can this technique be generalized to enumerate arbitrarily many clusterings where each clustering is non-redundant with respect the clusterings that have come before? At issue is the modeling of the known structure which in this case consists of two or more clusterings. We consider two approaches to representing this information: the cartesian product of the known clusterings may be taken and then supplied as categorical Z to the algorithm or the concatenated membership vectors may be treated as a binary vector and then supplied as continuous Z to the algorithm.

One might expect the continuous approach to outperform the categorical. This is because by taking the cartesian product, one ignores the relation between different combinations within the cartesian product. For example, with known cluster memberships in A and B, no information is shared in estimating the Y distribution for an instance in combination (a_1, b_1) and an instance in combination (a_1, b_2). This is in contrast to the GLM approach which learns a function in Y over all (a, b) and so can share information between combinations.

TABLE 11.2:   N = 200 instances, dimensions associated with clusterings A,B,D = [8 8 4]. We assume A and B are known. Results are over 5 random initializations.

| Algorithm | $Prec_D$ | | | time |
	mean	best	worst	mean
CCIB, cartesian product	0.9300	0.9300	0.9300	0.36s
CCIB, GLM	0.7300	0.7300	0.7300	64.42s

We first evaluate both approaches on synthetic data sets with three partitionings, $A, B,$ and D. Using the number of features associated with each partitioning, $m_A = 8, m_B = 8, m_D = 4$, we assume A and B are known and evaluate the ability of the approaches to discover partitioning D. We restrict attention to the CCIB approach as it tends to be less sensitive to initialization. Results are shown in Table 11.2. We further consider the approaches as the data sets vary according to size and dimension. Figures 11.15(a) and 11.15(b) show performance as the number of instances and relative strength of partitions vary. The results show for this variety of settings, the cartesian

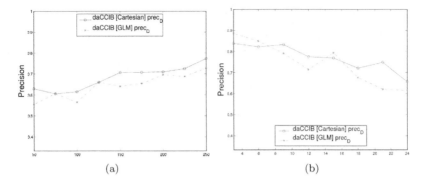

FIGURE 11.15: Obtaining successive non-redundant clusterings. For data sets containing independent partitionings A, B, D, comparing categorical representation (using cartesian product of A and B) versus continuous representation (concatenating A and B as binary vector). For (a), dimensions $[m_A\ m_B\ m_D] = [8\ 8\ 4]$, N varies, k = 3. For (b), $m_D = 6$, N=200, k=3, m_A varies.

product approach is in fact approximately as successful as the GLM approach while coming at a fraction of the computational cost. This rough equivalence holds up when the number of instances varies and when the relative strength of the desired clustering is varied.

11.5.4   Summary of Experimental Results

Over all the data sets considered, the CondEns approach frequently outperforms CCIB, while at a fraction of the computational cost. It does not, however, strictly dominate CCIB in terms of average performance. However, on several text data sets, CCIB does outperform CondEns. A potential concern is that CondEns is motivated by rather strong demands on the data set, namely that the structures be information-orthogonal (the so-called "orthogonality assumption"). Notably, despite this strict theoretical requirement, CondEns performs robustly even as the orthogonality assumption is challenged, outperforming CCIB on data sets where the two clusterings are substantially correlated. A further advantage of CondEns is the lack of tuning parameters, although CondEns is parameterized by the base clustering method, which potentially may require tuning parameters. As was shown in the experiments, typically performance was relatively consistent irregardless of which base clustering methods was employed. A potential disadvantage to CondEns is the sensitivity to initialization. While its mean performance is better than CCIB, the range of solutions obtained typically contains solutions which are of lower quality than any of those obtained by CCIB. One way to counter this tendency would be to run CondEns multiple times and select the solution which scores highest on a CCIB-like objective function.

In summary, both approaches performed well throughout the experimental settings. Selecting the best-performing technique depends upon the data set and the particular setting. CondEns often outperforms CCIB. CCIB, however, is less sensitive to initialization than CondEns and so the use of CCIB promises more consistent results.

11.6 Conclusion

We have proposed the problem of non-redundant clustering, presented three distinct approaches to solving the problem, evaluated their performance on synthetic and real data sets, and discussed extensions to related problems. Intuitively, the goal of non-redundant clustering is to obtain a clustering which is novel, or non-redundant, with respect to some given known structure. Using relevant concepts from information theory, we introduced the notion of information-orthogonal clusterings which is then used as a key constraint in the formal problem definition. The definition given is sufficiently general to apply to categorical or continuous known structure.

The first algorithm presented was CondEns, a framework which makes use of clustering ensembles. The framework makes use of base clustering techniques which are applied to a subset of the data selected according to the known structure. A wide variety of general or domain-specific base clustering techniques may be used, which gives this framework a broad applicability. Furthermore, the algorithm is efficient and typically requires less computation than if the base clustering technique were applied to the entire data set. Another benefit is that no tuning parameter is required. In practice, this approach achieves performance competitive with the other techniques, with the only drawback that results are more sensitive to initialization.

Then an approach was derived based on maximizing a conditional mutual information score. An information bottleneck approach, which we dub conditional information bottleneck (CIB) was derived. As stated, the CIB does not enforce coordination across the known structure and so we propose an enhanced coordinated conditional information bottleneck (CCIB) and a deterministic annealing approach to obtaining solutions. The resulting algorithm is capable of handling categorical or continuous known structure and a wide variety of distribution-based assumptions for the features, is insensitive to initialization, and requires no tuning parameter to trade off between cluster quality and redundancy. The approach to coordination does introduce a tuning parameter, however, we find performance to be quite insensitive to this parameter when the data set contains strong, highly orthogonal clusterings.

Two approaches to non-redundant clustering have been presented: condi-

TABLE 11.3: Comparison of non-redundant clustering algorithms.

Algorithm	CCIB Information Bottleneck (IB)	CondEns Clustering Ensembles
Categorical known structure	yes	yes
Continuous known structure	yes (with GLMs)	no
Distribution-based clustering	yes	yes
Distance-based clustering	no	yes
Tuning parameters	yes (coordination)	no
Successive non-redundant clustering	yes (continuous)	yes (cross-product)

tional ensembles (CondEns) and coordinated conditional information bottleneck. The experimental results show that the algorithms successfully discover novel, non-redundant structure over a variety of synthetic and real data sets.

While it has long been a well-known complication that data often contains multiple quality clusterings, existing work has largely concerned itself with tailoring objective functions to, or requiring the user to specify properties of, a desired clustering. We have formally derived non-redundant clustering approaches which allow a user to specify only what is not desired. This lends itself naturally to an interactive, exploratory clustering approach as well as a systematic method to enumerate multiple clusterings in a data set. The techniques we have presented for accomplishing this task handle a broad range of data types and settings. Furthermore, they are based on frequently used and well-studied clustering techniques which allow the leverage of a large body of research and practical experience.

References

[1] Leon Bottou and Yoshua Bengio. Convergence properties of the K-means algorithms. In G. Tesauro, D. Touretzky, and T. Leen, editors, *Advances in Neural Information Processing Systems*, volume 7, pages 585–592, 1995.

[2] G. Chechik and N. Tishby. Extracting relevant structures with side information. In *Advances in Neural Information Processing Systems 15*, pages 857–864, 2002.

[3] Thomas M. Cover and Joy A. Thomas. *Elements of Information Theory.* John Wiley & Sons, 1991.

[4] D. R. Cox and N. Reid. Parameter orthogonality and approximate conditional inference. In *Journal of the Royal Statistical Society, Series B*, volume 49, pages 1–39, 1987.

[5] Mark Craven, Dan DiPasquo, Dayne Freitag, Andrew K. McCallum, Tom M. Mitchell, Kamal Nigam, and Seán Slattery. Learning to extract symbolic knowledge from the World Wide Web. In *Proceedings of the 15th Conference of the American Association for Artificial Intelligence*, pages 509–516, 1998.

[6] Ian Davidson and Ashwin Satyanarayana. Speeding up k-means clustering by bootstrap averaging. In *Third IEEE International Conference on Data Mining, Workshop on Clustering Large Data Sets*, pages 16–25, 2003.

[7] Nir Friedman, Ori Mosenzon, Noam Slonim, and Naftali Tishby. Multivariate information bottleneck. In *Proceedings of the 17th Conference on Uncertainty in Artificial Intelligence*, pages 152–161, 2001.

[8] M. A. Gluck and J. E. Corter. Information, uncertainty, and the utility of categories. In *Proceedings of the Seventh Annual Conference of the Cognitive Science Society*, pages 283–287, 1985.

[9] David Gondek and Thomas Hofmann. Conditional information bottleneck clustering. In *Third IEEE International Conference on Data Mining, Workshop on Clustering Large Data Sets*, pages 36–42, 2003.

[10] David Gondek and Thomas Hofmann. Non-redundant data clustering. In *Proceedings of the Fourth IEEE International Conference on Data Mining*, pages 75–82, 2004.

[11] David Gondek and Thomas Hofmann. Non-redundant clustering with conditional ensembles. In *KDD '05: Proceeding of the 11th ACM SIGKDD International Conference on Knowledge Discovery in Data Mining*, pages 70–77, 2005.

[12] Anil K. Jain and Richard C. Dubes. *Algorithms for Clustering Data.* Prentice-Hall, 1988.

[13] Martin H. Law, Anil K. Jain, and Mário A. T. Figueiredo. Feature selection in mixture-based clustering. In *Advances in Neural Information Processing Systems 15*, pages 609–616, 2002.

[14] P. McCullagh and J. A. Nelder, editors. *Generalized Linear Models.* Chapman & Hall, 2nd edition, 1989.

[15] Marina Meilă. Comparing clusterings by the variation of information. In *16th Annual Conference on Computational Learning Theory*, pages 173–187, 2003.

[16] B. Minaei-Bidgoli, A. Topchy, and W. Punch. Ensembles of partitions via data resampling. In *Proceedings of the International Conference on Information Technology: Coding and Computing*, pages 188–192, 2004.

[17] Boris Mirkin. Reinterpreting the category utility function. *Machine Learning*, 45(2):219–228, 2001.

[18] K. Rose. Deterministic annealing for clustering, compression, classification, regression, and related optimization problems. In *Proceedings of the IEEE*, volume 86, pages 2210–2239, 1998.

[19] Noam Slonim. *The Information Bottleneck: Theory and Applications*. The Hebrew University, 2002.

[20] Alexander Strehl and Joydeep Ghosh. Cluster ensembles: A knowledge reuse framework for combining partitionings. *Journal of Machine Learning Research*, 3:583–617, 2002.

[21] Naftali Tishby, Fernando C. Pereira, and William Bialek. The information bottleneck method. In *Proceedings of the 37th Annual Allerton Conference on Communication, Control and Computing*, pages 368–377, 1999.

[22] Alexander Topchy, Anil K. Jain, and William Punch. Combining multiple weak clusterings. In *Third IEEE International Conference on Data Mining*, pages 331–338, 2003.

[23] Shivakumar Vaithyanathan and Byron Dom. Model selection in unsupervised learning with applications to document clustering. In *The 16th International Conference on Machine Learning*, pages 433–443, 1999.

[24] Shivakumar Vaithyanathan and David Gondek. Clustering with informative priors. Technical report, IBM Almaden Research Center, 2002.

Chapter 12

Joint Cluster Analysis of Attribute Data and Relationship Data

Martin Ester

Simon Fraser University, `ester@cs.sfu.ca`

Rong Ge

Simon Fraser University, `rge@cs.sfu.ca`

Byron J. Gao

University of Wisconsin, Madison, `byron@cs.wisc.edu`

Zengjian Hu

Simon Fraser University, `zhu@cs.sfu.ca`

Boaz Ben-moshe

Ben-Gurion University of the Negev, `benmoshe@cs.bgu.ac.il`

12.1 Introduction

Entities can be described by two principal types of data: attribute data and relationship data. Attribute data describe intrinsic characteristics of entities whereas relationship data represent extrinsic influences among entities. While attribute data have been the major data source in data analysis, more and more relationship data are becoming available. To name a few, acquaintance and collaboration networks are examples of social networks, and neural and metabolic networks are examples of biological networks. Consequently, network analysis [42, 52, 53] has been gaining popularity in the study of marketing, community identification, epidemiology, molecular biology and so on.

Depending on the application and the chosen data representation, the two types of data, attribute data and relationship data, can be more or less related. If the dependency between attribute data and relationship data is high enough such that one can be soundly deducted from or closely approximated by the other, a separate analysis on either is sufficient. However, often relationship data contains information that goes beyond the information represented in the attributes of entities, and vice versa. For example, two persons may have many characteristics in common but they never got to know each other; on the other hand, even with very different demographics, they may happen to become good acquaintances. In these cases, attribute and relationship data are neither redundant nor independent but complementary. We argue that in such scenarios joint cluster analysis of attribute and relationship data can achieve more accurate results than conventional methods that consider only one of the data types.

Given both attribute data and relationship data, it is intuitive to require clusters to be cohesive (within clusters) and distinctive (between clusters) in terms of attributes as well as relationships. Due to the profound differences in nature between the two data types, it is difficult to obtain a single combined objective measure for joint cluster analysis. Instead, we propose to optimize some objective derived from the continuous attribute data and to constrain the discrete relationship data. In this chapter, we introduce and study the Connected k-Center (CkC) problem which is essentially a k-Center problem with the constraint of internal connectedness on relationship data. The internal connectedness constraint requires that any two entities in a cluster are connected by an internal path, i.e., a path via entities only from the same cluster. The k-Center problem [14] is to determine k cluster centers such that the maximum distance of any entity to its closest cluster center, the radius of the cluster, is minimized. We base our clustering model on the k-Center problem, since it is more appropriate from the point of view of a theoretical analysis and since it allows the development of an approximation algorithm with performance guarantee. From a practical point of view, the related k-Means problem, minimizing the average distances, is more appropriate, and the proposed NetScan algorithm can easily be adapted to the Connected k-Means problem, the k-Means version of the CkC problem.

The CkC problem can be motivated by market segmentation, community identification, and many other applications such as document clustering, epidemic control, and gene expression profile analysis. In the following, we further discuss the first two driving applications.

Market segmentation is the process of dividing a market into distinct customer groups with homogeneous needs, such that firms can target groups effectively and allocate resources efficiently, as customers in the same segment are likely to respond similarly to a given marketing strategy. Traditional segmentation methods are based only on attribute data such as demographics (age, sex, ethnicity, income, education, religion, etc.) and psychographic profiles (lifestyle, personality, motives, etc.). Recently, social networks have become more and more important in marketing [26]. The relations in networks are channels and conduits through which resources flow [26]. Customers can hardly hear companies but they listen to their friends; customers are skeptical but they trust their friends [53]. By word-of-mouth propagation, a group of customers with similar attributes have much more chances to become like-minded. The CkC problem naturally models such scenarios: a customer is assigned to a market segment only if he has similar purchasing preferences (attributes) to the segment representative (cluster center) and can be reached by propagation from customers of similar interest in the segment.

Community identification is one of the major social network analysis tasks, and graph-based clustering methods have been the standard tool for the task [52]. In this application, clustering has generally been performed on relationship (network) data solely. Yet it is intuitive that attribute data can impact community formation in a significant manner [23, 42]. For example, given a scientific collaboration network, scientists can be separated into different research communities such that community members are not only connected (e.g., by co-author relationships) but also share similar research interests. As a natural assumption, a community should be at least internally connected with possibly more constraints on the intensity of connectivity.

This chapter is based on [15]. It is organized as follows. Related work is reviewed in Section 12.2. Section 12.3 introduces the CkC clustering problem and analyzes its complexity. In Section 12.4, we present an approximation algorithm for the proposed clustering problem. To provide more scalability, we also present an efficient heuristic algorithm in Section 12.5. We report experimental results in Section 12.6 and conclude the chapter with a discussion of interesting directions for future research in Section 12.7.

12.2   Related Work

In this section, we review related work from the areas of theory and algorithms, data mining, social network analysis and graph clustering, constrained and semi-supervised clustering and bioinformatics.

Theory and algorithms. Theoretical approaches to cluster analysis usually formulate clustering as optimization problems, for which rigorous complexity studies are performed and polynomial approximation algorithms are provided. Depending on the optimization objective, many clustering problems and their variants have been investigated, such as the k-Center problem [1, 17, 25, 19, 14], the k-Median problem [8, 28, 29, 33], the min-diameter problem (pairwise clustering) [6], the min-sum problem [21, 3], the min-sum of diameters (or radii) problem [9, 13], and the k-Means problem [46, 34]. These problems minimize the cluster radius, the cluster diameter, the sum of intra-cluster pairwise distances, the sum of diameters (or radii), and the compactness (sum of squared distances from data points to cluster centers), respectively.

The CkC problem we study is essentially the k-Center problem with the constraint of internal connectedness on relationship data. It is well known that both the k-Center and Euclidean k-Center problems are NP-Complete for d (dimensionality) ≥ 2 and arbitrary k [36]. In the case of $d = 1$, the Euclidean k-Center problem is polynomially solvable using dynamic programming techniques [37, 18]. For $d \geq 2$ and fixed k, the k-Center problem can also be easily solved by enumerating all the k centers. However, as we will see in Section 12.3, the CkC problem remains NP-Complete even for $k = 2$ and $d = 1$. In this sense, the CkC problem is harder than the Euclidean k-Center problem. It is NP-hard to approximate the k-Center problem for $d \geq 2$ within a factor smaller than 2 even under the L_∞ metric [17]. Hochbaum and Shmoys [25] gives a 2-approximation greedy algorithm for the k-Center problem in any metric space. Feder and Greene [17] also give a 2-approximation algorithm but improve the running time to $O(n \log k)$.

Many of the above-mentioned clustering models are closely related to the general facility location problem [49], which has been extensively studied in the operations research literature. Given a set of facilities and a set of customers, the problem is to decide which facilities should be opened and which customers should be served from which facilities so as to minimize the total cost of serving all the customers. Note that the recently studied Connected k-Median problem [47] is not closely related to our CkC problem. As a variant of the facility location problem, the Connected k-Median problem additionally considers the communication cost among facilities, whereas our CkC problem requires within-cluster connectedness. While all of these optimization problems are related to our study in the sense that they also study clustering from the theoretical perspective, they have no intention to perform joint cluster analysis, and they do not require clusters to be cohesive with respect to both attribute data and relationship data.

Data mining. In the data mining community, clustering research emphasizes real-life applications and development of efficient and scalable algorithms. Existing methods roughly fall into several categories, including partitioning methods such as k-Means [35], k-Medoids [31], and CLARANS [39]; hierarchical methods such as AGNES and DIANA [31]; and density-based methods such as DBSCAN [16] and OPTICS [2]. These clustering methods, in general, take only attribute data into consideration.

While almost all clustering algorithms assume data to be represented in a single table, recently multi-relational clustering algorithms have been explored which can deal with a database consisting of multiple tables related via foreign key references. [48] presents a multi-relational clustering method based on probabilistic relational models (PRMs). PRMs are a first-order generalization of the well-known Bayesian networks. [54] introduces an approach to multi-relational clustering based on user guidance in the form of the specification of some attributes that are known to be related to the (unknown) cluster labels. The problem addressed in this chapter, i.e., clustering a single table with attributes and relationships, can be understood as a special case of multi-relational clustering. However, the approach of [48] is not applicable in this scenario since PRMs do not allow cycles which often occur in relationships within a single table. The method of [54] requires additional user guidance which may not be available.

Social network analysis and graph clustering. Recently, the increasing availability of relationship data has stimulated research on network analysis [52, 42, 23]. Clustering methods for network analysis are mostly graph-based, separating sparsely connected dense subgraphs from each other as in [5]. A good graph clustering should exhibit few between-cluster edges and many within-cluster edges. More precisely, graph clustering refers to a set of problems whose goal is to partition nodes of a network into groups so that some objective function is minimized. Several popular objective functions, e.g., *normalized cut* [44] and *ratio cut* [7], have been well studied. Those graph clustering problems can be effectively solved by spectral methods that make use of eigenvectors. Recently, Dhillon et al. [12] discovered the equivalence between a general kernel k-means objective and a weighted graph clustering objective. They further utilize the equivalence to develop an effective multilevel algorithm, called GraClus, that optimizes several graph clustering objectives including the normalized cut. The experiments in [12] show that GraClus can beat the best spectral method on several clustering tasks.

Graph clustering methods can be applied to data that are originally network data. The original network can be weighted where weights normally represent the probability that two linked nodes belong to the same cluster [44]. In some cases, the probability is estimated by the distance between linked nodes on attribute data. Moreover, graph clustering methods can also be applied to similarity graphs representing similarity matrices, which are derived from attribute data. A similarity graph can be a complete graph as in the agglomerative hierarchical clustering algorithms, e.g., single-link, complete link, and average link [27], or incomplete retaining those edges whose corresponding similarity is above a threshold [20, 24]. CHAMELEON [30] generates edges between a vertex and its k nearest neighbors, which can be considered as relative thresholding.

There are two major differences between graph clustering, in particular the normalized cut, and CkC. On the one hand, the graph clustering model does not require the generated clusters to be internally connected which makes it somewhat more flexible than CkC. Yet, for some applications such as market segmentation and community identification, CkC fits better than the graph clustering model as these applications often require the generated clusters to be internally connected. On the other hand, in graph clustering, attribute data is used only indirectly by using distances between nodes as edges weights, which may lose important information since it reduces the d-dimensional attribute data of two connected nodes to a single, relative distance value. In CkC, attribute data are used directly, avoiding information loss.

Constrained and semi-supervised clustering. Early research in this direction allowed the user to guide the clustering algorithm by constraining cluster properties such as size or aggregate attribute values [50]. More recently, several frameworks have been introduced that represent available domain knowledge in the form of pairwise "must-links" and "cannot-links."

Objects connected by a must-link are supposed to belong to the same cluster, those with a cannot-link should be assigned to different clusters. [4] proposes a probabilistic framework based on hidden Markov random fields (HMRF), incorporating supervision into k-clustering algorithms. [32] shows that the objective function of the HMRF-based semi-supervised clustering model, as well as some graph clustering models, can be expressed as special cases of weighted kernel k-Means objective. Based on these theoretical connections, a unified algorithm is proposed to perform semi-supervised clustering on data given either as vectors or as a graph. [10] considers additional minimum separation and minimum connectivity constraints, but they are ultimately translated into must-link and cannot-link constraints. A k-Means-like algorithm is presented using a novel distance function which penalizes violations of both kinds of constraints. The above two papers are similar to our research in the sense that they also adopt a k-clustering approach under the framework of constrained clustering. Nevertheless, in semi-supervised clustering, links represent specific instance-level constraints on attribute data. They are provided by the user to capture some background knowledge. In our study, links represent relationship data. They are not constraints themselves, but data on which different constraints can be enforced, such as being "internally connected." Enforcing the connectedness constraint should lead to cohesion of clusters with respect to relationship data, so that clusters can be cohesive in both ways.

Bioinformatics. There have been several research efforts that consider both attribute and relationship data in the bioinformatics literature. With the goal of identifying functional modules, Hanisch et al. [22] propose a co-clustering method for biological networks and gene expression data by constructing a distance function that combines the expression distance and the network distance. However, their method cannot guarantee that the resulting clusters are connected. Segal et al. [43] introduce a probabilistic graphical model, combining a naive Bayes model for the expression data and a Markov random field for the network data. While the probabilistic framework has the advantage of representing the uncertainty of cluster assignments, it cannot ensure the connectedness of the resulting clusters. Ulitsky and Shamir [51] present an algorithmic framework for clustering gene data. Given a gene network and expression similarity values, they seek heavy subgraphs in an edge-weighted similarity graph. Similar to our model, this model requires the generated clusters to be connected. Different from the CkC model, their model does not search for a partition of the whole data set, i.e., not every gene needs to be assigned to a cluster.

12.3   Problem Definition and Complexity Analysis

In this section, we formally define the Connected k-Center (CkC) problem. We prove the NP-completeness of the decision version of the CkC problem through a reduction from the 3SAT problem. The key observation in this proof is the existence of so-called "bridge" nodes, which can be assigned to multiple centers and are crucial to link some other nodes to their corresponding centers within a certain radius.

12.3.1   Preliminaries and Problem Definition

Relationship data are usually modeled by networks comprised of nodes and links, which we call entity networks. In this chapter, we concentrate on symmetric binary relations, thereby entity networks can be naturally represented as simple graphs with edges (links) indicating the presence or absence of a relation of interest such as acquaintance, collaboration, or transmission of information or diseases.

Nodes in an entity network do not have meaningful locations. With attribute data available, attributes for each entity can be represented as a coordinate vector and assigned to the corresponding node, resulting in what we call an "informative graph." Informative graphs, with both attribute data and relationship data embedded, are used as input for our Connected k-Center problem.

In this chapter, the terms "vertex" and "node" are used interchangeably, so are "edge" and "link." In the following sections, "graph" will refer to "informative graph" since we always consider the two data types simultaneously.

The Connected k-Center (CkC) problem performs a joint cluster analysis on attribute data and relationship data, so that clusters are cohesive in both ways. The problem is to find a disjoint k-clustering (k-partitioning) of a set of nodes, such that each cluster satisfies the internal connectedness constraint (defined on the relationship data), and the maximum radius (defined on the attribute data) is minimized. The radius of a cluster is the maximum distance of any node in the cluster to the corresponding center node. A formal definition of the CkC problem is given in the following.

DEFINITION 12.1   (CkC problem) *Given an integer k, a graph $g = (V, E)$, a function $w : V \rightarrow \mathcal{X}$ mapping each node in V to a d-dimensional coordinate vector, and a distance function $||\cdot||$, find a k-partitioning $\{V_1, \ldots, V_k\}$ of V, i.e., $V_1 \cup \ldots \cup V_k = V$ and $\forall 1 \leq i < j \leq k, V_i \cap V_j = \phi$, such that the partitions satisfy the internal connectedness constraint, i.e., the induced subgraphs $g[V_1], \ldots, g[V_k]$ are connected, and the maximum radius defined on $||\cdot||$ is minimized.*

In this study, we assume the given graph g is connected, which is reasonable for many application scenarios, e.g., social networks. Even if the entire graph is not connected, the problem and the corresponding algorithms can still be applied to its connected components.

12.3.2 Complexity Analysis

Given the similarity of the CkC problem to the traditional k-Center problem, it is natural to ask how much the traditional k-Center problem has been changed in terms of hardness by adding the constraint of internal connectedness. To answer this question, we analyze the complexity of the CkC problem. In the following, we define the decision version of the CkC problem and prove its NP-completeness. Note that in this subsection of complexity analysis, the names of the problems refer to their decision versions.

DEFINITION 12.2 (*CkC problem, decision version*) *Given an integer k, a graph $g = (V, E)$, a function $w : V \to \mathcal{X}$ mapping each node in V to a d-dimensional coordinate vector, a distance function $||\cdot||$, and a radius threshold $r \in \mathbb{R}^+$, decide whether there exists a k-partitioning $\{V_1, \ldots, V_k\}$ of V, i.e., $V_1 \cup \ldots \cup V_k = V$ and $\forall 1 \leq i < j \leq k, V_i \cap V_j = \phi$, such that in addition to the internal connectedness constraint, the partitions also satisfy the radius constraint, i.e., $\forall 1 \leq i \leq k$, there exists a center node $c_i \in V_i$, such that $\forall v \in V_i, ||w(v) - w(c_i)|| \leq r$.*

We will prove an NP-completeness result for fixed k. As the formal analysis is rather technical, we precede it with an intuitive explanation. We say a solution (or partitioning) is *legal* if all the k partitions (or clusters) are disjoint and the corresponding induced subgraphs are connected. Since k is fixed as a constant, a naive algorithm would enumerate all the combinations of k centers, and for each combination assign the remaining nodes to the centers such that both the internal connectedness and radius constraints are satisfied. However, we note that there may exist some "bridge" node v which can connect to multiple centers within distance r and is critical to connect some other nodes to their corresponding centers. In a legal partitioning, every bridge node must be assigned to a unique center. If there are many such bridge nodes, it is difficult to assign each of them to the "right" center in order to maintain the connection for others. Therefore, the naive algorithm may fail to determine a legal partitioning. By intuition, the CkC problem is hard even for a fixed k. In the following, we prove a hardness result for the CkC problem by a reduction from 3SAT. For convenience, we state the 3SAT problem as follows:

DEFINITION 12.3 (3SAT problem) *Given a set $U = \{u_1, \ldots, u_n\}$ of variables, a boolean formula $I = \mathcal{C}_1 \wedge \mathcal{C}_2 \wedge \ldots \wedge \mathcal{C}_m$ where each clause $\mathcal{C}_i = l_i^1 \vee l_i^2 \vee l_i^3$ contains three literals and each literal l_i^j, $j = 1, 2, 3$, is a variable* *or negated variable, decide whether there exists a truth assignment of U that satisfies every clause of C.*

THEOREM 12.1
For any $k \geq 2$ and $d \geq 1$, the CkC problem is NP-Complete.

PROOF
We only construct a proof for the case of $k = 2$ and $d = 1$, the proof can be easily extended to any larger k and d.

First, we show $C2C$ is in NP. We can nondeterministically guess a partitioning of graph G and pick a node as center from each partition. For each partition, we can traverse the corresponding subgraph in polynomial time to verify whether it is a legal partitioning satisfying the radius constraint.

Next, we perform a reduction from 3SAT to show the NP-hardness of $C2C$. Let $L = \{u_1, \bar{u}_1, \ldots, u_n, \bar{u}_n\}$ be a set of literals. For any 3SAT instance $I = C_1 \wedge C_2 \wedge \ldots \wedge C_m$, we construct a $C2C$ instance $f(I) = (g, w, r)$, where $g = (V, E)$ is the underlying graph, $w : V \rightarrow R$ is the function mapping nodes to coordinate vectors, and $r \in \mathbb{R}^+$ is the radius constraint, by the following procedure:

1. Create a set of nodes $V = P \cup L \cup C \cup A \cup B$. $P = \{p_0, p_1\}$ where p_0 and p_1 are two center nodes. L and C are the sets of literals and clauses respectively. $A = \{a_1, \ldots, a_n\}$ and $B = \{b_1, \ldots, b_n\}$ are two sets of nodes introduced only for the purpose of the reduction.

2. Connect the nodes created in step (1). We link each literal $l \in L$ to both p_0 and p_1. For each literal $l \in L$ and clause $C_i \in C$, we link l to C_i if $l \in C_i$. For each $i \in [n]$, we link a_i and b_i to both u_i and $\bar{u}_i$.

3. Set r to an arbitrary positive value and assign each node $v \in V$ a coordinate as follows.

$$w(v) = \begin{cases} 0, & \text{if } v \in B; \\ r, & \text{if } v = p_0; \\ 2r, & \text{if } v \in L; \\ 3r, & \text{if } v = p_1; \\ 4r, & \text{if } v \in A \cup C. \end{cases}$$

Steps (1) and (2) construct the underlying graph g. A visual explanation of the construction method is provided in Figure 12.1. Note that every node in A, B, C can only connect to the center nodes p_0 and p_1 via some nodes in L.

Step (3) assigns each node in V a carefully chosen coordinate, such that each node in A, B, C is within distance r to one unique center node p_0 or p_1. Figure 12.2 illustrates the deployment of nodes on the line.

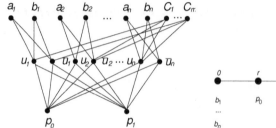

FIGURE 12.1: Constructed graph g.

FIGURE 12.2: Deployment of nodes on the line.

In order to have a legal partitioning (partitions are disjoint and satisfy the internal connectedness constraint), every node in L must be assigned to an appropriate center (cluster). For the reduction, we associate a truth value (true or false) to each cluster; accordingly, the allocations of these nodes can then be transferred back to a truth assignment for the input 3SAT instance I. Besides, we need to guarantee that the truth assignment for I is proper, i.e., $\forall i \in [n]$, node u_i and $\overline{u}_i$ belong to different clusters. Node sets A and B are two gadgets introduced for this purpose.

Clearly the above reduction is polynomial. Next, we show I is satisfiable if and only if $f(I) = (g, w, r)$ has a legal partitioning satisfying the radius constraint. We use V_0 and V_1 to refer to the clusters centered at p_0 and p_1 respectively.

If $f(I) = (g, w, r)$ has a legal partitioning satisfying the radius constraint, we have the following simple observations:

1. Both p_0 and p_1 must be selected as centers, otherwise some node cannot be reached within distance r.

2. For the same reason, each node in A and C must be assigned to cluster V_1 and each node in B must be assigned to V_0.

3. For any $i \in [n]$, u_i and $\overline{u}_i$ cannot be in the same cluster. If u_i and $\overline{u}_i$ are both assigned to cluster V_0 (or V_1), some node in A (or B) would not be able to connect to p_1 (or p_0).

4. For each clause $C_i \in C$, there must be at least one literal assigned to cluster V_1, otherwise C_i will be disconnected from p_1.

We construct a satisfying assignment for I as follows: For each variable $u_i \in U$, if u_i is assigned to V_1, set u_i to be true, otherwise false. Note by observation (3), u_i and $\overline{u}_i$ are always assigned different values, hence the assignment is proper. Moreover, the assignment satisfies I since by observation (4), all the clauses are satisfied.

If I is satisfiable, we construct a partitioning $\{V_0, V_1\}$ as follows:

$$V_0 = B \cup \{p_0\} \cup \{l_i \in L \mid l_i = false\}$$
$$V_1 = V \setminus V_0$$

It is easy to verify that the above partitioning is legal. In addition, the radius constraint is satisfied since every node in V is within distance r from its corresponding center node, p_0 or p_1.

Finally, we show that the above proof can be easily extended to any larger k and d. When $k > 2$, one can always add $k - 2$ isolated nodes (hence each of them must be a center) to graph g and apply the same reduction; when $d > 1$, one can simply add $d - 1$ coordinates with identical values to the existing coordinate for each node. ⬜

The traditional k-Center problem which is known to be NP-hard only when k is arbitrary and the dimensionality is greater than 1, but the CkC problem is NP-hard even for a fixed k or one dimensional data.

Theorem 12.1 implies that the optimization version of the CkC problem defined in Definition 12.1 is NP-hard.

Similar to the CkC problem, one can define the connected k-Median and connected k-Means problems. In fact, the proof of Theorem 12.1 can be extended to these problems to show their NP-Completeness.

12.4   Approximation Algorithms

In this section we study the optimization version of the CkC problem defined in Definition 12.1. We prove that the problem is not approximable within $2 - \epsilon$ for any $\epsilon > 0$ unless $P = NP$. When the distance function is metric, we provide approximation algorithms with ratios of 3 and 6, respectively, for the cases of fixed and arbitrary k. The idea is to tackle an auxiliary CkC' problem. Based on the solution of CkC', we show the gap between these two problems is at most 3, i.e., a feasible solution of CkC' with radius r can always be transferred to a feasible solution of CkC with radius at most $3r$.

12.4.1   Inapproximability Results for CkC

In the following, we prove an inapproximability result for the CkC problem.

THEOREM 12.2
For any $k \geq 2$, $\epsilon > 0$, the CkC problem is not approximable within $2 - \epsilon$ unless $P = NP$.

PROOF   (Sketch.) We can prove this theorem by applying a similar proof to that of Theorem 12.1 and noting that the distances are multiples of r.

$\Box$

12.4.2   Approximation Results for Metric CkC

In the following, we study approximation algorithms for the CkC problem in the metric space. Our approximation results rely on the triangle inequality. However, our hardness results presented in Section 12.3 remain valid even for non-metric spaces.

We provide approximations with ratios 3 and 6 for the cases of fixed and arbitrary k. For this purpose, we introduce the CkC' problem, which is a relaxed version of the CkC problem without stipulating the disjointness requirement on the clusters. Then we show that CkC' can be solved in polynomial time for fixed k and approximated within a factor of 2 for arbitrary k. We then show the gap between these two problems is at most 3.

DEFINITION 12.4   (*CkC' problem*) *Given an integer k, a graph $g = (V, E)$, a function $w : V \rightarrow \mathcal{X}$ mapping each node in V to a d-dimensional coordinate vector, and a distance function $||\cdot||$, find k node sets $V_1, \ldots, V_k \subseteq V$ with $V_1 \cup \ldots \cup V_k = V$, such that the node sets satisfy the internal connectedness constraint and the maximum radius defined on $|| \cdot ||$ is minimized.*

Complexity of CkC'. If k is treated as part of the input, CkC' is NP-Complete as it is an extension of the traditional k-center problem. On the contrary, if k is fixed as a constant, CkC' is in P (justification follows). **Solving CkC' for fixed k.** We propose an exact algorithm to solve the CkC' problem for fixed k in polynomial time. We define the reachability between any two nodes as follows:

DEFINITION 12.5   *Let $G = (V, E)$, for $u, v \in V$, v is reachable from u w.r.t. r, $r \in \mathbb{R}^+$, if there exists a path $p : \{u = s_0 \rightarrow s_1 \rightarrow \ldots \rightarrow s_l \rightarrow s_{l+1} = v\}$, $s_1, \ldots, s_l \in V$, such that $\forall 1 \leq i \leq l+1$, $(s_{i-1}, s_i) \in E$ and $||w(u) - w(s_i)|| \leq r$.*

Intuitively, v is reachable from u w.r.t. r if and only if v can be included in the cluster with center u and radius r. Clearly it can be decided in polynomial time by performing a breadth first search (BFS) for node v from node u. This forms the main idea of Algorithm 1 in Figure 12.3, which returns the optimal solution for CkC' in polynomial time.

Runtime complexity. Algorithm 1 in Figure 12.3 performs $O(n^k \log n)$ calls of BFS since it iterates over all possible sets of k centers, and a binary search is performed for all possible $r \in R$ where $|R| = \binom{n}{2}$. Since every BFS

Algorithm 1

1: Calculate all the pairwise distances for the nodes in V and store them in set R;
2: Sort R in increasing order;
3: $low = 0; high = |R|$;
4: **while** $low \leq high$
5:     $middle = (low + high)/2$;
6:     $r = R[middle]$;
7:     **for** each set of k centers $\{c_1, \ldots, c_k\} \subseteq V$
8:         Perform BFS from each center c_i and mark all the nodes that are reachable from c_i w.r.t. r;
9:     **if** all nodes are marked
10:       **if** $low = high$
11:         Return r and the k clusters;
12:       **else**
13:         $high = middle - 1$;
14:     **else**
15:       $low = middle + 1$;

FIGURE 12.3: Polynomial exact algorithm for CkC'.

takes $O(n^2)$ steps, the total running time of Algorithm 1 in Figure 12.3 is $O(n^{k+2} \log n)$.

Approximating CkC' for arbitrary k. For the case that k is arbitrary, we show an approach providing a 2 approximation for the CkC' problem. We define the *reaching distance* between any two nodes as follows:

DEFINITION 12.6   *Let G, u, v, p be defined as in Definition 12.5. The distance between u and v w.r.t p is defined as $D(u,v)_p = \max_{s_i, s_j \in p} \|w(s_i) - w(s_j)\|$. The reaching distance between u and v is defined as $D(u,v) = \min_{p \in P} D(u,v)_p$, where P is the set of all paths between u and v.*

Note that the reaching distance is symmetric, i.e., $\forall u, v \in V, D(u,v) = D(v,u)$. It also satisfies the triangle inequality, i.e., $\forall u, v, s \in V, D(u,s) \leq D(u,v) + D(v,s)$. We can obtain a $|V| \times |V|$ matrix, storing reaching distances for all the nodes in V. Then, we can apply the 2-approximation algorithm proposed in [25] on V with the reaching distance matrix replacing the pairwise distance matrix. The maximum radius of the k clusters resulting from this algorithm is at most twice as big as the optimal solution.

Back to CkC. In Algorithm 2 (Figure 12.4), we present a method transfer-

Algorithm 2

1: **for** i from 1 to k
2:     $V_i = \phi$, $c_i \leftarrow c_i'$;
3:     Add all the nodes reachable w.r.t. r from c_i in $G[V_i' \setminus \cup_{j=1}^{i-1} V_j]$ to V_i
       (by performing a BFS from c_i in $G[V_i' \setminus \cup_{j=1}^{i-1} V_j]$);
4:     **for** every node $v \in \left(\cup_{j=1}^{i-1} V_j\right) \cap V_i'$
5:         Add all the nodes connected to v in $G[V_i']$ to the cluster of v
           (by performing a BFS from v in $G[V_i']$);
6: Output clusters $V_1, \ldots, V_k$;

FIGURE 12.4: Converting a solution of CkC' to a solution of CkC.

ring a feasible solution of CkC' with radius r to a feasible solution of CkC with radius at most $3r$. Combining the CkC' results and Algorithm 2 gives approximations for the CkC problem.

Let $\{V_1', \ldots, V_k'\}$ be a clustering returned by Algorithm 2 or the approximation algorithm specified in Section 12.4.1 where $V_i' \subseteq V$ and the node sets (clusters) $V_1', \ldots, V_k'$ may not be disjoint. Algorithm 2 determines a clustering $\{V_1, \ldots, V_k\}$ with disjoint node sets $V_1, \ldots, V_k$. Let $c_1, \ldots, c_k$ be the centers of $V_1, \ldots, V_k$. Since the algorithm retains the cluster centers, they are also the centers of $V_1', \ldots, V_k'$. Algorithm 2 assigns every node in V to a unique cluster V_i for $1 \leq i \leq k$. For each iteration $1 \leq i \leq k$, line 3 assigns the nodes in V_i' that have not been assigned to any previous clusters $V_1, \ldots, V_{i-1}$ and are connected to c_i to V_i. Afterwards, there may still be some unassigned nodes in V_i', and line 5 assigns them to one of the clusters $V_1, \ldots, V_{i-1}$ to which they are connected.

Figure 12.5 provides an illustration for Algorithm 2. The circles with dashed lines represent the three initial (overlapping) clusters $V_1', V_2',$ and V_3' generated by Algorithm 1. Applying Algorithm 2, we obtain three new disjoint clusters $V_1, V_2,$ and V_3. The center nodes were not changed.

LEMMA 12.1

Let r be the maximum radius associated with a feasible solution for the CkC' problem. Algorithm 2 is guaranteed to find a feasible solution for the CkC problem with maximum radius at most $3r$.

PROOF

First we show that Algorithm 2 assigns each node $u \in V$ to a unique cluster. There are two cases. In case 1, u can be reached via a path from center node

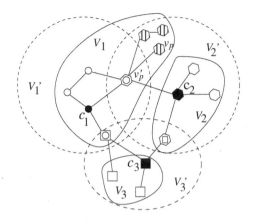

FIGURE 12.5: Illustration of Algorithm 2.

c_i without having any node previously assigned to $V_1, \ldots, V_{i-1}$ on the path; then, u is assigned to V_i in line 3 of Algorithm 2. In case 2, u is connected to c_i via some node $v \in \cup_{j=1}^{i-1} V_j$; then, in line 5 of Algorithm 2, u is assigned to the cluster that v belongs to.

Next, we bound the maximum radius of a node u to the corresponding center node. In case 1, since u is assigned to V_i, the distance between u and c_i is at most r. In case 2, observe that the distance between u and v is at most $2r$ due to the triangle inequality and the fact that u and v were in the same set V_i'. Besides, we observe that the distance between v and its corresponding center node c_j is at most r. Therefore, again by the triangle inequality, the distance between u and its corresponding center node is at most $3r$.

$\square$

Let *opt* and *opt'* be the optimal solutions for the CkC and CkC' problems, respectively. Clearly $opt' \leq opt$ since opt is also a feasible solution for CkC'. Based on this observation, we obtain the following approximation results for CkC:

THEOREM 12.3

Combining Algorithm 1 and Algorithm 2 gives a polynomial 3-approximation for the CkC problem for fixed k.

THEOREM 12.4

Combining the approach proposed in 12.4.1 and Algorithm 2 gives a polynomial 6-approximation for the CkC problem for arbitrary k.

12.5 Heuristic Algorithm

While the development of an approximation algorithm with guaranteed clustering quality is important from the theoretical point of view, the expensive enumeration operation makes the approach infeasible for application on large data sets. Therefore, in this section, we present *NetScan*, a heuristic algorithm that efficiently produces a "good" CkC clustering and scales to large real-life data sets.

12.5.1 Overview of NetScan

NetScan follows a three-step approach. It starts by picking k centers randomly, then assigns nodes to the best centers and refines the clusters iteratively.

- Step I: Randomly pick k initial cluster centers.

- Step II: Assign all nodes to clusters by traversing the input graph.

- Step III: Recalculate cluster centers.

The algorithm repeats steps II and III until no change of the cluster centers occurs or a certain number of iterations have been performed. In step III, finding the optimal center from a group of n nodes requires $O(n^2)$ time. For efficiency, we select the node closest to the mean of the cluster as the new center. Typically, the mean provides a reasonably good approximation for the center.

The three-step framework resembles the k-Means algorithm. However, unlike the straightforward assignment step in k-Means, given k centers, finding an optimal assignment satisfying the connectedness constraint requires a search through an exponential space, as shown in Section 12.3.2. Thus, the major challenge of NetScan is finding a good membership assignment, i.e., step II.

From the design principles of the approximation algorithm, we observe that the BFS-based approach provides an efficient way of generating clusters without violating the internal connectedness constraint. Therefore, we start the membership assignment from the centers, and neighboring nodes (directly connected by some edge of the graph) of already assigned nodes are gradually absorbed to the clusters. The whole step II may take multiple rounds to finish until all the nodes are assigned, and each round i is associated with a radius threshold R_i. For the first round, the assignment starts from cluster centers with the initial radius threshold R_0. Each node is tested and assigned to the first cluster for which its distance to the center is no larger than R_0. If all the centers have been processed but not all nodes have been assigned, the next assignment round tries to assign them with an incremented radius threshold

---

Algorithm 3

1: Empty working queue Q;
2: **for** every center c_j of cluster C_j
3:     Append all unassigned neighbors of c_j to Q;
4:     **while** Q is not empty
5:         Pop the first element q from Q;
6:         **if** $||q - c_j|| \leq R_i$
7:             **if** q is a potential bridge node
8:                 Invoke the look-ahead routine to decide the membership for q. If q should be assigned to C_j, append q's unassigned neighbors to Q; otherwise, only assign q to the right cluster without appending q's neighbors to Q; (Section 12.5.2 (c))
9:             **else**
10:                 Assign q to C_j and append q's unassigned neighbors to Q;
11: **if** all nodes are assigned to some C_j
12:     Stop;
13: **else**
14:     Increase R_i and goto 1;

FIGURE 12.6: Step II of NetScan.

R_1. The process continues until all the nodes are assigned. The pseudocode of step II is given in Algorithm 3 (Figure 12.6), and more details of NetScan will be discussed shortly.

12.5.2 More Details on NetScan

(a) How to choose initial cluster centers. The initialization has a direct impact on the NetScan results as in many similar algorithms. Instead of using a naive random approach, we weight each node with its degree so that nodes with higher degrees have higher probabilities to be chosen. Since NetScan relies on edges to grow clusters in step II, the weighted random approach allows clusters to grow fast. More importantly, due to the improved edge availability, true cluster contents can be absorbed during early rounds of membership assignment, reducing the possibility that they would be assigned to some other clusters inappropriately.

(b) How to choose R_i. In step II of NetScan, the radius threshold R_i is gradually incremented from round to round. R_i plays an important role in minimizing the maximum radius of the resulting clusters. Figure 12.7 gives an example where a larger threshold R_{i+1} allows node a to be assigned to cluster 1, resulting in a larger radius of cluster 1. A similar situation applies to node b whose assignment to cluster 2 would result in a larger radius of cluster 2. Instead, by using a smaller threshold R_i, these cases are avoided because a and b can only be assigned to cluster 2 and cluster 3, respectively. From the point of view of minimizing the maximum radius, we want the increment of R_i to be as small as possible. However, a too small increment of R_i may lead to the case that no additional node can be assigned for many rounds, which may greatly and unnecessarily increase the runtime.

As a trade-off, we propose the increment to be the average pairwise distance of nodes. That is, the radius threshold R_{i+1} is chosen as $R_i + \overline{D}$ where $\overline{D}$ is the average pairwise distance of nodes. This choice of increment makes it likely that at least some further nodes can be assigned in the next round. $\overline{D}$ can be obtained efficiently by drawing a small set of samples and calculating the average pairwise distance of the samples.

Our complexity analysis suggests that the nodes located in the overlapping area of two clusters w.r.t. a given radius threshold are more difficult to assign than the others. Thus, to start with, we choose R_0 to be half of the smallest distance among all pairs of cluster centers. This choice of R_0 does not create overlap that introduces any ambiguity in the node assignment.

(c) How to assign nodes. In step II of NetScan, nodes are assigned to clusters generally based on their distances to the cluster centers. Special attention, however, needs to be paid to those nodes in the overlap area of two or more clusters w.r.t. R_i. Inspired by the concept of bridge nodes introduced in Section 12.3, we call these nodes *potential bridge nodes*. We assign potential bridge nodes not only based on their distances to the different cluster centers, but also on their neighborhood situations. For example, in Figure 12.7, a is

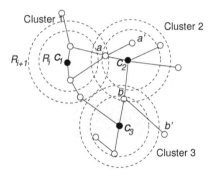

FIGURE 12.7: Radius increment.

a potential bridge node and its assignment has an impact on the assignment of its neighbor a'. If node a is assigned to cluster 1, a' has to be assigned to cluster 1, resulting in a larger radius compared to assigning both nodes to cluster 2. A similar situation applies to nodes b and b'.

Whether a node is a potential bridge node depends on three factors: (1) the node has neighbors who have been assigned membership and those neighbors are from more than one cluster, e.g., C_i and C_j, (2) the node is within R_i distance from both centers of C_i and C_j and (3) the node has unassigned neighbors.

We propose the following look-ahead approach for the cluster assignment of potential bridge nodes (line 8 of Algorithm 3). For the sake of efficiency, for each potential bridge node, we only check its unassigned neighbors (if any) which have a degree of 1, the so-called *unary neighbors*. These unary neighbors are especially critical since they can be connected to any cluster only via the node under consideration. A potential bridge node is assigned to its closest center unless the node has a direct unary neighbor which is closer to some other center. In the case that more than one unary neighbor exists, the cluster center leading to the smallest radius increase is chosen. Our algorithm could benefit from looking into indirect neighbors of potential bridge nodes as well, however, this would significantly increase the runtime without guarantee of quality improvement.

(d) Postprocessing to eliminate outliers. As in the traditional k-Center problem, the CkC problem faces the same challenge of "outliers," which may cause a significant increase in the radius of the resulting clusters. In many applications such as market segmentation, it is acceptable and desirable to give up a few customers to meet most customers' preference. We propose an optional step, which utilizes a graphical approach to eliminate outliers from the NetScan results. Each node remembers the radius threshold at which it was assigned, and all the nodes are sorted by these thresholds. We filter out the node (and its following nodes) which causes a sudden increase of the

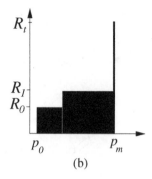

FIGURE 12.8: Outlier elimination by radius histogram.

radius. The "cut-off" point can be determined by automatic detection as well as manual inspection from a chart displaying the sorted nodes, as illustrated in Figure 12.8 (b). Only node p_m would be removed as an outlier in the example.

(e) Runtime complexity. In each iteration of step II and III, the NetScan algorithm generates k clusters one by one. During membership assignment of each cluster, the nodes sharing edges with the assigned nodes of that cluster are considered. The distances between these nodes and the cluster center are calculated. Thus, the overall runtime complexity is bounded by the total number of nodes being visited. For the purpose of minimizing the maximum radius, NetScan gradually increases the radius threshold R_i. Let $\overline{D}$ represent the amount of radius increment, the total number of radius increases in one iteration is a constant, $\frac{diam}{\overline{D}}$, where $diam$ is the longest distance among all pairs of nodes. In the worst case, every edge is visited k times for each R_i, hence the total number of node visits in an iteration is $O(k|E|\frac{diam}{\overline{D}})$, where $|E|$ is the total number of edges. We assume the NetScan algorithm converges after t iterations. Hence, the worst case runtime complexity of NetScan is $O(tk|E|\frac{diam}{\overline{D}})$. However, in each iteration, we only need to consider those edges connecting to the nodes in the *frontier*, i.e., a set of unassigned nodes that are direct neighbors of the assigned nodes. The worst case rarely happens, in which all the edges are connected to the frontier nodes. In practice, the number of edges visited in one iteration can be reasonably assumed to be $O(|E|)$ on average, and the expected runtime of NetScan would be $O(t|E|)$ under this assumption.

12.5.3 Adaptation of NetScan to the Connected k-Means Problem

As we have discussed in related work (Section 12.2), various clustering problems can be formulated depending on different objectives. The well-known k-Means problem [46, 34] minimizes the compactness, i.e., the sum of squared distances from data points to their corresponding cluster centers. The corresponding k-Means algorithm [35] is widely used as a practical and robust clustering method. As an analogue for joint cluster analysis, we can define the Connected k-Means problem, which finds a k-partitioning of nodes minimizing the compactness under the internal connectedness constraint.

As a straightforward extension, NetScan can be adapted to the Connected k-Means problem. We can simply use the means of clusters to replace the center nodes. Then in step II of NetScan, the radius is computed with respect to the means instead of the center nodes. Similarly in step III, the new cluster means are relocated instead of the center nodes. The algorithm terminates when there is no change in node membership or a certain number of iterations have been performed.

12.6 Experimental Results

In this section, we demonstrate the meaningfulness and accuracy of our joint cluster analysis model on a real-life data set (see Table 12.1 for a summary of the data set). The data set was generated based on papers published from 2000 to 2004 in nine major conferences of three communities: theory, databases and data mining, and machine learning. 1786 researchers were extracted as authors of those papers. The attributes of each researcher are vectors representing the keyword frequencies in the abstracts of his/her papers. After deleting stop words and applying stemming and word occurrence thresholding, we obtain a data set whose attribute vectors have 603 dimensions. We used term frequency inverse-document frequency [41], a state-of-the-art method in text mining, to normalize the data set. The relationship data is a connected subgraph extracted from the DBLP [11] coauthorship network. Note that the researchers were chosen so that the relationship graph is connected. We also removed researchers that make the true clusters unconnected, since otherwise, due to the connectedness constraint, NetScan will have no chance to achieve 100% accuracy. The task was to cluster researchers with the goal of identifying research communities in an unsupervised manner. A researcher's true community (cluster label) was determined by the community to which the majority of his/her papers belongs. These true labels were then compared to the labels determined by our algorithm.

The traditional k-Means algorithm is known to work well for document

TABLE 12.1: Summaries of the real data set.

Communities	Conferences	# of Researchers
Theory	FOCS, STOC, SODA	547
Databases and Data Mining	SIGMOD, VLDB, KDD	722
Machine Learning	ICML, NIPS, COLT	517

clustering [45] utilizing only the attribute data. We applied our adapted NetScan (for the Connected k-Means problem, see Section 12.5.3) to the data set and compared the results with k-Means. We used the cosine distance as the distance measure for the attributes, a standard measure for text data. Table 12.2 reports the clustering results averaged over 20 runs for both algorithms, recording the number of correctly identified researchers for each community together with the overall accuracy. In order to measure the accuracy, a cluster is labeled by a majority vote of its members. Compared to k-Means, NetScan significantly improved the accuracy from 79% to 89.7%. Note that we perform unsupervised learning, which accounts for the relatively low accuracy of both algorithms compared to supervised classification algorithms.

TABLE 12.2: Comparison of NetScan and k-Means

Communities	Size	k-Means	NetScan
Theory	547	417	514
Databases	722	575	691
Machine Learning	517	422	397
Sum	1786	1414	1602
Accuracy		79.2%	89.7%

The main reason why NetScan significantly outperforms k-Means is that both relationship and attribute data make contributions in the clustering process, and considering only one data type can mislead the clustering algorithm. For example, Jon Kleinberg published papers in KDD, NIPS, STOC, SODA, etc. From this attribute information, it seems reasonable to identify him as a researcher in databases and data mining or machine learning. Nevertheless, after taking his coauthorship information into consideration, NetScan clustered him into the theory community, which is a better match for his overall research profile. On the other hand, Rajeev Motwani has broad coauthorship connections, which alone cannot be used to confidently identify his community membership. However, the majority of his papers from 2000 to 2004 was published in conferences of the theory community, and NetScan correctly clustered him into the theory community.

12.7   Discussion

The framework of joint cluster analysis of attribute and relationship data suggests several interesting directions for future research, some of which are discussed in this section.

There are many applications where the connectivity constraint of the CkC model is appropriate, such as the driving applications (market segmentation and community identification) mentioned in Section 12.1. Yet, in other applications such as molecular biology the connectivity constraint becomes insufficient to capture the properties of clusters. In molecular biology, since data is often obtained from scientific measurements the requirement of simple connectivity of a cluster may not be strict enough and may make the resulting clustering too sensitive to noisy graph edges. In such scenarios, stronger connectivity constraints are desirable. So-called quasi-cliques, which have recently received a lot of attention in the literature [40], are one promising way of specifying such constraints. A quasi-clique is a subgraph where every node is directly connected to at least a specified percentage of the other subgraph nodes. As a quasi-clique is not necessarily connected, the quasi-clique property should be added on top of the simple connectivity constraint. While the CkC model assumes input graphs without edge labels, there are applications where it makes sense to weight the edges to indicate the strength of relationships. For example, the strength of a friendships can go from intimate and close to just nodding acquaintanceship. In a scientific application, edges might be labeled with probabilities of the corresponding relationship as computed by some underlying model. A simple connectivity constraint, requiring at least one path between any pair of nodes of a cluster, is not natural for such data, since it cannot distinguish between strong and weak connections. A joint cluster analysis model for such data has to constrain the strength of relevant paths. This introduces a multi-objective optimization problem where the radius in the attribute space and the diameter in the graph space have to be simultaneously optimized. The CkC model, like many other clustering models, assumes the number of clusters as input parameter. However, this information may be hard to provide a priori, and joint cluster analysis without a priori specification of the cluster number is desirable in many applications. With increasing number of clusters, the compactness and accuracy of clusterings trivially increases. In order to automatically determine a model with a good trade-off between model accuracy and complexity, a clustering quality measure is needed that is not biased toward larger numbers of clusters. [38] presents a first clustering method of this kind using an adaption of the silhouette coefficient as model selection criterion.

Acknowledgments

We would like to thank Dr. Binay Bhattacharya and Dr. Petra Berenbrink for the valuable discussions in the early stage of this study.

References

[1] P. K. Agarwal and C. M. Procopiuc. Exact and approximation algorithms for clustering. *Algorithmica*, 33(2):201–226, 2002.

[2] M. Ankerst, M. M. Breunig, H. P. Kriegel, and J. Sander. Optics: Ordering points to identify the clustering structure. In *Proceedings of the ACM International Conference on Management of Data (SIGMOD)*, pages 49–60, 1999.

[3] Y. Bartal, M. Charikar, and D. Raz. Approximating min-sum k-clustering in metric spaces. In *Proceedings of the 33rd Annual ACM Symposium on Theory of Computing (STOC)*, pages 11–20, 2001.

[4] S. Basu, M. Bilenko, and R. J. Mooney. A probabilistic framework for semi-supervised clustering. In *Proceedings of the 10th ACM International Conference on Knowledge Discovery and Data Mining (SIGKDD)*, 2004.

[5] U. Brandes, M. Gaertler, and D. Wagner. Experiments on graph clustering algorithms. In *Proceedings of the 11th Annual European Symposium (ESA)*, pages 568–579, 2003.

[6] P. Brucker. On the complexity of clustering problems. In R. Hehn, B. Korte, and W. Oettli, editors, *Optimization and Operations Research*, pages 45–54. Springer-Verlag, 1977.

[7] P. K. Chan, M. D. F. Schlag, and J. Y. Zien. Spectral k-way ratio-cut partitioning and clustering. *IEEE Transactions on Computer-Aided Design of Integrated Circuits and Systems*, 13(9):1088–1096, 1994.

[8] M. Charikar, S. Guha, É. Tardos, and D. B. Shmoys. A constant factor approximation algorithm for the k-median problem. In *Proceedings of the 31st Annual ACM Symposium on Theory of Computing*, pages 1–10, 1999.

[9] M. Charikar and R. Panigrahy. Clustering to minimize the sum of cluster diameters. *Journal of Computer and System Sciences*, 68(2):417–441, 2004.

[10] I. Davidson and S. S. Ravi. Clustering with constraints: Feasibility issues and the k-means algorithm. In *Proceedings of 2005 SIAM International Conference on Data Mining (SDM)*, pages 138–149, 2005.

[11] DBLP. Computer science bibliography. http://www.informatik.uni-trier.de/~ley/db/index.html.

[12] I. Y. Dhillon, Y. Guan, and B. Kulis. Weighted graph cuts without eigenvectors: A multilevel approach. *IEEE Transactions on Pattern Analysis and Machine Intelligence, To Appear*, 2007.

[13] S. Doddi, M. V. Marathe, S. S. Ravi, D. S. Taylor, and P. Widmayer. Approximation algorithms for clustering to minimize the sum of diameters. In *Proceedings of the 7th Scandinavian Workshop on Algorithm Theory*, pages 237–250, 2000.

[14] M. Dyer and A. M. Frieze. A simple heuristic for the p-center problem. *Operations Research Letters*, 3:285–288, 1985.

[15] M. Ester, R. Ge, B. J. Gao, Z. Hu, and B. Ben-moshe. Joint cluster analysis of attribute data and relationship data: the connected k-center problem. In *Proceedings of the 6th SIAM Conference on Data Mining (SDM)*, pages 246–257, 2006.

[16] M. Ester, H. P. Kriegel, J. Sander, and X. Xu. A density-based algorithm for discovering clusters in large spatial databases with noise. In *Proceedings of the 2nd International Conference on Knowledge Discovery and Data Mining(ICDM)*, pages 226–231, 1996.

[17] T. Feder and D. H. Greene. Optimal algorithms for approximate clustering. In *Proceedings of the 20th annual ACM symposium on Theory of computing*, pages 434–444, 1988.

[18] G. N. Frederickson and D. B. Johnson. Optimal algorithms for generating quantile information in $x + y$ and matrices with sorted columns. In *Proceedings of the 13th Annual Conference on Information Science and Systems*, pages 47–52, 1979.

[19] T. Gonzalez. Clustering to minimize the maximum inter-cluster distance. *Theoretical Computer Science*, 38(2-3):293–306, 1985.

[20] S. Guha, R. Rastogi, and K. Shim. Rock: a robust clustering algorithm for categorical attributes. In *Proceedings of the 15th International Conference on Data Engineering (ICDE)*, 1999.

[21] N. Guttman-Beck and R. Hassin. Approximation algorithms for min-sum p-clustering. *Discrete Applied Mathematics*, 89(1-3):125–142, 1998.

[22] D. Hanisch, A. Zien, R. Zimmer, and T. Lengauer. Co-clustering of biological networks and gene expression data. *Bioinformatics*, 18:S145–S154, 2002.

[23] R. A. Hanneman and M. Riddle. *Introduction to social network methods.* http://faculty.ucr.edu/~hanneman/, 2005.

[24] E. Hartuv and R. Shamir. A clustering algorithm based on graph connectivity. *Information Processing Letters*, 76(4-6):175–181, 2000.

[25] D. S. Hochbaum and D. B. Shmoys. A best possible heuristic for the k-center problem. *Mathematics of Operations Research*, 10:180–184, 1985.

[26] D. Iacobucci. *Networks in Marketing.* Sage Publications, London, 1996.

[27] A. K. Jain and R. C. Dubes. *Algorithms for Clustering Data.* Prentice Hall, 1988.

[28] K. Jain and V. Vazirani. Approximation algorithms for metric facility location and k-median problems using the primal-dual scheme and lagrangian relaxation. *Journal of the ACM*, 48(2):274–296, 2001.

[29] O. Kariv and S. L. Hakimi. An algorithmic approach to network location problems, part ii: p-medians. *SIAM Journal of Applied Mathematics*, 37:539–560, 1979.

[30] G. Karypis, E. H. Han, and V. Kumar. Chameleon: Hierarchical clustering using dynamic modeling. *IEEE Computer*, 32(8):68–75, 1999.

[31] L. Kaufman and P.J. Rousseeuw. *Finding Groups in Data: an Introduction to Cluster Analysis.* John Wiley & Sons, 1990.

[32] B. Kulis, S. Basu, I. S. Dhillon, and R. J. Mooney. Semi-supervised graph clustering: a kernel approach. In *Proceedings of the 22nd International Conference on Machine learning(ICML)*, pages 457–464, 2005.

[33] J. H. Lin and J. S. Vitter. Approximation algorithms for geometric median problems. *Information Processing Letters*, 44(5):245–249, 1992.

[34] S. P. Lloyd. Least squares quantization in pcm. *IEEE Transactions on Information Theory*, 28(2):129–136, 1982.

[35] J. MacQueen. Some methods for classification and analysis of multivariate observations. In *Proceedings of the 5th Berkeley Symposium on Mathematics, Statistics and Probability*, pages 281–297, 1967.

[36] N. Megiddo and K. J. Supowit. On the complexity of some common geometric location problems. *SIAM Journal on Computing*, 13(1):182–196, 1984.

[37] N. Megiddo, A. Tamir, E. Zemel, and R. Chandrasekaran. An $o(n \log^2 n)$ algorithm for the k-th longest path in a tree with applications to location problems. *SIAM Journal on Computing*, 10(2):328–337, 1981.

[38] F. Moser, R. Ge, and M. Ester. Joint cluster analysis of attribute and relationship data without a-priori specification of the number of clusters. In *Proceedings of the 13th ACM International Conference on Knowledge Discovery and Data Mining (SIGKDD)*, pages 510–519, 2007.

[39] R. T. Ng and J. Han. Efficient and effective clustering methods for spatial data mining. In *Proceedings of the 20th International Conference on Very Large Databases (VLDB)*, pages 144–155, 1994.

[40] J. Pei, D. Jiang, and A. Zhang. On mining cross-graph quasi-cliques. In *Proceedings of the 11th ACM International Conference on Knowledge Discovery in Data Mining (SIGKDD)*, pages 228–238, 2005.

[41] G. Salton and M. J. McGill. *Introduction to Modern Information Retrieval.* McGraw-Hill, 1983.

[42] J. Scott. *Social Network Analysis: A Handbook.* Sage Publications, London, 2000.

[43] E. Segal, H. Wang, and D. Koller. Discovering molecular pathways from protein interaction and gene expression data. In *Proceedings of the 11th International Conference on Intelligent Systems for Molecular Biology*, pages 264–272, 2003.

[44] J. Shi and J. Malik. Normalized cuts and image segmentation. *IEEE Transactions on Pattern Analysis and Machine Intelligence*, 22(8):888–905, 2000.

[45] M. Steinbach, G. Karypis, and V. Kumar. A comparison of document clustering techniques. In *Proceedings of the Text Mining Workshop, KDD'00*, 2000.

[46] H. Steinhaus. Sur la division des corp materiels en parties. *Bulletin L'Acadmie Polonaise des Science*, C1. III, IV:801–804, 1956.

[47] C. Swamy and A. Kumar. Primal-dual algorithms for connected facility location problems. *Algorithmica*, 40(4):245–269, 2004.

[48] B. Taskar, E. Segal, and D. Koller. Probabilistic classification and clustering in relational data. In *Proceedings of the 17th International Joint Conference On Artificial Intelligence (IJCAI)*, pages 870–878, 2001.

[49] C. Toregas, R. Swan, C. Revelle, and L. Bergman. The location of emergency service facilities. *Operations Research*, 19:1363–1373, 1971.

[50] A. K. H. Tung, R. T. Ng, L. V. S. Lakshmanan, and J. Han. Constraint-based clustering in large databases. In *Proceedings of the 8th International Conference on Database Theory (ICDT)*, pages 405–419, 2001.

[51] I. Ulitsky and R. Shamir. Identification of functional modules using network topology and high-throughput data. *BMC System Biology*, 1(8), 2007.

[52] S. Wasserman and K. Faust. *Social Network Analysis*. Cambridge University Press, 1994.

[53] C. M. Webster and P. D. Morrison. Network analysis in marketing. *Australasian Marketing Journal*, 12(2):8–18, 2004.

[54] X. Yin, J. Han, and P. S. Yu. Cross-relational clustering with user's guidance. In *Proceedings of the 11th ACM International Conference on Knowledge Discovery and Data Mining (SIGKDD)*, pages 344–353, 2005.

Chapter 13

Correlation Clustering

Nicole Immorlica

Northwestern University, `nickle@eecs.northwestern.edu`

Anthony Wirth

The University of Melbourne, `awirth@csse.unimelb.edu.au`

Abstract   CORRELATION CLUSTERING addresses clustering problems in which the algorithm has access to some information regarding whether pairs of items should be grouped together or not. Such problems arise in areas like database consistency and natural language processing. Traditional clustering problems such as k-means assume that there is some type of distance measure (metric) on the data items, and often specify the number of clusters that should be formed. In CORRELATION CLUSTERING, however, the number of clusters to be built need not be specified in advance: it can be an outcome of the objective function. Furthermore, instead of a distance function we are given advice as to which pairs of items are similar. This chapter formalizes the CORRELATION CLUSTERING model and presents several approximation algorithms for various clustering objectives.

13.1   Definition and Model

In its rawest form, CORRELATION CLUSTERING is the graph optimization problem. As such, we will use graph terminology in our discussion, denoting the input data X with the vertex set V of the corresponding graph, and letting n denote the cardinality of V. Consider a clustering Y to be a mapping from the elements to be clustered, V, to a set of cluster labels, so that u and v are in the same cluster if and only if $y_u = y_v$. *Given* a collection of items in which each pair (u, v) has two weights w_{uv}^+ and w_{uv}^-, we must *find* a clustering Y that minimizes

$$\sum_{y_u = y_v} w_{uv}^- + \sum_{y_u \neq y_v} w_{uv}^+ \,, \tag{13.1}$$

or, equivalently, maximizes

$$\sum_{y_u=y_v} w_{uv}^+ + \sum_{y_u \neq y_v} w_{uv}^- . \tag{13.2}$$

Note that although w_{uv}^+ and w_{uv}^- may be thought of as positive and negative evidence toward co-association, the actual weights are nonnegative. Also, we avoid the notation $w_=(u,v)$, as our *constraints* are soft.

Finding a clustering which agrees best with the inconsistent advice is an NP-HARD problem, and so work has focused on designing *approximation algorithms*, or algorithms whose solutions are guaranteed to be close to optimal. An α-approximation algorithm A for a minimization problem with cost function c is an algorithm such that, for every input I, the solution $A(I)$ of the algorithm satisfies $c(A(I)) \leq \alpha \min_S c(S)$ for some $\alpha \geq 1$, where S is a solution to I. Similarly, if the problem is a maximization problem, we require the algorithm's solutions to satisfy $c(A(I)) \geq \alpha \max_S c(S)$ for some $\alpha \leq 1$. The factor α is called the *approximation factor*.

13.2   Motivation and Background

Bansal et al [3] introduced the CORRELATION CLUSTERING problem to the theoretical computer science and machine learning communities. They were motivated by database consistency problems, in which the same entity appeared in different forms in various databases. Given a collection of such records from multiple databases, the aim is to cluster together the records that appear to correspond to the same entity. From this viewpoint, the log odds ratio from some classifier,

$$\log \left(\frac{P(\text{same})}{P(\text{different})} \right),$$

corresponds to a label w_{uv} for the pair. In many applications only one of the $+$ and $-$ weights for the pair is non-zero, that is

$$(w_{uv}^+, w_{uv}^-) = \begin{cases} (w_{uv}, 0) & \text{for } w_{uv} \geq 0 \\ (0, -w_{uv}) & \text{for } w_{uv} \leq 0 . \end{cases}$$

In addition, if every pair has weight $w_{uv} = \pm 1$, then the input is called *complete*, otherwise it is referred to as *general*. Demaine et al [10] suggest the following toy motivation. Suppose we have a set of guests at a party. Each guest has preferences for whom he/she would like to sit with, and for whom he/she would like to avoid. We must group the guests into tables in a way that enhances the amicability of the party.

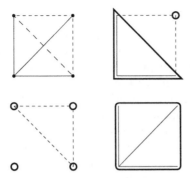

FIGURE 13.1: Top left is a toy CORRELATION CLUSTERING example showing three similar pairs (solid edges) and three dissimilar pairs (dashed edges). Bottom left is a clustering solution for this example with four singleton clusters, while bottom right has one cluster. Top right is a partitioning into two clusters that appears to best respect the advice.

The notion of producing good clusterings when given inconsistent advice first appeared in the work of Ben-Dor et al [4]. A canonical example of inconsistent advice is this: items u and v are similar, items v and w are similar, but u and w are dissimilar. It is impossible to find a clustering that satisfies all the advice. Figure 13.1 shows a very simple example of inconsistent advice.

While the optimal solutions to the minimization objective (13.1) and maximization objective (13.2) stated in the CORRELATION CLUSTERING definition are identical, their approximability varies greatly.

13.2.1 Maximizing Agreements

In setting out the CORRELATION CLUSTERING framework, Bansal et al [3] noted that the following algorithm produces a 0.5-approximation for the maximization problem:

If the total of the positive weights exceeds the total of the negative weights (i.e., $\sum_{u,v} w_{uv}^+ \geq \sum_{u,v} w_{uv}^-$), then place all the items in a single cluster; otherwise, make each item a singleton cluster.

Could it be that this trivial algorithm is the best possible? A result of Charikar et al, later extended by Tan [20], proves that this maximization problem is APX-hard: more precisely, they show that it is NP-hard to approximate the problem to a factor strictly better than $79/80 \approx 0.99$. This still leaves substantial room for improvement over Algorithm 13.2.1, and indeed some progress has been made in this direction. The 0.5 factor was improved to 0.7664 via semi-definite programming by Charikar et al [6]. Using the same semi-definite program, with improved rounding techniques, Swamy [19] showed how to solve the maximization problem within a factor of 0.7666. Interestingly, all known approximations for this problem operate by outputting the best of a highly restricted class of solutions. The trivial algorithm outputs either a single cluster or n clusters, whereas the semi-definite programming algorithms output at most a constant number of clusters.

All these algorithms work with no restriction on the input. If the input is known to be complete, the problem becomes significantly easier, although still NP-hard [3]. Bansal et al provided a PTAS (polynomial time approximation scheme) for the maximization objective in complete inputs.

13.2.2 Minimizing Disagreements

As is often the case in approximation algorithms, the minimization problem is significantly more difficult than the maximization problem. For the minimization objective, both general [3] and complete inputs [6] are known to be APX-hard. Designing sub-logarithmic approximations for general inputs involves solving a well-studied open question [11, 12].

The first constant-factor algorithms for complete inputs were provided by Bansal et al [3]. Their algorithm worked via local search, iteratively *cleaning* clusters until every cluster is *δ-clean*, where a cluster is δ-clean ($0 < \delta < 1$) if, for each item, at most a δ fraction of items inside its cluster have a negative relation with it, and at most a δ fraction of items outside its cluster have a positive relation with it. The constant for this combinatorial algorithm was rather large. At the expense of solving the natural linear program formulation of the problem, this constant can be significantly improved. Unfortunately, solving this linear program is very slow and has huge memory demands [5]. Nonetheless, Charikar et al [6] were able to harness it to design a 4-approximation for the problem via region-growing type rounding procedures. This was later lowered to 2.5, by Ailon random clusters around random items with probabilities guided by the solution to the linear program. Since solving the linear program is highly resource hungry, Ailon et al provided a very clever combinatorial alternative which we will sketch in the next section. Not only is this combinatorial algorithm very fast, it is also a factor 3 approximation.

For the general case, Demaine and Immorlica [11] and Emanuel and Fiat [12] proved that there is an approximation-preserving reduction to minimizing disagreements from the well-studied MINIMUM MULTICUT problem. That is, an α-approximate solution to the minimization problem in CORRELATION CLUSTERING induces an α-approximate solution to the minimum multicut problem. The minimum multicut problem is APX-hard and has an $O(\log n)$-

approximation, and it is a long-standing open question to improve this approximation factor. Hence, designing an $o(\log n)$-approximation algorithm for minimizing disagreements involves solving a difficult open question. Interestingly, Emanuel and Fiat [12] also show that minimizing disagreements is reducible to minimum multicut. This immediately implies an $O(\log n)$-approximation for minimizing disagreements by simply adapting the minimum multicut algorithm. Demaine and Immorlica [11] also give a direct analysis of an $O(\log n)$ approximation algorithm for minimizing disagreements using linear programming with region-growing techniques, as discussed in the following sections. In addition, they described an $O(r^3)$-approximation algorithm for graphs that exclude the complete bipartite graph $K_{r,r}$ as a minor.

13.2.3 Maximizing Correlation

A further variant in the CORRELATION CLUSTERING family of problems is the maximization of (13.2) − (13.1), known as *maximizing correlation*. Charikar and Wirth [7] proved an $\Omega(1/\log n)$ approximation for the general problem of maximizing

$$\sum_{i=1}^{n} \sum_{j=1}^{n} a_{ij} y_i y_j, \quad \text{s.t. } y_i \in \{-1, 1\} \text{ for all } i, \tag{13.3}$$

for a matrix A with null diagonal entries, by rounding the canonical semidefinite program relaxation. This effectively maximized correlation with the requirement that two clusters be formed. It is not hard to show that this is a constant factor approximation to the problem where the number of clusters is unspecified. The gap between the vector SDP solution and the integral solution to maximizing the quadratic program (13.3) was in fact shown to be $\Theta(1/\log n)$ in general [1]. However, in other inputs, such as those with a bounded number of non-zero weights for each item, a constant factor approximation was possible. Arora et al [2] went further and showed that it is *quasi*-NP-HARD to approximate the maximization to a factor better than $\Omega(1/\log^\gamma n)$ for some $\gamma > 0$.

13.3 Techniques

We now illustrate some of the standard techniques in CORRELATION CLUSTERING by sketching a few of the known results. The first technique is based on rounding a linear program (LP) using *region growing*, which was introduced in the seminal paper of Leighton and Rao [16] on multicommodity max-flow min-cut theorems. We will harness these techniques to design an $O(\log n)$-approximation for minimizing disagreements in CORRELATION CLUSTERING.

The second technique is a combinatorial approach that draws upon connections to sorting to give a 3-approximation for the minimization problem in complete inputs.

13.3.1 Region Growing

Each CORRELATION CLUSTERING solution can be represented by binary variables $\{x_{uv}\}$ where $x_{uv} = 1$ implies u and v's separation in the solution, while $x_{uv} = 0$ implies co-clustering. The cost of the solution can then be written as

$$\sum_{uv} w_{uv}^+ \cdot x_{uv} + w_{uv}^- \cdot (1 - x_{uv}).$$

In this formulation, each term w_{uv}^+ contributes to the cost exactly when $x_{uv} = 1$, i.e., the corresponding items u and v are separated in the solution. Similarly, each w_{uv}^- contributes exactly when $x_{uv} = 0$, i.e., the corresponding items u and v are co-clustered. To be feasible, a clustering that places item u with item v and item v with item w must also place item u with item w. That is, for every triple of items, u, v, w, the triangle inequality, $x_{uw} \leq x_{uv} + x_{vw}$, holds. Combining these observations and relaxing the x_{uv} to be quantities in the range $[0, 1]$, we obtain the following linear program:

$$
\begin{aligned}
\text{minimize} \quad & \sum_{uv} w_{uv}^+ \cdot x_{uv} + w_{uv}^- \cdot (1 - x_{uv}) \\
\text{subject to} \quad & x_{uw} \leq x_{uv} + x_{vw} && \text{for all } u, v, w \\
& x_{uv} \in [0, 1] && \text{for all } u, v.
\end{aligned}
\tag{13.4}
$$

The region-growing technique uses the optimal solution to this LP to build its clustering. Seeing the x_{uv} values as *distances* between the items, it iteratively grows *regions* or *balls* of, at most, some fixed radius around items until all items are included in some cluster. Since high x_{uv} values indicate that items should be separated, using a fixed radius guarantees that the resulting clustering solution does not pay much more than the optimum LP solution for pairs u and v that have $w_{uv}^+ > 0$. The region-growing technique itself guarantees that the clustering solution does not pay too much for pairs of items that should be separated ($w_{uv}^- > 0$).

To define the algorithm, we first must introduce some notation. It will be useful to imagine the items as nodes of a graph whose edges are those (u, v) for which w_{uv}^+ or w_{uv}^- are positive. A *ball* $\mathcal{B}(u, r)$ of radius r around node u consists of all nodes v such that $x_{uv} \leq r$, the subgraph induced by these vertices, and the fraction $(r - x_{uv})/x_{uv}$ of edges (u, v) with only one endpoint in $\mathcal{B}(u, r)$. The *cut* $\mathcal{C}(S)$ of a set S of nodes is the weight of the positive edges with exactly one endpoint in S, i.e.,

$$\mathcal{C}(S) = \sum_{|\{u,v\} \cap S| = 1} w_{uv}^+.$$

The *cut* of a ball is the cut induced by the set of vertices included in the ball. The *volume* $\mathcal{V}(S)$ of a set S of nodes is the weighted distance of the edges with both endpoints in S, i.e.,

$$\mathcal{V}(S) = \sum_{u,v \in S} w^+_{uv} x_{uv} \, .$$

Finally, the *volume* of a ball is the volume of $\mathcal{B}(u, r)$ including the fractional weighted distance of positive edges leaving $\mathcal{B}(u, r)$. In other words, if (v, w) has $v \in \mathcal{B}(u, r)$ and $w \notin \mathcal{B}(u, r)$, then (v, w) contributes $w^+_{vw} \cdot (r - x_{uv})$ weight to the volume of ball $\mathcal{B}(u, r)$. For technical reasons, we assign every ball an initial volume I, so that $\mathcal{V}(\mathcal{B}(u, 0)) = I$, for every u, and

$$\mathcal{V}(\mathcal{B}(u, r)) = I + \sum_{v, w \in \mathcal{B}(u, r)} w^+_{vw} x_{vw} + \sum_{v \in \mathcal{B}(u, r), w \notin \mathcal{B}(u, r)} w^+_{vw} (r - x_{uv}) \, .$$

We can now define the algorithm for rounding the LP. Suppose the volume of the entire graph is F (i.e., $F = \sum_{uv} w^+_{uv} x_{uv}$). Let the initial volume I of balls be F/n and let c be a constant larger than 2.

Region Growing:

1. Pick any node u.

2. Let $r = 0$.

3. Repeat until $\mathcal{C}(\mathcal{B}(u, r)) \leq c \ln(n + 1) \times \mathcal{V}(\mathcal{B}(u, r))$:

   Increase r by $\min\{(x_{uv} - r) > 0 : v \notin \mathcal{B}(u, r)\}$, so that $\mathcal{B}(u, r)$ includes another entire edge.

4. Output the vertices in $\mathcal{B}(u, r)$ as one of the clusters.

5. Remove the vertices in $\mathcal{B}(u, r)$ from consideration.

6. Repeat Steps 1–5 until all nodes are clustered.

This algorithm is clearly feasible and efficient. To analyze the approximation factor, we will prove that the algorithm's solution is a good approximation to the optimum *termwise*. We first consider pairs of items for which the advice suggests co-clustering ($w^+_{uv} > 0$), and then those that ought to be separated ($w^-_{uv} < 0$). Throughout, we refer to the rounded solution using variables $\{\bar{x}_{uv}\}$ and the optimal solution using variables $\{x^*_{uv}\}$. The fractional variables output by the LP are denoted by $\{x_{uv}\}$. Let B be the set of balls selected by the algorithm.

For pairs with $w_{uv}^+ > 0$, the termination condition guarantees the following inequality:

$$\sum_{uv} w_{uv}^+ \bar{x}_{uv} = \frac{1}{2} \sum_{b \in B} C(b)$$

$$\leq \frac{c}{2} \ln(n+1) \sum_{b \in B} V(b)$$

$$\leq \frac{c}{2} \ln(n+1) \left(\sum_{u,v} w_{uv}^+ x_{uv} + F \right)$$

$$\leq c \ln(n+1) \sum_{u,v} w_{uv}^+ x_{uv} .$$

For pairs in which $w_{uv}^- > 0$, the radius guarantee allows us to prove the approximation ratio. The analysis of this ratio relies on the *region-growing lemma*, which states that the balls returned by this algorithm have radius at most $1/c$.

LEMMA 13.1
For any vertex u and family of balls $\mathcal{B}(u, r)$, the condition $C(\mathcal{B}(u, r)) \leq c \ln(n+1) \times V(\mathcal{B}(u, r))$ is achieved for some $r \leq 1/c$.

The idea behind this lemma is that the volume grows provably faster than the cut, and so the inequality becomes true at some fixed radius. We refer the interested reader to the textbook by Vazirani [21] for a proof.

This radius guarantee implies that all the x_{uv} values of items co-clustered by our algorithm are at most $2/c$, i.e., the diameter of a ball. We can use this to bound the remaining component of our objective function:

$$\sum_{uv} w_{uv}^-(1 - x_{uv}) \geq \sum_{b \in B} \sum_{(u,v) \in b} w_{uv}^-(1 - x_{uv})$$

$$\geq \sum_{b \in B} \sum_{(u,v) \in b} w_{uv}^-(1 - 2/c)$$

$$\geq (1 - 2/c) \sum_{b \in B} \sum_{(u,v) \in b} w_{uv}^-$$

$$= \frac{c-2}{c} \sum_{uv} w_{uv}^- \bar{x}_{uv} .$$

Combining these two inequalities, with the fact that

$$\sum_{uv} w_{uv}^+ x_{uv}^* + w_{uv}^-(1 - x_{uv}^*) \geq \sum_{uv} w_{uv}^+ x_{uv} + w_{uv}^-(1 - x_{uv}),$$

we observe the following theorem:

THEOREM 13.1

Algorithm 13.3.1 is an $O(\log n)$-approximation for minimizing disagreements in CORRELATION CLUSTERING.

13.3.2 Combinatorial Approach

The combinatorial approach we discuss next gives a 3-approximation for *complete inputs* ($w_{uv} = \pm 1$). Simply select a random *pivot* item, divide the problem into two sub-problems based on whether an items should be co-clustered with or separated from the pivot, and recurse on the separated items. More precisely, if V is the set of items to be clustered, then call $PivotAlg(V)$.

$PivotAlg(V)$:

1. If $|V| = 0$, return $\emptyset$.

2. If $|V| = 1$, return $\{V\}$.

3. Choose u uniformly at random from V.

4. Let $S = \{u\}$, $T = \emptyset$.

5. For each v,

   (a) if $w_{uv}^+ = 1$, $S = S \cup \{v\}$.
   (b) else, $T = T \cup \{v\}$.

6. Return $\{S\} \cup \mathrm{PivotAlg}(T)$.

We can charge the *mistakes* of this algorithm to inconsistent triples u, v, w (i.e., $w_{uv}^+ = w_{vw}^+ = w_{uw}^- = 1$, or some permutation thereof). The algorithm makes a mistake on a pair u, v if and only if there is third item w which forms an inconsistent triple with u, v, and it is the choice of w as the pivot that separates u and v. Note that in this case all three items are in the input to the recursive call that chooses w as pivot. Let I be the set of inconsistent triples. For a triple $t \in I$, let A_t be the event that all three members of the triple were in the same recursive call and one of them was chosen as the pivot, with $p_t = \mathrm{P}(A_t)$. Since these events are disjoint, the expected number of mistakes (the cost of the algorithm's solution) is $\sum_{t \in I} p_t$.

We now compare this to the optimal cost. For any set J of *disjoint* inconsistent triples, the cardinality of J is clearly a lower bound on the optimal cost. The proof proceeds by using a fractional variant of this packing of inconsistent triangles as a tighter lower bound. We create new edge-based variables so that

$z_{uv} = x_{uv}$ if $w_{uv}^+ = 1$, and $z_{uv} = 1 - x_{uv}$ if $w_{uv}^- = 1$. Therefore, LP (13.4) can be rewritten as:

$$
\begin{aligned}
\text{minimize} \quad & \sum_{uv} z_{uv} \\
\text{subject to} \quad & z_{uv} + z_{vw} + z_{uw} \geq 1 \qquad \text{for all } u, v, w \in I \\
& z_{uv} \in [0,1] \qquad \text{for all } u, v.
\end{aligned}
\tag{13.5}
$$

The dual of (13.5) is

$$
\begin{aligned}
\text{maximize} \quad & \sum_{t \in I} \alpha_t \\
\text{subject to} \quad & \sum_{t \in I : (u,v) \in t} \alpha_t \leq 1 \qquad \text{for all } u, v \\
& \alpha_t \in [0,1] \qquad \text{for all } t \in I.
\end{aligned}
\tag{13.6}
$$

Clearly, the optimal solution to this dual LP (13.6) is a lower bound on the optimal cost; indeed, any feasible solution to the dual program is a lower bound on the optimal cost. We will use the probabilities p_t to define a feasible solution for the dual program.

Let t be an inconsistent triple containing u and v. Note that, conditioned on event A_t, each of the three members u, v, w of the triple is equally likely to be the pivot, and hence each of the three pairs is equally likely to be a mistake. Thus, the probability that (u, v) is a mistake, conditioned on A_t, is $1/3$. Let B_{uv} be the event that (u, v) is a mistake. Then we have argued that

$$
P(B_{uv} \text{ and } A_t) = P(B_{uv} \mid A_t)\,P(A_t) = p_t/3.
$$

Now u and v may be contained in another inconsistent triple, say t', but the events A_t and $A_{t'}$ are disjoint. Therefore,

$$
\sum_{t \in I : (u,v) \in t} p_t/3 = P(B_{uv}) \leq 1.
$$

Hence setting $\alpha_t = p_t/3$ results in a feasible solution to the dual program (13.6), which implies that $\sum_{t \in I} p_t/3$ is a lower bound on the optimal cost. This proves the following theorem.

THEOREM 13.2

Algorithm 13.3.2 is a 3-approximation for minimizing disagreements in complete inputs of CORRELATION CLUSTERING.

13.4   Applications

There are many applications of CORRELATION CLUSTERING, of which we now describe a few.

13.4.1   Location Area Planning

The work of Demaine and Immorlica [11] on CORRELATION CLUSTERING is closely linked with that of Bejerano et al on LOCATION AREA PLANNING. The latter problem concerns the assignment of cell towers in a cell phone network to clusters known as *location areas*. There are *hand-off* costs associated with traffic between the location areas (cuts between clusters). Such traffic causes messages to be sent to a centralized database which tracks the location area associated with each cell phone. There are further *paging* costs associated with the sizes of the location areas (cluster sizes), related to paging phones within location areas to identify a particular phone's current cell tower upon an incoming call. These costs drive the clustering solution in opposite directions. The authors design an $O(\log n)$ region-growing algorithm for LOCATION AREA PLANNING, which turns out to be closely related to the algorithms for minimizing CORRELATION CLUSTERING and MULTICUT.

13.4.2   Co-Reference

In many collections of data, there are often multiple references to the same concept or object. Co-reference analysis, for example, examines natural language text to find the "nouns, pronouns and general noun phrases that refer to the same entity, enabling the extraction of relations among entities" [17]. CORRELATION CLUSTERING has been directly applied to the co-reference problem in natural language processing and other problems in which there are multiple references to the same object [17, 8]. Assuming some sort of undirected graphical model, such as a CONDITIONAL RANDOM FIELD, algorithms for CORRELATION CLUSTERING are used to partition a graph whose edge weights corresponding to log-potentials between node pairs. The machine learning community has applied some of the algorithms for CORRELATION CLUSTERING to problems such as e-mail clustering and image segmentation. With similar applications in mind, Finley and Joachims [13] explore the idea of adapting the pairwise input information to fit example clusterings given by a user. Their objective function is the same as CORRELATION CLUSTERING (13.2), but their main tool is the SUPPORT VECTOR MACHINE.

13.4.3 Constrained Clustering

Traditional clustering problems assume a distance function between the input points. Constrained clustering incorporates constraints into the problem, usually in addition to this distance function. In this framework, the constraints are usually assumed to be consistent (non-contradictory) and hard. CORRELATION CLUSTERING, therefore, can be viewed as a clustering problem with *no* distance function, and only *soft* constraints. The constraints do not have to be obeyed, but there is a penalty for each infraction; consequently the constraints need not be consistent.

Davidson and Ravi [9] looked at a variant of constrained clustering in which various requirements on the distances between points in particular clusters were enforced, in addition to the usual must- and cannot-link constraints. They analyzed the computational feasibility of the problem of establishing the (in)feasibility of a set of constraints for various constraint types. Their constrained k-means algorithms were used to help a robot discover objects in a scene.

13.4.4 Cluster Editing

The CLUSTER EDITING problem is almost equivalent to CORRELATION CLUSTERING on complete inputs. The idea is to obtain a graph that consists only of cliques: a partitioning into sets is essentially a family of cliques. Letting the edges in the CLUSTER EDITING problem correspond to positive-weight edges in the CORRELATION CLUSTERING problem, and non-edges in correspond to negative-weight edges, we see that the problems are essentially the same.

Although CLUSTER DELETION requires us to delete the smallest number of edges to obtain such a graph, in CLUSTER EDITING we are permitted to add as well as remove edges. Another variant is CLUSTER COMPLETION in which edges can only be added. Each of these problems can be restricted to building a specified number of cliques.

Shamir et al [18] showed that CLUSTER EDITING and p-CLUSTER EDITING, in which p clusters must be formed, are NP-COMPLETE (for $p \geq 2$). Guo et al [15] took an innovative approach to solving the CLUSTERING EDITING problem exactly. They had previously produced an $O(2.27^K + n^3)$ time handmade search tree algorithm, where K is the number of edges that need to be modified. This "awkward and error-prone work" was then replaced with a computer program that itself designed a search tree algorithm, involving automated case analysis, that ran in $O(1.92^K + n^3)$ time.

13.4.5 Consensus Clustering

In CONSENSUS CLUSTERING, we are given several candidate clusterings and asked to produce a clustering which combines the candidate clusterings in a reasonable way. Gionis et al [14] note several sources of motivation for CONSENSUS CLUSTERING, including identifying the correct number of clusters and improving clustering robustness.

The CONSENSUS CLUSTERING problem is defined as follows: we are given a set of n objects V, and a set of m clusterings $\{Y^{(1)}, Y^{(2)}, ..., Y^{(m)}\}$ of the objects in V. The aim is to find a single clustering Y that *disagrees* least with the input clusterings, that is, Y minimizes

$$\sum_i d(Y, Y^{(i)}),$$

for some metric d on clusterings of V. The Mirkin metric is the most widely used. In this metric, $d(Y, Y')$ is the number of pairs of objects (u, v) that are clustered together in Y and apart in Y', or vice versa.

We can interpret each of the clusterings $Y^{(i)}$ in CONSENSUS CLUSTERING as evidence that pairs ought be together or separated. That is, w_{uv}^+ is the number of $Y^{(i)}$ in which $Y_u^{(i)} = Y_v^{(i)}$ and w_{uv}^- is the number of $Y^{(i)}$ in which $Y_u^{(i)} \neq Y_v^{(i)}$. It is clear that $w_{uv}^+ + w_{uv}^- = m$ and that CONSENSUS CLUSTERING is an instance of CORRELATION CLUSTERING in which the w_{uv}^- weights obey the triangle inequality.

Gionis et al [14] adapt the region-growing technique to create a 3-approximation that performs reasonably well in practice, though not as well as local search techniques. They also suggest using sampling as a tool for handling large data sets. Bertolacci and Wirth [5] extended this study by implementing the Ailon et al algorithms with sampling. They note that LP-based methods perform best, but place a significant strain on resources.

References

[1] N. Alon, K. Makarychev, Y. Makarychev, and A. Naor. Quadratic forms on graphs. *Inventiones Mathematicae*, 163(3):499–522, 2006.

[2] S. Arora, E. Berger, E. Hazan, G. Kindler, and S. Safra. On non-approximability for quadratic programs. In *Proceedings of 46th IEEE Symposium on Foundations of Computer Science*, pages 206–15, 2005.

[3] N. Bansal, A. Blum, and S. Chawla. Correlation clustering. In *Proceedings of 43rd IEEE Symposium on Foundations of Computer Science*, pages 238–47, 2002.

[4] A. Ben-Dor, R. Shamir, and Z. Yakhini. Clustering gene expression patterns. *Journal of Computational Biology*, 6:281–97, 1999.

326 Constrained Clustering: Advances in Algorithms, Theory, and Applications

[5] M. Bertolacci and A. Wirth. Are approximation algorithms for consensus clustering worthwhile? In *Proceedings of 7th SIAM Conference on Data Mining*, pages 437–42, 2007.

[6] M. Charikar, V. Guruswami, and A. Wirth. Clustering with qualitative information. In *Proceedings of 44th IEEE Symposium on Foundations of Computer Science*, pages 524–33, 2003.

[7] M. Charikar and A. Wirth. Maximizing quadratic programs: Extending Grothendieck's inequality. In *Proceedings of 45th IEEE Symposium on Foundations of Computer Science*, pages 54–60, 2004.

[8] H. Daume. *Practical Structured Learning Techniques for Natural Language Processing*. PhD thesis, University of Southern California, 2006.

[9] I. Davidson and S. Ravi. Clustering with constraints: Feasibility issues and the k-means algorithm. In *Proceedings of 5th SIAM Conference on Data Mining*, 2005.

[10] E. Demaine, D. Emanuel, A. Fiat, and N. Immorlica. Correlation clustering in general weighted graphs. *Theoretical Computer Science*, 361(2):172–87, 2006.

[11] E. Demaine and N. Immorlica. Correlation clustering with partial information. In *Proceedings of the 9th International Workshop on Approximation Algorithms for Combinatorial Optimization Problems*, pages 1–13, 2003.

[12] D. Emanuel and A. Fiat. Correlation clustering—minimizing disagreements on arbitrary weighted graphs. In *Proceedings of the 11th Annual European Symposium on Algorithms*, pages 208–20, 2003.

[13] T. Finley and T. Joachims. Supervised clustering with support vector machines. In *Proceedings of the 22nd Annual International Conference on Machine Learning*, 2005.

[14] A. Gionis, H. Mannila, and P. Tsaparas. Clustering aggregation. In *Proceedings of 21st International Conference on Data Engineering*, pages 341–52, 2005.

[15] J. Gramm, J. Guo, F. Hüffner, and R. Niedermeier. Automated generation of search tree algorithms for hard graph modification problems. *Algorithmica*, 39(4):321–47, 2004.

[16] T. Leighton and S. Rao. Multicommodity max-flow min-cut theorems and their use in designing approximation algorithms. *Journal of the ACM*, 46(6):787–832, 1999.

[17] A. McCallum and B. Wellner. Conditional models of identity uncertainty with application to noun coreference. In L. Saul, Y. Weiss, and

L. Bottou, editors, *Advances in Neural Information Processing Systems 17*, pages 905–12. MIT Press, Cambridge, MA, 2005.

[18] R. Shamir, R. Sharan, and D. Tsur. Cluster graph modification problems. *Discrete Applied Mathematics*, 144:173–82, 2004.

[19] C. Swamy. Correlation clustering: Maximizing agreements via semidefinite programming. In *Proceedings of the 15th ACM-SIAM Symposium on Discrete Algorithms*, pages 519–20, 2004.

[20] J. Tan. A note on the inapproximability of correlation clustering. Technical Report 0704.2092, eprint arXiv, 2007.

[21] V. Vazirani. *Approximation Algorithms*. Springer-Verlag, Berlin, 2001.

Chapter 14

Interactive Visual Clustering for Relational Data

Marie desJardins

University of Maryland Baltimore County, `mariedj@cs.umbc.edu`

James MacGlashan

University of Maryland Baltimore County, `jmac1@cs.umbc.edu`

Julia Ferraioli

Bryn Mawr College, `jferraio@brynmawr.edu`

14.1 Introduction

The goal of this research is to develop interactive clustering methods, which allow a user to partition a data set into clusters that are appropriate for their tasks and interests. The goal of traditional automated clustering is to partition a data set into clusters that have high *intra*-cluster similarity and low *inter*-cluster similarity. In general, there will be a single best clustering (or possibly several local maxima), which depends on the similarity metric used for clustering, the particular objective function being optimized by the clustering algorithm, and the search method. In practice, however, the "best" clusters may also depend on the user's goals and interests. For example, when performing clustering in a collection of student data, an admissions officer may be looking for patterns in student performance, whereas a registrar might want to track enrollment patterns for different course offerings. The appropriate clusters will not be the same for these two users. An automated clustering method might find one of these clusterings, but not both.

Recent work on constrained clustering addresses the issue of discovering multiple target clusterings, using additional knowledge provided by a user. Constrained clustering is based on the insight that although users may not be able to explicitly state the criteria for their desired clustering, they can often provide partial knowledge about the nature of the clusters. This additional information is typically given in the form of pairwise constraints on cluster membership, which are used to guide the system toward the desired solution.

Ideally, the user would provide a few initial constraints to "seed" the clusters, then add constraints as necessary to adjust and improve the resulting clusters. The difficulty with doing this in practice is that the clusters are not always easy to understand, particularly in high-dimensional domains, where the "shapes" of the clusters are also high dimensional and therefore difficult to visualize clearly. As a result, the user may not be able to tell *which* additional constraints would be most useful for improving the clustering.

In some domains, there may be other relational information in addition to the pairwise constraints. For example, links might exist between students who are in the same classes or Facebook group, scientific papers that cite the same references, or songs that were played during the same radio segment on a single day. This relational information, which can be represented as edges in the data graph, provides additional similarity information. However, these relations are generally weaker than pairwise constraints: they do not strictly imply shared cluster membership, although they may indicate a higher cluster correlation between the connected instances. Most clustering algorithms take into account either the attribute information on the data instances, or the relational information between instances, but not both.[1]

Our goal is to allow a user to explore a large relational data set interactively, in order to produce a clustering that satisfies their objectives. We achieve this goal by combining spring-embedded graph layout techniques with user interaction and constrained clustering.

Specifically, we present a novel approach called interactive visual clustering (IVC). In this approach, the relational data is initially displayed using a spring-embedded graph layout. The user can then move groups of instances together in order to form initial clusters. A constrained clustering algorithm is applied to generate clusters that combine the attribute information with the constraints implied by the instances that have been moved. These clusters are then used to generate additional graph edges, which are combined with the relational edges to produce a new layout, in which instances are relocated closer to the clusters to which they appear to belong. Based on the new layout, the user can identify instances that are "misplaced" and move these instances into the correct clusters.

We show experimentally, using several synthetic and real-world data sets, that IVC converges to the target clustering significantly faster than either manual adjustment, spring-embedded layout alone, or clustering alone.

---

[1]Note that there has been some recent work on relational clustering [4, 24, 15, 19], including our own ongoing research in this area [1, 2]. However, to our knowledge, none of the existing work explicitly combines relational data with pairwise constraints.

14.2 Background

Our work combines and extends standard force-directed graph layouts and the constrained clustering framework introduced by Wagstaff and Cardie [22], as described in Chapter 1.

Force-directed layout methods are among the most popular graph layout techniques [12]. We use a type of force-directed layout called *spring embedding* [9], specifically, the implementation provided by the Prefuse graph visualization system [17].

In spring embedding, nodes in a graph act on each other with two kinds of simulated forces, modeled on physical processes. The first force is a *node repulsion force* emitted from each node, simulating an inverse gravitational force. The repulsion force from a node exerts a "push" on every other node in the graph, with a magnitude inversely proportional to the square of the distance between the nodes. Consider two vertices in the graph, V_i and V_j, where V_i and V_j are represented as two-dimensional locations, so the vector from i to j can be described as $V_j - V_i$. The vector force on V_i that results from its interaction with V_j is:

$$\mathbf{f}_{ij}^n = \frac{V_i - V_j}{D(V_i, V_j)}^2 .$$ (14.1)

Note that V_i will exert the precise opposite of this force on V_j, so they are pushing each other apart.

The second force is a *spring force* that "pulls" (or pushes, if the nodes become too close) along the edges between the nodes. Each edge (V_i, V_j) is modeled as a spring with an ideal *spring length*, l_{ij}, and a *spring constant*, c_{ij}. The edge exerts a force on the nodes at either end, with magnitude proportional to the spring constant and to the difference between the ideal length and the current length:

$$\mathbf{f}_{ij}^s = c_{ij}(V_j - V_i)(D(V_i, V_j) - l_{ij}).$$ (14.2)

If the edge is longer than the ideal length, the spring force is an attracting force; if shorter than ideal, the force is a repelling force. As with the node repulsion force, the spring force exerts an equal and opposite force on each pair of nodes.

The spring-embedded layout is determined iteratively, by computing and summing the forces on each node (as given in Equations 14.1 and 14.2), then moving the nodes incrementally in the direction of the net resulting force. This "settling" process is repeated until the layout reaches an equilibrium. In the resulting layout, nodes with edges between them tend to be situated near each other, whereas nodes without edges between them tend to be spread apart.

14.3   Approach

Our visual clustering paradigm consists of the following steps:

1. **Initializing the display.** We use Prefuse's spring-embedded graph layout algorithm to produce the initial display.

2. **Interpreting user actions.** As the user moves instances, pairwise cluster membership constraints are generated.

3. **Constrained clustering.** After each instance is moved, the new constraints are added to the constraint set, and a constrained clustering algorithm is used to produce a new clustering of the data.

4. **Updating the display.** Using the clusters produced, the display is updated so that the new clusters are visually apparent.

The following subsections describe our approach to Steps 2, 3, and 4. We then discuss mechanisms for simulating user behavior for our experiments.

14.3.1   Interpreting User Actions

When the user moves an instance, it is "pinned" in place, and is not affected by the spring-embedded layout. These pinned instances do, however, exert forces on the other instances in the graph.

The constrained clustering process begins after the user has moved two instances. To generate the constraints, the screen distance between each pair of moved instances is computed. If the instances are less than ϵ units apart (where ϵ is a user-adjustable parameter), then they are considered to be in the same cluster, and a *must-link* constraint is added.[2] The transitive closure of these constraints results in a group of nodes that are used as seed clusters in the next step.

14.3.2   Constrained Clustering

We use a new constrained clustering algorithm called *seeded single link clustering* (SSLC), which is based on single-link clustering. Single-link clustering is an iterative, agglomerative graph-based clustering technique in which each data instance is initially treated as its own cluster. The distance between any two clusters is given by the attribute distance[3] between the instances for singleton clusters; for clusters of more than one instance, the cluster distance

---

[2]In our experiments, ϵ is set to 227 pixels.

[3]Note that the distance metric for PCK-Means is Euclidean distance in the attribute space, *not* the screen distance used to generate constraints.

is given by the shortest distance between any pair of instances in the two clusters. The result is a binary tree-structured clustering. A stopping criterion (e.g., a threshold distance or target number of clusters) is usually specified.

SSLC assumes that there is a target number of clusters, k, and that at least one instance has been assigned to each cluster. Each of the k initially specified instances is referred to as a *seed*. In IVC, these seed clusters are the groups of nodes resulting from the transitive closure of the *must-link* constraints, as described in the previous section. Single-link clustering then proceeds as described above, except that each step must merge one of the non-seed instances into one of the seed clusters. In effect, manually moved nodes in groups are separated by a gap larger than ϵ will be treated as having *cannot-link* constraints between them, since SSLC will never merge them into the same cluster.

Using the user's node movements to seed the clusters in this way allows the system to adapt to the user's goals interactively. The user may create more clusters (by using different "screen real estate" to move nodes near each other), and can relocate nodes from one cluster to another. In particular, the user can easily create "disjunctive" clusters (i.e., clusters that include non-contiguous regions of the original attribute space).

In our earlier publication on this work [8], we used MPCK-Means (metric pairwise constrained k-means), which is a k-means variation that incorporates metric learning [5]. However, we discovered that in several of our real-world data sets, the target clusters did not satisfy the Gaussian distribution that is assumed by this algorithm. SSLC does not rely solely on Euclidean spatial relationships to represent clusters, so it is more flexible in its ability to represent a wide range of target clusterings. SSLC also allows us to easily incorporate non-Euclidean distance metrics, such as Hamming distance for binary attributes, or cosine similarity for text data.

14.3.3   Updating the Display

Once the new constraints have been generated, and a new clustering produced, the display must be updated to reflect the groupings inherent in the new clustering. Ideally, the relational structure of the data should also be preserved. If the relational structure is correlated with cluster membership, then the graph edges and the cluster membership edges will reinforce each other, leading to rapid convergence of the interaction to the correct clusters.

To update the graph, we adapt an approach described by [6] for visualizing clusters in graphs. First, a new "dummy" node is generated to represent the center of each cluster. This node is located at the center of the instances that were manually placed in that cluster (i.e., the transitive closure that was computed in Step 2). Next, a *cluster edge* is added between this cluster center and every instance assigned to that cluster. The relational edges use Prefuse's default spring constant (2.0×10^{-5}). Cluster edges are set to have a spring constant equal to twice the default (4.0×10^{-5}). As a result, the cluster edges have a more significant effect on the layout than the relational edges, but do not completely dominate the layout.

The spring-embedded layout is then invoked on the combined graph (i.e., the graph with both the relational edges from the original data set and the new cluster edges). The resulting graph is displayed, but only the relational edges are shown to the user, and the cluster center nodes are not drawn. (It would be possible to also show the cluster edges, but this makes the graph very cluttered and obscures the relational edges.)

14.3.4 Simulating the User

We are currently running formal experiments on human users. For the experiments reported here, we simulate user behavior using one of two heuristics for instance selection: *random* and *farthest-first*. The random instance method simply selects a random instance to move at each step. The farthest-first method selects the instance that is farthest (on the screen) from its correct cluster. The intuition behind the latter heuristic is that the user will be most likely to notice anomalous instances, that is, the instances that appear farthest from where they should be. For both node heuristics, we use predefined locations (near the screen corners) for the cluster centers. Instances are moved to this location, with a small random (x, y) offset.

In the experiments with force-directed layout but no clustering, after each instance is moved, the layout is allowed to "settle" to an equilibrium before the next instance is moved.

14.4 System Operation

A series of screenshots is shown in Figures 14.1 to 14.5. In this sequence, a user is moving nodes to their target clusters. Figure 14.1 shows the initial display of the synthetic Overlapping Circles data set (described in "Data Sets," section 14.5.1). For the purposes of illustrating the process, the shades of gray of the nodes and numeric labels indicate the "true" (target) cluster membership. In order to simplify the displays for these small-scale screen captures, the relational edges are not shown. Notice that nodes from all of the clusters are interspersed in the display.

The circled nodes in Figure 14.1 are the first two nodes chosen by the user. The resulting display is shown in Figure 14.2. Here, the upper left and lower right clusters (where the first two nodes were placed) are starting to become apparent. Figures 14.3 and 14.4 show the display after the third and fourth nodes are moved. In Figure 14.4, all four clusters can be seen; however, there are still a number of "ambiguous" nodes in the center of the display, which

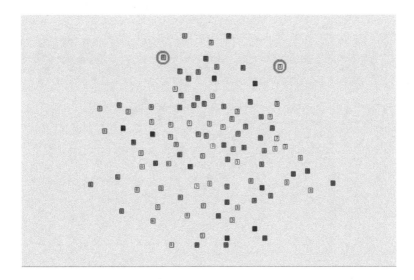

FIGURE 14.1: Initial display of the Overlapping Circles data set. The circled instances are the first two instances that will be moved by the user.

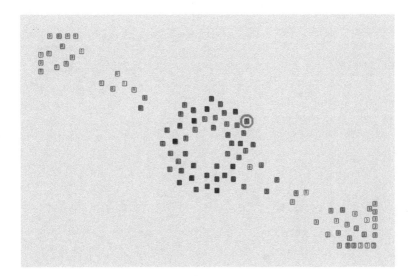

FIGURE 14.2: Layout of the Overlapping Circles data set, after the two instances shown in Figure 14.1 have been moved. The circled instance will be moved next.

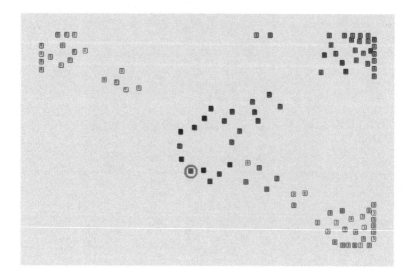

FIGURE 14.3: Layout of the Overlapping Circles data set after three instances have been moved. The circled instance will be moved next.

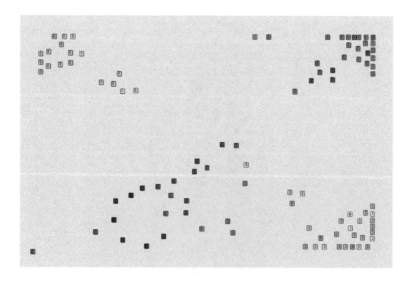

FIGURE 14.4: Layout of the Overlapping Circles data set after four instances have been moved.

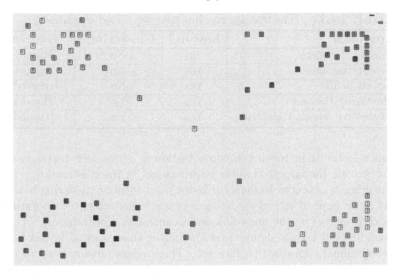

FIGURE 14.5: Layout of the Overlapping Circles data set after 14 instances have been moved.

are not clearly associated with any one cluster.

Figure 14.5 shows the display after 14 nodes have been moved. At this point, as seen in the results in Figure 14.9, most of the instances are grouped correctly into their target clusters. Visually, the clusters are very distinct, with only a few nodes scattered between the clusters.

14.5   Methodology

We compared our Interactive Visual Clustering method to several alternative approaches. The five approaches we tested are shown in Table 14.1. "Layout?" indicates whether force-directed layout is used. (If not, the layout only changes when instances are explicitly moved by the user.) "Clustering?" indicates whether constrained clustering is used. If so, each time an instance is moved, a new clustering is computed, and cluster edges are updated. If not, no cluster edges are used in the layout. "Heuristic" indicates the instance movement heuristic: either farthest-first or random.

Note that the fourth approach (clustering baseline) is equivalent to simply doing standard constrained clustering with random constraints, since the layout position is not taken into account in selecting which instance to move.

We hypothesize that the farthest-first instance heuristic will improve per-

TABLE 14.1: The five approaches that we tested empirically.

Approach	Layout?	Clustering?	Heuristic
Manual Baseline	No	No	Random
Layout Baseline	Yes	No	Random
Layout + FF	Yes	No	Farthest-First
Clustering Baseline	Yes	Yes	Random
Interactive Visual Clustering	Yes	Yes	Farthest-First

formance faster than moving random instances, since each instance moved should provide the largest possible improvement in the clustering.

Clustering is expected to perform faster than without clustering because it results in an explicit model of the user's target clustering, incorporating the feedback provided by the must-link and cannot-link constraints.

Force-directed layout should perform better than manual layout because of the relational edges in the data set. These edges already tend to cluster the instances visually, because they pull together instances that are related to each other. Therefore, when an incorrect instance is moved to its target cluster, it should also pull similar instances toward that cluster, resulting in the possibility of multiple instances being moved to the correct group. Furthermore, the cluster edges exert an even stronger influence (because their spring constant is higher), so as the clustering algorithm receives more constraints, the layout increasingly reflects the learned clustering. Therefore, the farthest-first heuristic primarily utilizes the relational knowledge from the data set when there are few constraints (few instances moved), but primarily utilizes the clustering structure when there are many constraints (many instances moved). As a result, the interaction shifts from creating an initial clustering toward repairing the learned clustering over time.

Note that the IVC paradigm relies on an assumption that the relational edges are correlated with the cluster membership of the instances. If there is no such correlation, then these edges may not be helpful, or could even hinder performance.

To measure the performance of the alternative approaches, we use the Adjusted Rand Index (ARI) [10]. The ARI is used to evaluate how close a given clustering is to the "correct" or target clustering. The Rand Index [18] measures the proportion of clustering matches. (A "match" is a pair of instances that are either grouped together in both the learned and the target clustering, or grouped separately in both the learned and the target clustering.) Using y_i to indicate the cluster labeling of instance x_i in the target clustering and y_i' to indicate x_i's cluster labeling in the learned clustering, the number of same-cluster matches is:

$$M_{\text{same}} = |\{x_i, x_j : (y_i = y_j) \wedge (y_i' = y_j')\}|$$

and the number of different-cluster matches is:

$$M_{\text{diff}} = |\{x_i, x_j : (y_i \neq y_j) \wedge (y_i' \neq y_j')\}|.$$

Then the Rand Index is given by:

$$RI = \frac{\#\text{ matches}}{\#\text{ pairs}}$$
$$= \frac{M_{\text{same}} + M_{\text{diff}}}{\binom{n}{2}}.$$

The Rand Index penalizes partitions with more clusters, so the Adjusted Rand Index is often used instead. The ARI normalizes the Rand Index to adjust for the number of clusters, by comparing the expected number of matches to the observed number of matches. (The derivation of the expected number of matches is mathematically nontrivial, and is omitted here for space. Details are given by Hubert and Arabie [10].) The ARI is bounded between 0 and 1. An ARI of 1 means that all instances are correctly clustered. We use the ARI implementation provided with the Weka system [21].

In the experimental results, clustering performance is always shown as a function of the number of instances moved. Both the layout and the cluster assignments use a random initialization step, so for each experiment, we show the average performance over 20 runs.

14.5.1 Data Sets

We tested our hypotheses experimentally using seven data sets: two synthetic data sets (Circles and Overlapping Circles); the Iris data set from the UC Irvine Machine Learning Repository [16]; a data set from the Internet Movie Data Base (IMDB) website; a music data set gathered from online sources; and two different data sets involving amino acid information, referred to as Amino Acid Indices and Amino Acid. The amino acid and IMDB data sets include relational edges already, as explained later. For the synthetic, Iris, and music data sets, we tested three methods for edge generation, resulting in three versions of each data set: one with no edges, one with edges generated by nearest-neighbor comparisons, and another version with edges generated probabilistically.

Nearest-neighbor edge generation creates an edge between each instance and that instance's nearest neighbor (using Euclidean distance in the attribute space). For data sets whose cluster membership is strongly related to the instances' distribution in Euclidean attribute space, this will result in edges that are well correlated with cluster membership. Nearest-neighbor edge generation results in a number of edges equal to or less than the number of instances (since one edge is created for each instance, but some pairs of instances may be each others' nearest neighbor, so only a single edge is added for the pair).

Probabilistic edge generation uses knowledge of shared membership in the true clusters to generate the edges. Specifically, for each pair of instances, if the instances belong to the same cluster, then an edge is created between them with probability 0.2. If the instances do not belong to the same group, then we create an edge between them with probability 0.05. This process results in a denser graph than nearest-neighbor edge generation: the expected number of edges is $O(\frac{N^2}{k})$, where N is the number of nodes and k is the number of clusters. The actual expected number of edges depends on the distribution of nodes among the clusters. For k equal-sized clusters, the expected number of edges is approximately $\frac{N^2}{8k}$.

14.5.2 Circles

The synthetic data sets are simple low-dimensional clusters that are included as benchmarks for the different approaches.

The synthetic Circles data set includes 120 instances in two distinct clusters. These clusters are generated by positioning circles of radius 50 at [50,50] and [150,150] on the (x, y) plane. Fifty points are randomly selected from inside each circle, and assigned to the corresponding cluster. Twenty additional "outlier" instances are generated by randomly sampling between the bounding circles. These outliers are then assigned to the nearest cluster. The two attributes for each instance are the (x, y) positions.

Because these clusters do not overlap and are well separated, in the nearest-neighbor version of this data set, there are no edges between instances from different cluster origins. In other words, if two points have an edge between them, they are in the same cluster. In the probabilistic-edge version of the data, there are more edges, some of which join instances of different clusters.

14.5.3 Overlapping Circles

The Overlapping Circles data set includes 100 instances in four overlapping clusters. This data is generated by creating random points from a uniform distribution within the radius of four circles—corresponding to the four clusters—whose centers lie on another circle's radius at each 45-degree mark. As shown in Figure 14.6, the four clusters overlap each other. Therefore, some of the instances' nearest neighbors in Euclidean space can be from a different cluster. In this data set, both the nearest-neighbor and the probabilistic edges sometimes connect instances from different clusters.

14.5.4 Iris

The Iris data set is a widely used classification database from the UC Irvine Machine Learning Repository [16]. The original data set consists of 150 instances; we selected 99 of these instances to create our data set by choosing 33 instances randomly from each cluster. Each instance is described by four numeric attributes (sepal length and width, petal length and width). The

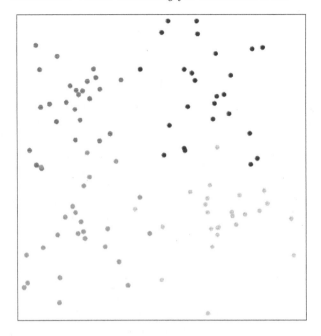

FIGURE 14.6: 2D view of the Overlapping Circles data set, with the four clusters shown in different shades of gray.

three clusters correspond to the three classes provided with the original data set (three different species of irises: Iris Setosa, Iris Versicolour, and Iris Virginica). This data set is known to be a difficult one for most clustering algorithms, because two of the classes are linearly separable from each other, but the third is not.

14.5.5 Internet Movie Data Base

In this data set, the instances represent actors retrieved from the IMDB web-based database. Each instance is described by eight binary attributes (has won an award, was most active in 1990s, most prevalent genre is drama, most prevalent genre is comedy, is experienced, is male, has high stock exchange rate, has many movies). An edge between two actors indicates that they have appeared in a movie together. There are four predefined classes in the data set, corresponding to to the four clusters that the simulated user partitions the data into (popular male actor [male and has high stock exchange rate], less popular male, popular female, and less popular female). Each of these four classes contains 25 instances. Because this data set consists entirely of binary attributes, it poses a difficult clustering problem for many clustering algorithms. The binary attributes also make use of a Euclidean distance metric problematic, so a Hamming distance metric is used in the SSLE clustering algorithm.

14.5.6 Classical and Rock Music

Each instance in the Classical and Rock Music data set represents a classical music composition or a modern rock music piece. Each piece of music has 25 associated attributes: tempo and 24 bark frequency scale values. There are no predefined edges in the data set, so for our experiments, edges are constructed synthetically using the methods described earlier. (One could imagine that this edge-construction process corresponds to a temporal relationship between pieces, e.g., indicating that the pieces were played within an hour of each other on a particular user's MP3 player.) This data set contains 98 total instances in two clusters: 48 classical pieces and 50 modern rock pieces.

14.5.7 Amino Acid Indices

The amino acid data set is a subset of the AAIndex database [13, 11]. Our data set is based on version 6.0 of the AAIndex database, which includes 494 *indices*, each of which measures a chemical property of amino acids. Each instance in the AAIndex database has 20 attributes, corresponding to the values of this index for each of the 20 amino acids used in the standard genetic code. Tomii and Kanehisa [20] identified six clusters of indices in the original database: A (measures of alpha and turn propensities), B (beta propensities), C (composition), H (hydrophobicity), P (physiochemical properties), and O (other). We use 100 of these indices, selected randomly from the A and H classes; the A/H classification is also used as the target clustering.

The edges in this data set were determined by measuring the correlations between the instances, then reducing the edges to a minimum spanning tree.

14.5.8 Amino Acid

In this data set, the attributes and instances are inverted from the Amino Acid Index data set. The Amino Acid data set includes 20 instances—one for each amino acid—whose attributes are the amino acid's chemical properties. Twenty-five of the 100 indices from the Amino Acid data set are used as attributes. We first removed binary indices, which do not yield good clustering performance. Since many of the indices are minor variations of the same basic measurement, we then asked a domain expert to select 25 indices that measured relatively "orthogonal" (uncorrelated) properties.

Edges were added to the data set based on three properties of amino acids: acidic side chains, basic side chains, and cyclic hydrocarbons. Edges are placed between pairs of instances that share one or more of these properties.

The target clustering has three clusters, also manually identified by our domain expert: polar, non-polar, and both. Polar amino acids show asym-

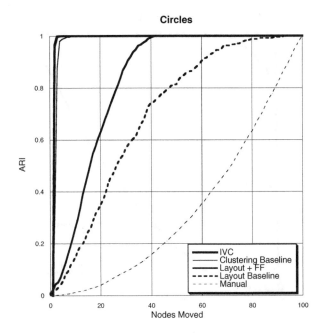

FIGURE 14.7: Experimental results on the Circles data set.

metrical electron charge on the amino acid side chain. Non-polar amino acids show symmetrical electron charge. Amino acids that have long side chains with both polar and non-polar regions are grouped into the "both" cluster.

14.6 Results and Discussion

Overall, our experimental results support our claim—that interactive visual clustering provides improved clustering performance, compared to the alternative approaches we tested. However, the Amino Acid Index data set does not yield the expected results, highlighting some of the open challenges.

14.6.1 Circles

As can be seen in Figure 14.7, the results on this data set are as predicted. Manually moving the instances shows the slowest improvement as a function of the number of instances moved (the lowest dashed line). The layout baseline (middle dashed line) shows significant improvement over the manual baseline.

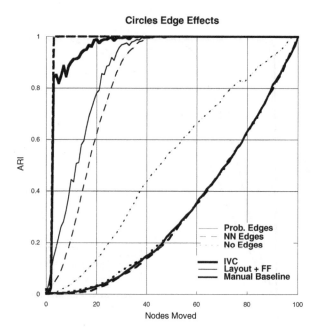

FIGURE 14.8: Effect of different types of edges on the experimental results for the Circles data set.

Adding the farthest-first heuristic provides yet more improvement (middle solid line). IVC performs the best; however, the clustering baseline yields nearly identical performance to IVC. We conclude that for this data set, when using clustering, the farthest-first heuristic does not provide any additional benefit. This is not surprising: the instances are well separated, so this a fairly easy clustering problem.

In this data set, we are also interested in understanding the effect of edge generation on performance (Figure 14.8). When no clustering is used, having edges increases the speed of convergence to the correct clustering. This can be seen in the middle, light-colored lines in the graph: The "No edges" version of the data set results in the worst performance, with some improvement for nearest-neighbor edges, and still more improvement for probabilistic edges.

Probabilistic edges most likely outperform nearest-neighbor edges on this data set simply because there are more edges. As a result, more instances are pulled toward a cluster when the user moves a single instance. However, when clustering is used (upper, thicker lines), the data sets with no edges or with nearest-neighbor edges perform better than the data set with probabilistic edges. The probabilistic edges on this data set contain edges between instances that do not belong to the same cluster, so the edges are only par-

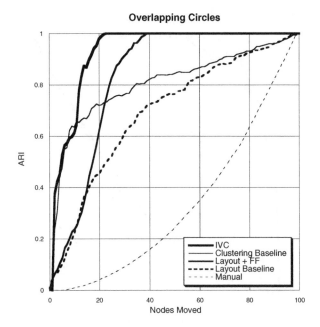

FIGURE 14.9: Experimental results on the Overlapping Circles data set.

tially correlated with cluster membership. As a result, the probabilistic edges may pull some instances into the incorrect cluster. By contrast, the nearest-neighbor edges for this data set only connect instances that are in the same cluster.

14.6.2 Overlapping Circles

Figure 14.9 shows the experimental results for the Overlapping Circles data set. Again, the methods perform as expected, with interactive visual clustering outperforming the other methods. In this case, IVC does provide a noticeable improvement beyond the clustering baseline, indicating that the farthest-first heuristic is helpful in identifying important instances for repairing the clustering.

As with the Circles data set, clustering performance is worse when using the probabilistic edges, which connect instances in different clusters (Figure 14.10). However, for IVC, the data set using nearest-neighbor edges actually results in slightly worse performance than using no edges. This happens because the nearest-neighbor edges connect some instances that are not in the same cluster. By contrast, for Layout + FF (i.e., without clustering), using edges yields better performance than no edges. In this case, the edges do

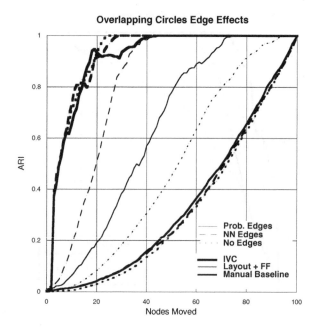

FIGURE 14.10: Effect of different types of edges on the experimental results for the Overlapping Circles data set.

provide some useful—if noisy—information about cluster membership.

14.6.3 Iris

As seen in Figure 14.11, the interactive visual clustering method also yields the best performance of any of the methods we tested on the Iris data set. The improvement provided by IVC is quite noticeable in this data set: after only 10 instances, with IVC, the clusters are nearly perfect, with an ARI close to 1.0. The next-best method (clustering baseline) has only reached an ARI of 0.75 at this point.

As in the Overlapping Clusters data set, when using clustering, probabilistic edges result in worse performance than nearest-neighbor edges (Figure 14.12). Again, this is likely due to the fact that the probabilistic set has more edges between instances in different clusters.

14.6.4 IMDB

As shown in Figure 14.13, all four of the methods require many instances to be moved before the clustering is correct. However, IVC still performs

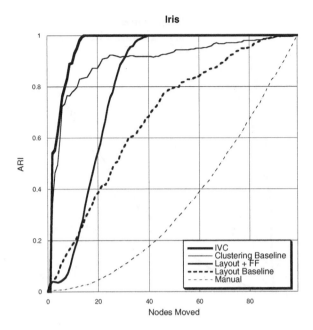

FIGURE 14.11: Experimental results on the Iris data set.

noticeably better than the other methods, achieving an ARI of 1.0 after about 78 instances have been moved. The next best method (clustering baseline) only achieves an ARI of about 0.77 at this point.

We conclude that the IMDB data set is a very difficult data set to cluster, but can still benefit from IVC.

14.6.5   Classical and Rock Music

Figure 14.14 shows that IVC also performs noticeably better on the music data set than the other methods. In this case, IVC achieves an ARI above 0.5 after only a handful of instances have been moved, reaching a correct clustering with (ARI = 1.0) after around 22 instances have been moved. While Layout + FF initially improves more slowly than the clustering baseline, it ultimately achieves the correct clustering much sooner than the clustering baseline, and is the next best method (after IVC) for this data set. However, by the time IVC has achieved a correct clustering, Layout + FF has only reached an ARI of around 0.56.

Interestingly, while the other data sets yield the best clustering when nearest-neighbor edges are included, with the music data set, the probabilistic edges yield better results.

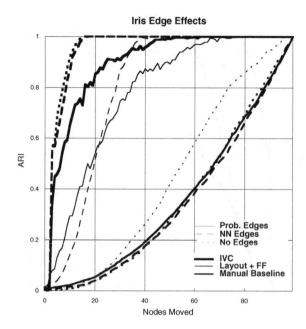

FIGURE 14.12: Effect of different types of edges on the experimental results for the Iris data set.

14.6.6 Amino Acid Indices

Figure 14.16 shows the results for the Amino Acid Indices data set. The results on this data set are as predicted: the best performance is given by the IVC method. After about 24 instances have been moved with IVC, clusters are correctly partitioned with an ARI of 1.0. The clustering baseline is the next best; after moving 24 instances, the ARI is about 0.6. Layout + FF, the next best method, has an ARI of only 0.3 at this point. Note also that Layout + FF and the layout baseline do not reach optimal performance (ARI = 1.0) until all 100 instances have been moved.

In our earlier experiments with MPCK-Means, we found that the clusters are not well separated in Euclidean space, so the underlying assumptions of MPCK-Means are violated. However, there *is* a higher statistical correlation among the attribute values within clusters than is seen across clusters. Therefore, using a different clustering method, such as SSLC, yields better performance. Our observation about the non-Euclidean space of the Amino Acid Indices data set also led us to develop the alternative (Amino Acid) data set.

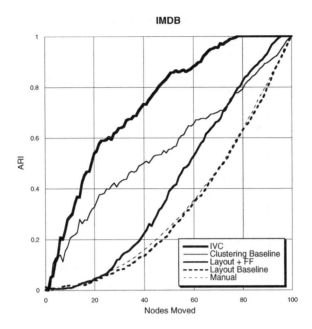

FIGURE 14.13: Experimental results on the IMDB data set.

14.6.7 Amino Acid

The results for the Amino Acid data set are shown in Figure 14.17. On this data set, many fewer instances have to be moved in order to achieve comparable performance to the Amino Acid Indices data set. This highlights the importance of choosing an appropriate representation for any given problem domain. IVC outperforms the other methods, but the Layout + FF approach is comparable. The latter method slightly outperforms IVC when only a few nodes have been moved, but IVC is slightly better for more nodes. These differences, however, are not statistically significant.

Similarly, the clustering baseline and layout baseline perform about equally, both outperforming the manual baseline. We conclude that the force-directed layout (taking advantage of the relational structure) and the farthest-first heuristic (identifying significant errors) help to guide the user toward the correct clustering. However, the clustering itself does not provide much, if any, additional benefit.

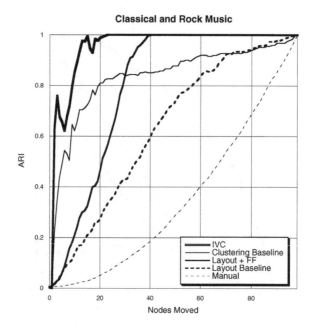

FIGURE 14.14: Experimental results on the music data set.

14.7 Related Work

Lesh, Marks, and Patrignani [14] presented an interactive graph partitioning method using their human-guided search (HuGS) framework. Similar to IVC, their approach used force-directed layout to create the visual representation of the data. There are a few differences between our problem setting and theirs. First, their underlying clustering method is purely graph-based, not attribute-based. Second, rather than using constrained clustering, their approach uses the modified clusters produced by the user as seeds for the local heuristic search. However, their results show that similar interactive approaches may be useful even for much larger data sets than we have studied.

In the constrained clustering literature, there has been some work on active (automatic) selection of constraints [3, 23, 7]. However, we are not aware of any previous work on interactive methods for enabling the user to select appropriate constraints more effectively.

Classical and Rock Music Edge Effects

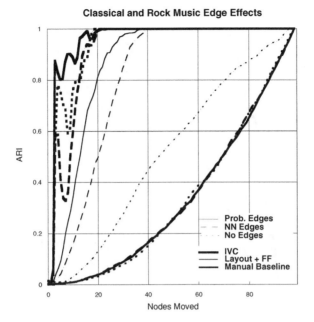

FIGURE 14.15: Effect of different types of edges on the experimental results for the music data set.

14.8 Future Work and Conclusions

We have shown that interactive visual clustering can improve clustering performance by integrating force-directed graph layout techniques with user interaction and constrained clustering. The methods we have described here are only the first step toward a more user-centered approach to clustering.

We are currently designing a user study to test the hypothesis that users will be able to identify anomalous (misplaced) instances in the display, and therefore converge more quickly to the correct clustering than without the force-directed layout. We also plan to analyze and test other models of user behavior (i.e., additional instance selection and placement heuristics). Other types of user feedback may prove to be useful, such as annotations describing why a particular instance was moved into a given cluster. Combining the user-guided approach of IVC with the system-guided methods of active constraint selection methods could result in a more mixed-initiative paradigm, where the user and the system jointly guide the clustering process.

The ultimate goal of our research is to design more integrated, interac-

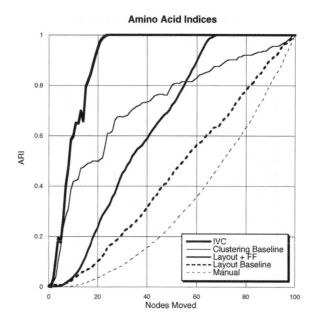

FIGURE 14.16: Experimental results on the Amino Acid Indices data set.

tive clustering methods for relational data sets than currently exist. The force-directed layout used in IVC incorporates the relational edges into the clustering process, but only indirectly. We are also developing relational constrained clustering algorithms, which cluster the data in attribute space and relational space simultaneously [1, 2].

Acknowledgments

Thanks to Adam Anthony, Blaz Bulka, Donald MacGlashan, and Penny Rheingans for their assistance and inputs. This work was partially supported by NSF awards #0325329 and #00000923, and by the Distributed Mentor Project (DMP) of the Computing Research Association's Committee on the Status of Women in Computing Research (CRA-W).

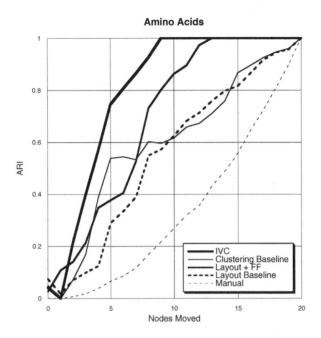

FIGURE 14.17: Experimental results on the Amino Acid data set.

References

[1] A. Anthony and M. desJardins. Open problems in relational clustering. In *ICML Workshop on Open Problems in Statistical Relational Learning*, 2006.

[2] A. Anthony and M. desJardins. Data clustering with a relational push-pull model (student abstract). In *Proceedings of the 26th National Conference on Artificial Intelligence (AAAI-2007)*, 2007.

[3] S. Basu, A. Banerjee, and R. Mooney. Active semi-supervision for pairwise constrained clustering. In *Proceedings of the 2004 SIAM International Conference on Data Mining*, pages 333–344, April 2004.

[4] I. Bhattacharya and L. Getoor. Relational clustering for multi-type en-

tity resolution. In *Proceedings of the Fourth International KDD Workshop on Multi-Relational Mining*, pages 3–12, 2005.

[5] M. Bilenko, S. Basu, and R. J. Mooney. Integrating constraints and metric learning in semi-supervised clustering. In *Proceedings of the Twenty-First International Conference on Machine Learning*, pages 11–18, 2004.

[6] R. Brockenauer and S. Cornelsen. Drawing clusters and hierarchies. In M. Kaufmann and D. Wagner, editors, *Drawing Graphs: Methods and Models*, pages 193–227. Springer, 2001.

[7] N. Cebron and M. R. Berthold. Mining of cell assay images using active semi-supervised clustering. In *Proceedings of the ICDM 2005 Workshop on Computational Intelligence in Data Mining*, pages 63–69, 2005.

[8] M. desJardins, J. MacGlash, and J. Ferraioli. Interactive visual clustering. In *Proceedings of the 2007 International Conference on Intelligent User Interfaces*, January 2007.

[9] P. Eades. A heuristic for graph drawing. *Congressus Numerantium*, 42:149–160, 1984.

[10] L. Hubert and P. Arabie. Comparing partitions. *Journal of Classification*, 2:193–218, 1988.

[11] Genome Net Japan. Aaindex: Amino acid index database, 2006.

[12] M. Kaufmann and D. Wagner, editors. *Drawing Graphs: Methods and Models*. Springer, 2001.

[13] S. Kawashima and M. Kanehisa. AAindex: Amino acid index database. *Nucleic Acids Research*, 28(1):374, 2000.

[14] N. Lesh, J. Marks, and M. Patrignani. Interactive partitioning. In *International Symposium on Graph Drawing*, pages 31–36, 2000.

[15] J. Neville, M. Adler, and D. Jensen. Clustering relational data using attribute and link information. In *Proceedings of the IJCAI Text Mining and Link Analysis Workshop*, 2003.

[16] D. J. Newman, S. Hettich, C. L. Blake, and C. J. Merz. UCI repository of machine learning databases, 1998.

[17] prefuse.org. Prefuse: Interactive information visualization toolkit, 2006.

[18] W. M. Rand. Objective criteria for the evaluation of clustering methods. *Journal of the American Statistical Association*, 66:846–850, 1971.

[19] B. Taskar, E. Segal, and D. Koller. Probabilistic classification and clustering in relational data. In B. Nebel, editor, *Proceedings of the 17th International Joint Conference on Artificial Intelligence (IJCAI-01)*, pages 870–878, Seattle, 2001.

[20] K. Tomii and M. Kanehisa. Analysis of amino acid indices and mutation matrices for sequence comparison and structure prediction of proteins. *Protein Engineering*, 9:27–36, 1996.

[21] University of Waikato. Weka 3: Data mining with open source machine learning software in Java, 2006.

[22] K. Wagstaff and C. Cardie. Clustering with instance-level constraints. In *Proceedings of the International Conference on Machine Learning (ICML-00)*, pages 1103–1110, 2000.

[23] Q. Xu, M. desJardins, and K. Wagstaff. Active constrained clustering by examining spectral eigenvectors. In *Proceedings of the 2005 Discovery Science Conference*, 2005.

[24] X. Yin, J. Han, and P. Yu. Cross-relational clustering with user's guidance. In *Proceedings of the Eleventh ACM SIGKDD International Conference on Knowledge Discovery in Data*, pages 344–353, 2005.

Chapter 15

Distance Metric Learning from Cannot-be-Linked Example Pairs, with Application to Name Disambiguation

Satoshi Oyama

Kyoto University, oyama@i.kyoto-u.ac.jp

Katsumi Tanaka

Kyoto University, ktanaka@i.kyoto-u.ac.jp

Abstract   Existing distance metric learning algorithms use only must-be-linked example pairs or both must-be-linked and cannot-be-linked example pairs. In some application problems, however, cannot-be-linked examples are readily available while must-be-linked examples are not. We describe a method for learning a distance metric from only cannot-be-linked example pairs. Unlike other metric learning algorithms, it does not require eigenvalue decompositions to enforce the positive semi-definiteness of the learned distance metric matrix. We apply the metric learning to a name disambiguation problem, in which clustering is used to determine whether the names of objects in documents or databases refer to the same object or not. Experiments using the DBLP data set show that the learned metric improves precision and recall for name disambiguation.

15.1   Background and Motivation

Similarity and distance are important factors in clustering, classification, and search. An appropriate similarity/distance measure must be used to achieve accurate results. Several methods have been proposed for learning a similarity measure or distance metric from humanly labeled data (e.g., Bilenko and Mooney [6]; Xing et al. [29]). One advantage of using a distance metric rather than a general similarity/dissimilarity measure is that it satisfies mathematical properties such as the triangle inequality and can be used in many existing algorithms.

One problem in learning a distance metric is that labeling by a person involves costs. In previous research, labeling was usually given as pairwise constraints, such as two data items are similar and must be in the same class ("must-be-linked") or dissimilar and cannot be in the same class ("cannot-be-linked"). The metric is modified so as to shorten the distance between must-be-linked examples and lengthen the distance between cannot-be-linked examples.

In some application problems, however, cannot-be-linked examples are readily available while must-be-linked examples are not. One case is where some example pairs are easily predicted to belong to different classes with high confidence. An example is name disambiguation, which is to determine whether names appearing documents or database records refer to the same real-world object. Although it is uncertain whether two J. Smiths in a bibliographic database refer to the same person or not, J. Smith and D. Johnson cannot be the same person. This enables us to use such example pairs as cannot-be-linked examples in metric learning (Figure 15.1). We will revisit this problem later in Section 15.9.

Another case is where only dissimilar items are stored in a collection. For example, patents and trademarks are registered in official databases only if they are significantly dissimilar to registered ones. It is helpful if a system can retrieve possible conflicts to a proposed item from databases according to some distance metric. However, only dissimilar example pairs are usually available from databases. This kind of problem can be considered as an anomaly detection that identifies unusually similar items. (See Section 15.5.)

In this chapter, we describe a method to learn a distance metric from only cannot-be-linked example pairs [16]. The metric learning method described in this chapter can be compared with constrained-based (semi-supervised) clustering [27, 2, 13, 3], in which pairwise constraints that specify whether two data items should be in the same cluster or not are placed on some portion of the data. Existing semi-supervised clustering methods use only must-be-linked constraints or both must-be-linked and cannot-be-linked constraints.

An additional merit of using only cannot-be-linked example pairs is that the learning process becomes much simpler than using both must-be-linked and cannot-be-linked examples. In the following sections, we formalize distance metric learning from cannot-be-linked examples as a quadratic programming problem [7] and describe its application to name disambiguation.

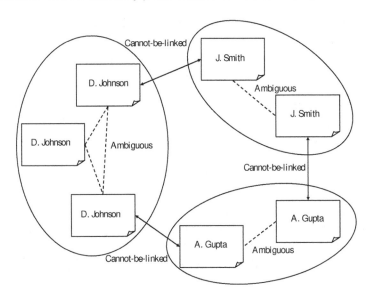

FIGURE 15.1: Using dissimilar (cannot-be-linked) example pairs in learning a metric for clustering ambiguous data

15.2   Preliminaries

In this chapter, $x_i \in \mathcal{X}$ denotes data such as documents or database records, where the subscript i is the index for each data item. Each data item x_i is represented as a d dimensional feature vector $\mathbf{x} = (x_{i1}, \ldots, x_{id})^\top$, in which each feature corresponds to, for example, a word in a document or an attribute in a database. The superscript $\top$ denotes the transpose of a vector or matrix.

Given vector representations of the data, we can define various distance metrics. For the function $D : \mathcal{X} \times \mathcal{X} \to \mathbb{R}$ to be a (pseudo) metric, it must satisfy the following conditions:[1]

$$D(x_i, x_j) \geq 0$$
$$D(x_i, x_j) = D(x_j, x_i)$$
$$D(x_i, x_k) + D(x_k, x_j) \geq D(x_i, x_j) \ .$$

---

[1]D becomes a metric in the strict sense when $D(x_i, x_j) = 0$ if and only if $x_i = x_j$.

One of the simplest metrics is the Euclidean distance:

$$D_E(x_i, x_j) = \left(\sum_{s=1}^{d} (x_{is} - x_{js})^2 \right)^{\frac{1}{2}} . \tag{15.1}$$

In the Euclidean metric, each feature equally contributes to the distance. We can also consider metrics in which each feature is given a weight ($w_i \geq 0$) based on its importance:

$$D_{\mathbf{w}}(x_i, x_j) = \left(\sum_{s=1}^{d} w_s (x_{is} - x_{js})^2 \right)^{\frac{1}{2}} . \tag{15.2}$$

In information retrieval, various weighting heuristics have been proposed [1]. Among them, the most commonly used weighting method is TF-IDF (term frequency - inverse document frequency). When each feature represents the number of times a particular word appears in the document (TF), IDF weighting is

$$w_s = (\text{IDF})^2 = \left(\frac{N}{\log \text{DF}_s + 1} \right)^2 , \tag{15.3}$$

where N denotes the number of documents, and DF_s denotes the number of documents that contain the sth word.

The feature weighting method of Equation (15.2) treats each feature independently and does not represent interaction among features. Using $d \times d$ matrix $\mathbf{A} = \{a_{st}\}$, we can define a distance metric in a more general form:

$$d_{\mathbf{A}}(x_i, x_j) = \left((\mathbf{x}_i - \mathbf{x}_j)^\top \mathbf{A} (\mathbf{x}_i - \mathbf{x}_j) \right)^{\frac{1}{2}}$$
$$= \left(\sum_{s=1}^{d} \sum_{t=1}^{d} a_{st} (x_{is} - x_{js})(x_{it} - x_{jt}) \right)^{\frac{1}{2}} .$$

The necessary and sufficient condition for $d_{\mathbf{A}}$ being a pseudo metric is that $\mathbf{A}$ be a positive semi-definite matrix, in other words, a symmetric matrix in which all eigenvalues are non-negative.

In their pioneering work on distance metric learning, Xing et al. [29] proposed a method in which similar and dissimilar pairs of examples are given, and a matrix $\mathbf{A}$ is found that minimizes the sum of the distances between similar pairs while keeping the distances between dissimilar pairs greater than a certain value. This is formalized as the following optimization problem:

$$\min_{\mathbf{A}} \sum_{c_= (i,j) \in C_=} D_{\mathbf{A}}^2(x_i, x_j)$$
$$\text{s.t.} \sum_{c_{\neq} (i,j) \in C_{\neq}} D_{\mathbf{A}}(x_i, x_j) \geq 1$$
$$\mathbf{A} \succeq 0 ,$$

where $C_=$ is the set of similar example pairs (must-link constraints) and $C_{\neq}$ is the set of dissimilar example pairs (cannot-link constraints). $\mathbf{A} \succeq 0$ is a constraint that matrix $\mathbf{A}$ must be positive semi-definite. We thus have a semi-definite programming problem [25]. To enforce this constraint, the method involves singular value decompositions, which is computationally intensive.

15.3   Problem Formalization

In the metric learning described in this chapter, only pairs of dissimilar (cannot-be-linked) examples $c_{\neq}(i,j) \in C_{\neq}$ are given. We want examples in such a pair to belong to different clusters. To ensure that, we use a matrix $\mathbf{A}$ that enlarges the distance $D_{\mathbf{A}}(x_i, x_j)$ between the two examples. However, multiplying $\mathbf{A}$ by a large scalar makes the distance between any two points long and thus not meaningful. Thus we divide the matrix by its norm and normalize the distance as:

$$\frac{D_{\mathbf{A}}^2(x_i, x_j)}{\|\mathbf{A}\|} = (\mathbf{x}_i - \mathbf{x}_j)^\top \frac{\mathbf{A}}{\|\mathbf{A}\|} (\mathbf{x}_i - \mathbf{x}_j) \ .$$

As the matrix norm, we use the Frobenius norm:

$$\|\mathbf{A}\|_F = \left(\sum_{s=1}^{d} \sum_{t=1}^{d} a_{st}^2 \right)^{\frac{1}{2}} \ .$$

We can now formalize distance metric learning from only dissimilar example pairs as an optimization problem:

$$\max_{\mathbf{A}} \ \min_{c_{\neq}(i,j) \in C_{\neq}} \frac{D_{\mathbf{A}}^2(x_i, x_j)}{\|\mathbf{A}\|_F} \tag{15.4}$$

$$\text{s.t. } \mathbf{A} \succeq 0 \ . \tag{15.5}$$

Objective function (15.4) requires finding the $\mathbf{A}$ that maximize the (normalized) distance between the closest example pair. This idea is similar to large margin principles in SVMs [26] and is justified because clustering errors most probably occur at the cannot-be-linked points closest to each other, and keeping these points far from each other reduces the risk of errors.

To simplify the subsequent calculation, we translate the above optimization problem into an equivalent one. The following derivation is similar to that for support vector machines [26]. We will look into the relationship between the metric learning and SVM learning in Section 15.5.

First, we introduce a variable r for the minimum distance and rewrite the original problem into the following form:

$$\max_{\mathbf{A}} \; r$$
$$\text{s.t.} \quad \frac{D_{\mathbf{A}}^2(x_i, x_j)}{\|\mathbf{A}\|_F} \geq r \; \forall c_{\neq}(i, j) \in C_{\neq}$$
$$\mathbf{A} \succeq 0 \; .$$

Using a variable transformation $r' = r\|\mathbf{A}\|_F$, we obtain the form:

$$\max_{\mathbf{A}} \; \frac{r'}{\|\mathbf{A}\|_F}$$
$$\text{s.t.} \quad D_{\mathbf{A}}^2(x_i, x_j) \geq r' \; \forall c_{\neq}(i, j) \in C_{\neq}$$
$$\mathbf{A} \succeq 0 \; .$$

Varying r' only scales the problem and its solution. Thus r' can be fixed by some constant, say, 1:

$$\max_{\mathbf{A}} \; \frac{1}{\|\mathbf{A}\|_F}$$
$$\text{s.t.} \quad D_{\mathbf{A}}^2(x_i, x_j) \geq 1 \; \forall c_{\neq}(i, j) \in C_{\neq}$$
$$\mathbf{A} \succeq 0 \; .$$

Noting that maximizing $\frac{1}{\|\mathbf{A}\|_F}$ is equivalent to minimizing $\frac{1}{2}\|\mathbf{A}\|_F^2$, we obtain the following optimization problem,

$$\min_{\mathbf{A}} \; \frac{1}{2}\|\mathbf{A}\|_F^2 \tag{15.6}$$
$$\text{s.t.} \quad D_{\mathbf{A}}^2(x_i, x_j) \geq 1 \quad \forall c_{\neq}(i, j) \in C_{\neq} \tag{15.7}$$
$$\mathbf{A} \succeq 0 \; , \tag{15.8}$$

which is equivalent to the original problem consisting of (15.4) and (15.5).

15.4   Positive Semi-Definiteness of Learned Matrix

We now consider an optimization problem consisting of only (15.6) and (15.7) without (15.8). To solve this problem, we introduce the Lagrangian

$$
\begin{aligned}
L(\mathbf{A}, \alpha) &= \frac{1}{2}\|\mathbf{A}\|_F^2 + \sum_{c_{\neq}(i,j)\in C_{\neq}} \alpha_{ij}\left(1 - D_{\mathbf{A}}^2(x_i, x_j)\right) \\
&= \frac{1}{2}\|\mathbf{A}\|_F^2 + \sum_{c_{\neq}(i,j)\in C_{\neq}} \alpha_{ij}\left(1 - (\mathbf{x}_i - \mathbf{x}_j)^\top \mathbf{A}(\mathbf{x}_i - \mathbf{x}_j)\right), \tag{15.9}
\end{aligned}
$$

with Lagrange multipliers $\alpha_{ij} \geq 0$.

In the solution of (15.6) and (15.7), the derivative of $L(\mathbf{A}, \alpha)$ with respect to $\mathbf{A}$ must vanish; that is, $\frac{\partial L}{\partial \mathbf{A}} = 0$. This leads to the following solution:

$$\mathbf{A} = \sum_{c_{\neq}(i,j) \in C_{\neq}} \alpha_{ij} (\mathbf{x}_i - \mathbf{x}_j)(\mathbf{x}_i - \mathbf{x}_j)^\top \ . \tag{15.10}$$

A necessary and sufficient condition for $d \times d$ matrix $\mathbf{A}$ being positive semi-definite is that for all d dimensional vectors $\mathbf{v}$, $\mathbf{v}^\top \mathbf{A} \mathbf{v} \geq 0$ holds. However, this is always the case for a matrix $\mathbf{A}$ in the form of (15.10). Noting that $\alpha_{ij} \geq 0$, we can confirm this as follows:

$$\mathbf{v}^\top \mathbf{A} \mathbf{v} = \sum_{c_{\neq}(i,j) \in C_{\neq}} \alpha_{ij} ((\mathbf{x}_i - \mathbf{x}_j)^\top \mathbf{v})^2 \geq 0 \ .$$

This means that without condition (15.8), the positive semi-definiteness of $\mathbf{A}$ is automatically satisfied. In fact, the optimization problem consisting of only (15.6) and (15.7) is a convex quadratic programming problem [7] and can be solved without computationally intensive singular value decompositions.

15.5   Relationship to Support Vector Machine Learning

Our formalization of learning a distance metric from only dissimilar example pairs is closely related to support vector machine learning. Actually, the optimization problem can be translated into an SVM learning problem [26] and can be solved by existing SVM software with certain settings.

The optimization problem for training an SVM that classifies the data into two classes is as follows [26]:

$$\min_{\mathbf{w},b} \ \frac{1}{2} \|\mathbf{w}\|_2^2 \tag{15.11}$$

$$\text{s.t.} \ \ y_i(\langle \mathbf{w}, \mathbf{x}_i \rangle + b) \geq 1 \ \ \forall (\mathbf{x}_i, y_i) \in \mathcal{T} \ . \tag{15.12}$$

$\mathcal{T}$ is the set of training examples $(\mathbf{x}_i, y_i)$, where $\mathbf{x}_i$ is a data vector and $y_i \in \{-1, +1\}$ is the class label. $\langle \mathbf{x}, \mathbf{z} \rangle$ is the inner product of vectors $\mathbf{x}$ and $\mathbf{z}$.

Using the Frobenius product

$$\langle \mathbf{A}, \mathbf{B} \rangle_F = \sum_{s=1}^{d} \sum_{t=1}^{d} a_{st} b_{st}$$

of two $d \times d$ matrices, we can rewrite the problem of (15.6) and (15.7):

$$\min_{\mathbf{A}} \ \frac{1}{2} \|\mathbf{A}\|_F^2 \tag{15.13}$$

$$\text{s.t.} \ \ \langle \mathbf{A}, (\mathbf{x}_i - \mathbf{x}_j)(\mathbf{x}_i - \mathbf{x}_j)^\top \rangle_F \geq 1 \ \ \forall c_{\neq}(i,j) \in C_{\neq} \ . \tag{15.14}$$

Comparison of (15.13) and (15.14) with (15.11) and (15.12) reveals that our problem corresponds to unbiased SVM learning ($b = 0$) from only positive data ($y_i = 1$), if we consider the examples and the learned weight of $d \times d$ matrices as d^2 dimensional vectors. The expansion form of the SVM solution

$$\mathbf{w} = \sum_i y_i \alpha_i \mathbf{x}_i$$

makes clear why our method can avoid semi-definite programming. We use only positive examples (cannot-be-linked pairs), thus all the coefficients for the examples become positive in the solution. If we also used negative examples (must-be-linked pairs), the coefficients for these examples become negative and the solution is not always positive semi-definite.

Substituting (15.10) into (15.9) gives us the dual form of the problem:

$$\max \sum_{c_{\neq}(i,j)\in C_{\neq}} \alpha_{ij}$$
$$-\frac{1}{2} \sum_{c_{\neq}(i,j)\in C_{\neq}} \sum_{c_{\neq}(i',j')\in C_{\neq}} \left(\alpha_{ij}\alpha_{i'j'} \langle \mathbf{x}_i - \mathbf{x}_j, \mathbf{x}_{i'} - \mathbf{x}_{j'} \rangle^2 \right)$$
$$\text{s.t.} \quad \alpha_{ij} \geq 0 \ .$$

These formulas indicate that our learning problem can be solved by using the quadratic polynomial kernel on d dimensional vectors and that we do not need to calculate the Frobenius products between the $d \times d$ matrices. As with standard SVMs, our method can be "kernelized" [20, 23]. By substituting a positive semi-definite kernel function $k(x, z) = \langle \Phi(x), \Phi(z) \rangle$ ($\Phi(x)$ is a map to a higher dimensional space) for the inner product $\langle \mathbf{x}, \mathbf{z} \rangle$, we can virtually learn the distance metric matrix for a very high (possibly infinite) dimensional feature space by the so-called "kernel trick." In addition, a distance metric for structured data, such as trees or graphs, can be learned with a kernel function defined on the space of such data.

Schultz and Joachims [21] proposed a method for learning a distance metric from relative comparison such as "A is closer to B than A is to C." They also formulated the metric learning as a constrained quadratic programming and solved it by SVMs. In their method, the interactions between features are fixed and optimization is applied to a diagonal matrix. The method using only cannot-be-linked pairs can learn a full distance metric matrix.

15.6 Handling Noisy Data

In SVM learning, there is the case where training data cannot be separated by any plane. In our setting, on the other hand, we can always find a matrix

$\mathbf{A}$ that satisfies the constraints (15.7) unless a pair with $\mathbf{x}_i - \mathbf{x}_j = \mathbf{0}$ exists, since by making the diagonal elements a_{ss} for $x_{is} - x_{js} \neq 0$ large enough, the conditions can always be fulfilled.

However, if there exists a pair such that $\mathbf{x}_i - \mathbf{x}_j$ is very close to the zero vector because of noise, the learned metric can be greatly affected by such outliers. To avoid this problem, we can introduce slack variables ξ_{ij} as soft-margin SVMs [26] and allow some constraint violations:

$$\min_{\mathbf{A},\xi} \frac{1}{2}\|\mathbf{A}\|_F^2 + C \sum_{c_{\neq}(i,j) \in C_{\neq}} \xi_{ij} \tag{15.15}$$

$$\text{s.t. } D_{\mathbf{A}}(x_i, x_j) \geq 1 - \xi_{ij} \quad \forall c_{\neq}(i,j) \in C_{\neq} . \tag{15.16}$$

C is a parameter for the trade-offs between the norm of the matrix and the constraint violations. It is straightforward to show that $\mathbf{A}$ is positive semi-definite as in the case without slack variables.

15.7 Relationship to Single-Class Learning

Our formalization can also be considered as a single-class learning problem like one-class SVM [19], which is used for detecting anomalies or outliers. In one-class SVM, examples $\mathbf{x}_i \in \mathcal{T}$ forming only one class are given to the learning algorithm. The optimization problem for training a one-class SVM is as follows:

$$\min_{\mathbf{w},\xi,\rho} \frac{1}{2}\|\mathbf{w}\|_2^2 + C \sum_i \xi_i - \rho \tag{15.17}$$

$$\text{s.t. } \langle \mathbf{w}, \mathbf{x}_i \rangle \geq \rho - \xi_i \quad \forall \mathbf{x}_i \in \mathcal{T} . \tag{15.18}$$

After training, a new example is classified as an outlier if $\langle \mathbf{w}, \mathbf{x}_i \rangle < \rho$.

By comparing (15.17) and (15.18) with (15.15) and (15.16), we can see that our learning problem corresponds to one-class SVM if the offset ρ in the latter is not a variable to be optimized but a constant. In our setting, dissimilar example pairs and similar pairs correspond to target class examples and outliers, respectively.

15.8 Relationship to Online Learning

The close relationship between online kernel machines [8, 9] and SVMs based on quadratic programming suggests an interesting problem: designing an online algorithm that learns a metric only from dissimilar examples.

Shalev-Shwartz et al. [22] proposed an online learning algorithm for learning a distance metric. Other than solving a constrained optimization problem, it finds successive approximate solutions using an iterative procedure that combines a perceptron-like update rule and the Lanczos method to find a negative eigenvalue. While designed for learning from both similar and dissimilar pairs, their algorithm can avoid the eigenvalue problem, if it uses only dissimilar example pairs. Given a pair of cannot-be-linked examples (x_i, x_j), the algorithm updates matrix A as:

$$\mathbf{A} \leftarrow \mathbf{A} + \alpha(\mathbf{x}_i - \mathbf{x}_j)(\mathbf{x}_i - \mathbf{x}_j)^\top \tag{15.19}$$

$$\alpha = \frac{1 - \langle \mathbf{A}, (\mathbf{x}_i - \mathbf{x}_j)(\mathbf{x}_i - \mathbf{x}_j)^\top \rangle_F}{\|(\mathbf{x}_i - \mathbf{x}_j)(\mathbf{x}_i - \mathbf{x}_j)^\top\|_F^2} \;, \tag{15.20}$$

if $\langle \mathbf{A}, (\mathbf{x}_i - \mathbf{x}_j)(\mathbf{x}_i - \mathbf{x}_j)^\top \rangle_F < 1$. (We eliminated the bias term from their original formalization.)

Actually, this coincides with the update rule in online kernel AdaTron [9]. Furthermore, the equality between kernel AdaTron and sequential minimal optimization (SMO) [17] for finding the SVM solution without the bias term is proved [12]. Therefore, if we solve the problem consisting of (15.13) and (15.14) by using SMO, it is identical to online learning with the update rule (15.19) and (15.20).

15.9 Application to Name Disambiguation

15.9.1 Name Disambiguation

Name disambiguation, which is used for example to determine whether the names of people in documents or databases refer to the same person or not, is an important problem in information retrieval and integration. It is most often used for personal name disambiguation, e.g., author identification in bibliographic databases. Citation and bibliographic databases are particularly troublesome because author first names are often abbreviated in citations. Resolving these ambiguities is necessary when evaluating the activity of researchers, but major citation databases such as the ISI Citation Index[2] and Citeseer's Most Cited Authors in Computer Science[3] cannot distinguish authors with the same first name initial and last name. Personal name disambiguation on the Web is now gaining attention as well [14, 4, 28].

Name disambiguation is a special case of object identification, which has been studied for a long time in the database community. Recently, these

---

[2] http://isiknowledge.com/
[3] http://citeseer.ist.psu.edu/mostcited.html

problems have attracted the interest of machine learning researchers. Several methods have been proposed to train a classifier for identifying data items referring to the same object [18, 24, 6, 15]. Other conventional approaches are summarized by Bilenko et al. [5].

Name disambiguation problems are generally solved by clustering data containing the target names based on some similarity measure or distance metric [14]. Metric learning can improve clustering accuracy but preparing training data is costly. Disambiguating two people with the same name or similar names is a subtle and time-consuming task even for a person. However, the following two assumptions enable us to prepare cannot-be-linked example pairs without manual labeling and to use the metric learning algorithm described in the preceding sections.

Different names refer to different objects. In many name disambiguation problems, pairs of different names presumably refer to different objects with few exceptions. For example, two J. Smiths are ambiguous, while J. Smith and D. Johnson cannot be the same person (neglecting, of course, the possibility of false names or nicknames).

Names are arbitrary. There is no reason to believe that the data for two people with the same name are more similar than the data for two people with different names. For example, the research papers written by two different J. Smiths are not assumed to be more similar than those written by J. Smith and D. Johnson. We assume that a pair of data items for two people with different names has the same statistical properties as a pair of data items for two people with the same name.

These two assumptions justify the use of pairs of data items collected for different names (for example, J. Smith and D. Johnson) as cannot-be-linked examples for learning a distance metric to be used for clustering data for people with the same or similar names (Figure 15.1). The learned distance metric that gives good separation of the data for people with different names can be expected to separate the data for different people with the same name as well. These cannot-be-linked example pairs can be formed mechanically without manual labeling. In this setting, no similar (must-be-linked) example pairs are used.

In the remainder of this section, we present experimental results for author identification using a bibliographic database.

15.9.2 Data Set and Software

We describe experiments on the DBLP data set, which is a bibliography of computer science papers.[4] The data is publicly available in XML format. We

---

[4]http://dblp.uni-trier.de/

TABLE 15.1: DBLP data set

Abbreviated name	Number of distinct authors
D. Johnson	17
A. Gupta	23
J. Smith	29
R. Johnson	29
L. Zhang	31
H. Zhang	26
R. Jain	10
J. Mitchell	11

used both journal papers and conference papers. The entries were made by people, and many author names include the full first name, not only an initial. We assume that the same first and last names refer to the same person.

From among the Most Cited Authors in Computer Science,[5] we selected eight cases of first-initial-plus-surname names, which involve a collapsing of many distinct author names. We selected names like J. Smith rather than ones like J. Ullman to ensure a high level of collapsing. We retrieved papers written by authors with the same last name and the same first initial from the DBLP data and randomly selected 100 examples for each abbreviated name. Then we abbreviated first names into initials and removed middle names. The number of distinct authors for each abbreviated name is shown in Table 15.1.

Training data were built by pairing examples of different abbreviated names, for example, J. Smith and D. Johnson, and test data were built by pairing examples with the same name. Thus the experimental setting here is not purely inductive but transductive as previous work on semi-supervised clustering [29, 27, 13, 3, 22], where "must-be-linked" or "cannot-be-linked" constraints are given to some portion of the (test) data. We used words in titles, journal names, and names of coauthors as features. Each feature represented the presence or absence of each word. Since few words appear more than once in a bibliographic entry, we used binary features. Each bibliographic entry was represented as a feature vector using these features.

To learn a distance metric, we used SVM^{light}, an implementation of the SVM learning algorithm [11]. We used the quadratic polynomial kernel for our experiments and the parameter C in Equation (15.15) is set to 1.

---

[5]http://citeseer.ist.psu.edu/mostcited.html

TABLE 15.2: Maximum F-measure values

Abbreviated	F-measure		
name	Learned	IDF	Euclidean
D. Johnson	.644	.390	.399
A. Gupta	.490	.170	.169
J. Smith	.417	.270	.292
R. Johnson	.508	.253	.227
L. Zhang	.278	.165	.158
H. Zhang	.423	.226	.226
R. Jain	.709	.569	.552
J. Mitchell	.640	.535	.536

15.9.3 Results

The learned metric was used in clustering the data from the same-first-initial-and-last author names. The results of clustering were evaluated by referring to the original full names. We used the single-linkage clustering algorithm [10]. When S is the set of pairs of examples in the same cluster (i.e., the clustering algorithms predict these pairs being the same person) and T is the set of pairs that have the same full name, precision, recall and F-measure are defined as follows:

$$\text{Precision} = \frac{|S \cap T|}{|S|}$$

$$\text{Recall} = \frac{|S \cap T|}{|T|}$$

$$\text{F-measure} = \frac{2}{\frac{1}{\text{Precision}} + \frac{1}{\text{Recall}}}.$$

The clustering algorithm enables us to specify the number of clusters. We measured the precision and recall for each number of clusters and drew a recall-precision curve. The results with the learned metric were compared to the results with two other metrics, one was the Euclidean distance of Equation (15.1) and the other was the IDF weighting of Equation (15.3). Since each bibliography entry is short and the same word rarely appears more than once in the entry, we did not apply TF weighting. We neither normalized the feature vectors because the lengths of bibliographic entries are rather uniform. Figure 15.2 shows the recall-precision curves for the 8 abbreviated names. The maximum F-measure for each combination of name and metric is given in Table 15.2. Table 15.3 also presents the values of precision, recall, and F-measure at the correct numbers of clusters, which is shown in Table 15.1.

In most cases, use of the learned metric resulted in the highest precision, recall, and F-measure, while the values varied for different names and the ab-

TABLE 15.3: Results with the correct cluster numbers

Abbreviated	Learned			IDF			Euclidean		
name	P	R	F	P	R	F	P	R	F
D. Johnson	.381	.757	.507	.242	.770	.368	.260	.771	.389
A. Gupta	.298	.620	.402	.081	.597	.142	.086	.635	.151
J. Smith	.197	.754	.312	.137	.769	.232	.131	.734	.222
R. Johnson	.159	.757	.263	.132	.688	.222	.136	.686	.227
L. Zhang	.157	.488	.238	.093	.594	.161	.082	.509	.142
H. Zhang	.195	.643	.299	.128	.575	.209	.128	.577	.128
R. Jain	.354	.914	.510	.360	.932	.520	.357	.922	.514
J. Mitchell	.418	.897	.570	.373	.876	.523	.373	.876	.523

breviated names with many distinct full names, for example, L. Zhang, tended to be more difficult to disambiguate. This confirms that learning a distance metric from dissimilar example pairs is effective and the two assumptions are appropriate.

15.10 Conclusion

Existing distance metric learning algorithms use only must-be-linked example pairs or both must-be-linked and cannot-be-linked example pairs. In this chapter, we described a distance metric learning method that uses only cannot-be-linked example pairs. We formalized the metric learning as a convex quadratic programming problem. Unlike other metric learning algorithms, it does not require eigenvalue decompositions to enforce the positive semi-definiteness of the learned matrix. The optimization problem can be translated into an SVM learning problem and can be efficiently solved by existing SVM software.

We applied the metric learning from cannot-be-linked examples to a name disambiguation problem, by introducing the two assumptions: different names refer to different objects and the data for two people with exactly the same name are no more similar than the data for two people with different names. The distance metric was learned from pairs of data items for different names, which are mechanically collected without human supervision. Experiments using the DBLP data set showed that the learned metric improves precision and recall for name disambiguation.

References

[1] Ricardo Baeza-Yates and Berthier Ribeiro-Neto. *Modern Information Retrieval.* Addison-Wesley, 1999.

[2] Sugato Basu, Arindam Banerjee, and Raymond J. Mooney. Semi-supervised clustering by seeding. In *Proceedings of the Nineteenth International Conference on Machine Learning (ICML 2002)*, pages 19–26, 2002.

[3] Sugato Basu, Mikhail Bilenko, and Raymond J. Mooney. A probabilistic framework for semi-supervised clustering. In *Proceedings of the Tenth ACM SIGKDD International Conference on Knowledge Discovery and Data Mining (KDD 2004)*, pages 59–68, 2004.

[4] Ron Bekkerman and Andrew McCallum. Disambiguating web appearances of people in a social network. In *Proceedings of the Fourteenth International World Wide Web Conference (WWW 2005)*, pages 463–470, 2005.

[5] Mikhail Bilenko, William W. Cohen, Stephen Fienberg, Raymond J. Mooney, and Pradeep Ravikumar. Adaptive name-matching in information integration. *IEEE Intelligent Systems*, 18(5):16–23, 2003.

[6] Mikhail Bilenko and Raymond J. Mooney. Adaptive duplicate detection using learnable string similarity measures. In *Proceedings of the Ninth ACM SIGKDD International Conference on Knowledge Discovery and Data Mining (KDD 2003)*, pages 39–48, 2003.

[7] Stephen Boyd and Lieven Vandenberghe. *Convex Optimization.* Cambridge University Press, 2004.

[8] Yoav Freund and Robert E. Schapire. Large margin classification using the perceptron algorithm. *Machine Learning*, 37(3):277–296, 1999.

[9] Thilo-Thomas Frieß, Nello Cristianini, and Colin Campbell. The Kernel-Adatron algorithm: a fast and simple learning procedure for support vector machines. In *Proceedings of the Fifteenth International Conference on Machine Learning (ICML 1998)*, pages 188–196, 1998.

[10] Anil K. Jain and Richard C. Dubes. *Algorithms for Clustering Data.* Prentice-Hall, 1988.

[11] Thorsten Joachims. Making large-scale SVM learning practical. In B. Schölkopf, C. Burges, and A. Smola, editors, *Advances in Kernel Methods: Support Vector Learning*, pages 169–184. MIT Press, 1999.

[12] Vojislav Kecman, Michael Vogt, and Te Ming Huang. On the equality of kernel AdaTron and sequential minimal optimization in classification and regression tasks and alike algorithms for kernel machines. In *Proceedings of the Eleventh European Symposium on Artificial Neural Networks (ESANN 2003)*, pages 215–222, 2003.

[13] Dan Klein, Sepandar D. Kamvar, and Christopher D. Manning. From instance-level constraints to space-level constraints: Making the most of prior knowledge in data clustering. In *Proceedings of the Nineteenth International Conference on Machine Learning (ICML 2002)*, pages 307–314, 2002.

[14] Gideon S. Mann and David Yarowsky. Unsupervised personal name disambiguation. In *Proceedings of the Seventh Conference on Computational Natural Language Learning (CoNLL 2003)*, pages 33–40, 2003.

[15] Satoshi Oyama and Christopher D. Manning. Using feature conjunctions across examples for learning pairwise classifiers. In *Proceedings of the Fifteenth European Conference on Machine Learning (ECML 2004)*, pages 322–333, 2004.

[16] Satoshi Oyama and Katsumi Tanaka. Learning a distance metric for object identification without human supervision. In *Proceedings of the Tenth European Conference on Principles and Practice of Knowledge Discovery in Databases (PKDD 2006)*, pages 609–616, 2006.

[17] John C. Platt. Fast training of support vector machines using sequential minimal optimization. In B. Schölkopf, C. Burges, and A. Smola, editors, *Advances in Kernel Methods: Support Vector Learning*, pages 185–208. MIT Press, 1999.

[18] Sunita Sarawagi and Anuradha Bhamidipaty. Interactive deduplication using active learning. In *Proceedings of the Eighth ACM SIGKDD International Conference on Knowledge Discovery and Data Mining (KDD 2002)*, pages 269–278, 2002.

[19] Bernhard Schölkopf, John C. Platt, John Shawe-Taylor, Alex J. Smola, and Robert C. Williamson. Estimating the support of a high-dimensional distribution. *Neural Computation*, 13(7):1443–1471, 2001.

[20] Bernhard Schölkopf and Alex Smola. *Learning with Kernels: Support Vector Machines, Regularization, Optimization and Beyond*. MIT Press, 2002.

[21] Matthew Schultz and Thorsten Joachims. Learning a distance metric from relative comparisons. In *Advances in Neural Information Processing Systems 16*, pages 41–48. MIT Press, 2004.

[22] Shai Shalev-Shwartz, Yoram Singer, and Andrew Y. Ng. Online and batch learning of pseudo-metrics. In *Proceedings of the Twenty-First International Conference on Machine Learning (ICML 2004)*, 2004.

[23] John Shawe-Taylor and Nello Cristianini. *Kernel Methods for Pattern Analysis*. Cambridge University Press, 2004.

[24] Sheila Tejada, Craig A. Knoblock, and Steven Minton. Learning domain-independent string transformation weights for high accuracy object identification. In *Proceedings of the Eighth ACM SIGKDD International Conference on Knowledge Discovery and Data Mining (KDD 2002)*, pages 350–359, 2002.

[25] Lieven Vandenberghe and Stephen Boyd. Semidefinite programming. *SIAM Review*, 38(1):49–95, 1996.

[26] Valdimir N. Vapnik. *Statistical Learning Theory*. John Wiley & Sons, 1998.

[27] Kiri Wagstaff, Claire Cardie, Seth Rogers, and Stefan Schroedl. Constrained k-means clustering with background knowledge. In *Proceedings of the Eighteenth International Conference on Machine Learning (ICML 2001)*, pages 577–584, 2001.

[28] Xiaojun Wan, Jianfeng Gao, Mu Li, and Binggong Ding. Person resolution in person search results: WebHawk. In *Proceedings of the Fourteenth ACM International Conference on Information and Knowledge Management (CIKM 2005)*, pages 163–170, 2005.

[29] Eric P. Xing, Andrew Y. Ng, Michael I. Jordan, and Stuart J. Russell. Distance metric learning, with application to clustering with side-information. In *Advances in Neural Information Processing Systems 15*, pages 505–512. MIT Press, 2003.

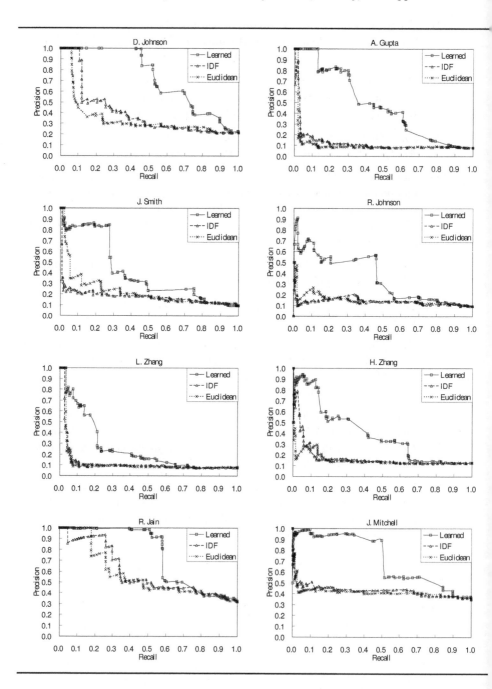

FIGURE 15.2: Results of author identification for DBLP data set.

Chapter 16

Privacy-Preserving Data Publishing: A Constraint-Based Clustering Approach

Anthony K. H. Tung

National University of Singapore, `anthony@comp.nus.edu.sg`

Jiawei Han

University of Illinois, Urbana-Champaign, `hanj@cs.uiuc.edu`

Laks V. S. Lakshmanan

University of British Columbia, `laks@cs.ubc.ca`

Raymond T. Ng

University of British Columbia, `rng@cs.ubc.edu`

Abstract

Privacy-preserving data publishing has drawn much research interest recently. In this chapter, we address this topic from the viewpoint of constrained clustering, i.e., the problem of finding clusters that satisfy certain user-specified constraints. More specifically, we begin with the problem of clustering under aggregate constraints (without privacy considerations) and explain how traditional algorithms for the unconstrained problem (e.g., the c-means algorithm) break down in the presence of constraints. From there, we develop scalable algorithms that overcome this problem and finally illustrate how our algorithm can also be used for privacy-preserving data publishing.

16.1 Introduction

Publishing personal data while protecting individual's privacy has now become an important and well-studied topic [14, 13, 1, 16, 11, 18, 19, 10, 12]. The input to such a problem is typically a table consisting of two types of attributes: *sensitive* attributes whose values must not be associated with any particular individual and *quasi-identifier (QI)* attributes which are attributes that are publishable but that must be generalized in such a way that the sensitive attributes of individuals cannot be inferred through a database join operation with any external table such as a voters list that is public.

Central to the idea of privacy preserving data publishing is the concept of k-anonymity [13] from which many other variants have been derived [16, 9, 11, 19, 10]. To compute a k-anonymous table from a raw table, the most common approach involves an iterative, bottom-up merging of tuples until the k-anonymity condition is satisfied [16, 9, 11, 19, 10]. During the merging, special care is taken to ensure that information loss (defined differently in different papers) is minimized due to the merging of tuples.

Interestingly, such an approach can also be seen as a form of clustering called *agglomerative clustering* [5] where objects are iteratively merged into larger clusters until a certain stopping condition becomes true. In the k-anonymity case, a simple abstraction is to allow merging of tuples to continue until each cluster contains at least k objects. A more subtle distinguishing feature of clustering for k-anonymity compared to the classical clustering framework lies in the fact that the QI attributes in the privacy preservation data publishing literature [16, 9, 11, 19, 10] are typically associated with a concept hierarchy that is used to guide the merging of the tuples. This, however, only helps simplify the clustering process compared to agglomerative clustering on numerical attributes with no given concept hierarchies.[1]

In this chapter, we continue to explore this analogous relationship between clustering and k-anonymity by looking at another type of clustering called *partitioning-based clustering*. A partitioning-based approach to clustering is known to have an advantage over an agglomerative one in at least two ways [5]:

1. Most agglomerative clustering algorithms have quadratic time complexity whereas many partitioning-based algorithms like c-means[2] complete in linear time.

2. Unlike agglomerative clustering which fixes the cluster membership of the tuples once they are merged, partitioning-based algorithms typically adopt an iterative refinement approach which could swap cluster membership to reduce information loss when the initial assignment of cluster membership is not optimal.

To facilitate our objective, we first introduce a constrained version of the partitioning-based clustering problem [15] in the next section. Besides mini-

---

[1]As a side note, the use of concept hierarchies in privacy-preserving publishing is sometimes the reason for privacy breach [19].

[2]We will use c to replace the k in k-means in order to avoid confusion with the k in k-anonymity.

mizing the total dispersion of the clusters, the constrained version also has the requirement that some *aggregate constraints* must be satisfied. The theoretical implications of introducing such constraints to clustering are then explained. In the next section we introduce our algorithm for clustering under aggregate constraints and explain how such an algorithm can be made scalable through the use of *micro-clustering*. We then explain how our algorithm for clustering under aggregate constraints can in fact be adopted for privacy-preserving data publishing. Finally, the last section concludes the chapter.

16.2   The Constrained Clustering Problem

Cluster analysis has been an active area of research in computational statistics and data mining with many algorithms developed. More specifically, the problem of clustering that many existing algorithms solve is defined as follows.

> **The Unconstrained Clustering (UC) Problem**: Given a data set D with n objects, a distance function $df : D \times D \longrightarrow \Re$, and a positive integer c, find a *c-clustering*, i.e., a partition of D into c pairwise disjoint clusters $(Cl_1, \ldots, Cl_c)$ such that $DISP = (\sum_{i=1}^{c} disp(Cl_i, rep_i))$ is minimized.

The "dispersion" of cluster Cl_i, $disp(Cl_i, rep_i)$, measures the total distance between each object in Cl_i and a *representative* rep_i of Cl_i, i.e., $disp(Cl_i, rep_i)$ defined as $\sum_{p \in Cl_i} df(p, rep_i)$. The representative of a cluster Cl_i is chosen such that $disp(Cl_i, rep_i)$ is minimized. Finding such a representative for each cluster is generally not difficult. For example, the c-means algorithm uses the centroid of the cluster as its representative which could be calculated in linear time. The c-medoids algorithm, on the other hand, uses the medoid of a cluster as its representative [8] which requires $O(|Cl_i|^2)$ time to compute.

In this chapter, we propose the *constrained clustering* (CC) problem, defined as follows.

> **The Constrained Clustering (CC) Problem**: Given a data set D with n objects, a distance function $df : D \times D \longrightarrow \Re$, a positive integer c, and *a set of constraints C*, find a *c-clustering* $(Cl_1, \ldots, Cl_c)$ such that $DISP = (\sum_{i=1}^{k} disp(Cl_i, rep_i))$ is minimized, and *each cluster Cl_i satisfies the constraints C*, denoted as $Cl_i \models C$.

Depending on the nature of the constraints, the CC problem can take on a different flavor and interested users are referred to [15] for a list. Here, within the theme of our study, we will focus on constraints formulated with SQL aggregates, formalized next.

Let each object O_i in the database D be associated with a set of m attributes $\{A_1, \ldots, A_m\}$. The value of an attribute A_j for an object O_i is denoted as $O_i[A_j]$.

DEFINITION 16.1 SQL Aggregate Constraints   Consider the aggregate functions $agg \in \{max(), min(), avg(), sum()\}$. Let θ be a comparator function, i.e., $\theta \in \{<, \leq, \neq, =, \geq, >\}$, and v be a numerical constant. Given a cluster Cl, an SQL aggregate constraint on Cl is a constraint in one of the following forms: (i) $agg(\{O_i[A_j] \mid O_i \in Cl\}) \; \theta \; v$; or (ii) $count(Cl) \; \theta \; v$.   □

Within SQL aggregate constraints, we are specially interested in a type of constraints, called **existential constraints**, defined as follows.

DEFINITION 16.2 Existential Constraints   Let $W \subseteq D$ be any subset of objects. We call them **pivot** objects. Let n be a positive integer. An **existential constraint** on a cluster Cl is a constraint of the form: $count(\{O_i | O_i \in Cl, O_i \in W\}) \geq n$.   □

Pivot objects are typically specified via constraints or other predicates. For example, in the market segmentation problem [8], frequent customers might be the pivot objects. More precisely, W is the subset of customers who are frequent.

Note that the definition of existential constraints is more general than it may appear as a number of SQL aggregate constraints can be reduced to it. Essentially, W can be seen as the extent of a predicate on individual members of D. Thus, an existential constraint $count(\{O_i \mid O_i \in Cl, O_i \in W\} \geq n$ says each cluster must have at least n objects that satisfies that predicate. As such, deriving an algorithm to solve the problem with existential constraints is thus a central problem.

A key complication is that these algorithms find clusterings satisfying what we call the *nearest rep(resentative) property* (NRP):

> **The Nearest Rep(resentative) Property** (NRP): Let $(Cl_1, \ldots, Cl_c)$ be the c-clustering computed by the algorithm, and let rep_i denote the representative of cluster Cl_i, $1 \leq i \leq c$. Then a data object $p \in D$ is placed in a cluster Cl_j iff rep_j is the closest to p among all the representatives. More precisely, $(\forall p \in D)(\forall 1 \leq j \leq c) \; [p \in Cl_j \; \Leftrightarrow \; (\forall i \neq j) \; df(p, rep_j) \leq df(p, rep_i)]$.

Before proceeding to develop an algorithm to perform constrained clustering, we first examine the theoretical implication of adding constraints to clustering w.r.t. the NRP. We pick the popular c-means algorithm as the target of our discussion, though the discussion generalizes to other algorithms, such as the c-medoids algorithm.

Given a set of constraints C, let us begin by defining a "solution space" for the CC problem:

$$ClSp(C, c, D) = \{(Cl_1, \ldots, Cl_c) \mid \forall 1 \le i, j \le c :$$
$$\emptyset \subset Cl_j \subset D \ \& \ Cl_j \models C \ \&$$
$$\cup Cl_j = D \ \& \ Cl_i \cap Cl_j = \emptyset, \text{ for } i \ne j\}$$

We refer to $ClSp(C, c, D)$ as the (constrained) clustering space. Clusterings found by the c-means algorithm satisfy the NRP. Accordingly, the *constrained mean solution space* is defined as:

$$MeanSp(C, c, D) = \{(Cl_1, \ldots, Cl_c) \mid$$
$$(Cl_1, \ldots, Cl_c) \in ClSp(C, c, D)$$
$$\& \ \forall 1 \le j \le c, \forall q \in D :$$
$$(q \in Cl_j \ \Leftrightarrow \ (\forall i \ne j :$$
$$df(q, p_j) \le df(q, p_i)))\}$$

where p_j is the centroid of cluster Cl_j. It should be clear by definition that the mean space $MeanSp()$ is a strict subset of the clustering space $ClSp()$. To understand the role played by the NRP, let us revisit the situation when the set of constraints C is empty. The c-means algorithm does the smart thing by operating in the smaller $MeanSp()$ space than in the $ClSp()$ space. More importantly, the following theorem says that there is no loss of quality.

We refer to the unconstrained version of clustering as the *unconstrained clustering* (UC) problem.

THEOREM 16.1
A clustering $\mathcal{UCL}$ is an optimal solution to the UC problem in the space $ClSp(\emptyset, k, D)$ iff it is an optimal solution to the UC problem in the mean space $MeanSp(\emptyset, k, D)$. □

Like virtually all existing clustering algorithms, the c-means algorithm does not attempt to find the global optimum. This is because the decision problem corresponding to c-clustering is NP-complete even for $c = 2$ [4]. Thus, the c-means algorithm focuses on finding local optima. Theorem 16.1 can be extended from the global optimum to a local optimum.

The point here is that $MeanSp(\emptyset, c, D)$ contains the "cream" of $ClSp(\emptyset, c, D)$, in that the global and local optima in $ClSp(\emptyset, c, D)$ are also contained in the smaller $MeanSp(\emptyset, c, D)$. This nice situation, however, does not generalize to the CC problem in general. Here is a simple example. Suppose there are only 4 customers and three of them are located close to each other at one end of a highway, and the remaining is at the other end. If the CC problem is to find two clusters with (at least) two customers each, it is easy to see that it is impossible to satisfy the constraint and the NRP simultaneously.

To resolve this conflict, we adopt the policy that the user-defined constraints take precedence over the NRP. Specifically, the algorithm to be presented next regards the set C to be hard constraints that must be satisfied. The NRP, on the other hand, is treated as a "soft" constraint in the sense that it is satisfied as much as possible by the minimization of ($\sum_{i=1}^{k} disp(Cl_i, rep_i)$). But there is no guarantee that every object is in the cluster corresponding to the nearest center.

16.3 Clustering without the Nearest Representative Property

In this section, we will derive an algorithm to perform CC under an existential constraint. Besides making the NRP a "soft" constraint, a more important implication of our analysis is that unlike UC, the NRP property is not usable in CC to enhance efficiency by restricting search to the mean space $MeanSp(C, c, D)$. This is because $MeanSp(C, c, D)$ consists of only solutions that satisfy the NRP but may not satisfy the user-specified constraint. An attempt to refine such a clustering to make it satisfy the user-specified constraint will subsequently invalidate the NRP, leading to the same problem as clustering without the NRP.

Instead, our algorithm tries to find a good solution by performing cluster refinement in the constraint space, $ClSp(C, c, D)$, which we represent using a *clustering locality graph*, $\mathcal{G} = (\mathcal{V}, \mathcal{E})$. $\mathcal{G}$ is described as follows:

- The set $\mathcal{V}$ of nodes is the set of all c-clusterings. More precisely, it is the unconstrained clustering space $ClSp(\emptyset, c, D)$, mentioned in the previous section. Nodes which satisfy existential constraint (EC) are called *valid nodes*, and those that do not are called *invalid nodes*.

- There is an edge between two nodes $\mathcal{CL}_1$, $\mathcal{CL}_2$ in the graph iff they are different from one another by one pivot object, i.e., $\mathcal{CL}_1$ of the form $(Cl_1, \ldots, Cl_i, \ldots, Cl_j, \ldots, Cl_c)$, whereas $\mathcal{CL}_2$ of the form $(Cl_1, \ldots, Cl_i - \{p\}, \ldots, Cl_j \cup \{p\}, \ldots, Cl_c)$ for some pivot object $p \in Cl_i$ & $j \neq i$. If a node $\mathcal{CL}_2$ is connected to $\mathcal{CL}_1$ by an edge, then $\mathcal{CL}_2$ is called a neighbor of $\mathcal{CL}_1$ and vice versa.

Note that the size of the above graph is huge and only part of it is materialized as the refinement of the clusters takes place. With such a graph, a naive algorithm to solve the CC problem given c and EC is to first pick a valid node in the locality graph and move to a valid neighboring node which gives the highest decrease in $DISP$. Intuitively, a movement from a node of higher $DISP$ to a node of lower $DISP$ is a cluster refinement process similar to the c-means algorithm which tries to refine the clustering by moving objects to the nearest center to reduce $DISP$. Our cluster refinement process terminates when no node of lower $DISP$ is found. The algorithm will then stop and output $\mathcal{CL}$ as the solution. However, such an algorithm is a generate-and-test algorithm which is very inefficient since the number of neighbors that a node has is potentially large. To improve the efficiency of such an algorithm, the number of nodes to be examined needs to be restricted.

16.3.1 Cluster Refinement under Constraints

To derive a more efficient algorithm for performing CC without NRP, let us first define a set of *unstable pivots* given a valid node $\mathcal{CL} = (Cl_1, \ldots, Cl_c)$ as follows.

DEFINITION 16.3 (Unstable Pivots)
A set of unstable pivots, S, with respect to $\mathcal{CL}$ is a collection of all pivots in D such that each $s \in S$ belongs to some Cl_i in $\mathcal{CL}$ but is in fact nearer to a representative of some Cl_j, $i \neq j$. □

Using S, we form an induced subgraph of G, $\mathcal{SG} = (\mathcal{SV}, \mathcal{SE})$ as follows.
- The set $\mathcal{SV}$ of nodes that induces the subgraph can be defined as follows:

  - (base case) the initial node $\mathcal{CL}$, representing the clustering is in $\mathcal{SV}$;
  - (inductive case) for any node $\mathcal{CL}$ in $\mathcal{SV}$, if (i) there is an object s from Cl_i whose nearest cluster representative is from Cl_j, $j \neq i$; and (ii) $\mathcal{CL}$ is of the form $(Cl_1, \ldots, Cl_i, \ldots, Cl_c)$, the node $\mathcal{CL}'$ of the form $(Cl_1, \ldots, Cl_i - \{s\}, \ldots, Cl_j \cup \{s\}, \ldots, Cl_c)$ is also in $\mathcal{SV}$; and
  - there is no other node in $\mathcal{SV}$.

Intuitively, once S is defined, the subgraph $\mathcal{SG}$ includes all the nodes that are reachable from $\mathcal{CL}$ via the movements of some $s \in S$ to their nearest cluster. Let us denote the $DISP$ of any node v with respect to a set of representatives REP as $DISP_{REP}(v)$.

THEOREM 16.2
$DISP_{REP'}(\mathcal{CL}') \leq DISP_{REP}(\mathcal{CL})$ *for any node $\mathcal{CL}'$ in $\mathcal{SG}$, REP and REP' being the set of representatives for $\mathcal{CL}$ and $\mathcal{CL}'$ respectively.*
Proof. *Let $REP = (rep_1, \ldots, rep_c)$ and $REP' = (rep'_1, \ldots, rep'_c)$. The dispersion of $\mathcal{CL}'$ calculated* **with respect to** *REP will be $DISP_{REP}(\mathcal{CL}') = (\sum_{i=1}^{k} disp(Cl'_i, rep_i))$. We first observe that*
$$DISP_{REP}(\mathcal{CL}') \leq DISP_{REP}(\mathcal{CL})$$
This is because the set of representatives is the same on both sides of the inequality and since $\mathcal{CL}'$ can be obtained by moving some $s \in S$ to their nearest representative in REP, the reduction in dispersion will result in the above observation. On the other hand, since REP' is a set of representatives

for $\mathcal{CL}'$, by definition they will minimize the dispersion for $Cl'_1, \ldots, Cl'_c$, we thus have the following inequality,

$$DISP_{REP'}(\mathcal{CL}') \leq DISP_{REP}(\mathcal{CL}')$$

By combining these two inequalities together, we have

$$DISP_{REP'}(\mathcal{CL}') \leq DISP_{REP}(\mathcal{CL}') \leq DISP_{REP}(\mathcal{CL})$$

$\square$

From Theorem 16.2, we conclude that our clusters can in fact be refined just by searching $\mathcal{SG}$. There are two advantages to doing this. First, the efficiency improves because the number of nodes to be searched is reduced, and these nodes will have lower $DISP$ than $\mathcal{CL}$ hence giving better quality clusters. What remains to be done is to ensure that these nodes are valid. Second, instead of considering only neighbors, $\mathcal{SG}$ allows us to consider nodes that are many steps away.

Given $\mathcal{SG}$, we adopt the steepest descending approach and try to plan a path along the valid nodes of $\mathcal{SG}$ which leads to a new valid node $\mathcal{CL}'$ with minimized dispersion in $\mathcal{SG}$. We call this problem the *best path (BP) problem*. Note that in UC, the BP problem is trivially solved by an algorithm like *c*-means which moves objects to their nearest representatives. In such a case, computing the best path is easy as there are no invalid nodes to avoid. For the CC case, however, if we want to plan a path through only valid nodes, we can move an unstable pivot to its nearest clusters only if it is originally in a *surplus* cluster, i.e., a cluster which has more pivot objects than required by the *EC*. We call an unstable pivot which is in a surplus cluster, a *movable* object.

To gain more insight into the BP problem and to derive an algorithm for solving it, we introduce a concept called *pivot movement graph* which could be used to represent the state of clustering in each node of $\mathcal{SG}$.

DEFINITION 16.4 (Pivot Movement Graph)
A *pivot movement graph* is a directed graph in which each cluster is represented by a node. An edge from Cl_i to Cl_j indicates that there is at least one unstable pivot object in Cl_i that has Cl_j as its nearest center. These objects are represented as labels on the edge. The reduction in $DISP$ when an unstable object is moved to its nearest center is shown next to each of these objects. $\square$

Figure 16.1 shows an example of a pivot movement graph which is under the constraint "$\forall i, count(Cl_i) \leq 50$." As such, the surplus clusters at this instance are Cl_1, Cl_3 and Cl_5. Figure 16.2 shows the actual situation depicted by the object movement graph in Figure 16.1. For clarity, only the unstable pivots and the cluster representatives (marked by a cross) are shown. Given a pivot movement graph, a *pivot movement (PM)* problem is the problem of computing a schedule of movements for the unstable objects in the pivot movement graph such that the total reduction in $DISP$ is maximized.

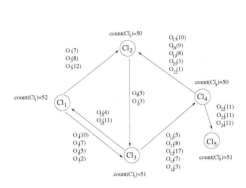

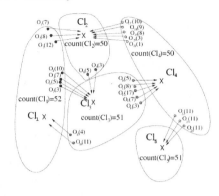

FIGURE 16.1: A pivot movement graph

FIGURE 16.2: The actual situation

THEOREM 16.3

The BP (i.e., best path) problem is equivalent to the PM (i.e., pivot movement) problem.

Proof. *Given an optimized solution for BP, we follow the path given in the solution and move the pivots in the corresponding pivot movement graph. This will give a maximized reduction in dispersion. Similarly, if an optimized schedule is give for PM, we can follow the schedule and move along a path where each node in the path corresponds to a state of the pivot movement graph when the schedule is followed. This will bring us to a node with minimized dispersion in $\mathcal{SG}$.* □

Given their equivalence, any result which we prove to be true for the PM problem can be applied to the BP problem. This is true also for any algorithm derived for the PM problem. We now proceed to define a decision version of the PM problem as follows.

DEFINITION 16.5 (The PM Decision Problem)

Given a pivot movement graph and an existential constraint EC, the PM decision problem is to determine whether there is a schedule of movements of objects around the clusters such that EC is satisfied at all times and the total dispersion being reduced is $\geq B$ where B is a numeric constant. □

By analyzing the graph, we make two observations which hint that the PM problem is a very difficult problem. First, the movement of an unstable pivot object could possibly trigger a series of movements of other unstable pivot objects. For example, by moving O_3 from Cl_1 to Cl_2, Cl_2 now has 51 pivot objects, and thus we could move O_8 from Cl_2 to Cl_3. We refer to such a series of triggerings as a **movement path**. Second, given a surplus cluster with more than one outgoing edge, it is not obvious which outgoing edge should be picked so that $DISP$ is minimized in the resultant movement path.

True to our observation, we prove the following theorem:

THEOREM 16.4
The PM decision problem is NP-complete.
Proof. *See Appendix A.*

Furthermore, by using a result given in [6], we can show that it is not possible to compute in polynomial time a constant factor approximation for the PM problem. In view of this, our next alternative is to use heuristics which could work well in practice and efficient enough for handling a large dataset. The purpose of the heuristic is to iteratively pick an edge in the pivot movement graph and move an unstable object on the edge to its nearest representative thus forming a schedule of movements for the unstable pivots. It is clear that once an edge has been chosen, the unstable pivot with the largest reduction in $DISP$ should be moved. This is because at each iteration of the loop, the key change is whether the surplus status of a cluster changes as a result of the current movement. Once an edge has been selected, this status is kept fixed; in this case, moving the object with the biggest reduction is the appropriate action to take. We experiment with two heuristics.

The first heuristic is a **random heuristic** in which a random edge is selected from those edges that originate from a surplus cluster. Using Figure 16.2 as an example, only edges outgoing from Cl_1 and Cl_3 can be picked. Suppose that the edge from Cl_3 to Cl_4 is picked, and object O_{12} is moved. Then, in the next iteration of the loop, Cl_3 will be a non-surplus cluster, while Cl_4 will be a surplus one.

The second heuristic is a **look-ahead** l heuristic which looks ahead at all possible movement paths originating from a surplus cluster of up to length l, and selects the best among them. The selected movement path is then activated, resulting in a movement of up to l objects depending on the length of the path. When $l = 2$, the heuristic examines all outgoing paths from Cl_1 or from Cl_3 of length 2. These include $\langle Cl_3, Cl_4, Cl_5 \rangle$, $\langle Cl_3, Cl_1, Cl_3 \rangle$, etc. Since there are at most $k(k-1)$ edges, there are at most $O(k(k-1)^{l+1})$ movement paths. While there exist optimization strategies that can avoid examining all the qualifying movement paths of length l, the worst case complexity of this heuristic remains $O(k(k-1)^{l+1})$. Thus, the value of l is designed to be a small integer.

Using these heuristics, our corresponding movement in $\mathcal{SG}$ will eventually reach a node $\mathcal{CL}''$ where future movement is no longer possible. We then repeat the process and form a new subgraph $\mathcal{SG}$ for processing.

16.3.2 Handling Tight Existential Constraints

While the cluster refinement algorithm discussed earlier works well under most constraints, problem arises when the constraint EC is tight, i.e., when it

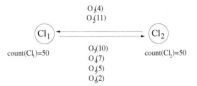

FIGURE 16.3: An example of a deadlock cycle

is nearly impossible to be satisfied. For example, given $k = 5$, $|D| = 100$ and $EC = \{count(Cl_i) \geq 20\}, 1 \leq i \leq 5$, our algorithm will not work well because such a tight constraint will result in what we call a *deadlock cycle*. A sequence of clusters $\langle Cl_1, \ldots, Cl_c, Cl_1 \rangle$ is said to be in a *deadlock cycle* of length c if (a) all the clusters are non-surplus; and (b) there is an edge in the pivot movement graph from Cl_i to $Cl_{i+1}, 1 \leq i \leq k - 1$, and one from Cl_c to Cl_1, respectively. Figure 16.3 shows a deadlock cycle of length 2. It is obvious although both Cl_1 and Cl_2 are non-surplus, the constrained c-means algorithm can reduce $DISP$ by moving O_1 and O_2 from Cl_2 to Cl_1 and moving O_3 and O_4 from Cl_1 to Cl_2 without invalidating the constraint.

In terms of the graph, $\mathcal{SG}$, a tight EC means that $\mathcal{SG}$ contains a large number of invalid nodes and refining the clusters by movement through only valid nodes is not possible. In view of this, a deadlock resolution phase is added before computing a new subgraph $\mathcal{SG}$. The objective of the deadlock resolution phase is to provide a mechanism to jump over a set of invalid nodes by resolving deadlock in the pivot movement graph. Similar to the PM problem, we can prove that resolving deadlock optimally is NP hard.

The proof is rather similar to the proof for Theorem 16.4. Similarly, we can show that there is also no constant factor approximation algorithm for the deadlock resolution problem which runs in polynomial time. Thus, we resort to the following heuristic based on a randomized strategy. It conducts a depth-first search on the pivot movement graph to find any deadlock cycle. This step is efficient and takes time linear in the number of edges. Suppose the deadlock cycle detected is $\langle Cl_1, \ldots, Cl_c, Cl_1 \rangle$. Let n_i denote the number of unstable pivot objects appearing as labels on the edge from Cl_i to Cl_{i+1}. Then let n_{max} denote the minimum n_i value among the edges in the cycle, i.e., $n_{max} = min_{1 \leq i \leq k}\{n_i\}$. This marks the *maximum* number of unstable objects that can be moved across the *entire* cycle without violating EC. Furthermore, once this movement has taken place, those edges in the cycle with $n_i = n_{max}$ can be deleted, thus breaking the cycle. Once the n_{max} value has been determined, the heuristic would move the unstable pivot objects with the top-n_{max} highest reduction in $DISP$ across each edge of the cycle.

16.3.3 Local Optimality and Termination

Having introduced our algorithm, we will now look at its formal properties by analyzing the two main phases of the algorithm. These two phases are, namely, the pivot movement phase in which we try to move only through valid nodes and the deadlock resolution phase. Our algorithm essentially iterates through these two phases and computes a new subgraph $\mathcal{SG}$ at the end of each iteration.

16.3.3.1 Local Optimality Result

Having modeled our cluster refinement algorithm as a graph search, we would like to establish that at the end of each iteration, the clustering obtained corresponds to a local minimum in the subgraph $\mathcal{SG}$. However, one subtle fact here is that all dispersions of nodes in $\mathcal{SG}$ is actually computed with respect to the cluster representatives of $\mathcal{CL}$. The critical aspect here is that when there is a pivot movement, say object p moved from Cl_i to Cl_j, both the representatives of Cl_i and that of Cl_j change. When this occurs, the set of unstable pivots S can also change, which means that $\mathcal{SG}$ itself must be recomputed. This process is time-consuming, especially for our look-ahead heuristic which must recompute $\mathcal{SG}$ every step it looks ahead. Because of this, we choose to freeze the representative of each cluster and avoid the re-computation of $\mathcal{SG}$. As such, the cost of each node $\mathcal{CL}$ in the subgraph $\mathcal{SG}$ is not the true dispersion but rather the "approximated" dispersion, denoted as $\widehat{disp}(\mathcal{CL})$, relative to the fixed representatives. Now we can establish the following result. Intuitively, at the end of the pivot movement phase, no surplus cluster in the pivot movement graph has an outgoing edge. Thus, it is not possible to find a valid node neighboring to the current one that has a lower dispersion.

LEMMA 16.1
The clustering obtained at the end of the pivot movement phase is a local minimum in the subgraph $\mathcal{SG}$, where cost is based on approximated dispersion $\widehat{disp}(\mathcal{CL})$. $\qquad\square$

Interestingly, a deadlock cycle of length c corresponds to a path $\langle \mathcal{CL}_1, \ldots, \mathcal{CL}_{c+1} \rangle$ in $\mathcal{SG}$, such that the first node/clustering $\mathcal{CL}_1$ and the last node $\mathcal{CL}_{c+1}$ are valid, but *all the other nodes are not*. This is a very interesting phenomenon because resolving a deadlock cycle amounts to jumping from one valid node to another via a sequence of invalid nodes in $\mathcal{SG}$. In particular, if deadlock cycles are resolved after the pivot movement phase as in our algorithm, then we jump from a valid local minimum to another valid local minimum (which is not a neighbor) with a strictly lower value of dispersion.

LEMMA 16.2
The clustering obtained at the end of the deadlock resolution phase is a local minimum in the subgraph $\mathcal{SG}$, where cost is based on approximated dispersion $\widehat{disp}(\mathcal{CL})$. $\qquad\square$

16.3.3.2 Termination of the Algorithm

While the above analysis sheds some light on the quality of the results computed by pivot movement and deadlock resolution, we examine another important property, *termination*, below.

Since each move in the graph $\mathcal{SG}$ corresponds to a reduction in the number of unstable pivot objects, and the number of unstable pivot objects is finite, we are guaranteed that both the object movement phase and deadlock resolution phase will terminate. Indeed, both pivot movement and deadlock resolution take polynomial time in the size of the graph $\mathcal{SG}$.

To guarantee termination of the algorithm itself, the only remaining issue is whether the algorithm will iterate through the two phases indefinitely. Since we move to a node of lower $DISP$ for every iteration, and $\mathcal{G}$ is a finite clustering space, it is impossible to have the $DISP$ value decreasing forever. Thus, the algorithm will not iterate through the two phases indefinitely.

16.4 Scaling the Algorithm for Large Databases

In the previous section, we introduced a cluster refinement algorithm that solves the CC problem under an existential constraint. While the algorithm terminates and gives results with good quality (e.g., local minima), it may require a huge number of object movements for large databases, resulting in high CPU as well as I/O costs. In this section, we examine how our algorithm can be scaled up for large, disk-resident databases.

16.4.1 Micro-Clustering and Its Complication

For clustering large, disk-resident databases, many studies have adopted a *micro-clustering* methodology, e.g., [20, 17, 2, 3, 7]. Essentially, the data objects are "compressed" into micro-clusters in a pre-clustering phase so that the subsequent clustering activities can be accomplished at the micro-cluster level and in main memory. Intuitively, objects which are in the same micro-cluster are objects which are so close together that they are most likely to be in the same cluster anyway. As such, grouping them together and moving them as a group represents a good trade-off between quality and efficiency. Typically, to ensure that not much quality is lost, a maximum radius on a micro-cluster is imposed (by a predefined maximal number of micro-clusters as a threshold or by the user). For our cluster refinement algorithm, adopting the micro-clustering strategy means that instead of moving one unstable object across the edges of a pivot movement graph at a time, we have to move one micro-cluster.

However, since each micro-cluster can contain more than one pivot object,

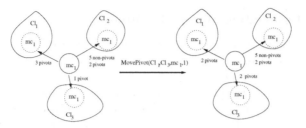

FIGURE 16.4: An example of micro-cluster sharing

it may not be possible to move a micro-cluster away from a surplus cluster without invalidating the constraint. For example, any micro-cluster that contains more that 2 pivot objects cannot be moved away from Cl_1 in Figure 16.1. Similar complication arises when resolving deadlock since there is no guarantee that for each edge in a cycle, the total number of pivot objects in the micro-clusters to be moved are added up to exactly n_{max}.

16.4.2 Micro-Cluster Sharing

To resolve the above problems, we introduce a novel concept called *micro-cluster sharing*. Given a micro-cluster with n non-pivot objects and m pivot objects, the n non-pivot objects will always be allocated to the nearest cluster, while the m pivot objects can be shared among multiple clusters. For example, consider Figure 16.4 in which micro-cluster mc_1 is formed from 5 non-pivot objects and 6 pivot objects. It is shared by three clusters, Cl_1, Cl_2 and Cl_3. Since Cl_2 is the nearest to mc_1, it owns all 5 of mc_1's non-pivot objects and also 2 pivot objects from mc_1. Cl_1, on the other hand, contains 3 pivot objects from mc_1, while Cl_3 has 1 pivot object from mc_1.

To record the sharing or "splitting" of mc_1 into multiple clusters, we use the notation $Cl_i.mc_1$ to represent the part of mc_1 that are in Cl_i. Notice that at this stage, we only record the number of pivot objects from mc_1, and are not concerned with the *exact* identities of these objects. This issue will be examined more closely at the end of this section.

During the pivot movement and deadlock resolution phases, if p objects of $Cl_i.mc_1$ are to be moved to Cl_j, the algorithm calls a function MovePivot(Cl_i, Cl_j, mc_1, p) which updates the numbers in $Cl_i.mc_1$ and $Cl_j.mc_1$ accordingly. In Figure 16.4, MovePivot(Cl_1, Cl_3, mc_1, 1) moves one pivot object from $Cl_1.mc_1$ to $Cl_3.mc_1$.

Since it is possible for $Cl_i.mc_1$ to consist of a single pivot object, one may suggest that we put each pivot object into its own micro-cluster. This would simplify bookkeeping. However, the problem is that this defeats the original purpose of micro-clustering. Essentially, micro-cluster sharing allows a micro-cluster to be as large as possible, and splits a micro-cluster only *on-demand*. Furthermore, the MovePivot() function can cause split micro-clusters to be re-united again, thereby maximizing the effect of micro-clustering.

Given the MovePivot() function, the problem of being unable to shift micro-clusters around the clusters is effectively solved since the micro-clusters can now be dynamically split and combined to cater to the condition for swapping. Since the number of objects in a micro-cluster is small enough for all of them to fit in main memory, the above heuristic requires a minimum amount of I/O.

The remaining issue that we need to address is at the end of clustering, how to determine the actual objects in a micro-cluster mc that are to be assigned to $Cl_1, \ldots, Cl_q$, where these are all the clusters for which $Cl_i.mc$ is positive. We adopt the following greedy heuristic:

- For all the non-pivot objects in mc, they are all assigned to the nearest center/cluster. This is to reduce $DISP$ as much as possible.

- Consider the set of distances defined as: $\{df(O, Cl_i) \mid O \text{ is a pivot object in } mc, \text{ and } 1 \le i \le q\}$. Sort this set of distances in ascending order. Based on this order, the pivot objects are assigned to the cluster as near as possible, while satisfying the numbers recorded in $Cl_1.mc, \ldots, Cl_q.mc$.

16.5 Privacy Preserving Data Publishing as a Constrained Clustering Problem

Having developed a solution for the CC problem, we are now ready to model the privacy preserving data publishing problem as a constrained clustering problem. To facilitate discussion, we will first try to formalize a generic version of the privacy preserving data publishing problem as follows.

We have a raw data table T with d QI attributes A_1, ..., A_d and one sensitive attribute A_s which we assume to be categorical with domain values s_1, ..., s_v. Our aim is to compute a generalized version of T, T', which contains a generalized tuple $m(t)$ for each tuple t in T. In addition, T' must satisfy two criteria:

1. Privacy Constraints
   For any t' in T', let us denote the set of tuples that have exactly the same values as t' for the QI attributes as $group(t')$. We will use the term *equivalence group* to refer to the union of groups of tuples together with t'. We want $group(t')$ to satisfy a certain set of hard constraints $\mathcal{P}$, where $\mathcal{P}$ is a set of privacy constraints which must be satisfied in order to protect the privacy of people whose record is in T.

2. Minimizing Loss Function
   To measure the information loss due to the generalization, we define a

loss function $L(T, T')$ which is typically an aggregate function computed over each t in T and the corresponding $m(t)$ in T'. $L(T, T')$ must be minimized subject to the condition that the privacy constraints C are satisfied.

To reduce this generic problem to our CC problem, we will set $m(t)$ (the generalized version of t) to be the cluster center that t is assigned to in the CC problem, i.e., each tuple t is represented by its cluster center in T'. The loss function in this case is the dispersion which measures the total amount of information loss by representing each tuple with their cluster center. Two important issues remain. First, depending on the privacy constraint $\mathcal{P}$, the corresponding set of constraints C on the clustering must be determined. Second, the appropriate value of c, the number of clusters, must also be set such that information loss is minimized (the larger value of c, the better) while the privacy constraint can still be satisfied (the lower value of c, the better). We next consider these two issues in detail.

16.5.1   Determining C from $\mathcal{P}$

In privacy preserving data publishing, the set of constraints in $\mathcal{P}$ is the most important component that determines the amount of privacy protection that is given to the people in the database. Here, we will give two examples of $\mathcal{P}$ from the privacy preserving data publishing literature and show how they can be converted into C, a set of constraints on the clusters in our CC problem.

1. The k-anonymity model.

The k-anonymity model [14, 13] is one of the fundamental models for protecting privacy. Here, $\mathcal{P}$ is a single constraint which states that each tuple in the generalized table must have at least $k - 1$ other tuples that share the same QI values in all the QI attributes. In this simple case, all data objects in the table are pivots, and the corresponding clustering constraint is to view all data objects in the raw table as pivots and require that each cluster, Cl, must satisfy the existence constraint that $count(Cl) \geq k$.

2. The l-diversity model.

Although k-anonymity ensures that a tuple is indistinguishable from at least $k-1$ other tuples based on the QI attributes, no constraints are enforced on the sensitive values in each group. Thus, privacy breach can occur if an adversary has certain background knowledge. For example, if an adversary knows that a particular person must be in the table and this person happens to be in the same group of k (or more) tuples that have the *same* disease, then it is still possible for the adversary to deduce that this particular person has a certain disease.

In view of this, the l-diversity model is introduced in [11]. The l-diversity model imposes a constraint that each equivalent group in the generalized table must contain at least l "well-represented" sensitive values. In [11], three interpretations are given to the term "well-represented", giving rise to three versions of l-diversity. The first version is **distinct l-diversity** which simply states that there should be at least l distinct sensitive values within each equivalence group. The second, **entropy l-diversity**, requires the entropy of each equivalence group to be greater than $log(l)$; whereas the third, **recursive (m, l)-diversity**, has the restriction that for each equivalence group, the number of occurrences for the most frequent sensitive domain value should be less than m times the total number of occurrences of the l least frequent sensitive domain values in the group.

To cater to l-diversity, the corresponding CC problem must have one class of pivots for each sensitive domain value. Again, all objects are pivots and each must belong to a pivot class that is associated with its corresponding sensitive value. Let us denote the pivot class associated with a sensitive value, s_i, as $class(s_i)$ and that of an object O_i as $class(O_i[A_s])$. Given a cluster Cl, we denote the number of objects with sensitive value s_i in Cl as $count(s_i, Cl)$. The distinct l-diversity simply means that for each cluster Cl, there must exist l distinct sensitive values s'_1, ..., s'_l such that $count(s'_j, Cl) > 0$ for $1 \leq j \leq l$. Likewise, the entropy l-diversity and recursive (m, l)-diversity have corresponding aggregation constraints which can be computed based on $count(s_j, Cl)$ and thus the swapping procedure for constrained clustering described in the earlier section can simply be applied as long as care is taken to ensure that these aggregation constraints are not invalidated.

As can be seen from the above examples, the set of privacy constraints $\mathcal{P}$ can in fact be effectively transformed into a set of constraints in the CC problem, thus making it possible to adopt a constrained-based clustering approach for privacy-preserving data publishing.

16.5.2   Determining c

Next, we look at the setting of c, the number of clusters which is very important in determining the amount of information loss. Note that unlike the unconstrained version of clustering where information loss will be reduced with a high value of c, the relationship between c and the amount of information loss is not clear in the constrained clustering problem. This is because a high value of c will make it difficult or even impossible to satisfy the privacy constraint and thereby result in poor quality clusters with large information loss. For example, if c is larger than n/k, then it is not possible to ensure that every equivalence group will contain more than k tuples. Here, we propose two solutions.

The first and straightforward solution is to adopt an existing hierarchical algorithm which will terminate at a certain value of c when all clusters satisfy the privacy constraint. The result can then be used as an initial clustering for our algorithm which can help reduce information loss through iterative clustering. The setting of c in this case can thus be automatically determined.

However, this means that the quality of the output is in many ways dependent on the existence of a good hierarchical algorithm, an assumption which might not be true all the time.

The second approach is to perform the clustering for a range of possible values of c. Note that a single scan of the database can be used to update multiple instances of the clustering algorithm in parallel and thus computing the clustering result for a range of values for c will not increase the number of scans on the database substantially. At the same time, it is also possible to deduce an upper bound for c in the form of n/k and n/l for the k-anonymity and distinct l-diversity models, respectively, thus reducing the range of possible values. Among the constrained clustering results with different c's, the clustering result with the minimum information loss can then be chosen to compute the final generalized table.

Once the appropriate C and c have been determined, our constrained clustering algorithm can then be used for privacy-preserving data publishing.

16.6 Conclusion

In this chapter, we have introduced and studied the constrained clustering problem and linked it to an important application: privacy-preserving data publishing. For constraint-based clustering, our focus was mainly on existential constraints, whose presence complicates traditional algorithms. We have developed a (constrained) cluster refinement algorithm, which includes two phases of movement in a clustering locality graph: the pivot movement phase and the deadlock resolution phase. Experimental results, reported in [15], clearly show that both phases are valuable. Given that the optimal searches in both pivot movement and deadlock resolution are hard to compute, we have proposed various heuristics. Moreover, micro-cluster sharing is proposed as a key to scale up the algorithm for large databases. As a deep insight on its new, potential applications, we examine the applicability of our algorithm for privacy-preserving data publishing. As indicated in our discussion, using constrained clustering for privacy-preserving data publishing is simply a matter of setting the correct clustering constraints and the number of clusters. Therefore, this study builds up an important linkage between constraint-based clustering and privacy-preserving data publishing. Applying constrained clustering for other models of anonymity [19] is an interesting direction for future work.

Appendix A: Proof Sketch

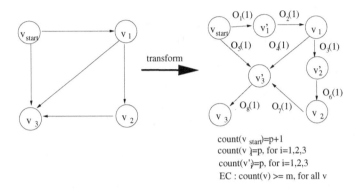

FIGURE 16.5: Transforming DHP to PM

THEOREM 16.5
The PM decision problem is NP-complete.

Proof Sketch. Given a pivot movement graph, we can simply guess a schedule of a set of pivots to be moved and verify that the schedule results in a total decrease in $DISP$ which is $\geq B$ without invalidating EC at any time. As such, $PM \in NP$.

Next, we will transform a known NP-complete problem, the direct Hamiltonian path (DHP) problem [4] into the PM problem. In a DHP problem, a directed graph $G = (V, E)$ is given, and the objective is to decide whether G contains a Hamiltonian path starting from a node v_{start}. Given an instance of DHP, we transform the graph G into a pivot movement graph $G' = (V', E')$ by first removing all incoming edges to v_{start}. A dummy node v' is then added for each $v \in V$ and all incoming edges of v are directed into v' instead. In addition, an edge is added from v' into v. Each node of G' contains p objects except for v_{start} which has $p + 1$ objects. For each edge, only one object is to be moved along it. Each pivot that is successfully moved through the edge reduces $DISP$ by 1. We set the constraint EC to be $count(V') \geq p$, i.e., each node must contain at least p objects. The bound B is set to $2(|V| - 1)$. We illustrate this transformation with an example in Figure 16.5 which should be self-explanatory. Note that the numeric constant p is an arbitrary positive integer which is used to ensure that only one node is eligible to move its object at any one time.

Given that a solution could be found in the transformed instance, this implies that at least $2(|V| - 1)$ nodes have been triggered. Since all the edges are between a dummy node and a non-dummy one, half of the nodes must be non-dummy nodes, i.e., there are $|V| - 1$ non-dummy nodes being triggered. There is no repeating node within these $|V| - 1$ non-dummy nodes as each of them can only be triggered by their corresponding dummy nodes and each dummy node has only one object to be moved along the edge. As such, by following the order of triggering of these $|V| - 1$ from v_{start}, a Hamiltonian path can be formed.

Correspondingly, if there exists a Hamiltonian path in the original instance, the remaining $|V - 1|$ nodes can be trigged from v_{start} in the transformed instance by going through the inserted dummy nodes. As such, if we add in the dummy nodes, $2|V - 1|$ nodes will have been triggered. Since each node triggered causes a reduction of 1 in $DISP$, the total reduction in $DISP$ will be $\geq B$.

Since the PM problem has a solution if and only if the DHP problem has a solution, PM must be NP-complete. $\quad\square$

References

[1] R. J. Bayardo and R. Agrawal. Data privacy through optimal k-anonymization. In *ICDE '05: Proceedings of the 21st International Conference on Data Engineering (ICDE'05)*, pages 217–228, 2005.

[2] P. Bradley, U. Fayyad, and C. Reina. Scaling clustering algorithms to large databases. In *Proceedings of the International Conference of Knowledge Discovery and Data Mining (KDD'98)*, pages 9–15, Aug. 1998.

[3] V. Ganti, J. Gehrke, and R. Ramakrishnan. Mining very large databases. *COMPUTER*, 32:38–45, 1999.

[4] M. Garey and D. Johnson. *Computers and Intractability: A Guide to the Theory of NP-Completeness*. Freeman and Company, New York, 1979.

[5] J. Han and M. Kamber. *Data Mining: Concepts and Techniques*. Morgan Kaufmann, 2006.

[6] D. Karger, R. Motwani, and G. D. S. Ramkumar. On approximating the longest path in a graph. *Algorithmica*, 18:99–110, 1997.

[7] G. Karypis, E.-H. Han, and V. Kumar. CHAMELEON: A hierarchical clustering algorithm using dynamic modeling. *COMPUTER*, 32:68–75, 1999.

[8] L. Kaufman and P. J. Rousseeuw. *Finding Groups in Data: An Introduction to Cluster Analysis*. John Wiley & Sons, 1990.

[9] K. LeFevre, D. J. DeWitt, and R. Ramakrishnan. Incognito: Efficient full-domain k-anonymity. In *Proceedings of the ACM SIGMOD International Conference on Management of Data*, pages 49–60, 2005.

[10] N. Li, T. Li, and S. Venkatasubramanian. t-closeness: Privacy beyond k-anonymity and l-diversity. In *Proceedings of the 23rd International Conference on Data Engineering, ICDE'07*, pages 106–115, 2007.

[11] A. Machanavajjhala, J. Gehrke, D. Kifer, and M. Venkitasubramaniam. l-diversity: Privacy beyond k-anonymity. In *Proceedings of the 22nd International Conference on Data Engineering (ICDE'06)*, page 24, 2006.

[12] D. J. Martin, D. Kifer, A. Machanavajjhala, J. Gehrke, and J. Y. Halpern. Worst-case background knowledge for privacy-preserving data publishing. In *Proceedings of the 23rd International Conference on Data Engineering, ICDE'07*, pages 126–135, 2007.

[13] L. Sweeney. Achieving k-anonymity privacy protection using generalization and suppression. *International Journal of Uncertainty,Fuzziness Knowlege-Based Systems*, 10(5):571–588, 2002.

[14] L. Sweeney. k-anonymity: a model for protecting privacy. *International Journal of Uncertainty,Fuzziness Knowlege-Based Systems*, 10(5):557–570, 2002.

[15] A. K. H. Tung, R. T. Ng, L. V. S. Lakshmanan, and J. Han. Constraint-based clustering in large databases. In *ICDT*, pages 405–419, 2001.

[16] K. Wang, P. S. Yu, and S. Chakraborty. Bottom-up generalization: a data mining solution to privacy protection. In *Proceedings of the 4th IEEE International Conference on Data Mining (ICDM 2004)*, November 2004.

[17] W. Wang, J. Yang, and R. Muntz. STING: A statistical information grid approach to spatial data mining. In *Proceedings of the 1997 International Conference on Very Large Data Bases (VLDB'97)*, pages 186–195, Athens, Greece, Aug. 1997.

[18] X. Xiao and Y. Tao. Anatomy: Simple and effective privacy preservation. In *Proceedings of the 32nd International Conference on Very Large Data Bases*, pages 139–150, 2006.

[19] X. Xiao and Y. Tao. Personalized privacy preservation. In *Proceedings of the ACM SIGMOD International Conference on Management of Data*, pages 229–240, 2006.

[20] T. Zhang, R. Ramakrishnan, and M. Livny. BIRCH: an efficient data clustering method for very large databases. In *Proceedings 1996 ACM-SIGMOD International Conference Management of Data (SIGMOD'96)*, pages 103–114, Montreal, Canada, June 1996.

Chapter 17

Learning with Pairwise Constraints for Video Object Classification

Rong Yan

IBM TJ Watson Research Center, `yanr@us.ibm.com`

Jian Zhang

Purdue University, `jianzhan@stat.purdue.edu`

Jie Yang

Carnegie Mellon University, `yang@cs.cmu.edu`

Alexander G. Hauptmann

Carnegie Mellon University, `alex@cs.cmu.edu`

Abstract   To deal with the problem of insufficient labeled data in video object classification, one solution is to utilize additional pairwise constraints that indicate the relationship between two examples, i.e., whether these examples belong to the same class or not. In this chapter, we propose a discriminative learning approach which can incorporate pairwise constraints into a conventional margin-based learning framework. Different from previous work that usually attempts to learn better distance metrics or estimate the underlying data distribution, the proposed approach can directly model the decision boundary and thus require fewer model assumptions. Moreover, the proposed approach can handle both labeled data and pairwise constraints in a unified framework. In this work, we investigate two families of pairwise loss functions, namely convex and non-convex pairwise loss functions, and then derive three pairwise learning algorithms by plugging in the hinge loss and the logistic loss functions. We also extend the learning framework to support multi-class learning and noisy pairwise constraints. The proposed learning algorithms were evaluated using a people identification task on two surveillance video data sets. The experiments demonstrated that the proposed pairwise learning

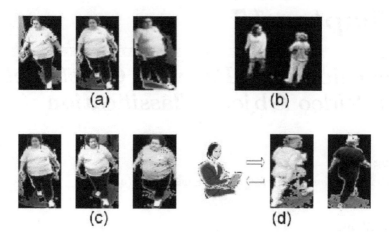

FIGURE 17.1: Examples of various pairwise constraints: (a) Temporal constraints from a single tracked sequence. (b) Temporal constraints of different regions extracted at the same time. (c) Constraints provided by comparing faces. (d) Constraints provided by user feedback.

algorithms considerably outperform the baseline classifiers using only labeled data and two other pairwise learning algorithms with the same amount of pairwise constraints.

17.1 Introduction

Learning with insufficient training data in classifying or recognizing objects or people in videos [2, 22, 25] has recently become an interesting topic for a lot of researchers [17, 9, 27, 29, 33]. To address this problem, one solution is to integrate new knowledge sources that are complementary to the insufficient training data. In this chapter, we are particularly interested in how to incorporate additional pairwise constraints to improve classification performance for video objects. The inherent characteristics of video streams, that is, the sequential continuity and multi-modalities, allow us to pose different types of constraints to boost the learning performance. Moreover, these constraints can often be obtained automatically or only with little human effort.

Figure 17.1 illustrates several examples of pairwise constraints in a scenario of classifying people's identities from surveillance video. First, pairwise constraints can be obtained from knowledge of temporal relations. For instance, two spatially overlapping regions extracted from temporally adjacent frames can be assumed to share the same labels whereas two regions appearing simultaneously in a camera cannot be labeled as the same. Second, we can extract constraints from various modalities such as visual (face) [19] and auditory (voice) cues [10]. For example, if we want to automatically identify a person's face from video sequences, conventionally we need to learn from many training examples of the same person with different head poses and under different lighting conditions. However, with the representation of pairwise constraints, we only need a face comparison algorithm to provide the pairwise relation between examples without building statistical models for every possible subject under every possible circumstance. This provides an alternative way to aggregate different modalities, especially when the training examples of people of interest are limited or not available at all. Finally, constraints can also come from human feedback. Typically the system can select and show some pairs of video sequences to a human annotator who can judge whether these examples depict the same subjects or not. Unlike the general relevance feedback process which forces users to annotate with the exact labels, asking feedback in the form of pairwise constraints does not require users to have prior knowledge or experience with the data set and in some degree it helps to protect the privacy of human subjects in the video.

In recent years, researchers have realized the usefulness of incorporating pairwise constraints into different kinds of learning algorithms. As discussed in the next section, a large amount of previous work managed to use pairwise constraints to achieve reasonable performance improvement in various tasks such as clustering [35, 30, 3, 16] and distance metrics learning (e.g. Mahalanobis, cosine distance, Bregman divergence) [24, 15, 32, 4]. However, relatively less attention has been placed on using additional pairwise constraints to support the classification (supervised learning) task. In this case, the most general method to leverage pairwise constraints is to learn a better distance metric before applying the supervised learning algorithm. But for classification, it is more natural to directly model the decision boundaries as has been done in discriminative classifiers, because the decision boundaries might be simpler to estimate even when true underlying distance metrics are either complex or against the model assumption. Moreover, since extant work usually focuses on the unsupervised learning problem, it does not need to provide a principled way to handle the labeled data. But in our case, we have to consider incorporating the labeled data into the learning framework since they are the most useful information sources available. It is infeasible to convert every pair of labeled data into pairwise constraints because this usually leads to a prohibitive computation with an unreasonably large number of constraints.

In this work, we propose a regularized discriminative learning framework which naturally incorporates pairwise constraints into a conventional margin-based learning algorithm. The proposed framework is able to use additional pairwise constraints together with labeled data to model the decision boundary directly, instead of resorting to estimating an underlying distance metric which could be much more complex. We investigate two families of pairwise loss functions, i.e., convex and non-convex pairwise loss functions under the proposed learning framework. Analogous to kernel logistic regression (KLR) [37] and support vector machines (SVMs)[28], we derive three pairwise learning algorithms by plugging in the hinge loss and the logistic loss functions into this framework. These algorithms are evaluated in the context of classifying people's identities from surveillance video.

17.2 Related Work

The classification of visual objects is a perceptual and cognitive task which is fundamental to human vision. Despite the fact that these objects may vary somewhat in shape, color, texture, etc., a human can detect and recognize a multitude of familiar and novel objects through vision without any effort. However, it is a very challenging problem for machines. Object classification has been an active research area in the computer vision community for last two decades, though problems of interest have been changing over time, from automatic target recognition (ATR) [12, 20], to optical character recognition (OCR) [26], to face detection and recognition [7]. Visual object recognition has made great progress in recent years because of advances in learning theories, which is evident in several recent chapters [9, 27, 29, 17, 25, 22].

Along another research direction, efforts have been made to help both supervised and unsupervised learning with pairwise constraints [35, 30, 24, 23, 3, 14, 15, 32, 34]. In the context of graph partitioning, Yu and Shi [35] have successfully integrated pairwise constraints into a constrained grouping framework, leading to improved segmentation results. Wagstaff et al. [30] introduced pairwise constraints into the k-means clustering algorithm for unsupervised learning problems. In more closely related work by Xing et al. [32], a distance metric learning method is proposed to incorporate pairwise information and solved by convex optimization. However, the method contains an iterative procedure with projection and eigenvalue decomposition which is computationally expensive and sensitive to parameter tuning. By comparison, relevant component analysis (RCA) [24] is a simpler and more efficient approach for learning a full Mahalanobis metric. A whitening transformation of the covariance matrix of all the center-points in the chunklets is computed as a Mahalanobis distance. However, only positive constraints can be utilized in this algorithm. In [23], Shental et al. propose a constrained Gaussian mixture model which incorporates both positive and negative pairwise constraints into a GMM model using the expectation-maximization (EM) algorithm. Basu et al. [3] studied a new approach for semi-supervised clustering by adding additional penalty terms into the objective function. They also proposed an approach to actively select the most informative constraints rather than selecting them at random. In [4], they also used pairwise constraints to learn more advanced metrics such as parameterized Bregman distances or directional distances. Kumar and Hebert [14] presented a discriminative learning framework for the classification of the image regions by incorporating interactions from neighborhood nodes together with the observed examples. Pairwise constraints have also been found useful in the context of kernel learning. Kwok and Tsang [15] formulated the kernel adaptation problem as a distance metric learning problem that searches for a suitable linear transform in the kernel-induced feature space, even if it is of infinite dimensionality.

Learning with pairwise constraints is also related to the semi-supervised learning problem, which attempts to leverage a large number of unlabeled data to boost the classifier built from a small number of labeled data. Work by Nigam et al. [18] handled the unlabeled data by using a combination of the EM algorithm [8] and a naive Bayes classifier to augment text classifiers, and demonstrated that unlabeled data can be used to improve the accuracy of text classification. Co-training [5] is one of the most well-known multi-view semi-supervised learning algorithms. The idea of co-training is to incrementally update the classifiers of multiple views which allows the redundant information across views to improve the learning performance. Lafferty et al. [38] represented the labeled and unlabeled data as the vertices in the weighted graph, where the edge weights encode the similarity between instances. For learning the part-based appearance models, Xie et al. [31] extended the GMM model to the semi-supervised case where most of positive examples are corrupted with cluster but a small fraction are uncorrupted. Compared with these semi-supervised learning algorithms, the algorithms leveraging pairwise constraints can utilize additional information about the relationship between pairs of examples other than the unlabeled data itself. Recently, Zhang and Yan [36] proposed a transformation-based learning method for learning with pairwise constraints and showed that optimal decision boundary can be consistently found as the number of pairwise constraints approaches infinity.

17.3 Discriminative Learning with Pairwise Constraints

Formally, the goal of classification is to produce a hypothesis $f : \mathcal{X} \to \mathcal{Y}$, where $\mathcal{X}$ denotes the domain of possible examples and $\mathcal{Y}$ denotes a finite set of classes. A learning algorithm typically takes a set of training examples $(x_1, y_1), ..., (x_n, y_n)$ as input, where $y_i \in \mathcal{Y}$ is the label assigned to the example $x_i \in \mathcal{X}$. In this section, we mainly consider the case of binary classes while leaving the discussions of multiple classes to Section 17.5. In addition to the data with explicit labels, there is another set of pairwise constraints (x_i, x_j, c_{ij}) constructed from both labeled and unlabeled data, where $c_{ij} \in \{-1, 1\}$ is the pairwise constraint assigned to two examples $x_i, x_j \in \mathcal{X}$. For the sake of simplicity, $(x_i, x_j, 1)$ will be called the positive constraints which means the example pair (x_i, x_j) belongs to the same class, and $(x_i, x_j, -1)$ the negative constraints which means the pair (x_i, x_j) belongs to different classes.

17.3.1   Regularized Loss Function with Pairwise Information

In the following discussion, we pay particular attention to supervised learning algorithms that attempt to minimize a margin-based loss function, called margin-based learning algorithms [11]. This includes a large family of well-studied algorithms with different loss functions and minimization algorithms, such as decision trees, logistic regression, support vector machines, and AdaBoost. The margin-based learning algorithms minimize the loss function with respect to the margin, which is,

$$\min_f R_{reg}(f) = \sum_{i=1}^{n} \widetilde{L}(y_i, f(x_i)) + \lambda \Omega(\|f\|_{\mathcal{H}}), \qquad (17.1)$$

where $\widetilde{L}$ is the empirical loss function, $\Omega(\cdot)$ is some monotonically increasing regularization function on the domain $[0, +\infty]$ which controls the complexity of the hypothesis space, $\mathcal{H}$ denotes a reproducing kernel Hilbert space (RKHS) generated by some positive definite kernel K, $\|\cdot\|_{\mathcal{H}}$ is the corresponding norms and λ is the regularization constant. The empirical loss function $\widetilde{L}(y_i, f(x_i))$ is usually set to a function of "margin" $yf(x)$ [11], i.e., $\widetilde{L}(y_i, f(x_i)) = L(y_i f(x_i))$. With different choices of loss functions and regularization terms, we can derive a large family of well-studied algorithms from equation (17.1). For example, the support vector machines (SVMs) can be viewed as a binary margin-based learning algorithm with loss function $L(z) = max(1 - z, 0)$ and regularization factor $\|w\|_2^2$ where w is the margin. To illustrate, Figure 17.2(a) shows a comparison of four different loss functions against the margin $yf(x)$, including misclassification loss $I(sgn(f) \neq y)$, exponential loss $\exp(-yf)$, hinge loss $(1 - yf)_+$, and logistic loss $\log(1 + \exp(-yf(x))$.

Under this learning framework, pairwise constraints can be introduced as another set of empirical loss functions in an attempt to penalize the violation of the given constraints,

$$\mathcal{O}(f) = \sum_{i=1}^{n} L(y_i f(x_i)) + \mu \sum_{(i,j) \in C} L'(f(x_i), c_{ij} f(x_j)) + \lambda \Omega(\|f\|_{\mathcal{H}}), \quad (17.2)$$

where we call μ pairwise factors and $L'(f(x_i), c_{ij} f(x_j))$ pairwise loss functions. In the rest of this chapter, we simplify the notation of $f(x_i)$ to be f_i and thus $L'(f(x_i), c_{ij} f(x_j))$ can be written as $L'(f_i, c_{ij} f_j)$. Eqn(17.2) enjoys the nice property that when the number of pairwise constraints n is zero, it trivially degrades to a margin-based learning problem with only the labeled data. To complete the definition of the learning framework in Eqn(17.2), we still need to determine a family of appropriate pairwise loss functions for the pair of examples. Although there are lots of ways to design the pairwise loss functions, we want to seek a family of loss functions that satisfy the following properties:

1. L' is commutable, i.e., L' have the same value when f_i and f_j exchange their positions, or equally $L'(f_i, c_{ij}f_j) = L'(f_j, c_{ij}f_i)$, because the constraints would not change if the examples exchange their positions.

2. L' is even, i.e., L' have the same value when f_i and f_j reverse their signs, or equally $L'(f_i, c_{ij}f_j) = L'(-f_i, -c_{ij}f_j)$, because the constraints would not change if the predictions reverse their signs.

3. L' has correct decision boundaries, i.e., $L' \geq L'(0,0)$ when f_i and $c_{ij}f_j$ have different signs but $L' \leq L'(0,0)$ when they have the same signs. This property ensures that the goal of minimizing the objective functions $\mathcal{O}(f)$ could provide predictions consistent with most of the given pairwise constraints.[1]

4. L' is a convex function for both f_i and $c_{ij}f_j$, i.e., the value L' at the midpoint of every interval in $[-\infty, \infty]$ does not exceed the average of its value at the end of its interval. This property indicates the existence of a unique global optimum and allows simpler parameter estimation methods.

Both property 3 and 4 are important. Property 3 essentially implies that the desired solution can be obtained by seeking the minimum expected loss, where the expectation is taken with respect to the distribution of pairwise constraints. On the other hand, property 4 implies that we are able to find the optimal solution as the number of pairwise constraints approaches infinity. Unfortunately, it can be shown that the last two properties conflict with each other. That is to say, no matter how you design pairwise loss functions, it is impossible for them to have correct decision boundaries and be convex at the same time [34].[2] As a trade-off, we have to determine which of these two properties is supposed to be satisfied. In the rest of this section, we describe two possible families of pairwise loss functions and discuss their relationships: one is the non-convex pairwise loss functions which have correct decision boundaries, the other is the convex pairwise loss functions with incorrect decision boundaries.

---

[1]Note that we only consider the non-trivial case that for each inequality there is at least one point where the inequality is strictly satisfied.

[2]However, in our recent work [36] we constructed a transformation-based method which can find the optimal classification boundary consistently. This method cannot be covered by the formulation in Eqn(17.2).

17.3.2 Non-Convex Pairwise Loss Functions

In order to provide a family of pairwise loss functions which are commutable, even, and also have the correct decision boundary, the simplest case is to choose the binary loss function analogous to the misclassification loss,

$$L'_{binary} = I(sgn[f_i] \neq sgn[c_{ij}f_j]),$$

which gives a unit penalty for violation of pairwise constraints and no penalties otherwise. Although minimizing this exact misclassification loss may be worthwhile, it is generally intractable to optimize because of its discontinuity. Even worse, it is not able to penalize large errors more heavily.

To provide a continuous family of pairwise loss functions, we introduce the following non-convex pairwise loss functions,

$$L'_{nonconv} = L''(f_i) + L''(c_{ij}f_j) - L''(f_i + c_{ij}f_j)$$

where $L''(x) = L'(x) + L'(-x)$ and $L'(x)$ can be any convex loss function such as the logistic loss and the hinge loss function. To ensure the empirical loss function and pairwise loss function are comparable, we usually choose L' in the same form as L and thus $L''(x) = L(x) + L(-x)$. Therefore the primal optimization problem has the following form,

$$\sum_{i=1}^{n} L(y_i f_i) + \mu \sum_{(i,j) \in C} (L''(f_i) + L''(c_{ij}f_j) - L''(f_i + c_{ij}f_j)) + \lambda\Omega(\|f\|_{\mathcal{H}}). \quad (17.3)$$

It has been proven that $L'_{nonconv}$ is commutable, even, and has correct decision boundaries under some general conditions [34]. Two additional advantages make it a preferred choice compared to the binary loss function. First, $L'_{nonconv}$ is able to place more penalties on larger errors. Second, its continuity allows efficient optimization approaches to be applied such as the EM algorithm and quadratic programming. However, the function of $L'_{nonconv}$ is no longer convex and thus it is possible for the optimization algorithm to get trapped in a local optimum.

17.3.3 Convex Pairwise Loss Functions

This section considers the family of convex pairwise loss functions based on the intuition that the prediction difference of two examples, i.e., $f_i - c_{ij}f_j$, can be a "soft" measure of how possible the pairwise constraints would be violated. Therefore we choose loss function L' to be a monotonic decreasing function of prediction difference $f_i - c_{ij}f_j$, i.e., $\widehat{L}'(f_i - c_{ij}f_j)$, which plays a similar role as the residues $y - f(x)$ in regression. Meanwhile, the pairwise loss function should be symmetric for any example pair and therefore $\widehat{L}'$ could be represented as $\widehat{L}'(x) = \widehat{L}(x) + \widehat{L}(-x)$, where $\widehat{L}$ now can be any monotonic decreasing function $f : \mathcal{X} \to \mathbf{R}$. By choosing $\widehat{L}$ to be empirical loss function L, we obtain the convex pairwise loss function[3]

$$L'_{conv} = L(f_i - c_{ij}f_j) + L(c_{ij}f_j - f_i),$$

and the corresponding primal optimization problem,

$$\sum_{i=1}^{n} L(y_i f_i) + \mu \sum_{(i,j)\in C} (L(f_i - c_{ij}f_j) + L(c_{ij}f_j - f_i)) + \lambda\Omega(\|f\|_{\mathcal{H}}).\ (17.4)$$

When $L(x)$ is convex to x (true for most loss functions), it is not difficult to verify that the pairwise loss function L'_{conv} is also convex to f_i and f_j, which allows us to apply standard convex optimization techniques to solve the primal optimization problem. Generally speaking, minimizing a convex pairwise loss function is much more efficient than minimizing a non-convex pairwise loss function, which comes at the price that L'_{conv} cannot provide the correct decision boundaries. But this disadvantage can be largely overcome by the fact that L'_{conv} actually serves as a convex upper bound of $L'_{nonconv}$ [34]. The upper bound is usually tight because L'_{conv} and $L'_{nonconv}$ are equal if and only if $f_i = -c_{ij}f_j$. This property guarantees the global optimum of the corresponding convex objective functions in Eqn(17.4), although they have incorrect decision boundaries, can still provide a reasonable approximation for the optimum of the non-convex objective functions in Eqn(17.3).

A special case for Eqn(17.4) is to fit a linear decision boundary on the input feature space, i.e., $f(x)$ can be expressed in the form of $w^T x$ and $\|f\|_{\mathcal{H}} = \|w\|$ in the L_2 space. Substituting $f(x) = w^T x$ and $\|f\|_{\mathcal{H}} = \|w\|$ into Eqn(17.4), we have

$$\sum_{i=1}^{n} L(y_i w^T x_i) + \mu \sum_{(i,j)\in C} \left\{ L(w^T(x_i - c_{ij}x_j)) + L(w^T(c_{ij}x_j - x_i)) \right\} + \lambda\Omega(\|w\|).$$

It can be shown that this objective function with $\mu = 1$ is equivalent to the objective function of Eqn(17.1) with an expanded labeled data set, which includes $2n$ pseudo-labeled data $(x = x_i - c_{ij}x_j, y = 1)$ and $(x = x_i - c_{ij}x_j, y = -1)$ in addition to the original labeled data. This property is intriguing because it allows an easier implementation for linear kernel classifiers by means of adding $2n$ new training examples without modifying existing algorithms or software packages.

---

[3]This function has another interpretation as follows. For a pairwise constraint (x_i, x_j, c_{ij}), we would like to penalize two cases based on the predictions: 1. $f_i > 0$ and $c_{ij}f_j < 0$; 2. $f_i < 0$ and $c_{ij}f_j > 0$. If we use $L(f_i - c_{ij}f_j)$ to penalize the first case and $L(c_{ij}f_j - f_i)$ for the second case, we have exactly the pairwise loss function described above.

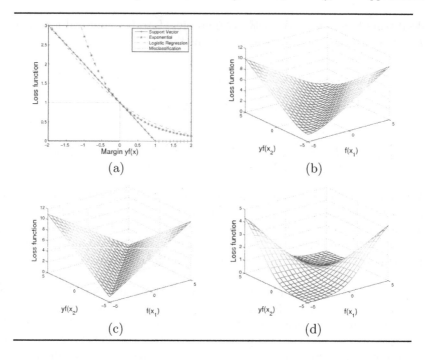

FIGURE 17.2: A comparison of loss functions: (a) A comparison of four different loss functions against margin $yf(x)$. The losses are misclassification loss $I(sgn(f) \neq y)$, exponential loss $exp(-yf)$, support vector loss $(1 - yf)_+$ and logistic regression loss $log(1 + exp(-yf(x)))$. (b) The pairwise loss function in CPKLR against $f(x_1)$ and $yf(x_2)$. (c) The pairwise loss function in CPSVM against $f(x_1)$ and $yf(x_2)$. (d) The pairwise loss function in NPKLR against $f(x_1)$ and $yf(x_2)$.

17.4 Algorithms

In this section, we substitute two widely applied loss functions, i.e., the logistic loss function and hinge loss function, into both the non-convex pairwise objective functions in Eqn(17.3) and the convex pairwise objective functions in Eqn(17.4). We derive three different but closely related learning algorithms from the proposed discriminative learning framework, i.e., convex pairwise kernel logistic regression (CPKLR), convex pairwise support vector machines (CPSVM) and non-convex pairwise kernel logistic regression (NPKLR). In the following, we describe these three algorithms in more details, present their optimization approaches, and conclude with an illustrative example.

17.4.1   Convex Pairwise Kernel Logistic Regression (CPKLR)

We begin our discussion by considering convex pairwise objective functions in Eqn(17.4), which can be easily solved by convex optimization techniques. In the first algorithm, we adopt the logistic regression loss function $L(x) = \log(1 + e^{-x})$ as the empirical loss function, yielding

$$\mathcal{O}(f) = \sum_{i=1}^{n} \log(1 + e^{-y_i f(x_i)}) + \mu \sum_{(i,j) \in C} \log(1 + e^{f(x_i) - c_{ij} f(x_j)})$$

$$+ \mu \sum_{(i,j) \in C} \log(1 + e^{c_{ij} f(x_j) - f(x_i)}) + \lambda \Omega(\|f\|_{\mathcal{H}}). \quad (17.5)$$

Figure 17.2(b) depicts the pairwise loss function used in Eqn(17.5). In the following discussions, we present the kernelized representation of the primal problem Eqn(17.5) using the representer theorem [13]. This representation allows simple learning algorithms to construct a complex decision boundary by projecting the original input space to a high dimensional feature space, even infinitely dimensional in some cases. This seemingly computationally intensive task can be easily achieved through a positive definite reproducing kernel K and the well-known "kernel trick." To begin, let $R(\cdot)$ represent the empirical loss and $\Omega(\|f\|_{\mathcal{H}}) = \|f\|_{\mathcal{H}}^2$. Therefore, the primal problem Eqn(17.5) can be rewritten as,

$$\min_{f \in \mathcal{H}} R(\{y_i, f(x_i)\}, \{c_{ij}, f(x_i), f(x_j)\}) + \lambda \|f\|_{\mathcal{H}}^2. \quad (17.6)$$

The loss function $R(\cdot)$ is pointwise, which only depends on the value of f at the data points $\{f(x_i), f(x_i), f(x_j)\}$. Therefore by the representer theorem, the minimizer $f(x)$ admits a representation of the form

$$f(\cdot) = \sum_{i=1}^{n'} \alpha_i K(\cdot, \bar{x}_i)), \quad (17.7)$$

where $n' = n + 2|C|$, $\bar{x}_i \in \{x_i\}_{i=1...n} \cup \{(x_i, x_j)\}_{(i,j) \in C}$ is an expanded training set including labeled examples x_i and examples from every pairwise constraints $\{x_i, x_j\}$.

In the following, denote by $\mathbf{K}$ the $n' \times n'$ Gram matrix. Moreover, denote by $\mathbf{K}_l$ an $n \times n'$ matrix containing top n rows of $\mathbf{K}$ corresponding to x_i, i.e., $\mathbf{K}_l = [\mathbf{K}(x_i, \bar{x}_j)]_{n \times n'}$. Similarly, denote by $\mathbf{K}_{l1}$ and $\mathbf{K}_{l2}$ the $|C| \times n'$ matrices containing $|C|$ rows of $\mathbf{K}$ corresponding to x_i and x_j, respectively. We derive the kernelized representation of logistic regression loss function by substituting Eqn(17.7) into Eqn(17.5),

$$R(\alpha) = \vec{\mathbf{1}}^T \log(1 + e^{-\mathbf{K}_p \alpha}) + \mu \cdot \vec{\mathbf{1}}^T \log(1 + e^{\mathbf{K}'_p \alpha})$$

$$+ \mu \cdot \vec{\mathbf{1}}^T \log(1 + e^{-\mathbf{K}'_p \alpha}) + \lambda \alpha \mathbf{K} \alpha, \quad (17.8)$$

where $\alpha = \{\alpha_1 \ldots \alpha_{n+2|C|}\}$, the regressor matrix $\mathbf{K}_p = diag(y_1 \ldots y_n)\mathbf{K}_l$, and the pairwise regressor matrix $\mathbf{K}'_p = \mathbf{K}_{l1} - diag(c_1 \ldots c_{|C|})\mathbf{K}_{l2}$.

To find the minimizer α, we derive the parameter estimation method using the interior-reflective Newton method to iteratively solve the equation. Since the optimization function is convex, the Newton method can guarantee the finding of the global optimum. The gradient and Hessian of the objective function are as follows,

$$\frac{\partial R(\alpha)}{\partial \alpha} = \mathbf{K}_p^T \mathbf{p} + \mu(\mathbf{K}'^T_p \mathbf{p} - \mathbf{K}'^T_p(1 - \mathbf{p})) + 2\lambda \mathbf{K}^T \alpha, \qquad (17.9)$$

$$\frac{\partial^2 R(\alpha)}{\partial \alpha^2} = \mathbf{K}_p^T \mathbf{W} \mathbf{K}_p + 2\mu \mathbf{K}'^T_p \mathbf{W}' \mathbf{K}_p + 2\lambda \mathbf{K}^T, \qquad (17.10)$$

where $p(x), p'(x)$ denote the logistic model

$$\mathbf{p}(x) = \frac{e^{\mathbf{K}_p \alpha}}{1 + e^{\mathbf{K}_p \alpha}}, \mathbf{p}'(x) = \frac{e^{\mathbf{K}'_p \alpha}}{1 + e^{\mathbf{K}'_p \alpha}},$$

and $\mathbf{W}, \mathbf{W}'$ denote the corresponding weighted matrices $diag(\mathbf{p}(x_i)(1 - \mathbf{p}(x_i)))$ and $diag(\mathbf{p}'(x_i)(1 - \mathbf{p}'(x_i)))$. It can be shown that the Newton updates are

$$\alpha \leftarrow \alpha - \left(\frac{\partial^2 R(\alpha)}{\partial \alpha^2}\right)^{-1} \frac{\partial R(\alpha)}{\partial \alpha}.$$

In practice, we solve this optimization problem with a subspace trust region method based on the interior-reflective Newton method described in [6]. Finally, the prediction is made by,

$$Pred(x) = \log \left\{ 1 + \exp\left(-\sum_{i=1}^{n'} \alpha_i \mathbf{K}(\bar{x}_i, x)\right) \right\}.$$

In the rest of this chapter, we will call this learning algorithm convex pairwise kernel logistic regression (CPKLR).

17.4.2   Convex Pairwise Support Vector Machines (CPSVM)

The second type of convex pairwise objective functions to be discussed is derived from the hinge loss function $L(x) = (1-x)_+$ by analogy to the SVMs. As the first step of construction, we plug the hinge loss into the convex pairwise loss function, yielding

$$\begin{aligned} L_{conv} &= (1 + f_i - c_{ij}f_j)_+ + (1 - f_i + c_{ij}f_j)_+ \\ &= \max(2, 1 + f_i - c_{ij}f_j, 1 - f_i + c_{ij}f_j). \end{aligned} \qquad (17.11)$$

It can be found that the loss function of Eqn(17.11) is invariant to the shifts of f_i, f_j as long as the condition $-1 \le f_i - c_{ij}f_j \le 1$ holds. However, we prefer the pairwise loss function to be more sensitive to the violation of constraints even when their decision outputs are close to each other. Therefore we modify the L_{conv} to be the following form,

$$L_{conv} = \max((1 + f_i - c_{ij}f_j)_+, (1 - f_i + c_{ij}f_j)_+)$$
$$= \max(1 + f_i - c_{ij}f_j, 1 - f_i + c_{ij}f_j) = 1 + |f_i - c_{ij}f_j|. \quad (17.12)$$

Obviously, we can show that L_{conv} in Eqn(17.12) are still convex but more sensitive to the constraint violation. Figure 17.2(c) plots the pairwise loss function used in Eqn(17.12). By substituting this pairwise loss function into the optimization objective function and ignoring the constant terms, we have,

$$\mathcal{O}(f) = \sum_{i=1}^{n} (1 - y_i f(x_i))_+ +$$
$$\mu \sum_{(i,j) \in C} |f(x_i) - c_{ij}f(x_j)| + \lambda \Omega(\|f\|_{\mathcal{H}}). \quad (17.13)$$

Let us first consider the family of linear prediction functions where $f(x) = w^T x$. In this case, by replacing the absolute and the hinge loss functions, we can get the primal optimization form as follows,

$$\min \sum_{i=1}^{n} \xi_i + \mu \sum_{(i,j) \in C} \eta_{ij} + \lambda w^T w$$
$$s.t. \ \xi_i \geq 1 - y_i w^T x_i, \ \xi_i \geq 0, \ i = 1..n$$
$$\eta_{ij} \geq w^T x_i - c_{ij} w^T x_j,$$
$$\eta_{ij} \geq -w^T x_i + c_{ij} w^T x_j, \ (i, j) \in C. \quad (17.14)$$

We take the Lagrangian as usual to get the dual form,

$$\mathcal{L}(w, \xi, \eta, \alpha, \beta, \gamma) = \sum_{i=1}^{n} \xi_i + \mu \sum_{(i,j) \in C} \eta_{ij} + \lambda w^T w + \sum_{i=1}^{n} \alpha_i (1 - y_i w^T x_i - \xi_i) - \sum_{i=1}^{n} \beta_i \xi_i$$
$$+ \sum_{(i,j) \in C} \gamma_{ij}^+ (w^T x_i - c_{ij} w^T x_j - \eta_{ij}) + \sum_{(i,j) \in C} \gamma_{ij}^- (-w^T x_i + c_{ij} w^T x_j - \eta_{ij}).$$

By setting all the derivatives of the Lagrangian with respect to the primal variables to be zero, we have

$$1 = \alpha_i + \beta_i, \quad (17.15)$$
$$\mu = \gamma_{ij}^+ + \gamma_{ij}^-, \quad (17.16)$$
$$-2\lambda w = -\sum_{i=1}^{n} \alpha_i y_i x_i + \sum_{(i,j) \in C} (\gamma_{ij}^+ - \gamma_{ij}^-) x_i + \sum_{(i,j) \in C} (-c_{ij}\gamma_{ij}^+ + c_{ij}\gamma_{ij}^-) x_j$$
$$= -\sum_{i=1}^{n} \alpha_i y_i x_i + \sum_{(i,j) \in C} (\gamma_{ij}^+ - \gamma_{ij}^-)(x_i - c_{ij}x_j). \quad (17.17)$$

According to the Karush-Kuhn-Tucker (KKT) dual-complementarity condition, we have $\alpha_i, \beta_i, \gamma_{ij}^+, \gamma_{ij}^- > 0$. By plugging the above equations back into the Lagrangian and denoting $\gamma_{ij} = \gamma_{ij}^+ - \gamma_{ij}^-$, the dual form can be rewritten as,

$$\sum_{i=1}^{n} \alpha_i - \frac{1}{4\lambda} \sum_{i,j=1}^{n} \alpha_i \alpha_j y_i y_j \mathbf{K}(x_i, x_j)$$

$$+ \frac{1}{4\lambda} \sum_{(i,j),(i',j') \in C}$$

$$\{\gamma_{ij} \gamma_{i'j'} [\mathbf{K}(x_i, x_{i'}) + c_{ij} c_{i'j'} \mathbf{K}(x_j, x_{j'}) - c_{ij} \mathbf{K}(x_j, x_{i'}) - c_{i'j'} \mathbf{K}(x_i, x_{j'})]\}$$

$$- \frac{1}{2\lambda} \sum_{i=1}^{n} \sum_{(i',j') \in C} \alpha_i y_i \gamma_{i'j'} [\mathbf{K}(x_i, x_{i'}) - c_{i'j'} \mathbf{K}(x_i, x_{j'})], \qquad (17.18)$$

subject to the following conditions,

$$0 \leq \alpha_i, \alpha_j \leq 1, \quad i, j = 1..n$$

$$-\mu \leq \gamma_{ij}, \gamma_{i'j'} \leq \mu, \quad (i,j), (i',j') \in C$$

where the kernel function $\mathbf{K}(x_i, x_j)$ is the inner product of x_i and x_j, i.e., $\langle x_i, x_j \rangle$. We can find that the dual objective function only relies on the inner product of the input variables. Therefore we can place any kind of positive definite kernel function into Eqn(17.18) and allow it to produce non-linear predictions even in infinite dimensions. This quadratic programming problem can be solved by modifying the sequential minimal optimization (SMO) algorithm [21]. After the dual objective is optimized, w can be computed with Eqn(17.17) and the prediction is made by,

$$Pred(x) = \frac{1}{2\lambda} \left\{ \sum_{i=1}^{n} \alpha_i y_i \mathbf{K}(x_i, x) - \sum_{(i,j) \in C} \gamma_{ij} [\mathbf{K}(x_i, x) - c_{ij} \mathbf{K}(x_j, x)] \right\}.$$

In the rest of this chapter, we will call this learning algorithm convex pairwise support vector machines (CPSVM). This algorithm is efficient because its dual form only contains $n + |C|$ number of variables.

17.4.3 Non-Convex Pairwise Kernel Logistic Regression (NPKLR)

Until now, we mainly studied the variants of the convex pairwise loss functions and their corresponding pairwise learning algorithms, i.e., the CPKLR and CPSVM algorithms. Both algorithms are computationally efficient and guaranteed to converge to the global optimum because of the convexity of their loss functions. However, their classification performances are likely to be degraded due to the drawback that they cannot provide correct decision boundaries.

In this section, we investigate the third type of the pairwise objective functions which is derived from the family of non-convex pairwise loss functions $L_{nonconv}$ with the logistic loss function $L(x) = \log(1 + e^{-x})$. By substituting the logistic loss into Eqn(17.3), our optimization goal becomes minimizing the following objective function

$$\mathcal{O}(f) = \sum_{i=1}^{n} \log(1 + e^{-y_i f(x_i)}) + \lambda\Omega(\|f\|_{\mathcal{H}})$$
$$+ \mu \sum_{(i,j)\in C} \left\{ \log(1 + e^{c_{ij}f(x_j)}) + \log(1 + e^{f(x_i)}) - \log(1 + e^{f(x_i)+c_{ij}f(x_j)}) \right\}.$$

In contrast to convex pairwise loss functions, the non-convex pairwise loss function above can provide correct decision boundaries and hopefully produce more accurate predictions than its convex counterpart. With some further manipulations for the objective function, we can derive an equivalent form as follows,

$$\mathcal{O}(f) = -\sum_{i=1}^{m} \log\left(\frac{1}{1 + e^{-y_i f(x_i)}}\right) + \lambda\Omega(\|f\|_{\mathcal{H}}) \tag{17.19}$$
$$-\mu \sum_{(i,j)\in C} \log\left(\frac{1}{1 + e^{f(x_i)}} \frac{1}{1 + e^{c_{ij}f(x_j)}} + \frac{1}{1 + e^{-f(x_i)}} \frac{1}{1 + e^{-c_{ij}f(x_j)}}\right).$$

This formulation naturally provides a Bayesian interpretation for the proposed objective function. Let $P(y|x)$ denote the conditional probability for an example pair (x, y), $P(c|x_1, x_2)$ denote the conditional probability for a constraint pair (x_1, x_2, c), and y_1, y_2 denote the labels of (x_1, x_2). The posterior mode of the parameters θ can be written as,

$$\arg\max_{\theta} p(\theta|x, y, c) = \arg\max_{\theta} p(\theta)\mathcal{L}(\theta)$$
$$= \arg\max_{\theta} \left(\log p(\theta) + \log \mathcal{L}(\theta)\right). \tag{17.20}$$

The first term $\log p(\theta)$ is the logarithm of the prior probability for parameters θ. If we assume the prior probability $p(\theta)$ to be proportional to the exponential function $e^{-n\lambda\Omega(\|f\|_{\mathcal{H}})}$, we can recover the regularization term in Eqn(17.19). The second term above is the log-likelihood for all examples and constraints where,

$$\log \mathcal{L}(\theta) = \sum_{i=1}^{n} \log P(y_i|x_i; \theta) + \sum_{(i,j)\in C} \log P(c_{ij}|x_i, x_j; \theta). \tag{17.21}$$

The sample space which satisfy the constraint (x_1, x_2, c) can be partitioned into two mutually exclusive events. One is the event of $y_1 = 1$ and $y_2 = c$, and the other is the event of $y_1 = -1$ and $y_2 = -c$. By assuming the prediction of x_1 and x_2 are independent to each other, we obtain

$$P(c_{ij}|x_i, x_j; \theta) = P(y_i = 1|x_i; \theta)P(y_j = c_{ij}|x_j; \theta)$$
$$+ P(y_i = -1|x_i; \theta)P(y_j = -c_{ij}|x_j; \theta). \qquad (17.22)$$

Similar to logistic regression, the conditional probability $P(y|x)$ can be represented as the sigmoid function $1/(1+\exp(-yf(x)))$. By substituting Eqn(17.22) and Eqn(17.21) into Eqn(17.20) we can exactly recover to the formulation of the non-convex pairwise loss function in Eqn(17.19) except the additional weight μ in Eqn(17.19) allows more flexibility in the implementation.

The major difficulty for explicitly minimizing the optimization objectives lies in the log-sum form of the pairwise loss function. Therefore, we apply the expectation-maximization (EM) algorithm [8] to iteratively optimize the objective function. For each constraint pair (x_i, x_j, c_{ij}) we define z_i, z_j as the hidden variable where only one of them is 1 and the other is 0. So $E(z_i) + E(z_j) = 1$ where $E(z)$ is the expectation of z and here $E(z) = P(z = 1)$. The EM algorithm can proceed as follows,

E-step: For each $(i, j) \in C$, set the hidden variables to be

$$E(z_i) = \left(1 + e^{f(x_i)} \cdot e^{f(z_i x_j)}\right)^{-1},$$

$$E(z_j) = \left(1 + e^{-f(x_i)} \cdot e^{-f(z_i x_j)}\right)^{-1}.$$

M-step: Maximize the objective function $-\mathcal{O}(f)$ given hidden variables,

$$\theta = \arg\max_{\theta} \sum_{i=1}^{n} \log\left(\frac{1}{1 + e^{-y_i f(x_i)}}\right) - \lambda\Omega(\|f\|_{\mathcal{H}})$$

$$+ \mu \sum_{(i,j)\in C} \left[E(z_i) \log\left(\frac{1}{1 + e^{f(x_i)}} \frac{1}{1 + e^{c_{ij}f(x_j)}}\right)\right]$$

$$+ \mu \sum_{(i,j)\in C} \left[E(z_j) \log\left(\frac{1}{1 + e^{-f(x_i)}} \frac{1}{1 + e^{-c_{ij}f(x_j)}}\right)\right].$$

The M-step can actually be solved as a weighted logistic regression problem. If $f(x)$ belongs to the family of linear prediction functions the M-step can be solved by any gradient descent method. The kernel version of the algorithm can be derived by modifying the M-step to be weighted kernel logistic regression using the same technique presented in Section 17.4.1.

In the rest of this chapter, we will call the learning algorithm above non-convex pairwise kernel logistic regression (NPKLR). The NPKLR algorithm is less efficient than its convex counterpart because it needs to run multiple iterations of kernel logistic regression containing $n + 4|C|$ examples.

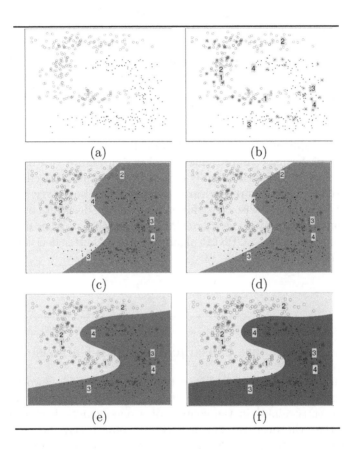

FIGURE 17.3: An illustration of the pairwise learning algorithms applied to the synthetic data: (a) The synthetic data set. (b) The labeled examples and pairwise constraints. "o" and "·" denote positive and negative examples, "∗" denotes training data, and each pair of framed numbers denotes positive constraints. (c) The decision boundary of KLR. (d) The decision boundary of KLR in the metric space learned by RCA. (e) The decision boundary of CPKLR. (f) The decision boundary of NPKLR.

17.4.4 An Illustrative Example

To show the advantages of incorporating pairwise constraints into the framework of discriminative learning, we prepared a synthetic spiral data set shown in Figure 17.3(a) which is non-linearly separable. There are a total of 201 positive examples and 199 negative examples. Forty training examples are randomly sampled from each class. An additional 4 pairs of positive constraints are also provided on the data set as shown in 17.3(b). We use kernel logistic regression(KLR) as the underlying learning algorithm.

As shown in Figure 17.3(c), with only the labeled data the conventional KLR algorithm misclassifies the tails of two spirals due to insufficient labeled data. The additional positive constraints might be useful to correct the bias. However, applying the RCA algorithm [24] with these constraints only leads to slight performance improvement as shown in Figure 17.3(d), since the true distance metric cannot be simply modeled by a Mahalanobis distance. In contrast, the CPKLR algorithm learns a much better boundary shown in Figure 17.3(e) by using pairwise constraints to model the decision boundary directly. The non-convex cousin, i.e., the NPKLR algorithm, further provides a slight improvement over the CPKLR algorithm with a better decision boundary as shown in Figure 17.3(f).

17.5 Multi-Class Classification with Pairwise Constraints

In the following discussions we extend our learning framework to the multi-class classification. As a first step, it is worthwhile to consider how to present pairwise constraints[4] in the context of a one-against-all classifier, where it means that the positive class is a certain object and the negative class is less-defined anything else. Positive constraints still hold in this case because if data pairs are considered the same object they must belong to the same class. However, negative constraints, which means two examples are different objects, can no longer be interpreted as that two examples are in different classes because it might be the case they both belong to the negative class. Therefore for negative constraints, we can only penalize the cases where they are both labeled as positive. Thus, the modified convex pairwise loss function

---

[4]Note that in multi-class object classification, a pairwise constraint indicates whether a pair of examples are the same object or not, instead of whether they belong to the same positive/negative class in a one-against-all classifier.

can be defined as,

$$\mathcal{O}(f) = \sum_i L(y_i f_i) + \mu \sum_{c_{ij}=-1} L(-f_i - f_j)$$
$$+ \mu \sum_{c_{ij}=1} (L(f_i - f_j) + L(f_j - f_i)) + \lambda\Omega(\|f\|_{\mathcal{H}}), \qquad (17.23)$$

where f_i denotes $f(x_i)$. Similarly the modified non-convex pairwise loss function can be defined as,

$$\mathcal{O}(f) = \sum_i L(y_i f_i) + \mu \sum_{c_{ij}=-1} (L(-f_i) + L(-f_j) - \frac{1}{2}L''(f_i - f_j))$$
$$+ \mu \sum_{c_{ij}=1} (L''(f_i) + L''(f_j) - L''(f_i + f_j)) + \lambda\Omega(\|f\|_{\mathcal{H}}). \qquad (17.24)$$

One-against-all classifiers allow the learning algorithm to handle new types of objects in the test set by classifying every unseen object into the negative class. This is important because in the testing phase there are always some unseen objects to predict especially when the number of the training examples is small.

Under this one-against-all representation, we can simply extend our algorithm to multi-class classification with some output coding schemes. We choose a loss-based output coding scheme to construct a multi-class classifier using multiple binary classifiers [1],

$$\hat{y} = \arg\min_r \sum_{s=1}^{S} L_M (m_{rs} f_s(x)),$$

where S is the number of binary classification problems, s is their indices, r is the class index, m_{rs} is the elements of coding matrix, and $f_s(x)$ is the prediction for x using classifier s. The loss function L_M we choose is the same as $L(x)$. M is the one-against-all coding matrix here. Note that if only positive constraints are available, we can also use the other coding schemes as long as there are no zero entries in the coding matrices, such as ECOC coding schemes.

17.6 Noisy Pairwise Constraints

We extend the proposed algorithms to incorporate noisy pairwise constraints. This extension is important for video object classification, because pairwise constraints can be mistakenly constructed due to automatic recognition errors or manual annotation errors. To handle noisy constraints, we introduce an additional noise factor, w_{ij}, to model the confidence on how likely the constraint (x_i, x_j, c_{ij}) will be correctly identified. The noise factor can simply be multiplied with the pairwise loss function in order to degrade their influence when the pairwise constraints are not sufficiently accurate. For example, if we plug the noise factor into CPKLR as shown in Eqn(17.5), the modified optimization objective function can be rewritten as,

$$\mathcal{O}(f) = \sum_{i=1}^{n} \log(1 + e^{-y_i f(x_i)}) + \mu \sum_{(i,j) \in C} w_{ij} \log(1 + e^{f(x_i) - c_{ij} f(x_j)})$$
$$+ \mu \sum_{(i,j) \in C} w_{ij} \log(1 + e^{c_{ij} f(x_j) - f(x_i)}) + \lambda \Omega(\|f\|_{\mathcal{H}}), \quad (17.25)$$

The idea of noise factors can also be applied in the other forms of pairwise learning algorithms proposed in this chapter, but we are not going to elaborate here. These factors are usually determined before the learning process. In practice, we can obtain the values of w_{ij} based on user studies on the manual labeling process or performance analysis on automatic tracking algorithms. The kernelized representation of the empirical loss function can be derived based on the representer theorem as follows,

$$R(\alpha) = \vec{\mathbf{1}}^T \log(1 + e^{-\mathbf{K}_p \alpha}) + \mu \cdot \vec{\mathbf{w}}^T \log(1 + e^{\mathbf{K}'_p \alpha})$$
$$+ \mu \cdot \vec{w}^T \log(1 + e^{-\mathbf{K}'_p \alpha}) + \lambda \alpha \mathbf{K} \alpha, \quad (17.26)$$

where $\vec{\mathbf{w}}$ is the vector of all the noise factors, $\alpha = \{\alpha_1 \ldots \alpha_{n+2|C|}\}$, the regressor matrix $\mathbf{K}_p = diag(y_1 \ldots y_n)\mathbf{K}_l$, and the pairwise regressor matrix $\mathbf{K}'_p = \mathbf{K}_{l1} - diag(c_1 \ldots c_{|C|})\mathbf{K}_{l2}$. To solve the optimization problem, we apply the interior-reflective Newton methods to obtain a global optimum. In the rest of this chapter, we term this type of learning algorithms as weighted pairwise kernel logistic regression (WPKLR).

17.7 Experiments

In the experiments that follow, we applied the three proposed pairwise learning algorithms to the task of classifying people identities on two data sets from real-world surveillance video. First, we introduce how we collect and preprocess the data of people identities, followed by discussing the strategies to select a limited number of pairwise constraints from the video. Finally we describe the experimental setting and evaluate the results using various pairwise learning algorithms.

17.7.1   Data Collections and Preprocessing

To examine the performance of the proposed algorithms, we collected two different data sets from a geriatric nursing home surveillance video. One data set was extracted from a 6 hour long, single-day and single view video. The other data set was extracted from video across 6 consecutive days from the same camera view. Both collections were sampled at a resolution of 320 × 240 and a rate of 30 frames per second. The moving sequences of subjects were automatically extracted using a background subtraction tracker. The silhouette images, each of which corresponds to the extracted silhouette of a moving subject, are sampled from the tracking sequence every half second. In this experiment, we mainly experimented on images that did not have any foreground segments containing two or more people. Finally, we obtain the single-day data set with 63 tracking sequences or 363 silhouette images for 6 subjects, and the multiple-day data set with 156 tracking sequences or 1118 silhouette images for 5 subjects.

Because of the relative robustness of color histograms to appearance variations, we represent the silhouette images using a histogram of HSV color spaces in all of our experiments, where each color channel has a fixed number of 32 bins. Thus we have a total of 96 one-dimensional features in the histogram. Sample images from both data sets are depicted in Figure 17.4. Taking a closer look at these examples, it can be found that the silhouette images are collected from various lighting environments and the subjects walked in arbitrary directions. For each subject, the color representation is relatively stable in the single-day data set, but it is much more diverse in the multiple-day data set which makes learning more difficult. Note that the specific color histogram representation seems to be quite simplistic from the viewpoint of the video-based people identification problem, but we adopt these sets of features due to their robustness to our applications and sufficiency to illustrate the power of the proposed learning algorithms.

17.7.2   Selecting Informative Pairwise Constrains from Video

As mentioned in Section 17.1, there are several types of pairwise constraints that can be extracted from a video stream. In this chapter, we pay particular attention to two types of pairwise constraints:

- Temporal Constraints: This type of constraint is obtained by knowing the temporal relation in video sequences. For example, a sequence of extracted regions generated from tracking a single moving object can be assumed to indicate a single person. On the other hand, two regions extracted simultaneously from a camera cannot be the same person.

- Active Constraints: In analogy to active learning paradigms, this type of constraint is obtained from users' feedback. Typically, the system

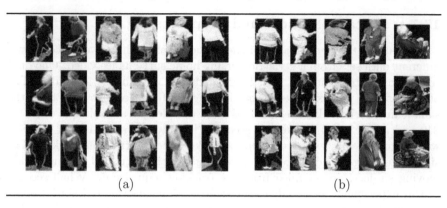

(a)   (b)

FIGURE 17.4: Examples of images from the data sets collected from a geriatric nursing home. (a) Examples of 6 subjects in the single-day data set. Each column refers to a different subject. (b) Examples of 5 subjects in the multiple-day data set.

gives users the most ambiguous pairs of examples and users provide the label of positive/negative constraints as feedback.

However, even only considering two types of constraints, there are always too many pairwise constraints available for the video data. For example, if there are 10^3 training images in the data set, all possible pairwise constraints between them is close to $5 * 10^5$ which is unaffordable for most of the learning algorithms. To address this, we would like to select the most informative pairwise constraints before applying the proposed learning algorithm. One useful observation to reduce the number of constraints is that surveillance video data generally arrive in the form of image tracking sequences. If we want to model all the constraints between every image pair of tracking sequences G_1 and G_2 for convex pairwise loss functions, Eqn(17.3) will be expanded to a sum of $|G_1||G_2|$ terms,

$$L'(f(G_1), cf(G_2)) = \sum_{i=1}^{|G_1|} \sum_{j=1}^{|G_2|} L'(f(x_i), c_{ij} f(x_j))$$

for every $x_i \in G_1$ and $x_j \in G_2$.[5] In the case when either $|G_1|$ or $|G_2|$ is large, the computational effort will be very prohibitive. However, it is reasonable to assume that the images in a single sequence are similar to each other and thus the pairwise constraints $(x_i, x_j), x_i \in G_1, x_j \in G_2$ are probably redundant.

---

[5]Note that G_1 and G_2 can be the same sequence G, which refers to modeling the self-similarity of sequence G.

Given this assumption, we approximate all of the sequence constraints with the centroids μ_i which is the mean color histogram of every sequence of images. Therefore, we have the following pairwise loss function: when $G_1 = G_2 = G$,

$$L'(f(G_1), cf(G_2)) = \sum_{i=1}^{|G|} L(f(x_i), f(\mu)),$$

or when $G_1 \neq G_2$,

$$L'(f(G_1), cf(G_2)) = L(f(\mu_1), cf(\mu_2)).$$

Another observation can help to further reduce the number of pairwise constraints, i.e., it is not necessary to incorporate the constraints for which the learning algorithm already provides correct predictions. But since true constraints are not known for unlabeled sequence pairs, we choose the most ambiguous sequences in analogy to the active learning algorithms and construct the corresponding pairwise constraints based on the predictions of learning algorithms with labeled data. Since our experiments are dealing with multi-class classification, we adopt a sample selection strategy called best-worst case model proposed in [33], of which the rationale is to choose the most ambiguous sequences by maximizing the expected loss of sequence G,

$$G^* = arg \max_G L(G), \tag{17.27}$$

where $L(G) = \max_{x \in G} \min_{s \in S} L(f_s(x))$ is the loss of classification prediction for the sequence G, and $f_s(x)$ is the sth binary classifier for the example x. Figure 17.5 summarizes the learning process with the selection strategy for pairwise constraints. The kernel logistic regression or support vector machines are first applied with no constraints. The top K ambiguous sequences $\{G_1, ..., G_i, ..., G_K\}$ are selected based on Eqn(17.27). For each sequence G_i, we add a temporal constraint $(G_i, G_i, 1)$ into the constraint set. For any pairs of sequences that overlap, a negative constraint $(G_i, G_j, -1)$ will be constructed.

We can also construct a number of active constraints based on the prediction of the tracking sequences. Here we want to point out that until now constructing the optimal pairwise constraints is still an open research direction without clear theoretical guidelines available. To address this problem to some extent, we have designed three different sampling strategies as follows:

1. **MIN:** couple each top ambiguous example G_i with the nearest training sequence G_j, i.e., the sequence with minimal kernel distance $K(G_i, G_i) + K(G_j, G_j) - 2K(G_i, G_j)$

2. **MAX:** couple each top ambiguous example G_i with the farthest training sequence G_j, i.e., the sequence with maximal kernel distance $K(G_i, G_i) + K(G_j, G_j) - 2K(G_i, G_j)$

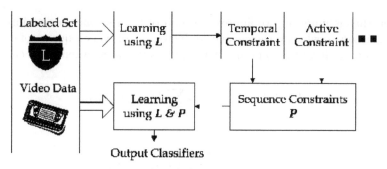

FIGURE 17.5: The flowchart of the learning process. The pairwise learning algorithm is first applied with only labeled data. The top K ambiguous sequences are selected based on Eqn(17.27). For each sequence G_i, we add the related temporal constraints and active constraints into the constraint set. Finally, the pairwise learning algorithm is trained with both existing labeled data and additional pairwise constraints.

3. **COM:** couple two testing examples G_i, G_j together that maximizes the criterion of $L(G_i) + L(G_j) - K(G_i, G_j)$. This criterion intends to maximize the ambiguities of selected examples and meanwhile make them distinguishable from each other.

For each pair of constraints provided by these above strategies, we request the pairwise labels c_{ij} from users and use it to generate an active constraint (G_i, G_j, c_{ij}). After all these constraints are available, the learning algorithm can be easily re-learned using both the existing labeled data and the additional pairwise constraints.

17.7.3 Experimental Setting

Our experiments are carried out in the following way. Each data set is first split into two disjoint sets based on temporal order. Training images are randomly drawn from the first set, which contains 50% of its video sequences. The rest images are used as test images. For every specific parameter setting, we increase the number of sequence constraints from 0 to N until the classification performance is relatively stable. N was chosen to be 20 in the single-day data set and 40 in the multiple-day data set. In terms of active constraints, we simulated the human labeling process using true pairwise constraints without actually asking a human to label each iteration. The MIN sampling strategy is applied unless stated otherwise.

For evaluation, the prediction error on testing data is reported. The baseline performance of the CPKLR and NPKLR algorithms uses KLR with a majority voting scheme, i.e., each image is predicted independently and then the majority label for each sequence is predicted as true labels. Similarly, the baseline performance of the CPSVM algorithm uses SVMs with a majority voting scheme. We used the RBF kernel $K(x_i, x_j) = e^{-\rho\|x_i - x_j\|^2}$ with $\rho = 0.08$ in all of our experiments, which was chosen by maximizing the accuracy with cross-validation in the training set. Also, we empirically set the regularization parameters λ to be 0.01, and pairwise coefficient μ to be 1.

We also compared the proposed approaches with the following two learning algorithms utilizing pairwise constraints. The first one is called relevant component analysis (RCA) [24], which is an efficient algorithm for learning a full Mahalanobis metric by linear transformation. In this work, the authors define a chunklet as a subset of points that belong to the same class but the identity of this class is unknown. Given the chunklets, the covariance matrix S_{ch} of all the center-points in the chunklets is computed. The Mahalannobis distance is generated from the whitening transformation of S_{ch}. In the implementation, we added an identity matrix ϵI to the covariance matrix S_{ch} in order to avoid the issue of singularity. Since RCA is a metric learning algorithm, it cannot handle supervised learning directly. In the following experiments, we first apply RCA to transform the feature space and then apply the same baseline classifiers as before to predict the testing data. One drawback for this algorithm is that it can only work with positive constraints.

The other approach we compared is a constrained Gaussian mixture model [23] which incorporates both positive and negative pairwise constraints into a GMM model using the EM algorithm. In the following we call this algorithm pairwise Gaussian mixture model (PGMM), where more details can be found in the work done by Shental et al. [23]. To apply PGMM for classification, we chose 2 Gaussian mixtures to model the positive data and 3 mixtures to model the negative data. The number of mixtures is determined by using cross validation in the training set and picking the best configuration from 1 mixture to 5 mixtures. Similar to the RCA algorithm, an identity matrix ϵI was added to the covariance matrix for the purpose of regularization. Finally, the posterior probability for a testing example being positive $P(y = 1|x)$ can be computed from the data likelihoods $P(x|y = +1)$ and $P(x|y = -1)$.

17.7.4   Performance Evaluation

The first series of experiments compare the effectiveness of the proposed pairwise learning algorithms using different types of pairwise constraints as well as the baseline classifiers shown in Figure 17.6. Three different curves are plotted in each subgraph, indicating the performance of the CPKLR, CPSVM, and NPKLR algorithms. From Figure 17.6, we can observe that the classification error can be considerably reduced even with a small number of constraints. By comparing the performance of pairwise learning algorithms in different settings, we find that NPKLR usually outperforms the algorithms using convex loss functions (namely CPKLR and CPSVM), because the non-

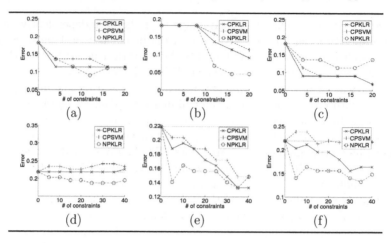

FIGURE 17.6: Summary of the experimental results: (a) The classification error of pairwise learning algorithms against the number of constraints using temporal constraints alone in the single-day data set. The number of constraints is growing from 0 to 20 at step 4. Three proposed algorithms are compared including the CPKLR, CPSVM, and NPKLR algorithms. (d) is similar to (a) except the results are from the multiple-day data set. The number of constraints is growing from 0 to 40 at an increment of 5. (b) The classification error learned using active constraints alone in the single-day data set and (e) in the multiple-day data set. (c) The classification error learned with the combination of temporal constraints and active constraints in the single-day data set and (f) in the multiple-day data set.

convex pairwise loss functions can provide correct decision boundaries which cannot be done by the convex pairwise loss functions. However, the performance improvement comes at a price of higher computational intensity. Since the computational time of each iteration in solving NPKLR is similar to that of solving CPKLR, the overall computational time of NPKLR is N_{EM} times higher than the time of CPKLR if N_{EM} denotes the number of EM iterations in NPKLR. Moreover, it shows that sometimes NPKLR tends to degrade its performance especially when a large number of constraints are incorporated. This can be explained by the fact that as more constraints are introduced, the surface of the non-convex objective function becomes more "bumpy" and thus NPKLR is more likely to get trapped in a local minimum instead of reaching the global optimum. In contrast, both the CPKLR and CPSVM algorithms achieve a relatively smaller performance boost than NPKLR. However, the improvement is usually more stable than NPKLR. Among these two learning algorithms with convex pairwise loss functions, their performances are close to each other but on average the CPKLR algorithm is slightly superior to the

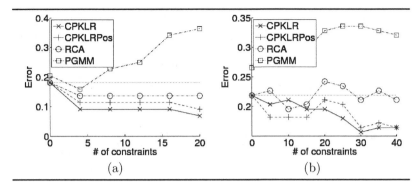

FIGURE 17.7: The classification error of various algorithms against the number of temporal constraints and active constraints. We compare CPKLR with all constraints, CPKLR with positive constraints, KLR with RCA algorithms, and PGMM with all constraints. (a) is reported in the single-day data set and (b) is reported in the multiple day data set.

CPSVM algorithm.

Along another direction, it is also useful to compare the classification performances across various constraint types. As can be seen, learning with temporal constraints is effective in the single-day data set but unable to get any improvement in the multiple day data set. This is partially due to the diverse color representation in the multi-day video sequences. It degrades the effectiveness of temporal constraints which cannot capture long term relations between image examples. However, active constraints, if available from users, can be more effective to reduce the error in both data sets. Moreover, the combination of both constraints often produces a higher performance. For the first data set when using NPKLR, it reduces the error rate from 18% down to 6% with 20 pairs of both types of constraints. For the second data set, it again reduces the error rate from 22% down to 12% with 40 pairs of both type of constraints.

In Figure 17.7, we compare the performance of the CPKLR algorithm with two baseline algorithms as mentioned before, i.e., the RCA algorithm and PGMM using the same amounts of pairwise constraints. In this experiment, we adopted kernel logistic regression (KLR) as the underlying classifier except for PGMM. A combination of temporal and active constraints is applied for each learning algorithm. Because RCA can only take the positive constraints as input, another curve is depicted for PKLR algorithm with the presence of only positive constraints. The results show that our algorithm achieves a superior performance to both the RCA algorithm and the PGMM even without negative constraints. The degrading performance of PGMM suggests that our data might violate the model assumption of the Gaussian mixture model.

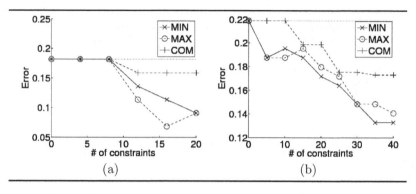

FIGURE 17.8: The classification error of the CPKLR algorithm against the number of temporal constraints and active constraints using three different sampling strategies as described in Section 17.7.2. (a) is reported in the single-day data set and (b) is reported in the multiple-day data set.

Also, it corroborates the advantage of the proposed discriminative framework which requires fewer assumptions about the underlying distributions. On the other hand, the results also demonstrate the usefulness of incorporating negative constraints.

Finally, Figure 17.8 analyzes the performance of using three different sampling strategies described in Section 17.7.2, i.e., MIN, MAX, and COM. We can observe that all these sampling strategies can boost the classification performance over the baseline by using additional pairwise constraints. Specifically, the MAX and MIN sampling strategies provide more significant improvement than the COM strategy. This might be related to the fact that MAX/MIN strategies impose constraints between training examples and testing examples, while the COM strategy only considers the coupling between testing examples.

17.7.5 Results for Noisy Pairwise Constraints

In order to show how noisy pairwise constraints can be obtained in practice, we describe a user study that attempts to manually collect constraints between human subjects. Different from the traditional labeling process, we intentionally masked the faces of each subject before presenting them to the users so as to protect their privacy, but this also increased the difficulty of manually judging the correctness of given constraints.

A screen shot of the interface is shown in Figure 17.9. The image on the top left side is the sample image, while the other images are all candidates to be compared with. In the experiments, the volunteers were requested to label whether the candidate images were of the same person with the sample image.

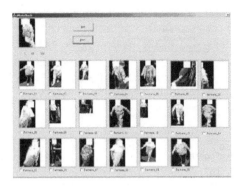

FIGURE 17.9: The labeling interface for the user study for noisy pairwise constraints.

All images were randomly selected from pre-extracted silhouette images and all candidate images do not belong to the same sequence as to the sample image. In more detail, these images were randomly selected from a pool of 102 images, each of which was sampled from a different sequence of video. Nine human subjects took a total of 180 runs to label the pairwise constraints. In all 160 labeled pairwise constraints, 140 constraints correctly correspond to the identities of the subjects and 20 of them are errors, which achieved an overall accuracy around 88.89%. The result shows that human annotators could label the pairwise constraints with a reasonable accuracy from face-obscured video data. But it also indicates that these pairwise constraints are not perfect, which can pose a challenge for the learning algorithm.

Therefore we applied the weighted pairwise kernel logistic regression (WP-KLR) algorithm to identify the human subject from video. The parameter setting is similar to the previous experiments. Our first experiment is to examine the effectiveness of noisy pairwise constraints for labeling identities as shown in Figure 17.10(a). The learning curve of "Noisy Constraint" is completely based on the labeling result from the user study, but weighted all the constraints with 1. "Weighted Noisy Constraint" uses different weights for each constraint. In current experiments, we simulated and smoothed the weights based on the user study. Therefore, the noise factor w_i is set to the labeling accuracy for each human subject. "True Constraint" assumes the ground truth is available and thus the correct constraints are always weighted as 1 while wrong constraints are ignored. Although the true constraints is unknown in practice, we intentionally show its performance to serve as an upper bound of incorporating noisy constraints.

Figure 17.10(a) demonstrated the performance with three types of constraint learning approaches. In contrast to the accuracy of 0.7375 without using any constraints, the accuracy of "Weighted Noisy Constraint" grows to 0.8125 with 140 weighted constraints, achieving a significant performance

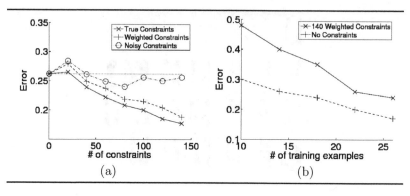

(a) (b)

FIGURE 17.10: (a) The classification errors with different numbers of pairwise constraints. We compare CPKLR with noisy constraints, WPKLR with noisy constraints, and CPKLR with true constraints. (b) The classification errors with different numbers of labeled examples. We compare KLR without any constraints and WPKLR with noisy constraints.

improvement of 10.17%. Also, "Weighted Noisy Constraint" substantially outperforms "Noisy Constraint," and it can achieve performance close to "True Constraint." Note that, when given only 20 constraints, the accuracy is slightly degraded in each setting. A possible explanation is that the decision boundary does not change stably with a small number of constraints. But the performance always goes up after a sufficient number of constraints are introduced. Our next experiment explores the effect of varying the number of labeled examples with 140 additional pairwise constraints. In general, we hope to minimize the labeling effort without severely affecting the overall accuracy. Figure 17.10(b) illustrates the learning performance with different numbers of training examples. For all the settings, introducing more constraints could always improve classification accuracy. More importantly, pairwise constraints could even make more noticeable improvements when fewer training examples are present.

17.8 Conclusion

We have presented a discriminative classification framework which can directly model the decision boundary with labeled data as well as additional pairwise constraints without explicitly estimating the underlying data distribution. Two families of pairwise loss functions, i.e., convex and non-convex pairwise loss functions, were investigated and three pairwise learning algorithms were derived by plugging in the hinge loss and the logistic loss functions. The experiments with two surveillance video data sets demonstrated the proposed pairwise learning algorithms could achieve considerable improved performance with pairwise constraints, compared to the baseline classifier which uses labeled data alone and a majority voting scheme. The proposed algorithms also outperformed the RCA algorithm and the Gaussian mixture model with constraints when the same number of pairwise constraints are used. A comparison among the proposed algorithms showed that the algorithms with non-convex loss functions could achieve a higher classification accuracy but the algorithms with convex loss functions are more efficient and robust. Finally, we also evaluated the performance of weighted pairwise kernel logistic regression algorithms using noisy pairwise constraints provided by human feedback. It showed that the weighted algorithms can achieve higher accuracy than the non-weighted counterpart.

In this work, we mainly focused on developing new pairwise learning algorithms and leave the exploration of more advanced visual features to future research. We also want to point out that although our learning framework and previous work on learning distance metric exploit the pairwise constraints in different ways, they can be complementary to each other. For example, it is possible to apply the proposed learning framework in a new distance metric learned from other algorithms.

References

[1] E. L. Allwein, R. E. Schapire, and Y. Singer. Reducing multiclass to binary: A unifying approach for margin classifiers. In *Proceedings of the 17th International Conference on Machine Learning*, pages 9–16, 2000.

[2] S. Antania, R. Kasturi, and R. Jain. A survey on the use of pattern recognition methods for abstraction, indexing and retrieval of images and video. *Pattern Recognition*, 4:945–65, April 2002.

[3] S. Basu, A. Banerjee, and R. J. Mooney. Active semi-supervision for pairwise constrained clustering. In *Proceedings of the 20th International Conference on Machine Learning*, Washington, DC, Aug 2003.

[4] S. Basu, M. Bilenko, and R. Mooney. A probabilistic framework for semi-supervised clustering. In *Proceedings of SIGKDD*, pages 59–68, 2004.

[5] A. Blum and T. Mitchell. Combining labeled and unlabeled data with

co-training. In *Proceedings of the Workshop on Computational Learning Theory*, 1998.

[6] T. F. Coleman and Y. Li. An interior, trust region approach for nonlinear minimization subject to bounds. *SIAM Journal on Optimization*, 6:418–445, 1996.

[7] A. J. Comenarez and T. S. Huang. Face detection with information-based maximum discrimination. In *Proceedings of CVPR*, 1997.

[8] A. Dempster, N. Laird, and D. Rubin. Maximum likelihood from incomplete data via the EM algorithm. *Journal of the Royal Statistical Society, Series B*, 39(1):1–38, 1977.

[9] R. Fergus, P. Perona, and A. Zisserman. Object class recognition by unsupervised scale-invariant learning. In *Proceedings of CVPR*, 2003.

[10] H. Gish and M. Schmidt. Text-independent speaker identification. *IEEE Signal Proceedingsssing Magazine*, 11(4):18–32, 1994.

[11] T. Hastie, R. Tibshirani, and J. Friedman. *The Elements of Statistical Learning. Springer Series in Statistics.* Springer Verlag, Basel, 2001.

[12] M. Hewish. Automatic target recognition. *International Defense Review*, 24(10), 1991.

[13] G. Kimeldorf and G. Wahba. Some results on tchebycheffian spline functions. *Journal of Mathematical Analysis and Applications*, 33:82–95, 1971.

[14] S. Kumar and M. Hebert. Discriminative random fields: A discriminative framework for contextual interaction in classification. In *IEEE International Conference on Computer Vision (ICCV)*, 2003.

[15] J. T. Kwok and I. W. Tsang. Learning with idealized kernel. In *Proceedings of the 20th International Conference on Machine Learning*, Washington, DC, Aug 2003.

[16] T. Lange, M. H. Law, A. K. Jain, and J. Buhmann. Learning with constrained and unlabeled data. In *Proceedings of CVPR*, 2005.

[17] F. Li, R. Fergus, and P. Perona. A bayesian approach to unsupervised one-shot learning of object categories. In *Proceedings of the International Conference on Computer Vision*, Oct 2003.

[18] K. Nigam, A. K. McCallum, S. Thrun, and T. M. Mitchell. Text classification from labeled and unlabeled documents using EM. *Machine Learning*, 39:103–134, 2000.

[19] A. Pentland, B. Moghaddam, and T. Starner. View-based and modular eigenspaces for face recognition. In *Proceedings of IEEE Conference on*

Computer Vision and Pattern Recognition 94 (CVPR'94), pages 568–574, Seattle, WA, June 1994.

[20] W. E. Pierson and T. D. Ross. Automatic target recognition (atr) evaluation theory: a survey. In *Proceedings of the SPIE - The International Society for Optical Engineering 4053*, 2000.

[21] J. Platt. Fast training of support vector machines using sequential minimal optimization. In B. Schölkopf, C. Burges, and A. Smola, editors, *Advances in Kernel Methods - Support Vector Learning*. MIT Press, 1998.

[22] G. Shakhnarovich, L. Lee, and T. Darrell. Integrated face and gait recognition from multiple views. In *Proceedings IEEE Conference on Computer Vision and Pattern Recognition*, 2001.

[23] N. Shental, A. Bar-Hillel, T. Hertz, and D. Weinshall. Computing gaussian mixture models with em using side information. In *Workshop on 'The Continuum from Labeled to Unlabeled Data in Machine Learning and Data Mining,' ICML 2003*, Washington, DC, Aug 2003.

[24] N. Shental, A. Bar-Hillel, T. Hertz, and D. Weinshall. Enhancing image and video retrieval: Learning via equivalence constraints. In *Proceedings of IEEE Conference on Computer Vision and Pattern Recognition*, Madison, WI, June 2003.

[25] J. Sivic and A. Zisserman. Video google: A text retrieval approach to object matching in videos. In *Proceedings of the International Conference on Computer Vision*, Oct 2003.

[26] O. Trier, A. Jain, and T. Taxt. Feature extraction methods for character recognition - a survey. *Pattern Recognition*, 29, 1993.

[27] Z. Tu, X. Chen, A. L. Yuille, and S. Zhu. Image parsing. unifying segmentation, detection and recognition. In *Proceedings of ICCV*, 2003.

[28] V. N. Vapnik. *The Nature of Statistical Learning Theory*. Springer, 1995.

[29] P. Viola, M. J. Jones, and D. Snow. Detecting pedestrians using patterns of motion and appearance. In *Proceedings of ICCV*, 2003.

[30] K. Wagstaff, C. Cardie, S. Rogers, and S. Schroedl. Constrained k-means clustering with background knowledge. In *Proceedings of the 18th International Conference on Machine Learning*, pages 577–584. Morgan Kaufmann Publishers Inc., 2001.

[31] L. Xie and P. Pérez. Slightly supervised learning of part-based appearance models. In *IEEE Workshop on Learning in Computer Vision and Pattern Recognition, in conjunction with CVPR 2004*, June 2004.

[32] E. P. Xing, A. Y. Ng, M. I. Jordan, and S. Russel. Distance metric learning with applications to clustering with side information. In *Advances in Neural Information Proceedings Systems*, 2002.

[33] R. Yan, J. Yang, and A. G. Hauptmann. Automatically labeling data using multi-class active learning. In *Proceedings of the International Conference on Computer Vision*, pages 516–523, 2003.

[34] R. Yan, J. Zhang, J. Yang, and A. G. Hauptmann. A discriminative learning framework with pairwise constraints for video object classification. *IEEE Transactions on Pattern Analysis Machine Intelligence*, 28(4):578–593, 2006.

[35] S. X. Yu and J. Shi. Grouping with directed relationships. *Lecture Notes in Computer Science*, 2134:283–291, 2001.

[36] J. Zhang and R. Yan. On the value of pairwise constraints in classification and consistency. In *Proceedings of the 24th International Conference on Machine Learning*, Corvallis, OR, June 2007.

[37] J. Zhu and T. Hastie. Kernel logistic regression and the import vector machine. In *Advances in Neural Information Proceedingsssing Systems*, 2001.

[38] X. Zhu, Z. Ghahramani, and J. Lafferty. Semi-supervised learning using gaussian fields and harmonic functions. In *Proceedings of 20th International Conference on Machine Learning*, 2003.

Index

T - #0073 - 101024 - C0 - 234/156/25 [27] - CB - 9781584889960 - Gloss Lamination